C0-DYF-054

Ms Lynne Torres
2340 Washington Rd
Lansing, MI 48911

Jehovah's Witnesses
Proclaimers of God's Kingdom

© 1993
WATCH TOWER
BIBLE AND TRACT SOCIETY OF PENNSYLVANIA
All rights reserved

Publishers
WATCHTOWER BIBLE AND TRACT SOCIETY OF NEW YORK, INC.
INTERNATIONAL BIBLE STUDENTS ASSOCIATION
Brooklyn, New York, U.S.A.

First Printing in English:
500,000 Copies

Unless otherwise indicated,
Scripture quotations are from the modern-language
New World Translation of the Holy Scriptures—With References, 1984 Edition

Jehovah's Witnesses—Proclaimers of God's Kingdom
English (*jv*-E)
Made in the United States of America

Foreword

Jehovah's Witnesses are a people widely known. Their preaching and way of worship have penetrated national and racial groups worldwide and have been embraced by people young and old, at every economic and educational level. Their zeal as proclaimers of God's Kingdom has impressed even their critics. Their love toward one another makes some non-Witnesses wish that more people acted that way.

Yet, many still wonder, 'Who really are Jehovah's Witnesses?' Others have written about them, not always impartially. Probably they were not aware of all the facts. Certainly, no one knows their modern-day history better than they themselves do. The editors of this volume have endeavored to be objective and to present a candid history. To all who are aware of what the Bible foretells for the last days, this history of a people who intensely believe and preach what the Bible says will be especially enlightening.

The Publishers

Contents

SECTION 1

"You Are My Witnesses," Says Jehovah

CHAPTER			
	1	Why Should Jehovah Have Witnesses?	10
	2	Jesus Christ, the Faithful Witness	19
	3	Christian Witnesses of Jehovah in the First Century	26
	4	The Great Apostasy Develops	33
	5	Proclaiming the Lord's Return (1870-1914)	42
	6	A Time of Testing (1914-1918)	61
	7	Advertise the King and the Kingdom! (1919-1941)	72
	8	Declaring the Good News Without Letup (1942-1975)	90
	9	Jehovah's Word Keeps Moving Speedily (1976-1992)	108

SECTION 2

Gaining Accurate Knowledge of God's Word and Applying It

CHAPTER			
	10	Growing in Accurate Knowledge of the Truth	120
	11	How We Came to Be Known as Jehovah's Witnesses	149
	12	The Great Crowd—To Live in Heaven? Or on Earth?	159
	13	Recognized by Our Conduct	172
	14	"They Are No Part of the World"	188

SECTION 3

An Association of Brothers

CHAPTER			
	15	Development of the Organization Structure	204
	16	Meetings—For Worship, Instruction, and Encouragement	236
	17	Conventions—Proof of Our Brotherhood	254
	18	"Seeking First the Kingdom"	283
	19	Growing Together in Love	304
	20	Building Together on a Global Scale	318
	21	How Is It All Financed?	340

SECTION 4

Proclaiming the Good News in All the Inhabited Earth

CHAPTER	22	WITNESSES TO THE MOST DISTANT PART OF THE EARTH	404
	23	MISSIONARIES PUSH WORLDWIDE EXPANSION	521
	24	BY HUMAN POWER? OR BY GOD'S SPIRIT?	547

SECTION 5

Kingdom Preaching Furthered by Production of Bible Literature

CHAPTER	25	PREACHING PUBLICLY AND FROM HOUSE TO HOUSE	556
	26	PRODUCING BIBLE LITERATURE FOR USE IN THE MINISTRY	575
	27	PRINTING AND DISTRIBUTING GOD'S OWN SACRED WORD	603

SECTION 6

Exposed to Reproaches and Tribulations

CHAPTER	28	TESTING AND SIFTING FROM WITHIN	618
	29	"OBJECTS OF HATRED BY ALL THE NATIONS"	642
	30	'DEFENDING AND LEGALLY ESTABLISHING THE GOOD NEWS'	678

SECTION 7

A People Distinctively His Own, Zealous for Fine Works

CHAPTER	31	HOW CHOSEN AND LED BY GOD	704
	32	"BY THIS ALL WILL KNOW THAT YOU ARE MY DISCIPLES"	710
	33	CONTINUING TO KEEP ON THE WATCH	713

WORLD HEADQUARTERS
AND PRINCIPAL OFFICES OF JEHOVAH'S WITNESSES—IN PICTURES 352

NOTEWORTHY EVENTS
IN THE MODERN-DAY HISTORY OF JEHOVAH'S WITNESSES 718

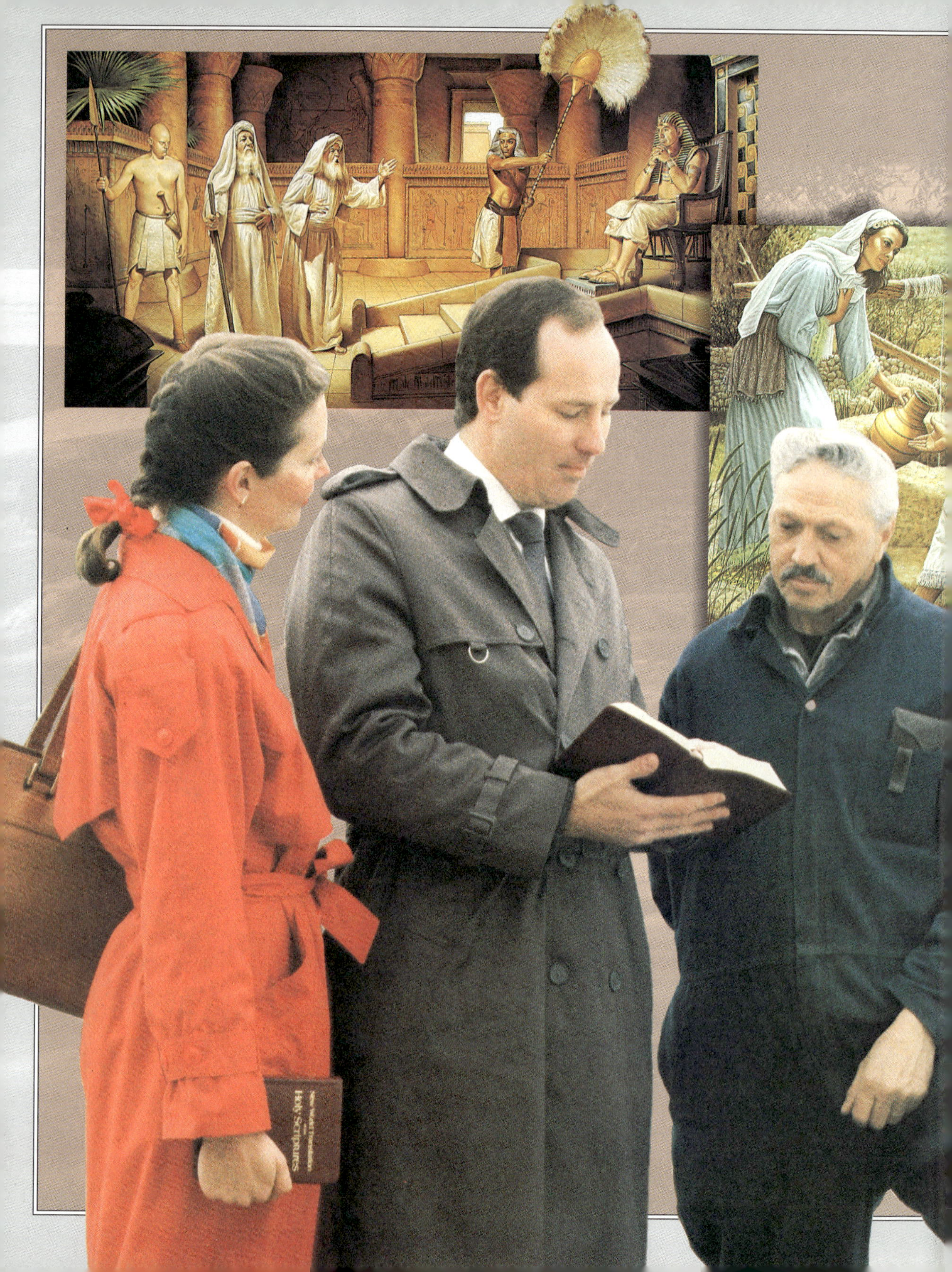
Holy Scriptures

SECTION 1

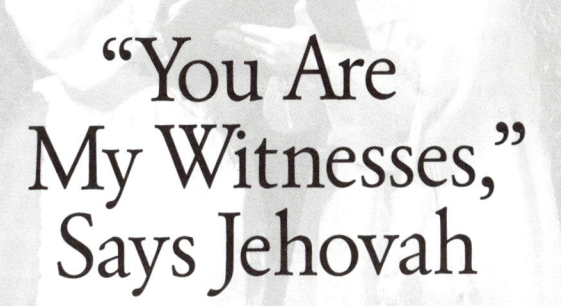

"You Are My Witnesses," Says Jehovah

Why would Jehovah have witnesses? Who are they? This section (Chapters 1 to 9) provides a concise review of Jehovah's use of witnesses from ancient times right down to our day.

Each succeeding section contains an in-depth discussion on a specific aspect of that history.

CHAPTER 1

WHY SHOULD JEHOVAH HAVE WITNESSES?

JEHOVAH'S WITNESSES are known worldwide for their persistence in talking to people everywhere about Jehovah God and his Kingdom. They also have the reputation of being a people who hold to their beliefs despite all manner of opposition, even death.

The events in Eden raised important issues: Is Jehovah's sovereignty righteous? Will his creatures be faithful to him?

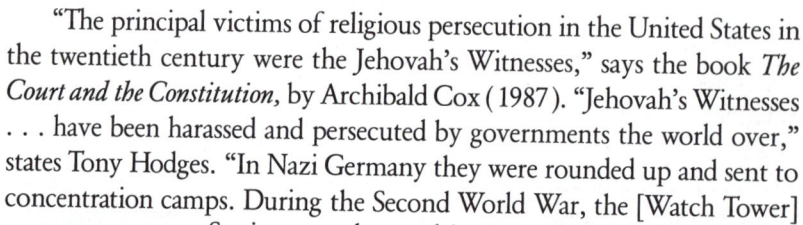

"The principal victims of religious persecution in the United States in the twentieth century were the Jehovah's Witnesses," says the book *The Court and the Constitution,* by Archibald Cox (1987). "Jehovah's Witnesses . . . have been harassed and persecuted by governments the world over," states Tony Hodges. "In Nazi Germany they were rounded up and sent to concentration camps. During the Second World War, the [Watch Tower] Society was banned in Australia and Canada. . . . Now [in the 1970's] the Jehovah's Witnesses are being hounded in Africa."—*Jehovah's Witnesses in Africa,* 1985 Edition.

Why the persecution? What is the objective of the preaching? Have Jehovah's Witnesses really been commissioned by God? Why would Jehovah have *witnesses* anyway—and imperfect human witnesses at that? The answers have to do with issues being tried in a universal court case—by far the most crucial case ever to be argued. We must examine these issues in order to understand why Jehovah has witnesses and why these witnesses are willing to endure even the most intense opposition.

Jehovah's Sovereignty Challenged

These vital issues involve the rightfulness of the sovereignty, or supreme rulership, of Jehovah God. He is the Universal Sovereign by reason of his Creatorship, his Godship, and his Almightiness. (Gen. 17:1; Ex. 6:3; Rev. 4:11) He thus has rightful domination over everything in heaven and on earth. (1 Chron. 29:12, ftn.) But he always administers his sovereignty in love. (Compare Jeremiah 9:24.) What, then, does he ask in return from his intelligent creatures? That they love him and show appreciation for his sovereignty. (Ps. 84:10) Yet, thousands of years ago a challenge was hurled against Jehovah's rightful sovereignty. How? By whom? Genesis, the first book of the Bible, sheds light on the matter.

It reports that God created the first human pair, Adam and Eve, and gave them a beautiful garden home. He also laid this command upon them: "From every tree of the garden you may eat to satisfaction. But as for the tree of the knowledge of good and bad you must not eat from it, for in the day you eat from it you will positively die." (Gen. 2:16, 17) What was "the tree of the knowledge of good and bad," and what would eating of its fruit signify?

It was a literal tree, but God employed it for a symbolic purpose. Because he called it "the tree of the knowledge of good and bad" and because he commanded that the first human pair not eat from it, the tree fittingly symbolized God's right to determine for humans what is "good" (pleasing to God) and what is "bad" (displeasing to God). The presence of this tree thus tested man's respect for God's sovereignty. Sadly, the first human pair disobeyed God and ate of the forbidden fruit. They failed this simple yet profound test of obedience and appreciation.—Gen. 3:1-6.

This seemingly small act constituted rebellion against Jehovah's sovereignty. How so? Understanding the way we humans are made is a key to understanding the significance of what Adam and Eve did. When Jehovah created the first human pair, he gave them a remarkable gift—free will. Complementing this gift, Jehovah gave them mental abilities that included the powers of perception, reason, and judgment. (Heb. 5:14) They were not like mindless robots; nor were they like animals, which act mainly on instinct. Their freedom, though, was relative, subject to the rule of God's laws. (Compare Jeremiah 10:23, 24.) Adam and Eve *chose* to eat of the forbidden fruit. They thus abused their freedom. What led them to this course?

The Bible explains that a spirit creature of God had taken a willful course of opposition and resistance to God. This one, who later came to be known as Satan, spoke through a serpent in Eden and led Eve and, through her, Adam away from subjection to God's sovereignty. (Rev. 12:9) By eating of the tree, Adam and Eve placed their judgment above God's, indicating that they wanted to judge for themselves what is good and what is bad. —Gen. 3:22.

The issue thus raised was, Does Jehovah have the right to rule humankind, and does he exercise his sovereignty in the best interests of his

Humans can choose to benefit from Jehovah's sovereignty. But first they must hear about it

subjects? This issue was clearly implied by the Serpent's words to Eve: "Is it really so that God said you must not eat from every tree of the garden?" The implication was that God was wrongfully withholding something good from the woman and her husband.—Gen. 3:1.

The rebellion in Eden raised another issue: Can humans under test be faithful to God? This related issue was put in clear focus 24 centuries later in connection with faithful Job. Satan, the 'voice' behind the serpent, challenged Jehovah to His face, saying: "Is it for nothing that Job has feared God?" Satan charged: "Have not you yourself put up a hedge about him and about his house and about everything that he has all around? The work of his hands you have blessed, and his livestock itself has spread abroad in the earth." Satan thus intimated that Job's uprightness was motivated by self-interest. He further charged: "Skin in behalf of skin, and everything that a man has he will give in behalf of his soul." Since, as Jehovah had noted, 'there was no one like Job in the earth,' Satan was really claiming that he could turn *any servant of God* away from Him. (Job 1:8-11; 2:4) All of God's servants were thus indirectly challenged regarding their integrity and loyalty to His sovereignty.

Once raised, the issues had to be settled. The passage of time—about 6,000 years now—and the miserable failure of human governments clearly demonstrate that humans *need* God's sovereignty. But do they *want* it? Are there humans who will manifest heartfelt recognition of Jehovah's righteous sovereignty? Yes! Jehovah has his witnesses! But before we consider their testimony, let us first examine what is involved in being a witness.

What It Means to Be a Witness

The original-language words translated "witness" provide insight into what it means to be a witness for Jehovah. In the Hebrew Scriptures, the noun rendered "witness" (*'edh*) is derived from a verb (*'udh*) meaning "return" or "repeat, do again." Regarding the noun (*'edh*), the *Theological Wordbook of the Old Testament* says: "A witness is one, who by reiteration, emphatically affirms his testimony. The word [*'edh*] is at home in the language of the court." *A Comprehensive Etymological Dictionary of the Hebrew Language for Readers of English* adds: "The orig[inal] meaning [of the verb *'udh*] prob[ably] was 'he said repeatedly and forcefully.'"

In the Christian Scriptures, the Greek words rendered "witness" (*mar'-tys*) and "bear witness" (*mar·ty·re'o*) also had a legal connotation, although in time they took on a broader meaning. According to the *Theological Dictionary of the New Testament*, "the concept of witness [is used] both in the sense of witness to ascertainable facts and also in that of witness to truths, i.e., the making known and confessing of convictions." So a witness relates facts from direct personal knowledge, or he proclaims views or truths of which he is convinced.*

The faithful course of first-century Christians carried the meaning of "witness" a step farther. Many of those early Christians witnessed under persecution and in the face of death. (Acts 22:20; Rev. 2:13) As a result, by about the second century C.E., the Greek word for witness (*mar'tys*, from which is also derived the word "martyr") acquired the meaning that applied to persons who were willing to "seal the seriousness of their witness or confession by death." They were not called witnesses because they died; they died because they were loyal witnesses.

Who, then, were the early witnesses of Jehovah? Who were willing to proclaim "repeatedly and forcefully"—in words and by the way they lived—that Jehovah is the rightful, worthy Sovereign? Who were willing to maintain integrity to God, even to death?

Early Witnesses of Jehovah

The apostle Paul says: "We have so great a cloud [Gr., *ne'phos*, denoting a cloud mass] of witnesses surrounding us." (Heb. 12:1) This 'cloud mass' of witnesses began forming shortly after rebellion against God's sovereignty in Eden.

At Hebrews 11:4, Paul identifies Abel as the first witness of Jehovah, saying: "By faith Abel offered God a sacrifice of greater worth than Cain, through which faith he had witness borne to him that he was righteous, God bearing witness respecting his gifts; and through it he, although he died, yet speaks." In what way did Abel serve as a witness for Jehovah? The answer centers around why Abel's sacrifice was of "greater worth" than Cain's.

Put simply, Abel made the right offering with the right motive and backed it up by right works. As his gift, he gave a blood sacrifice representing the life of the firstlings of his flock—whereas Cain offered lifeless produce. (Gen. 4:3, 4) Cain's sacrifice lacked the motivation of faith that made Abel's offering acceptable. Cain needed to modify his worship. Instead, he manifested his bad heart attitude by rejecting God's counsel and warning and by murdering faithful Abel.—Gen. 4:6-8; 1 John 3:11, 12.

Abel was the first witness of Jehovah

Abel displayed the faith that his parents lacked. By his faithful course, he made known his conviction that Jehovah's sovereignty is righteous and worthy. During the century or so that he lived, Abel demonstrated that a man can be faithful to God to the point of sealing his testimony by death. And Abel's blood continues to 'speak,' for the inspired record of his martyrdom was preserved in the Bible for future generations!

---

* For example, some first-century Christians could bear witness to historical facts about Jesus —concerning his life, death, and resurrection—from firsthand knowledge. (Acts 1:21, 22; 10: 40, 41) However, persons who later put faith in Jesus could bear witness by proclaiming to others the significance of his life, death, and resurrection.—Acts 22:15.

Enoch bore witness about God's judgment against the ungodly

About five centuries after Abel's death, Enoch began 'walking with God,' pursuing a course in harmony with Jehovah's standards of good and bad. (Gen. 5:24) By then, rejection of God's sovereignty had led to a proliferation of ungodly practices among humankind. Enoch was convinced that the Supreme Sovereign would act against ungodly persons, and God's spirit moved him to proclaim their future destruction. (Jude 14, 15) Enoch remained a faithful witness even to death, for Jehovah "took him," apparently sparing him a violent death at the hands of his enemies. (Heb. 11:5) Enoch's name could thus be added to the growing list of the 'great cloud of witnesses' of pre-Christian times.

A spirit of ungodliness continued to pervade human affairs. During the lifetime of Noah, who was born about 70 years after Enoch's death, angelic sons of God came to the earth, evidently materializing in human form, and cohabited with attractive women. The offspring they produced were known as Nephilim; they were giants among men. (Gen. 6:1-4) What was the result of this unnatural union of spirit creatures with humans and of the hybrid race thus produced? The inspired record answers: "Consequently Jehovah saw that the badness of man was abundant in the earth and every inclination of the thoughts of his heart was only bad all the time. So God saw the earth and, look! it was ruined, because all flesh had ruined its way on the earth." (Gen. 6:5, 12) How sad that the earth, God's footstool, was "full of violence."—Gen. 6:13; Isa. 66:1.

In contrast, "Noah was a righteous man," one who "proved himself faultless among his contemporaries." (Gen. 6:9) He demonstrated his submission to God's sovereignty by doing 'just as God commanded.' (Gen. 6:22) Acting in faith, he "constructed an ark for the saving of his household." (Heb. 11:7) But Noah was more than a builder; as "a preacher [or herald] of righteousness," he warned of the coming destruction. (2 Pet. 2:5) Despite Noah's bold witnessing, however, that wicked generation "took no note until the flood came and swept them all away."—Matt. 24:37-39.

Following Noah's day, Jehovah had witnesses among the post-Flood patriarchs. Abraham, Isaac, Jacob, and Joseph are mentioned as an early part of the cloud of pre-Christian witnesses. (Heb. 11:8-22; 12:1) They demonstrated their support of Jehovah's sovereignty, doing so by keeping integrity. (Gen. 18:18, 19) They thus contributed to the sanctification of Jehovah's name. Rather than seek security in some earthly kingdom, they "publicly declared that they were strangers and temporary residents in the land," in faith "awaiting the city having real foundations, the builder and maker of which city is God." (Heb. 11:10, 13) They accepted Jehovah as their Ruler, anchoring their hope in the promised heavenly Kingdom as an expression of his rightful sovereignty.

Noah was a preacher of righteousness before God destroyed the world by means of a deluge

In the 16th century B.C.E., Abraham's descendants were slaves needing deliverance from Egyptian bondage. It was then that Moses and his brother Aaron became key figures in a 'battle of the gods.' They appeared before Pharaoh and delivered Jehovah's ultimatum: "Send my people away." But proud Pharaoh hardened his heart; he did not want to lose a great nation of slave workers. "Who is Jehovah," he replied, "so that I should obey his voice to send Israel away? I do not know Jehovah at all and, what is more, I am not going to send Israel away." (Ex. 5:1, 2) By that disdainful response, Pharaoh, who was believed to be a living god himself, refused to recognize Jehovah's Godship.

The issue of godship having been raised, Jehovah now proceeded to prove that he is the true God. Pharaoh, through his magic-practicing

Moses and Aaron testified forcefully to Pharaoh about Jehovah's Godship

priests, summoned the combined power of the gods of Egypt in defiance of Jehovah's power. But Jehovah sent ten plagues, each announced by Moses and Aaron, to demonstrate his dominion over earth's elements and creatures as well as his supremacy over Egypt's gods. (Ex. 9:13-16; 12:12) Following the tenth plague, Jehovah brought Israel out of Egypt by "a strong hand."—Ex. 13:9.

It took much courage and faith for Moses, the 'meekest of all men,' to appear before Pharaoh, not once, but many times. (Num. 12:3) Moses, however, never watered down the message that Jehovah commanded him to deliver to Pharaoh. Not even the threat of death could silence his testimony! (Ex. 10:28, 29; Heb. 11:27) Moses was a witness in the true sense of the word; he testified "repeatedly and forcefully" to the Godship of Jehovah.

Following that deliverance from Egypt in 1513 B.C.E., Moses wrote the book of Genesis. Thus began a new era—the era of Bible writing. Since

Moses evidently wrote the book of Job, he had some discernment of the issue between God and Satan. But as Bible writing progressed, the issues involving God's sovereignty and man's integrity would be put clearly on the record; thus all concerned could gain full knowledge of the great issues involved. Meanwhile, in 1513 B.C.E., Jehovah laid the groundwork for producing a nation of witnesses.

A Nation of Witnesses

In the third month after their leaving Egypt, Jehovah brought the Israelites into an exclusive covenant relationship with him, making them his "special property." (Ex. 19:5, 6) Through Moses, he now dealt with them as a nation, giving them a theocratic government founded on the Law covenant as their national constitution. (Isa. 33:22) They were Jehovah's chosen people, organized to represent him as their Sovereign Lord.

However, in the centuries that followed, the nation did not always acknowledge Jehovah's sovereignty. After becoming settled in the Promised Land, Israel at times fell away to worshiping the demonistic gods of the nations. Because of their failure to obey him as rightful Sovereign, Jehovah allowed them to be plundered, and thus it appeared that the gods of the nations were stronger than Jehovah. (Isa. 42:18-25) But in the eighth century B.C.E., Jehovah openly challenged the gods of the nations in order to clear up that misimpression and settle the question, Who is the true God?

Through the prophet Isaiah, Jehovah issued the challenge: "Who is there among them [the gods of the nations] that can tell this [prophesy accurately]? Or can they cause us to hear even the first things [that is, things in advance]? Let them [as gods] furnish their witnesses, that they may be declared righteous, or let them [the peoples of the nations] hear and say, 'It is the truth!'" (Isa. 43:9) Yes, let the gods of the nations furnish

Jehovah made clear to an entire nation their responsibility as his witnesses

witnesses who could testify regarding the prophecy of their gods, "It is the truth!" But none of such gods could produce true witnesses to their godship!

Jehovah made clear to Israel their responsibility in settling the question, Who is the true God? He said: "You are my witnesses, . . . even my servant whom I have chosen, in order that you may know and have faith in me, and that you may understand that I am the same One. Before me there was no God formed, and after me there continued to be none. I—I am Jehovah, and besides me there is no savior. I myself have told forth and have saved and have caused it to be heard, when there was among you no strange god. So you are my witnesses, . . . and I am God."—Isa. 43:10-12.

"You are my witnesses, . . . and I am God"

So Jehovah's people Israel constituted a nation of witnesses. They could emphatically affirm Jehovah's rightful, worthy sovereignty. On the basis of their past experiences, they could proclaim with conviction that Jehovah is the Great Deliverer of his people and the God of true prophecy.

Witnessing Concerning the Messiah

Despite the abundant testimony of that 'cloud mass' of pre-Christian witnesses, God's side of the issues was not completely settled. Why not? Because at God's own appointed time, after it has been clearly demonstrated that humans *need* Jehovah's rulership and that they cannot rule successfully on their own, Jehovah must execute judgment upon all who refuse to respect his rightful authority. Furthermore, the issues raised reach far beyond the human sphere. Since an angel had rebelled in Eden, the question of integrity to God's sovereignty reached up to and involved God's heavenly creatures. Hence, Jehovah purposed for a spirit son to come to the earth, where Satan would have full opportunity to put him to the test. That spirit son would be given the opportunity to settle, in a perfect way, the question, Will anyone be faithful to God under whatever trial may be brought against him? Having thus proved his loyalty, this son of God would be empowered as Jehovah's great vindicator, who would destroy the wicked and fully accomplish God's original purpose regarding the earth.

But how would this one be identified? In Eden, Jehovah had promised a "seed" that would bruise the serpentlike Adversary in the head and vindicate God's sovereignty. (Gen. 3:15) Through the Hebrew prophets, Jehovah provided many details about that Messianic "seed"—his background and activities, even the time he would appear.—Gen. 12:1-3; 22:15-18; 49:10; 2 Sam. 7:12-16; Isa. 7:14; Dan. 9:24-27; Mic. 5:2.

By the middle of the fifth century B.C.E., with the completion of the Hebrew Scriptures, the prophecies were in place, waiting for the arrival of the Messiah to fulfill them. The testimony of this witness—in fact, God's greatest witness—will be considered in the following chapter.

CHAPTER 2

JESUS CHRIST, THE FAITHFUL WITNESS

FOR some 4,000 years, a long line of pre-Christian witnesses had offered their testimony. But the issues involving God's sovereignty and the integrity of his servants were far from settled. The time now arrived for the promised royal "seed," the Messiah, to appear on earth.—Gen. 3:15.

Out of all of his millions of spirit sons, whom did Jehovah select for this assignment? All of them had witnessed what happened in Eden and were no doubt aware of the universal issues raised. But who was the most anxious to serve in clearing Jehovah's name and vindicating his sovereignty? Who could provide the most conclusive answer to Satan's challenge that no one would maintain integrity to God's sovereignty under test? The one Jehovah selected was his Firstborn, his only-begotten Son, Jesus. —John 3:16; Col. 1:15.

Jesus eagerly and humbly accepted this assignment, although it meant leaving the heavenly home he had shared with his Father longer than anyone else. (John 8:23, 58; Phil. 2:5-8) His motive? Deep love for Jehovah and a zealous desire to see His name cleared of all reproach. (John 14:31) Jesus also acted out of love for humankind. (Prov. 8:30, 31; compare John 15:13.) His birth on earth, in early autumn of the year 2 B.C.E., was made possible by holy spirit—by means of which Jehovah transferred Jesus' life from heaven to the womb of the Jewish virgin Mary. (Matt. 1:18; Luke 1:26-38) Jesus was thus born into the nation of Israel.—Gal. 4:4.

More than any other Israelite, Jesus knew that he had to be a witness of Jehovah. Why? He was a member of the nation to which Jehovah by the prophet Isaiah had said: "You are my witnesses." (Isa. 43:10) In addition to that, at Jesus' baptism in the Jordan River in 29 C.E., Jehovah anointed him with holy spirit. (Matt. 3:16) Thus Jesus was empowered, as he later testified, to "proclaim the year of goodwill on the part of Jehovah." —Isa. 61:1, 2; Luke 4:16-19.

Jesus faithfully carried out his assignment and became Jehovah's greatest witness ever on earth. With every right, then, the apostle John, who stood near Jesus at the time of his death, calls Jesus "the Faithful Witness." (Rev. 1:5) And at Revelation 3:14, the glorified Jesus calls himself "the

Amen" and "the faithful and true witness." What testimony did this "Faithful Witness" offer?

'Bearing Witness to the Truth'

When on trial before Roman governor Pilate, Jesus stated: "For this I have been born, and for this I have come into the world, that I should bear witness to the truth. Everyone that is on the side of the truth listens to my voice." (John 18:37) To what truth did Jesus bear witness? It was God's truth, the revelation of Jehovah's eternal purposes.—John 18:33-36.

How, though, did Jesus bear witness to this truth? The Greek verb for "bear witness to" also means "declare, confirm, testify favorably, speak well (of), approve (of)." In ancient Greek papyri, the common occurrence of another form of the verb (*mar·ty·ro'*) was after a signature, such as in business transactions. By his ministry, then, Jesus had to confirm God's truth. This certainly required that he declare, or preach, that truth to others. However, much more than talking was needed.

"I *am* . . . the truth," Jesus said. (John 14:6) Yes, he *lived* in such a way as to fulfill God's truth. God's purpose in connection with the Kingdom and its Messianic Ruler had been spelled out in prophecy. Jesus, by his entire earthly life course, which culminated in his sacrificial death, fulfilled all the things prophesied about him. He thus confirmed and guaranteed the truth of Jehovah's prophetic word. For this reason the apostle Paul could say: "No matter how many the promises of God are, they have become Yes by means of him. Therefore also through him is the 'Amen' [meaning, "so be it," or "surely"] said to God for glory through us." (2 Cor. 1:20) Yes, Jesus is the one in whom God's promises find fulfillment.—Rev. 3:14.

Bearing Witness to God's Name

Jesus taught his followers to pray: "Our Father in the heavens, let your name be sanctified [or, "be held sacred; be treated as holy"]." (Matt. 6:9, ftn.) On the final night of his earthly life, in prayer to his heavenly Father, Jesus also said: "I have made your name manifest to the men you gave me out of the world. They were yours, and you gave them to me, and they have observed your word. And I have made your name known to them and will make it known, in order that the love with which you loved me may be in them and I in union with them." (John 17:6, 26) This, in fact, was Jesus' primary purpose in coming to earth. What was involved in his making God's name known?

Jesus' followers already knew and used God's name. They saw and read it in the Hebrew Bible scrolls available in their synagogues. They also saw

'Born to bear witness to the truth'

and read it in the *Septuagint*—a Greek translation of the Hebrew Scriptures, which they used in teaching and writing. If they knew the divine name, in what sense did Jesus make it manifest, or known, to them?

In Bible times, names were not mere labels. Says *A Greek-English Lexicon of the New Testament,* by J. H. Thayer: "*The name of God* in the N[ew] T[estament] is used for all those qualities which to his worshippers are summed up in that name, and by which God makes himself known to men." Jesus made known God's name not just by using it but by revealing the Person behind the name—his purposes, activities, and qualities. As the one 'who had been in the bosom position with the Father,' Jesus could explain the Father in a way that no one else could. (John 1:18) Moreover, so perfectly did Jesus reflect his Father that Jesus' disciples could 'see' the Father in the Son. (John 14:9) By what he said and did, Jesus bore witness to God's name.

He Witnessed About God's Kingdom

As "the Faithful Witness," Jesus was outstandingly a proclaimer of God's Kingdom. He emphatically said: "I must declare the good news of the kingdom of God, because for this I was sent forth." (Luke 4:43) He proclaimed that heavenly Kingdom throughout Palestine, covering hundreds of miles on foot. He preached wherever there were people who would listen: at lakeshores, on hillsides, in cities and villages, in synagogues and the temple, in the marketplaces, and at the people's homes. But Jesus knew that there was a limit to the area he could cover and the number of people to whom he could witness. (Compare John 14:12.) So with a view to covering the world field, Jesus trained and sent out his disciples to be proclaimers of the Kingdom.—Matt. 10:5-7; 13:38; Luke 10:1, 8, 9.

Jesus was a hardworking, zealous witness, and he did not allow himself to be sidetracked. Although he showed personal concern for the needs of the people, he did not get so wrapped up in doing things that would bring short-term relief that he neglected his God-given assignment of pointing people to the lasting solution to their problems—God's Kingdom. On one occasion, after he miraculously fed about 5,000 men (perhaps well over 10,000 people counting also women and children), a group of Jews wanted to seize him and make him an earthly king. What did Jesus do? He "withdrew again into the mountain all alone." (John 6:1-15; compare Luke 19: 11, 12; Acts 1:6-9.) Although he performed many miracles of healing, Jesus was not primarily known as the Miracle Worker, but, rather, he was recognized by both believers and unbelievers as "Teacher."—Matt. 8:19; 9:11; 12:38; 19:16; 22:16, 24, 36; John 3:2.

Clearly, bearing witness to God's Kingdom was the most important work that Jesus could do. It is Jehovah's will that everyone know what His

Jesus made the Kingdom of God the theme of his preaching

Kingdom is and how it will fulfill His purposes. It is very dear to His heart, for it is the means by which He will sanctify His name, clearing it of all reproach. Jesus knew that, and so he made that Kingdom the theme of his preaching. (Matt. 4:17) By sharing wholeheartedly in proclaiming it, Jesus upheld Jehovah's rightful sovereignty.

A Witness Faithful Even to Death

No one could love Jehovah and His sovereignty more than Jesus does. As "the firstborn of all creation," Jesus 'fully knew' the Father from his intimate association with him as a spirit creature in the heavens. (Col. 1:15; Matt. 11:27) He had willingly subjected himself to God's sovereignty during countless ages of time prior to the creation of the first man and woman. (Compare John 8:29, 58.) How deeply hurt he must have felt when Adam and Eve turned their backs on God's sovereignty! Yet, he patiently waited in the heavens for some 4,000 years, and then, at last, the time arrived for him to serve as Jehovah's greatest witness ever on earth!

Jesus Christ was the greatest witness of Jehovah ever on earth

Jesus was fully aware that the universal issues directly involved him. It might have appeared that Jehovah had put a hedge about him. (Compare Job 1:9-11.) True, he had demonstrated his faithfulness and devotion in the heavens, but would he maintain integrity as a human on earth under any type of test? Could he resist Satan in a setting in which his enemy apparently had the upper hand?

The serpentlike Adversary wasted no time. Shortly after Jesus' baptism and anointing, Satan tempted him to display selfishness, to elevate himself, and, finally, to reject his Father's sovereignty. But Jesus' unequivocal statement to Satan, "It is Jehovah your God you must worship, and it is to him alone you must render sacred service," showed where he stood on the issues. How unlike Adam!—Matt. 4:1-10.

The course appointed for Jesus meant suffering and death, and Jesus well knew this. (Luke 12:50; Heb. 5:7-9) Nevertheless, "when he found himself in fashion as a man, he humbled himself and became obedient as far as death, yes, death on a torture stake." (Phil. 2:7, 8) Jesus thereby proved Satan a monstrous liar, completely settling the question, Will anyone maintain integrity to God's sovereignty if Satan is allowed to put him to the test? But Jesus' death accomplished much more.

By his death on the torture stake, Jesus also gave "his soul a ransom in exchange for many." (Matt. 20:28; Mark 10:45) His perfect human life had sacrificial value. Jesus' sacrificing his life not only makes it possible for us to receive forgiveness of sins but also opens to us the opportunity for eternal life on a paradise earth, in harmony with God's original purpose. —Luke 23:43; Acts 13:38, 39; Heb. 9:13, 14; Rev. 21:3, 4.

Jehovah proved his love for and approval of Jesus as "the Faithful

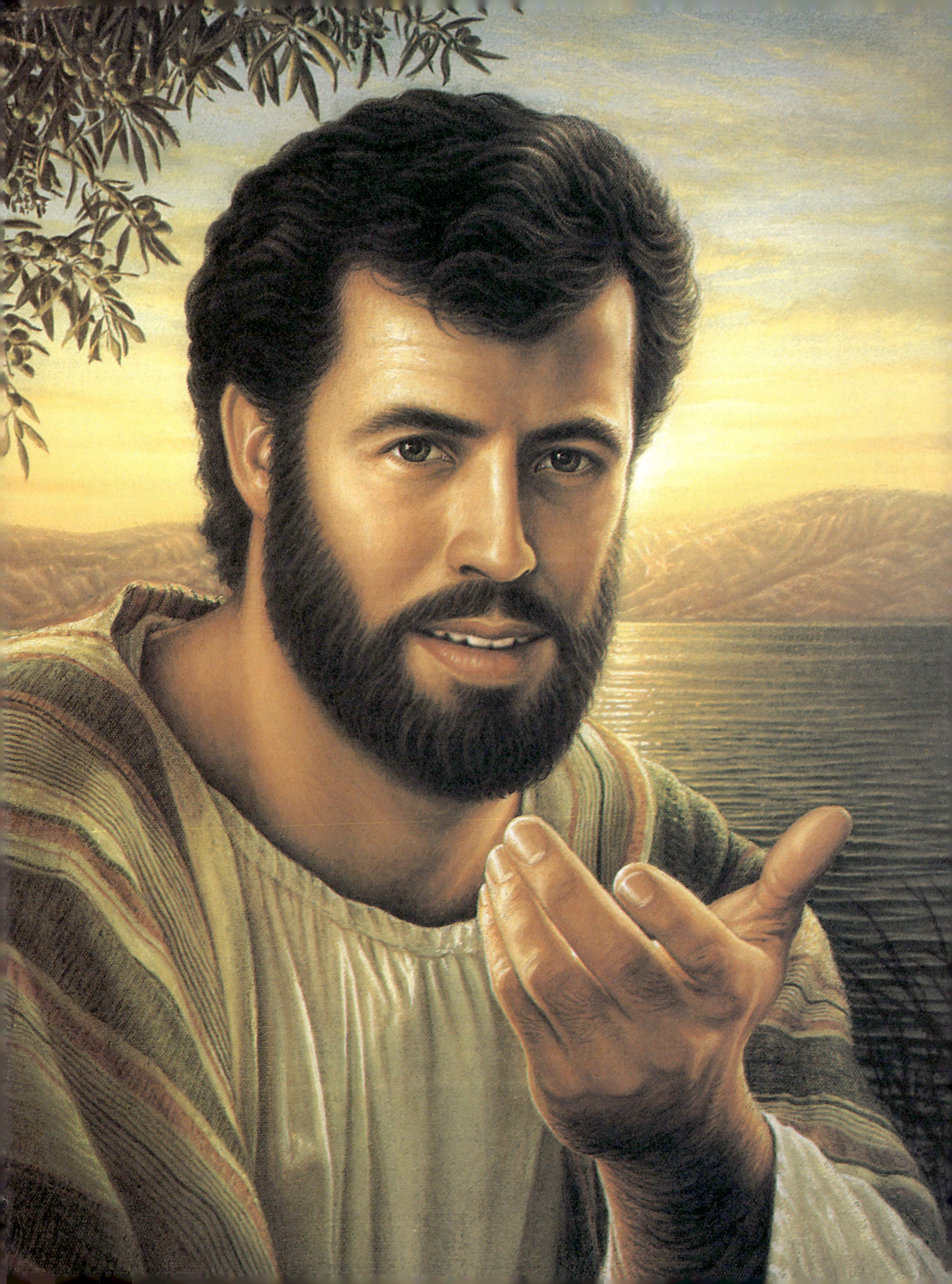

Witness" by raising him from the dead on the third day. This confirmed that the witness Jesus had given pertaining to the Kingdom was true. (Acts 2:31-36; 4:10; 10:36-43; 17:31) After remaining in the vicinity of the earth for 40 days, during which time he appeared to his apostles on numerous occasions, Jesus ascended to heaven.—Acts 1:1-3, 9.

Jesus had indicated that the establishment of the Messianic Kingdom of God would be in the far distant future. (Luke 19:11-27) That event would also mark the start of Jesus' "presence and of the conclusion of the system of things." (Matt. 24:3) But how could his followers on earth discern when these things would occur? Jesus gave them a "sign"

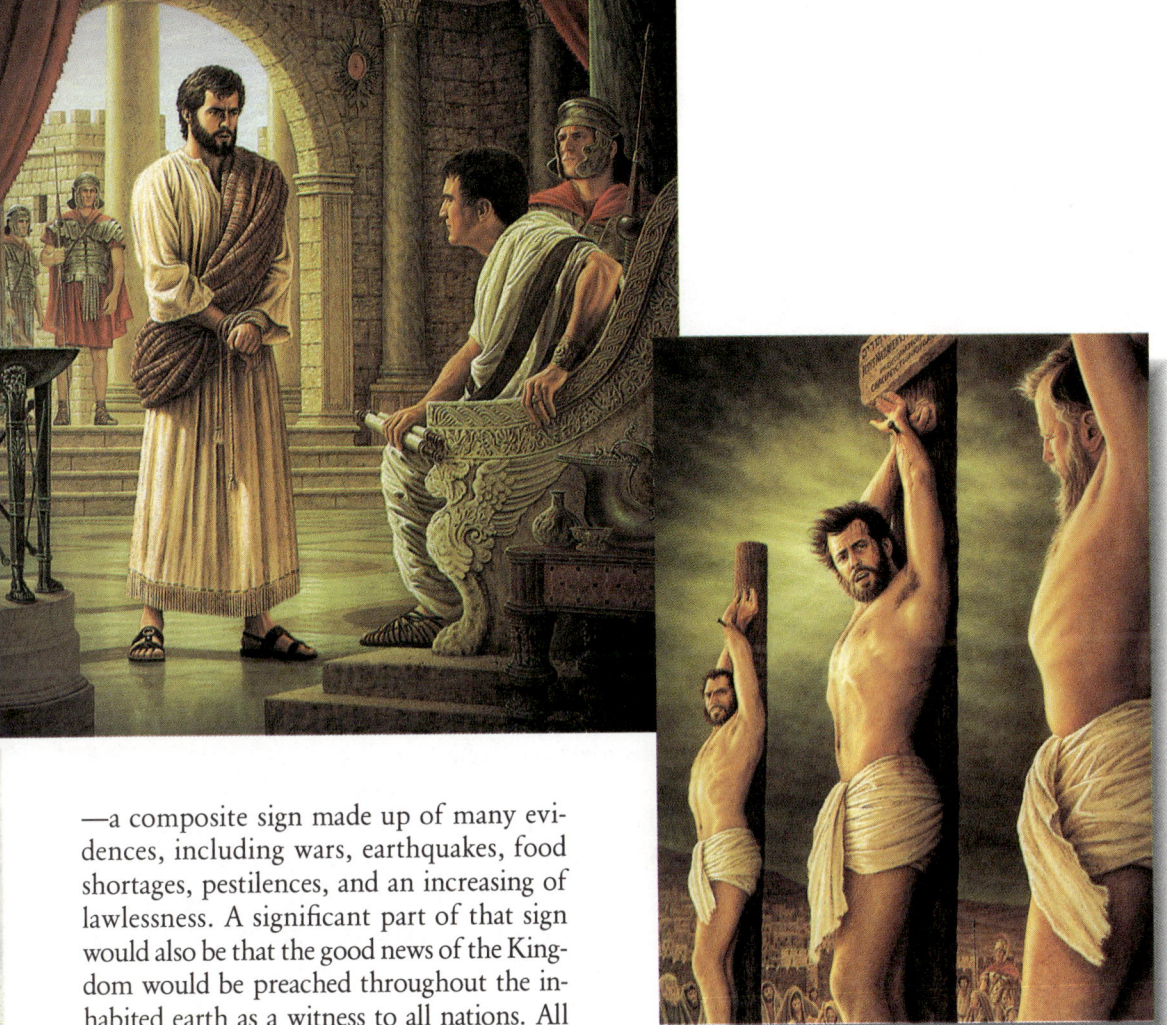

—a composite sign made up of many evidences, including wars, earthquakes, food shortages, pestilences, and an increasing of lawlessness. A significant part of that sign would also be that the good news of the Kingdom would be preached throughout the inhabited earth as a witness to all nations. All the features of that remarkable sign can be observed in our day, indicating that we are living in the time of Jesus' presence as heavenly King and of the conclusion of the system of things.*—Matt. 24:3-14.

What, though, about Jesus' followers? During this time of Jesus' presence, individuals adhering to many different churches claim to follow Christ. (Matt. 7:22) Yet, the Bible says there is but "one faith." (Eph. 4:5) So how can you identify the true Christian congregation, the one that has God's approval and direction? You can do so by examining what the Scriptures say about the first-century Christian congregation and then seeing who today follow that same pattern.

* See chapter 10, "A Bible Prophecy You Have Seen Fulfilled," in the book *The Bible—God's Word or Man's?* published by the Watchtower Bible and Tract Society of New York, Inc.

CHAPTER 3

CHRISTIAN WITNESSES OF JEHOVAH IN THE FIRST CENTURY

"YOU will be witnesses of me . . . to the most distant part of the earth." (Acts 1:8) With those parting words, Jesus commissioned his disciples to be witnesses. But witnesses of whom? "Witnesses of *me*," said Jesus. Do these words mean that they were not to be witnesses of Jehovah? Far from it!

Actually, Jesus' disciples were given an unprecedented privilege—that of being witnesses of *both* Jehovah and Jesus. As faithful Jews, Jesus' early disciples were already witnesses of Jehovah. (Isa. 43:10-12) But now they were to witness also concerning Jesus' vital role in sanctifying Jehovah's name by means of His Messianic Kingdom. Their thus bearing witness to Jesus was with Jehovah's glory in view. (Rom. 16:25-27; Phil. 2:9-11) They testified that Jehovah had not lied, that after more than 4,000 years he had at last raised up the long-promised Messiah, or Christ!

Christian witnesses of Jehovah in the first century were also given a unique responsibility—one that rests upon genuine Christians to this day.

"Go . . . Make Disciples"

After Jesus' resurrection from the dead, he appeared to his disciples who had gathered at a mountain in Galilee. There, Jesus outlined their responsibility: "Go therefore and make disciples of people of all the nations, baptizing them in the name of the Father and of the Son and of the holy spirit, teaching them to observe all the things I have commanded you. And, look! I am with you all the days until the conclusion of the system of things." (Matt. 28:19, 20) Consider what was involved in this weighty commission.

"Go," said Jesus. But to whom? To "people of all the nations." This was a new command, especially challenging for Jewish believers. (Compare Acts 10:9-16, 28.) Prior to Jesus' day, Gentiles were welcomed when *they* came to Israel because of interest in true worship. (1 Ki. 8:41-43) Earlier in his ministry, Jesus had told the apostles to "go, preach," but only to

New disciples were to be, not mere passive believers, but obedient followers

"the lost sheep of the house of Israel." (Matt. 10:1, 6, 7) Now they were commanded to go to people of *all* nations. For what purpose?

"Make disciples," commanded Jesus. Yes, his disciples were commissioned to make disciples of others. What does this involve? A disciple is a learner, a taught one—not just a pupil, however, but an adherent. A disciple accepts Jesus' authority not just *inwardly* by believing in him but *outwardly* by obeying him. According to the *Theological Dictionary of the New Testament,* the Greek word rendered "disciple" (*ma·the·tes'*) "implies the existence of a personal attachment which shapes the whole life of the one described as [a disciple]."

"Teaching them," added Jesus, "to observe all the things I have commanded you." To develop a personal attachment to Jesus, a person must be taught to "observe all the things" Christ has commanded, including his command to preach the "good news of the kingdom." (Matt. 24:14) Only in this way can he become a disciple in the true sense of the word. And only those who accept the teaching and become genuine disciples get baptized.

"I am with you," Jesus assured them, "all the days until the conclusion of the system of things." Jesus' teaching is always relevant, never outmoded. On that basis, Christians to this very day are under obligation to make disciples of others.

A responsible commission was thus conferred upon Christ's followers, namely, to do a disciple-making work among all nations. To make disciples of Christ, though, they had to witness concerning Jehovah's name and Kingdom, for that is what their Exemplar, Jesus, had done. (Luke 4:43; John 17:26) Those who accepted Christ's teaching and became disciples thus became Christian witnesses of Jehovah. Becoming a witness of Jehovah was a matter no longer of birth—into the Jewish nation—but of choice. Those who became witnesses did so because they loved Jehovah and sincerely wanted to submit to his sovereign rule.—1 John 5:3.

But did the Christian witnesses of Jehovah in the first century fulfill their commission to serve as witnesses of God and Christ and to 'make disciples of people of all nations'?

"To the Most Distant Part of the Earth"

Shortly after giving his disciples their commission, Jesus returned to the heavenly courts of his Father. (Acts 1:9-11) Ten days later, on the day of

Becoming a witness of Jehovah was a matter no longer of birth but of choice

---

Christianity Spread Through Zealous Preaching

Fired by a zeal that could not be quenched, the early Christian witnesses of Jehovah exercised the greatest vigor in giving the good news the widest possible proclamation. Edward Gibbon, in "The Decline and Fall of the Roman Empire," notes that the "zeal of the Christians . . . diffused them through every province and almost every city of the [Roman] empire." Says Professor J. W. Thompson in "History of the Middle Ages": "Christianity had spread with remarkable rapidity over the Roman world. By the year 100 probably every province that bordered the Mediterranean had a Christian community within it."

Pentecost 33 C.E., the extensive disciple-making work got under way. Jesus poured out the promised holy spirit upon his waiting disciples. (Acts 2: 1-4; compare Luke 24:49 and Acts 1:4, 5.) This filled them with zeal to preach about the resurrected Christ and his future return with Kingdom power.

True to Jesus' instructions, those first-century disciples started their testifying about God and Christ right there in Jerusalem. (Acts 1:8) Taking the lead, at the Festival of Pentecost, the apostle Peter "bore thorough witness" to thousands of Jewish celebrators from many nations. (Acts 2: 5-11, 40) Soon the number of believing men alone was about 5,000. (Acts 4:4; 6:7) Later, to the Samaritans, Philip declared "the good news of the kingdom of God and of the name of Jesus Christ."—Acts 8:12.

By the end of the first century, the Christian witnesses of Jehovah had made disciples in Asia, Europe, and Africa!

But there was much more work to be done. Starting in 36 C.E., with the conversion of Cornelius, an uncircumcised Gentile, the good news began to spread to non-Jewish people of all nations. (Acts, chap. 10) In fact, so rapidly did it spread that by about 60 C.E., the apostle Paul could say that the good news had been "preached in all creation that is under heaven." (Col. 1:23) Thus, by the end of the first century, Jesus' faithful followers had made disciples throughout the Roman Empire—in Asia, Europe, and Africa!

Since the Christian witnesses of Jehovah in the first century accomplished so much in such a short time, the questions arise: Were they organized? If so, how?

Organization of the Christian Congregation

From the time of Moses onward, the Jewish nation was in a unique position—it served as the congregation of God. That congregation was highly organized by God under older men, heads, judges, and officers. (Josh. 23:1, 2) But the Jewish nation lost its privileged position because it rejected Jehovah's Son. (Matt. 21:42, 43; 23:37, 38; Acts 4:24-28) On Pentecost 33 C.E., the Christian congregation of God replaced the congregation of Israel.* How was this Christian congregation organized?

Already on the day of Pentecost, the disciples were "devoting themselves to the teaching of the apostles," indicating that they began with a unity based on teaching. From that first day, they met together "with one accord." (Acts 2:42, 46) As the disciple-making work spread, congregations of believers began to form, first in Jerusalem and then outside Jerusalem. (Acts 8:1; 9:31; 11:19-21; 14:21-23) It was their custom to assemble together in public places as well as in private homes.—Acts 19:8, 9; Rom. 16:3, 5; Col. 4:15.

---

* In the Christian Greek Scriptures, "congregation" is at times used in a collective sense, referring to the Christian congregation in general (1 Cor. 12:28); it may also refer to a local group in some city or in someone's home.—Acts 8:1; Rom. 16:5.

What kept the expanding Christian congregation from becoming a loose association of independent local congregations? They were united under one Leader. From the beginning, Jesus Christ was the appointed Lord and Head of the congregation, and he was recognized as such by all the congregations. (Acts 2:34-36; Eph. 1:22) From the heavens, Christ actively directed the affairs of his congregation on earth. How? By means of holy spirit and angels, put at his disposal by Jehovah.—Acts 2:33; compare Acts 5:19, 20; 8:26; 1 Pet. 3:22.

Christ had something else at his disposal for maintaining the unity of the Christian congregation—a visible governing body. At first, the governing body was made up of the faithful apostles of Jesus. Later, it included other older men of the Jerusalem congregation as well as the apostle Paul, even though he did not reside in Jerusalem. Each congregation recognized the authority of this central body of older men and looked to it for direction when organizational or doctrinal issues arose. (Acts 2:42; 6:1-6; 8:14-17; 11:22; 15:1-31) With what result? "Therefore, indeed, the congregations continued to be made firm in the faith and to increase in number from day to day."—Acts 16:4, 5.

The governing body, under the direction of holy spirit, supervised the appointment of overseers and assistants, ministerial servants, to care for each congregation. These were men who met spiritual qualifications that applied in all the congregations, not merely standards set locally. (1 Tim. 3:1-13; Titus 1:5-9; 1 Pet. 5:1-3) Overseers were urged to follow the Scriptures and submit to the leading of holy spirit. (Acts 20:28; Titus 1:9) All in the congregation were encouraged to 'be obedient to those taking the lead.' (Heb. 13:17) In this way unity was maintained not only within each congregation but within the Christian congregation as a whole.

There was no clergy-laity distinction among the first-century Christians

Even though some men held positions of responsibility, there was no clergy-laity distinction among the first-century Christian witnesses of Jehovah. They were all brothers; there was but one Leader, the Christ. —Matt. 23:8, 10.

Identified by Holy Conduct and Love

The testimony of the first-century witnesses of Jehovah was not limited to "the fruit of lips." (Heb. 13:15) Discipleship shaped the entire life of a Christian witness. Hence, not only did those Christians proclaim their beliefs but their beliefs transformed their lives. They put away the old personality with its sinful practices and endeavored to clothe themselves with the new personality created according to God's will. (Col. 3:5-10) They were truthful and honest, as well as hardworking and dependable. (Eph. 4:25, 28) They were morally clean—sexual immorality was strictly prohibited. So were drunkenness and idolatry. (Gal. 5:19-21) For good reason, then, Christianity became known as "The Way," a way or manner of life that centered around faith in Jesus, following closely in his footsteps.—Acts 9:1, 2; 1 Pet. 2:21, 22.

One quality, though, stands out above all others—*love*. The early Christians demonstrated loving concern for the needs of fellow believers. (Rom. 15:26; Gal. 2:10) They loved one another not *as* themselves but *more than* themselves. (Compare Philippians 2:25-30.) They were willing even to die for one another. But this was not surprising. Was not Jesus willing to die for them? (John 15:13; compare Luke 6:40.) He could tell his disciples: "I am giving you a new commandment, that you love one another; just as I have loved you, that you also love one another. By this all will know that you are my disciples, if you have love among yourselves." (John 13:34, 35) Christ commanded that his followers show such self-sacrificing love; and this command his first-century disciples closely observed.—Matt. 28:20.

"No Part of the World"

To fulfill their responsibility to make disciples and to be witnesses of God and Christ, first-century Christians could not allow themselves to be distracted by worldly affairs; they had to keep their commission in clear focus. Jesus certainly had done so. To Pilate he said: "My kingdom is no part of this world." (John 18:36) And to his disciples he plainly stated: "You are no part of the world." (John 15:19) Like Jesus, then, the early Christians kept separate from the world; they did not get involved in politics or wars. (Compare John 6:15.) Neither did they get caught up in the ways of the world—its eager pursuit of material things and its overindulgence in pleasure.—Luke 12:29-31; Rom. 12:2; 1 Pet. 4:3, 4.

Because they kept separate from the world, the first-century Christian witnesses were a distinctive people. Notes historian E. G. Hardy in his book *Christianity and the Roman Government:* "The Christians were strangers and pilgrims in the world around them; their citizenship was in heaven; the kingdom to which they looked was not of this world. The consequent want of interest in public affairs came thus from the outset to be a noticeable feature in Christianity."

Persecuted for Righteousness' Sake

"A slave is not greater than his master," warned Jesus. "If they have persecuted me, they will persecute you also." (John 15:20) Before his death on the torture stake, Jesus suffered severe persecution. (Matt. 26:67; 27:26-31, 38-44) And true to his warning,

---

'The Triumphs of Christianity'

Extra-Biblical sources confirm the fine conduct and love that characterized the early Christians. Historian John Lord stated: "The true triumphs of Christianity were seen in making good men of those who professed her doctrines.... We have testimony to their blameless lives, to their irreproachable morals, to their good citizenship, and to their Christian graces."—"The Old Roman World."

his disciples soon experienced similar treatment. (Matt. 10:22, 23) But why?

It did not take long for the early Christians to be noticed by others. They were people with high principles of morality and integrity. They carried out a disciple-making work with outspokenness and zeal; as a result, literally thousands of persons abandoned false religious systems and became Christians. These refused to get involved in worldly affairs. They would not join in worship of the emperor. It is not surprising, then, that they quickly became the target of vicious persecution instigated by false religious leaders and misinformed political rulers. (Acts 12:1-5; 13:45, 50; 14:1-7; 16:19-24) These, though, were only the human agents of the real persecutor—"the original serpent," Satan. (Rev. 12:9; compare Revelation 12:12, 17.) His objective? The suppression of Christianity and its bold witnessing.

But no amount of persecution could shut the mouths of the first-century Christian witnesses of Jehovah! They had received their commission to preach from God through Christ, and they were determined to obey God rather than men. (Acts 4:19, 20, 29; 5:27-32) They relied on

A central governing body helped to provide direction for the congregations, but they all looked to Christ as their one Leader

Jehovah's strength, confident that he would reward his loyal witnesses for their endurance.—Matt. 5:10; Rom. 8:35-39; 15:5.

History confirms that persecution by authorities of the Roman Empire failed to stamp out the early Christian witnesses of Jehovah. Says Josephus, a Jewish historian of the first century C.E.: "And the tribe of the Christians, so called after [Jesus], has still to this day [about 93 C.E.] not disappeared."—*Jewish Antiquities*, XVIII, 64 (iii, 3).

The record of the testimony of the Christian witnesses of Jehovah in the first century thus reveals several clearly identifiable characteristics: They boldly and zealously fulfilled their commission to witness concerning God and Christ and to do a disciple-making work; they had an organizational structure in which all were brothers, with no clergy-laity distinction; they held to high principles of morality and loved one another; they kept separate from worldly ways and affairs; and they were persecuted for righteousness' sake.

By the end of the first century, though, the one united Christian congregation was threatened by a grave and insidious danger.

Early Christians were the target of vicious persecution

CHAPTER 4

THE GREAT APOSTASY DEVELOPS

"ONE Lord, one faith." (Eph. 4:5) When the apostle Paul under inspiration penned those words (about 60-61 C.E.), there was but one Christian faith. Yet, today we see a profusion of denominations, sects, and cults that claim to be Christian, though they teach conflicting doctrines and hold to different standards of conduct. What a far cry from the one united Christian congregation that started on Pentecost 33 C.E.! How did these divisions come about? For the answer, we must go back to the first century of our Common Era.

From the very beginning, the Adversary, Satan, tried to silence the testimony of the Christian witnesses of Jehovah by bringing upon them persecution from those outside the congregation. (1 Pet. 5:8) First it came from the Jews and then from the Gentile Roman Empire. The early Christians successfully endured all manner of opposition. (Compare Revelation 1:9; 2:3, 19.) But the Adversary did not give up. If he could not silence them by pressure from those on the outside, why not corrupt them *from within*? While the Christian congregation was still in its infancy, its very existence was threatened by an internal enemy—apostasy.*

Apostasy, however, did not creep into the congregation unannounced. As Head of the congregation, Christ saw to it that his followers were warned in advance.—Col. 1:18.

"There Will . . . Be False Teachers Among You"

"Be on the watch," cautioned Jesus, "for the false prophets that come to you in sheep's covering." (Matt. 7:15) Jesus knew that Satan would try to divide and corrupt His followers. So from early in his ministry, he warned them about false teachers.

From where would these false teachers come? "From among you yourselves," said the apostle Paul about 56 C.E., when speaking to overseers of Ephesus. Yes, from within the congregation, men would "rise and speak

While still in its infancy, the Christian congregation was threatened by apostasy

---

* In the Christian Greek Scriptures, the noun "apostasy" (Gr., *a·po·sta·si'a*) has the sense of "desertion, abandonment or rebellion." (Acts 21:21, ftn.) There it primarily has reference to *religious* defection; a withdrawal from or abandonment of true worship.

twisted things to draw away the disciples after themselves." (Acts 20: 29, 30) Such self-seeking apostates would not be content to make their *own* disciples; they would endeavor "to draw away *the* disciples," that is, Christ's disciples.

The apostle Peter (about 64 C.E.) also foretold internal corruption and even described the way such apostates would operate: "There will . . . be false teachers among you. These very ones will quietly bring in destructive sects . . . With covetousness they will exploit you with counterfeit words." (2 Pet. 2:1, 3) Like spies or traitors in an enemy's camp, the false teachers, though arising from within the congregation, would infiltrate their corrupting views in a secret or camouflaged way.

These warnings of Jesus and his apostles were not in vain. Internal opposition had small beginnings, but it surfaced early in the Christian congregation.

"Already at Work"

Less than 20 years after Jesus' death, the apostle Paul indicated that efforts of Satan to cause division and turn men away from the true faith were "already at work." (2 Thess. 2:7) As early as about 49 C.E., in a letter sent out to the congregations, the governing body noted: "We have heard that some from among us have caused you trouble with speeches, trying to subvert your souls, although we did not give them any instructions." (Acts 15:24) So some *within* the congregation were vocal about their opposing viewpoint—in this case evidently over the issue of whether Gentile Christians needed to get circumcised and observe the Mosaic Law.—Acts 15:1, 5.

As the first century progressed, divisive thinking spread like gangrene. (Compare 2 Timothy 2:17.) By about 51 C.E., some in Thessalonica were wrongly predicting that "the presence" of the Lord Jesus was imminent. (2 Thess. 2:1, 2) By about 55 C.E., some in Corinth had rejected the clear Christian teaching regarding the resurrection of the dead. (1 Cor. 15:12) About 65 C.E., others said that the resurrection had already taken place, it being of a symbolic kind that living Christians experience.—2 Tim. 2: 16-18.

There are no inspired records as to what took place within the Christian congregation during the next 30 years. But by the time the apostle John wrote his letters (about 98 C.E.), there were "many antichrists" —persons who denied that "Jesus is the Christ" and that Jesus is the Son of God who came "in the flesh."—1 John 2:18, 22; 4:2, 3.

For over 60 years, the apostles had 'acted as a restraint,' endeavoring to hold back the tide of apostasy. (2 Thess. 2:7; compare 2 John 9, 10.)

Internal opposition had small beginnings

But as the Christian congregation was about to enter the second century, the last surviving apostle, John, died, about 100 C.E. The apostasy that had slowly begun to creep into the congregation was now ready to burst forth unrestrained, with devastating organizational and doctrinal repercussions.

Clergy and Laity

"All you are brothers," Jesus had said to his disciples. "Your Leader is one, the Christ." (Matt. 23:8, 10) So there was no clergy class within Christian congregations of the first century. As spirit-anointed brothers of Christ, all the early Christians had the prospect of being heavenly priests with Christ. (1 Pet. 1:3, 4; 2:5, 9) As to organization, each congregation was supervised by a body of overseers, or spiritual elders.* All the elders had equal authority, and not one of them was authorized to 'lord it over' the flock in their care. (Acts 20:17; Phil. 1:1; 1 Pet. 5:2, 3) However, as the apostasy unfolded, things began to change—quickly.

Among the earliest deviations was a separation between the terms "overseer" (Gr., *e·pi'sko·pos*) and "older man," or "elder" (Gr., *pres·by'te·ros*), so that they were no longer used to refer to the same position of responsibility. Just a decade or so after the death of the apostle John, Ignatius, "bishop" of Antioch, in his letter to the Smyrnaeans, wrote: "See that you all follow the bishop [overseer], as Jesus Christ follows the Father, and the presbytery [body of older men] as if it were the Apostles." Ignatius thus advocated that each congregation be supervised by one bishop,# or overseer, who was to be recognized as distinct from, and having greater authority than, the presbyters, or older men.

How, though, did this separation come about? Augustus Neander, in his book *The History of the Christian Religion and Church, During the Three First Centuries,* explains what happened: "In the second century . . . , the standing office of president of the presbyters must have been formed, to whom, inasmuch as he had especially the oversight of every thing, was the name of [*e·pi'sko·pos*] given, and he was thereby distinguished from the rest of the presbyters."

The groundwork was thus laid for a clergy class gradually to emerge. About a century later, Cyprian, "bishop" of Carthage, North Africa, was a strong advocate of authority of the bishops—as a group separate from

Cyprian, "bishop" of Carthage, saw the bishops as being a class separate from the presbyters, the deacons, and the laity

---

* In the Scriptures the terms "overseer" and "older man," or "elder," refer to the same position. (Acts 20:17, 28; Titus 1:5, 7) "Older man" indicates the mature qualities of the one so appointed, and "overseer" the responsibility inherent in the appointment—watching over the interests of those persons entrusted to one's care.

The English word "bishop" derives from the Greek term *e·pi'sko·pos* ("overseer") as follows: from Middle English *bisshop,* from Old English *biscop,* from Vulgar Latin *biscopus,* variant of Late Latin *episcopus,* from Greek *e·pi'sko·pos.*

the presbyters (later known as priests*), the deacons, and the laity. But he did not favor the primacy of one bishop over the others.#

As bishops and presbyters ascended the hierarchical ladder, they left below it the rest of the believers in the congregation. This resulted in a separation between clergy (those taking the lead) and laity (the passive body of believers). Explains McClintock and Strong's *Cyclopedia*: "From the time of Cyprian [who died about 258 C.E.], the father of the hierarchical system, the distinction of clergy and laity became prominent, and very soon was universally admitted. Indeed, from the third century onward, the term *clerus* . . . was almost exclusively applied to the ministry to distinguish it from the laity. As the Roman hierarchy was developed, the clergy came to be not merely a distinct order . . . but also to be recognised as the only priesthood."

Thus, within 150 years or so of the death of the last of the apostles, two significant organizational changes found their way into the congregation: first, the separation between the bishop and the presbyters, with the bishop occupying the top rung of the hierarchical ladder; second, the separation between the clergy and the laity. Instead of all spirit-begotten believers forming "a royal priesthood," the clergy were now "recognised as the only priesthood."△—1 Pet. 2:9.

Plato and "Christianity"

The Greek philosopher Plato (born about 428 B.C.E.) had no way of knowing that his teachings would eventually find their way into apostate Christianity. Plato's principal contributions to "Christianity" were in connection with the teachings of the Trinity and the immortality of the soul.

Plato's ideas about God and nature influenced Christendom's Trinity doctrine. Explains the "Nouveau Dictionnaire Universel": "The Platonic trinity, itself merely a rearrangement of older trinities dating back to earlier peoples, appears to be the rational philosophic trinity of attributes that gave birth to the three hypostases or divine persons taught by the Christian churches. . . . This Greek philosopher's conception of the divine trinity . . . can be found in all the ancient [pagan] religions."—Volume 2, page 1467.

Regarding the immortal-soul doctrine, the "New Catholic Encyclopedia" says: "The Christian concept of a spiritual soul created by God and infused into the body at conception to make man a living whole is the fruit of a long development in Christian philosophy. Only with Origen [died about 254 C.E.] in the East and St. Augustine [died 430 C.E.] in the West was the soul established as a spiritual substance and a philosophical concept formed of its nature. . . . [Augustine's] doctrine . . . owed much (including some shortcomings) to Neoplatonism."—Volume XIII, pages 452, 454.

---

* The English word "priest" derives from *pre-sby′te-ros* ("older man," or "elder") as follows: from Middle English *pre(e)st*, from Old English *prēost*, from Vulgar Latin *prester*, contracted from Late Latin *presbyter*, from Greek *pre-sby′te-ros*.

\# In time the bishop of Rome, claiming to be a successor of Peter, was thought of as the supreme bishop and pope.—See *Mankind's Search for God*, published by the Watchtower Bible and Tract Society of New York, Inc., 1990, pages 270-2.

△ Interestingly, Dr. Neander observes: "The false conclusion was drawn, that as there had been in the Old Testament a visible priesthood joined to a particular class of men, there must also be the same in the New [Testament] . . . The false comparison of the Christian priesthood with the Jewish furthered again the rise of episcopacy above the office of presbyters."—*The History of the Christian Religion and Church*, translated by Henry John Rose, Second Edition, New York, 1848, p. 111.

The Great Apostasy Develops

Such changes marked a defection from the Scriptural method of governing the congregations in apostolic days. Organizational changes, though, were not the only consequences of the apostasy.

Pagan Teachings Infiltrate

Christ's pure teachings are a matter of record—they are preserved in the Holy Scriptures. For example, Jesus clearly taught that Jehovah is "the only true God" and that the human soul is mortal. (John 17:3; Matt. 10:28) Yet, with the death of the apostles and the weakening of the organizational structure, such clear teachings were corrupted as pagan doctrines infiltrated Christianity. How could such a thing happen?

A key factor was the subtle influence of Greek philosophy. Explains *The New Encyclopædia Britannica:* "From the middle of the 2nd century AD Christians who had some training in Greek philosophy began to feel the need to express their faith in its terms, both for their own intellectual satisfaction and in order to convert educated pagans." Once philosophically minded persons became Christians, it did not take long for Greek philosophy and "Christianity" to become inseparably linked.

As a result of this union, pagan doctrines such as the Trinity and the immortality of the soul seeped into tainted Christianity. These teachings, however, go back much farther than the Greek philosophers. The Greeks actually acquired them from older cultures, for there is evidence of such teachings in ancient Egyptian and Babylonian religions.

As pagan doctrines continued to infiltrate Christianity, other Scriptural teachings were also distorted or abandoned.

Kingdom Hope Fades

Jesus' disciples were well aware that they had to keep on the watch for Jesus' promised "presence" and the coming of his Kingdom. In time, it was appreciated that this Kingdom will rule over the earth for a thousand years and transform it into a paradise. (Matt. 24:3; 2 Tim. 4:18; Rev. 20:4, 6) The Christian Bible writers exhorted first-century witnesses to keep spiritually awake and to keep separate from the world. (Jas. 1:27; 4:4; 5:7, 8; 1 Pet. 4:7) But once the apostles died, Christian expectation of Christ's presence and the coming of his Kingdom faded. Why?

One factor was the spiritual contamination caused by the Greek doctrine of the immortality of the soul. As it took hold among Christians, the millennial hope was gradually abandoned. Why? *The New International Dictionary of New Testament Theology* explains: "The doctrine of the immortality of the soul came in to take the place of NT [New Testament]

Not only did apostates transfer millennial blessings from earth to heaven but they shifted the Kingdom from heaven to earth eschatology [the teaching on the "Last Things"] with its hope of the resurrection of the dead and the new creation (Rev. 21 f.), so that the soul receives judgment after death and attains to paradise now thought of as other-worldly." In other words, apostate Christians thought that the soul survived the body at death and that the blessings of Christ's Millennial Reign must therefore relate to the spirit realm. They thus transferred Paradise from earth to heaven, which, they believed, the saved soul attains at death. There was, then, no need to watch for Christ's presence and the coming of his Kingdom, since at death they all hoped to join Christ in heaven.*

Another factor, though, actually made it seem to be pointless to watch for the *coming* of Christ's Kingdom. *The New Encyclopædia Britannica* explains: "The [apparent] delay of the Parousia resulted in a weakening of the imminent expectation in the early church. In this process of 'de-eschatologizing' [weakening of the teaching on the "Last Things"], *the institutional church increasingly replaced the expected Kingdom of God.* The formation of the Catholic Church as a hierarchical institution is directly connected with the declining of the imminent expectation." (Italics ours.) So not only were millennial blessings transferred from earth to heaven but the Kingdom was shifted from heaven to earth. This "relocation" was completed by Augustine of Hippo (354-430 C.E.). In his famous work *The City of God,* he stated: "The Church even now is the kingdom of Christ, and the kingdom of heaven."

Meanwhile, in about 313 C.E., during the rule of Roman Emperor Constantine, legal recognition was given to Christianity, much of which by this time had become apostate in its thinking. Religious leaders were willing to be put into the service of the State, and at first the State controlled religious affairs. (Before long, religion would control State affairs.) Thus began Christendom,# part of which (the Catholic religion) in time became the official State religion of Rome. Now, the "kingdom" not only was *in* the world but was *part* of the world. What a far cry from the Kingdom that Christ preached!—John 18:36.

The Reformation—A Return to True Worship?

Like weeds flourishing in among strangled wheat, the Church of Rome, under its papal ruler, dominated worldly affairs for centuries.

"The Church even now is the kingdom of Christ, and the kingdom of heaven" (*Augustine of Hippo*)

---

* This view mistakenly presumes that at death all Christians go to heaven. However, the Bible teaches that only 144,000 persons are called to rule with Christ in heaven. (Rev. 7:4-8; 20:4-6) Countless others can have the hope of everlasting life on a paradise earth under Christ's Kingdom. —Matt. 6:10; Rev. 7:9, 15.

\# As used in this publication, the term "Christendom" refers to professed Christianity, in contrast with the true Christianity of the Bible.

Martin Luther

John Calvin

Ulrich Zwingli

Reformers who attacked the church on various issues

(Matt. 13:24-30, 37-43) As it became more and more a part of the world, the church grew further and further away from first-century Christianity. Through the centuries "heretical" sects called for reforms within the church, but the church continued to abuse power and amass wealth. Then, in the 16th century, the Protestant Reformation, a religious revolt, burst forth in all its fury.

Reformers such as Martin Luther (1483-1546), Ulrich Zwingli (1484-1531), and John Calvin (1509-64) attacked the church on various issues: Luther on the sale of indulgences, Zwingli on clerical celibacy and Mariolatry, and Calvin on the need for the church to return to the original principles of Christianity. What did such efforts accomplish?

To be sure, the Reformation accomplished some good things, most notably the translation of the Bible into languages of the common people. The free spirit of the Reformation led to more objective Bible research and an increased understanding of Bible languages. The Reformation did not, however, mark a return to true worship and doctrine.* Why not?

The effects of the apostasy had penetrated deep, to the very foundations of Christendom. Thus, although various Protestant groups broke free from the papal authority of Rome, they carried over some of the basic flaws of the Roman Catholic Church, features that resulted from the

---

* For a fuller discussion of the Reformation and what it accomplished, see chapter 13, "The Reformation—The Search Took a New Turn," in the book *Mankind's Search for God*.

abandonment of true Christianity. For example, although the governing of the Protestant churches varied somewhat, the basic division of the church into a dominating clergy class and a subjugated laity was retained. Also retained were unscriptural doctrines such as the Trinity, the immortal soul, and eternal torment after death. And like the Roman Church, the Protestant churches continued to be part of the world, being closely involved with the political systems and the elite ruling classes.

Meanwhile, what about Christian expectation—watching for Jesus' presence and the coming of his Kingdom? For centuries after the Reformation, the churches—both Catholic and Protestant—were deeply committed to secular power and tended to push off expectations of the coming of Christ's Kingdom.

Stirrings of Watchfulness

In the 19th century, though, the religious climate led to stirrings of Christian watchfulness. As a result of Bible research on the part of some clergymen and Bible scholars, such teachings as the immortal soul, eternal torment after death, predestination, and the Trinity were restudied. In addition, some students of the Bible were closely examining Bible prophecies pertaining to the last days. Consequently, various groups of persons began thinking seriously about the Lord's promised return.—Matt. 24:3.

In the United States, William Miller predicted the return of Christ in visible form in 1843 or 1844. The German theologian J. A. Bengel set the date for 1836; the Irvingites in England looked first to 1835, then 1838, 1864, and 1866. There was a Mennonite group in Russia that looked first to 1889, then to 1891.

Such efforts to keep on the watch served to awaken many to the prospect of our Lord's return. However, these efforts at Christian watchfulness ended up in disappointment. Why? For the most part, because they relied too much on men and not enough on the Scriptures. After a few decades, most of those groups faded out of existence.

Meanwhile, during this period other developments had an impact on human hopes and expectations.

An Age of "Enlightenment" and Industrialization

In 1848, Karl Marx and Friedrich Engels published *The Communist Manifesto*. Instead of advocating religion, which Marx called "the opium of the people,"

Karl Marx's "Communist Manifesto" actually fostered worship of the State. Charles Darwin's "Origin of Species" deeply influenced the scientific and religious thinking of the time

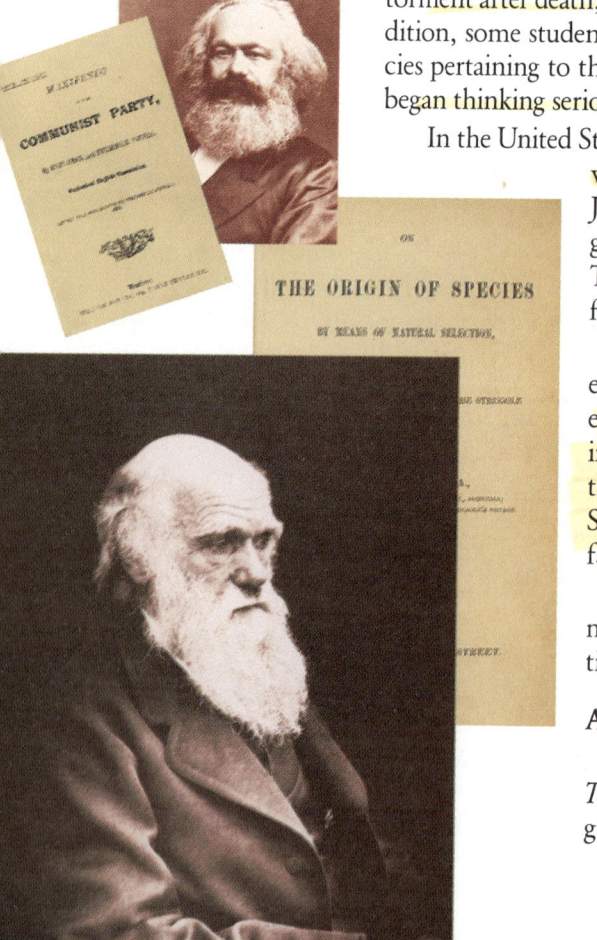

The steam locomotive

The electric light

The first telephone

Early Linotype

they advocated atheism. While ostensibly against all religion, they actually fostered the religion, or worship, of the State and its leaders.

About a decade later, in 1859, Charles Darwin's *Origin of Species* was published; it deeply influenced the scientific and religious thinking of the time. The theories of evolution led to a challenging of the truthfulness of the Bible's account of creation and of the introduction of sin through the disobedience of the first human pair. (Gen., chaps. 1-3) As a result, faith of many in the Bible was undermined.

The phonograph

Meanwhile, the industrial revolution was under way and gaining momentum. Emphasis switched from agriculture to industry and machine manufacture. The development of the steam locomotive (early 19th century) was leading to expansion of countrywide railroads. The latter half of the 19th century saw the invention of the telephone (1876), the phonograph (1877), the electric light (1878-79), as well as use of the Linotype in producing lines of type for printing (1884).

Mankind was entering a period of the greatest development of rapid transportation and communication in history. Although these benefits would be used to advance commercial and political ends, they would also be available to the religious field. The stage was thus set for a modest initiative by a small group of Bible students that would have worldwide effects.

CHAPTER 5

PROCLAIMING THE LORD'S RETURN (1870-1914)

"The following history is given not merely because I have been urged to give a review of God's leadings in the path of light, but specially because I believe it to be needful that the truth be modestly told, that misapprehensions and prejudicial misstatements may be disarmed, and that our readers may see how hitherto the Lord has helped and guided."*

FOLLOWING those words Charles Taze Russell proceeded to outline the developments that led to his publishing *Millennial Dawn* (later called *Studies in the Scriptures*) and *Zion's Watch Tower and Herald of Christ's Presence* (now known as *The Watchtower Announcing Jehovah's Kingdom*). This history is of special interest to Jehovah's Witnesses. Why? Because their present understanding of Bible truths and their activities can be traced back to the 1870's and the work of C. T. Russell and his associates, and from there to the Bible and early Christianity.

Who was Charles Taze Russell? Does the history of his work give evidence of the Lord's help and guidance?

A Search for Truth

C. T. Russell was born in the United States, in Allegheny (now part of Pittsburgh), Pennsylvania, on February 16, 1852. He was the second son of Joseph L. and Ann Eliza (Birney) Russell, who were Presbyterians of Scottish-Irish descent. Charles' mother died when he was only nine years old, but from an early age, Charles was influenced by both of his religiously-minded parents. As a later associate of C. T. Russell put it, "they trained the small twig; and it grew in the direction of the Lord." Although brought up as a

Charles Taze Russell

---
* The *Watch Tower*, July 15, 1906, p. 229.

Presbyterian, Charles eventually joined the Congregational Church because he preferred its views.

Young Charles was evidently quite a businessman. At just 11 years of age, he became a partner with his father in a thriving men's clothing store. Charles enlarged the business, eventually operating a number of different stores himself. Although things went well for him in business, spiritually he was very troubled. Why was this?

Charles' parents sincerely believed the creeds of Christendom's churches and brought him up to accept them too. Young Charles was thus taught that God is love, yet that he had created men inherently immortal and had provided a fiery place in which he would eternally torment all except those who had been predestined to be saved. Such an idea repulsed the honest heart of teenage Charles. He reasoned: "A God that would use his power to create human beings whom he foreknew and predestinated should be eternally tormented, could be neither wise, just nor loving. His standard would be lower than that of many men."

But young Russell was no atheist; he simply could not accept the commonly understood teachings of the churches. He explained: "Gradually I was led to see that though each of the creeds contained some elements of truth, they were, on the whole, misleading and contradictory of God's Word." Indeed, in the creeds of the churches, "elements of truth" were buried under a morass of pagan teachings that had infiltrated tainted Christianity during the centuries-long apostasy. Turning away from church creeds and searching for truth, Russell examined some leading Oriental religions, only to find these unsatisfying.

Joseph L. Russell, Charles' father, was a member of the Allegheny Bible study class and a close associate of his son in the activities of the Watch Tower Society until his death in 1897

Reestablished in Faith

The twig, though, had been trained by God-fearing parents; it was inclined "in the direction of the Lord." While he was still searching for truth, one evening in 1869, something happened that reestablished Charles' wavering faith. Walking along near the Russells' store on Federal Street, he heard religious singing coming from a basement hall. In his own words, this is what took place:

"Seemingly by accident, one evening I dropped into a dusty, dingy hall, where I had heard religious services were held, to see if the handful who met there had anything more sensible to offer than the creeds of the great churches. There, for the first time, I heard something of the views of Second Adventists [Advent Christian Church], the preacher being Mr. Jonas Wendell . . . Thus, I confess indebtedness to Adventists as well as to other denominations. Though his Scripture exposition was not entirely clear, . . . it was sufficient, under God, to re-establish my wavering faith in the divine inspiration of the Bible, and to show that the records of the apostles and prophets are indissolubly linked. What I heard sent me to my Bible to study with more zeal and care than ever before, and I shall ever thank the Lord for that leading; for though Adventism helped me to no single truth, it did help me greatly in the unlearning of errors, and thus prepared me for the Truth."

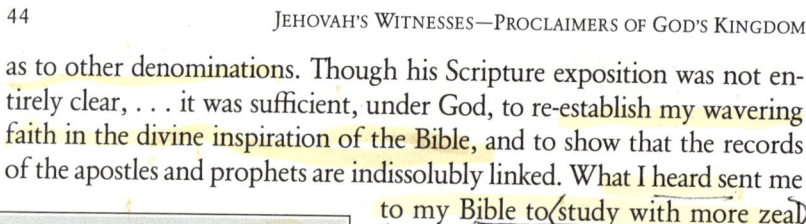

That meeting renewed young Russell's determination to search for Scriptural truth. It sent him back to his Bible with more eagerness than ever before. Russell soon came to believe that the time was near for those who served the Lord to come to a clear knowledge of His purpose. So, in 1870, fired by enthusiasm, he and a few acquaintances in Pittsburgh and nearby Allegheny got together and formed a class for Bible study. According to a later associate of Russell, the small Bible class was conducted in this manner: "Someone would raise a question. They would discuss it. They would look up all related scriptures on the point and then, when they were satisfied on the harmony of these texts, they would finally state their conclusion and make a record of it." As Russell later acknowledged, the period "from 1870 to 1875 was a time of constant growth in grace and knowledge and love of God and his Word."

As they researched the Scriptures, a number of things became clearer to these sincere truth seekers. They saw the Scriptural truths pertaining to the mortality of the human soul and that immortality was a gift to be attained by

---

"Let Both Grow Together Until the Harvest"

What happened to true Christianity after the first century? In an illustration, Jesus had warned that the Devil would sow "weeds," imitation Christians, in among "the wheat," true Christians, "the sons of the kingdom." Both would grow together until "the harvest," the "conclusion of a system of things." (Matt. 13:24-30, 36-43) During the great apostasy that developed after the death of the apostles, "the weeds" predominated for many centuries.

But what about "the wheat"? Who were among "the sons of the kingdom" during the centuries-long apostasy? We cannot say for a certainty. The literal weeds of Jesus' illustration are generally considered to be bearded darnel, which very much resembles wheat until maturity, when it can readily be distinguished from wheat by its smaller black seeds. Similarly, only at "the harvest" would a clear distinction be made between imitation Christians and the true "sons of the kingdom." Nevertheless, Jesus said: "Let both grow together until the harvest." True Christianity, then, was never completely stamped out.

Throughout the centuries there have always been truth lovers. To mention just a few: John Wycliffe (c. 1330-1384) and William Tyndale (c. 1494-1536) furthered the work of Bible translation even at the risk of their life or freedom. Wolfgang Fabricius Capito (1478-1541), Martin Cellarius (1499-1564), Johannes Campanus (c. 1500-1575), and Thomas Emlyn (1663-c. 1741) accepted the Bible as God's Word and rejected the Trinity. Henry Grew (1781-1862) and George Storrs (1796-1879) not only accepted the Bible and rejected the Trinity but also expressed appreciation for the ransom sacrifice of Christ.

Although we cannot positively identify any of such persons as "the wheat" of Jesus' illustration, certainly "Jehovah knows those who belong to him."—2 Tim. 2:19.

PROCLAIMING THE LORD'S RETURN (1870 - 1914)

those who became joint heirs with Christ in his heavenly Kingdom. (Ezek. 18:20; Rom. 2:6, 7) They began to grasp the doctrine of the ransom sacrifice of Jesus Christ and the opportunity that this provision made possible for humankind. (Matt. 20:28) They came to recognize that although Jesus first came to the earth as a man in the flesh, at his return he would be invisibly present as a spirit person. (John 14:19) They further learned that the object of Jesus' return was, not to destroy everyone, but to bless the obedient families of the earth. (Gal. 3:8) Russell wrote: "We felt greatly grieved at the error of Second Adventists, who were expecting Christ in the flesh, and teaching that the world and all in it except Second Adventists would be burned up."

The Scriptural truths that became clear to this little Bible class were certainly a departure from the pagan doctrines that had filtered into Christianity during the centuries-long apostasy. But did Russell and his spiritually-minded associates gain these truths from the Bible unaided by others?

Influence of Others

Russell referred quite openly to the assistance in Bible study he had received from others. Not only did he acknowledge his indebtedness to Second Adventist Jonas Wendell but he also spoke with affection about two other individuals who had aided him in Bible study. Russell said of these two men: "The study of the Word of God with these dear brethren led, step by step, into greener pastures." One, George W. Stetson, was an earnest student of the Bible and pastor of the Advent Christian Church in Edinboro, Pennsylvania.

The other, George Storrs, was publisher of the magazine *Bible Examiner,* in Brooklyn, New York. Storrs, who was born on December 13, 1796, was initially stimulated to examine what the Bible says about the condition of the dead as a result of reading something published (though at the time anonymously) by a careful student of the Bible, Henry Grew, of Philadelphia, Pennsylvania. Storrs became a zealous advocate of what was called conditional immortality—the teaching that the soul is mortal and that immortality is a gift to be attained by faithful Christians. He also reasoned that since the wicked do not have immortality, there is no eternal torment. Storrs traveled extensively, lecturing on the subject of no immortality for the wicked. Among his published works was the *Six Sermons,*

George W. Stetson
—"A Man of Marked Ability"

C. T. Russell gratefully acknowledged the assistance that was given him by George W. Stetson, of Edinboro, Pennsylvania, in studying the Scriptures. Stetson died on October 9, 1879, at the age of 64. The following month the "Watch Tower" carried an announcement of Stetson's death that revealed 27-year-old Russell's deep respect for him. "Our brother was a man of marked ability," wrote Russell, "and surrendered bright prospects of worldly and political honors to be permitted to preach Christ." Stetson's dying request was that C. T. Russell preach his funeral sermon; Russell complied with the request. "About twelve hundred persons attended the funeral services," reported Russell, "thus giving evidence of the high esteem in which our brother was held."—The "Watch Tower," November 1879.

> ### George Storrs
> ### —"A Friend and Brother"
>
> C. T. Russell felt a sense of indebtedness to George Storrs, who was some 56 years his senior. Russell had learned much from Storrs about the mortality of the soul. So when Storrs lay seriously ill late in 1879, Russell offered to print in the "Watch Tower" a statement of Storrs' condition. "Our brother," Russell wrote, "so long the editor of 'The Bible Examiner' is known to most of our readers; also that he has been obliged by severe illness to discontinue his paper." In Russell's estimation, Storrs had "much reason to thank God for being privileged to spend so long a life and one so consecrated to the Master." Storrs died on December 28, 1879, at the age of 83. An announcement of his death appeared in the February 1880 issue of the "Watch Tower," which said: "We mourn the loss of a friend and brother in Christ yet, 'not as those who have no hope.'"
>
> *George Storrs*

which eventually attained a distribution of 200,000 copies. Without a doubt, Storrs' strong Bible-based views on the mortality of the soul as well as the atonement and restitution (restoration of what was lost due to Adamic sin; Acts 3:21) had a strong, positive influence on young Charles T. Russell.

Yet, another man who had a profound effect on Russell's life also caused his loyalty to Scriptural truth to be put to the test.

Time Prophecies and the Presence of the Lord

One morning in January 1876, 23-year-old Russell received a copy of a religious periodical called *Herald of the Morning*. From the picture on the cover, he could see that it was identified with Adventism. The editor, Nelson H. Barbour, of Rochester, New York, believed that the object of Christ's return was not to destroy the families of the earth but to bless them and that his coming would be not in the flesh but as a spirit. Why, this was in agreement with what Russell and his associates in Allegheny had believed for some time!* Curiously, though, Barbour believed from Biblical time-prophecies that Christ was already present (invisibly) and that the harvest work of gathering "the wheat" (true Christians making up the Kingdom class) was already due.—Matt., chap. 13.

Russell had shied away from Biblical time prophecies. Now, however, he wondered: "Could it be that the *time prophecies* which I had so long despised, because of their misuse by Adventists, were really meant to indicate when the Lord would be *invisibly present* to set up his Kingdom?" With his insatiable thirst for Scriptural truth, Russell had to learn more. So he arranged to meet with Barbour in Philadelphia. This meeting confirmed their agreement on a number of Bible teachings and provided an opportunity for them to exchange views. "When we first met," Russell later stated, "he had much to learn from me on the fulness of *restitution* based upon the sufficiency of the ransom given for all, as I had much to

---

* Neither Barbour nor Russell was the first to explain the Lord's return as an invisible presence. Much earlier, Sir Isaac Newton (1642-1727) had written that Christ would return and reign "invisible to mortals." In 1856, Joseph Seiss, a Lutheran minister in Philadelphia, Pennsylvania, had written about a two-stage second advent—an invisible *pa·rou·siʹa*, or presence, followed by a visible manifestation. Then, in 1864, Benjamin Wilson had published his *Emphatic Diaglott* with the interlinear reading "presence," not "coming," for *pa·rou·siʹa*, and B. W. Keith, an associate of Barbour, had drawn it to the attention of Barbour and his associates.

learn from him concerning *time.*" Barbour succeeded in convincing Russell that Christ's invisible presence had begun in 1874.*

"Resolved Upon a Vigorous Campaign for the Truth"

C. T. Russell was a man of positive convictions. Convinced that Christ's invisible presence had begun, he was determined to proclaim it to others. He later said: "The knowledge of the fact that we were already in the harvest period gave to me an impetus to spread the Truth such as I never had before. I therefore at once resolved upon a vigorous campaign for the Truth." Russell now decided to curtail his business interests so as to devote himself to preaching.

To counteract wrong views regarding the Lord's return, Russell wrote the pamphlet *The Object and Manner of Our Lord's Return.* It was published in 1877. That same year Barbour and Russell jointly published *Three Worlds, and the Harvest of This World.* This 196-page book discussed the subjects of restitution and Biblical time prophecies. Though each subject had been treated by others before, in Russell's view this book was "the first to *combine* the idea of restitution with time-prophecy." It presented the view that Jesus Christ's invisible presence dated from the autumn of 1874.

As Russell traveled and preached, it became evident to him that something more was needed to keep the seeds of truth he was sowing alive and watered. The answer? "A monthly journal," said Russell. So he and Barbour decided to revive publication of the *Herald,* which had been suspended because of canceled subscriptions and exhausted funds. Russell contributed his own funds to revive the journal, becoming one of its co-editors.

All went well for a while—until 1878, that is.

Russell Breaks With Barbour

In the August 1878 issue of *Herald of the Morning,* there appeared an article by Barbour that denied the substitutionary value of Christ's death. Russell, who was nearly 30 years younger than Barbour, could see that this was, in fact, denying the essential part of the ransom doctrine. So in the very next issue (September 1878), Russell, in an article entitled "The Atonement," upheld the ransom and contradicted Barbour's statements. The controversy continued in the pages of the journal for the next few months. Finally, Russell decided to withdraw from fellowship with Mr. Barbour and discontinued further financial support to the *Herald.*

C. T. Russell, though, felt that to withdraw from the *Herald* was not enough; the ransom doctrine must be defended and Christ's presence must be proclaimed. Hence, in July 1879, Russell began publishing *Zion's*

---

* A clearer understanding of Bible chronology was published in later years. See Chapter 10, "Growing in Accurate Knowledge of the Truth."

"I Leave the 'Herald' With You"

In the spring of 1879, C. T. Russell withdrew all support from the magazine "Herald of the Morning," which he had shared in publishing with N. H. Barbour. In a letter to Barbour dated May 3, 1879, Russell explained his reason: "There has arisen a difference of view between us as to the teaching of our Father's word [regarding the substitutionary value of the ransom] and while giving you credit for all sincerity and honesty in your views, which I claim for myself in the opposite view, yet I must be guided by my own understanding of our Father's word, and consequently think you to be in error. . . . The points of variance seem to me to be so fundamental and important that the full fellowship and sympathy such as should exist among publishers and editors of a paper or magazine, no longer obtains between you and me, and because this is the case, I feel that our relationship should cease."

In a follow-up letter dated May 22, 1879, Russell wrote: "Now I leave the 'Herald' with you. I withdraw entirely from it, asking nothing from you. . . . Please announce in next No. of the 'Herald' the dissolution and withdraw my name," Starting with the June 1879 issue, Russell's name no longer appeared as an assistant editor of the "Herald."

Barbour continued to publish the "Herald" until 1903, when, according to available library records, it ceased publication. Barbour died a few years later, in 1906.

Nelson H. Barbour

Watch Tower and Herald of Christ's Presence.* Russell was the editor and publisher, with five others originally listed as contributors to its columns. The first issue had a printing of 6,000 copies. By 1914 the printing of each issue was about 50,000 copies.

"Not as *New,* Not as *Our Own,* But as the Lord's"

C. T. Russell used the *Watch Tower* and other publications to uphold Bible truths and to refute false religious teachings and human philosophies that contradicted the Bible. He did not, however, claim to discover new truths.

From the latter part of the 18th century, many ministers and Bible scholars had been exposing the false teachings of the immortality of the soul and eternal punishment for the wicked. This exposé had been thoroughly reported in the book *Bible Vs. Tradition*, by Aaron Ellis, originally published in England and then in the United States in 1853 by George Storrs. But no one at that time did more than C. T. Russell and his associates to make this truth known.

What about other Bible doctrines that were discussed in the *Watch Tower* and other publications? Did Russell take full credit for uncovering these gems of truth? Explained Russell: "We found that for centuries various sects and parties had split up the Bible doctrines amongst them, blending them with more or less of human speculation and error . . . We found the important doctrine of justification by faith and not by works had been clearly enunciated by Luther and more recently by many Christians; that divine justice and power and wisdom were carefully guarded tho not clearly discerned by Presbyterians; that

---

* The expression "Watch Tower" is not unique to Russell's writings or to Jehovah's Witnesses. George Storrs published a book in the 1850's called *The Watch Tower: Or, Man in Death; and the Hope for a Future Life*. The name was also incorporated in the title of various religious periodicals. It stems from the idea of keeping on the watch for the outworking of God's purposes.—Isa. 21: 8, 11, 12; Ezek. 3:17; Hab. 2:1.

Methodists appreciated and extolled the love and sympathy of God; that Adventists held the precious doctrine of the Lord's return; that Baptists amongst other points held the doctrine of baptism symbolically correctly, even tho they had lost sight of the real baptism; that some Universalists had long held vaguely some thoughts respecting 'restitution.' And so, nearly all denominations gave evidence that their founders had been feeling after truth: but quite evidently the great Adversary had fought against them and had wrongly divided the Word of God which he could not wholly destroy."

Concerning the chronology he often presented, Russell stated: "When we say 'our' chronology we merely mean the one we use, the Bible chronology, which belongs to all of God's people who approve it. As a matter of fact it was used in practically the form we present it long before our day, just as various prophecies we use were used to a different purpose by Adventists, and just as various doctrines we hold and which seem so new and fresh and different were held in some form long ago: for instance—Election, Free Grace, Restitution, Justification, Sanctification, Glorification, Resurrection."

Then how did Russell perceive the role that he and his associates played in publishing Scriptural truth? He explained: "Our work . . . has been to bring together these long scattered fragments of truth and present them to the Lord's people—not as *new*, not as *our own*, but as the Lord's. . . . We must disclaim any credit even for the finding and rearrangement of the jewels of truth." He further stated: "The work in which the Lord has been pleased to use our humble talents has been less a work of origination than of reconstruction, adjustment, harmonization."

Russell thus was quite modest about his accomplishments. Nevertheless, the "scattered fragments of truth" that he brought together and presented to the Lord's people were free of the God-dishonoring pagan doctrines of the Trinity and immortality of the soul, which had become entrenched in the churches of Christendom as a result of the great apostasy. Like no one at that time, Russell and his associates proclaimed worldwide the meaning of the Lord's return and of the divine purpose and what it involved.

'Building Each Other Up in the Most Holy Faith'

Honesthearted persons quickly responded to the liberating truths that C. T. Russell and his associates were proclaiming both through the printed page and in lectures. Russell, still less than 30 years of age, soon realized that there was a need for the readers of the *Watch Tower* to get acquainted with fellow believers and encourage one another. The Bible Students in Pittsburgh were doing this by regularly meeting together, but what could be done to help *Watch Tower* readers in other places?

The answer came in the *Watch Tower* issues of May and June 1880. There Russell announced his plans to visit a number of towns and cities in Pennsylvania, New Jersey, Massachusetts, and New York. For what purpose? "Our readers," the announcement explained, "are much scattered, some places 2 and 3, and on up to 50. Many places they are totally unacquainted with each other, and thus lose the sympathy and comfort which our Father designed should come to them by 'The assembling of themselves together as the manner of some is.' It is His design that we should 'Edify one another,' and build each other up in the most holy faith. The proposed meetings we would hope, might conduce to personal acquaintance."—Heb. 10:24, 25.

The "proposed meetings" were held during Russell's trip, and they proved very successful; readers of the *Watch Tower* were drawn closer together. These and other trips to visit "little bands of waiting ones" soon resulted in the forming of a number of classes, or ecclesias (later called congregations), located in the aforementioned areas as well as in Ohio and Michigan. These classes were encouraged to hold regular meetings. But what kind of meetings?

The Pittsburgh class had established the custom of meeting together at least twice each week. One meeting of the Pittsburgh class often included a lecture by a qualified speaker to the entire ecclesia, perhaps in a rented hall. But at the other meetings, usually held in private homes, those in attendance were invited to bring Bible, concordance, paper, and pencil—and to participate.

The warm spiritual fellowship experienced at those regular weekly meetings was a refreshing change from the cold, impersonal atmosphere at the services of many of the churches of Christendom. But Russell and his associates did not pioneer the idea of regularly meeting together. That custom of assembling, even in private homes, was established by the first-century Christians.—Rom. 16:3, 5; Col. 4:15.

The Bible Students distributed tens of millions of copies of tracts that exposed religious error, explained Scriptural truths, and proclaimed the significant year 1914

"Are You Preaching?"

C. T. Russell and his associates strongly believed that they were in a time of harvest and that people needed to hear liberating truth. Yet, they were few in number. The *Watch Tower* was filling a vital need, but could more be done? Russell and his coworkers thought so. During 1880 they began to produce *Bible Students' Tracts* (later also called *Old Theology Quarterly*), and these were provided to readers of the *Watch Tower* for free distribution to the public.

Yes, readers of the *Watch Tower* were encouraged to share with others the precious truths they were learning. "Are you preaching?" was the question raised in the combined *Watch Tower* issue of July and August 1881. How important was it for them to preach? The article went on to state: "We believe that none will be of the little flock except preachers. . . . Yes, we were called to suffer with him and to proclaim that *good news* now, that in due time we might be glorified and perform the things now preached. We were not *called, nor anointed* to receive honor and amass wealth, but to spend and be spent, and to *preach* the good news."

It is appropriate that those early Bible Students felt keenly the need to preach the good news. In fact, the commission to preach was placed upon the first-century Christians; it is a responsibility that rests upon all genuine Christians to this day. (Matt. 24:14; 28:19, 20; Acts 1:8) But what was the objective of the preaching done by Russell and the early readers of the *Watch Tower*? Was it simply to distribute Bible literature or awaken churchgoers to Scriptural truths?

"You Must . . . Leave Her"

"Get out of her, my people," the Bible long ago warned. Out of what? "Babylon the Great, the mother of the harlots and of the disgusting things of the earth." (Rev. 17:5; 18:4) Why get out of Babylon? "For her sins have massed together clear up to heaven, and God has called her acts of injustice to mind." (Rev. 18:5) Who is this mother harlot from whom people should separate themselves?

Martin Luther and other leaders of the Reformation identified the Catholic Church and its papacy as Babylon the Great. What about the Protestant churches that sprang up as a result of the Reformation? The fact is, apart from their rejection of the primacy of the pope, some were not much different from Catholicism in church structure, and they retained unscriptural doctrines, such as the Trinity, immortality of the soul, and eternal torment. For this reason some preachers urged people to break free not only from the Catholic Church but also from the main Protestant church systems.

'Called to preach the good news'

C. T. Russell penned six volumes of "Millennial Dawn" (1886 to 1904) as well as tracts, booklets, and "Watch Tower" articles over a period of about 37 years

C. T. Russell and his associates also realized that this infamous harlot was not merely the Catholic Church. Thus, while the *Watch Tower* of November 1879 identified Babylon the Great with the *"Papacy as a* SYSTEM," the article added: "We must go further and implicate, (not the individual members, but the church systems) other churches united to the Empires of earth. Every church claiming to be a chaste virgin espoused to Christ, but in reality united to and supported by the world (beast) we must condemn as being in scripture language a *harlot church*."

What, therefore, were readers of the *Watch Tower* encouraged to do? Russell wrote: "If the church with which you are connected, lives in adulterous union with the world, you must, if you would keep your garments white, leave her." Russell and his associates did not then understand the full range of the influence of Babylon the Great. Nevertheless, readers of the *Watch Tower* were urged to separate themselves from church systems that were corrupt and worldly.—John 18:36.

"Its Truth Captured My Heart At Once"

The publishing of Bible truths took a significant step forward in 1886 with the release of the first volume of a promised series of books called *Millennial Dawn*, written by C. T. Russell. Volume I was called *The Divine Plan of the Ages*. It contained studies on 16 subjects, such as "The Existence of a Supreme Intelligent Creator Established," "The Bible as a Divine Revelation Viewed in the Light of Reason," "Our Lord's Return—Its Object, the Restitution of All Things," and "The Permission of Evil and Its Relation to God's Plan." Eventually,

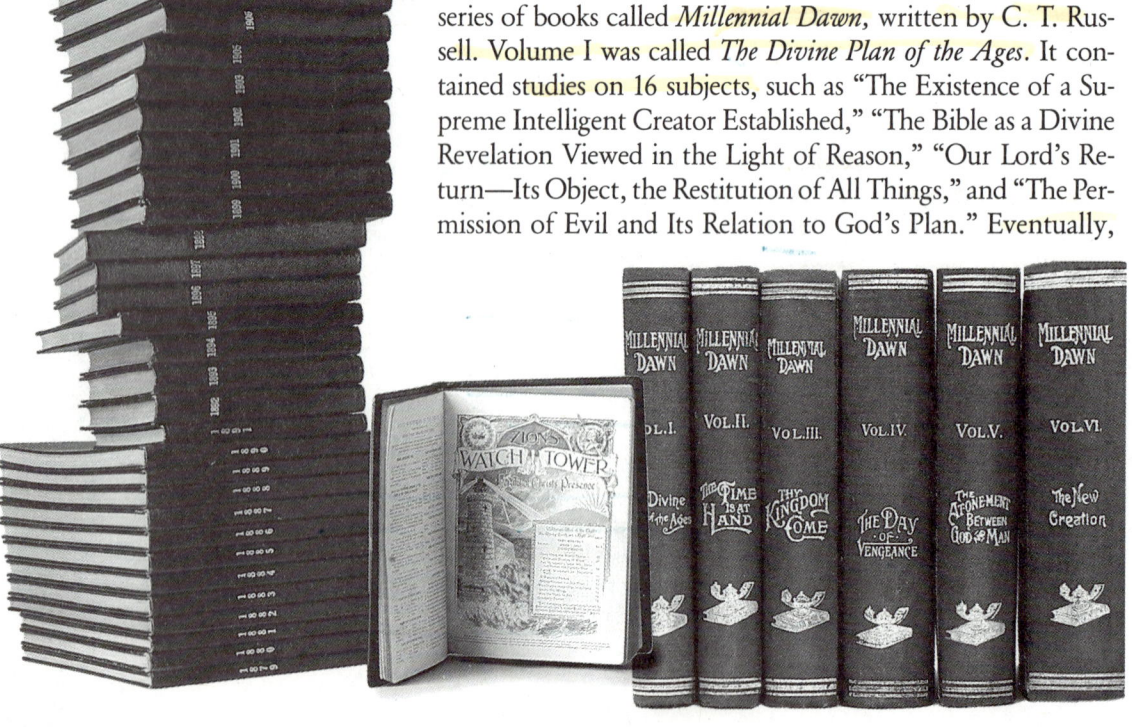

PROCLAIMING THE LORD'S RETURN (1870 - 1914)   53

C. T. Russell wrote five other books of the *Millennial Dawn* series.*

Russell did not survive to write an intended seventh volume of the series, but the widespread distribution of the six volumes that he did complete struck a responsive chord in honesthearted persons. "Your book MILLENNIAL DAWN came to me last Fall," wrote one woman in 1889, "the first hint I ever had of such a work. I received it on a Saturday evening, commenced to read it immediately and never laid it aside, except when obliged, until finished. Its truth captured my heart at once; forthwith I withdrew from the Presbyterian Church where I had so long been groping in the dark for the truth, and found it not."

It took real courage in those days to withdraw from one's church. Demonstrating this was a woman in Manitoba, Canada, who came into possession of *Millennial Dawn* in 1897. At first, she tried to stay with her church and teach in local Sunday schools. The day came, in 1903, when she decided to make a break. She stood up and told all present why she felt she must separate from the church. The nearest neighbor (dear to people in small communities in those days) tried to persuade her to go back to church. But she stood firm, even though there was no congregation of Bible Students nearby. As her son later described her situation: "No study servant [elder] to lean on. No meetings. A contrite heart. A worn Bible. Long prayerful hours."

What was it about *Millennial Dawn*, the *Watch Tower*, and other publications of the Society that captured the hearts of people and moved them to take such decisive action? C. T. Russell took an approach to explaining Bible teachings that was distinct from many writers of his day. He believed the Bible to be the infallible Word of God and that its teachings should be

When he gave public lectures, Brother Russell did not use any notes, and he was always on the move—gesturing with his arms and stepping about the platform

---

* They were: Volume II, *The Time Is at Hand* (1889); Volume III, *Thy Kingdom Come* (1891); Volume IV, *The Day of Vengeance* (1897; later called *The Battle of Armageddon*); Volume V, *The At-one-ment Between God and Man* (1899); and Volume VI, *The New Creation* (1904). When the *Millennial Dawn* volumes began to be called *Studies in the Scriptures*, Volume I was designated as "Series I," Volume II as "Series II," and so forth. The name *Studies in the Scriptures* was adopted in limited editions beginning about October 1904, and the new name was more generally used beginning in 1906.

Why Called Pastor

Charles Taze Russell was referred to by his associates as Pastor Russell. Why? Because of his activities in shepherding the flock of God. Ephesians 4:11 states that Christ would give to his congregation some as "pastors" ("KJ"), or "shepherds." Brother Russell certainly did serve as a spiritual shepherd in the Christian congregation.

In view of the pastoral work that he was doing under the Chief Shepherd, Jesus Christ, certain congregations acknowledged by vote that he was their pastor. It was not a self-assumed title. The first group to vote him their pastor was the congregation in Pittsburgh, Pennsylvania, in 1882. Thereafter, he was voted pastor by some 500 other congregations, in the United States and Britain.

Back then, it was customary for the congregations to vote each year for those who would preside among them. Today, Christian elders among Jehovah's Witnesses are not elected by local congregations but are appointed by the Governing Body of Jehovah's Witnesses. Care is also exercised not to use expressions such as "pastor" or "elder" as titles.

---

harmonious. Therefore, if any part of the Bible is difficult to understand, he felt, it should be clarified and interpreted by another part of the inspired Word. He did not try to support the explanations he presented with the testimony of theologians of his day or with the views of the so-called early church fathers. As he wrote in Volume I of *Millennial Dawn:* "We believe it to be a common failing of the present and all times for men to believe certain doctrines because others did so, in whom they had confidence.... Truth-seekers should empty their vessels of the muddy waters of tradition and fill them at the fountain of truth —God's Word."

As a growing number of such truth seekers responded to what they read in publications of the Watch Tower Society, some unexpected changes became necessary in Allegheny.

Headquarters at the Bible House

The Bible Students in Allegheny, associated with the publishing of the *Watch Tower,* were considered the most experienced in doing the Lord's work and were looked to by all the ecclesias, or congregations, as those taking the lead. At first they had headquarters offices at 101 Fifth Avenue, Pittsburgh, and later at 44 Federal Street, Allegheny. In the late 1880's, however, expansion became necessary. So Russell arranged to build larger facilities. In 1889 a four-story brick building at 56-60 Arch Street, Allegheny, was completed. Valued at $34,000, it was known as the Bible House. It served as the Society's headquarters for some 19 years.

As of 1890, the small Bible House family was serving the needs of several hundred active associates of the Watch Tower Society. But as the decade of the 1890's progressed, more showed interest in what these were doing. In fact, according to an incomplete report published in the *Watch Tower,* on March 26, 1899, the Memorial of Christ's death was observed at 339 separate meetings with 2,501 participants. What, though, would help to keep the growing number of Bible Students united?

Unifying the Growing Flock

C. T. Russell encouraged all readers of the *Watch Tower* to come together wherever they could to form groups, small or large, in order to build one another up spiritually. Scriptural counsel was provided through the columns of the *Watch Tower*. Traveling representatives of the Watch Tower Society were also sent out from headquarters to keep in touch with the various groups and to build them up spiritually.

At intervals, there were also special assemblies attended by Bible Students from many places. "This is a SPECIAL INVITATION to every reader who can come," urged the March 1886 issue of the *Watch Tower*. What was the occasion? The annual commemoration of the Lord's Evening Meal, to be held on Sunday, April 18, 1886, at Allegheny. More, though, was planned: A series of special meetings was scheduled during the evenings of the week that followed. The Bible Students in Allegheny opened their homes—and their hearts,—free of charge for the visiting delegates. For the next few years, similar assemblies were held in Allegheny at the time of the Memorial of the Lord's death.

During the late 1890's, conventions began to be organized in many places. C. T. Russell frequently spoke on these occasions. What was it like to listen to him?

Ralph Leffler, who heard C. T. Russell speak, recalled: "When on the platform before an audience, he always wore a long black cloak and a white necktie. His voice was not loud, and he would never use a microphone or a loudspeaker, for they had not been invented; yet, somehow his voice always carried to the most distant part of the auditorium. He could hold the attention of a large audience for not just one hour but sometimes two or three hours. He would always begin his lecture with a gentle bow to the audience. While speaking, he did not stand still like a statue, but he was always on the move, gesticulating with his arms and stepping from side to side or from front to back. I never once saw him carry any notes or a manuscript in his hands—only the Bible, which he used very frequently. He spoke from the heart and in a manner that was very convincing. Usually the only article on the platform in those days was a small table with a Bible on it and a pitcher of water and a glass from which the speaker occasionally took a sip of water."

Those early conventions were periods of warm fellowship and spiritual refreshment. They served to strengthen the unity of all the Bible Students and to publicize Bible truths. Meanwhile, as the decade of the 1890's drew to a close, it was evident to the Bible Students that much more needed to be done in disseminating Bible truth. But they were still relatively few in number. Was there a way of reaching millions more people than could be contacted by the methods then being used? Indeed there was!

Opening the Door of "Newspaper Gospelling"

By the end of the 19th century, the world was crisscrossed with telegraph lines. Telegraphic communication was inexpensive and fast; it

The "Photo-Drama of Creation"

The "Photo-Drama of Creation" combined motion pictures and a slide presentation, synchronized with sound. This striking presentation took the audience from the time of creation to the end of the Millennium.

At least 20 four-part sets were prepared, making it possible for a part of the "Photo-Drama" to be shown in 80 different cities each day. It was a real challenge to fill those 80 engagements. Train schedules were not always convenient. Congregations could not always rent exhibition locations on the desired dates. Yet, by the end of 1914, the "Photo-Drama" had been presented to audiences totaling over 9,000,000 in North America, Europe, and Australia.

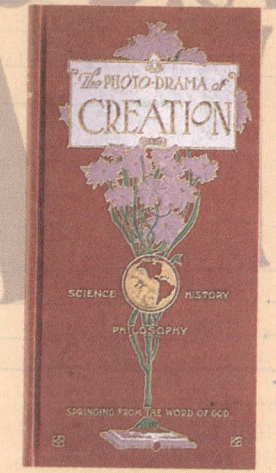

Film projector

"Scenario" of the "Photo-Drama," containing the lectures and many illustrations

{ Theaters used full-time for showings of the "Photo-Drama" }

Chicago

Slide projector

Phonograph records

New York

Slides from the "Photo-Drama"

MOTHER EVE CREATED

FLOOD DESTROYING MAN AND BEAST

CONFUSION OF TONGUES

"WHEN I CONSIDER THY HEAVENS"—DAVID

TYNDALE TRANSLATING NEW TESTAMENT

ARMAGEDDON

Isa. 11:6

THE MILLENNIUM SYMBOLIZED

Advertising folder

in 1913 It was estimated that one year, through 2,000 newspapers, C. T. Russell's sermons were reaching 15,000,000 readers

JEHOVAH'S WITNESSES—PROCLAIMERS OF GOD'S KINGDOM

revolutionized the press. News could be quickly transmitted over long distances and printed in newspapers. In the early part of the 20th century, C. T. Russell and his associates saw newspapers as an effective way of reaching large numbers of people. Russell later said: "The newspaper has become the great factor in the daily life of the civilized world."

The December 1, 1904, issue of the *Watch Tower* announced that sermons by C. T. Russell were appearing in three newspapers. The next issue of the *Watch Tower,* under the heading "Newspaper Gospelling," reported: "Millions of sermons have thus been scattered far and near; and some at least have done good. If the Lord wills we shall be glad to see this 'door' keep open, or even open still wider." The door of "newspaper gospelling" did open still wider. In fact, by 1913 it was estimated that through 2,000 newspapers Russell's sermons were reaching 15,000,000 readers!

How, though, did Russell manage to get a weekly sermon printed even when he was traveling? Each week he telegraphed a sermon (about two newspaper columns long) to a newspaper syndicate. The syndicate, in turn, retelegraphed it to newspapers in the United States, Canada, and Europe.

Russell was convinced that the Lord had pushed the door of newspaper preaching wide open. During the first decade of the

20th century, the Bible message that Russell and his associates proclaimed became widely known through such newspaper sermons. A publication called *The Continent* once stated concerning Russell: "His writings are said to have greater newspaper circulation every week than those of any other living man; a greater, doubtless, than the combined circulation of the writings of all the priests and preachers in North America."

Moving to Brooklyn

As the newspaper preaching gained momentum, the Bible Students looked for another location from which to originate the sermons. Why? The Bible House in Allegheny had become too small. It was also thought that if Russell's sermons emanated from a larger, better-known city, it would result in the publication of the sermons in more newspapers. But which city? The *Watch Tower* of December 15, 1908, explained: "Altogether we concluded, after seeking Divine guidance, that Brooklyn, N.Y., with a large population of the middle class, and known as 'The City of Churches,' would, for these reasons, be our most suitable center for the harvest work during the few remaining years."

In 1908, therefore, several representatives of the Watch Tower Society, including its legal counsel, Joseph F. Rutherford, were sent to New York City. Their objective? To secure property that C. T. Russell had located on an earlier trip. They purchased the old "Plymouth Bethel," located at 13-17 Hicks Street, Brooklyn. It had served as a mission structure for the nearby Plymouth Congregational Church, where Henry Ward Beecher once served as pastor. The Society's representatives also purchased Beecher's former residence, a four-story brownstone at 124 Columbia Heights, a few blocks away.

The Hicks Street building was remodeled and named the Brooklyn Tabernacle. It housed the Society's offices and an auditorium. After considerable repairs, Beecher's former residence at 124 Columbia Heights became the new home of the Society's headquarters staff. What would it be called? *The Watch Tower* of March 1, 1909, explained: "The new home we shall call 'Bethel' [meaning, "House of God"]."*

"Newspaper gospelling," as it was called, gained momentum after the move to Brooklyn. But it was not the only way of reaching masses of people.

Expanding the Proclamation of the Good News

In 1912, Russell and his associates embarked on a bold educational venture that was far ahead of its time. In fact, it was to reach millions of people

---
* Later, the adjoining property, 122 Columbia Heights, was purchased, thus enlarging the Bethel Home. Also, in 1911 an additional building was added to the rear of the Bethel Home, providing new housing accommodations.

worldwide. It was the "Photo-Drama of Creation"—a combination motion picture and slide presentation, synchronized with musical recordings and phonograph-record talks. It was about eight hours in length and was presented in four parts. Besides the regular "Photo-Drama," the "Eureka Drama," consisting of either the recorded lectures and musical recordings or the records plus the slides, was also made available. Though it lacked motion pictures, it was successfully presented in less densely populated areas.

Imagine the historic scene: In January 1914, during the era of silent movies,* an audience of 5,000 gathered at The Temple, a building on West 63rd Street, in New York City. Many others had to be turned away. The occasion? Why, the premiere in New York of the "Photo-Drama of Creation"! Before the audience was a large motion-picture screen. As they watched—and listened—something truly amazing happened. C. T. Russell, then in his early 60's, appeared on the screen. His lips began to move, and his words could be heard! As the presentation continued, it took those in attendance—by means of words, color pictures, and music—from earth's creation to the end of Christ's Millennial Reign. During the presentation they also saw (by means of time-lapse photography) other things that astounded them—the unfolding of a flower and the hatching of a chick. They were truly impressed!

By the end of 1914, the "Photo-Drama" had been presented before millions of persons in North America, Europe, New Zealand, and Australia. The "Photo-Drama" certainly proved to be an effective means of reaching masses of people in a relatively short period of time.

Meanwhile, what about October 1914? For decades Russell and his associates had been proclaiming that the Gentile Times would end in 1914. Expectations were high. C. T. Russell had been critical of those who had set various dates for the Lord's return, such as William Miller and some Second Adventist groups. Yet, from the time of his early association with Nelson Barbour, he was convinced that there was an accurate chronology, based on the Bible, and that it pointed to 1914 as the end of the Gentile Times.

As that significant year approached, there were great expectations among the Bible Students, but not all that they expected had been directly stated in Scripture. What would happen?

"Look Out for 1914!"

When World War I broke out in 1914, "The World," then a leading newspaper in New York City, stated in its magazine section: "The terrific war outbreak in Europe has fulfilled an extraordinary prophecy.... 'Look out for 1914!' has been the cry of the hundreds of travelling evangelists, who, representing this strange creed [associated with Russell], have gone up and down the country enunciating the doctrine that 'the Kingdom of God is at hand.'"—"The World Magazine," August 30, 1914.

---

* Although there were early attempts to combine motion pictures with sound, the era of sound pictures was introduced in August 1926 with the release of *Don Juan* (with music but no speech), followed by *The Jazz Singer* (with speech) in the fall of 1927.

CHAPTER 6

A TIME OF TESTING (1914-1918)

"Let us remember that we are in a testing season.... If there is any reason that would lead any to let go of the Lord and His Truth and to cease sacrificing for the Lord's Cause, then it is not merely the love of God in the heart which has prompted interest in the Lord, but something else; probably a hoping that the time was short; the consecration was only for a certain time. If so, now is a good time to let go."

THOSE words, appearing in *The Watch Tower* of November 1, 1914, could not have been more appropriate. The years from 1914 to 1918 did, indeed, prove to be "a testing season" for the Bible Students. Some of the tests came from within; others came from outside. All of them, though, tested the Bible Students in ways that revealed whether they really had 'the love of God in their hearts.' Would they hold on to "the Lord and His Truth" or let go?

Great Expectations

On June 28, 1914, Archduke Francis Ferdinand of Austria-Hungary was struck down by an assassin's bullet. That assassination triggered the outbreak of the Great War, as World War I was originally called. The fighting began in August 1914 when Germany swept into Belgium and France. By the autumn of that year, the bloodbath was well under way.

"The Gentile Times have ended; their kings have had their day"! So exclaimed Brother Russell as he entered the dining room at the Brooklyn headquarters of the Watch Tower Society the morning of Friday, October 2, 1914. Excitement was high. Most of those present had for years been looking forward to 1914. But what would the end of the Gentile Times bring?

World War I was raging, and at that time it was believed that the war was leading into a time of global anarchy that would result in the end of the existing system of things. There were also other expectations concerning 1914. Alexander H. Macmillan, who had been baptized in September 1900, later recalled: "A few of us seriously thought we were going to heaven during the first week of that October."* In fact, recalling the morning that Russell

---

* Quotations from A. H. Macmillan in this chapter are taken from his book *Faith on the March*, published in 1957 by Prentice-Hall, Inc.

"Some of Us Had Been a Bit Too Hasty"

As October 1914 approached, some of the Bible Students expected that at the end of the Gentile Times they, as spirit-anointed Christians, would receive their heavenly reward. Illustrating this is an incident that took place at a convention of the Bible Students in Saratoga Springs, New York, September 27-30, 1914. A. H. Macmillan, who had been baptized 14 years earlier, gave a discourse on Wednesday, September 30. In it he stated: "This is probably the last public address I shall ever deliver because we shall be going home [to heaven] soon."

However, two days later (on Friday, October 2), Macmillan came in for some good-natured teasing back in Brooklyn, where the conventioners were to reconvene. From his seat at the head of the table, C. T. Russell announced: "We are going to make some changes in the program for Sunday [October 4]. At 10:30 Sunday morning Brother Macmillan will give us an address." The response? Macmillan later wrote: "Everybody laughed heartily, recalling what I had said on Wednesday at Saratoga Springs—my 'last public address'!"

"Well," Macmillan continued, "then I had to get busy to find something to say. I found Psalm 74:9, 'We see not our signs: there is no more any prophet: neither is there among us any that knoweth how long.' Now that was different. In that talk I tried to show the friends that perhaps some of us had been a bit too hasty in thinking that we were going to heaven right away, and the thing for us to do would be to keep busy in the Lord's service until he determined when any of his approved servants would be taken home to heaven."

announced the end of the Gentile Times, Macmillan admitted: "We were highly excited and I would not have been surprised if at that moment we had just started up, that becoming the signal to begin ascending heavenward—but of course there was nothing like that."

Disappointed expectations as to the return of the Lord Jesus had in the 19th century caused many followers of William Miller and various Adventist groups to lose faith. But what about the Bible Students associated with Russell? Had some been attracted by the thought of their own early salvation rather than love for God and a strong desire to do his will?

'Brother Russell, Were You Not Disappointed?'

Brother Russell had been encouraging the Bible Students to keep on the watch and to be determined to continue in the Lord's work even if matters did not culminate as soon as they might have expected.

October 1914 passed, and C. T. Russell and his associates were still on earth. Then October 1915 passed. Was Russell disappointed? In *The Watch Tower* of February 1, 1916, he wrote: "'But, Brother Russell, what is your thought as to the time of our change? Were you not disappointed that it did not come when we hoped that it would?' you will ask. No, we reply, we were not disappointed. . . . Brethren, those of us who are in the right attitude toward God are not disappointed at any of His arrangements. We did not wish our own will to be done; so when we found out that we were expecting the wrong thing in October, 1914, then we were glad that the Lord did not change His Plan to suit us. We did not wish Him to do so. We merely wish to be able to apprehend His plans and purposes."

No, the Bible Students were not 'taken home' to heaven in October 1914. Nevertheless, the Gentile Times did end in that year. Clearly, the Bible

A TIME OF TESTING (1914-1918)

Students had more to learn as to the significance of 1914. Meanwhile, what were they to do? Work! As *The Watch Tower* of September 1, 1916, put it: "We imagined that the Harvest work of gathering the Church [of anointed ones] would be accomplished before the end of the Gentile Times; but nothing in the Bible so said.... Are we regretful that the Harvest work continues? Nay, verily... Our present attitude, dear brethren, should be one of great gratitude toward God, increasing appreciation of the beautiful Truth which He has granted us the privilege of seeing and being identified with, and increasing zeal in helping to bring that Truth to the knowledge of others."

But was there much more to be done in the harvest work? Brother Russell evidently thought so. Indicating this was a conversation he had with Brother Macmillan in the fall of 1916. Calling Macmillan to his study at Brooklyn Bethel, Russell told him: "The work is increasing rapidly, and it will continue to increase, for there is a world-wide work to be done in preaching the 'gospel of the kingdom' in all the world." Russell spent three and a half hours outlining to Macmillan what he saw from the Bible to be the great work yet ahead.

The Bible Students had come through a difficult test. But with the help of *The Watch Tower*, they were strengthened to triumph over disappointment. The testing season, however, was far from over.

"What Is Going to Happen Now?"

On October 16, 1916, Brother Russell and his secretary Menta Sturgeon departed on a previously arranged lecture tour of western and southwestern parts of the United States. Russell, though, was seriously ill at the time. The tour took them first to Detroit, Michigan, by way of Canada. Then, after stops in Illinois, Kansas, and Texas, the two men arrived in California, where Russell delivered his last talk on Sunday, October 29, in Los Angeles. Two days later, in the early afternoon of Tuesday, October 31, 64-year-old Charles Taze Russell died on a train at Pampa, Texas. Notice of his death appeared in *The Watch Tower* of November 15, 1916.

What was the effect on the Bethel family when news of Brother Russell's death was announced? A. H. Macmillan, who served as Russell's assistant in the office while Russell was away, later recalled the morning he read the telegram to the Bethel family: "A moan went up all over that dining room. Some wept audibly. None ate breakfast that morning. All were greatly upset. At the end of the meal period they met in little groups to talk and whisper, 'What is going to happen now?' Little work was done that day. We did not know what to do. It was so unexpected, and yet Russell had tried to prepare us for it. What *would* we do? The first shock of our loss of C. T. Russell was the worst. For those first few days our future was a blank wall. Throughout his life Russell had been 'the Society.' The work centered around his dynamic determination to see God's will done."

On October 31, 1916, 64-year-old Charles Taze Russell died on a train at Pampa, Texas; many newspapers reported on the funeral

After funeral services at The Temple in New York and at Carnegie Hall in Pittsburgh, Brother Russell was buried at Allegheny, in the Bethel family plot, according to his request. A brief biography of Russell along with his will and testament was published in *The Watch Tower* of December 1, 1916, as well as in subsequent editions of the first volume of *Studies in the Scriptures*.

What would happen now? It was difficult for the Bible Students to imagine someone else in Brother Russell's place. Would their understanding of the Scriptures continue to be progressive, or would it stop where it was? Would they become a sect centered around him? Russell himself had made it quite clear that he expected the work to go on. So following his death, some obvious questions soon arose: Who will supervise the contents of *The Watch Tower* and other publications? Who should succeed Russell as president?

A Change in Administration

In his will Brother Russell outlined an arrangement for an Editorial Committee of five to determine the contents of *The Watch Tower*.* In ad-

---

* The five members of the Editorial Committee as named in Russell's will were William E. Page, William E. Van Amburgh, Henry Clay Rockwell, E. W. Brenneisen, and F. H. Robison. In addition, to fill any vacancies, others were named—A. E. Burgess, Robert Hirsh, Isaac Hoskins, G. H. Fisher, J. F. Rutherford, and John Edgar. Page and Brenneisen, however, promptly resigned—Page because he could not take up residence in Brooklyn, and Brenneisen (later the spelling was changed to Brenisen) because he had to take up secular work to support his family. Rutherford and Hirsh, whose names were listed in the December 1, 1916, *Watch Tower*, replaced them as members of the Editorial Committee.

A TIME OF TESTING (1914-1918)

dition, the board of directors of the Watch Tower Bible and Tract Society made arrangements for an Executive Committee of three—A. I. Ritchie, W. E. Van Amburgh, and J. F. Rutherford—to have general supervision of all the work of the Society, subject to the control of the board of directors.* Who, though, would become the new president? That decision would be made at the next annual meeting of the Society, about two months later, on January 6, 1917.

At first, the Executive Committee did its best to hold things together, encouraging the Bible Students to keep active and not lose courage. *The Watch Tower* continued to be published, containing articles that Russell had written before his death. But as the annual meeting approached, tension began to mount. Some were even doing a little electioneering to get a man of their choice selected to be president. Others, on account of their deep respect for Brother Russell, seemed more concerned with trying to copy his qualities and develop a sort of cult around him. Most of the Bible Students, however, were primarily interested in getting on with the work into which Russell had poured himself.

As the time for the election approached, the question remained, Who would succeed Russell as president? *The Watch Tower* of January 15, 1917, reported the outcome of the annual meeting, explaining: "Brother Pierson, with very appropriate remarks and expressions of appreciation and love for Brother Russell, stated that he had received word as proxy-holder from friends all over the land to the effect that he cast their votes for Brother J. F. Rutherford for President, and he further stated that he was in full sympathy with this." After Rutherford's name was placed in nomination and seconded, there were no further nominations, so "the Secretary cast the ballot as directed, and Brother Rutherford was declared the unanimous choice of the Convention as President."

With the election decided, how was the new president received? *The Watch Tower* mentioned above reported: "The friends everywhere had prayed earnestly for the Lord's guidance and direction in the matter of the election; and when it was concluded, everyone was content and happy, believing that the Lord had directed their deliberations and answered their prayers. Perfect harmony prevailed amongst all present."

That "perfect harmony," however, did not last very long. The new president was warmly received by many but not by all.

---

* According to the charter of the Watch Tower Society, the board of directors was to be composed of seven members. The charter provided for the surviving members of the board of directors to fill a vacancy. So, two days after Russell's death, the board of directors met and elected A. N. Pierson to be a member. The seven members of the board at that point were A. I. Ritchie, W. E. Van Amburgh, H. C. Rockwell, J. D. Wright, I. F. Hoskins, A. N. Pierson, and J. F. Rutherford. The seven-member board then elected the Executive Committee of three.

J. F. Rutherford had a commanding appearance, standing six feet two inches tall and weighing about 225 pounds

The New President Moves Ahead

Brother Rutherford was inclined, not to change the direction of the organization, but to continue in the forward-moving pattern established by Russell. Traveling representatives of the Society (known as pilgrims) were increased from 69 to 93. Distribution of the Society's free tracts was accelerated on occasional Sundays in front of the churches and regularly in the house-to-house ministry.

The "pastoral work," which had been started prior to Russell's death, was now stepped up. This was a follow-up work, similar to the return-visit activity now carried on by Jehovah's Witnesses. To further revitalize the preaching work, the Society's new president expanded the colporteur work. Colporteurs (forerunners of today's pioneers) were increased from 372 to 461.

"The year 1917 opened with rather a discouraging outlook," stated *The Watch Tower* of December 15, 1917. Yes, following the death of C. T. Russell, there were some misgivings, some doubts, and some fears. Yet, the year-end report was encouraging; field activity had increased. Clearly, the work was moving ahead. Had the Bible Students passed another test —the death of C. T. Russell—successfully?

Efforts to Gain Control

Not everyone was supportive of the new president. C. T. Russell and J. F. Rutherford were very different men. They had different personalities and came from different backgrounds. These differences were hard for some to accept. In their minds, no one could 'fill Brother Russell's shoes.'

A few, especially at headquarters, actually resented Brother Rutherford. The fact that the work was moving ahead and that he was making every effort to follow the arrangements that had been put in place by Russell did not seem to impress them. Opposition soon mounted. Four members of the board of directors of the Society went so far as to endeavor to wrest administrative control from Rutherford's hands. The situation came to a head in the summer of 1917, with the release of *The Finished Mystery*,

A TIME OF TESTING (1914-1918)

the seventh volume of *Studies in the Scriptures*.

Brother Russell had been unable to produce this volume during his lifetime, though he had hoped to do so. Following his death, the Executive Committee of the Society arranged for two associates, Clayton J. Woodworth and George H. Fisher, to prepare this book, which was a commentary on Revelation, The Song of Solomon, and Ezekiel. In part, it was based on what Russell had written about these Bible books, and other comments and explanations were added. The completed manuscript was approved for publication by officers of the Society and was released to the Bethel family at the dining table on Tuesday, July 17, 1917. On that same occasion, a startling announcement was made—the four opposing directors had been removed, and Brother Rutherford had appointed four others to fill the vacancies. What was the reaction?

It was as if a bombshell had exploded! The four ousted directors seized upon the occasion and stirred up a five-hour controversy before the Bethel family over the administration of the Society's affairs. A number of the Bethel family sympathized with the opposers. The opposition continued for several weeks, with the disturbers threatening to "overthrow the existing tyranny," as they put it. But Brother Rutherford had a sound basis for the action he had taken. How so?

It turned out that although the four opposing directors had been appointed by Brother Russell, these appointments had never been confirmed by vote of the corporation members at the annual meeting of the Society. Therefore, the four of them were not legal members of the board of

---

J. F. Rutherford's Background

Joseph Franklin Rutherford was born of Baptist parents on a farm in Morgan County, Missouri, U.S.A., on November 8, 1869. When Joseph was 16, his father consented to his attending college, provided that he pay his own way and that he pay for a hired laborer to take his place on the farm. A determined young man, Joseph secured a loan from a friend and managed to go to college while also studying law.

After completing his academy education, Rutherford spent two years under the tutelage of Judge E. L. Edwards. By the time he was 20, he became the official court reporter for the courts of the Fourteenth Judicial Circuit in Missouri. On May 5, 1892, his license to practice law in Missouri was granted. Rutherford later served for four years as public prosecutor for Boonville, Missouri. Still later, he served on occasion as a special judge in the Eighth Judicial Circuit Court of Missouri. That is why he came to be known as "Judge" Rutherford.

Interestingly, to help pay his way through school, Rutherford sold encyclopedias from house to house. It was not an easy job—there were many rebuffs. On one occasion he almost died when he fell into an icy stream while calling on farms. He promised himself that when he became a lawyer, if anyone ever came to his office selling books, he would buy them. True to his word, he accepted three volumes of "Millennial Dawn" from two colporteurs who appeared at his office early in 1894. Several weeks later he read the books and promptly wrote a letter to the Watch Tower Society, in which he said: "My dear wife and myself have read these books with the keenest interest, and we consider it a God-send and a great blessing that we have had the opportunity of coming in contact with them." In 1906, Joseph F. Rutherford was baptized, and a year later he became the Watch Tower Society's legal counsel.

directors at all! Rutherford had been aware of this but had not mentioned it at first. Why not? He had wanted to avoid giving the impression that he was going against Brother Russell's wishes. However, when it became evident that they would not discontinue their opposition, Rutherford acted within his authority and responsibility as president to replace them with four others whose appointments were to be confirmed at the next annual meeting, to be held in January 1918.

On August 8, the disgruntled ex-directors and their supporters left the Bethel family; they had been asked to leave because of the disturbance they had been creating. They soon began spreading their opposition by an extensive speaking and letter-writing campaign throughout the United States, Canada, and Europe. As a result, after the summer of 1917, a number of congregations of Bible Students were split into two groups—those loyal to the Society and those who were easy prey to the smooth talk of the opposers.

Rutherford asked the opposers to leave Bethel

But might the ousted directors, in an effort to gain control of the organization, try to influence those attending the annual meeting? Anticipating such a reaction, Rutherford felt it advisable to take a survey of all the congregations. The results? According to the report published in *The Watch Tower* of December 15, 1917, those voting indicated their overwhelming support of J. F. Rutherford and the directors cooperating with him! This was confirmed at the annual meeting.* The opposers' efforts to gain control had failed!

What became of those opposers and their supporters? After the January 1918 annual meeting, the opposing ones splintered off, even choosing to celebrate the Memorial, on March 26, 1918, on their own. Any unity they enjoyed was short-lived, and before long they broke up into various sects. In most cases their numbers dwindled and their activity diminished or ceased entirely.

Clearly, following Brother Russell's death, the Bible Students faced a real test of loyalty. As Tarissa P. Gott, who was baptized in 1915, put it: "Many of those who had seemed so strong, so devoted to the Lord, began to turn away.... All of this just did not seem right, yet it was happening and it upset us. But I said to myself: 'Was not this organization the one that Jehovah used to free us from the bonds of false religion? Have we not tasted of his goodness? If we were to leave now, where would we go? Would we not wind up following some man?' We could not see why we

---

* At the annual meeting held on January 5, 1918, the seven persons receiving the highest number of votes were J. F. Rutherford, C. H. Anderson, W. E. Van Amburgh, A. H. Macmillan, W. E. Spill, J. A. Bohnet, and G. H. Fisher. From these seven board members, the three officers were chosen—J. F. Rutherford as president, C. H. Anderson as vice president, and W. E. Van Amburgh as secretary-treasurer.

A TIME OF TESTING (1914-1918)   69

should go with the apostates, so we stayed."—John 6: 66-69; Heb. 6:4-6.

Some who withdrew from the organization later repented and associated with the Bible Students in worship once again. By far the majority, like Sister Gott, continued to cooperate with the Watch Tower Society and Brother Rutherford. The love and unity that bound them together had been built up through years of association together at meetings and conventions. They would allow nothing to break up that bond of union.—Col. 3:14.

By 1918 the Bible Students had survived testing from within. What, though, if opposition arose from those on the outside?

Objects of Attack

Through the close of 1917 and into 1918, the Bible Students energetically distributed the new book, *The Finished Mystery*. By the end of 1917, the printers were busy on the 850,000 edition. *The Watch Tower* of December 15, 1917, reported: "The sale of the Seventh Volume is unparalleled by the sale of any other book known, in the same length of time, excepting the Bible."

But not everyone was thrilled with the success of *The Finished Mystery*. The book contained some references to the clergy of Christendom that were very cutting. This so angered the clergy that they urged the government to suppress the publications of the Bible Students. As a result of this clergy-inspired opposition, early in 1918, *The Finished Mystery* was banned in Canada. Opposition soon mounted against the Bible Students in the United States.

To expose this clergy-inspired pressure, on March 15, 1918, the Watch Tower Society released the tract *Kingdom News* No. 1. Its message? The six-column-wide headline read: "Religious Intolerance—Pastor Russell's Followers Persecuted Because They Tell the People the Truth." Below the heading "Treatment of Bible Students Smacks of the 'Dark Ages'" were set forth the facts of the persecution and the ban that had begun in

> **'No Men on Earth More Highly Favored'**
>
> On June 21, 1918, J. F. Rutherford and several of his close associates were sentenced to 20 years' imprisonment, having been falsely convicted of conspiracy. Their feelings? In a handwritten note dated June 22-23 (shown below), from the Raymond Street jail in Brooklyn, New York, Brother Rutherford wrote: "There are probably no men on earth today more highly favored and who are happier than the seven brethren now in prison. They are conscious of their entire innocence of intentional wrongdoing, and rejoice to be suffering with Christ for loyally serving Him."

Written with his own hand by Brother Joseph F. Rutherford, June 22-23, 1918, while confined in the Raymond Street Jail, Brooklyn, NY

The Raymond Street jail, in Brooklyn, New York, where Brother Rutherford and several of his close associates were held for seven days immediately following their sentencing

Victims of Clergy-Inspired Persecution

By the middle of 1918, J. F. Rutherford and seven of his associates were in prison—victims of clergy-inspired opposition. But those eight men were not the only targets of such hatred. During earlier years it had been C. T. Russell who was primarily the object of attack by the clergy and the press. Now the Bible Students themselves were victims. "The Golden Age" (now "Awake!") of September 29, 1920, published a graphic, extensive report of vicious persecution they endured in the United States. It read like something out of the Inquisition.* Included were the following accounts:

"April 22, 1918, at Wynnewood, Oklahoma, Claud Watson was first jailed and then deliberately released to a mob composed of preachers, business men and a few others that knocked him down, caused a negro to whip him and, when he had partially recovered, to whip him again. They then poured tar and feathers all over him, rubbing the tar into his hair and scalp."

"April 29, 1918, at Walnut Ridge, Arkansas, W. B. Duncan, 61 years of age, Edward French, Charles Franke, a Mr. Griffin and Mrs. D. Van Hoesen were jailed. The jail was broken into by a mob that used the most vile and obscene language, whipped, tarred, feathered and drove them from town. Duncan was compelled to walk twenty-six miles to his home and barely recovered. Griffin was virtually blinded and died from the assault a few months later."

"April 30, 1918, . . . at Minerva, Ohio, S. H. Griffin was first jailed and then released to a mob, then lectured fifteen minutes by the minister, then struck repeatedly, cursed, kicked, trodden upon, threatened with hanging and with drowning, driven from town, spit upon, tripped repeatedly, jabbed repeatedly with an umbrella, forbidden to ride, followed five miles to Malvern, Ohio, rearrested, jailed for safety at Carrollton and finally taken home by brave and faithful officials who, after examining his literature, said, in so many words, 'We find no fault in this man.'"

---

* Pp. 712-17.

Canada. The instigators? The tract pulled no punches in pointing to the clergy, who were described as "a bigoted class of men who have systematically endeavored to prevent the people from understanding the Bible and to throttle all Bible teaching unless it comes through them."* What a hard-hitting message!

How did the clergy respond to such an exposé? They had already stirred up trouble against the Watch Tower Society. But now they got vicious! In the spring of 1918, a wave of violent persecution was launched against the Bible Students in both North America and Europe. The clergy-inspired opposition came to a head on May 7, 1918, when U.S. federal warrants were issued for the arrest of J. F. Rutherford and several of his close associates. By mid-1918, Rutherford and seven associates found themselves in the federal penitentiary in Atlanta, Georgia.

But with Judge Rutherford and his associates in prison, what happened to the operation of headquarters?

Keeping the Home Fires Burning

Back in Brooklyn an Executive Committee was appointed to take charge of the work. A chief concern of the brothers appointed was to keep *The Watch Tower* in circulation. The Bible Students everywhere certainly

---

* Two other hard-hitting tracts followed. *Kingdom News* No. 2, dated April 15, 1918, contained an even stronger message under the headline "'The Finished Mystery' and Why Suppressed." Then, *Kingdom News* No. 3, of May 1918, carried the significant headline "Two Great Battles Raging—Fall of Autocracy Certain."

A Time of Testing (1914-1918)

needed all the spiritual encouragement that could be given them. In fact, during this entire "testing season," not one issue of *The Watch Tower* failed to appear in print!*

What was the spirit at headquarters? Thomas (Bud) Sullivan, who later served as a member of the Governing Body, recalled: "It was my privilege to visit Brooklyn Bethel in the late summer of 1918 during the brothers' incarceration. The brothers in charge of the work at Bethel were in no wise fearful or downhearted. In fact, the reverse was true. They were optimistic and confident that Jehovah would give his people the victory ultimately. I was privileged to be at the breakfast table on Monday morning when the brothers sent out on weekend appointments gave their reports. A fine picture of the situation was obtained. In every case the brothers were confident, waiting for Jehovah to direct their activities further."

Many problems, however, were encountered. World War I was still raging. There were shortages of paper supplies and coal, which were vitally needed for the work at headquarters. With patriotism at fever pitch, there was considerable animosity against the Society; the Bible Students were viewed as traitors. Under these extreme circumstances, it appeared impossible to continue operations at Brooklyn. So, the Executive Committee, after consulting with other brothers, sold the Brooklyn Tabernacle and closed the Bethel Home. On August 26, 1918, the operations were transferred back to Pittsburgh to an office building at Federal and Reliance streets.

Nevertheless, a good spirit prevailed. Martha Meredith recalled: "We in Pittsburgh got together and decided we were going to keep 'the home fires burning' until the brethren got out of prison. At that time the Brooklyn office was moved to Pittsburgh, so the brethren got busy writing articles for *The Watch Tower* and had it printed. When *The Watch Towers* were ready to be sent out, we sisters wrapped them and sent them out to the people."

The Bible Students had faced some severe trials since the Gentile Times had ended in the fall of 1914. Could they continue to survive? Did they really have 'the love of God in their hearts' or not? Would they firmly hold on to "the Lord and His Truth," as Russell had cautioned, or would they let go?

Thomas (Bud) Sullivan visited headquarters in 1918 and later served on the Governing Body of Jehovah's Witnesses

---

* On earlier occasions, issues of the *Watch Tower* had been combined, but this was not done during 1914-18.

CHAPTER 7

ADVERTISE THE KING AND THE KINGDOM! (1919-1941)

"Do you believe that the King of glory has begun his reign? Then back to the field, O ye sons of the most high God! Gird on your armor! Be sober, be vigilant, be active, be brave. Be faithful and true witnesses for the Lord. Go forward in the fight until every vestige of Babylon lies desolate. Herald the message far and wide. The world must know that Jehovah is God and that Jesus Christ is King of kings and Lord of lords. This is the day of all days. Behold, the King reigns! You are his publicity agents. Therefore advertise, advertise, advertise, the King and his kingdom."

THAT dramatic call to action delivered by J. F. Rutherford at the international convention at Cedar Point, Ohio, in 1922, had a profound influence on those in attendance. The Bible Students left that convention with a burning desire to advertise the Kingdom. But just a few short years earlier, the prospect of serving as publicity agents of the Kingdom seemed bleak indeed. J. F. Rutherford and seven of his associates were in prison, and their future role within the organization seemed uncertain. How were these difficulties overcome?

"I Know Something About the *Law* of the *Loyal*"

A convention was scheduled in Pittsburgh, Pennsylvania, January 2-5, 1919, during the time that Brother Rutherford and his associates were in prison. But this was no ordinary convention—it was combined with the annual meeting of the Watch Tower Society, on Saturday, January 4, 1919. Brother Rutherford was well aware of the significance of this meeting. That Saturday afternoon he searched for Brother Macmillan and found him at the prison tennis court. According to Macmillan, this is what happened:

"Rutherford said, 'Mac, I want to talk to you.'

"'What do you want to talk to me about?'

"'I want to talk to you about what's going on at Pittsburgh.'

"'I'd like to play this tournament out here.'

ADVERTISE THE KING AND THE KINGDOM! (1919 - 1941)

"'Aren't you interested in what's going on? Don't you know it's the election of officers today? You might be ignored and dropped and we'll stay here forever.'

"'Brother Rutherford,' I said, 'let me tell you something perhaps you haven't thought of. This is the first time since the Society was incorporated that it can become clearly evident whom Jehovah God would like to have as president.'

"'What do you mean by that?'

"'I mean that Brother Russell had a controlling vote and he appointed the different officers. Now with us seemingly out of commission the matter's different. But, if we got out in time to go up to that assembly to that business meeting, we would come in there and would be accepted to take Brother Russell's place with the same honor he received. It might look then like man's work, not God's.'

"Rutherford just looked thoughtful and walked away."

That day a tense meeting was in progress back at Pittsburgh. "Confusion, dissension, and arguments reigned for a while," recalled Sara C. Kaelin, who was raised in the Pittsburgh area. "Some wanted to postpone the meeting for six months; others questioned the legality of electing officers who were in prison; others suggested all new officers."

After a lengthy discussion, W. F. Hudgings, a director of the Peoples Pulpit Association,* read to the audience a letter from Brother Rutherford. In it he sent love and greetings to those assembled. *"Satan's chief weapons are PRIDE, AMBITION and FEAR,"* he warned. Showing a desire to submit to Jehovah's will, he even humbly suggested suitable men in the event that the shareholders should decide to elect new officers for the Society.

Discussion continued for a while longer, and then E. D. Sexton, who had been appointed chairman of a nominating committee, spoke up, saying:

"I just arrived. My train was forty-eight hours late, having been snowbound. I have something to say and for my own comfort I better say it now. My dear brethren, I have come here, as the balance of you have, with certain ideas in mind—pro and con. . . . There is no legal obstacle in the way. If we desire to re-elect our brethren in the South to any office they can hold, I cannot see, or find from any [legal] advice I have received, how this will, in any shape or form, interfere with the aspect of their case before the Federal Court or before the public.

"I believe that the greatest compliment we can pay to our dear brother Rutherford would be to re-elect him as president of the W[atch] T[ower]

"Satan's chief weapons are PRIDE, AMBITION and FEAR"

---

* A New York corporation formed in 1909 in connection with the Society's moving of its principal offices to Brooklyn, New York.

B[ible] & T[ract] Society. I do not think there is any question in the mind of the public as to where we stand on the proposition. If our brethren in any way technically violated a law they did not understand, we know their motives are good. And before Almighty [God] they have neither violated any law of God or of man. We could manifest the greatest confidence if we re-elected Brother Rutherford as president of the Association.

"I am not a lawyer, but when it comes to the legality of the situation I know something about the *law* of the *loyal*. Loyalty is what God demands. I cannot imagine any greater confidence we could manifest than to have an election AND RE-ELECT BROTHER RUTHERFORD AS PRESIDENT."

Well, Brother Sexton evidently expressed the sentiments of most of those in attendance. There were nominations; a vote was taken; and J. F. Rutherford was elected president, C. A. Wise vice president, and W. E. Van Amburgh secretary-treasurer.

The next day Brother Rutherford knocked on Macmillan's cell wall and said: "Poke your hand out." He then handed Macmillan a telegram saying that Rutherford had been reelected president. "He was very happy," Macmillan later recalled, "to see this display of assurance that Jehovah was running the Society."

The election was over, but Brother Rutherford and the seven others were still in prison.

"A Country-Wide Agitation" in Behalf of the Prisoners

"During the past few weeks a country-wide agitation has been started in behalf of these brethren," stated *The Watch Tower* of April 1, 1919. Certain newspapers were calling for the release of J. F. Rutherford and his associates. The Bible Students in all parts of the United States indicated their support by writing letters to newspaper editors, congressmen, senators, and governors, urging them to take action in behalf of the eight prisoners. Clearly, the Bible Students would not rest until their eight brothers were free.

By March 1919, Bible Students in the United States were circulating a petition in which they asked President Woodrow Wilson to use his influence to accomplish one of the following in behalf of the imprisoned brothers:

"FIRST: A complete pardon, if that now be possible, OR

"SECOND: That you direct the Department of Justice to dismiss the prosecution against them, and that they be fully released, OR

"THIRD: That they be immediately admitted to bail pending a final decision of their case by the higher courts."

Within two weeks the Bible Students obtained 700,000 signatures. The petition, though, was never presented to the president or the government.

"Assurance that Jehovah was running the Society"

Why not? Because before that could be done, the eight men were released on bail. What, then, did the petition work accomplish? *The Watch Tower* of July 1, 1919, stated: "The evidence is overwhelming that the Lord desired this work to be done, not so much to get the brethren out of prison, as for the purpose of a witness to the truth."

"Welcome Home, Brethren"

On Tuesday, March 25, the eight brothers left Atlanta for Brooklyn. News of their release spread quickly. It was truly a touching scene—Bible Students gathering at train stations along the route with the hope of seeing them and expressing joy at their release. Others rushed to the Bethel Home in Brooklyn, which had been closed down, to arrange for a welcome-home banquet. Back in Brooklyn, on March 26, the brothers were admitted to bail of $10,000 each, and they were released.

"Immediately they were accompanied by a number of friends to the Bethel Home, where between five and six hundred friends had assembled to welcome them," reported *The Watch Tower* of April 15, 1919. In the dining room, there was a large banner that said, "Welcome Home, Brethren." Nearly 50 years later, Mabel Haslett, who was present for that banquet, recalled: "I remember making a hundred doughnuts, which the brothers seemed to enjoy after nine months of prison fare. I can still see Brother Rutherford reaching out for them. It was an unforgettable occasion as he and the others related their experiences. I also remember short-statured Brother DeCecca standing on a chair so that all could see and hear him."

On Tuesday morning, April 1, Brother Rutherford arrived in Pittsburgh, where the headquarters offices were now located. Here, too, the brothers, learning that he was due to arrive, scheduled a banquet, which was held that evening at the Hotel Chatham. The conditions in prison, though, had taken their toll on Brother Rutherford. He had developed a weakened lung condition, and as a result, after his release he contracted a severe case of pneumonia. So, shortly afterward his ill health made it necessary for him to go to California, where he had some relatives.

The Test in Los Angeles

Now that Brother Rutherford and the others were free, the question arose, What about the work of proclaiming God's Kingdom? During the time that these brothers were in prison, organizational oversight of the witnessing work had largely been shut down. The Brooklyn Tabernacle had been sold and the Bethel Home closed. The headquarters offices in Pittsburgh were small, and funds were limited. Besides, how much interest really was there in the Kingdom message? From California, Brother Rutherford decided to arrange for a test.

'Out of prison, not so much for themselves, as for the purpose of a witness to the truth'

"House of the Princes"

Brother Rutherford had a severe case of pneumonia after his release from unjust imprisonment in 1919. Thereafter, he had only one good lung. In the 1920's, under a doctor's treatment, he went to San Diego, California, and the doctor urged him to spend as much time as possible there. From 1929 on, Brother Rutherford spent the winters working at a San Diego residence he had named Beth-Sarim. Beth-Sarim was built with funds that were a direct contribution for that purpose. The deed, which was published in full in "The Golden Age" of March 19, 1930, conveyed this property to J. F. Rutherford and thereafter to the Watch Tower Society.

Concerning Beth-Sarim, the book "Salvation," published in 1939, explains: "The Hebrew words 'Beth Sarim' mean 'House of the Princes'; and the purpose of acquiring that property and building the house was that there might be some tangible proof that there are those on earth today who fully believe God and Christ Jesus and in His kingdom, and who believe that the faithful men of old will soon be resurrected by the Lord, be back on earth, and take charge of the visible affairs of earth."

A few years after Brother Rutherford's death, the board of directors of the Watch Tower Society decided to sell Beth-Sarim. Why? "The Watchtower" of December 15, 1947, explained: "It had fully served its purpose and was now only serving as a monument quite expensive to keep; our faith in the return of the men of old time whom the King Christ Jesus will make princes in ALL the earth (not merely in California) is based, not upon that house Beth-Sarim, but upon God's Word of promise."*

---

* At the time, it was believed that faithful men of old times, such as Abraham, Joseph, and David, would be resurrected before the end of this system of things and would serve as "princes in all the earth," in fulfillment of Psalm 45:16. This view was adjusted in 1950, when further study of the Scriptures indicated that those earthly forefathers of Jesus Christ would be resurrected after Armageddon.—See "The Watchtower," November 1, 1950, pages 414-17.

A meeting was arranged at Clune's Auditorium in Los Angeles, on Sunday, May 4, 1919. "The Hope for Distressed Humanity" was the title of the lecture to which the public was invited. But the talk was to be given by J. F. Rutherford—a man who had just got out of prison. Through extensive newspaper advertising, Rutherford promised a candid presentation of the facts, including an explanation of the reasons for the illegal convictions of the Society's officers. Would anyone be interested enough to attend?

The response was overwhelming. In fact, 3,500 turned out to hear the lecture, and about 600 others had to be turned away. Brother Rutherford was thrilled! He agreed to speak to the overflow crowd on Monday night, and 1,500 showed up. He was so ill, though, that he could not finish that lecture. After an hour he had to be replaced by an associate. Nevertheless, the test in Los Angeles was a success. Brother Rutherford was convinced that there was considerable interest in the Kingdom message, and he was determined to see it proclaimed.

On With the Work!

By July 1919, Brother Rutherford was back on the job at the headquarters in Pittsburgh. Things happened quickly during the next few months. Arrangements were made for a convention of the Bible Students to be held at Cedar Point, Ohio, September 1-8, 1919. The Society's offices were moved back to Brooklyn and were operating there by October 1.

What were they to do now? Their mission was clearly emphasized at the

Cedar Point convention. On Tuesday, September 2, Brother Rutherford explained: "A Christian's mission on earth . . . is to proclaim the message of the Lord's kingdom of righteousness, which will bring blessings to the whole groaning creation." Three days later, on Friday, September 5, which was called Co-Laborers' Day, Brother Rutherford further stated: "In sober moments a Christian naturally asks himself, Why am I on the earth? And the answer of necessity must be, The Lord has graciously made me his ambassador to bear the divine message of reconciliation to the world, and my privilege and duty is to announce that message."

Yes, it was time to get on with the work of proclaiming God's Kingdom! And to assist in carrying out this commission, Brother Rutherford announced: "Under the Lord's providence we have arranged for the publication of a new magazine under the name and title THE GOLDEN AGE." Little did the conventioners know what a courageous journal *The Golden Age* would prove to be.

"That first post World War I convention was a great boost for all of us," recalled Herman L. Philbrick, who traveled to the convention from his home in Boston, Massachusetts. Truly, that Cedar Point convention stirred the Bible Students to action. They were ready to get on with the work of proclaiming the good news. It was as though they had come back to life from the dead.—Compare Ezekiel 37:1-14; Revelation 11:11, 12.

Meanwhile, significant things were happening on the world scene. The Treaty of Versailles was signed on June 28, 1919, and went into effect on January 10, 1920. Officially ending military actions against Germany in World War I, the treaty also provided for the formation of the League of Nations—an international association created to keep peace in the world.

'Advertise the King and the Kingdom'

In 1922 the Bible Students returned to Cedar Point for a nine-day program, from September 5 to 13. Excitement ran high as the delegates arrived for this international convention. The climax of the convention was reached on Friday, September 8, when Brother Rutherford delivered the talk "The Kingdom."

Thomas J. Sullivan later recalled: "Those who were privileged to attend that meeting can even yet visualize Brother Rutherford's earnestness when he told the few restless people that were walking around because of the intense heat to 'SIT DOWN' and 'LISTEN' to the talk at any cost." Those who did were not disappointed, for that was the historic discourse in which Brother Rutherford urged his listeners to 'advertise the King and the Kingdom.'

The audience responded with great enthusiasm. *The Watch Tower* reported: "Each one present was thoroughly impressed with the fact that the

"A Christian's mission on earth . . . is to proclaim the message of the Lord's kingdom"

obligation is laid upon every one of the consecrated from this time forward to act as a publicity agent for the King and the kingdom." The Bible Students came away from that convention with a burning zeal for the preaching work. As Sister Ethel Bennecoff, a colporteur then in her late 20's, said, "we were aroused to 'advertise, advertise, advertise the King and his kingdom'—Yes, with more zeal and love in our hearts than ever before."

As the spiritual light of understanding grew brighter, the Bible Students began to perceive some thrilling Bible truths. (Prov. 4:18) The understanding of these precious truths gave a powerful impetus to their work of proclaiming God's Kingdom. At the same time, they had to adjust their thinking—and for some this was a real test.

"Unrealized Hopes Are Not Unique to Our Day"

"We may confidently expect," stated the booklet *Millions Now Living Will Never Die,* back in 1920, "that 1925 will mark the return [from the dead] of Abraham, Isaac, Jacob and the faithful prophets of old . . . to the condition of human perfection." Not only was the resurrection of faithful men of old expected in 1925 but some hoped that anointed Christians might receive their heavenly reward in that year.*

The year 1925 came and went. Some abandoned their hope. But the vast majority of the Bible Students remained faithful. "Our family," explained Herald Toutjian, whose grandparents had become Bible Students about the turn of the century, "came to appreciate that unrealized hopes are not unique to our day. The apostles themselves had similar misplaced expectations. . . . Jehovah is worthy of loyal service and praise with or without the ultimate reward."—Compare Acts 1:6, 7.

Which Organization—Jehovah's or Satan's?

"Birth of the Nation"—that was the title of a dramatic article appearing in the March 1, 1925, issue of *The Watch Tower.* It presented an enlightened understanding of Revelation chapter 12 that some found difficult to accept.

The symbolic characters mentioned in this chapter of Revelation were identified as follows: the "woman" that gives birth (vss. 1, 2) as "God's [heavenly] organization"; the "dragon" (vs. 3) as "the devil's organization"; and the "man child" (vs. 5, *KJ*) as "the new kingdom, or new government." On the basis of this, something was clearly explained for the first time: There are two distinct and opposing organizations—Jehovah's and Satan's. And following the "war in heaven" (vs. 7, *KJ*), Satan and his demon supporters were cast out of heaven and hurled down to the earth.

"We sat down and studied it all night until I could understand it very

'Advertise the Kingdom with more zeal and love than ever before'

---

* See Chapter 28, "Testing and Sifting From Within."

ADVERTISE THE KING AND THE KINGDOM! (1919 - 1941)

well," wrote Earl E. Newell, who later served as a traveling representative of the Watch Tower Society. "We went to an assembly in Portland, Oregon, and there we found the friends all upset and some of them were ready to discard *The Watch Tower* because of this article." Why was this explanation of Revelation chapter 12 so difficult for some to accept?

For one thing, it was a striking departure from what had been published in *The Finished Mystery*, which was largely a posthumous compilation of Brother Russell's writings.* Walter J. Thorn, who served as a traveling pilgrim, explained: "The article on 'The Birth of the Nation' was . . . difficult to take hold of because of a previous interpretation by dear Brother Russell, which we believed to be the final word on Revelation." Little wonder, then, that some stumbled over the explanation. "Unquestionably this interpretation may prove a sifting medium," noted J. A. Bohnet, another pilgrim, "but the really earnest and sincere ones of the faith will stand firm and rejoice."

J. A. Bohnet

Indeed, the really earnest and sincere ones did rejoice over the new explanation. It was now so clear to them: everyone belongs either to Jehovah's organization or to Satan's. "Remember," the article "Birth of the Nation" explained, "it will be our privilege . . . to valiantly fight for the cause of our King by proclaiming his message, which he has given us to proclaim."

As the 1920's and then the 1930's progressed, more flashes of Bible understanding followed. Worldly celebrations and holidays, such as Christmas, were put away. Other practices and beliefs were also discarded when it was seen that they had God-dishonoring roots.# More than abandoning wrong practices and beliefs, though, the Bible Students continued to look to Jehovah for progressive revelations of truth.

"You Are My Witnesses"

"'You are my witnesses,' is the utterance of Jehovah, 'and I am God.'" (Isa. 43:12) Starting in the 1920's, the Bible Students became increasingly aware of the deep significance of these words of the prophet Isaiah. Through the pages of *The Watch Tower*, attention was repeatedly drawn to our responsibility to bear witness to Jehovah's name and his Kingdom. A milestone, though, was reached at a convention held in Columbus, Ohio, in 1931.

On Sunday, July 26, at noon, Brother Rutherford delivered the public discourse "The Kingdom, the Hope of the World," which was broadcast over a vast radio hookup, with more than 300 additional stations later

---

* According to the interpretation set out in *The Finished Mystery*, the woman of Revelation chapter 12 was "the early Church," the dragon was "the Pagan Roman Empire," and the man child was "the papacy."

See Chapter 14, "They Are No Part of the World."

Broadcasting the Kingdom Message

Within two years after regular commercial radio broadcasting began, radio was being used to transmit the Kingdom message. Thus on February 26, 1922, Brother Rutherford delivered his first radio broadcast, in California. Two years later, on February 24, 1924, the Watch Tower Society's own radio station WBBR, on Staten Island, New York, began broadcasting. Eventually, the Society organized worldwide networks to broadcast Bible programs and lectures. By 1933 a peak of 408 stations were carrying the Kingdom message to six continents!

WBBR, in New York, was operated by the Watch Tower Society from 1924 until 1957

WBBR orchestra in 1926

J. F. Rutherford delivering the lecture "Face the Facts," at the Royal Albert Hall, in London, England, on September 11, 1938; more than 10,000 jammed the auditorium (below), while millions more heard by radio

WBBR opening program

STATION
W B B R
International Bible Students Association
Opening Program
8:30 p.m.
Sunday, February 24, 1924
[244 meters]

Piano Solos.................Prof. L. W. Jackson
  (a) "Minuet in G" (Paderewski)
  (b) "Soaring" (Schumann)
Vocal Trio................Prof. John T. Read, Messrs.
W. P. Mockridge and F. W. Franz
"I Heard the Voice of Jesus Say"
Solos

Staff at station 2HD, Newcastle, NSW, Australia

Radio station CHCY in Edmonton, Alberta, was one of several stations the Society owned and operated in Canada

Broadcasting to Finland via a radio station in Estonia

Broadcasting equipment at station WORD, near Chicago, Illinois; owned and operated by the Society

rebroadcasting the message. At the end of the discourse, Brother Rutherford served notice on Christendom by reading a stinging resolution entitled "Warning From Jehovah," which was addressed "To the Rulers and to the People." To his invitation that they adopt the resolution, the entire visible audience stood and shouted, "Aye!" Telegrams later received indicated that many of those listening on the radio likewise raised their voices in agreement.

From one o'clock, when the public discourse was finished, until four o'clock, when Brother Rutherford reentered the auditorium, the atmosphere was charged with excitement. Brother Rutherford had specially requested that everyone who was really interested in the noonday warning to Christendom be in his seat at four o'clock.

Promptly at four, Brother Rutherford began by stating that he regarded what he was about to say as of vital importance to everyone who could hear his voice. His listeners were keenly interested. During his discourse he presented another resolution, this one entitled "A New Name," which was climaxed by the declaration: "We desire to be known as and called by the name, to wit, *Jehovah's witnesses.*" The thrilled conventioners again jumped to their feet with the ringing shout "Aye!" They would henceforth be known as Jehovah's Witnesses!

"We desire to be known as . . . Jehovah's witnesses"

"Jehovah's Spirit Made Us Fearless"

During 1927, Jehovah's people were encouraged to spend a portion of every Sunday in group witnessing. Immediate legal opposition was raised. Within a few years, arrests began to mount—268 in the United States alone in 1933, 340 in 1934, 478 in 1935, and 1,149 in 1936. On what charge? Actually, on various charges, including selling without a license, disturbing the peace, and violating Sunday sabbath laws. The local groups of Witnesses were not versed in how to deal with police officials and courts. Getting legal help locally was either too expensive or not possible because of prejudice. So the Watch Tower Society wisely established a legal department in Brooklyn to render counsel.

A strong legal defense, though, was not enough. These sincere Witnesses of Jehovah were determined to live up to the name they had embraced. So, early in the 1930's, they struck back by going on the offensive. How? By means of special preaching missions known as divisional campaigns. Thousands of volunteers throughout the United States were organized into divisions. When Witnesses were arrested in one town for house-to-house preaching, a division of volunteers from other areas soon arrived and "besieged" the town, giving a thorough witness.*

Those divisional campaigns did much to strengthen the local Witnesses. In each division, there were qualified brothers who had been trained to

---

* See Chapter 30, "Defending and Legally Establishing the Good News."

deal with the authorities. It was a great encouragement to the brothers living in a trouble area, perhaps in a small town, to know that they were not alone in proclaiming God's Kingdom.

It took a great deal of courage to share in the divisional campaigns of the 1930's. In the midst of the Great Depression period, jobs were scarce. Yet, Nicholas Kovalak, Jr., a traveling overseer for some 40 years, recalls: "When the call came to cover a trouble spot, the 'service director' would ask for volunteers. Individuals were told *not* to volunteer if they were afraid of losing their jobs.... But we were always happy to see 100% affirmative response!" Observed John Dulchinos, an overseer from Springfield, Massachusetts: "Indeed, those were thrilling years and their memories are precious. Jehovah's spirit made us fearless."

Meanwhile, a flash of Bible understanding was developing that would have a tremendous impact on the work.

What About the Jonadabs?

In 1932 it was explained that Jehonadab (Jonadab), King Jehu's associate, prefigured a class of persons who would enjoy everlasting life on earth.* (2 Ki. 10:15-28) The Jonadabs, as they came to be known, counted it a privilege to be associated with Jehovah's anointed servants and to have some share with them in advertising the Kingdom. But at that time, there was no special effort to gather and organize these individuals with an earthly hope.

However, real encouragement was given to the Jonadabs in *The Watchtower* of August 15, 1934. The article "His Kindness" stated: "Should a Jonadab consecrate himself to the Lord and be baptized? Answer: Most assuredly it is proper for a Jonadab to consecrate himself to do the will of God. No one will ever get life without doing that. Water immersion is merely a symbol of having made a consecration [or, as we would now say, dedication] to do God's will, and that would not be out of order." The Jonadabs were thrilled!

Yet, even greater joy was near for them. The following spring, several issues of *The Watchtower*, beginning with the April 1, 1935, issue, carried this announcement: "Again *The Watchtower* reminds its readers that a convention of Jehovah's witnesses and Jonadabs# will be held at Washington, D.C., beginning May 30 and ending June 3, 1935." The Jonadabs eagerly awaited the convention.

Yes! Jonadabs should be baptized

---
* *Vindication*, Book Three, page 77. See also Chapter 12, "The Great Crowd—To Live in Heaven? or on Earth?"
# At that time the Jonadabs were not considered to be "Jehovah's witnesses." (See *The Watchtower*, August 15, 1934, page 249.) However, a few years later, *The Watchtower* of July 1, 1942, stated: "These 'other sheep' [Jonadabs] become witnesses for Him, on the same wise that the faithful men before Christ's death, from John the Baptist all the way back to Abel, were the never-quitting witnesses for Jehovah."

'Searching for sheeplike people yet to be gathered'

The "great multitude," foretold in Revelation 7:9-17 (*KJ*), was the subject of a talk Brother Rutherford delivered on the second afternoon of the convention. In that discourse he explained that the great multitude was made up of the modern-day Jonadabs and that these Jonadabs had to show the same degree of faithfulness to Jehovah as the anointed. Well, the audience was excited! At the speaker's request, the Jonadabs arose. "There was at first a hush," recalled Mildred Cobb, who had been baptized in the summer of 1908, "then a gladsome cry, and the cheering was loud and long."

This flash of Bible understanding had a profound effect upon the activity of Jehovah's Witnesses. "With enthusiasm running high," remarked Sadie Carpenter, a full-time preacher for over 60 years, "we went back to our territories to search for these sheeplike people who were yet to be gathered." Later the *Yearbook of Jehovah's Witnesses for 1936* reported: "This revelation stirred the brethren and stimulated them to renewed activities, and everywhere throughout the earth come the reports exhibiting joy in the fact that the remnant now have the privilege of carrying the message to the great multitude, and these together working to the honor of the Lord's name." To help them in this work, the book *Riches*, published in 1936, contained an extensive discussion of the prospects held out in the Scriptures for the great multitude.

At last, the dedicated, baptized members of the great multitude were finding their proper place alongside the anointed in advertising God's Kingdom!

'Tanning the Old Lady's Hide'

In the 1930's, the message these zealous Witnesses proclaimed included a stinging exposé of false religion. A helpful tool in this regard was released at the general convention of Jehovah's Witnesses, September 15-20, 1937, in Columbus, Ohio.

On Saturday, September 18, following his morning discourse, Brother Rutherford released the tan-colored book *Enemies*. It denounced false religion as "a great enemy, always working injury to mankind." False religionists were identified as "agents of the Devil, whether they are aware of that fact or not." When presenting the book to the audience, Brother Rutherford said: "You will notice that its cover is tan, and we will tan the old lady's* hide with it." To this the audience gave loud and enthusiastic approval.

---

* A reference to "the great harlot," mentioned in Revelation chapter 17. The book *Enemies* stated: "All organizations on the earth that are in opposition to God and his kingdom . . . take the name of 'Babylon' and 'harlot,' and those names specifically apply to the leading religious organization, the Roman Catholic church." (Page 198) Years later it was seen that the harlot actually represents the world empire of all false religion.

For some years the phonograph had played a part in 'tanning the old lady.' But in connection with the phonograph work, there was a surprise at the 1937 convention. "At this assembly the work using the portable phonograph on the doorstep was introduced," recalls Elwood Lunstrum, who was just 12 years old at the time. "Formerly we had been carrying the phonograph with us in the service, but we had only played it when invited inside. . . . An organization of 'Special Pioneers' was outlined at the Columbus convention to spearhead the use of the doorstep setup with the phonograph and the follow-up work with interested persons (first then called 'back-calls') and Bible studies with an arrangement called 'model study.'"

Jehovah's people left that convention well equipped for the work of proclaiming God's Kingdom. They certainly needed all the encouragement they could get. The rising tide of nationalism in the 1930's brought opposition, in some cases mob violence, from individuals who were determined to stop Jehovah's Witnesses from meeting together and from preaching.

"A Bunch of Hijackers"

A strong force of opposition came from certain Catholic Action groups. On October 2, 1938, Brother Rutherford was straightforward in delivering the lecture "Fascism or Freedom," which later appeared in booklet form and was distributed by the millions. Brother Rutherford in this speech detailed a number of incidents of unlawful acts to demonstrate collusion between certain public officials and representatives of the Roman Catholic Church.

After presenting the facts, Rutherford noted: "When the people are told the facts about a crowd that is operating under a religious cloak to steal their rights, the Hierarchy howls and says: 'Lies! Put a gag in the mouths of those and do not permit them to speak.'" Then he asked: "Is it wrong to publish the truth concerning a bunch of hijackers that are robbing the people? No! . . . Shall honest men be gagged and compelled to remain silent while this bunch of hijackers destroy the liberties of the people? Above all, shall the people be denied their God-given privileges of peaceable assembly and freedom of worship of Almighty God, and freedom of speech concerning his kingdom and those who oppose it?"

Following this stinging rebuke, opposition continued from Catholic Action groups across the United States. Jehovah's Witnesses waged legal battles for freedom of worship and their right to proclaim God's Kingdom. But the situation only worsened as the world went to war. Legal restrictions and imprisonment also came upon Jehovah's Witnesses in country after country in Europe, Africa, and Asia.

Rutherford was straightforward in rebuking religious opposers

"Everyone Wanted to Go to St. Louis"

"In 1941," recalls Norman Larson, who had recently entered the full-time ministry, "we all felt we were in for some critical days ahead with the war now going on in Europe. So everyone wanted to go to St. Louis." For what? Why, for the Theocratic Assembly of Jehovah's Witnesses in St. Louis, Missouri, August 6-10, 1941! And "everyone" came. The convention facilities were filled to overflowing. According to a police estimate, a peak of 115,000 persons attended.

From the first day, the convention program provided timely encouragement. Brother Rutherford's opening discourse, "Integrity," sounded the keynote of the convention. "We realized more clearly than ever before why Jehovah was permitting such intense persecution of his people world wide," recalled Hazel Burford, who served as a missionary for nearly 40 years, until her death in 1983. Reporting on the convention, the *1942 Yearbook of Jehovah's Witnesses* added: "All could see clearly that there lay ahead of them a great work of witnessing to be done, and that by so doing they would maintain their integrity, though they be hated of all men and worldly organizations."

A touching scene at the convention came on Sunday, August 10, which was "Children's Day." When the morning session opened, 15,000 children —between 5 and 18 years of age—were assembled in the main arena directly in front of the platform and in a place similarly set aside at a trailer city where an overflow crowd listened. As Brother Rutherford, then in his early 70's, stepped onto the platform, the children cheered and applauded. He waved his handkerchief, and the children waved back. Then, in a clear, kind voice, he addressed the entire audience on the theme "Children of the King." After talking for over an hour to the audience in general, he directed his remarks to the children seated in the reserved sections.

"All of you . . . children," he said, fixing his attention on the young beaming faces before him, "who have agreed to do the will of God and have taken your stand on the side of his Theocratic Government by Christ Jesus and who have agreed to obey God and his King, please stand up." The children rose as one body. "Behold," exclaimed the enthusiastic speaker, "more than 15,000 new witnesses to the Kingdom!" There was a burst of applause. "All of you who will do what you can to tell others about God's kingdom and its attending blessings, please say 'Aye.'" A thunderous cry, "Aye!"

To climax it all, Brother Rutherford announced the release of the new book *Children*, which was received with shouts of joy and tremendous applause. Afterward, the speaker, a tall man, shared in distributing free copies of the book as a long line of children walked up on the platform and filed past him. Many wept at the sight.

15,000 children take their stand on the side of the Kingdom

Preaching With Phonographs

In 1933, Jehovah's Witnesses began to employ another innovative method of preaching. A transportable transcription machine with an amplifier and loudspeaker was used to broadcast 33 1/3-rpm recordings of Brother Rutherford's radio lectures, in halls, parks, and other public places. Sound cars and sound boats also were used to let the Kingdom message ring out.

The effective use of transcription machines led to yet another innovation—preaching from house to house with a lightweight phonograph. In 1934 the Society began producing portable phonographs and a series of 78-rpm discs containing 4 1/2-minute Bible lectures. Eventually, recordings covering 92 different subjects were in use. In all, the Society produced more than 47,000 phonographs to trumpet the Kingdom message. However, in time, greater emphasis was laid on oral presentations of the Kingdom message, so the phonograph work was phased out.

With a sound car on a hilltop, the Kingdom message could be heard miles away (above)

Using the transcription machine in Mexico (right)

A sound boat broadcasting on the River Thames, in London, England (above)

Using a phonograph in field service (left)

Demonstrating how to use a vertical-style phonograph, in 1940 (right)

From 1917, when J. F. Rutherford became president, to 1941, the Watch Tower Society produced a flood of publications, including 24 books, 86 booklets, and annual "Yearbooks," as well as articles for "The Watch Tower" and "The Golden Age" (later called "Consolation")

In the audience that Sunday morning were many children who lived up to their shout of "Aye!" LaVonne Krebs, Merton Campbell, and Eugene and Camilla Rosam were among the young ones who received a *Children* book on that occasion. Still serving at the Society's headquarters in 1992, they have devoted 51, 49, 49, and 48 years respectively to the full-time ministry. Some of the children went on to serve in foreign missionary assignments, including Eldon Deane (Bolivia), Richard and Peggy Kelsey (Germany), Ramon Templeton (Germany), and Jennie Klukowski (Brazil). Indeed, that Sunday morning program in St. Louis made a lasting impression on many young hearts!

On Sunday afternoon Brother Rutherford had some parting words for the conventioners. He encouraged them to carry forward the work of proclaiming God's Kingdom. "I feel absolutely certain," he told them, "that from henceforth . . . those who will form the great multitude will grow by leaps and bounds." He urged them to return to their respective parts of the land and "put on more steam . . . put in all the time you can." Then came his final words to the audience: "Well, my dear brethren, the Lord bless you. Now I won't say Good-bye, because I expect to see you at some time again."

But for many it was the last time they would see Brother Rutherford.

Closing Days of J. F. Rutherford

Brother Rutherford had developed cancer of the colon and was in poor health at the St. Louis convention. Still, he managed to give five strong discourses. Following the convention, however, his condition worsened, and he was compelled to have a colostomy. Arthur Worsley recalls the day Brother Rutherford said good-bye to the Bethel family. "He confided in us that he was going to undergo a serious operation and that whether he lived through it or not, he was confident that we would keep on proclaiming Jehovah's name. He . . . concluded by saying, 'So, if God wills, I will see you again. If not, keep up the fight.' There was not a dry eye in the family."

Brother Rutherford, 72 years of age, survived the surgery. Shortly thereafter he was taken to a residence in California he had named Beth-Sarim. It was evident to his loved ones, and to medical experts, that he would not recover. In fact, he required further surgery.

About the middle of December, Nathan H. Knorr, Frederick W. Franz, and Hayden C. Covington arrived from Brooklyn. Hazel Burford, who cared for Brother Rutherford during those sad and trying days, later recalled: "They spent several days with him going over the annual report for the *Yearbook* and other organizational matters. After their departure, Brother Rutherford continued to weaken and, about three weeks later, on Thursday, January 8, 1942, he faithfully finished his earthly course."*

How was news of Brother Rutherford's death received at Bethel? "I will never forget the day we learned of Brother Rutherford's passing," recalled William A. Elrod, who had been a member of the Bethel family for nine years. "It was at noontime when the family was assembled for lunch. The announcement was brief. There were no speeches. No one took the day off to mourn. Rather, we went back to the factory and worked harder than ever."

Those were extremely trying times for Jehovah's Witnesses. The war had become a global conflict. The fighting spread from Europe to Africa, then to what was known as the Soviet Union. On December 7, 1941, just a month before Brother Rutherford's death, Japan's attack on Pearl Harbor had drawn the United States into the war. In many places the Witnesses were the objects of mob violence and other forms of intense persecution.

What would happen now?

"If God wills, I will see you again. If not, keep up the fight"

---

* Brother Rutherford was survived by his wife, Mary, and their son, Malcolm. Because Sister Rutherford had poor health and found the winters in New York (where the Watch Tower Society's headquarters were located) difficult to endure, she and Malcolm had been residing in southern California, where the climate was better for her health. Sister Rutherford died December 17, 1962, at the age of 93. Notice of her death, appearing in the Monrovia, California, *Daily News-Post*, stated: "Until poor health confined her to her home, she took an active part in the ministerial work of Jehovah's Witnesses."

CHAPTER 8

DECLARING THE GOOD NEWS WITHOUT LETUP (1942-1975)

"TO ALL LOVERS OF THE THEOCRACY:
On January 8, 1942, our beloved brother, J. F. Rutherford, faithfully finished his earthly course . . . To him it was a joy and comfort to see and know that all the witnesses of the Lord are following, not any man, but the King Christ Jesus as their Leader, and that they will move on in the work in complete unity of action."
—A letter announcing the death of Brother Rutherford.*

NEWS of Brother Rutherford's death came as a momentary shock to Jehovah's Witnesses around the world. Many knew that he had been ill, but they did not expect him to die so soon. They were saddened over the loss of their dear brother but were determined to "move on in the work"—the work of proclaiming God's Kingdom. They did not view J. F. Rutherford as their leader. Charles E. Wagner, who had worked in Brother Rutherford's office, observed: "The brothers everywhere had developed a strong conviction that Jehovah's work did not depend on any man." Still, someone was needed to shoulder the responsibilities that Brother Rutherford had carried as president of the Watch Tower Society.

"Determined to Keep Close to the Lord"

It was Brother Rutherford's heartfelt wish that Jehovah's Witnesses declare the good news without letup. So in mid-December 1941, several weeks before his death, he called together four directors of the two principal legal corporations used by Jehovah's Witnesses and suggested that as soon after his death as possible, all the members of the two boards be called in joint session and a president and a vice president be elected.

On the afternoon of January 13, 1942, just five days after Rutherford's death, all the board members of the two corporations met jointly at Brooklyn Bethel. Several days earlier, the Society's vice president, 36-year-old

---

* *The Watchtower,* February 1, 1942, p. 45; *Consolation,* February 4, 1942, p. 17.

Nathan H. Knorr, had suggested that they earnestly seek divine wisdom by prayer and meditation. The board members recognized that while the brother elected president would administer the legal affairs of the Watch Tower Society, he would also serve as a principal overseer of the organization. Who had the needed spiritual qualifications for this weighty responsibility in caring for Jehovah's work? The joint meeting was opened with prayer, and after careful consideration, Brother Knorr was unanimously elected president of the two corporations and 30-year-old Hayden C. Covington, the Society's lawyer, vice president.*

Later that day, W. E. Van Amburgh, the Society's secretary-treasurer, announced to the Bethel family the results of the election. R. E. Abrahamson, who was present on that occasion, recalled that Van Amburgh said: 'I can remember when C. T. Russell died and was replaced by J. F. Rutherford. The Lord continued to direct and prosper His work. Now, I fully expect the work to move ahead with Nathan H. Knorr as president, because this is the Lord's work, not man's.'

How did the Bethel family members in Brooklyn feel about the results of the election? A touching letter from them dated January 14, 1942, the day after the election, answers: "His [Rutherford's] change shall not slow us up in the performance of the task the Lord has assigned to us. We are determined to keep close to the Lord and to one

---

* In September 1945, Brother Covington graciously declined to serve further as vice president of the Watch Tower Bible and Tract Society (of Pennsylvania), explaining that he wished to comply with what was then understood to be Jehovah's will for all members of the directorate and officers—that they be spirit-anointed Christians, whereas he professed to be one of the "other sheep." On October 1, Lyman A. Swingle was elected to the board of directors, and on October 5, Frederick W. Franz was selected as vice president. (See *1946 Yearbook of Jehovah's Witnesses*, pp. 221-4; *The Watchtower*, November 1, 1945, pp. 335-6.)

Background of N. H. Knorr

Nathan Homer Knorr was born in Bethlehem, Pennsylvania, U.S.A., on April 23, 1905. When he was 16 years old, he became associated with the Allentown Congregation of Bible Students. In 1922 he attended the convention at Cedar Point, Ohio, where he made up his mind to resign from the Reformed Church. The following year, on July 4, 1923, after Frederick W. Franz, from Brooklyn Bethel, delivered a baptism talk, 18-year-old Nathan was among those who were baptized in the Little Lehigh River, in Eastern Pennsylvania. On September 6, 1923, Brother Knorr became a member of the Bethel family in Brooklyn.

Brother Knorr applied himself diligently in the Shipping Department, and before long his natural abilities in organizing were recognized. When the Society's factory manager, Robert J. Martin, died on September 23, 1932, Brother Knorr was appointed to replace him. On January 11, 1934, Brother Knorr was elected to be a director of the Peoples Pulpit Association (now Watchtower Bible and Tract Society of New York, Inc.), and the following year he was made the Association's vice president. On June 10, 1940, he became the vice president of the Watch Tower Bible and Tract Society (Pennsylvania corporation). His election to the presidency of both societies and of the British corporation, International Bible Students Association, came in January 1942.

In the years that followed, one of Brother Knorr's closest associates and trusted counselors was Frederick W. Franz, a man older in years than he was and one whose knowledge of languages and whose background as a Bible scholar had already proved to be of great value to the organization.

another, firmly pushing the battle to the gate, fighting shoulder to shoulder. . . . Our intimate association with Brother Knorr for approximately twenty years . . . enables us to appreciate the Lord's direction in the choice of Brother Knorr as president and thereby the loving watch-care of the Lord over His people." Letters and cablegrams of support soon poured into headquarters from around the world.

There was no feeling of uncertainty as to what to do. A special article was prepared for the February 1, 1942, *Watchtower*, the very same issue that announced the death of J. F. Rutherford. "The final gathering by the Lord is on," it declared. "Let nothing for one instant interrupt the onward push of his covenant-people in His service. . . . Now to hold fast our integrity toward the Almighty God is the ALL-IMPORTANT thing." Jehovah's Witnesses were urged to continue declaring the good news with zeal.

But 'holding fast their integrity' was a real challenge in the early 1940's. The world was still at war. Wartime restrictions in many parts of the earth made it difficult for Jehovah's Witnesses to preach. Arrests and mob action against the Witnesses continued unabated. Hayden Covington, as the Society's legal counsel, directed the legal fight, sometimes from his office at Brooklyn headquarters and sometimes from trains as he traveled caring for legal cases. Working with local lawyers, such as Victor Schmidt, Grover Powell, and Victor Blackwell, Brother Covington fought hard to establish the constitutional rights of Jehovah's Witnesses to preach from house to house and to distribute Bible literature without restraint from local officials.*

Sounding the "Go Ahead" Signal

Despite wartime rationing of food and gasoline, early in March 1942, plans were announced for the New World Theocratic Assembly, to be held September 18-20. To facilitate travel, 52 convention cities were selected across the United States, many of them tied in by telephone to Cleveland, Ohio, the key city. About the same time, Jehovah's Witnesses convened in 33 other cities throughout the earth. What was the objective of this assembly?

'We are not here gathered to meditate on the past or what individuals have done,' stated the chairman, Brother Covington, in his introductory words for the opening session. Then, he introduced the keynote speech, "The Only Light," based on Isaiah chapters 59 and 60, which was delivered by Brother Franz. Referring to Jehovah's prophetic command recorded by Isaiah, the speaker rousingly declared: "Here, then, is the 'Go ahead' signal from the Highest Authority to keep going on in his [work] of witness no

Preaching despite arrests and mob action

---

* See Chapter 30, "Defending and Legally Establishing the Good News."

matter what happens before Armageddon comes." (Isa. 6:1-12) It was no time to slack the hand and relax.

"There is further work to be done; much work!" declared N. H. Knorr in the next talk on the program. To aid his listeners in their response to the "Go ahead" signal, Brother Knorr announced the release of an edition of the King James version of the Bible, printed on the Society's own presses and complete with a concordance specially designed for use by Jehovah's Witnesses in their field ministry. That release reflected Brother Knorr's keen interest in printing and distributing the Bible. In fact, after he had become president of the Society earlier that year, Brother Knorr had moved quickly to secure the printing rights for this translation and to coordinate the preparation of the concordance and other features. Within months this special edition of the *King James Version* was ready for release at the convention.

On the final day of the assembly, Brother Knorr delivered the discourse "Peace—Can It Last?" In it he set out powerful evidence from Revelation 17:8 that World War II, which was then raging, would not lead into Armageddon, as some thought, but that the war would end and a period of peace would set in. There was still work to be done in proclaiming God's Kingdom. The conventioners were told that in order to help care for the anticipated growth in the organization, starting the next month the Society would send "servants to the brethren" to work with the congregations. Each congregation would be visited every six months.

"That New World Theocratic Assembly welded Jehovah's organization together solidly for the work ahead," says Marie Gibbard, who attended in Dallas, Texas, with her parents. And there was much work to do. Jehovah's Witnesses looked ahead to the period of peace to come. They were determined to plow right on through opposition and persecution, declaring the good news without letup!

An Era of Increased Education

They had been using the testimony card and the phonograph in their house-to-house preaching, but could each witness of Jehovah improve in his ability to explain from the Scriptures the reasons for his hope? The Society's third president, N. H. Knorr, thought so. C. James Woodworth, whose father was

---

An Encouraging Look Ahead

Delegates to the New World Theocratic Assembly in Cleveland, Ohio, in September 1942, were delighted when the aged secretary-treasurer of the Society, W. E. Van Amburgh, addressed the convention. Brother Van Amburgh recalled that the first convention he attended was in Chicago in 1900, and it was a "big" one.—there were about 250 in attendance. After enumerating other "big" conventions over the years, he concluded with this encouraging look ahead: "This convention* looks large to us now, but as this convention is large in comparison with the ones that I have attended in the past, so I anticipate this convention will be a very small one in comparison to those just in the future when the Lord begins to assemble his people from all corners of the globe."

* A peak of 26,000 attended in Cleveland, with a total attendance of 129,699 for the 52 convention cities scattered across the United States.

for years the editor of *The Golden Age* and *Consolation*, put it this way: "Whereas in Brother Rutherford's day the emphasis was on 'Religion Is a Snare and a Racket,' now the era of global expansion was dawning, and education—Biblical and organizational—commenced on a scale heretofore not known by Jehovah's people."

The era of education got under way almost immediately. On February 9, 1942, about a month after N. H. Knorr was elected president of the Society, a far-reaching announcement was made at Brooklyn Bethel. Arrangements were made at Bethel for an Advanced Course in Theocratic Ministry—a school that featured Bible research and public speaking.

By the following year, the groundwork was laid for a similar school to be conducted in the local congregations of Jehovah's Witnesses. At the "Call to Action" Assembly held throughout the United States on April 17 and 18, 1943, the booklet *Course in Theocratic Ministry* was released. Each congregation was urged to start the new school, and the Society appointed instructors to act as chairmen and to offer constructive counsel on student talks delivered by male enrollees. As quickly as possible, the course was translated and put into operation in other lands.

As a result, qualified speakers trained in this ministry school began to share in a worldwide public speaking campaign to proclaim the Kingdom message. Many of these were later able to put their training to good use as convention speakers and in caring for heavy organizational responsibilities.

Among them was Angelo C. Manera, Jr., a traveling overseer for some 40 years. He was one of the first enrollees in the school in his congregation, and he observed: "Those of us who attended the meetings and went out in field service for many years without this provision have come to look upon it as a great step in our personal and organizational progress."

Regarding his training in the school inaugurated at Brooklyn Bethel in 1942, George Gangas, a Greek translator at the time, later noted: "I recall the time I gave my first six-minute talk. I was not confident in myself so I wrote it down. But when I got up to give it, audience fear gripped me and I stuttered and muttered, losing my thoughts. Then I resorted to reading from the manuscript. But my hands were trembling so much that the lines were jumping up and down!" Yet, he did not quit. In time, he was giving talks before large convention audiences and even serving as a member of the Governing Body of Jehovah's Witnesses.

A School Founded on Faith

On September 24, 1942, a further stride was taken in the era of increased education. At a joint meeting of the boards of directors of the two legal corporations, Brother Knorr suggested that the Society establish an-

'Global expansion and education on a scale not previously known'

other school, using a building that had been constructed at Kingdom Farm, at South Lansing, New York, 255 miles northwest of New York City. The purpose of this school would be to train missionaries for service in foreign countries where there was a great need for Kingdom proclaimers. The suggestion was unanimously approved.

Albert D. Schroeder, who was then 31 years of age, was designated registrar and served as chairman of the committee to get the new school organized. "My, did our hearts leap for joy at this amazing new assignment!" he says. The instructors got busy right away; they had just four months to develop the courses, work up the lectures, and gather a library. "The course of advanced Christian education covered 20 weeks, the Bible being the major textbook," explains Brother Schroeder, who now serves as a member of the Governing Body.

On Monday, February 1, 1943, a cold winter day in upstate New York, the first class, with 100 students, commenced. Here was a school truly founded on faith. In the midst of World War II, there were only a few areas of the world to which missionaries could be sent. Yet, with full confidence that there would be a period of peace during which they could be used, prospective missionaries were trained.

Gilead School at South Lansing, New York

Postwar Reorganizing

In May 1945 the hostilities of World War II in Europe came to an end. Four months later, in September, the fighting ceased in the Pacific. World War II was over. On October 24, 1945, a little over three years after the Society's president delivered the talk "Peace—Can It Last?" the Charter of the United Nations went into effect.

Reports about the activity of Jehovah's Witnesses had already begun trickling out of Europe. To an extent that amazed their brothers and sisters around the world, the Kingdom proclamation work had forged ahead in European countries in spite of the war. *The Watchtower* of July 15, 1945, reported: "In 1940 France had 400 publishers; now there are 1,100 that talk the Kingdom. . . . In 1940 Holland had 800 publishers. Four hundred of them were whisked off to concentration camps in Germany. Those left behind talked the Kingdom. The result? In that land there are now 2,000 Kingdom publishers." The open door of freedom now presented opportunities of further declaring the good news, not just in Europe but around the world. First, though, much reconstruction and reorganization were needed.

N. H. Knorr's Service Tours, 1945-56

1945-46: Central America, South America, North America, Europe, the Caribbean

1947-48: North America, Pacific islands, the Orient, the Middle East, Europe, Africa

1949-50: North America, Central America, South America, the Caribbean

1951-52: North America, Pacific islands, the Orient, Europe, the Middle East, Africa

1953-54: South America, the Caribbean, North America, Central America

1955-56: Europe, Pacific islands, the Orient, North America, the Middle East, North Africa

Anxious to survey the needs of Jehovah's Witnesses in the war-ravaged countries, the Society's president, along with his secretary, Milton G. Henschel, set out on a tour of Britain, France, Switzerland, Belgium, the Netherlands, and Scandinavia in November 1945 to encourage the brothers and to inspect the branch offices of the Society.* Their objective was postwar reorganization. Arrangements were made for literature supplies as well as food and clothing to be shipped to the brothers in need. Branch offices were reestablished.

Brother Knorr well realized that good branch organization was needed

---

* Detailed reports of the trip were published in *The Watchtower* during 1946.—See pages 14-16, 28-31, 45-8, 60-4, 92-5, 110-12, 141-4.

DECLARING THE GOOD NEWS WITHOUT LETUP (1942 - 1975)

to keep pace with the forward movement of the preaching work. His natural abilities in organizing were fully used in expanding the Society's branch facilities worldwide. In 1942, when he became president, there were 25 branch offices. By 1946, despite the bans and hindrances of World War II, there were branches in 57 lands. Over the next 30 years, down to 1976, the number of branches increased to 97.

Equipped to Be Teachers

From his international travels shortly after the war, the Society's president determined that Jehovah's Witnesses needed to be better equipped to be teachers of God's Word. Further Bible education was necessary as well as suitable instruments for use in the field ministry. Those needs were met early in the postwar period.

At the Glad Nations Theocratic Assembly, held in Cleveland, Ohio, August 4-11, 1946, Brother Knorr delivered the talk "Equipped for Every Good Work." The entire audience was intrigued as he posed such questions as: "Would it not be of tremendous aid to have information on each one of the sixty-six books of the Bible? Would it not aid in understanding the Scriptures if we knew who wrote each book of the Bible? when each book was written? where it was written?" Expectancy ran high as he then declared: "Brethren, you have all that information and much more in the new book entitled 'Equipped for Every Good Work'!" A burst of applause followed that announcement. The new publication would serve as a textbook for the ministry school held in the congregations.

Not only were Jehovah's Witnesses equipped with a publication to deepen their knowledge of the Scriptures but they were also given some excellent aids for use in the field. The 1946 convention will long be remembered for the release of the first issue of *Awake!* This new magazine replaced *Consolation* (formerly known as *The Golden Age*). Also released was the book "*Let God Be True.*"* Henry A. Cantwell, who later served as a traveling overseer, explains: "For some time we had very much needed a book that could be used effectively in conducting Bible studies with newly interested persons, one that would cover the basic Bible doctrines and truths. Now with the release of '*Let God Be True,*' we had just what was needed."

Equipped with such valuable teaching aids, Jehovah's Witnesses expected further rapid expansion. Addressing the convention on the subject "The Problems of Reconstruction and Expansion," Brother Knorr explained that during the years of global war, no standstill had occurred in

Brother Knorr, shown here visiting Cuba, traveled the world many times over

---

* Within a few years, this Bible study aid became known around the world. Revised as of April 1, 1952, more than 19,000,000 copies were printed in 54 languages.

efforts at witnessing. From 1939 to 1946, the number of Kingdom proclaimers had increased by over 110,000. To meet the growing worldwide demand for Bible literature, the Society planned to expand the factory and the Bethel Home in Brooklyn.

The anticipated period of world peace had set in. The era of global expansion and Bible education was well under way. Jehovah's Witnesses returned home from the Glad Nations Theocratic Assembly better equipped to be teachers of the good news.

Kingdom Proclamation Surges Ahead

With a view to worldwide expansion, on February 6, 1947, the Society's president and his secretary, Milton G. Henschel, embarked on a 47,795-mile world service tour. The trip took them to islands of the Pacific, New Zealand, Australia, Southeast Asia, India, the Middle East, the Mediterranean area, Central and Western Europe, Scandinavia, England, and Newfoundland. It was the first time since 1933 that representatives of the Society's headquarters staff in Brooklyn had been able to visit their brothers in Germany. Jehovah's Witnesses around the world followed the two travelers as reports of the trip were published in issues of *The Watchtower* throughout 1947.*

"It was the first opportunity for us to get acquainted with the brothers in Asia and other places and to see what the needs were," explains Brother Henschel, now a member of the Governing Body of Jehovah's Witnesses. "We had in mind sending out missionaries, so we had to know what they were getting into and what they would need." Following the tour, a steady stream of Gilead-trained missionaries reached foreign soil to spearhead the work of Kingdom proclamation. And the results were impressive. Over the next five years (1947-52), the number of Kingdom preachers worldwide more than doubled, from 207,552 to 456,265.

Theocracy's Increase

On June 25, 1950, military forces from the Democratic People's Republic of Korea invaded the Republic of Korea to the south. Eventually, troops were sent in from 16 other lands. But as the war pitted major nations against one another, Jehovah's Witnesses prepared to gather for an international convention that would demonstrate not only their worldwide unity but also that Jehovah was blessing them with increase.—Isa. 60:22.

England

Lebanon

Brother Knorr felt that every Witness should be able to preach from house to house

---

* See pages 140-4, 171-6, 189-92, 205-8, 219-23, 236-40, 251-6, 267-72, 302-4, 315-20, 333-6, 363-8.

The Theocracy's Increase Assembly was scheduled for July 30 through August 6, 1950. This was to be by far the biggest convention ever held up to that time by Jehovah's Witnesses at one site. Some 10,000 foreign delegates from Europe, Africa, Asia, Latin America, islands of the Pacific—altogether 67 different lands—converged on Yankee Stadium in New York City. The peak attendance of over 123,000 for the public lecture—compared with the peak of 80,000 who attended the Glad Nations Theocratic Assembly just four years earlier—was itself impressive evidence of increase.

A significant factor in the increase experienced by Jehovah's Witnesses has been the printing and distribution of God's Word. A milestone in this regard was reached on August 2, 1950, when Brother Knorr announced the release of the modern-language *New World Translation of the Christian Greek Scriptures* in English. The conventioners were thrilled to learn that this new translation restored the divine name Jehovah 237 times in the main text from Matthew to Revelation! In concluding his discourse, the speaker made this stirring appeal: "Take this translation. Read it through. Study it, for it will help you to better your understanding of God's Word. Put it in the hands of others." Other installments would follow over the next decade, so that eventually Jehovah's Witnesses would have an accurate, easy-to-read translation of the entire Bible that they could enthusiastically offer to others.

Before leaving the convention city, the delegates were invited to tour the new Bethel headquarters at 124 Columbia Heights and the greatly expanded printing factory at 117 Adams Street. Constructed with the financial support of Witnesses from around the world, the new facilities completed the vast expansion program announced and enthusiastically approved at the 1946 Cleveland convention. Little did Jehovah's Witnesses then realize how much expansion there would yet be, not just in Brooklyn, but worldwide. More and larger printeries would be needed to care for the constantly increasing ranks of Kingdom publishers.

As president of the Society, Brother Knorr worked closely with Brother Franz for over 35 years

Intensified Training in House-to-House Ministry

At the New World Society Assembly, held in New York City, July 19-26, 1953, new publications were provided for Jehovah's Witnesses themselves and for use especially in the house-to-house proclamation of the Kingdom. For example, the release of *"Make Sure of All Things"* brought forth thunderous applause from the 125,040 present on Monday, July 20. A handy field service tool, the 416-page pocket-size book assembled more than 4,500 scriptures under 70 main themes. Jehovah's Witnesses now had at their fingertips the Scriptural answers to questions raised in their house-to-house preaching.

On Wednesday morning during the talk "Principal Work of All Servants," Brother Knorr announced a further step in the ongoing education of Jehovah's Witnesses—an extensive house-to-house training program to be put into operation in all congregations. More experienced publishers were asked to help less experienced ones to become regular, effective house-to-house proclaimers of the Kingdom. This far-reaching program began September 1, 1953. Jesse L. Cantwell, a traveling overseer who took part in the training work, observed: "This program really helped the publishers to become more efficient."

In the months following July 1953, extension conventions were held on all five continents, with locally adapted forms of the same program. The intensified training in the house-to-house ministry was thus initiated in congregations of Jehovah's Witnesses around the world. That same year the number of Kingdom proclaimers peaked at 519,982.

Meeting the Needs of Global Expansion

In the mid-1950's, further arrangements were made to care for the rapid growth in the organization. For more than a decade, N. H. Knorr had traveled the globe to inspect the operation of the branches. These trips did much to ensure proper supervision of the work in each country and to strengthen the worldwide unity of Jehovah's Witnesses. Brother Knorr had a deep love for the missionaries and those serving in the branches around the world. Wherever he went, he took time to talk with them about their

Board of directors of the Watch Tower Bible and Tract Society of Pennsylvania, in mid-1950's. (From left to right) Lyman A. Swingle, Thomas J. Sullivan, Grant Suiter, Hugo H. Riemer, Nathan H. Knorr, Frederick W. Franz, Milton G. Henschel

DECLARING THE GOOD NEWS WITHOUT LETUP (1942 - 1975)   101

problems and needs and to encourage them in their ministry. But in 1955, there were 77 branch offices of the Watch Tower Society and 1,814 Gilead-trained missionaries serving in 100 different lands. Realizing that it was more than he could handle alone, Brother Knorr took steps to include others in this important work of visiting the branches and the missionary homes.

Arrangements were made to divide the earth into ten zones, each zone embracing a number of the Society's branches. Qualified brothers from the office in Brooklyn and experienced branch overseers were appointed to be zone servants (now called zone overseers) and were trained for this work by Brother Knorr. On January 1, 1956, the first of these zone servants inaugurated this new service of visiting branches. As of 1992, upwards of 30 brothers, including members of the Governing Body, were serving as zone overseers.

Education in the Divine Will

In the summer of 1958, the threat of war loomed in the Middle East. Despite the strain in international relations, Jehovah's Witnesses prepared to gather for an international convention that would further educate them in the divine will. It would also prove to be their largest convention in any one city.

A peak of 253,922 delegates from 123 lands flooded New York City's Yankee Stadium and the Polo Grounds for the Divine Will International Assembly, July 27 through August 3. "Jehovah's Witnesses Pour in by the Stadiumful," said New York's *Daily News* of July 26, 1958. "Eight special trains, 500 chartered buses and 18,000 auto pools are bringing the members, besides the two chartered ships and 65 chartered planes."

Gilead-trained missionaries had made known to the Society's headquarters the challenge they faced in teaching Bible truth to those not acquainted with the beliefs and doctrines of Christendom's churches. If only they could have a publication that would set forth just the true Biblical teachings, yet would be easy to read and understand! To the delight of the 145,488 delegates present on Thursday afternoon, July 31, Brother Knorr announced the release of the new book *From Paradise Lost to Paradise Regained*.

Brother Knorr urged all to use the new book in their field ministry. He also suggested that parents would find it helpful in teaching their children Bible truth. Many parents took the suggestion to heart. Grace A. Estep, a schoolteacher who was raised in a small town near Pittsburgh, Pennsylvania, noted: "A whole generation of children have grown up fingering the *Paradise* book, carrying it to meetings with them, sharing it

In 1958, delegates from 123 lands converged on Yankee Stadium for the Divine Will International Assembly

with their little playmates, being able to relate, long before they were old enough to read, a whole series of Bible stories just from the pictures."

Meaty material for advanced students of God's Word was also provided. At the conclusion of his stirring discourse "Let Your Will Come to Pass," Brother Knorr thrilled the audience when he announced the release of a new book entitled *"Your Will Be Done on Earth."* This new publication, containing an extensive study of the book of Daniel, educated its readers in how the divine will has been done and is now being done. "You are going to enjoy tremendously this book!" declared the speaker. By thunderous applause the vast audience of 175,441 expressed their delight at receiving this new instrument to deepen their appreciation of the divine will!

In his closing remarks, Brother Knorr announced further special educational programs that would benefit the worldwide organization. "The educational work is not on the decline," Knorr declared, "but rather it is on the move forward." He outlined plans for providing a ten-month training course in Brooklyn for overseers from the Society's branches all over the world. Also, in many countries around the world, there would be training courses of one month for traveling overseers and those having oversight in the congregations. Why all this education? "We want to move to higher levels of understanding," he explained, "so that we can get deeper into the thoughts of Jehovah as he has expressed them in his Word."

Work began immediately on the courses of study for these training programs. Seven months later, on March 9, 1959, the first class of a new school, the Kingdom Ministry School, began at South Lansing, New

York, home of the Gilead School. What started there soon reached out around the world as the new school was used to train those having oversight in the congregations.

Fortified to "Stand Firm in the Faith"

During the 1960's, human society was engulfed by a tidal wave of religious and social changes. Clergymen labeled portions of the Bible as mythical or outmoded. The "God is dead" ideology became increasingly popular. Human society sank deeper and deeper into the morass of sexual immorality. Through *The Watchtower* and other publications as well as convention programs, Jehovah's people were fortified to "stand firm in the faith" during that turbulent decade.—1 Cor. 16:13.

At a series of conventions held around the world in 1963, the talk "The Book of 'Everlasting Good News' Is Beneficial" defended the Bible against the onslaught of critics. "Critics of the Bible do not need to point out that mere men wrote this book," explained the speaker. "The Bible itself honestly informs us of that fact. But what makes this book different from any other book written by men is that the Holy Bible is 'inspired of God.'" (2 Tim. 3:16, 17) This stirring talk led up to the release of the book *"All Scripture Is Inspired of God and Beneficial."* The new publication included a discussion of each book of the Bible, giving the background of the book, such as who wrote it, when and where it was written, and evidence of its authenticity. Then came a summary of the Bible book, followed by a section called "Why Beneficial," which showed how this particular Bible book is of great value to the reader. A valuable instrument in the continuing Bible education of Jehovah's Witnesses, this publication is still featured as a textbook in the Theocratic Ministry School some 30 years after its release!*

Defending the Bible against the onslaught of critics

Jehovah's Witnesses were not unaffected by the sexual revolution of the 1960's. In fact, several thousand—a small percentage of their total number—had to be disfellowshipped each year, the majority for sexual immorality. With good reason, then, Jehovah's people were given direct counsel at a series of district conventions held in 1964. Lyle Reusch, a traveling overseer originally from Saskatchewan, Canada, recalls the talk "Keeping the Organization of Public Servants Pure, Chaste." Said Reusch: "Frank, straight language on morals spelled things out in plain talk."

The contents of the talk were published in *The Watchtower* of November 15, 1964. Among other things, it stated: "Girls, do not make yourselves a dirty towel for public use, available to the dirty hands of any whoremonger, any symbolic 'dog.'"—Compare Revelation 22:15.

---

* The book *"All Scripture Is Inspired of God and Beneficial"* was updated in 1990.

Such frank counsel was designed to help Jehovah's Witnesses as a people to keep in clean moral condition, fit to continue proclaiming the Kingdom message.—Compare Romans 2:21-23.

"Say, What Does This 1975 Mean?"

The Witnesses had long shared the belief that the Thousand Year Reign of Christ would follow after 6,000 years of human history. But when would 6,000 years of human existence end? The book *Life Everlasting—In Freedom of the Sons of God,* released at a series of district conventions held in 1966, pointed to 1975. Right at the convention, as the brothers examined the contents, the new book triggered much discussion about 1975.

At the convention held in Baltimore, Maryland, F. W. Franz gave the concluding talk. He began by saying: "Just before I got on the platform a young man came to me and said, 'Say, what does this 1975 mean?'" Brother Franz then referred to the many questions that had arisen as to whether the material in the new book meant that by 1975 Armageddon would be finished, and Satan would be bound. He stated, in essence: 'It could. But we are not saying. All things are possible with God. But we are not saying. And don't any of you be specific in saying anything that is going to happen between now and 1975. But the big point of it all is this, dear friends: Time is short. Time is running out, no question about that.'

'The big point of it all is this, dear friends: Time is short'

In the years following 1966, many of Jehovah's Witnesses acted in harmony with the spirit of that counsel. However, other statements were published on this subject, and some were likely more definite than advisable. This was acknowledged in *The Watchtower* of March 15, 1980 (page 17). But Jehovah's Witnesses were also cautioned to concentrate mainly on doing Jehovah's will and not to be swept up by dates and expectations of an early salvation.*

An Instrument for Speeding Up the Work

In the late 1960's, Jehovah's Witnesses were declaring the good news with a feeling of expectancy and urgency. During 1968 the number of Kingdom publishers had increased to 1,221,504 in 203 lands. Still, it was not uncommon for some persons to study the Bible year after year without acting upon the knowledge they gained. Was there a way of speeding up the work of making disciples?

---

* For example, the following articles were published in *The Watchtower:* "Making Wise Use of the Remaining Time" (May 1, 1968); "Serve With Eternity in View" (June 15, 1974); "Why We Have Not Been Told 'That Day and Hour'" and "How Are You Affected by Not Knowing the 'Day and Hour'?" (May 1, 1975). Earlier, in 1963, the book *"All Scripture Is Inspired of God and Beneficial"* had stated: "It does no good to use Bible chronology for speculating on dates that are still future in the stream of time.—Matt. 24:36."

DECLARING THE GOOD NEWS WITHOUT LETUP (1942 - 1975)

The answer came in 1968 with the release of a new Bible study aid, *The Truth That Leads to Eternal Life*. This 192-page pocket-size book was prepared with newly interested ones in mind. It contained 22 absorbing chapters dealing with such subjects as "Why It Is Wise to Examine Your Religion," "Why We Grow Old and Die," "Where Are the Dead?" "Why Has God Permitted Wickedness Until Our Day?" "How to Identify the True Religion," and "Building a Happy Family Life." The *Truth* book was designed to encourage the Bible student to reason on the material being considered and to apply it in his own life.

This new publication was to be used in connection with a six-month Bible study program. The September 1968 issue of the *Kingdom Ministry* explained how the new program would work: "It would be good to try to study *a whole chapter of the 'Truth' book each week*, though this may not be possible with all householders or with all the chapters in the book. . . . If, at the end of six months of intensive study and conscientious efforts to get them to meetings, they are not yet associating with the congregation, then it may be best to use your time to study with someone else who really wants to learn the truth and make progress. Make it your goal to present the good news on Bible studies in such a way that interested ones will act within six months!"

And act they did! In a short period of time, the six-month Bible study program had astounding success. For the three service years beginning September 1, 1968, and ending August 31, 1971, a total of 434,906 persons were baptized—more than double the number baptized during the previous three service years! Coming as it did at a time when there was a feeling of expectancy and urgency among Jehovah's Witnesses, the *Truth* book and the six-month Bible study campaign greatly aided in speeding up the disciple-making work.—Matt. 28:19, 20.

"It Has to Work; It Is From Jehovah"

For many years the congregations of Jehovah's Witnesses were organized so that one spiritually qualified man was appointed by the Society to be congregation servant, or "overseer," and was assisted by other appointed "servants."* (1 Tim. 3:1-10, 12, 13) These men were to serve the flock, not to rule over it. (1 Pet. 5:1-4) But could the congregations more closely conform to the structure of the first-century Christian congregations?

---

* See Chapter 15, "Development of the Organization Structure."

"Today I Started Thinking Again"

Released in 1968, the book "The Truth That Leads to Eternal Life" was widely used by Jehovah's Witnesses in studying the Bible with interested persons. This timely provision helped hundreds of thousands of thinking persons to gain an accurate knowledge of the Scriptures. A letter of appreciation received in 1973 from a reader in the United States said: "A very nice lady came to my door today and gave me a book called 'The Truth That Leads to Eternal Life.' I just finished it. The first time I've read 190 pages of anything in one day of my life. On June 29, 1967, I stopped believing in God. Today I started thinking again."

In 1971, at a series of conventions held throughout the earth, the talk "Theocratic Organization Amidst Democracies and Communism" was presented. On July 2, F. W. Franz delivered the talk at Yankee Stadium in New York City. In it he pointed out that where enough qualified men were available, first-century congregations had more than one overseer. (Phil. 1:1) "The congregational group of overseers," he stated, "would compose a 'body of older men'. . . The members of such a 'body [or, assembly] of older men' were all equal, having the same official status, and none of them was the most important, most prominent, most powerful member in the congregation." (1 Tim. 4:14) That talk really stirred the entire convention. What impact would this information have on the congregations of Jehovah's Witnesses around the world?

The answer came two days later, in the concluding talk, given by N. H. Knorr. Beginning October 1, 1972, adjustments in the oversight of the congregations worldwide would become effective. No longer would there be just one congregation servant, or overseer. But during the months leading up to October 1, 1972, responsible, mature men in each congregation would recommend to the Society for appointment the names of those who would serve as a *body* of elders (and the names of those who would serve as ministerial servants). One elder would be designated chairman,* but all the elders would have equal authority and share the responsibility for making decisions. "These organization adjustments," explained Brother Knorr, "will help to bring the operation of the congregations into closer conformity with God's Word, and surely that will result in greater blessings from Jehovah."

> *"An encouragement to all mature men to take hold of responsibility"*

How was this information about organization adjustments received by the assembled delegates? One traveling overseer was moved to say: "It has to work; it is from Jehovah." Another Witness of long experience added: "It will be an encouragement to all mature men to take hold of responsibility." Indeed, as many men as were qualified could now 'reach out' and be appointed to the "office of overseer." (1 Tim. 3:1) A greater number of brothers could thus gain valuable experience in shouldering congregation responsibility. Though they did not realize this at first, all of these would be needed to shepherd the great influx of new ones in the years to come.

The material presented at the convention also led to some clarifications and adjustments that involved the Governing Body. On September 6, 1971, it was resolved that the chairmanship of the Governing Body should rotate among its members, doing so alphabetically. Several weeks later, on

---

* The speaker also explained that beginning October 1, 1972, there would be a yearly rotating of chairmanship within each congregation's body of elders. This arrangement was adjusted in 1983, when each body of elders was asked to recommend a presiding overseer who, after appointment by the Society, would serve for an indefinite period of time as the chairman of the body of elders.

Publications for training Jehovah's Witnesses for the ministry

Some of the publications for use in the field ministry

Books that provided solid food to strengthen Jehovah's people spiritually

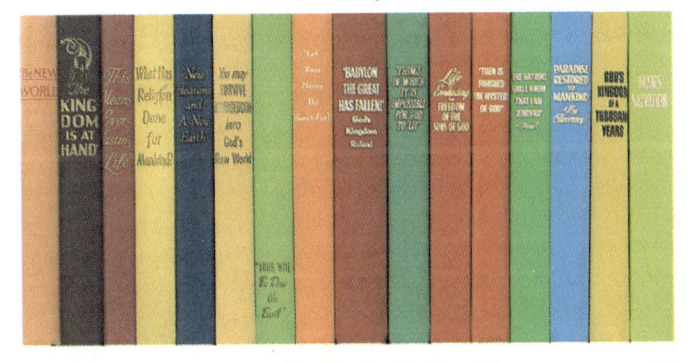

October 1, 1971, F. W. Franz became the chairman of the Governing Body for one year.

The following year, in September 1972, the first shifting of responsibilities in the congregations began, and by October 1 the rotation in most congregations was completed. During the next three years, Jehovah's Witnesses experienced impressive growth—over three quarters of a million persons getting baptized. But now they were facing the autumn of 1975. If all the expectations concerning 1975 were not realized, how would this affect their zeal for the global preaching activity as well as their worldwide unity?

Also, for decades Nathan H. Knorr, a man with a dynamic personality and outstanding ability as an organizer, had played a key role in advancing education within the organization and getting the Bible into the hands of people and helping them to understand it. How would the change to closer supervision by the Governing Body affect these objectives?

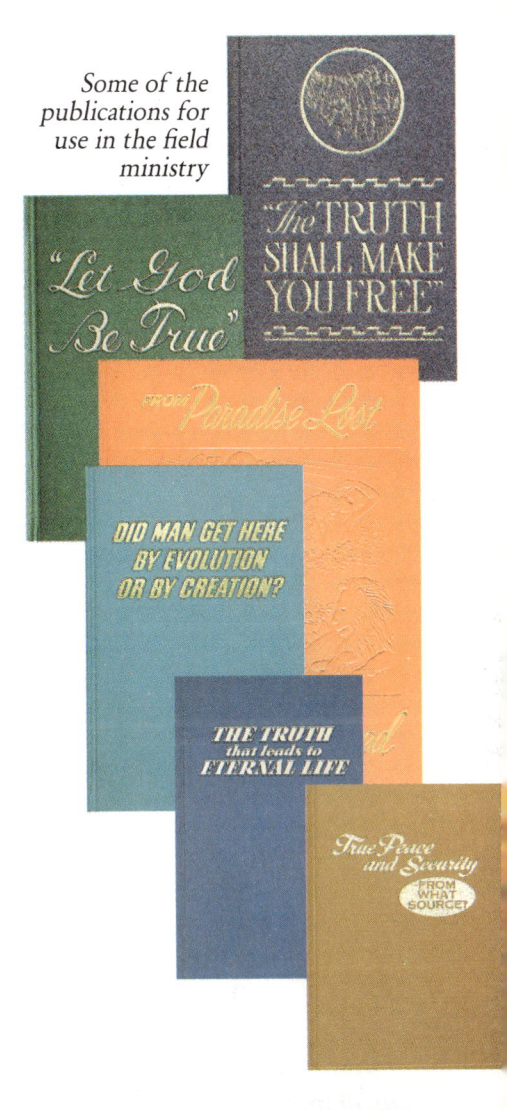

Research and study aids

CHAPTER 9

JEHOVAH'S WORD KEEPS MOVING SPEEDILY (1976-1992)

"Finally, brothers, carry on prayer for us, that the word of Jehovah may keep moving speedily [or, 'may be running'] and being glorified just as it is in fact with you."—2 Thess. 3:1, "Kingdom Interlinear."

WITH those words the apostle Paul asked his fellow believers in Thessalonica to pray that he and his companions might be successful in proclaiming Jehovah's word without hindrance. Jehovah answered that prayer. But this does not mean that the apostle did not have to deal with problems. He faced severe opposition from the world and had to reckon with false brothers who dealt deceitfully. (2 Cor. 11:23-27; Gal. 2:4, 5) Yet, in spite of this, after about ten years, Paul could write that as a result of God's blessing, the good news was "bearing fruit and increasing in all the world."—Col. 1:6.

In a similar way in our day—but on a scale never before experienced—the good news is bearing fruit. More people are being reached with the good news and are embracing it than at any time in the past. The accomplishment of what God's Word foretold is moving speedily, like a runner in a race.—Isa. 60:22.

Organizational Readjustments

By 1976, Brother Knorr had worked diligently as president of the Watch Tower Society for over three decades. He had traveled the globe many times over, visiting and encouraging missionaries, teaching and instructing branch-office personnel. He was privileged to see the number of active Witnesses increase from 117,209 in 1942 to 2,248,390 in 1976.

But by the summer of 1976, 71-year-old N. H. Knorr had noticed that he had a tendency to bump into things. Subsequent tests indicated that he was suffering from an inoperable brain tumor. He struggled to continue to carry a work load for some months, but his physical prognosis was poor. Would his failing health impede the forward movement of the work?

Enlargement of the Governing Body had already begun in 1971. During 1975, there were 17 members. Throughout much of that year, the Governing Body had given serious and prayerful consideration to how they could best care for all that is involved in the global preaching and teaching work outlined in God's Word for our day. (Matt. 28:19, 20) On December 4, 1975, the Governing Body had unanimously approved one of the most significant organizational readjustments in the modern-day history of Jehovah's Witnesses.

Starting January 1, 1976, all the activities of the Watch Tower Society and of the congregations of Jehovah's Witnesses around the earth had been brought under the supervision of six administrative committees of the Governing Body. In harmony with that arrangement, on February 1, 1976, changes had been put into effect in all branch offices of the Society around the earth. No longer was each branch supervised by one branch overseer, but three or more mature men served as a Branch Committee, with one member serving as the permanent coordinator.* After the committees had been operating for some months, the Governing Body observed: "It has proved beneficial to have a number of brothers taking counsel together to consider the interests of the Kingdom work.—Prov. 11:14; 15:22; 24:6."

In the fall of 1976, despite the fact that his physical prognosis remained poor, Brother Knorr shared in giving instruction at meetings held at headquarters with Branch Committee members and other branch personnel from around the world. In addition to sharing in the meetings during the day, Brother Knorr invited these brothers, in small groups, to his room in the evenings. In this way he and his wife, Audrey, shared close fellowship with the men who knew and loved him and with whom he had had such close dealings over the years. Following these meetings, Brother Knorr's health deteriorated steadily until his death on June 8, 1977.

On June 22, 1977, two weeks after Brother Knorr's death, 83-year-old Frederick W. Franz was elected president of the Watch Tower Society. Regarding Brother Franz, *The Watchtower* of August 1, 1977, stated: "His outstanding reputation as an eminent Bible scholar and his tireless work in behalf of Kingdom interests has won him the confidence and loyal support of Jehovah's Witnesses everywhere."

By the time of this transition, new organizational arrangements were already in operation that ensured the forward movement of the work.

Each branch office of the Society is supervised by a committee of brothers, like this one that oversees the work in Nigeria

------
* See Chapter 15, "Development of the Organization Structure."

Filling Spiritual Needs With Bible Literature

Jehovah's Witnesses were well fed spiritually before 1976. But an examination of what has taken place since then under the direction of the Governing Body and its Writing Committee reveals that the waters of truth have flowed out in ever greater quantities and in more diversified forms.

Many of the publications produced have filled specific needs of the Witnesses themselves. Special concern was shown for young people. To help them to apply Bible principles to the situations they face in life, *Your Youth—Getting the Best Out Of It* was published in 1976, and *Questions Young People Ask—Answers That Work*, in 1989. The illustrated publication *My Book of Bible Stories*, prepared with children in mind, was released in 1978. That same year practical counsel and guidance for strengthening families was presented in *Making Your Family Life Happy*.

At times, specific needs of Jehovah's people have been addressed by means of timely counsel in the pages of *The Watchtower*. For example, the worldwide report of the activity of Jehovah's Witnesses for 1977/78 reflected a *decrease* in the number sharing in the preaching work. Was the decrease at least partly due to disappointed expectations concerning 1975? Perhaps. But there were other influencing factors. What could be done?

The Governing Body took steps to strengthen the conviction among Jehovah's Witnesses that there was a need to continue zealously proclaiming the Kingdom from house to house. *The Watchtower* of July 15, 1979, contained the articles "Zeal for Jehovah's House," "Preaching in a Lawless World," "They Preached From House to House," and "What Others Have

From 1976 to 1992, there was an increase of 42 percent in the number of languages in which "The Watchtower" was produced

1976: 78
1992: 111

Said About House-to-House Witnessing." These and other articles reaffirmed that house-to-house preaching has a solid Scriptural basis and urged zealous and whole-souled participation in this important activity.*—Acts 20:20; Col. 3:23.

Another situation also needed attention. By 1980, a number of persons who had shared in the activities of Jehovah's Witnesses for some years, including some who had served prominently in the organization, had been in various ways trying to cause division and oppose the work Jehovah's Witnesses were doing. To fortify Jehovah's people against such apostate influence, *The Watchtower* carried such articles as "Remain 'Solid in the Faith'" (August 1, 1980), "Quietly Bringing in Destructive Sects" (September 15, 1983), and "Reject Apostasy, Cling to the Truth!" (April 1, 1983), while the book *"Let Your Kingdom Come"* (1981) emphasized the reality that the Kingdom is at hand, having been established in the heavens in 1914. The Governing Body did not allow the efforts of opposers to distract it from the primary objective of Jehovah's Witnesses—proclaiming God's Kingdom!

> ### Background of F. W. Franz
>
> Frederick William Franz was born in Covington, Kentucky, U.S.A., on September 12, 1893. In 1899 the family moved to Cincinnati, where Frederick graduated from high school in 1911. He then entered the University of Cincinnati, taking a liberal arts course. He had decided that he would become a Presbyterian preacher, so he vigorously applied himself to the study of Bible Greek. At the university Frederick was chosen to receive a Rhodes scholarship, qualifying him for admission to Oxford University in England. However, before an announcement could be made, Frederick lost all interest in the scholarship and asked that his name be dropped from the list of contestants.
>
> Previously, his brother Albert had sent him a booklet that he had obtained from the International Bible Students. Later Albert gave him the first three volumes of "Studies in the Scriptures." Frederick was delighted with what he was learning and decided to sever his connection with the Presbyterian Church and associate with the congregation of Bible Students. On November 30, 1913, he was baptized. In May 1914 he left the university, and he immediately made arrangements to become a colporteur (pioneer).
>
> In June 1920 he became a member of the Bethel family in Brooklyn. Following the death of N. H. Knorr, in June 1977, Brother Franz was elected to the office of president of the Society. He served faithfully as a member of the Governing Body down till his death, on December 22, 1992, at the age of 99.

However, what of the need of Jehovah's Witnesses to continue to broaden their knowledge of Bible truth? For serious Bible study, in 1984 a revised reference edition of the *New World Translation* was issued, containing extensive marginal references, footnotes, and appendix material. Four years later, in 1988, Jehovah's people were thrilled to receive an up-to-date commentary on every verse in Revelation, in the book *Revelation—Its Grand Climax At Hand!*, also the two-volume Bible encyclopedia *Insight on the Scriptures*. Then, in 1991, there was published the beautifully illustrated book *The Greatest Man Who Ever Lived*, a thorough study of the life and teachings of Jesus Christ.

---

* From 1980 to 1985, there was a 33-percent increase in the number sharing in the preaching work, and from 1985 to 1992, there was a further 47.9-percent increase.

But what about the needs of persons who are not Jehovah's Witnesses? As an instrument to instruct newly interested ones, the publication *You Can Live Forever in Paradise on Earth* was released in 1982. It was designed to help Bible students to meet Jehovah's requirements for life in an earthly paradise. To help people who may have questions about the origin and purpose of life on earth, the book *Life—How Did It Get Here? By Evolution or by Creation?* was provided in 1985. This was followed, in 1989, by the faith-strengthening book *The Bible—God's Word or Man's?*

Attention was also given to humble persons who might need special help because of their cultural or religious background. To teach the truth about Jehovah's Kingdom to those who are illiterate or who read poorly, the 32-page brochure *Enjoy Life on Earth Forever!* was released in 1982. By 1992, over 76,000,000 copies had been printed, and it was being distributed in 200 languages around the world, making it the most widely translated of any publication of the Watch Tower Society.

In 1983, three booklets were produced for the special purpose of helping Muslims, Buddhists, and Hindus. To reach people with these and other religious backgrounds, it is helpful to understand something about their religion—its teachings and history. To fill this need, the book *Mankind's Search for God* was released in 1990.

The Governing Body was keenly interested in reaching as many people as possible with the Kingdom message—people "of all nations and tribes and . . . tongues." (Rev. 7:9) To that end, arrangements were made to translate the literature into many more languages. For example, from 1976 to 1992, there was an increase of about 42 percent in the number of languages in which *The Watchtower* was produced. In October 1992, the number was 111. To make speedy translation possible, that same year over 800 translators around the world were sharing in the work.

Programs of Education Enriched and Diversified

Under the direction of the Governing Body and its Teaching Committee, programs of instruction for the headquarters staff and for Bethel families in the branches around the world were enriched and given greater variety. In addition to reading the Bible and the *Yearbook* as part of their morning worship, there was introduced an in-depth analysis of the portion of the Bible read during

Expanding Ranks of Pioneers

the preceding week, with application of the material to those serving at Bethel. Regular reports from various Bethel departments as well as more frequent reports from zone overseers were also introduced.

To meet the needs of those with added responsibilities within the organization, further educational programs were designed and put into operation. During 1977, arrangements were made for all elders to attend a 15-hour course of the Kingdom Ministry School. (Acts 20:28) Since then, similar sessions of varying lengths have been arranged every few years; and beginning in 1984, ministerial servants also received training in the Kingdom Ministry School. In Brooklyn, starting in December 1977, a special five-week school for Branch Committee members began.

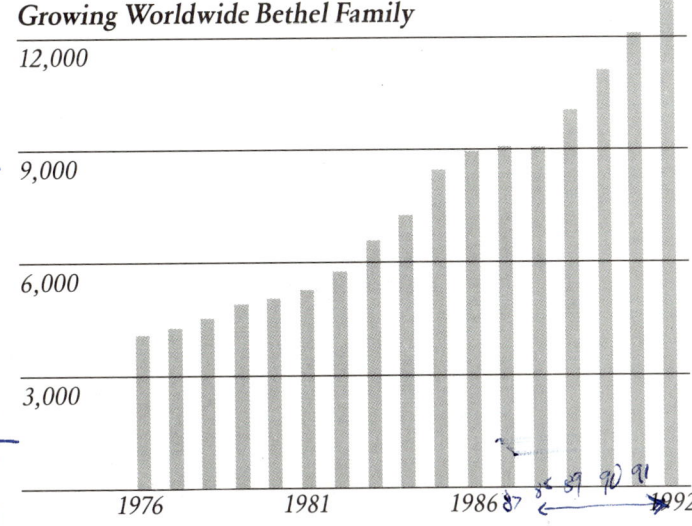

Special concern was also shown for those who were expending themselves in the full-time ministry as pioneers. In December 1977 the Pioneer Service School, a two-week course of training for pioneer ministers, was inaugurated in the United States and eventually extended to all parts of the earth. During the next 14 years, the number of pioneers increased more than fivefold—from 115,389 to 605,610!

In the fall of 1987, another new school was opened—the Ministerial Training School. This school was established to train qualified single brothers who had some experience as elders or ministerial servants and who were willing to serve wherever there was a need in the worldwide field. By 1992, classes had been held in Australia, Austria, Britain, El Salvador, France, Germany, Italy, Mexico, Nigeria, Spain, Sweden, and the United States. The result has been, not a class of individuals who are viewed as superior to others in the congregation, but rather an increase in the number of men well qualified to serve their brothers.

To further the global work of Bible education, international conventions were scheduled in strategically located cities—some in lands where Jehovah's Witnesses had been under ban. These conventions served to strengthen the brothers in those areas and to give strong impetus to the preaching of the good news in those lands.*

Facilities to Care for the Growth

As the word of Jehovah continued to move speedily, some thrilling

Growing Worldwide Bethel Family

---

* See Chapter 17, "Conventions—Proof of Our Brotherhood."

Multiplying Congregations

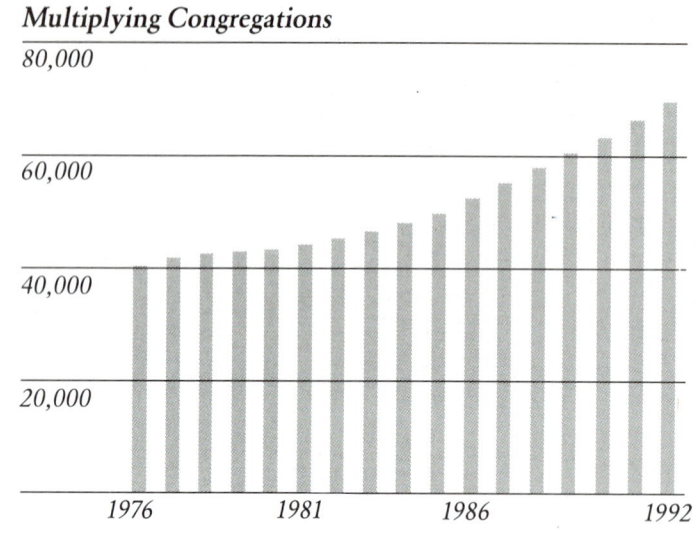

[Bar chart showing congregation growth from 1976 to 1992, with values ranging from approximately 40,000 in 1976 to over 70,000 in 1992. Y-axis shows values: 20,000, 40,000, 60,000, 80,000. X-axis shows years: 1976, 1981, 1986, 1992.]

developments became necessary in construction and printing—fields under the supervision of the Governing Body and its Publishing Committee.

Witnesses with experience in construction volunteered their services, and their efforts were coordinated to assist in building new and larger branch facilities around the world. From 1976 to 1992, the building of completely new branch facilities was undertaken in some 60 lands. In addition to that, projects to expand existing facilities got under way in 30 lands. The way the work was done (with volunteers coming from many congregations—sometimes from other lands) served to strengthen the bonds of love and unity among Jehovah's people.*

In order to meet the Society's expanding multilanguage printing needs, Witnesses with experience in the computer field developed a computerized prepress system called MEPS (Multilanguage Electronic Phototypesetting System). The project was completed in 1986. As a result, by 1992, *The Watchtower* was being printed simultaneously in 66 languages. The vast majority of Jehovah's Witnesses were thus able to receive the same spiritual food at the same time.#

As the facilities of the Watch Tower Society continued to expand, more volunteers were needed at the headquarters in Brooklyn as well as in the branch offices around the world. From 1976 to 1992, the international Bethel family tripled in size, from about 4,000 to over 12,900 members serving throughout the earth. The Governing Body and its Personnel Committee have looked after the personal and spiritual needs of this large army of full-time volunteers.

Caring for Congregations and the Work of Evangelizing

As the word of Jehovah moved ahead speedily, the Governing Body and its Service Committee directed their energies to building up the congregations worldwide and to expanding the global evangelizing work.

Was there more that could be done to help the many new ones who were getting baptized each year? Early in 1977, arrangements were made to

---

* See Chapter 20, "Building Together on a Global Scale."
# See Chapter 26, "Producing Bible Literature for Use in the Ministry."

strengthen new Witnesses spiritually. Explained *Our Kingdom Service:* "We believe that at least two books should be studied with all persons who come into the truth. . . . So the study should continue after baptism until the second book has been completed." In this way newly baptized Witnesses were given a fuller opportunity to gain knowledge and understanding and to have a growing appreciation for what it means to be baptized. The new arrangement also encouraged further close association between new ones and the Witnesses who helped them in their home Bible study.

To care for those streaming into Jehovah's organization, over 29,000 new congregations were formed worldwide between 1976 and 1992. (Mic. 4:1) More circuit and district overseers were appointed by the Governing Body and sent out to help. The number of these traveling overseers went from about 2,600 in 1976 to some 3,900 in 1992.

As the number of congregations increased, there was also a growing need for more meeting halls. Was there a quicker way to build Kingdom Halls? In the 1970's, Jehovah's Witnesses in the United States organized a building program whereby skilled construction workers from neighboring parts of the country were invited to help local Witnesses build a Kingdom Hall. With hundreds assisting, a hall could be completed quickly—often in just two or three days. By the 1980's, quickly built Kingdom Halls were going up in other parts of the earth.

Political changes in Eastern Europe also affected Jehovah's Witnesses. What a thrill for our brothers in such countries as East Germany (as it was then known), Hungary, Poland, Romania, and what was then called the Soviet Union to learn that they had been granted legal recognition, in some cases after 40 years of ban! The increased freedom in those countries now made it easier for them to reach some 380,000,000 persons with the good news! Jehovah's Witnesses wasted no time in availing themselves of their newfound freedom to share in their public preaching activity.

And the results? The word of Jehovah has moved speedily! For example, in April 1992 the number of Kingdom proclaimers reporting in Poland was 106,915. And the prospects for future growth were outstanding: That same month the attendance at the Memorial of Christ's death was

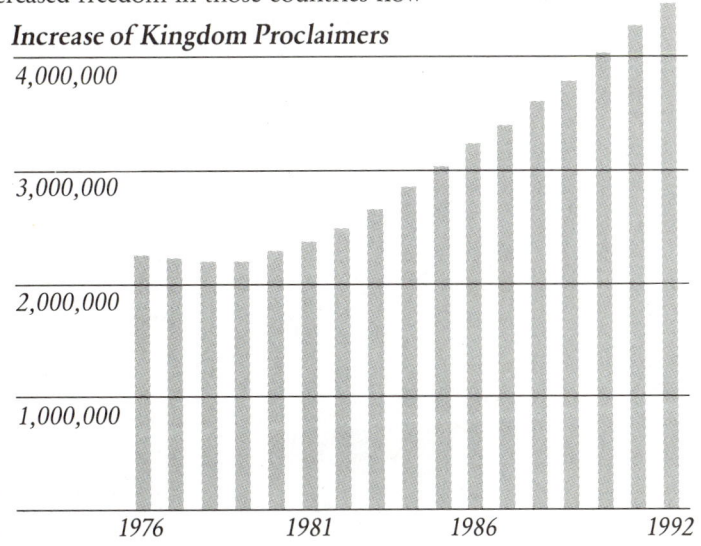

Increase of Kingdom Proclaimers

Carey W. Barber

John E. Barr

W. Lloyd Barry

John C. Booth

Frederick W. Franz

George D. Gangas

Milton G. Henschel

Theodore Jaracz

Karl F. Klein

Albert D. Schroeder

Lyman A. Swingle

Daniel Sydlik

The Governing Body of Jehovah's Witnesses
January 1992

214,218. Similarly, in the lands that formerly made up the Soviet Union, a total of 173,473 attended the Memorial in 1992, an increase of 60 percent over the year before.

In some lands, however, continued persecution and natural disasters have presented obstacles. In 1992 the activities of Jehovah's Witnesses were still under government restrictions in 24 lands. The Chairman's Committee of the Governing Body does what is possible to provide assistance and to inform the international brotherhood of ways that they can come to the aid of fellow Witnesses serving under adversity. (Compare 1 Corinthians 12: 12-26.) Neither campaigns of persecution nor natural disasters have been able to stop the preaching of the word of Jehovah!

"A People Peculiarly His Own"

So, in the years from 1976 to 1992, Jehovah's word has indeed moved ahead speedily. The organization nearly doubled in size, to over 4,470,000 Kingdom publishers!

Jehovah's people have continued to zealously proclaim God's Kingdom, now in more languages than ever before. Using the publications that have been provided, they have deepened their knowledge of the Bible and helped interested ones to learn Bible truths. They have benefited from the educational programs that have been instituted for those with added responsibilities within the organization. Jehovah has without doubt blessed their proclamation of his Kingdom.

From the 1870's down to the present, certain men have made outstanding contributions to the advancement of the Kingdom work, men such as Charles T. Russell, Joseph F. Rutherford, Nathan H. Knorr, and Frederick W. Franz, as well as others who have served as members of the Governing Body. But in no way have Jehovah's Witnesses become a sect built around the personalities of any of these men. Instead, they have but one leader, "the Christ." (Matt. 23:10) He is the Head of these organized Witnesses of Jehovah, the one to whom "all authority has been given" for directing this work "all the days until the conclusion of the system of things." (Matt. 28: 18-20) They are determined to submit to Christ's headship, keep close to God's Word, and cooperate with the leading of the holy spirit, that they may continue moving ahead in the worship of the only true God and in proving themselves to be "a people peculiarly his own, zealous for fine works."—Titus 2:14.

But what are some of the basic teachings and standards of conduct that distinguish Jehovah's Witnesses from all other religions? How did they come to be known as Jehovah's Witnesses? How are their activities financed? Why do they maintain strict separateness from other churches and from the world in general? Why have they been the objects of intense persecution in so many parts of the earth? These and many other questions will be answered in the chapters that follow.

Not a sect built around the personalities of any men

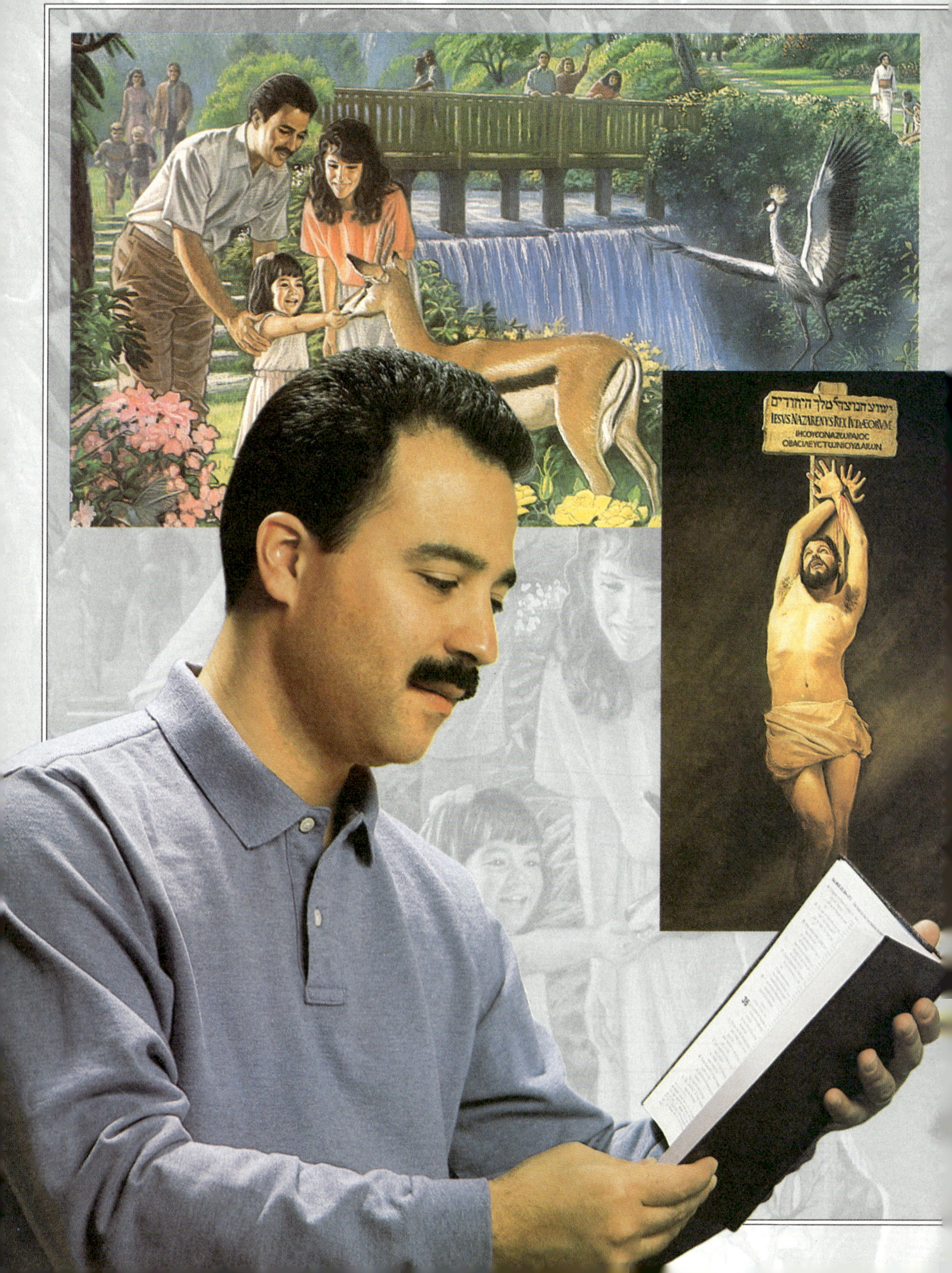
IESVS NAZARENVS REX IVDAEORVM

SECTION 2

Gaining Accurate Knowledge of God's Word and Applying It

How did the beliefs of Jehovah's Witnesses develop? How did they get their name? What distinguishes them from other religious groups? These questions are answered in Chapters 10 to 14.

Jehovah se Getuies
شهود يهوه
Mga Saksi ni Jehova
Mboni za Yehova
耶和華見證人
svědkové Jehovovi
Jehovas Vidner
Jehovah's Getuigen
Jehovah's Witnesses
Jehovan todistajat
Témoins de Jéhovah
Jehovas Zeugen
Μάρτυρες του Ιεχωβά
Jehova Tanúi
Dagiti Saksi ni Jehova
Saksi-Saksi Yehuwa
エホバの証人
여호와의 증인
Jehovas vitner
Testemunhas de Jeová
Dihlatse tša Jehofa
Lipaki tsa Jehova
Zvapupu zvaJehovha
Jehovovi svedkovia
Testigos de Jehová
Mashahidi wa Yehova
Timbhoni ta Yehova
Basupi ba ga Jehofa
Yehowa Adansefo
amaNgqina ka Yehova
oFakazi BakaJehova

CHAPTER 10

GROWING IN ACCURATE KNOWLEDGE OF THE TRUTH

JEHOVAH'S WITNESSES have not set out to introduce new doctrines, a new way of worship, a new religion. Instead, their modern-day history reflects conscientious effort to teach what is found in the Bible, the inspired Word of God. They point to it as the basis for all their beliefs and their way of life. Instead of developing beliefs that reflect the permissive trends of the modern world, they have sought to conform ever more closely to the Biblical teachings and practices of first-century Christianity.

In the early 1870's, Charles Taze Russell and his associates undertook an earnest study of the Bible. It became obvious to them that Christendom had strayed far from the teachings and practices of early Christianity. Brother Russell did not claim to be the first to discern this, and he freely acknowledged his indebtedness to others for the assistance they rendered during his early years of study of the Scriptures. He spoke with appreciation for the good work that various movements in the Reformation had done with a view to letting the light of truth shine more brightly. He mentioned by name older men such as Jonas Wendell, George Stetson, George Storrs, and Nelson Barbour, who personally contributed to his understanding of God's Word in various ways.*

He also stated: "Various doctrines we hold and which seem so new and fresh and different were held in some form long ago: for instance—Election, Free Grace, Restitution, Justification, Sanctification, Glorification, Resurrection." It was often the case, however, that one religious group was distinguished by a clearer understanding of one Bible truth; another group, by a different truth. Their further progress was frequently hindered because they were shackled to doctrines and creeds that embodied beliefs that had flourished in ancient Babylon and Egypt or that were borrowed from Greek philosophers.

But which group, with the help of God's spirit, would gradually lay hold again on the entire "pattern of healthful words" that had been cher-

C. T. Russell freely acknowledged the help that came from others during his early years of Bible study

---

* *Zion's Watch Tower and Herald of Christ's Presence,* July 15, 1906, pp. 229-31.

120

GROWING IN ACCURATE KNOWLEDGE OF THE TRUTH

ished by first-century Christians? (2 Tim. 1:13) For whom would it prove true that their path was "like the bright light that is getting lighter and lighter until the day is firmly established"? (Prov. 4:18) Who would really do the work that Jesus commanded when he said: "You will be witnesses of me . . . to the most distant part of the earth"? Who would not only make disciples but also 'teach them to observe all the things' that Jesus had commanded? (Acts 1:8; Matt. 28:19, 20) Indeed, was the time at hand when the Lord would make a clear distinction between those true Christians that he likened to wheat and the imitation ones that he referred to as weeds (actually, weeds of a sort that very much resemble wheat until they reach maturity)?* (Matt. 13:24-30, 36-43) Who would prove to be "the faithful and discreet slave" to whom the Master, Jesus Christ, at his presence in Kingdom power, would entrust further responsibility in connection with the work foretold for the conclusion of this system of things? —Matt. 24:3, 45-47.

Letting the Light Shine

Jesus instructed his disciples to share with others the light of divine truth that they had received from him. "You are the light of the world," he said. "Let your light shine before men." (Matt. 5:14-16; Acts 13:47) Charles Taze Russell and his associates recognized that they had an obligation to do that.

Did they believe that they had all the answers, the full light of truth? To that question Brother Russell pointedly answered: "Certainly not; nor will we have until the 'perfect day.'" (Prov. 4:18, KJ) Frequently they referred to their Scriptural beliefs as "present truth"—not with any idea that truth itself changes but rather with the thought that their understanding of it was progressive.

These earnest students of the Bible did not shy away from the idea that there is such a thing as *truth in matters of religion*. They recognized Jehovah as "the God of truth" and the Bible as his Word of truth. (Ps. 31:5; Josh. 21:45; John 17:17) They realized that there was still much that they did not know, but they did not hold back from stating with conviction what they had learned from the Bible. And when traditional religious doctrines and practices contradicted what they found to be clearly

C. T. Russell began to publish "Zion's Watch Tower" in 1879, when he was 27 years old

---

* See *Insight on the Scriptures*, published by the Watchtower Bible and Tract Society of New York, Inc., Volume 2, page 1176.

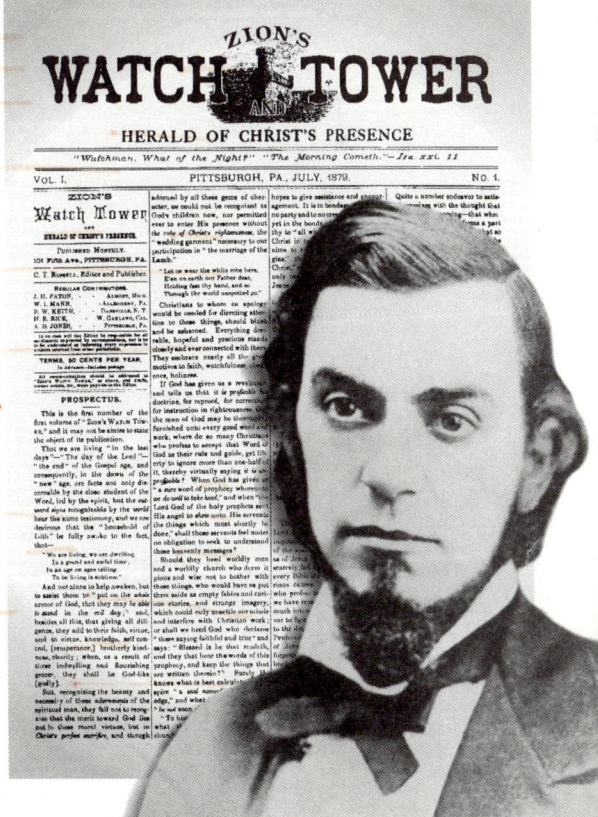

stated in God's inspired Word, then, in imitation of Jesus Christ, they exposed the falsehood, even though this brought ridicule and hatred upon them from the clergy.—Matt. 15:3-9.

To reach and feed others spiritually, C. T. Russell began publication, in July 1879, of the magazine *Zion's Watch Tower and Herald of Christ's Presence.*

The Bible—Truly the Word of God

Charles Taze Russell's confidence in the Bible was not simply a matter of accepting a traditional viewpoint that was popular at the time. On the contrary, what was popular among many at that time was higher criticism. Those who advocated it challenged the reliability of the Bible record.

As a youth, Russell had joined the Congregational Church and was active in its work, but the unreasonableness of traditional dogmas led to his becoming a skeptic. He found that what he had been taught could not be defended from the Bible in a satisfying way. So he discarded the dogmas of church creed and, with them, the Bible. Next, he explored leading Oriental religions, but they too proved unsatisfying. Then he began to wonder if perhaps the Bible was being misrepresented by Christendom's creeds. Encouraged by what he heard one evening at an Adventist meeting, he began a systematic study of the Scriptures. What he saw unfolding before him was indeed the inspired Word of God.

He came to be profoundly impressed by the harmony of the Bible with itself and with the personality of the One identified as its Divine Author. To help others to benefit from this, he later wrote the book *The Divine Plan of the Ages,* which he published in 1886. In it he included a major discussion on "The Bible as a Divine Revelation Viewed in the Light of Reason." Toward the end of that chapter, he stated unequivocally: "The depth and power and wisdom and scope of the Bible's testimony convince us that not man, but the Almighty God, is the author of its plans and revelations."

Confidence in the entire Bible as God's Word continues to be a cornerstone of the beliefs of Jehovah's modern-day Witnesses. Worldwide, they have study aids that enable them personally to examine the evidence of its inspiration. Aspects of this subject are frequently discussed in their magazines. In 1969 they published the book *Is the Bible Really the Word of God?* Twenty years later the book *The Bible—God's Word or Man's?* took a fresh look at the subject of Bible authenticity, drew attention to added evidence, and came to the same conclusion: The Bible is, indeed, the inspired Word of God. Another one of their books, printed first in 1963 and updated in 1990, is *"All Scripture Is Inspired of God and Beneficial."* Further detail is found in their Bible encyclopedia, *Insight on the Scriptures,* published in 1988.

They have personally examined the evidence that the Bible is truly God's Word

From their personal and congregational study of such material, they are convinced that although some 40 humans over a period of 16 centuries were used to record what is in the 66 books of the Bible, God himself actively directed the writing by his spirit. The apostle Paul wrote: "All Scripture is inspired of God." (2 Tim. 3:16; 2 Pet. 1:20, 21) This conviction is a powerful factor in the lives of Jehovah's Witnesses. Commenting on this, a British newspaper remarked: "Behind everything a Witness does lies a Scriptural reason. Indeed, their one basic tenet is recognition of the Bible as . . . true."

Getting to Know the True God

As Brother Russell and his associates studied the Scriptures, it did not take them long to see that the God portrayed in the Bible is not the god of Christendom. This was an important matter because, as Jesus Christ said, people's prospects for eternal life depend on their knowing the only true God and the one whom he sent forth, his Chief Agent of salvation. (John 17:3; Heb. 2:10) C. T. Russell and the group that shared with him in Bible study discerned that the justice of God is in perfect balance with divine wisdom, love, and power, and that these attributes are displayed in all of his works. On the basis of the knowledge that they then had of God's purpose, they prepared a discussion of why evil is permitted and included this in one of their earliest and most widely distributed publications, the 162-page book *Food for Thinking Christians*, issued first as a special edition of *Zion's Watch Tower* in September 1881.

Their study of God's Word helped them to realize that the Creator has a personal name and that he makes it possible for humans to know him and to enjoy a close relationship with him. (1 Chron. 28:9; Isa. 55:6; Jas. 4:8) The *Watch Tower* of October-November 1881 pointed out: "JEHOVAH is the name applied to none other than the Supreme Being—our Father, and him whom Jesus called Father and God."—Ps. 83:18; John 20:17.

The following year, in response to the question, "Do you claim that the Bible *does not* teach that there are three persons in one God?" the answer was given: "Yes: On the contrary, it does tell us that there is one God and Father of our Lord Jesus Christ of whom are all things (or who created all things). We believe then in One God and Father, and also in one Lord Jesus Christ . . . But these are *two* and not one being. They are *one* only in the sense of being in harmony. We believe also in a *spirit of God* . . . But it is no more a *person* than is the *spirit of devils* and the *spirit of the World* and the *spirit of Anti-Christ*."—*Zion's Watch Tower*, June 1882; John 17:20-22.

Growing Appreciation for God's Name

Gradually those Bible Students became increasingly aware of the prominence that the inspired Scriptures give to the personal name of

The Bible Students discerned that God's justice is in perfect balance with his wisdom, love, and power

God. That name had been obscured in English by the Roman Catholic Douay and the Protestant King James versions of the Bible, as it later was by most translations in many languages in the 20th century. But a variety of translations as well as Bible reference works testified that the name Jehovah occurs in the original-language text thousands of times—actually, far more often than any other name, and more often than the combined total of appearances of such titles as God and Lord. As "a people for his name," their own appreciation for the divine name grew. (Acts 15:14) In *The Watch Tower* of January 1, 1926, they presented what they recognized to be an issue that each individual must face, namely, "Who Will Honor Jehovah?"

The emphasis that they placed on the name of God was not merely a matter of religious knowledge. As explained in the book *Prophecy* (published in 1929), the paramount issue facing all intelligent creation involves the name and word of Jehovah God. Jehovah's Witnesses emphasize that the Bible shows that everyone must know God's name and treat it as something sacred. (Matt. 6:9; Ezek. 39:7) It must be cleared of all the reproach that has been heaped upon it, not only by those who have been openly defiant of Jehovah but also by those who have misrepresented him by their doctrines and deeds. (Ezek. 38:23; Rom. 2:24) On the basis of the Scriptures, the Witnesses recognize that the well-being of all the universe and its inhabitants depends upon the sanctification of Jehovah's name.

They realize that before Jehovah takes action to destroy the wicked, it is the duty and privilege of his witnesses to tell others the truth about him. Jehovah's Witnesses have been doing that earth wide. So zealous have they been in carrying out that responsibility that, internationally, anyone who freely uses the name Jehovah is quickly identified as being one of Jehovah's Witnesses.

Exposing the Trinity

As witnesses of Jehovah, C. T. Russell and his associates felt a keen responsibility to expose teachings that misrepresented God, to help lovers of truth realize that these are not based on the Bible. They were not the first to recognize that the Trinity is unscriptur-

---

Making Known the Name of God

• Since 1931 the name Jehovah's Witnesses has been used to designate those who worship and serve Jehovah as the only true God.

• Since October 15, 1931, God's personal name, Jehovah, has appeared on the front cover of each issue of the "Watchtower" magazine.

• At a time when God's personal name was being omitted from most modern translations of the Bible, Jehovah's Witnesses began to publish, in 1950, the "New World Translation," which restored the divine name to its rightful place.

• In addition to the Bible itself, much other literature has been published by the Watch Tower Bible and Tract Society to focus special attention on the divine name—for example, the books "Jehovah" (1934), "Let Your Name Be Sanctified" (1961), and "'The Nations Shall Know That I Am Jehovah'—How?" (1971), as well as the brochure "The Divine Name That Will Endure Forever" (1984).

al,* but they did appreciate that if they were to be faithful servants of God, they had a responsibility to make known the truth about it. Courageously, for the benefit of all lovers of truth, they laid bare the pagan roots of this central doctrine of Christendom.

The *Watch Tower* of June 1882 stated: "Many pagan philosophers finding that it would be policy to join the ranks of the rising religion [an apostate form of Christianity endorsed by Roman emperors in the fourth century C.E.], set about paving an easy way to it by trying to discover correspondencies between Christianity and Paganism, and so to blend the two together. They succeeded only too well. . . . As the old theology had a number of chief gods, with many demi-gods of both sexes, the Pago-christians (if we may coin a word) set themselves to reconstruct the list for the new theology. At this time, therefore, the doctrine of *three* Gods was invented—God the Father, God the Son, and God the Holy Ghost."

Some of the clergy endeavored to give Biblical flavor to their teaching by quoting such texts as 1 John 5:7, but Brother Russell presented evidence showing that it was well-known by scholars that a portion of that text was an interpolation, a spurious insertion made by a scribe to support a teaching that is not found in the Scriptures. Other apologists for the Trinity appealed to John 1:1, but the *Watch Tower* analyzed that scripture on the basis of both content and context to show that this in no way supported belief in the Trinity. In harmony with this, in its issue of July 1883, the *Watch Tower* said: "More Bible and less hymn-book theology would have made the subject clearer to all. The doctrine of the trinity is totally opposed to Scripture."

Sir Isaac Newton and Henry Grew were among those who had earlier rejected the Trinity as unscriptural

---

* For example: (1) By the 16th century, antitrinitarian movements were strong in Europe. For example, Ferenc Dávid (1510-79), a Hungarian, knew and taught that the dogma of the Trinity was not Scriptural. Because of his beliefs, he died in prison. (2) The Minor Reformed Church, which flourished in Poland for about a hundred years during the 16th and 17th centuries, also rejected the Trinity, and adherents of that church spread literature all over Europe, until the Jesuits succeeded in having them banished from Poland. (3) Sir Isaac Newton (1642-1727), in England, rejected the doctrine of the Trinity and wrote detailed historical and Scriptural reasons for doing so, but he did not have these published during his lifetime, evidently out of fear of the consequences. (4) Among others in America, Henry Grew exposed the Trinity as unscriptural. In 1824 he dealt with this matter at length in *An Examination of the Divine Testimony Concerning the Character of the Son of God*.

Brother Russell outspokenly exposed the foolishness of professing to believe the Bible while at the same time teaching a doctrine such as the Trinity, which contradicts what the Bible says. Thus he wrote: "In what a jumble of contradictions and confusion do they find themselves who say that Jesus and the Father are one God! This would involve the idea that our Lord Jesus acted the hypocrite when on earth and only pretended to address God in prayer, when He Himself was the same God. . . . Again, the Father has always been immortal, hence could not die. How, then, could Jesus have died? The Apostles are all false witnesses in declaring Jesus' death and resurrection if He did not die. The Scriptures declare, however, that He did die."*

Thus, at an early point in their modern-day history, Jehovah's Witnesses firmly rejected Christendom's Trinity dogma in favor of the reasonable, heartwarming teaching of the Bible itself.# The work that they have done to publish these truths and to give people everywhere opportunity to hear them has taken on proportions never attained by any other individual or group, past or present.

What Is the Condition of the Dead?

What the future holds for people who have not accepted God's provision for salvation was of deep concern to C. T. Russell from the time he was a young man. When just a lad, he believed what the clergy said about hellfire; he thought they were preaching God's Word. He would go out at night to chalk up Bible texts in conspicuous places so that workingmen who passed there might be warned and be saved from the awful doom of eternal torment.

Later, after he had seen for himself what the Bible really does teach, he was quoted by one of his associates as stating: "If the Bible does teach that eternal torture is the fate of all except the saints, it should be preached —yea, thundered from the housetops weekly, daily, hourly; if it does not so teach, the fact should be made known, and the foul stain dishonoring God's holy name removed."

At an early point in his study of the Bible, C. T. Russell saw clearly that

---

> **'Shall We Contradict Christ Himself?'**
>
> *After exposing the unscripturalness and unreasonableness of the doctrine of the Trinity, C. T. Russell expressed righteous indignation when he asked: "Shall we thus contradict the Apostles and Prophets and Jesus Himself, and ignore reason and common sense, in order to hold to a dogma handed to us from the dark, superstitious past, by a corrupt apostate Church? Nay! 'To the Law and to the testimony! If they speak not according to this Word, it is because there is no light in them.'"*
> —*The Watch Tower,* August 15, 1915.

---

* See also *Studies in the Scriptures,* Series V, pages 41-82.
# Thorough discussions of historical and Scriptural evidence bearing on this subject have been published by the Watchtower Bible and Tract Society at various times. See *"The Word"—Who Is He? According to John* (1962), *"Things in Which It Is Impossible for God to Lie"* (1965), *Reasoning From the Scriptures* (1985), and *Should You Believe in the Trinity?* (1989).

hell is not a place of torment for souls after death. He was most likely helped in this by George Storrs, editor of the *Bible Examiner*, whom Brother Russell mentioned with warm appreciation in his writings and who had himself written much about what he discerned from the Bible as to the condition of the dead.

But what about the soul? Did the Bible Students support the belief that it is a spirit part of man, something that lives on after the death of the body? On the contrary, in 1903 the *Watch Tower* stated: "We must notice carefully that the lesson is not that man *has* a soul, but that man *is* a soul, or being. Let us take an illustration from nature—the air we breathe: it is composed of oxygen and nitrogen, neither of which is atmosphere, or air; but when the two combine, as they do in proper chemical proportions, the resulting thing is atmosphere. Just so with soul. God speaks to us from this standpoint, of our being each a soul. He does not address our bodies nor our breath of lives, but he does address *us* as intelligent beings, or souls. In pronouncing the penalty of violating his law, he did not address Adam's body specifically, but the man, the soul, the intelligent being: 'Thou!' 'In the day that *thou* eatest thereof *thou* shalt surely *die*.' 'The *soul* that sinneth it shall *die*.'—Gen 2:17; Ezek. 18:20." This was in harmony with what the *Watch Tower* had stated as early as April 1881.*

How, then, did belief in the inherent immortality of human souls develop? Who was its author? After carefully examining both the Bible and religious history, Brother Russell wrote in the *Watch Tower* of April 15, 1894: "Evidently it came not from the Bible . . . The Bible distinctly declares that man is *mortal*, that death is possible to him. . . . Scanning the pages of history, we find that, although the doctrine of human immortality is not taught by God's inspired witnesses, it is the very essence of all heathen religions. . . . It is not true, therefore, that Socrates and Plato were the first to teach the doctrine: it had an earlier teacher than either of them, and a yet more able one. . . . The first record of this false teaching is found in the oldest history known to man—the Bible. The false teacher was Satan."#

Russell saw clearly that hell is not a place of torment after death

---

* What the Scriptures say regarding the soul is known by Jewish scholars as well as those of Christendom, but it is rarely taught in their places of worship. See *New Catholic Encyclopedia* (1967), Volume XIII, pages 449-50; *The Eerdmans Bible Dictionary* (1987), pages 964-5; *The Interpreter's Dictionary of the Bible*, edited by G. Buttrick (1962), Volume 1, page 802; *The Jewish Encyclopedia* (1910), Volume VI, page 564.

\# In a more detailed discussion of the subject, in 1955, the booklet *What Do the Scriptures Say About "Survival After Death"*? pointed out that the Bible record shows that Satan actually encouraged Eve to believe that she would not die *in the flesh* as a result of ignoring God's prohibition on eating fruit from "the tree of the knowledge of good and bad." (Gen. 2:16, 17; 3:4) In time, that obviously proved false, but there were further developments that had their root in that first lie. People adopted the view that an invisible part of man lived on. Following the Flood of Noah's day, this was fortified by demonic spiritistic practices emanating from Babylon.—Isa. 47:1, 12; Deut. 18:10, 11.

In public debate, Russell argued that the dead are really dead, not alive with the angels nor with demons in a place of despair

Turning the "Hose" on Hell

In harmony with Brother Russell's strong desire to remove from God's name the foul stain that resulted from the teaching of a hellfire of eternal torment, he wrote a tract featuring the subject, "Do the Scriptures Teach That Eternal Torment Is the Wages of Sin?" (*The Old Theology,* 1889) In it he said:

"The eternal torment theory had a heathen origin, though as held by the heathen it was not the merciless doctrine it afterward became, when it began gradually to attach itself to nominal Christianity during its blending with heathen philosophies in the second century. It remained for the great apostasy to tack to heathen philosophy the horrid details now so generally believed, to paint them upon the church walls, as was done in Europe, to write them in their creeds and hymns, and to so pervert the Word of God as to give a *seeming* divine support to the God-dishonoring blasphemy. The credulity of the present day, therefore, receives it as a legacy, not from the Lord, or the apostles, or the prophets, but from the compromising spirit which sacrificed truth and reason, and shamefully perverted the doctrines of Christianity, in an unholy ambition and strife for power and wealth and numbers. Eternal torment as the penalty for sin was unknown to the patriarchs of past ages; it was unknown to the prophets of the Jewish age; and it was unknown to the Lord and the apostles; but it has been the chief

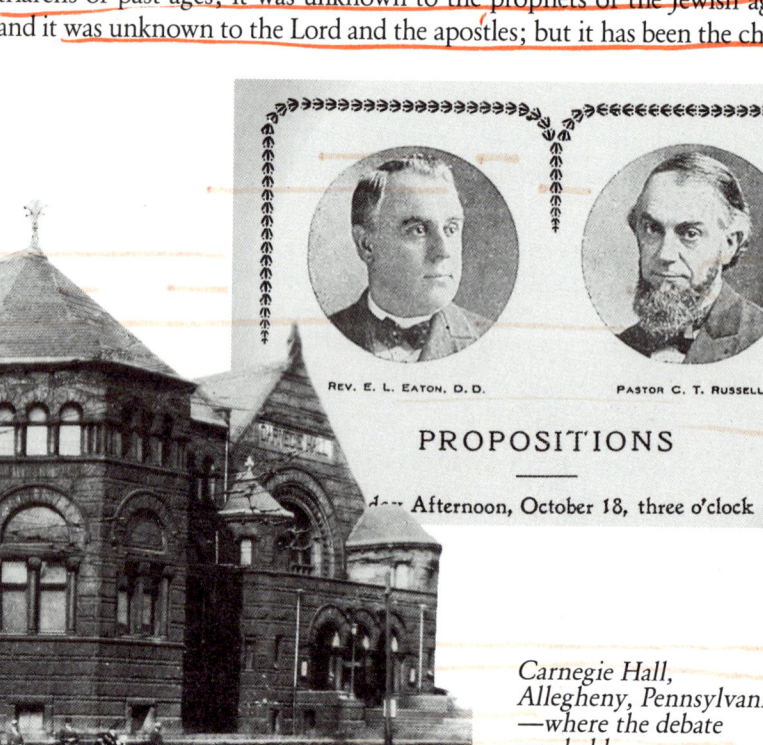

Carnegie Hall, Allegheny, Pennsylvania —where the debate was held

doctrine of Nominal Christianity since the great apostasy—the scourge wherewith the credulous, ignorant and superstitious of the world have been lashed into servile obedience to tyranny. Eternal torment was pronounced against all who offered resistance to or spurned Rome's authority, and its infliction in the present life was begun so far as she had power."

Brother Russell was well aware that the majority of sensible people did not really believe the doctrine of hellfire. But, as he pointed out, in 1896, in the booklet *What Say the Scriptures About Hell?*, "since they *think that the Bible teaches it,* every step they progress in real intelligence and brotherly kindness . . . is in most cases a step away from God's Word, which they falsely accuse of this teaching."

To draw such thinking people back to God's Word, he presented in this booklet every text in the *King James Version* in which the word hell was found, so readers could see for themselves what these said, and then he stated: "Thank God, we find no such place of everlasting torture as the creeds and hymn-books, and many pulpits, erroneously teach. Yet we have found a 'hell,' *sheol, hades,* to which all our race were condemned on account of Adam's sin, and from which all are redeemed by our Lord's death; and that 'hell' is the tomb—the death condition. And we find another 'hell' (*gehenna*—the second *death*—utter destruction) brought to our attention as the final penalty upon all who, after being redeemed and brought to the full knowledge of the truth, and to *full* ability to obey it, shall yet choose death by choosing a course of opposition to God and righteousness. And our hearts say, Amen. True and righteous are thy ways, thou King of nations. Who shall not venerate thee, O Lord, and glorify thy name? For thou art entirely holy. And all nations shall come and worship before thee, because thy righteous dealings are made manifest."—Rev. 15:3, 4.

What he was teaching was a source of irritation and embarrassment to the clergy of Christendom. In 1903 he was challenged to public debate. The condition of the dead was one of the issues in the resulting series of debates between C. T. Russell and Dr. E. L. Eaton, who served as spokesman for an unofficial alliance of Protestant ministers in the western part of Pennsylvania.

During those debates Brother Russell firmly upheld the proposition that "death is death, and that our dear ones, when they pass from us, are really dead, that they are neither alive with the angels nor with demons in a place of despair." In support of this, he referred to such scriptures as Ecclesiastes 9:5, 10; Romans 5:12; 6:23; and Genesis 2:17. He also said: "The scriptures are in full harmony with what you and I and every other sane, reasonable person in the world shall concede to be the reasonable and proper character of our God. What is declared of our heavenly Father? That he

Most sensible people did not believe the doctrine of hellfire

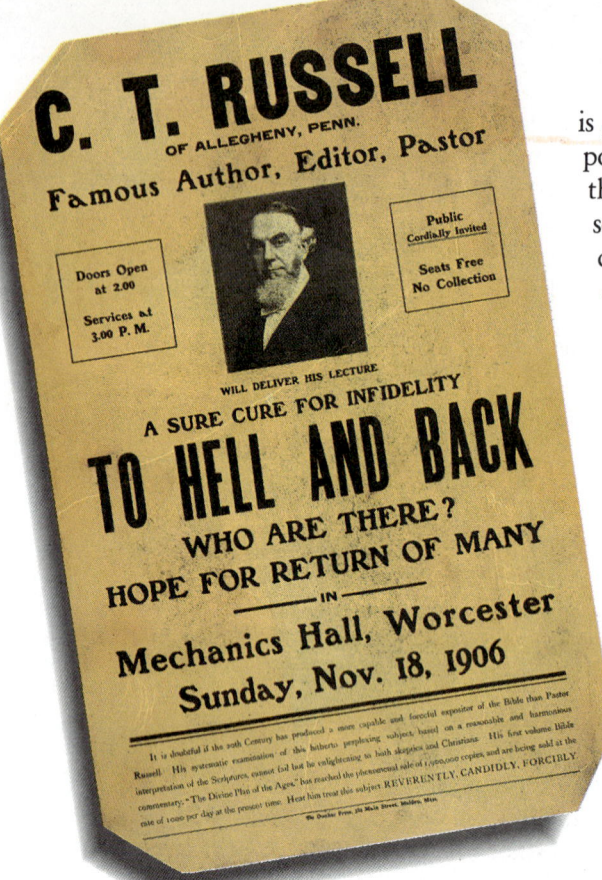

C. T. RUSSELL
OF ALLEGHENY, PENN.
Famous Author, Editor, Pastor

Doors Open at 2.00
Services at 3.00 P. M.

Public Cordially Invited
Seats Free No Collection

WILL DELIVER HIS LECTURE
A SURE CURE FOR INFIDELITY
TO HELL AND BACK
WHO ARE THERE?
HOPE FOR RETURN OF MANY
IN
Mechanics Hall, Worcester
Sunday, Nov. 18, 1906

Russell traveled to cities both large and small to tell the truth about hell

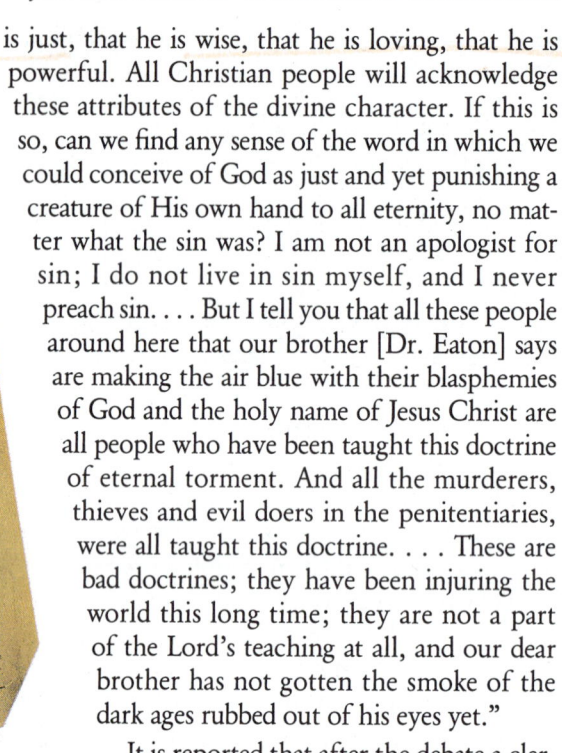

is just, that he is wise, that he is loving, that he is powerful. All Christian people will acknowledge these attributes of the divine character. If this is so, can we find any sense of the word in which we could conceive of God as just and yet punishing a creature of His own hand to all eternity, no matter what the sin was? I am not an apologist for sin; I do not live in sin myself, and I never preach sin. . . . But I tell you that all these people around here that our brother [Dr. Eaton] says are making the air blue with their blasphemies of God and the holy name of Jesus Christ are all people who have been taught this doctrine of eternal torment. And all the murderers, thieves and evil doers in the penitentiaries, were all taught this doctrine. . . . These are bad doctrines; they have been injuring the world this long time; they are not a part of the Lord's teaching at all, and our dear brother has not gotten the smoke of the dark ages rubbed out of his eyes yet."

It is reported that after the debate a clergyman who was in attendance approached Russell and said: "I am glad to see you turn the hose on hell and put out the fire."

To give even more widespread publicity to the truth about the condition of the dead, Brother Russell served an extensive series of one-day conventions, from 1905 through 1907, at which he featured the public discourse "To Hell and Back! Who Are There? Hope for Return of Many." The title was intriguing, and it attracted much attention. Audiences packed out assembly halls in cities both large and small in the United States and Canada to hear the talk.

Among those who were deeply moved by what the Bible says about the condition of the dead was a university student in Cincinnati, Ohio, who was preparing to become a Presbyterian minister. In 1913 he received from his fleshly brother the booklet *Where Are the Dead?*, written by John Edgar, a Bible Student who was also a medical doctor in Scotland. The student who received that booklet was Frederick Franz. After reading it carefully, he firmly declared: "This is the truth." Without hesitation, he changed his goals in life and got into the full-time ministry as a colporteur evangelizer. In 1920 he became a member of the Watch Tower Society's headquarters staff. Many years later he became a member of the Governing

Body of Jehovah's Witnesses and, later, the president of the Watch Tower Society.

The Ransom Sacrifice of Jesus Christ

In 1872, in connection with his examination of the Scriptures, Brother Russell and his associates took a fresh look at the subject of restitution, from the standpoint of the ransom given by Jesus Christ. (Acts 3:21, *KJ*) He was thrilled when he saw at Hebrews 2:9 that 'Jesus by the grace of God tasted death for every man.' That did not lead him to believe in universal salvation, for he knew that the Scriptures also say that one must exercise faith in Jesus Christ to be saved. (Acts 4:12; 16:31) But he began to grasp —though not all at once—what a marvelous opportunity the ransom sacrifice of Jesus Christ made possible for humankind. It opened the way for them to have what Adam had lost, the prospect of eternal life in human perfection. Brother Russell was not passive about the matter; he discerned the profound significance of the ransom and vigorously upheld it, even when close associates allowed their thinking to be corrupted by philosophical views.

By mid-1878, Brother Russell had, for about a year and a half, been an assistant editor of the magazine *Herald of the Morning*, of which N. H. Barbour was principal editor. But when Barbour, in the August 1878 issue of their magazine, belittled the Scriptural teaching of the ransom, Russell responded with a vigorous defense of that vital Bible truth.

Under the heading "The Atonement," Barbour had illustrated how he felt about the teaching, saying: "I say to my boy, or to one of the servants, when James bites his sister, you catch a fly, stick a pin through its body and impale it to the wall, and I'll forgive James. *This* illustrates the doctrine of substitution." Though professing to believe in the ransom, Barbour referred to the idea that Christ by his death paid the penalty for sin for the offspring of Adam as being "unscriptural, and obnoxious to all our ideas of justice."*

In the very next issue of *Herald of the Morning* (September 1878), Brother Russell took strong exception to what Barbour had written. Russell analyzed what the Scriptures really say and their consistency with "the perfection of [God's] justice, and finally his great mercy and love" as expressed by means of the ransom provision. (1 Cor. 15:3; 2 Cor. 5:18, 19; 1 Pet. 2:24; 3:18; 1 John 2:2) By the following spring, after repeated efforts to help Barbour to see things Scripturally, Russell withdrew his support from the *Herald;* and as of the issue of June 1879, his name no longer appeared as an assistant editor of that publication. His bold,

When Frederick Franz, a university student, learned the truth about the condition of the dead, he completely changed his goals in life

---

* Barbour claimed to believe in the ransom, that Christ died *for* us. What he rejected was the idea of "substitution"—that Christ died *instead of* us, that by his death Christ paid the penalty for sin for Adam's offspring.

uncompromising stand in connection with this central Bible teaching had far-reaching effects.

Throughout their modern-day history, Jehovah's Witnesses have consistently championed the Scriptural teaching of the ransom. The very first issue of *Zion's Watch Tower* (July 1879) emphasized that "merit toward God lies . . . in *Christ's perfect sacrifice.*" In 1919, at a convention sponsored by the International Bible Students Association at Cedar Point, Ohio, the printed program featured prominently the words "Welcome! All Believers in the Great Ransom Sacrifice." The inside front cover of *The Watchtower* continues to draw attention to the ransom, saying concerning the purpose of the magazine: "It encourages faith in God's now-reigning King, Jesus Christ, whose shed blood opens the way for mankind to gain eternal life."

Russell's firm stand on the ransom had far-reaching effects

Progressive, Not Creed-Bound

Clear understanding of God's Word did not come all at once. In many cases the Bible Students grasped one detail of the pattern of truth but did not yet see the complete picture. Nevertheless, they were willing to learn. They were not creed-bound; they were progressive. What they learned they shared. They did not take credit for the things they taught; they sought to be "taught by Jehovah." (John 6:45) And they came to appreciate that Jehovah makes possible the understanding of the details of his purpose in his own time and in his own way.—Dan. 12:9; compare John 16: 12, 13.

Learning new things requires adjustments in viewpoint. If mistakes are going to be admitted and beneficial changes made, humility is needed. This quality and its fruits are desirable to Jehovah, and such a course strongly appeals to lovers of truth. (Zeph. 3:12) But it is ridiculed by those who glory in creeds that have remained unchanged for many centuries, though these were formulated by imperfect men.

Manner of the Lord's Return

It was in the mid-1870's that Brother Russell and those who were diligently examining the Scriptures along with him discerned that when the Lord returned he would be invisible to human eyes.—John 14:3, 19.

Brother Russell later said: "We felt greatly grieved at the error of Second Adventists, who were expecting Christ in the flesh, and teaching that the world and all in it except Second Adventists would be burned up in 1873 or 1874, whose time-settings and disappointments and crude ideas generally as to the object and manner of his coming brought more or less reproach upon us and upon all who longed for and proclaimed his coming Kingdom. These wrong views so generally held of both the object and manner of the Lord's return led me to write a pamphlet—*The Object and Manner of Our Lord's*

Return.'" This pamphlet was published in 1877. Brother Russell had some 50,000 copies of it printed and distributed.

In that pamphlet, he wrote: "We believe the scriptures to teach, that, at His coming and for a time after He has come, He will remain invisible; afterward manifesting or showing Himself in judgments and various forms, so that 'every eye shall see Him.'" In support of this, he discussed such texts as Acts 1:11 ('he will come in the same manner as you have beheld him go'—that is, unobserved by the world) and John 14:19 ("a little longer and the world will behold me no more"). Brother Russell also referred to the fact that *The Emphatic Diaglott*, which had first been published in complete form in 1864 with an interlinear word-for-word English translation, gave evidence that the Greek expression *pa·rou·si'a* meant "presence." In analyzing the Bible's use of that term, Russell explained in this pamphlet: "The Greek word generally used in referring to the second advent—*Parousia*, frequently translated *coming*—invariably signifies *personal presence*, as having come, arrived and never signifies to *be on the way*, as we use the word *coming*."

When discussing the purpose of Christ's presence, Russell made it clear that this was not something that would be accomplished in a single world-shattering moment. "The second advent, like the first," he wrote, "covers a period of time, and is not the event of a moment." During that time, he wrote, the "little flock" would be given their reward with the Lord as joint heirs in his Kingdom; others, perhaps billions, would be given opportunity for perfect life on an earth restored to Edenic beauty.—Luke 12:32.

Within just a few years, on the basis of further study of the Scriptures, Russell realized that Christ would not only *return* invisibly but also *remain invisible*, even when manifesting his presence by judgment upon the wicked.

In 1876, when Russell had first read a copy of *Herald of the Morning*, he had learned that there was another group who then believed that Christ's return would be invisible and who associated that return with blessings for all families of the earth. From Mr. Barbour, editor of that publication, Russell also came to be persuaded that Christ's invisible presence had begun in 1874.* Attention was later drawn to this by the

> **Progressive Truth**
>
> In 1882, C. T. Russell wrote: "The Bible is our only standard, and its teachings our only creed, and recognizing the progressive character of the unfolding of Scriptural truths, we are ready and prepared to add to or modify our creed (faith—belief) as we get increase of light from our Standard."—"Watch Tower," April 1882, p. 7.

---

* This was influenced by the belief that the seventh millennium of human history had begun in 1873 and that a period of divine disfavor (of equal length to a former period considered to be one of favor) upon natural Israel would end in 1878. The chronology was flawed because of relying on an inaccurate rendering of Acts 13:20 in the *King James Version*, belief that there was a transcription error at 1 Kings 6:1, and failure to take into account Biblical synchronisms in the dating of reigns of the kings of Judah and of Israel. A clearer understanding of Biblical chronology was published in 1943, in the book "*The Truth Shall Make You Free*," and it was then refined the following year in the book "*The Kingdom Is at Hand*," as well as in later publications.

subtitle "Herald of Christ's Presence," which appeared on the cover of *Zion's Watch Tower*.

Recognition of Christ's presence as being invisible became an important foundation on which an understanding of many Bible prophecies would be built. Those early Bible Students realized that the presence of the Lord should be of primary concern to all true Christians. (Mark 13:33-37) They were keenly interested in the Master's return and were alert to the fact that they had a responsibility to publicize it, but they did not yet clearly discern all the details. Yet, what God's spirit did enable them to understand at a very early time was truly remarkable. One of these truths involved a highly significant date marked by Bible prophecy.

End of the Gentile Times

The matter of Bible chronology had long been of great interest to Bible students. Commentators had set out a variety of views on Jesus' prophecy about "the times of the Gentiles" and the prophet Daniel's record of Nebuchadnezzar's dream regarding the tree stump that was banded for "seven times."—Luke 21:24, *KJ;* Dan. 4:10-17.

As early as 1823, John A. Brown, whose work was published in London, England, calculated *the "seven times" of Daniel chapter 4 to be 2,520 years in length*. But he did not clearly discern the date with which the prophetic time period began or when it would end. He did, however, *connect these "seven times" with the Gentile Times of Luke 21:24*. In 1844, E. B. Elliott, a British clergyman, drew attention to 1914 as a possible date for the end of the "seven times" of Daniel, but he also set out an alternate view that pointed to the time of the French Revolution. Robert Seeley, of London, in 1849, handled the matter in a similar manner. At least by 1870, a publication edited by Joseph Seiss and associates and printed in Philadelphia, Pennsylvania, was setting out calculations that *pointed to 1914 as a significant date*, even though the reasoning it contained was based on chronology that C. T. Russell later rejected.

Then, in the August, September, and October 1875 issues of *Herald of the Morning*, N. H. Barbour helped to harmonize details that had been pointed out by others. Using chronology compiled by Christopher Bowen, a clergyman in England, and published by E. B. Elliott, Barbour identified *the start of the Gentile Times with King Zedekiah's removal from kingship as foretold at Ezekiel 21:25, 26*, and he pointed to 1914 as marking the end of the Gentile Times.

Early in 1876, C. T. Russell received a copy of *Herald of the Morning*. He promptly wrote to Barbour and then spent time with him in Philadelphia during the summer, discussing, among other things, prophetic time periods. Shortly thereafter, in an article entitled "Gentile Times: When Do

They could see that 1914 was clearly marked by Bible prophecy

They End?", Russell also reasoned on the matter from the Scriptures and stated that the evidence showed that "the seven times will end in A.D. 1914." This article was printed in the October 1876 issue of the *Bible Examiner*.* The book *Three Worlds, and the Harvest of This World*, produced in 1877 by N. H. Barbour in cooperation with C. T. Russell, pointed to the same conclusion. Thereafter, early issues of the *Watch Tower*, such as the ones dated December 1879 and July 1880, directed attention to 1914 C.E. as being a highly significant year from the standpoint of Bible prophecy. In 1889 the entire fourth chapter of Volume II of *Millennial Dawn* (later called *Studies in the Scriptures*) was devoted to discussion of "The Times of the Gentiles." But what would the end of the Gentile Times mean?

The Bible Students were not completely sure what would happen. They were convinced that it would not result in a burning up of the earth and a blotting out of human life. Rather, they knew it would mark a significant point in regard to divine rulership. At first, they thought that by that date the Kingdom of God would have obtained full, universal control. When that did not occur, their confidence in the Bible prophecies that marked the date did not waver. They concluded that, instead, the date had marked only a starting point as to Kingdom rule.

Similarly, they also first thought that global troubles culminating in anarchy (which they understood would be associated with the war of "the great day of God the Almighty") would precede that date. (Rev. 16:14) But then, ten years before 1914, the *Watch Tower* suggested that worldwide turmoil that would result in the annihilating of human institutions would come right *after* the end of the Gentile Times. They expected the year 1914 to mark a significant turning point for Jerusalem, since the prophecy had said that 'Jerusalem would be trodden down' until the Gentile Times were fulfilled. When they saw 1914 drawing close and yet they had not died as humans and been 'caught up in the clouds' to meet the Lord—in harmony with earlier expectations—they earnestly hoped that their change might take place at the end of the Gentile Times.—1 Thess. 4:17.

As the years passed and they examined and reexamined the Scriptures, their faith in the prophecies remained strong, and they did not hold back from stating what they expected to occur. With varying degrees of success, they endeavored to avoid being dogmatic about details not directly stated in the Scriptures.

1914 as the end of the Gentile Times was given wide publicity by the Bible Students, as in this I.B.S.A. tract distributed during 1914

Did the "Alarm Clock" Go Off Too Soon?

Great turmoil certainly burst forth upon the world in 1914 with the outbreak of World War I, which for many years was called simply the

---
* A magazine published by George Storrs, Brooklyn, New York.

Great War, but it did not immediately lead to an overthrow of all existing human rulerships. As events in connection with Palestine developed following 1914, the Bible Students thought they saw evidence of significant changes for Israel. But months and then years passed, and the Bible Students did not receive their heavenly reward as they had anticipated. How did they react to that?

The Watch Tower of February 1, 1916, specifically drew attention to October 1, 1914, and then said: "This was the last point of time that Bible chronology pointed out to us as relating to the Church's experiences. Did the Lord tell us that we would be taken [to heaven] there? No. What did He say? His Word and the fulfil[l]ments of prophecy seemed to point unmistakably that this date marked the end of the Gentile Times. We *inferred* from this that the Church's 'change' would take place on or before that date. But God did not *tell us* that it would be so. He permitted us to draw that inference; and we believe that it has proven to be a necessary test upon God's dear saints everywhere." But did these developments prove that their glorious hope had been in vain? No. It simply meant that not everything was taking place as soon as they had expected.

Several years before 1914, Russell had written: "Chronology (time prophecies in general) was evidently not intended to give God's people accurate chronological information all the way down the path of the centuries. Evidently it is intended more to serve as an alarm clock to awaken and energize the Lord's people at the proper time. . . . But let us suppose, for instance, that October, 1914, should pass and that no serious fall of Gentile power would occur. What would this prove or disprove? It would not disprove any feature of the Divine Plan of the Ages. The ransom-price finished at Calvary would still stand the guarantee of the ultimate fulfillment of the great Divine Program for human restitution. The 'high calling' of the Church to suffer with the Redeemer and to be glorified with him as his members or as his Bride would still be the same. . . . The only thing [a]ffected by the chronology would be the time for the accomplishment of these glorious hopes for the Church and for the world. . . . And if that date pass it would merely prove that our chronology, our 'alarm clock,' went off a little before the time. Would we consider it a great calamity if our alarm clock awakened us a few moments earlier in the morning of some great day full of joy and pleasure? Surely not!"

But that "alarm clock" had not gone off too soon. Actually, it was the experiences to which the "clock" had awakened them that were not exactly what they had expected.

Some years later, when the light had grown brighter, they acknowledged: "Many of the dear saints thought that all the work was done. . . . They rejoiced because of the clear proof that the world had ended, that the kingdom of heaven was at hand, and that the day of their deliverance drew

Not everything took place as soon as they expected

GROWING IN ACCURATE KNOWLEDGE OF THE TRUTH 137

nigh. But they had overlooked something else that must be done. The good news that they had received must be told to others; because Jesus had commanded: 'This gospel of the kingdom shall be preached in all the world for a witness unto all nations: and then shall the end come.' (Matthew 24:14)"—*The Watch Tower,* May 1, 1925.

As the events following 1914 began to unfold and the Bible Students compared these with what the Master had foretold, they gradually came to appreciate that they were living in the last days of the old system and that they had been since 1914. They also came to understand that it was in the year 1914 that Christ's invisible presence had begun and that this was, not by his personally returning (even invisibly) to the vicinity of the earth, but by his directing his attention toward the earth as ruling King. They saw and accepted the vital responsibility that was theirs to proclaim "this good news of the kingdom" for a witness to all nations during this critical time of human history.—Matt. 24:3-14.

What exactly was the message about the Kingdom that they were to preach? Was it any different from the message of the first-century Christians?

In 1931, using the most extensive radio network that had ever been on the air, J. F. Rutherford showed that only God's Kingdom can bring lasting relief to humankind

The discourse "The Kingdom, the Hope of the World," was broadcast by 163 stations simultaneously and was repeated by another 340 stations later

God's Kingdom, the Only Hope of Mankind

As a result of careful study of God's Word, the Bible Students associated with Brother Russell understood that God's Kingdom was the government that Jehovah had promised to set up by means of his Son for the blessing of mankind. Jesus Christ, in heaven, would have associated with him as rulers a "little flock" selected by God from among humankind. They understood that this government would be represented by faithful men of old who would serve as princes in all the earth. These were referred to as "ancient worthies."—Luke 12:32; Dan. 7:27; Rev. 20:6; Ps. 45:16.

Christendom had long taught 'the divine right of kings,' as a means of holding the people in subjection. But these Bible Students saw from the Scriptures that the future of human governments was not secured by any divine guarantee. In harmony with what they were learning, the *Watch Tower* of December 1881 stated: "The setting up of this kingdom will of course, involve the overthrow of all the kingdoms of earth, as they are all—even the best of them—founded on injustice and unequal rights and the oppression of many and favor of the few—as we read: 'It shall break in pieces and consume all these kingdoms and it shall stand forever.'"—Dan. 2:44.

As to the way in which those oppressive kingdoms would be broken, the Bible Students still had much to learn. They did not yet understand clearly how the benefits of God's Kingdom would spread to all mankind. But they were not confusing the Kingdom of God with a vague feeling within one's heart or with rule by a religious hierarchy that used the secular State as its arm.

By 1914, the faithful pre-Christian servants of God had not been resurrected on earth as princely representatives of the Messianic King, as had been expected, nor had the remaining ones of the "little flock" joined Christ in the heavenly Kingdom in that year. Nevertheless, *The Watch Tower* of February 15, 1915, confidently stated that 1914 was the due time "for our Lord to take up His great power and reign," thus ending the millenniums of uninterrupted Gentile domination. In its issue of July 1, 1920, *The Watch Tower* reaffirmed that position and associated it with the good news that Jesus had foretold would be proclaimed earth wide before the end. (Matt. 24:14) At the convention of the Bible Students at Cedar Point, Ohio, in 1922, this understanding was restated in a general resolution, and Brother Rutherford urged the conventioners: "Advertise, advertise, advertise, the King and his kingdom."

However, at that time the Bible Students felt that the setting up of the Kingdom, its *full establishment* in heaven, would not take place until the final members of Christ's bride were glorified. A real milestone was reached, therefore, in 1925, when *The Watch Tower* of March 1 featured the article "Birth of the Nation." It presented an eye-opening study of Revelation chapter 12. The article set forth evidence that the Messianic Kingdom had been born—established—in 1914, that Christ had then begun to rule on his heavenly throne, and that thereafter Satan had been hurled from heaven down to the vicinity of the earth. This was the good news that was to be proclaimed, the news that God's Kingdom was already in operation. How this enlightened understanding stimulated these Kingdom proclaimers to preach to the ends of the earth!

By every appropriate means, Jehovah's people gave witness that only God's Kingdom could bring lasting relief and solve the deep-seated problems that afflicted humankind. In 1931 this message was featured in a radio broadcast by J. F. Rutherford on the most extensive international network that had ever been on the air. The text of that broadcast was also published in many languages in the booklet *The Kingdom, the Hope of the World*—millions of copies of which were distributed within a few months. In addition to widespread distribution to the public, special effort was put forth to get copies into the hands of politicians, prominent businessmen, and the clergy.

Among other things, that booklet said: "The present unrighteous governments of the world can hold out no hope whatsoever to the people. God's judgment against them declares they must go down. The hope of the world, therefore, and the only hope is the righteous kingdom or government of God with Christ Jesus as invisible Ruler thereof." That Kingdom, they realized, would bring true peace and security to mankind. Under its rule the earth would become a real paradise, and sickness and death would be no more.—Rev. 21:4, 5.

The good news of God's Kingdom continues to be central to the beliefs of Jehovah's Witnesses. Since the issue of March 1, 1939, their principal magazine, now published in over 110 languages, has borne the title *The Watchtower Announcing Jehovah's Kingdom*.

But before the Kingdom rule would transform the earth into a paradise, the present wicked system would have to go. How would that be accomplished?

The War of the Great Day of God the Almighty

The world war that began in 1914 rocked the existing system of things to its foundations. For a time it appeared that events would develop as the Bible Students had expected.

Back in August 1880, Brother Russell had written: "We understand that before the human family are restored or even begin to be blessed the present kingdoms of earth which now bind and oppress mankind will all be overturned and that the kingdom of God will assume control and that

Good news to be proclaimed: God's Kingdom is already in operation!

the blessing and restitution come through the new kingdom." How would that 'overturning of kingdoms' take place? Based on conditions that he could then see developing in the world, Russell believed that during the war of Armageddon, God would use contending factions of mankind to overthrow existing institutions. He said: "The work of demolishing human empire is beginning. The power that will overthrow them is now at work. The people are already organizing their forces under the name of Communists, Socialists, Nihilists, etc."

The book *The Day of Vengeance* (later called *The Battle of Armageddon*), published in 1897, further enlarged on the way the Bible Students then understood the matter, saying: "The Lord, by his overruling providence, will take a general charge of this great army of discontents—patriots, reformers, socialists, moralists, anarchists, ignorants and hopeless—and use their hopes, fears, follies and selfishness, according to his divine wisdom, to work out his own grand purposes in the overthrow of present institutions, and for the preparation of man for the Kingdom of Righteousness." Thus they understood the war of Armageddon to be associated with violent social revolution.

But was Armageddon going to be merely a struggle between contending factions of mankind, a social revolution used by God to overthrow existing institutions? As further attention was given to the scriptures bearing on this matter, *The Watch Tower* of July 15, 1925, drew attention to Zechariah 14:1-3 and said: "By this we would understand that all the nations of earth, under Satan's direction, would be gathered to battle against the Jerusalem class, viz., those who take their stand on the Lord's side . . . Revelation 16:14, 16."

The following year, in the book *Deliverance*, attention was focused on the real purpose of this war, saying: "Now Jehovah, according to his Word, will make a demonstration of his power so clearly and unequivocally that the people may be convinced of their ungodly course and may understand that Jehovah is God. That is the reason why God brought the great flood, threw down the Tower of Babel, destroyed the army of Sennacherib the Assyrian king, and swallowed up the Egyptians; and it is also the reason why he is now going to bring another great trouble upon the world. The former calamities were but shadows of the one now impending. The gathering is to the great day of God Almighty. It is 'the great and the terrible day of the Lord' (Joel 2:31), when God will make for himself a name. In this great and final conflict the peoples of every nation, kindred and tongue will learn that Jehovah is the all-powerful, all-wise and just God." But Jehovah's servants on earth were cautioned: "In this great battle no Christian will strike a blow. The reason they do not is that Jehovah has said: 'For the battle is not yours, but God's.'" The war here being discussed was

Was Armageddon to be merely a social revolution?

definitely not the one that was fought among the nations, beginning in 1914. It was yet to come.

There were yet other questions that needed to be resolved on the basis of the Scriptures. One of these involved the identity of the Jerusalem that was to be trampled underfoot until the end of the Gentile Times, as stated at Luke 21:24; and related to this was identification of the Israel referred to in so many prophecies of restoration.

Would God Restore the Jews to Palestine?

The Bible Students were well aware of the many prophecies of restoration that were delivered to ancient Israel by God's prophets. (Jer. 30:18; 31:8-10; Amos 9:14, 15; Rom. 11:25, 26) Down till 1932, they understood these to apply specifically to the natural Jews. Thus, they believed that God would show Israel favor again, gradually restoring the Jews to Palestine, opening their eyes to the truth regarding Jesus as Ransomer and Messianic King, and using them as an agency for extending blessings to all nations. With this understanding, Brother Russell spoke to large Jewish audiences in New York as well as in Europe on the subject "Zionism in Prophecy," and Brother Rutherford, in 1925, wrote the book *Comfort for the Jews*.

But it gradually became evident that what was taking place in Palestine with regard to the Jews was not the fulfillment of Jehovah's grand restoration prophecies. Desolation came on first-century Jerusalem because the Jews had rejected God's Son, the Messiah, the one sent in Jehovah's name. (Dan. 9:25-27; Matt. 23:38, 39) It was becoming increasingly obvious that *as a people* they had not changed their attitude. There was no repentance over the wrongful act committed by their forefathers. The return of some to Palestine was not motivated by any love for God or desire for his name to be magnified by fulfillment of his Word. This was clearly explained in the second volume of *Vindication*, which was published by the Watch Tower Bible and Tract Society in 1932.* The correctness of this position was confirmed in 1949, when the State of Israel, then recently formed as a nation and as a homeland for the Jews, became a member of the United Nations, thus showing that its trust was not in Jehovah but in the political nations of the world.

What had been taking place in fulfillment of those restoration prophecies pointed in another direction. Jehovah's servants began to realize that it was *spiritual* Israel, "the Israel of God," composed of spirit-anointed Christians, who, in fulfillment of God's purpose, were enjoying peace

At last, in 1932, the real "Israel of God" was identified

---

* In 1978, when asked for a statement for the press as to the position of Jehovah's Witnesses regarding Zionism, the Governing Body said: "Jehovah's Witnesses continue to take the Biblical stand of being neutral as to all political movements and governments. They are convinced that no human movement will achieve what only God's heavenly kingdom can accomplish."

A. H. Macmillan was sent by ship to Palestine in 1925 because of special interest in the role of the Jews in connection with Bible prophecy

with God through Jesus Christ. (Gal. 6:16) Now their eyes were opened to discern in God's dealings with such true Christians a marvelous spiritual fulfillment of those restoration promises. In time they also came to realize that the Jerusalem that was exalted at the end of the Gentile Times was not a mere earthly city, or even a people on earth represented by that city, but, rather, "heavenly Jerusalem," where Jehovah installed his Son, Jesus Christ, with ruling authority in 1914. —Heb. 12:22.

With these matters clear, Jehovah's Witnesses were in better position to fulfill without partiality toward any group the assignment to preach the Kingdom good news "in all the inhabited earth for a witness to all the nations."—Matt. 24:14.

Who is to be credited for all these explanations of the Bible that have appeared in the Watch Tower publications?

The Means by Which Jehovah's Servants Are Taught

Jesus Christ foretold that after his return to heaven, he would send his disciples the holy spirit. This would serve as a helper, guiding them "into all the truth." (John 14:26; 16:7, 13) Jesus also said that as the Lord or Master of true Christians, he would have a "faithful and discreet slave," a "faithful steward," that would give spiritual "food at the proper time" to the domestics, the workers in the household of faith. (Matt. 24:45-47; Luke 12:42) Who is this faithful and discreet slave?

The very first issue of the *Watch Tower* alluded to Matthew 24:45-47 when it stated that the aim of the publishers of that magazine was to be alert to events in connection with Christ's presence and to give spiritual "meat in due season" to the household of faith. But the editor of the magazine was not himself claiming to be the faithful and discreet slave, or the "faithful and wise servant" (according to the rendering of the *King James Version*).

Thus, in the October-November 1881 issue of the magazine, C. T. Russell stated: "We believe that every member of this body of Christ is engaged in the blessed work, either directly or indirectly, of giving meat in due season to the household of faith. 'Who then is that *faithful* and *wise servant* whom his Lord hath made ruler over his household,' to give them meat in due season? Is it not that 'little flock' of consecrated servants who are *faithfully* carrying out their consecration vows—the body of Christ— and is not the whole body individually and collectively, giving the meat in due [s]eason to the household of faith—the great company of believers? Blessed is that servant (the whole body of Christ) whom his Lord when he has come (Gr. *elthon*) shall find so doing. 'Verily, I say unto you, that he shall make him ruler over all his goods.'"

Over a decade later, however, Brother Russell's wife publicly expressed the idea that Russell himself was the faithful and wise servant.* The view that she voiced concerning the identity of the 'faithful servant' came to be generally held by the Bible Students for some 30 years. Brother Russell did not reject their view, but he personally avoided making such an application of the text, emphasizing his opposition to the idea of a clergy class commissioned to teach God's Word in contrast to a lay class that was not thus commissioned. The understanding expressed by Brother Russell in 1881 that the faithful and wise servant was in reality a collective servant, made up of all the members of the spirit-anointed body of Christ on earth, was reaffirmed in *The Watch Tower* of February 15, 1927.—Compare Isaiah 43:10.

How did Brother Russell view his own role? Did he claim some special revelation from God? In the *Watch Tower* of July 15, 1906 (page 229), Russell humbly replied: "No, dear friends, I claim nothing of superiority, nor supernatural power, dignity or authority; nor do I aspire to exalt myself in the estimation of my brethren of the household of faith, except in the sense that the Master urged it, saying, 'Let him who would be great among you be your servant.' (Matt. 20:27.) . . . The truths I present, as God's mouthpiece, were not revealed in visions or dreams, nor by God's audible voice, nor all at once, but gradually . . . Neither is this clear unfolding of truth due to any human ingenuity or acuteness of perception, but to the simple fact that God's due time has come; and if I did not speak, and no other agent could be found, the very stones would cry out."

It was to Jehovah as their Grand Instructor that readers of the *Watch Tower* were encouraged to look, even as all of Jehovah's Witnesses are today. (Isa. 30:20) This was strongly emphasized in *The Watchtower* of November 1, 1931, in the article "Taught of God," which stated: "*The Watchtower* recognizes the truth as belonging to Jehovah, and not to any creature. *The Watchtower* is not the instrument of any man or set of men, nor is it published according to the whims of men. . . . Jehovah God is the great Teacher of his children. To be sure, the publication of these truths is put forth by imperfect men, and for this reason they are not absolutely perfect in form; but they are put forth in such form as reflects God's truth that he teaches his children."

In the first century, when questions as to doctrine or procedure arose, these were referred to a central governing body made up of spiritually older

"The faithful and discreet slave"—a person or a class?

---

* Sadly, it was only a short time after this that she parted from him because of her own desire for personal prominence.

Beliefs of Jehovah's Witnesses

♦ **The Bible is God's inspired Word. (2 Tim. 3: 16, 17)**

What it contains is not mere history or human opinion but the word of God, recorded to benefit us. (2 Pet. 1:21; Rom. 15:4; 1 Cor. 10:11)

♦ **Jehovah is the only true God. (Ps. 83:18; Deut. 4:39)**

Jehovah is the Creator of all things, and as such, he alone deserves to be worshiped. (Rev. 4:11; Luke 4:8)

Jehovah is the Universal Sovereign, the one to whom we owe full obedience. (Acts 4:24; Dan. 4:17; Acts 5:29)

♦ **Jesus Christ is the only-begotten Son of God, the only one created directly by God himself. (1 John 4:9; Col. 1:13-16)**

Jesus was the first of God's creations; thus, before he was conceived and born as a human, Jesus lived in heaven. (Rev. 3:14; John 8:23, 58)

Jesus worships his Father as the only true God; Jesus never claimed equality with God. (John 17:3; 20:17; 14:28)

Jesus gave his perfect human life as a ransom for humankind. His sacrifice makes possible everlasting life for all who truly exercise faith in it. (Mark 10:45; John 3:16, 36)

Jesus was raised from the dead as an immortal spirit person. (1 Pet. 3:18; Rom. 6:9)

Jesus has returned (having directed his attention as King toward the earth) and is now present as a glorious spirit. (Matt. 24:3, 23-27; 25:31-33; John 14:19)

♦ **Satan is the invisible "ruler of this world." (John 12:31; 1 John 5:19)**

Originally he was a perfect son of God, but he allowed feelings of self-importance to develop in his heart, craved worship that belonged only to Jehovah, and enticed Adam and Eve to obey him rather than listen to God. Thus he made himself Satan, which means "Adversary." (John 8:44; Gen. 3:1-5; compare Deuteronomy 32:4, 5; James 1:14, 15; Luke 4:5-7.)

Satan "is misleading the entire inhabited earth"; he and his demons are responsible for increased distress on the earth in this time of the end. (Rev. 12:7-9, 12)

At God's appointed time, Satan and his demons will be destroyed forever. (Rev. 20:10; 21:8)

♦ **God's Kingdom under Christ will replace all human governments and will become the one government over all humankind. (Dan. 7:13, 14)**

The present wicked system of things will be completely destroyed. (Dan. 2:44; Rev. 16:14, 16; Isa. 34:2)

The Kingdom of God will rule with righteousness and will bring real peace to its subjects. (Isa. 9:6, 7; 11:1-5; 32:17; Ps. 85:10-12)

Wicked ones will be cut off forever, and worshipers of Jehovah will enjoy lasting security. (Prov. 2:21, 22; Ps. 37:9-11; Matt. 25:41-46; 2 Thess. 1:6-9; Mic. 4:3-5)

♦ **We are living now, since 1914,* in "the time of the end" of this wicked world. (Matt. 24:3-14; 2 Tim. 3:1-5; Dan. 12:4)**

During this time period, a witness is being given to all nations; after that will come the end, not of the globe, but of the wicked system and of ungodly people. (Matt. 24:3, 14; 2 Pet. 3:7; Eccl. 1:4)

♦ **There is only one road to life; not all religions or religious practices are approved by God. (Matt. 7:13, 14; John 4:23, 24; Eph. 4:4, 5)**

True worship emphasizes not ritual and outward show but genuine love for God, shown by obedience to his commandments and by love for one's fellowman. (Matt. 15:8, 9; 1 John 5:3; 3:10-18; 4:21; John 13:34, 35)

People out of all nations, races, and language groups can serve Jehovah and have his approval. (Acts 10:34, 35; Rev. 7:9-17)

Prayer is to be directed only to Jehovah through Jesus; images are not to be used either as objects of devotion or as aids in worship. (Matt. 6:9; John 14:6, 13, 14; 1 John 5:21; 2 Cor. 5:7; 6:16; Isa. 42:8)

Spiritistic practices must be shunned. (Gal. 5:19-21; Deut. 18:10-12; Rev. 21:8)

There is no clergy-laity distinction among true Christians. (Matt. 20:25-27; 23:8-12)

True Christianity does not include keeping a weekly sabbath or conforming to other requirements of

---

* For details, see the book "Let Your Kingdom Come."

the Mosaic Law in order to gain salvation; doing so would be a rejection of Christ, who fulfilled the Law. (Gal. 5:4; Rom. 10:4; Col. 2:13-17)

Those who practice true worship do not engage in interfaith. (2 Cor. 6:14-17; Rev. 18:4)

All who are truly disciples of Jesus get baptized by complete immersion. (Matt. 28:19, 20; Mark 1: 9, 10; Acts 8:36-38)

All who follow Jesus' example and obey his commandments bear witness to others about the Kingdom of God. (Luke 4:43; 8:1; Matt. 10:7; 24:14)

♦ **Death is a result of inheritance of sin from Adam. (Rom. 5:12; 6:23)**

At death, it is the soul itself that dies. (Ezek. 18:4)

The dead are conscious of nothing. (Ps. 146:4; Eccl. 9:5, 10)

Hell (Sheol, Hades) is mankind's common grave. (Job 14:13, "Dy"; Rev. 20:13, 14, "KJ," margin)

The 'lake of fire' to which the incorrigibly wicked are consigned signifies, as the Bible itself says, "second death," death forever. (Rev. 21:8)

Resurrection is the hope for the dead and for those who have lost loved ones in death. (1 Cor. 15: 20-22; John 5:28, 29; compare John 11:25, 26, 38-44; Mark 5:35-42.)

Death due to Adamic sin will be no more. (1 Cor. 15:26; Isa. 25:8; Rev. 21:4)

♦ **A "little flock," only 144,000, go to heaven. (Luke 12:32; Rev. 14:1, 3)**

These are the ones who are "born again" as spiritual sons of God. (John 3:3; 1 Pet. 1:3, 4)

God selects these out of all peoples and nations to rule as kings with Christ in the Kingdom. (Rev. 5: 9, 10; 20:6)

♦ **Others who have God's approval will live forever on earth. (Ps. 37:29; Matt. 5:5; 2 Pet. 3:13)**

Earth will never be destroyed or depopulated. (Ps. 104:5; Isa. 45:18)

In harmony with God's original purpose, all the earth will become a paradise. (Gen. 1:27, 28; 2: 8, 9; Luke 23:42, 43)

There will be suitable homes and an abundance of food for the enjoyment of everyone. (Isa. 65: 21-23; Ps. 72:16)

Sickness, all kinds of disability, and death itself will become things of the past. (Rev. 21:3, 4; Isa. 35: 5, 6)

♦ **Secular authorities are to be treated with due respect. (Rom. 13:1-7; Titus 3:1, 2)**

True Christians do not share in rebellion against governmental authority. (Prov. 24:21, 22; Rom. 13:1)

They obey all laws that do not conflict with the law of God, but obedience to God comes first. (Acts 5:29)

They imitate Jesus in remaining neutral as to the world's political affairs. (Matt. 22:15-21; John 6:15)

♦ **Christians must conform to Bible standards regarding blood as well as sexual morality. (Acts 15:28, 29)**

Taking blood into the body through mouth or veins violates God's law. (Gen. 9:3-6; Acts 15: 19, 20)

Christians are to be morally clean; fornication, adultery, and homosexuality must have no place in their lives, neither should drunkenness or drug abuse. (1 Cor. 6:9-11; 2 Cor. 7:1)

♦ **Personal honesty and faithfulness in caring for marital and family responsibilities are important for Christians. (1 Tim. 5:8; Col. 3: 18-21; Heb. 13:4)**

Dishonesty in speech or in business, as well as playing the hypocrite, are not consistent with being a Christian. (Prov. 6:16-19; Eph. 4:25; Matt. 6:5; Ps. 26:4)

♦ **Acceptable worship of Jehovah requires that we love him above all else. (Luke 10:27; Deut. 5:9)**

Doing Jehovah's will, thus bringing honor to his name, is the most important thing in the life of a true Christian. (John 4:34; Col. 3:23; 1 Pet. 2:12)

While doing good to all persons as they are able, Christians recognize a special obligation toward fellow servants of God; so their help in times of illness and disaster is directed especially toward these. (Gal. 6:10; 1 John 3:16-18)

Love of God requires of true Christians not only that they obey his commandment to love their neighbor but also that they not love the immoral and materialistic way of life of the world. True Christians are no part of the world and so refrain from joining in activities that would identify them as sharing its spirit. (Rom. 13:8, 9; 1 John 2: 15-17; John 15:19; Jas. 4:4)

men. Decisions were made after considering what the inspired Scriptures said as well as evidence of activity that was in harmony with those Scriptures and that was prospering as a result of the operation of the holy spirit. The decisions were conveyed in writing to the congregations. (Acts 15:1–16:5) That same procedure is in operation among Jehovah's Witnesses today.

Spiritual instruction is provided by means of magazine articles, books, convention programs, and outlines for congregation discourses—all of which are prepared under the direction of the Governing Body of the faithful and discreet slave. Their content clearly demonstrates that what Jesus foretold is true today—that he does, indeed, have a faithful and discreet slave class that is loyally teaching 'all the things that he commanded'; that this agency is "on the watch," alert to events in fulfillment of Bible prophecy and particularly with regard to Christ's presence; that it is helping God-fearing people to understand what is involved in 'observing' the things commanded by Jesus and thus proving that they truly are his disciples.—Matt. 24:42; 28:20; John 8:31, 32.

Progressively, over the years, practices that might have the effect of drawing undue attention to certain humans in connection with the preparation of spiritual food have been eliminated. Down till the death of C. T. Russell, his name as editor was listed in nearly every issue of the *Watch Tower*. Names or initials of others who contributed material often appeared at the end of articles they prepared. Then, starting with the issue of December 1, 1916, instead of showing the name of one man as editor, *The Watch Tower* listed the names of an editorial committee. In the issue of October 15, 1931, even this list was removed, and Isaiah 54:13 took its place. As quoted from the *American Standard Version*, it reads: "And all thy children shall be taught of Jehovah; and great shall be the peace of thy children." Since 1942 it has been the general rule that literature published by the Watch Tower Society does not draw attention to any individual as the writer.* Under the supervision of the Governing Body, dedicated Christians in North and South America, Europe, Africa, Asia, and islands of the sea have had a part in preparing such material for use by congregations of Jehovah's Witnesses worldwide. But all credit is given to Jehovah God.

Progressively, practices that might draw undue attention to certain humans have been eliminated

The Light Shines More and More

As reflected in their modern-day history, the experience of Jehovah's Witnesses has been like that described at Proverbs 4:18: "The path of the righteous ones is like the bright light that is getting lighter and lighter until the day is firmly established." The shining of the light has been progressive, just as the light of early dawn gives way to sunrise and the full light of a

---

* In lands where the law requires it, however, a local representative may be named as one responsible for what is published.

new day. Viewing matters in the light that was available, they have at times had incomplete, even inaccurate, concepts. No matter how hard they tried, they simply could not understand certain prophecies until these began to undergo fulfillment. As Jehovah has shed more light on his Word by means of his spirit, his servants have been humbly willing to make needed adjustments.

Such progressive understanding was not limited to the early period of their modern-day history. It continues right down to the present. For example, in 1962 there was an adjustment of understanding regarding "the superior authorities" of Romans 13:1-7.

For many years the Bible Students had taught that "the higher powers" (*KJ*) were Jehovah God and Jesus Christ. Why? In *The Watch Towers* of June 1 and June 15, 1929, a variety of secular laws were cited, and it was shown that what was permitted in one land was forbidden in another. Attention was also drawn to secular laws that required people to do what God prohibited or that forbade what God commanded his servants to do. Because of their earnest desire to show respect for the supreme authority of God, it seemed to the Bible Students that "the higher powers" must be Jehovah God and Jesus Christ. They still obeyed secular laws, but the emphasis was on obedience to God first. That was an important lesson, one that fortified them during the years of world turmoil that followed. But they did not clearly understand what Romans 13:1-7 was saying.

Years later, a careful reanalysis of the scripture was made, along with its context and its meaning in the light of all the rest of the Bible. As a result, in 1962 it was acknowledged that "the superior authorities" are the secular rulers, but with the help of the *New World Translation*, the principle of *relative subjection* was clearly discerned.* This did not call for any major change in the attitude of Jehovah's Witnesses toward the governments of the world, but it did correct their understanding of an important portion of the Scriptures. In the process, there was opportunity for the Witnesses individually to consider carefully whether they were truly living up to their responsibilities toward both God and the secular authorities. This clear understanding of "the superior authorities" has served as a protection to Jehovah's Witnesses, especially in those lands where surges of nationalism and clamoring for greater freedom have resulted in outbreaks of violence and the formation of new governments.

The following year, 1963, an enlarged application of "Babylon the Great" was presented.# (Rev. 17:5) A review of secular and religious history pointed to the conclusion that the influence of ancient Babylon had permeated not only Christendom but every part of the earth. Babylon the

---

* *The Watchtower,* November 1, November 15, and December 1, 1962.
# *The Watchtower,* November 15 and December 1, 1963.

Great was thus seen to be the entire world empire of false religion. An awareness of this has enabled Jehovah's Witnesses to help many more people, from diverse backgrounds, to respond to the Biblical command: "Get out of her, my people."—Rev. 18:4.

Indeed, the unfolding of events foretold in the entire book of Revelation has provided an abundance of spiritual illumination. In 1917 a study of Revelation was published in the book *The Finished Mystery*. But "the Lord's day," referred to at Revelation 1:10, was just beginning back then; much of what was foretold had not yet occurred and was not clearly understood. However, developments during the years that followed cast greater light on the meaning of that part of the Bible, and these events had a profound effect on the very illuminating study of Revelation that was published in 1930 in the two volumes entitled *Light*. During the 1960's a further update appeared in the books *"Babylon the Great Has Fallen!" God's Kingdom Rules!* and *"Then Is Finished the Mystery of God."* Two decades later another in-depth study was made of that part of the Bible. The figurative language of Revelation was carefully analyzed in the light of similar expressions in other parts of the Bible. (1 Cor. 2:10-13) Twentieth-century events in fulfillment of the prophecies were reviewed. The results were published in 1988 in the thrilling book *Revelation—Its Grand Climax At Hand!*

During the early years of their modern-day history, foundations were being laid. Much valuable spiritual food was provided. In recent years a greater diversity of Bible study material has been provided to satisfy the needs of both mature Christians and new students from many backgrounds. Continued study of the Scriptures, along with fulfillment of divine prophecy, has in many instances made it possible to express Bible teachings with greater clarity. Because their study of God's Word is progressive, Jehovah's Witnesses have spiritual food in abundance, even as the Scriptures foretold would be true of God's servants. (Isa. 65:13, 14) Adjustments in viewpoint are never made with a view to becoming more acceptable to the world by adopting its declining moral values. On the contrary, the history of Jehovah's Witnesses shows that changes are made with a view to adhering even more closely to the Bible, being more like the faithful first-century Christians, and so being more acceptable to God.

Thus, their experience is in harmony with the prayer of the apostle Paul, who wrote to fellow Christians: "We . . . have not ceased praying for you and asking that you may be filled with the accurate knowledge of his will in all wisdom and spiritual comprehension, in order to walk worthily of Jehovah to the end of fully pleasing him as you go on bearing fruit in every good work and increasing in the accurate knowledge of God."—Col. 1:9, 10.

That increase of accurate knowledge of God also had a bearing on their name—Jehovah's Witnesses.

Changes made are with a view to adhering even more closely to God's Word

CHAPTER 11

How We Came to Be Known as Jehovah's Witnesses

DURING the early decades of their modern-day history, they were frequently referred to simply as Bible Students. When others asked about the name of the organization, our brothers would often answer, "We are Christians." Brother Russell replied to such a question by saying, in the *Watch Tower:* "We do not separate ourselves from other Christians by taking any distinctive or peculiar name. We are satisfied with the name, Christian, by which the early saints were known."—Issue of September 1888.

How, then, did it come about that we are known today as Jehovah's Witnesses?

The Name Christian

True followers of Jesus Christ, both in the first century and in modern times, have referred to themselves and to fellow believers as "the brothers," "the friends," and "the congregation of God." (Acts 11:29; 3 John 14; 1 Cor. 1:2) They have also spoken of Christ as "the Master" and of themselves as "slaves of Christ Jesus" and "slaves of God." (Col. 3:24; Phil. 1:1; 1 Pet. 2:16) Such designations have been used freely within the congregation, and there they have been well understood.

In the first century, the manner of life that centered around faith in Jesus Christ (and, by extension, the congregation itself) was referred to as "The Way." (Acts 9:2; 19:9) A number of translations of Acts 18:25 indicate that it was also called "the way of Jehovah."* On the other hand, some who were outside the congregation derisively referred to it as "the sect of the Nazarenes."—Acts 24:5.

By 44 C.E. or not long thereafter, faithful followers of Jesus Christ began to be known as Christians. Some claim that it was outsiders who dubbed them Christians, doing so in a derogatory way. However, a number of Biblical lexicographers and commentators state that a verb used at Acts 11:26 implies divine direction or revelation. Thus, in the *New World*

"The disciples were by divine providence called Christians"

---

* *New World Translation of the Holy Scriptures; A Literal Translation of the New Testament . . . From the Text of the Vatican Manuscript,* by Herman Heinfetter; and six translations into Hebrew. See also the footnote on Acts 19:23 in the *New World Translation of the Holy Scriptures.*

Translation, that scripture reads: "It was first in Antioch that the disciples *were by divine providence called* Christians." (Similar renderings are found in Robert Young's *Literal Translation of the Holy Bible,* Revised Edition, of 1898; *The Simple English Bible,* of 1981; and Hugo McCord's *New Testament,* of 1988.) By about 58 C.E., the name Christian was well-known even to Roman officials.—Acts 26:28.

While the apostles of Christ were still alive, the name Christian was distinctive and specific. (1 Pet. 4:16) All who professed to be Christians but whose beliefs or conduct belied their claim were expelled from the Christian community. However, as Jesus had foretold, after the death of the apostles Satan sowed seeds that produced imitation Christians. These counterfeits also claimed the name Christian. (Matt. 13:24, 25, 37-39) When apostate Christianity resorted to forced conversions, some claimed to be Christians simply to avoid being persecuted. In time, any European who did not claim to be a Jew, a Muslim, or an atheist was frequently considered to be a Christian, regardless of his beliefs or conduct.

The name Christian became distorted in the public mind

Derisive Nicknames

From the 16th century onward, this situation posed a problem for the Reformers. Since the name Christian was being used so loosely, how could they distinguish themselves from others who claimed to be Christians?

Often they simply acquiesced to the use of a derisive nickname given to them by their enemies. Thus theological opponents of Martin Luther, in Germany, were the ones that first applied his name to his followers, calling them Lutherans. Those associated with John Wesley, in England, were labeled Methodists because they were unusually precise and methodical in the observance of religious duties. Baptists at first resisted the nickname Anabaptist (meaning, "Rebaptizer") but gradually adopted the name Baptist as a sort of compromise.

What about the Bible Students? They were dubbed Russellites and Rutherfordites by the clergy. But adopting such a name would have fostered a sectarian spirit. It would have been inconsistent with the reproof given to early Christians by the apostle Paul, who wrote: "When one says: 'I belong to Paul,' but another says: 'I to Apollos,' are you not simply men [that is, fleshly in outlook instead of spiritual]?" (1 Cor. 3:4) Some people labeled them "Millennial Dawnists"; but Christ's Millennial Reign was only one of their teachings. Others called them "Watch Tower People"; but that too was inappropriate, for the *Watch Tower* was merely one of the publications that they used to disseminate Bible truth.

Need for a Distinctive Name

In time, it became increasingly evident that in addition to the designation Christian, the congregation of Jehovah's servants truly did need a dis-

The Name Jehovah's Witnesses in
The Americas

Arabic	شهود يهوه
Armenian	Եհովայի Վկաներ
Chinese	耶和華見證人
English	Jehovah's Witnesses
French	Témoins de Jéhovah
Greek	Μάρτυρες του Ιεχωβά
Greenlandic	Jehovap Nalunaajaasui
Italian	Testimoni di Geova
Japanese	エホバの証人
Korean	여호와의 증인
Papiamento	Testigonan di Jehova
Polish	Świadkowie Jehowy
Portuguese	Testemunhas de Jeová
Samoan	Molimau a Ieova
Spanish	Testigos de Jehová
Sranantongo	Jehovah Kotoigi
Tagalog	Mga Saksi ni Jehova
Vietnamese	Nhân-chứng Giê-hô-va

tinctive name. The meaning of the name Christian had become distorted in the public mind because people who claimed to be Christians often had little or no idea who Jesus Christ was, what he taught, and what they should be doing if they really were his followers. Additionally, as our brothers progressed in their understanding of God's Word, they clearly saw the need to be separate and distinct from those religious systems that fraudulently claimed to be Christian.

True, our brothers often referred to themselves as Bible Students, and starting in 1910, they used the name International Bible Students' Association with reference to their meetings. In 1914, in order to avoid confusion with their recently formed legal corporation called International Bible Students Association, they adopted the name Associated Bible Students for their local groups. But their worship involved more than studying the Bible. Furthermore, there were others who also studied the Bible—some, devoutly; others, as critics; and not a few, as persons who viewed it simply as fine literature. Then, after the death of Brother Russell, some former associates refused to cooperate with the Watch Tower Society and the International Bible Students Association, even opposing the work of these societies. Such fragmented groups used a variety of names, some of them clinging to the designation Associated Bible Students. This caused further confusion.

But then, in 1931, we embraced the truly distinctive name Jehovah's Witnesses. Author Chandler W. Sterling refers to this as "the greatest stroke

They were more than Bible Students

> **Others Saw It**
>
> *It was not only "The Watch Tower" that pointed out from the Bible that Jehovah would have witnesses on the earth. As an example, H. A. Ironside, in the book "Lectures on Daniel the Prophet" (first published in 1911), referred to those toward whom the precious promises of Isaiah chapter 43 would be fulfilled and said: "These shall be Jehovah's witnesses, testifying to the power and glory of the one true God, when apostate Christendom shall have been given up to the strong delusion to believe the lie of the Antichrist."*

of genius" on the part of J. F. Rutherford, then president of the Watch Tower Society. As that writer viewed the matter, this was a clever move that not only provided an official name for the group but also made it easy for them to interpret all the Biblical references to "witness" and "witnessing" as applying specifically to Jehovah's Witnesses. In contrast, A. H. Macmillan, an administrative associate of three presidents of the Watch Tower Society, said concerning that announcement by Brother Rutherford: "There is no doubt in my mind—not then nor now—that the Lord guided him in that, and that is the name Jehovah wants us to bear, and we're very happy and very glad to have it." Which viewpoint do the facts support? Was the name 'a stroke of genius' on the part of Brother Rutherford, or was it the result of divine providence?

Developments Pointing to the Name

It was in the eighth century B.C.E. that Jehovah caused Isaiah to write: "'You are my witnesses,' is the utterance of Jehovah, 'even my servant whom I have chosen, in order that you may know and have faith in me, and that you may understand that I am the same One. Before me there was no God formed, and after me there continued to be none. . . . You are my witnesses,' is the utterance of Jehovah, 'and I am God.'" (Isa. 43:10, 12) As shown in the Christian Greek Scriptures, many prophecies recorded by Isaiah have fulfillment in connection with the Christian congregation. (Compare Isaiah 8:18 with Hebrews 2:10-13; Isaiah 66:22 with Revelation 21: 1, 2.) Yet, Isaiah 43:10, 12 was never discussed in any detail in *The Watch Tower* during its first 40 years of publication.

After that, however, their study of the Scriptures directed the attention of Jehovah's servants to significant new developments. God's Kingdom with Jesus as Messianic King had been brought to birth in the heavens in 1914. In 1925, the year that this was made clear in *The Watch Tower*, the prophetic command, in Isaiah chapter 43, to be witnesses of Jehovah was given attention in 11 different issues of the magazine.

In *The Watch Tower* of January 1, 1926, the principal article featured the challenging question: "Who Will Honor Jehovah?" During the next five years, *The Watch Tower* discussed some portion of Isaiah 43:10-12 in 46 separate issues and each time made application of it to true Christians.* In 1929

---

* Among the principal *Watch Tower* articles published during this period were "Jehovah and His Works," "Honor His Name," "A People for His Name," "His Name Exalted," "True and Faithful Witness," "Praise Jehovah!" "Delight Thyself in Jehovah," "Jehovah Supreme," "Vindication of His Name," "His Name," and "Sing Unto Jehovah."

The Name Jehovah's Witnesses in The Orient and Islands of the Pacific

Bengali	যিহোবার সাক্ষীদের
Bicol, Cebuano, Hiligaynon, Samar-Leyte, Tagalog	Mga Saksi ni Jehova
Bislama	Ol Wetnes blong Jeova
Chinese	耶和華見證人
English	Jehovah's Witnesses
Fijian	Vakadinadina i Jiova
Gujarati	યહોવાહના સાક્ષીઓ
Hindi	यहोवा के गवाह
Hiri Motu	Iehova ena Witness Taudia
Iloko	Dagiti Saksi ni Jehova
Indonesian	Saksi-Saksi Yehuwa
Japanese	エホバの証人
Kannada	ಯೆಹೋವನ ಸಾಕ್ಷಿಗಳು
Korean	여호와의 증인
Malayalam	യഹോവയുടെ സാക്ഷികൾ
Marathi	यहोवाचे साक्षीदार
Marshallese	Dri Kennan ro an Jeova
Myanmar	ယေဟောဝါသက်သေများ
Nepali	यहोवाका साक्षीहरू
New Guinea Pidgin	Ol Witnes Bilong Jehova
Niuean	Tau Fakamoli a Iehova
Palauan	reSioning er a Jehovah
Pangasinan	Saray Tasi nen Jehova
Ponapean	Sounkadehde kan en Siohwa
Rarotongan	Au Kite o Iehova
Russian	Свидетели Иеговы
Samoan, Tuvaluan	Molimau a Ieova
Sinhalese	යෙහෝවා දෙවිගේ සාක්ෂිකරුවෝ
Solomon Islands Pidgin	all'gether Jehovah's Witness
Tahitian	Ite no Iehova
Tamil	யெகோவாவின் சாட்சிகள்
Telugu	యెహోవా సాక్షులు
Thai	พยานพระยะโฮวา
Tongan	Fakamo'oni 'a Sihova
Trukese	Ekkewe Chon Pwarata Jiowa
Urdu	یہوواہ کے گواہ
Vietnamese	Nhân-chứng Giê-hô-va
Yapese	Pi Mich Rok Jehovah

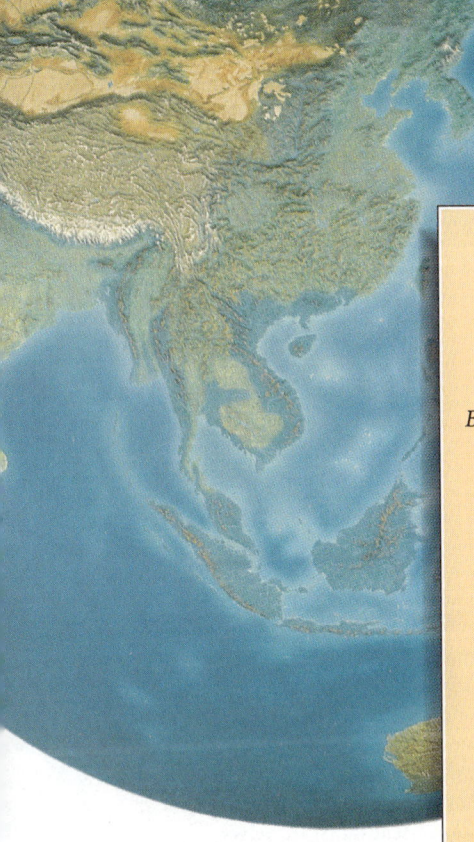

it was pointed out that the outstanding issue facing all intelligent creation involves the honoring of Jehovah's name. And in connection with the responsibility that Jehovah's servants have regarding this issue, Isaiah 43:10-12 repeatedly came up for consideration.

Thus the facts show that as a result of study of the Bible, attention was repeatedly being drawn to their obligation to be *witnesses of Jehovah*. It was not the *name* of a group that was under consideration but the *work* that they were to do.

But by what name should those witnesses be known?

The Name Jehovah's Witnesses in Africa

Afrikaans	Jehovah se Getuies
Amharic	የይሖዋ ምሥክሮች
Arabic	شهود يهوه
Chichewa	Mboni za Yehova
Cibemba	Inte sha kwa Yehova
Efịk	Mme Ntiense Jehovah
English	Jehovah's Witnesses
Ewe	Yehowa Ðasefowo
French	Témoins de Jéhovah
Ga	Yehowa Odasefoi
Gun	Kunnudetọ Jehovah tọn lẹ
Hausa	Shaidun Jehovah
Igbo	Ndịàmà Jehova
Kiluba	Ba Tumoni twa Yehova
Kinyarwanda	Abahamya ba Yehova
Kirundi	Ivyabona vya Yehova
Kisi	Seiyaa Jɛhowaa
Kwanyama	Eendombwedi daJehova
Lingala	Batemwe ya Jéhovah
Luganda	Abajulirwa ba Yakuwa
Malagasy	Vavolombelon'i Jehovah
Moore	A Zeova Kaset rãmba
Ndonga	Oonzapo dhaJehova
Portuguese	Testemunhas de Jeová
Sango	A-Témoin ti Jéhovah
Sepedi	Dihlatse tša Jehofa
Sesotho	Lipaki tsa Jehova
Shona	Zvapupu zvaJehovha
Silozi	Lipaki za Jehova
Swahili	Mashahidi wa Yehova
Tigrinya	ናይ የሆዋ መሰኻኽር
Tshiluba	Bantemu ba Yehowa
Tsonga	Timbhoni ta Yehova
Tswana	Basupi ba ga Jehofa
Twi	Yehowa Adansefo
Venda	Ṱhanzi dza Yehova
Xhosa	amaNgqina kaYehova
Yoruba	Ẹlẹ́rìí Jehofa
Zulu	oFakazi BakaJehova

The Name Jehovah's Witnesses in Europe and the Middle East

Albanian	Dëshmitarët e Jehovait
Arabic	شهود يهوه
Armenian	Եհովայի Վկաներ
Bulgarian	Свидетелите на Йехова
Croatian	Jehovini svjedoci
Czech	svědkové Jehovovi
Danish	Jehovas Vidner
Dutch	Jehovah's Getuigen
English	Jehovah's Witnesses
Estonian	Jehoova tunnistajad
Finnish	Jehovan todistajat
French	Témoins de Jéhovah
German	Jehovas Zeugen
Greek	Μάρτυρες του Ιεχωβά
Hebrew	עדי־יהוה
Hungarian	Jehova Tanúi
Icelandic	Vottar Jehóva
Italian	Testimoni di Geova
Macedonian, Serbian	Јеховини сведоци
Maltese	Xhieda ta' Jehovah
Norwegian	Jehovas vitner
Polish	Świadkowie Jehowy
Portuguese	Testemunhas de Jeová
Romanian	Martorii lui Iehova
Russian	Свидетели Иеговы
Slovak	Jehovovi svedkovia
Slovenian	Jehovove priče
Spanish	Testigos de Jehová
Swedish	Jehovas vittnen
Turkish	Yehova'nın Şahitleri
Ukrainian	Свідки Єгови

What would be appropriate in view of the work they were doing? To what conclusion did God's own Word point? This matter was discussed at a convention in Columbus, Ohio, U.S.A., on July 24-30, 1931.

A New Name

The large letters JW appeared prominently on the front cover of the convention program. What did they mean? It was not until Sunday, July 26, that their significance was explained. On that day Brother Rutherford delivered the public discourse "The Kingdom, the Hope of the World." In that discourse, when identifying those who are the proclaimers of God's Kingdom, the speaker made special reference to the name Jehovah's Witnesses.

Later that day Brother Rutherford followed this up with another talk, during which he discussed reasons why a distinctive name was needed.* To what name did the Scriptures themselves point? The speaker quoted Acts 15: 14, which directs attention to God's purpose to take out of the nations "a people for his name." In his discourse he highlighted the fact that as stated at Revelation 3:14, Jesus Christ is "the faithful and true witness." He referred to John 18:37, where Jesus declared: "For this I have come into the world, that I should bear witness to the truth." He directed attention to 1 Peter 2:9, 10, which says that God's servants are to 'declare abroad the excellencies of the one that called them out of darkness into his wonderful light.' He reasoned on a number of texts from Isaiah, not all of which were understood clearly at that time, but then he climaxed his presentation with Isaiah 43:8-12, which includes the divine commission: "'You are my witnesses,' is the utterance of Jehovah, 'and I am God.'" To what conclusion, then, was Jehovah's own Word directing them? What name would be in harmony with the way God was in fact using them?

The obvious answer was embodied in a resolution enthusiastically adopted on that occasion.# That resolution said, in part:

"In order that our true position may be made known, and believing that this is in harmony with the will of God, as expressed in his Word, BE IT RESOLVED, as follows, to wit:

The initials JW (with no explanation) were prominent at the 1931 convention. Their meaning was disclosed in a thrilling talk on the new name

---

* See the article "A New Name," in *The Watch Tower* of October 1, 1931.
# *The Watch Tower,* September 15, 1931, pp. 278-9.

"THAT we have great love for Brother Charles T. Russell, for his work's sake, and that we gladly acknowledge that the Lord used him and greatly blessed his work, yet we cannot consistently with the Word of God consent to be called by the name 'Russellites'; that the Watch Tower Bible and Tract Society and the International Bible Students Association and the Peoples Pulpit Association are merely names of corporations which as a company of Christian people we hold, control and use to carry on our work in obedience to God's commandments, yet none of these names properly attach to or apply to us as a body of Christians who follow in the footsteps of our Lord and Master, Christ Jesus; that we are students of the Bible, but, as a body of Christians forming an association, we decline to assume or be called by the name 'Bible Students' or similar names as a means of identification of our proper position before the Lord; we refuse to bear or to be called by the name of any man;

"THAT, having been bought with the precious blood of Jesus Christ our Lord and Redeemer, justified and begotten by Jehovah God and called to his kingdom, we unhesitatingly declare our entire allegiance and devotion to Jehovah God and his kingdom; that we are servants of Jehovah God commissioned to do a work in his name, and, in obedience to his commandment, to deliver the testimony of Jesus Christ, and to make known to the people that Jehovah is the true and Almighty God; therefore we joyfully embrace and take the name which the mouth of the Lord God has named, and we desire to be known as and called by the name, to wit, *Jehovah's witnesses.*—Isa. 43:10-12."*

Following the presentation of the full resolution, loud, sustained applause indicated the full agreement of the audience with what had been stated.

They were proud to let others know that they were Jehovah's Witnesses

Accepting the Responsibility

What an honor it is to bear the name of the only true God, the Sovereign of the universe! But with that name goes responsibility. It is a responsibility that other religious groups do not want. As Brother Rutherford said in his discourse: "Happy are they that can take a name that nobody under the sun wants except

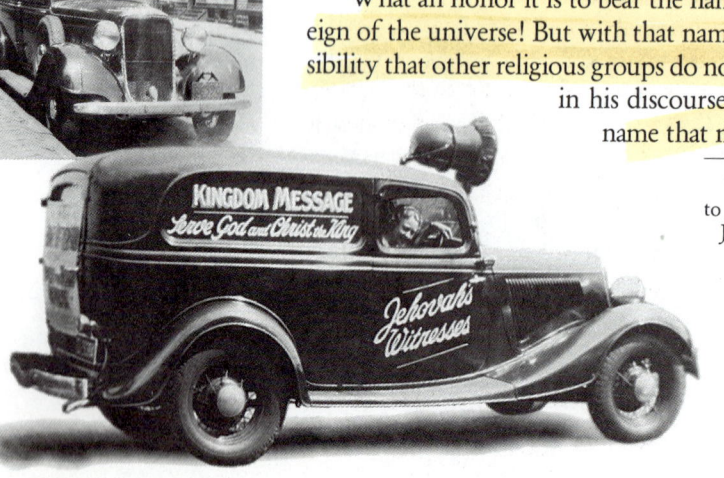

---

* Although the evidence points persuasively to Jehovah's direction in selection of the name Jehovah's Witnesses, *The Watchtower* (February 1, 1944, pp. 42-3; October 1, 1957, p. 607) and the book *"New Heavens and a New Earth"* (pp. 231-7) later pointed out that this name is not the "new name" referred to at Isaiah 62:2; 65:15; and Revelation 2:17, though the name harmonizes with the new relationship referred to in the two texts in Isaiah.

those who are wholly and unreservedly devoted to Jehovah." Yet, how fitting it is that Jehovah's servants bear God's personal name, that they make it known, and that it be prominently associated with the proclamation of his purpose!

Any group or individuals that speak in the name of Jehovah put themselves under obligation to convey his word truthfully. (Jer. 23:26-28) They must make known not only Jehovah's provisions for the blessing of lovers of righteousness but also his judgments upon practicers of unrighteousness. As Jehovah commanded his prophets in times past, so today, his witnesses must not take away anything from God's word by failing to make it known. (Jer. 1:17; 26:2; Ezek. 3:1-11) They must proclaim both "the year of goodwill on the part of Jehovah and the day of vengeance on the part of our God." (Isa. 61:1, 2) Those adopting the above resolution recognized that responsibility, and in the latter part of the resolution, they declared:

"As Jehovah's witnesses our sole and only purpose is to be entirely obedient to his commandments; to make known that he is the only true and Almighty God; that his Word is true and that his name is entitled to all honor and glory; that Christ is God's King, whom he has placed upon his throne of authority; that his kingdom is now come, and in obedience to the Lord's commandments we must now declare this good news as a testimony or witness to the nations and inform the rulers and the people of and concerning Satan's cruel and oppressive organization, and particularly with reference to 'Christendom', which is the most wicked part of that visible organization, and of and concerning God's purpose to shortly destroy Satan's organization, which great act will be quickly followed by Christ the King's bringing to the obedient peoples of earth peace and prosperity, liberty and health, happiness and everlasting life; that God's kingdom is the hope of the world, and there is no other, and that this message must be delivered by those who are identified as Jehovah's witnesses.

"We humbly invite all persons who are wholly devoted to Jehovah and his kingdom to join in proclaiming this good news to others, that the righteous standard of the Lord may be lifted up, that the peoples of the world may know where to find the truth and hope for relief; and, above all, that the great and holy name of Jehovah God may be vindicated and exalted."

It was not only in Columbus, Ohio, in America, but as far away as Australia that audiences burst into applause when they heard announcement of that new name. In Japan, after hours of effort, just a brief portion of the program was picked up on a shortwave radio in the middle of the night. Immediately it was translated. Thus the small group there heard the resolution and the thunderous applause. Matsue Ishii was there with them, and as she later wrote, they 'raised a shout of joy in harmony with their brothers in America.' Following the convention in Columbus, assemblies and congregations of Jehovah's Witnesses in all the lands where they were

"'You are my witnesses,' is the utterance of Jehovah, 'and I am God'"

carrying on their ministry expressed themselves as being in full agreement with that resolution. From Norway, as but one example, came the report: "At our year-convention . . . in Oslo we all arose on our feet and with great enthusiasm shouted 'Ja', when adopting our new name 'Jehovah's witnesses.'"

More Than a Label

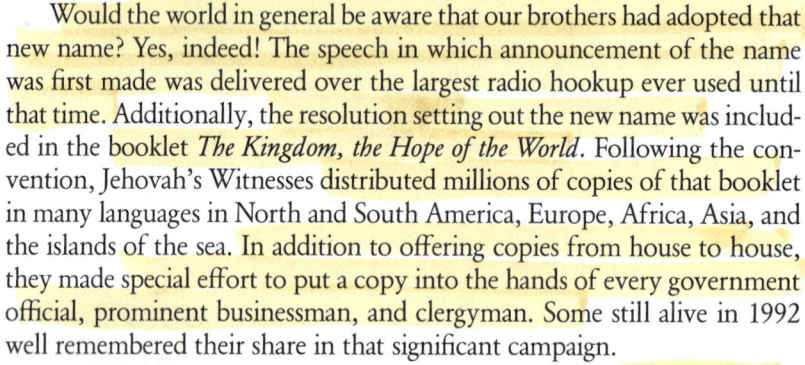

Would the world in general be aware that our brothers had adopted that new name? Yes, indeed! The speech in which announcement of the name was first made was delivered over the largest radio hookup ever used until that time. Additionally, the resolution setting out the new name was included in the booklet *The Kingdom, the Hope of the World*. Following the convention, Jehovah's Witnesses distributed millions of copies of that booklet in many languages in North and South America, Europe, Africa, Asia, and the islands of the sea. In addition to offering copies from house to house, they made special effort to put a copy into the hands of every government official, prominent businessman, and clergyman. Some still alive in 1992 well remembered their share in that significant campaign.

Not all received the booklet graciously. Eva Abbott recalls that as she left the house of a clergyman in the United States, the booklet came sailing past her and landed on the ground. She did not want to leave it there, so she proceeded to pick it up; but a large dog growled, snatched it from her hand, and took it to his master, the preacher. She said: "What I could not deliver, the dog did!"

Martin Poetzinger, who later served as a member of the Governing Body of Jehovah's Witnesses, recalled: "Astonished faces appeared at every door when we introduced ourselves with the words: 'I have come to you today as one of Jehovah's witnesses.' People would shake their heads or ask: 'But you are still Bible students, are you not? Or have you joined a new sect?'" Gradually that situation changed. Several decades after they began to use their distinctive name, Brother Poetzinger wrote: "What a change! Before I say a word people will remark: 'You must be one of Jehovah's witnesses.'" Yes, they know the name now.

That name is not just a label. Whether young or old, male or female, all of Jehovah's Witnesses share in the work of bearing witness to Jehovah and his grand purpose. As a result, C. S. Braden, a professor of religious history, wrote: "Jehovah's Witnesses have literally covered the earth with their witnessing."—*These Also Believe*.

Although the witnessing done by our brothers before they adopted the name Jehovah's Witnesses was globe encircling, in retrospect it appears that Jehovah was preparing them for an even greater work—the gathering of a great crowd who would be preserved alive through Armageddon, with the opportunity to live forever on a paradise earth.

CHAPTER 12

THE GREAT CROWD
TO LIVE IN HEAVEN?
OR ON EARTH?

IN CONTRAST to members of the religions of Christendom, the majority of Jehovah's Witnesses look forward to an eternity of life, not in heaven, but on earth. Why is this?

It has not always been that way. First-century Christians had the expectation that in time they would rule with Jesus Christ as heavenly kings. (Matt. 11:12; Luke 22:28-30) Jesus had told them, however, that the Kingdom heirs would be only a "little flock." (Luke 12:32) Who would be included? How many would there be? They did not learn the details until later.

At Pentecost 33 C.E., the first Jewish disciples of Jesus were anointed with holy spirit to be joint heirs with Christ. In the year 36 C.E., the operation of God's spirit made it clear that uncircumcised Gentiles would also share in that inheritance. (Acts 15:7-9; Eph. 3:5, 6) Another 60 years passed before it was revealed to the apostle John that only 144,000 would be taken from earth to share the heavenly Kingdom with Christ.—Rev. 7: 4-8; 14:1-3.

Charles Taze Russell and his associates shared that hope, as did most of Jehovah's Witnesses down till the mid-1930's. They also knew, from their study of the Scriptures, that anointing with holy spirit signified not only that persons were in line for future service as kings and priests with Christ in heaven *but also that they had a special work to do while still in the flesh.* (1 Pet. 1:3, 4; 2:9; Rev. 20:6) What work? They knew well and often quoted Isaiah 61:1, which states: "The spirit of the Sovereign Lord Jehovah is upon me, for the reason that Jehovah has anointed me to tell good news to the meek ones."

Preaching With What Objective?

Although they were few in number, they endeavored to convey to everyone possible the truth about God and his purpose. They printed and distributed vast amounts of literature telling the good news concerning his provision for salvation through Christ. But their objective was by no means the conversion of all those to whom they preached. Then, why did they preach to them? The *Watch Tower* of July 1889 explained: "We are his

Most of Jehovah's Witnesses look forward to eternal life on earth

[Jehovah's] representatives in the earth; the honor of his name is to be vindicated in the presence of his enemies and before many of his deceived children; his glorious plan is to be published broadcast in opposition to all the worldly-wise schemes which men are and have been trying to invent."

Special attention was given to those who claimed to be the Lord's people, many of whom were members of Christendom's churches. What was the objective in preaching to these? As Brother Russell often explained, the desire of the early Bible Students was not to draw church members away to some other organization but to help them to draw closer to the Lord as members of the one true church. The Bible Students knew, however, that in obedience to Revelation 18:4, such ones must get out of "Babylon," which they understood to be manifest in the nominal church, the churches of Christendom with all their unscriptural teachings and sectarian divisions. In the very first issue of the *Watch Tower* (July 1879), Brother Russell stated: "We understand that the object of the present witnessing is 'To take out a *people* for His name'—the Church—who at Christ's coming are united to Him, and receive His name. Rev. iii. 12."

They realized that, at that time, just one "calling" was being extended to all true Christians. This was an invitation to be members of the bride of Christ, which would finally be just 144,000 in number. (Eph. 4:4; Rev. 14:1-5) They sought to stir up all who professed faith in Christ's ransom sacrifice, whether these were church members or not, to appreciate "the precious and very grand promises" of God. (2 Pet. 1:4; Eph. 1:18) They endeavored to move them to zeal in conforming to the requirements for the little flock of Kingdom heirs. For the spiritual strengthening of all such, whom they viewed as constituting "the household of faith" (because they professed faith in the ransom), Brother Russell and his associates diligently sought to make available spiritual 'food in due season' through the columns of the *Watch Tower* and other Bible-based publications.—Gal. 6:10; Matt. 24:45, 46, *KJ*.

They could see, however, that not all who professed to have made a "consecration" (or, 'to have given themselves fully to the Lord,' as they understood it to mean) thereafter continued to pursue a life of willing self-sacrifice, making the Lord's service their first concern in life. Yet, as they explained, consecrated Christians had agreed to give up human nature willingly, with a heavenly inheritance in view; there was

---

A Time for Understanding

Over 250 years ago, Sir Isaac Newton wrote an interesting item about understanding prophecy, including the one about the "great crowd" of Revelation 7:9, 10. In his "Observations Upon the Prophecies of Daniel, and the Apocalypse of St. John," published in 1733, he stated: "These Prophecies of Daniel and John should not be understood till the time of the end: but then some should prophesy out of them in an afflicted and mournful state for a long time, and that but darkly, so as to convert but few.... Then, saith Daniel, many shall run to and fro, and knowledge shall be encreased. For the Gospel must be preached in all nations before the great tribulation, and end of the world. The palm-bearing multitude, which come out of this great tribulation, cannot be innumerable out of all nations, unless they be made so by the preaching of the Gospel before it comes."

no turning back; if they did not gain life in the spirit realm, second death would await them. (Heb. 6:4-6; 10:26-29) But many seemingly consecrated Christians were taking the easy road, failing to manifest true zeal for the Lord's cause and shunning self-sacrifice. Nevertheless, they apparently had not repudiated the ransom and were leading reasonably clean lives. What would become of such persons?

For many years the Bible Students thought that this was the group described at Revelation 7:9, 14 (*KJ*), which refers to "a great multitude" that come out of great tribulation and stand "before the throne" of God and before the Lamb, Jesus Christ. They reasoned that although these shunned a life of self-sacrifice, they would be confronted with trials of faith ending in death during a time of tribulation after the glorification of the final ones of the bride of Christ. They believed that if these who were said to be of the great multitude were faithful at that time, they would be resurrected to heavenly life—not to rule as kings but to take a position *before* the throne. It was reasoned that they would be given such secondary positions because their love for the Lord had not been sufficiently fervent, because they had not shown enough zeal. It was thought that these were people who had been begotten by God's spirit but had been negligent about obeying God, possibly continuing to cling to Christendom's churches.

They also thought that perhaps—just perhaps—the "ancient worthies" who would serve as princes on the earth during the millennial era would, at the end of that time, somehow be granted heavenly life. (Ps. 45:16) They reasoned that a similar prospect might await any who "consecrated" themselves after the 144,000 Kingdom heirs had all been finally chosen but before the time of restitution on earth began. In a limited way, this was a carryover from Christendom's view that all those who are good enough go to heaven. But there was a belief that the Bible Students cherished from the Scriptures that set them apart from all of Christendom. What was that?

Living Forever in Perfection on Earth

They recognized that while a limited number taken from among humankind would be granted heavenly life, there would be many more who would be favored with eternal life on earth, under conditions like those that had existed in the Paradise of Eden. Jesus had taught his followers to pray: "Let your will take place, as in heaven, *also upon earth*." He had also said: "Happy are the mild-tempered ones, since they will *inherit the earth*." —Matt. 5:5; 6:10.

In harmony with that, a chart* published as a supplement to the July-August 1881 *Watch Tower* indicated that there would be many from among humankind that would gain God's favor during Christ's Millennial Reign and

A belief that set them apart from all of Christendom

---
* This "Chart of the Ages" was later reproduced in the book *The Divine Plan of the Ages*.

CHART OF THE AGES

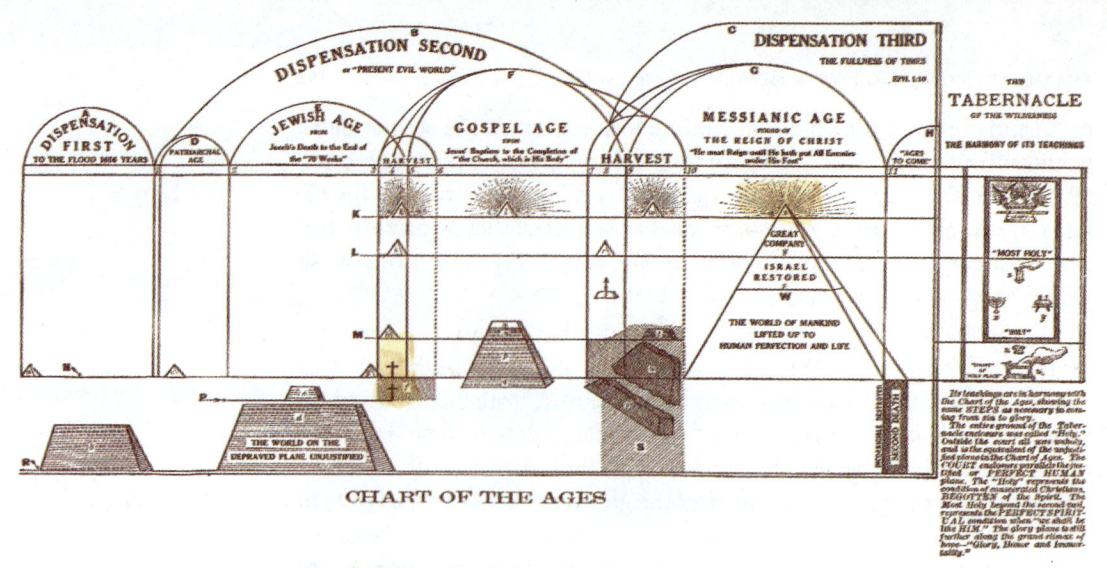

that would make up "the world of mankind lifted up to human perfection and life." This chart was used for many years as the basis for discourses to groups both large and small.

Under what conditions would people on earth live during that millennial era? *The Watch Tower* of July 1, 1912, explained: "Before sin had entered into the world, the Divine provision for our first parents was the Garden of Eden. As we think of this, let our minds turn to the future, guided by the Word of God; and in mental vision we see Paradise restored—not a *garden* merely, but the *entire earth* made beautiful, fruitful, sinless, happy. Then we recall the inspired promise so familiar to us—'And God shall wipe away all tears from their eyes; and there shall be no more death, neither sorrow nor crying, neither shall there be any more pain,' for the former things of sin and death will have passed away, and all things will have been made new!—Rev. 21:4, 5."

Who Would Live Forever on Earth?

There was no thought on the part of Brother Russell that God was offering mankind a choice—heavenly life for those who wanted it and life in an earthly paradise for those who thought they would prefer that. The *Watch Tower* of September 15, 1905, pointed out: "Our feelings or aspirations are not the call. Otherwise it would imply that we do our own calling. Speaking of our priesthood, the Apostle declares, 'No man taketh this honor to himself but he that is called of God,' (Heb. 5:4), and the place to ascertain what is God's call is not in our feelings but in God's own Word of revelation."

As for the opportunity to live in a restored earthly paradise, the Bible Students believed that this would be extended to people only after all the little flock had received their reward and the millennial age had been fully ushered in. That, they understood, would be the time of "restitution of all things," as referred to at Acts 3:21. (*KJ*) Even the dead would then be raised so that all could share in that loving provision. The brothers envisioned all of humankind (apart from those who had been called to heavenly life) as being given their opportunity then to choose life. As they understood it, that would be the time when Christ, on his heavenly throne, would separate the people one from another, as a shepherd separates sheep from goats. (Matt. 25:31-46) The obedient ones, whether born as Jews or as Gentiles, would prove to be the Lord's "other sheep."—John 10:16.*

After the Gentile Times ended, they thought that the time of restitution was very near; so from 1918 down till 1925, they proclaimed: "Millions now living will never die." Yes, they understood that people then living—mankind in general—had the opportunity to survive right into the time of restitution and that they would then be educated in Jehovah's requirements for life. If obedient, they would gradually attain to human perfection. If rebellious, they would, in time, be destroyed forever.

During those early years, the brothers had no idea that the Kingdom message would be proclaimed as extensively and for as many years as it has been. But they continued to examine the Scriptures and endeavored to respond to what these indicated as to the work that God would have them do.

"Sheep" at the Right Hand of Christ

A truly significant step in understanding Jehovah's purpose centered

---
* *Zion's Watch Tower,* March 15, 1905, pp. 88-91.

around Jesus' parable of the sheep and the goats, at Matthew 25:31-46. In that parable Jesus said: "When the Son of man arrives in his glory, and all the angels with him, then he will sit down on his glorious throne. And all the nations will be gathered before him, and he will separate people one from another, just as a shepherd separates the sheep from the goats. And he will put the sheep on his right hand, but the goats on his left." As the parable goes on to show, the "sheep" are those who help Christ's "brothers," even seeking to bring them relief when they are persecuted and in prison.

Time of fulfillment of the parable of the sheep and the goats

It had long been thought that this parable applied during the millennial era, in the time of restitution, and that the final judgment referred to in the parable was the one that would take place at the end of the Millennium. But in 1923, reasons for another view of matters were set forth by J. F. Rutherford, the president of the Watch Tower Society, in an enlightening discourse in Los Angeles, California. This was published later that year in the October 15 issue of *The Watch Tower*.

When discussing the time that this prophetic parable would be fulfilled, the article showed that Jesus included it as part of his response to a request for 'the sign of his presence and of the conclusion of the system of things.' (Matt. 24:3) The article explained why the "brothers" referred to in the parable could not be the Jews of the Gospel age nor humans who show faith during the millennial period of testing and judgment but must be those who are heirs with Christ of the heavenly Kingdom, thus why the parable's fulfillment must be at a time when some of Christ's joint heirs are still in the flesh.—Compare Hebrews 2:10, 11.

The experiences of those anointed brothers of Christ when they endeavored to witness to the clergy and to the common people associated with the churches of Christendom also indicated that the prophecy embodied in Jesus' parable was already being fulfilled. How so? The reaction of many of the clergy and prominent members of their churches was hostile—no refreshing cup of water, either literally or figuratively; instead, some of these instigated mobs to tear clothing from the brothers and beat them, or they demanded that officials imprison them. (Matt. 25:41-43) In contrast, many humble church members gladly received the Kingdom message, offered refreshment to those who brought it, and did what they could to help them even when the anointed ones were imprisoned for the sake of the good news.—Matt. 25:34-36.

As far as the Bible Students could see, those whom Jesus spoke of as the sheep were still in the churches of Christendom. These, they reasoned, were people who did not claim to be consecrated to the Lord but did have great respect for Jesus Christ and for his people. Yet, could they remain in the churches?

Taking a Firm Stand for Pure Worship

A study of the Bible's prophetic book of Ezekiel shed light on this. The first of a three-volume commentary entitled *Vindication* was published in 1931. It explained the significance of what Ezekiel wrote about Jehovah's rage against ancient apostate Judah and Jerusalem. Although the people of Judah claimed to serve the living and true God, they adopted the religious rites of surrounding nations, offered incense to lifeless idols, and immorally put their trust in political alliances, instead of demonstrating faith in Jehovah. (Ezek. 8:5-18; 16:26, 28, 29; 20:32) In all of this, they were exactly like Christendom; so, consistently, Jehovah would execute judgment upon Christendom just as he did upon unfaithful Judah and Jerusalem. But chapter 9 of Ezekiel shows that before the divine execution of judgment, some would be marked for preservation. Who are these?

The prophecy says that the ones marked would be "sighing and groaning over all the detestable things that are being done" in the midst of Christendom, or antitypical Jerusalem. (Ezek. 9:4) Surely, then, they could not be deliberately sharing in those detestable things. The first volume of *Vindication* therefore identified those having the mark as being people who refuse to be part of the church organizations of Christendom and who in some way take their stand on the Lord's side.

This material was followed up in 1932 by a discussion of the Bible record concerning Jehu and Jonadab and its prophetic implications. Jehu was commissioned by Jehovah to be king over the ten-tribe kingdom of Israel and to execute Jehovah's judgment on the wicked house of Ahab and Jezebel. When Jehu was en route to Samaria to eradicate Baal worship, Jehonadab (Jonadab), the son of Rechab, went out to meet him. Jehu asked Jehonadab: "Is your heart upright with me?" and Jehonadab answered: "It is." "Do give me your hand," Jehu invited, and he took Jehonadab up into his chariot. Then Jehu urged: "Do go along with me and look upon my toleration of no rivalry toward Jehovah." (2 Ki. 10:15-28) Jehonadab, though not an Israelite, agreed with what Jehu was doing; he knew that Jehovah, the true God, should be given exclusive devotion. (Ex. 20:4, 5) Centuries later, Jehonadab's descendants were still demonstrating a spirit that Jehovah approved, so He promised: "There will not be cut off from Jonadab the son of Rechab a man to stand before me always." (Jer. 35:19) The question thus arose, Are there people on earth today who are not spiritual Israelites with a heavenly inheritance but who are like Jehonadab?

The Watchtower of August 1, 1932, explained: "Jehonadab represented or foreshadowed that class of people now on the earth . . . [who] are out of harmony with Satan's organization, who take their stand on the side of righteousness, and are the ones whom the Lord will preserve during the time of Armageddon, take them through that trouble, and give them everlasting life on the earth. These constitute the 'sheep' class that favor God's

They came to be known as Jonadabs

anointed people, because they know that the anointed of the Lord are doing the Lord's work." Those manifesting such a spirit were invited to have a share in taking the Kingdom message to others just as the anointed were doing.—Rev. 22:17.

There were some (though relatively few at that time) associating with Jehovah's Witnesses who realized that the spirit of God had not engendered in them the hope of heavenly life. They came to be known as Jonadabs, for, like ancient Jonadab (Jehonadab), they counted it a privilege to be identified with Jehovah's anointed servants, and they were glad to share in the privileges to which God's Word pointed them. Would such persons who had the prospect of never dying become numerous before Armageddon? Was it possible, as had been said, that they could number into the millions?

The "Great Crowd"—Who Are They?

When announcement was made of arrangements for Jehovah's Witnesses to hold a convention in Washington, D.C., from May 30 to June 3, 1935, *The Watchtower* said: "Heretofore not many Jonadabs have had the privilege of attending a convention, and the convention at Washington may be a real comfort and benefit to them." That certainly proved true.

On May 31, 1935, the "great multitude" was clearly identified

At that convention special attention was given to Revelation 7:9, 10, which reads: "After these things I saw, and, look! a great crowd, which no man was able to number, out of all nations and tribes and peoples and tongues, standing before the throne and before the Lamb, dressed in white robes; and there were palm branches in their hands. And they keep on crying with a loud voice, saying: 'Salvation we owe to our God, who is seated on the throne, and to the Lamb.'" Who make up this great crowd, or "great multitude"?—*KJ*.

For years, even down till 1935, they were not understood to be the same as the sheep in Jesus' parable of the sheep and the goats. As already noted, it was thought that they were a secondary heavenly class—secondary because they had been negligent about obeying God.

However, that view gave rise to persistent questions. Some of these were discussed early in 1935 at the noon meal at the Watch Tower Society's headquarters. Some among those who expressed themselves at that time suggested that the great multitude was an earthly class. Grant Suiter, who later became a member of the Governing Body, recalled: "At one Bethel study, conducted by Brother T. J. Sullivan, I asked: 'Since the great multitude gain everlasting life, do those who make up that group maintain integrity?' There were many comments but no definitive answer." Well, on Friday, May 31, 1935, at the Washington, D.C., convention, a satisfying answer was given. Brother Suiter was sitting in the balcony looking down over the crowd, and how thrilled he was as the talk unfolded!

THE GREAT CROWD—TO LIVE IN HEAVEN? OR ON EARTH?

Shortly after the convention, *The Watchtower,* in its issues of August 1 and 15, 1935, published what was stated in that talk. It pointed out that an important factor in properly understanding matters is appreciation of the fact that Jehovah's chief purpose is not the salvation of men but the vindication of his own name (or, as we would now say, the vindication of his sovereignty). Thus Jehovah's approval is upon those who maintain integrity to him; he does not reward those who agree to do his will but then bring reproach on his name by compromising with the Devil's organization. This requirement of faithfulness applies to *all* who would have God's approval.

In harmony with this, *The Watchtower* said: "Revelation 7:15 really is the key to the identification of the great multitude. . . . This description in Revelation of the great multitude is that 'they are before the throne of God, and publicly serve him' . . . They see and understand and obey the words of Jesus, the Lamb of God, saying to them: 'Thou shalt worship the Lord thy God, and him only shalt thou serve'; which words apply to all creatures whom Jehovah approves." (Matt. 4:10) So, what the Bible says about the great multitude, or great crowd, could not be properly construed as providing a safety net for people who professed love for God but were indifferent about doing his will.

Then, is the great crowd a heavenly class? *The Watchtower* showed that the language of the scripture did not point to such a conclusion. As to their location "before the throne," it showed that Matthew 25:31, 32 tells of all nations being gathered before the throne of Christ, yet those nations are on earth. The great crowd, however, are "standing" before the throne because they have the approval of the One on the throne.—Compare Jeremiah 35:19.

But where could such a group be found—people "out of all nations," people who were no part of spiritual Israel (described earlier, in Revelation 7:4-8), people who exercised faith in the ransom (having figuratively

At the Washington, D.C., convention, 840 were baptized

The Earth, Man's Eternal Home

What was God's original purpose for humankind?

"God blessed them and God said to them: 'Be fruitful and become many and fill the earth and subdue it, and have in subjection the fish of the sea and the flying creatures of the heavens and every living creature that is moving upon the earth.'"—Gen. 1:28.

Has God's purpose regarding the earth changed?

"My word . . . will not return to me without results, but it will certainly do that in which I have delighted, and it will have certain success in that for which I have sent it."—Isa. 55:11.

"This is what Jehovah has said, the Creator of the heavens, He the true God, the Former of the earth and the Maker of it, He the One who firmly established it, who did not create it simply for nothing, who formed it even to be inhabited: 'I am Jehovah, and there is no one else.'"—Isa. 45:18.

"You must pray, then, this way: 'Our Father in the heavens, let your name be sanctified. Let your kingdom come. Let your will take place, as in heaven, also upon earth.'"—Matt. 6:9, 10.

"Evildoers themselves will be cut off, but those hoping in Jehovah are the ones that will possess the earth. The righteous themselves will possess the earth, and they will reside forever upon it."—Ps. 37:9, 29.

What conditions will exist on earth under God's Kingdom?

"There are new heavens and a new earth that we are awaiting according to his promise, and in these righteousness is to dwell."—2 Pet. 3:13.

"They will not lift up sword, nation against nation, neither will they learn war anymore. And they will actually sit, each one under his vine and under his fig tree, and there will be no one making them tremble; for the very mouth of Jehovah of armies has spoken it."—Mic. 4:3, 4.

"They will certainly build houses and have occupancy; and they will certainly plant vineyards and eat their fruitage. They will not build and someone else have occupancy; they will not plant and someone else do the eating. For like the days of a tree will the days of my people be; and the work of their own hands my chosen ones will use to the full."—Isa. 65:21, 22.

"No resident will say: 'I am sick.'"—Isa. 33:24.

"God himself will be with them. And he will wipe out every tear from their eyes, and death will be no more, neither will mourning nor outcry nor pain be anymore. The former things have passed away."—Rev. 21:3, 4; see also John 3:16.

"Who will not really fear you, Jehovah, and glorify your name, because you alone are loyal? For all the nations will come and worship before you, because your righteous decrees have been made manifest."—Rev. 15:4.

Those Who Go to Heaven

How many humans will go to heaven?
"Have no fear, little flock, because your Father has approved of giving you the kingdom."—Luke 12:32.

"I saw, and, look! the Lamb [Jesus Christ] standing upon the [heavenly] Mount Zion, and with him a hundred and forty-four thousand having his name and the name of his Father written on their foreheads. And they are singing as if a new song before the throne and before the four living creatures and the elders; and no one was able to master that song but the hundred and forty-four thousand, who have been bought from the earth."—Rev. 14:1, 3.

Are the 144,000 all Jews?
"There is neither Jew nor Greek, there is neither slave nor freeman, there is neither male nor female; for you are all one person in union with Christ Jesus. Moreover, if you belong to Christ, you are really Abraham's seed, heirs with reference to a promise."—Gal. 3:28, 29.

"He is not a Jew who is one on the outside, nor is circumcision that which is on the outside upon the flesh. But he is a Jew who is one on the inside, and his circumcision is that of the heart by spirit, and not by a written code."—Rom. 2:28, 29.

Why does God take some to heaven?
"They will be priests of God and of the Christ, and will rule as kings with him for the thousand years."—Rev. 20:6.

---

washed their robes in the blood of the Lamb), people who hailed Christ as King (with palm branches in their hands, like the crowd that greeted Jesus as King when he entered Jerusalem), people who truly were presenting themselves before Jehovah's throne to serve him? Was there such a group of people on earth?

By fulfilling his own prophetic word, Jehovah himself provided the answer. Webster Roe, who was in attendance at the Washington convention, recalled that at a climactic point in his discourse, Brother Rutherford asked: "Will all those who have the hope of living forever on the earth please stand." According to Brother Roe, "over half of the audience stood." In agreement with this, *The Watchtower* of August 15, 1935, stated: "Now we see a company that exactly fits the description given in Revelation seven concerning the great multitude. During the past few years, and within the time when 'this gospel of the kingdom is preached as a witness', there have come forward great numbers (and they are still coming) who confess the Lord Jesus as their Savior and Jehovah as their God, whom they worship in spirit and in truth and joyfully serve. These are otherwise called 'the

Jonadabs'. These are being baptized in symbol, thus testifying that they . . . have taken their stand on the side of Jehovah and serve him and his King."

At that time it was seen that the great crowd of Revelation 7:9, 10 are included among the "other sheep" to which Jesus referred (John 10:16); they are the ones that come to the aid of Christ's "brothers" (Matt. 25: 33-40); they are the people marked for survival because they are appalled at the disgusting things done in Christendom and shun these (Ezek. 9:4); they are like Jehonadab, who openly identified himself with Jehovah's anointed servant in carrying out that one's God-given commission (2 Ki. 10:15, 16). Jehovah's Witnesses understand that these are loyal servants of God who will survive Armageddon with the prospect of living forever on an earth restored to the condition of Paradise.

An Urgent Work to Be Done

Their understanding these scriptures had far-reaching effects on the activity of Jehovah's servants. They realized that they were not the ones who would select and gather the members of the great crowd; it was not up to them to tell people whether their hope should be a heavenly one or an earthly one. The Lord would direct matters in harmony with his will. But as Jehovah's Witnesses, they had a serious responsibility. They were to serve as proclaimers of the Word of God, sharing the truths that He enabled them to understand, so that people could know of Jehovah's provisions and have opportunity to respond appreciatively to these.

Furthermore, they recognized that there was great urgency to their work. In a series of articles entitled "Gathering the Multitude," published in 1936, *The Watchtower* explained: "The Scriptures strongly support the conclusion that at Armageddon Jehovah will destroy the peoples of the earth, saving only those who obey his commandments to stand by his organization. In times past millions upon millions of persons have gone into the grave without ever hearing of God and Christ, and these in due time must be awakened out of death and given a knowledge of the truth, that they may make their choice. The situation is different, however, concerning the people now on earth. . . . Those of the great multitude must receive this gospel message before the day of the battle of the great day of God Almighty, which is Armageddon. If the great multitude are not now given the message of truth, it will be too late when the slaughter work begins."—See 2 Kings 10:25; Ezekiel 9:5-10; Zephaniah 2:1-3; Matthew 24:21; 25:46.

As a result of this understanding of the Scriptures, Jehovah's Witnesses were infused with renewed zeal for the work of witnessing. Leo Kallio, who later served as a traveling overseer in Finland, said: "I cannot recall ever experiencing such joy and zeal, nor can I remember ever riding my bicycle as fast as I did in those days, when I hastened to bring interested ones the news that because of Jehovah's undeserved kindness, they were offered everlasting life on earth."

A heavenly hope or an earthly one—who determines it?

During the next five years, as the number of Jehovah's Witnesses grew, those who partook of the emblems at the annual Memorial of Christ's death gradually declined in number. Still, the influx of the great crowd was not as rapid as what Brother Rutherford had expected. At one point he even said to Fred Franz, who became the Society's fourth president: "It looks as if the 'great multitude' is not going to be so great after all." But since then, the number of Jehovah's Witnesses has mushroomed into the millions, while the number who expect a heavenly inheritance has, in general, continued to decline.

One Flock Under One Shepherd

There is no rivalry between the anointed class and the great crowd. Those who have a heavenly hope do not look down on those who eagerly anticipate receiving eternal life in an earthly paradise. Each accepts with gratitude the privileges extended to him by God, not reasoning that his position somehow makes him a better person or in some way inferior to someone else. (Matt. 11:11; 1 Cor. 4:7) As Jesus foretold, the two groups have truly become "one flock," serving under him as their "one shepherd."—John 10:16.

The feeling that Christ's anointed brothers have toward their companions of the great crowd is well expressed in the book *Worldwide Security Under the "Prince of Peace"*: "Since World War II, the fulfillment of Jesus' prophecy for 'the conclusion of the system of things' is largely due to the role that the 'great crowd' of 'other sheep' carry out. The illumination from the lighted lamps of the remnant has brightened the eyes of their hearts, and they have been helped to reflect the light to others yet remaining in the darkness of this world.... They have come to be inseparable companions of the remnant of the bride class.... Profuse thanks, therefore, to the international, multilingual 'great crowd' for the overwhelming part that they have played in the fulfilling of the Bridegroom's prophecy at Matthew 24:14!"

However, as Jehovah's Witnesses, including the great crowd, have shared unitedly in proclaiming the glorious news of God's Kingdom, the public has come to recognize them for something in addition to their zealous witnessing.

Memorial Report

▪ *Partakers*
■ *Attendance*

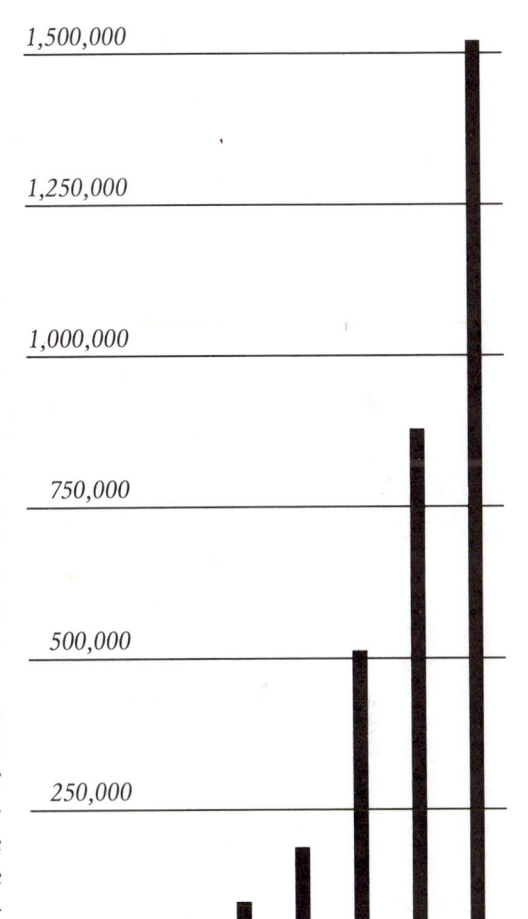

Within 25 years, Memorial attendance was over 100 times the number of partakers

CHAPTER 13

RECOGNIZED BY OUR CONDUCT

WE LIVE in an era in which moral standards that were long respected have been discarded by large segments of mankind. Most religions of Christendom have followed suit, either in the name of tolerance or with the argument that times are different and the taboos of earlier generations no longer apply. As to the result, Samuel Miller, a dean of Harvard Divinity School, said: "The church simply does not have a cutting edge. It has taken the culture of our time and absorbed it." The effect on the lives of those who looked to such churches for guidance has been devastating.

In contrast, when discussing Jehovah's Witnesses, *L'Eglise de Montréal*, the weekly bulletin of the Catholic archdiocese of Montreal, Canada, said: "They have remarkable moral values." Large numbers of schoolteachers, employers, and government officials agree with that. What accounts for this reputation?

Being one of Jehovah's Witnesses involves much more than holding to a certain framework of doctrinal beliefs and witnessing to others about these beliefs. Early Christianity was known as "The Way," and Jehovah's Witnesses realize that true religion today must be a way of life. (Acts 9:2) As was true in other things, however, the modern-day Witnesses did not immediately achieve a balanced appreciation of what this involves.

"Character or Covenant—Which?"

Although they started with sound Scriptural counsel about the need to be Christlike, the emphasis that some of the early Bible Students gave to "character development," as they called it, tended to minimize certain aspects of real Christianity. Some of them seemed to be of the opinion that being genteel—always appearing to be kind and good, speaking softly, avoiding any display of anger, reading the Scriptures daily—would guarantee their entrance into heaven. But these lost sight of the fact that Christ had given his followers a work to do.

This problem was firmly addressed in the article "Character or Covenant—Which?" in the May 1, 1926, issue of *The Watch Tower*.* It

"They have remarkable moral values"

---

* In *The Watchtower* of October 15, 1941, the subject was discussed again, in somewhat shortened form, under the heading "Character or Integrity—Which?"

showed that efforts to develop a "perfect character" while in the flesh caused some to give up in discouragement, but at the same time, it produced a "more holy than thou" attitude in others and tended to cause them to lose sight of the merit of Christ's sacrifice. After emphasizing faith in the shed blood of Christ, the article highlighted the importance of *'doing things'* in the active service of God to give evidence that one was pursuing a course pleasing to God. (2 Pet. 1:5-10) At that time, when much of Christendom still made a pretense of holding to Biblical moral standards, this emphasis on activity strengthened the contrast between Jehovah's Witnesses and Christendom. The contrast became even more evident as moral issues that were becoming common had to be dealt with by all who professed to be Christians.

"Abstain From Fornication"

The Christian standard regarding sexual morality was set out long ago in plain language in the Bible. "This is what God wills, the sanctifying of you, that you abstain from fornication . . . For God called us, not with allowance for uncleanness, but in connection with sanctification. So, then, the man that shows disregard is disregarding, not man, but God." (1 Thess. 4:3-8) "Let marriage be honorable among all, and the marriage bed be without defilement, for God will judge fornicators and adulterers." (Heb. 13:4) "Do you not know that unrighteous persons will not inherit God's kingdom? Do not be misled. Neither fornicators, . . . nor adulterers, nor men kept for unnatural purposes, nor men who lie with men . . . will inherit God's kingdom."—1 Cor. 6:9, 10.

In the *Watch Tower*, attention was drawn to this standard for true Christians as early as November of 1879. But it was not discussed repeatedly or at length as if this were a major problem among the early Bible Students. However, as the attitude of the world became more permissive, increased attention was directed to this requirement, especially in the years surrounding World War II. This was needed because some among Jehovah's Witnesses were adopting the view that as long as they were busy witnessing, a little laxness in sexual morality was just a personal matter. It is true that *The Watchtower* of March 1, 1935, had clearly stated that participation in the field ministry gave no license for immoral conduct. But not everyone took it to heart. So, in its issue of May 15, 1941, *The Watchtower* again discussed the matter, and at

> **'Character Development'—The Fruitage Was Not Always Good**
>
> *A report from Denmark:* 'Many, especially among the older friends, in their sincere efforts to put on a Christian personality, endeavored to avoid everything that had the slightest taint of worldliness and in this way make themselves more worthy of the heavenly Kingdom. Often, it was considered unsuitable to smile during meetings, and many of the older brothers wore only black suits, black shoes, black ties. They were often content to live quiet and peaceful lives in the Lord. They believed it was enough to hold meetings and let the colporteurs do the preaching.'

considerable length, in an article entitled "Noah's Day." It pointed out that the sexual debauchery in Noah's day was one reason why God destroyed the world of that time, and it showed that what God did then set a pattern for what he would do in our day. In plain language it warned that an integrity-keeping servant of God could not devote part of his day to doing the Lord's will and then, after hours, indulge in "the works of the flesh." (Gal. 5:17-21) This was followed up, in *The Watchtower* of July 1, 1942, with another article that condemned conduct that was out of line with the Bible's moral standards for single and for married persons. No one was to conclude that sharing in public preaching of the Kingdom message as one of Jehovah's Witnesses gave license for loose living. (1 Cor. 9:27) In time, even firmer measures would be taken to safeguard the moral cleanness of the organization.

Some who were then expressing a desire to be Jehovah's Witnesses had grown up in areas where trial marriage was accepted, where sex relations between engaged persons were tolerated, or where consensual relationships between persons not legally married were viewed as normal. A few married couples were endeavoring to practice celibacy. Other individuals, though not divorced, were unwisely separated from their mates. To provide needed direction, *The Watchtower,* during the 1950's, considered all these situations, discussed marital responsibilities, emphasized the Bible's prohibition of fornication, and explained what fornication is, so there would be no misunderstanding.*—Acts 15:19, 20; 1 Cor. 6:18.

In places where people beginning to associate with Jehovah's organization were not taking seriously the Bible's moral standards, this was given special attention. Thus, in 1945, when N. H. Knorr, the third president of the Watch Tower Society, was in Costa Rica, he gave a discourse on Christian morality in which he said: "All of you here tonight who are living with a woman but haven't got your marriage legally arranged, I'm giving you some advice. Go to the Catholic Church and put your name down as a member, because there you can practice these things. But this is God's organization, and you can't practice these things here."

Was there ever a question as to how homosexuality would be viewed?

Beginning with the 1960's, when homosexuals became more open about their practices, many churches debated the matter, then accepted them as members. Some churches now even ordain homosexuals as clergymen. In order to help sincere persons who had questions on these matters, the publications of Jehovah's Witnesses also discussed these issues. But among the Witnesses, there was never any question as to how homosexu-

---

* *The Watchtower* of April 15, 1951, defined fornication as "willing sexual intercourse on the part of an unmarried person with a person of the opposite sex." The issue of January 1, 1952, added that Scripturally the term could also apply to sexual immorality on the part of a married person.

ality would be viewed. Why not? Because they do not treat the Bible's requirements as if these were merely the opinions of men of another era. (1 Thess. 2:13) They gladly conduct Bible studies with homosexuals so these can learn Jehovah's requirements, and such persons may attend meetings of the Witnesses to listen, but no one who continues to practice homosexuality can be one of Jehovah's Witnesses.—1 Cor. 6:9-11; Jude 7.

In recent years sexual indulgence by unmarried youths became commonplace in the world. Youths in the families of Jehovah's Witnesses felt the pressure, and some began to adopt the ways of the world around them. How did the organization deal with this situation? Articles designed to help parents and youths to view things Scripturally were published in *The Watchtower* and *Awake!* Real-life dramas were presented at conventions to help everyone to be aware of the fruitage of rejecting the Bible's moral standards and of the benefits of obeying God's commands. One of the first of these, staged in 1969, was entitled "Thorns and Traps Are in the Way of the Independent One." Special books were prepared to help young folks appreciate the wisdom of Bible counsel. These included *Your Youth—Getting the Best Out Of It* (published in 1976) and *Questions Young People Ask —Answers That Work* (published in 1989). Local elders gave personal spiritual help to individuals and to families. The congregations of Jehovah's Witnesses were also safeguarded by expulsion of unrepentant wrongdoers.

The world's breakdown in morals has not led to a more permissive viewpoint among Jehovah's Witnesses. On the contrary, the Governing Body of Jehovah's Witnesses has placed increased emphasis on the necessity to avoid not only illicit sexual acts but also influences and situations that erode moral values. During the past three decades, it has provided instruction to fortify individuals against such "secret sins" as masturbation and to alert them to the danger of pornography, soap operas, and music that has a debasing effect. Thus, while the world's moral trend has been downward, that of Jehovah's Witnesses has been upward.

The world's moral breakdown has not caused the Witnesses to become more permissive

Family Life Governed by Godly Standards

Holding firmly to the Bible's standard of sexual morality has greatly benefited the family life of Jehovah's Witnesses. But being one of Jehovah's Witnesses is no guarantee that a person will not have domestic problems. Nevertheless, the Witnesses are convinced that God's Word gives the very best counsel on how to cope with such problems. They have available many provisions made by the organization to help them apply that counsel; and when they follow through on it, the results are, indeed, beneficial.

As early as 1904, the sixth volume of *Studies in the Scriptures* provided an extensive discussion of marital responsibilities and parental obligations. Since that time, hundreds of articles have been published and numerous discourses have been delivered in every congregation of Jehovah's Witnesses to help each family member to appreciate his God-given role. This education in wholesome family life is not merely for newlyweds but is an ongoing program that involves the entire congregation.—Eph. 5:22–6:4; Col. 3:18-21.

Would Polygamy Be Accepted?

Even though customs affecting marriage and family life differ from one land to another, Jehovah's Witnesses recognize that the standards set out in the Bible apply everywhere. As their work got under way in Africa in this 20th century, the Witnesses taught there, as they do everywhere, that Christian marriage allows for just one marriage mate. (Matt. 19:4, 5; 1 Cor. 7:2; 1 Tim. 3:2) Yet, there were hundreds who accepted the Bible's exposure of idolatry and gladly embraced what Jehovah's Witnesses taught concerning the Kingdom of God but who got baptized without abandoning polygamy. To correct this situation, *The Watchtower* of January 15, 1947, emphasized that Christianity makes no allowance for polygamy, regardless of local custom. A letter sent to the congregations notified any who professed to be Jehovah's Witnesses but who were polygamists that six months was being allowed for them to bring their marital affairs into harmony with the Bible standard. This was reinforced by a discourse given by Brother Knorr during a visit to Africa that same year.

In Nigeria, there were not a few people of the world who predicted that efforts to abolish polygamy from the ranks of Jehovah's Witnesses would mean abolishing the ranks. And it is true that not all practicers of polygamy who had earlier been baptized as Witnesses made the required changes even in 1947. For example, Asuquo Akpabio, a traveling overseer, relates that a Witness with whom he was staying at Ifiayong woke him at midnight and demanded that he change what had been announced regarding the requirement of monogamy. Because he refused to do so, his host threw him out into the pouring rain that night.

But love for Jehovah has given others the strength needed to obey his commandments. Here are just a few of them. In Zaire a man who had been both a Catholic and a polygamist dismissed two of his wives in order to become one of Jehovah's Witnesses, even though sending away the most-loved one because she was not the 'wife of his youth' was a severe test of his faith. (Prov. 5:18) In Dahomey (now Benin) a former Methodist who still had five wives overcame very difficult legal obstacles in order to obtain needed divorces so that he could qualify for baptism. Nevertheless, he continued to provide for his former wives and their children, as did others who dismissed secondary wives. Warigbani Whittington, a Nigerian, was the

Some tried to be Witnesses without abandoning polygamy

second of her husband's two wives. When she decided that pleasing Jehovah, the true God, was the most important thing to her, she faced the wrath of her husband and then of her own family. Her husband let her go, along with her two children, but with no financial help—not even for transportation. Yet, she said: 'None of the material benefits that I left behind can be compared to pleasing Jehovah.'

What About Divorce?

In Western lands polygamy is not widely practiced, but other attitudes that conflict with the Scriptures are in vogue. One of these is the idea that it is better to get a divorce than to have an unhappy marriage. In recent years some of Jehovah's Witnesses began to imitate this spirit, suing for divorce on such grounds as "incompatibility." How have the Witnesses dealt with this? A vigorous campaign of education as to Jehovah's view of divorce is regularly conducted by the organization to benefit longtime Witnesses as well as the hundreds of thousands who are being added to their ranks each year.

To what Bible guidelines has *The Watchtower* directed attention? The following, among others: In the Bible record of the first human marriage, the oneness of husband and wife is emphasized; it says: 'A man must stick to his wife, and they must become one flesh.' (Gen. 2:24) Later, in Israel, the Law prohibited adultery and prescribed death for any who engaged in it. (Deut. 22:22-24) Divorce on grounds other than adultery was allowed, but only 'because of their hardheartedness,' as Jesus explained. (Matt. 19: 7, 8) How did Jehovah view the practice of discarding one's marriage mate in order to marry another? Malachi 2:16 states: "He has hated a divorcing." Yet, he allowed those who got a divorce to remain in the congregation of Israel. There, if they accepted Jehovah's disciplining of his people, their heart of stone might in time be replaced with a softer heart, one that could express genuine love for his ways.—Compare Ezekiel 11:19, 20.

The Watchtower has frequently stated that when Jesus was discussing divorce as it was practiced in ancient Israel, he showed that a higher standard was to be instituted among his followers. He said that if anyone divorced his wife except on the ground of fornication (*por·nei′a*, "unlawful intercourse") and married another, he would be committing adultery; and even if he did not remarry, he would be making his wife a subject for adultery. (Matt. 5:32; 19:9) Thus, *The Watchtower* has pointed out that for Christians any divorce is a far more serious matter than it was in Israel. While the Scriptures do not direct that everyone obtaining a divorce be expelled from the congregation, those who also commit adultery and are unrepentant are disfellowshipped by the congregations of Jehovah's Witnesses.—1 Cor. 6:9, 10.

A vigorous program to teach Jehovah's view of divorce

Revolutionary changes have taken place in recent years in the world's attitudes regarding marriage and family life. Despite this, Jehovah's Witnesses have continued to adhere to the standards provided by God, the Originator of marriage, as set out in the Bible. Using those guidelines, they have endeavored to help honesthearted persons to cope with the difficult circumstances in which so many find themselves.

Dramatic changes in the lives of people

As a result, dramatic changes have been made in the lives of many who have accepted Bible instruction from Jehovah's Witnesses. Men who were formerly wife beaters, men who did not shoulder their responsibilities, men who provided materially but not emotionally and spiritually—many thousands of such have become loving husbands and fathers who care well for their households. Women who were fiercely independent, women who neglected their children and did not take care of themselves or their home —many of these have become wives who respect headship and pursue a course that causes them to be dearly loved by their husbands and children. Youths who were brazenly disobedient to their parents and rebels against society in general, youths who were ruining their own lives by the things they were doing and thus bringing heartbreak to their parents—not a few of these have come to have a godly purpose in life, and this has helped to transform their personality.

Of course, an important factor in success within the family is honesty with one another. Honesty is also vital in other relationships.

How Far Does the Requirement of Honesty Reach?

Jehovah's Witnesses recognize that honesty is required in everything they do. As the basis for their view, they point to such scriptures as the following: Jehovah himself is "the God of truth." (Ps. 31:5) On the other hand, as Jesus said, the Devil is "the father of the lie." (John 8:44) Understandably, then, among the things that Jehovah hates is "a false tongue." (Prov. 6:16, 17) His Word tells us: "Now that you have put away falsehood, speak truth." (Eph. 4:25) And not only must Christians *speak* truth but, like the apostle Paul, they need to 'conduct themselves honestly in all things.' (Heb. 13:18) There are no areas of life where Jehovah's Witnesses can legitimately apply some other set of values.

When Jesus visited the home of the tax collector Zacchaeus, the man acknowledged that his business practices had been improper, and he took steps to make amends for former acts of extortion. (Luke 19:8) In recent years, in order to have a clean conscience before God, some persons who began to associate with Jehovah's Witnesses have taken similar action. For example, in Spain a confirmed thief began to study the Bible with Jehovah's Witnesses. Soon his conscience began to bother him; so he returned stolen goods to his former employer and to his neighbors, then took other items to the police. He was required to pay a fine and serve a short time in jail, but now he has a clean conscience. In England, after just two months of Bible study with one of Jehovah's Witnesses, a former diamond thief turned himself over to the police, who were astonished; they had been looking for him for six months. During the two and a half years that he then spent in prison, he studied the Bible diligently and learned to share Bible truths with others. After his release he presented himself for baptism as one of Jehovah's Witnesses.—Eph. 4:28.

The reputation of Jehovah's Witnesses for honesty is well-known. Employers have learned that not only will Witnesses not steal from them but they will not lie or falsify records at their employers' direction—no, not even if threatened with loss of their job. To Jehovah's Witnesses a good relationship with God is far more important than the approval of any human. And they realize that, no matter where they are or what they are doing, "all things are naked and openly exposed to the eyes of him with whom we have an accounting."—Heb. 4:13; Prov. 15:3.

In Italy the newspaper *La Stampa* said regarding Jehovah's Witnesses: "They practice what they preach ... The moral ideals of love for neighbor, refusal of power, non-violence and personal honesty (which for most Christians are 'Sunday rules' only good for being preached from the pulpit) enter into their 'daily' way of life." And in the United States, Louis Cassels, religion editor for United Press International, Washington, D.C., wrote: "Witnesses adhere to their beliefs with great fidelity, even when doing so is very costly."

Why Gambling Has Not Been an Issue Among Them

In times past, honesty was generally associated with willingness to do hard work. Gambling, that is, risking a sum of money in a bet on the outcome of a game or other event, was looked down on by society in general. But as a selfish, get-rich spirit began to pervade the 20th century, gambling—legal and illegal—became widespread. It is sponsored not only by the underworld but often also by churches and secular

---

What Others See in the Witnesses

• "Münchner Merkur," a German newspaper, reported regarding Jehovah's Witnesses: "They are the most honest and the most punctual taxpayers in the Federal Republic. Their obedience to the laws can be seen in the way they drive as well as in crime statistics.... They obey those in authority (parents, teachers, government).... The Bible, basis for all their actions, is their support."

• The mayor in Lens, France, said to the Witnesses after they had used the local stadium for one of their conventions: "What I like is that you keep your promises and your agreements, on top of which, you are clean, disciplined, and organized. I like your society. I'm against disorder, and I don't like people who go around dirtying and breaking things."

• The book "Voices From the Holocaust" contains memoirs from a Polish survivor of the Auschwitz and the Ravensbrück concentration camps who wrote: "I saw people who became very, very good and people who became absolutely mean. The nicest group were the Jehovah's Witnesses. I take my hat off to those people.... They did marvelous things for other people. They helped the sick, they shared their bread, and gave everyone near them spiritual comfort. The Germans hated them and respected them at the same time. They gave them the worst work but they took it with their heads high."

governments in order to raise money. How have Jehovah's Witnesses dealt with this change of attitude in society? On the basis of Bible principles.

As has been pointed out in their publications, there is no specific commandment in the Bible that says, You must not gamble. But the fruitage of gambling is consistently bad, and this rotten fruitage has been exposed by *The Watchtower* and *Awake!* for half a century. Furthermore, these magazines have shown that gambling in any form involves attitudes that the Bible warns against. For example, *love of money:* "The love of money is a root of all sorts of injurious things." (1 Tim. 6:10) *And selfishness:* "Neither must you selfishly crave . . . anything that belongs to your fellowman." (Deut. 5:21; compare 1 Corinthians 10:24.) *Also greed:* "Quit mixing in company with anyone called a brother that is . . . a greedy person." (1 Cor. 5:11) In addition, the Bible warns against *appeals to "Good Luck"* as if it were some kind of supernatural force that could bestow favors. (Isa. 65:11) Because they take these Scriptural warnings to heart, Jehovah's Witnesses firmly shun gambling. And since 1976 they have put forth special effort to avoid having in their ranks any whose secular employment would clearly identify them as part of a gambling establishment.

Gambling has never been a real issue among Jehovah's Witnesses. They know that instead of fostering a spirit of gain at the expense of others, the Bible encourages them to work with their hands, to be faithful in caring for what is entrusted to them, to be generous, to share with those in need. (Eph. 4:28; Luke 16:10; Rom. 12:13; 1 Tim. 6:18) Is this readily recognized by others who have dealings with them? Yes, particularly by those with whom they have business dealings. It has not been unusual for secular employers to seek out Jehovah's Witnesses as employees because they know of their conscientiousness and dependability. They realize that it is the religion of the Witnesses that makes them the kind of people they are.

What About Tobacco and Drug Abuse?

The Bible does not mention tobacco, nor does it name the many other drugs that are abused in our day. But it does provide guidelines that have helped Jehovah's Witnesses to determine what course of conduct would be pleasing to God. Thus, as far back as 1895, when the *Watch Tower* commented on use of tobacco, it directed attention to 2 Corinthians 7:1, which says: "Therefore, since we have these promises, beloved ones, let us cleanse ourselves of every defilement of flesh and spirit, perfecting holiness in God's fear."

For many years that counsel seemed to suffice. But as tobacco companies used advertising to glamorize smoking, and then abuse of "illegal" drugs became widespread, more was needed. Other Bible principles were highlighted: respect for Jehovah, the Giver of life (Acts 17:24, 25); love for neighbor (Jas. 2:8), and the fact that a person who does not love his fellowman does not really love God (1 John 4:20); also obedience to secular rulers (Titus 3:1). It was pointed out that the Greek word *phar·ma·ki'a*, which basically signifies "druggery," was used by Bible writers to refer to "practice of spiritism" because of the use of drugs in spiritistic practices. —Gal. 5:20.

Back in 1946, *Consolation* magazine exposed the often fraudulent nature of paid testimonials used in cigarette ads. As scientific evidence became available, *Consolation's* successor, *Awake!*, also publicized proof that tobacco use causes cancer, heart disease, damage to the unborn child of a pregnant woman, and injury to nonsmokers who are forced to breathe smoke-filled air, as well as evidence that nicotine is addictive. Attention has been drawn to the intoxicating effect of marijuana and to evidence that its use can result in brain damage. Likewise the grave dangers of other addictive drugs have been discussed repeatedly for the benefit of the readers of Watch Tower publications.

Long before government agencies agreed on the extent to which they should alert people to the harm from tobacco use, *The Watchtower*, in its issue of March 1, 1935, made it clear that no one who was a user of tobacco could be a member of the headquarters staff of the Watch Tower Bible and Tract Society or be one of its appointed representatives. After all servants in the congregations of Jehovah's Witnesses were appointed by the Society (which arrangement began in 1938), *The Watchtower* of July 1, 1942, stated that the prohibition on tobacco use also applied to all these appointed servants. In some areas a number of years passed before this was fully implemented. However, the majority of Jehovah's Witnesses responded favorably to the Scriptural counsel and the good example of those taking the lead among them.

Tobacco—No!

As a further forward step in consistent application of that Bible counsel, none who were still smoking were accepted for baptism from 1973 onward. During the following months, those who were actively involved in tobacco production or in promoting the sale of tobacco were helped to realize that they could not continue to do that and be accepted as Jehovah's Witnesses. The counsel of God's Word must be applied consistently in every aspect of life. Such application of Bible principles to the use of tobacco, marijuana, and the so-called hard drugs has protected the Witnesses. With the use of the Scriptures, they have also been able to help many thousands of persons whose lives were being ruined by drug abuse.

Are Alcoholic Drinks Different?

Watch Tower publications have not adopted the view that use of alcoholic beverages is the same as drug abuse. Why not? They explain: The

Creator knows how we are made, and his Word permits moderate use of alcoholic drinks. (Ps. 104:15; 1 Tim. 5:23) But the Bible also warns against 'heavy drinking,' and it strongly condemns drunkenness.—Prov. 23:20, 21, 29, 30; 1 Cor. 6:9, 10; Eph. 5:18.

Because immoderate consumption of intoxicating drinks was ruining the lives of many people, Charles Taze Russell himself favored total abstinence. Yet, he acknowledged that Jesus did use wine. During the 19th century and the early part of the 20th century, there was much public agitation for legal prohibition of liquor in the United States. The *Watch Tower* freely expressed sympathy with those who were trying to combat the harm from liquor, but it did not join their campaign to have prohibition laws passed. However, the magazine did point firmly to the damage resulting from overindulgence and often stated that it would be better to avoid wine and liquor altogether. Those who felt that they could use liquor moderately were encouraged to consider Romans 14:21, which says: "It is well not to eat flesh or to drink wine or do anything over which your brother stumbles."

However, in 1930, when the superintendent of the Anti-Saloon League in the United States went so far as to claim publicly that his organization was "born of God," J. F. Rutherford, then president of the Watch Tower Society, used the occasion to give radio discourses showing that such a claim amounted to slander against God. Why? Because God's Word does not outlaw all use of wine; because prohibition laws were not putting an end to drunkenness, which God does condemn; and because the prohibition laws had, instead, given rise to a backlash of bootlegging and government corruption.

Alcoholic drinks —moderately, if at all

Use of alcoholic beverages or abstinence from them is viewed as a personal matter among Jehovah's Witnesses. But they adhere to the Scriptural requirement that overseers must be "moderate in habits." That expression is translated from the Greek ne·pha′li·on, which means, literally, 'sober, temperate; abstaining from wine, either entirely or at least from its immoderate use.' Ministerial servants too must be men "not giving themselves to a lot of wine." (1 Tim. 3:2, 3, 8) So, heavy drinkers do not qualify for special service privileges. The fact that those taking the lead among Jehovah's Witnesses set a good example gives them freeness of speech in helping others who may be inclined to rely on alcoholic beverages to cope with stress or may, in fact, need to be total abstainers in order to remain sober. What are the results?

As an example, a news report from south-central Africa states: "From all accounts, those areas in which Jehovah's Witnesses are strongest among Africans are now areas more trouble-free than the average. Certainly they have been active against agitators, witchcraft, drunkenness and violence of any kind."—*The Northern News* (Zambia).

Another important way in which the conduct of Jehovah's Witnesses differs from that of the world is with regard to—

Respect for Life

Such respect is rooted in recognition of the fact that life is a gift from God. (Ps. 36:9; Acts 17:24, 25) It includes a realization that even the life of the unborn is precious in the eyes of God. (Ex. 21:22-25; Ps. 139:1, 16) It takes into account that "each of us will render an account for himself to God."—Rom. 14:12.

In line with these Bible principles, Jehovah's Witnesses have consistently shunned the practice of abortion. To provide sound direction to its readers, *Awake!* magazine has helped them to appreciate that chastity is a divine requirement; it has discussed at length the marvels of the procreative process as well as the psychological and physiological factors involved in childbirth. In the post-World War II era, as abortions became more commonplace, *The Watchtower* showed clearly that this practice is contrary to the Word of God. Mincing no words, the issue of December 15, 1969, said: "Abortion simply to get rid of an unwanted child is the same as willfully taking a human life."

Why Blood Transfusions Are Refused

The respect for life shown by Jehovah's Witnesses has also affected their attitude toward blood transfusions. When transfusions of blood became an issue confronting them, *The Watchtower* of July 1, 1945, explained at length the Christian view regarding the sanctity of blood.* It showed that both animal blood and that of humans were included in the divine prohibition that was made binding on Noah and all his descendants. (Gen. 9:3-6) It pointed out that this requirement was emphasized again in the first century in the command that Christians 'abstain from blood.' (Acts 15:28, 29) That same article made it clear from the Scriptures that only sacrificial use of blood has ever been approved by God, and that since the animal sacrifices offered under the Mosaic Law foreshadowed the sacrifice of Christ, disregard for the requirement that Christians 'abstain from blood' would be an evidence of gross disrespect for the ransom sacrifice of Jesus Christ. (Lev. 17:11, 12; Heb. 9:11-14, 22) Consistent with that understanding of matters, beginning in 1961 any who ignored the divine requirement, accepted blood transfusions, and

Firmly resolved not to accept blood

---

* Earlier discussions of the sanctity of blood appeared in *The Watch Tower* of December 15, 1927, as well as *The Watchtower* of December 1, 1944, which specifically mentioned blood transfusions.

manifested an unrepentant attitude were disfellowshipped from the congregations of Jehovah's Witnesses.

At first, physical side effects of blood transfusions were not discussed in the Watch Tower publications. Later, when such information became available, it too was published—not as the reason why Jehovah's Witnesses refuse blood transfusions but in order to strengthen their appreciation for the prohibition that God himself had put on the use of blood. (Isa. 48:17) To that end, in 1961 the carefully documented booklet *Blood, Medicine and the Law of God* was published. In 1977 another booklet was printed. This one, entitled *Jehovah's Witnesses and the Question of Blood*, again emphasized the fact that the position taken by Jehovah's Witnesses is a religious one, based on what the Bible says, and does not depend on medical risk factors. A further updating of the subject was presented in 1990 in the brochure *How Can Blood Save Your Life?* Using these publications, Jehovah's Witnesses have put forth much effort to win the cooperation of doctors and to help them to understand the Witnesses' position. However, for many years use of blood transfusions has been held in high esteem by the medical profession.

Even though Jehovah's Witnesses told doctors that they had no religious objection to alternative treatment, rejecting blood transfusions was not easy. Often, great pressure was brought to bear on the Witnesses and their families to submit to what was then customary medical practice. In Puerto Rico, in November of 1976, 45-year-old Ana Paz de Rosario agreed to surgery and needed medication but requested that because of her religious beliefs, no blood be used. Nevertheless, armed with a court order, five policemen and three nurses went to her hospital room after midnight, strapped her to the bed, and forced a blood transfusion on her, contrary to her wishes and those of her husband and children. She went into shock and died. This was by no means an isolated case, and it was not only in Puerto Rico that such outrages occurred.

In Denmark, Witness parents were pursued by the police in 1975 because they refused to allow a blood transfusion to be forced on their young son but, instead, sought alternative treatment. In Italy, in 1982, a couple who had lovingly sought medical help in four countries for their incurably ill daughter were sentenced to 14 years in prison on the charge of murder after the girl died while being given a court-ordered transfusion.

Frequently, in connection with attempts to force transfusions on the children of Jehovah's Witnesses, great public hostility has been whipped up by the press. In some instances, even without a legal hearing at which the parents could speak, judges have ordered that their children be transfused. In more than 40 cases in Canada, however, the transfused children were returned dead to their parents.

Not all doctors and judges agree with these high-handed methods. A few began to urge a more helpful attitude. Some doctors used their skills to provide treatment without blood. In the process, they gained much experience in all types of bloodless surgery. It gradually was demonstrated that *all types of surgery* could be performed successfully, on both adults and infants, without blood transfusions.*

In order to prevent needless confrontations in emergency situations, early in the 1960's Jehovah's Witnesses began to make special visits to their doctors to discuss their position and provide them with appropriate literature. Later they requested that a written statement be placed in their individual medical files stating that no blood transfusions were to be given to them. By the 1970's, they made it a general practice to carry on their person a card to alert medical personnel to the fact that no blood was to be administered to them under any circumstances. After consultation with doctors and lawyers, the nature of the card was adjusted in order to make it a legal document.

To support Jehovah's Witnesses in this determination to prevent their being given blood transfusions, to clear away misunderstandings on the part of doctors and hospitals, and to establish a more cooperative spirit between medical institutions and Witness patients, Hospital Liaison Committees have been established at the direction of the Governing Body of Jehovah's Witnesses. From a handful of such committees in 1979, their number has grown to more than 800 in upwards of 70 lands. Selected elders have been trained and are providing such service in North America, the Far East, major lands of the South Pacific, Europe, and Latin America. In addition to explaining the position of Jehovah's Witnesses, these elders alert hospital staffs to the fact that there are valid alternatives to infusions of blood. In emergency situations they assist in setting up consultations between primary-care physicians and surgeons who have handled similar cases for the Witnesses without blood. Where necessary, these committees have visited not only hospital staffs but also judges who have been involved in cases where hospitals have sought court orders for transfusions.

When respect for their religious belief regarding the sanctity of blood could not be assured by other means, Jehovah's Witnesses have, on occasion, taken doctors and hospitals to court. They have usually sought simply a restraining order or an injunction. In recent years, however, they have even filed damage suits against doctors and hospitals that have acted high-handedly. In 1990 the Ontario Court of Appeal, in Canada, upheld

---

* *Contemporary Surgery*, March 1990, pp. 45-9; *The American Surgeon*, June 1987, pp. 350-6; *Miami Medicine*, January 1981, p. 25; *New York State Journal of Medicine*, October 15, 1972, pp. 2524-7; *The Journal of the American Medical Association*, November 27, 1981, pp. 2471-2; *Cardiovascular News*, February 1984, p. 5; *Circulation*, September 1984.

such a damage suit because the doctor had ignored a card in the patient's purse that clearly stated that the Witness would not accept blood transfusions under any circumstances. In the United States, since 1985, at least ten of such damage suits have been instituted in various parts of the country, and frequently the ones being sued have decided to settle out of court for a stipulated amount instead of facing the possibility that a jury would award even more in damages. Jehovah's Witnesses are fully determined to obey the divine prohibition on the use of blood. They would rather not take doctors to court, but they will do it when necessary to stop them from forcing on the Witnesses treatment that is morally repugnant to them.

The public is becoming more and more aware of the dangers inherent in blood transfusions. This is, in part, because of fear of AIDS. The Witnesses, however, are motivated by an earnest desire to please God. In 1987 the French medical daily *Le Quotidien du Médecin* stated: "Maybe Jehovah's Witnesses are right in refusing the use of blood products, for it is true that an important number of pathogenic agents can be transmitted by transfused blood."

The position taken by Jehovah's Witnesses is not based on superior medical knowledge originating with them. They simply have confidence that Jehovah's way is right and that 'he will not hold back anything good' from his loyal servants. (Ps. 19:7, 11; 84:11) Even if a Witness should die as a result of blood loss—and this has happened on occasion—Jehovah's Witnesses have full confidence that God does not forget his faithful ones but will restore them to life by means of a resurrection.—Acts 24:15.

When Individuals Choose to Ignore Bible Standards

Millions of persons have studied the Bible with Jehovah's Witnesses, but not all of them have become Witnesses. When some persons learn the high standards that apply, they decide that this is not the sort of life that they want. All who do get baptized are first given thorough instruction in basic Bible teachings, and thereafter (especially since 1967) elders in the congregation review such teachings with each baptismal candidate. Every effort is made to be sure that those being baptized clearly understand not only doctrine but also what Christian conduct involves. However, what if some of these later allow love of the world to entice them into serious wrongdoing?

As early as 1904, in the book *The New Creation,* attention was given to the need to take appropriate action so as not to allow a demoralizing of the congregation. The understanding that the Bible Students then had of the procedure for dealing with wrongdoers as outlined at Matthew 18:15-17 was discussed. In harmony with this, there were, on rare occasions, 'church trials' in which the evidence of wrongdoing in serious cases was presented to the entire congregation. Years later, *The Watchtower,* in its issue of May 15, 1944, reviewed the matter in the light of the entire Bible and showed that such matters affecting the congregation should be handled by responsible brothers charged with congregation oversight. (1 Cor. 5:1-13; compare Deuteronomy 21:18-21.) This was followed, in *The Watchtower* of March 1, 1952, with articles that emphasized not only proper procedure but the need to *take action to keep the organization clean.* Repeatedly since then, the subject has been given consideration. But the objectives have always remained the same: (1) to keep the organization clean and (2) to impress on the wrongdoer the need for sincere repentance, with a view to recovering him.

Disfellowshipping —to maintain a morally clean organization

In the first century, there were some who abandoned the faith for loose living. Others were turned aside because of apostate doctrines. (1 John 2:19) The same thing continues to occur among Jehovah's Witnesses in this 20th century. Sadly, in recent times it has been necessary to disfellowship tens of thousands of unrepentant wrongdoers each year. Prominent elders have been included among them. The same Scriptural requirements apply to all. (Jas. 3:17) Jehovah's Witnesses realize that maintaining a morally clean organization is vital in order to continue to have Jehovah's approval.

Putting On the New Personality

Jesus urged people to be clean not only on the outside but also on the inside. (Luke 11:38-41) He showed that the things that we say and do are a reflection of what is in our heart. (Matt. 15:18, 19) As the apostle Paul explained, if we are truly taught by Christ, we will 'be made new in the force that actuates our mind' and will 'put on the new personality, which is created according to God's will in true righteousness and loyalty.' (Eph. 4:17-24) Those being taught by Christ seek to acquire "the same mental attitude that Christ Jesus had" so that they think and act as he did. (Rom. 15:5) The conduct of Jehovah's Witnesses as individuals is a reflection of the extent to which they have actually done that.

Jehovah's Witnesses make no claim that their conduct is flawless. But they are earnest in their endeavors to be imitators of Christ as they conform to the Bible's high standard of conduct. They do not deny that there are other *individuals* who apply high moral standards in their lives. But in the case of Jehovah's Witnesses, it is not only as individuals but also as an *international organization* that they are easily recognized because of conduct that conforms to Bible standards. They are motivated by the inspired counsel recorded at 1 Peter 2:12: "Maintain your conduct fine among the nations, that . . . they may as a result of your fine works of which they are eyewitnesses glorify God."

CHAPTER 14

"They Are No Part of the World"

MODERN-DAY religion is, for the most part, very much a part of the world, so it shares in the world's celebrations and reflects its nationalistic spirit. Its clergy often acknowledge that fact, and many of them like it that way. In sharp contrast, Jesus said of his true followers: "They are no part of the world, just as I am no part of the world."—John 17:16.

What does the record show as to Jehovah's Witnesses in this regard? Have they given convincing evidence that they are no part of the world?

Attitude Toward Their Fellowmen

The early Bible Students were well aware that true Christians would be no part of the world. *The Watch Tower* explained that because Christ's anointed followers were sanctified and begotten by holy spirit so that they might share in the heavenly Kingdom, they were by this act of God set apart from the world. Additionally, it pointed out that they were under obligation to shun the spirit of the world—its aims, ambitions, and hopes, as well as its selfish ways.—1 John 2:15-17.

Did this affect the attitude of the Bible Students toward people who did not share their beliefs? It certainly did not make them recluses. But those who truly applied what they were learning from the Scriptures did not seek the fellowship of worldly people in such a way as to share their manner of life. *The Watch Tower* pointed God's servants to the Bible counsel to "work what is good toward all." It also counseled that when persecuted they should endeavor to avoid vengeful feelings and, instead, as Jesus had said, should 'love their enemies.' (Gal. 6:10; Matt. 5:44-48) Especially did it urge them to seek to share with others the precious truth regarding God's provision for salvation.

Not recluses, yet not sharing the world's manner of life

Understandably, their doing these things would cause them to be viewed by the world as different. But being no part of the world involves more—much more.

Separate and Distinct From Babylon the Great

To be no part of the world, they had to be no part of religious systems that were deeply involved in the affairs of the world and that had absorbed

"THEY ARE NO PART OF THE WORLD"

doctrines and customs from ancient Babylon, the longtime enemy of true worship. (Jer. 50:29) When the first world war erupted, the Bible Students had for decades been exposing the pagan roots of such doctrines of Christendom as the Trinity, immortality of the human soul, and hellfire. They had also laid bare the churches' record of trying to manipulate governments for their own selfish ends. Because of Christendom's doctrines and practices, the Bible Students had identified it with "Babylon the Great." (Rev. 18:2) They pointed out that it mixed truth with error, lukewarm Christianity with outright worldliness, and that the Biblical designation "Babylon" (meaning, "Confusion") well described that condition. They urged lovers of God to get out of "Babylon." (Rev. 18:4) To that end, late in December 1917 and early in 1918, they distributed 10,000,000 copies of the issue of *The Bible Students Monthly* that featured the subject "The Fall of Babylon," which was a hard-hitting exposé of Christendom. This, in turn, resulted in bitter animosity from the clergy, who exploited wartime hysteria in an endeavor to crush the work of Jehovah's Witnesses.

Ten million copies were distributed

Of necessity, getting out of Babylon the Great involved withdrawing from membership in organizations that advocated her false doctrines. The Bible Students did that, although for many years they viewed as Christian brothers those individuals in the churches who professed full consecration and faith in the ransom. Nevertheless, not only did the Bible Students write letters of withdrawal from Christendom's churches but, when possible, some would read theirs aloud at church meetings where it was in order for members to speak up. If this was not possible, they might send a copy of their letter of withdrawal—a kindly one containing an appropriate witness—to every member of the congregation.

They withdrew from Christendom's churches

Were they also making sure that they did not take along with them any of the ungodly customs and practices of those organizations? What was the situation in the period leading up to World War I?

Should Religion Mix in Politics?

In the political arena, rulers of many of the leading nations, because of their connections with a Catholic or a Protestant church, had long claimed to rule 'by divine right,' as representatives of the Kingdom of God and by God's special favor. The church gave its blessing to the government; in turn, the government gave its support to the church. Did the Bible Students also indulge in this?

Instead of imitating the churches of Christendom, they sought to learn from the teachings and example of Jesus Christ and his apostles. What did their study of the Bible show them? Early Watch Tower publications reveal that they were aware that when Jesus was questioned by the Roman governor Pontius Pilate, he stated: "My kingdom is no part of this world." In response to a question as to Jesus' role, he told the governor: "For this I have been born, and for this I have come into the world, that I should bear witness to the truth." (John 18:36, 37) The Bible Students knew that Jesus stuck unwaveringly to that assignment. When the Devil offered him all the kingdoms of the world and their glory, he refused. When the people wanted to make him king, he withdrew. (Matt. 4:8-10; John 6:15) The Bible Students did not sidestep the fact that Jesus referred to the Devil as "the ruler of the world" and said that the Devil 'had no hold on him.' (John 14:30) They could see that Jesus did not seek involvement for himself or his followers in Rome's political system but that he was fully occupied with declaring "the good news of the kingdom of God."—Luke 4:43.

Did their believing these things recorded in God's Word encourage disrespect for government authority? Not at all. Instead, it helped them to understand why the problems facing rulers are so overwhelming, why there is so much lawlessness, and why government programs to improve the lot of the people are often frustrated. Their belief caused them to be patient in the face of hardship, because they had confidence that God would in his due time bring lasting relief by means of his Kingdom. At that time they understood that "the higher powers," referred to at Romans 13: 1-7 (*KJ*), were the secular rulers. In accord with that, they urged respect for government officials. In discussing Romans 13:7, C. T. Russell, in the book *The New Creation* (published in 1904), stated that true Christians "would naturally be the most sincere in their recognition of the great of this world, and most obedient to the laws and the requirements of law, except where these would be found in conflict with the heavenly demands and commands. Few if any earthly rulers in our day will find fault with the recognition of a supreme Creator and a supreme allegiance to his commands. Hence, [true Christians] should be found amongst the most law-abiding of the present time—not agitators, not quarrelsome, not fault-finders."

"Christians stood aloof and distinct from the state"

As Christians, the Bible Students knew that the work to which they should be devoting themselves was the preaching of the Kingdom of God. And, as stated in the first volume of *Studies in the Scriptures*, "if this is faithfully done, there will be no time nor disposition to dabble in the politics of present governments."

In this respect they were, to a considerable extent, like those early Christians described by Augustus Neander in the book *The History of the Christian Religion and Church, During the Three First Centuries:* "The Christians stood aloof and distinct from the state, . . . and Christianity seemed able to influence civil life only in that manner which, it must be confessed, is the purest, by practically endeavouring to instil more and more of holy feeling into the citizens of the state."

"They Are No Part of the World"

When the World Went to War

Around the globe the events of World War I severely tested the claims of those who professed to be Christians. It was the most ghastly war fought down to that time; nearly the entire world population was involved in one way or another.

Pope Benedict XV, in spite of Vatican sympathies for the Central Powers, endeavored to maintain an appearance of neutrality. However, within each nation the clergy, Catholic and Protestant, maintained no such neutral stance. Regarding the situation in the United States, Dr. Ray Abrams, in his book *Preachers Present Arms,* wrote: "The churches assumed a unity of purpose hitherto unknown in religious annals. . . . The leaders lost no time in getting thoroughly organized on a war-time basis. Within twenty-four hours after the declaration of war, the Federal Council of the Churches of Christ in America laid plans for the fullest cooperation. . . . The Roman Catholic Church, organized for similar service under the National Catholic War Council, directed by fourteen archbishops and with Cardinal Gibbons as president, demonstrated an equal devotion to the cause. . . . Many of the churches went much further than they were asked. They became recruiting stations for the enlistment of troops." What did the Bible Students do?

Although they endeavored to do what they felt was pleasing to God, their position was not always one of strict neutrality. What they did was influenced by the belief, shared in common with other professed Christians, that "the higher powers" were "ordained of God," according to the wording of the *King James Version*. (Rom. 13:1) Thus, in accord with a proclamation of the president of the United States, *The Watch Tower* urged the Bible Students to join in observing May 30, 1918, as a day of prayer and supplication in connection with the outcome of the world war.*

During the war years, the circumstances into which individual Bible Students were thrust varied. The way they dealt with these situations also varied. Feeling obligated to obey "the powers that be," as they referred to the secular rulers, some went into the trenches at the front with guns and bayonets. But having in mind the scripture, "Thou shalt not kill," they would fire their weapons into the air or try simply to knock the weapon from the hands of an opponent. (Ex. 20:13, *KJ*) A few, such as Remigio Cuminetti, in Italy, refused to put on a military uniform. The Italian government at that time

Some went into the trenches with guns, but others, including A. P. Hughes of England and R. Cuminetti of Italy, refused such involvement

---
* *The Watch Tower,* June 1, 1918, p. 174.

made no allowance for anyone who for reasons of conscience would not take up arms. He stood trial five times and was confined in prisons and a mental institution, but his faith and determination remained unshaken. In England some who applied for exemption were assigned to work of national importance or to a noncombatant corps. Others, such as Pryce Hughes, adopted a position of strict neutrality, regardless of the consequences to them personally.

At least at that point, the overall record of the Bible Students was not quite like that of the early Christians described in *The Rise of Christianity*, by E. W. Barnes, who reported: "A careful review of all the information available goes to show that, until the time of Marcus Aurelius [Roman emperor from 161 to 180 C.E.], no Christian became a soldier; and no soldier, after becoming a Christian, remained in military service."

But then, at the end of World War I, another situation arose that called on religious groups to show where their loyalties were.

A Political Expression of God's Kingdom?

A peace treaty, including the Covenant of the League of Nations, was signed in Versailles, France, on June 28, 1919. Even before that peace treaty was signed, the Federal Council of the Churches of Christ in America went on record as proclaiming that the League would be "the political expression of the Kingdom of God on earth." And the U.S. Senate received an avalanche of mail from religious groups urging it to ratify the Covenant of the League of Nations.

Jehovah's Witnesses did not jump on the bandwagon. Even before the peace treaty was confirmed (in October), J. F. Rutherford gave a discourse at Cedar Point, Ohio, on September 7, 1919, in which he showed that not the League of Nations but the Kingdom set up by God himself is the only hope for distressed humanity. While acknowledging that a human alliance to improve conditions could accomplish much good, those Bible Students were not turning their backs on God's own Kingdom in exchange for a political expedient set up by politicians and blessed by the clergy. Instead, they undertook the work of giving a global witness concerning the Kingdom that God had placed in the hands of Jesus Christ. (Rev. 11:15; 12:10) In *The Watch Tower* of July 1, 1920, it was explained that this was the work that Jesus had foretold at Matthew 24:14.

Once again, following World War II, Christians were faced with a similar issue. This time, it involved the United Nations, successor to the League. While World War II was still under way, in 1942, Jehovah's Witnesses had already discerned from the Bible, at Revelation 17:8, that the world peace organization would rise again, also that it would fail to bring lasting peace. This was explained by N. H. Knorr, then president of the Watch Tower Society, in the convention discourse "Peace—Can It Last?" Boldly Jehovah's Witnesses proclaimed that view of the developing world situation. On the other hand, Catholic, Protestant, and Jewish leaders actually shared in the deliberations in San Francisco in 1945 during which the UN Charter was drafted. To observers of these developments, it was plain who wanted to be "a friend of the world" and who was endeavoring to be "no part of the world," as Jesus had said would be true of his disciples.—Jas. 4:4; John 17:14.

Jehovah's Witnesses refused to endorse the League of Nations or the UN as being from God but advocated only God's Kingdom through Christ

A Record of Christian Neutrality

Though Jehovah's Witnesses quickly discerned some issues that involve a Christian's relationship to the world, other matters required more time. However, as World War II gathered momentum in Europe, a significant article in *The Watchtower* of November 1, 1939, helped them to appreciate the meaning of Christian neutrality. Followers of Jesus Christ, the article stated, are obligated before God to be wholly devoted to him and his Kingdom, the Theocracy. Their prayers should be for God's Kingdom, not for the world. (Matt. 6:10, 33) In the light of what Jesus Christ disclosed as to the identity of the invisible ruler of the world (John 12:31; 14:30), the article reasoned, how could a person who is devoted to God's Kingdom favor one side or the other in a conflict between factions of the world? Had not Jesus said of his followers: "They are no part of the world, just as I am no part of the world"? (John 17:16) This

Christian neutrality put to the test

position of Christian neutrality was not one that the world in general would understand. But would Jehovah's Witnesses really live up to it?

Their neutrality was put to a grueling test during World War II, outstandingly in Germany. Historian Brian Dunn stated: 'Jehovah's Witnesses were incompatible with Nazism. Most important of the Nazi objections to them was their political neutrality. This meant that no believer would bear arms, hold office, take part in public festivals, or make any sign of allegiance.' (*The Churches' Response to the Holocaust,* 1986) In *A History of Christianity,* Paul Johnson added: "Many were sentenced to death for refusing military service . . . or they ended in Dachau or lunatic asylums." How many Witnesses in Germany were imprisoned? Jehovah's Witnesses in Germany later reported that 6,262 of them had been arrested and 2,074 of that number had been put into concentration camps. Secular writers usually opt for higher figures.

In Britain, where both men and women were regimented, the law provided for exemption; but this was refused to Jehovah's Witnesses by many tribunals, and judges imposed on them prison-sentence time exceeding 600 years in total. In the United States, hundreds of Jehovah's Witnesses as Christian ministers were exempted from military service. Over 4,000 others, denied the exemption provided by the Selective Service Act, were arrested and imprisoned for terms that ranged up to five years. In every country on earth, Jehovah's Witnesses held to the same position of Christian neutrality.

However, the test of the genuineness of their neutrality did not cease with the end of the war. Although the crisis of 1939-45 was past, other conflicts came; and even during times of relative peace, many nations chose to maintain compulsory military service. Jehovah's Witnesses, as Christian ministers, continued to face imprisonment where they were not granted exemption. In 1949, when John Tsukaris and George Orphanidis would not take up arms against their fellowmen, the Greek government ordered their execution. The treatment (of various kinds) meted out to Jehovah's Witnesses in Greece was repeatedly so harsh that in time the Council of Europe (Human Rights Committee) endeavored to use its influence in their behalf, but as a result of pressure from the Greek Orthodox Church, down till 1992 their urgings had, with few exceptions, been circumvented. However, some governments found it distasteful to continue punishing Jehovah's Witnesses for their conscientious religious beliefs. As of the 1990's, in a few countries, such as Sweden, Finland, Poland, the Netherlands, and Argentina, the government was not pressing active Witnesses to engage in military service or in alternative compulsory national service, though each case was carefully examined.

In one place after another, Jehovah's Witnesses have had to face situations that challenged their Christian neutrality. Governments in power in Latin America, Africa, the Middle East, Northern Ireland, and elsewhere have met with violent opposition from revolutionary forces. As a result, both the governments and opposition forces have pressured Jehovah's Witnesses for active support. But Jehovah's Witnesses have maintained complete neutrality. Some have been cruelly beaten, even executed, because of the stand taken. Often, though, the genuine Christian neutrality of Jehovah's Witnesses has won the respect of officers on both sides, and the Witnesses are permitted to proceed unmolested in their work of telling others the good news about Jehovah's Kingdom.

In the 1960's and the 1970's, the Witnesses' neutrality underwent brutal tests in connection with the demand that all citizens of Malawi buy a card signifying membership in the ruling political party. Jehovah's Witnesses saw it as contrary to their Christian beliefs to share in this. As a result, they were subjected to persecution that was unprecedented in its sadistic cruelty. Tens of thousands were forced to flee the country, and many were in time forcibly repatriated to face further brutality.

Although violently persecuted, Jehovah's Witnesses have not reacted in a spirit of rebellion. Their beliefs do not endanger any government under which they live. In contrast, the World Council of Churches has helped to finance revolutions, and Catholic priests have backed guerrilla forces. But if one of Jehovah's Witnesses were to engage in subversive activity, it would amount to renouncing his faith.

It is true that Jehovah's Witnesses believe that all human governments will be removed by God's Kingdom. This is what the Bible states at Daniel 2:44. But, as the Witnesses point out, instead of saying that humans would set up that Kingdom, the scripture declares that *"the God of heaven* will set up a kingdom." Likewise, they explain, the scripture does not say that humans are authorized by God to clear the way for that Kingdom by removing human rulerships.

No Threat to Any Government

• *When writing about the treatment of Jehovah's Witnesses in a Latin American land, an editorial in the Omaha, Nebraska, U.S.A., "World-Herald" said: "It takes a bigoted and paranoid imagination to believe that the Jehovah's Witnesses pose any kind of threat to any political regime; they are as non-subversive and peace-loving as a religious body can be, and ask only to be left alone to pursue their faith in their own way."*

• *"Il Corriere di Trieste," an Italian newspaper, stated: "Jehovah's Witnesses should be admired for their firmness and coherence. Contrary to other religions, their oneness as a people prevents them from praying to the same God, in the name of the same Christ, to bless two opposing sides of a conflict, or from mixing politics with religion to serve the interests of Heads of State or political parties. Last but not least, they are ready to face death rather than violate . . . the commandment THOU SHALT NOT KILL!"*

• *After Jehovah's Witnesses had endured a 40-year ban in Czechoslovakia, the newspaper "Nová Svoboda" said, in 1990: "The faith of Jehovah's Witnesses prohibits the use of weapons against humans, and those who refused basic military service and didn't get to work in the coal mines went to prison, even for four years. Just from this it is obvious that they have tremendous moral strength. We could use such unselfish people even in the highest political functions—but we are never going to get them there. . . . Of course, they recognize governmental authorities but believe that only God's Kingdom is capable of solving all human problems. But watch it—they are not fanatics. They are people who are absorbed in humanity."*

Jehovah's Witnesses recognize that the work of true Christians is to preach and to teach. (Matt. 24:14; 28:19, 20) In harmony with their respect for God's Word, the record shows that none of them have ever attempted to overthrow a government of any kind anywhere in the world, nor have they ever plotted to harm a public official. The Italian newspaper *La Stampa* said regarding Jehovah's Witnesses: "They are the most loyal citizens anyone could wish for: they do not dodge taxes or seek to evade inconvenient laws for their own profit." Nevertheless, because of recognizing the seriousness of the matter in the eyes of God, each one of them is firmly determined to remain "no part of the world."—John 15:19; Jas. 4:4.

When National Emblems Became Objects of Devotion

With the rise of Adolf Hitler to power in Germany, a wave of patriotic hysteria swept the world. In order to regiment the people, participation in patriotic ceremonies was made compulsory. In Germany everyone was required to give a prescribed salute and cry out, *"Heil Hitler!"* This was a lauding of Hitler as savior; it was meant to convey the idea that all the hopes of the people were centered on his leadership. But Jehovah's Witnesses could not join in such sentiments. They knew that their worship must go only to Jehovah and that He had raised up Jesus Christ as mankind's Savior.—Luke 4:8; 1 John 4:14.

Even before Hitler became dictator in Germany, Jehovah's Witnesses, in the booklet *The Kingdom, the Hope of the World* (published in 1931), reviewed the Scriptural example of the prophet Daniel's three courageous Hebrew companions in Babylon. When ordered by the king to bow before an image at the playing of certain music, those faithful Hebrews had refused to compromise, and Jehovah had made plain his approval by delivering them. (Dan. 3:1-26) The booklet pointed out that patriotic ceremonies confronted Jehovah's Witnesses in modern times with a similar challenge to their faithfulness.

Gradually, agitation for compulsory patriotic ceremonies spread beyond Germany. On June 3, 1935, at a convention in Washington, D.C., when J. F. Rutherford was asked to comment on flag saluting in the schools, he emphasized the matter of faithfulness to God. A few months later, when eight-year-old Carleton B. Nichols, Jr., of Lynn, Massachusetts, declined to salute the American flag and join in singing a patriotic song, it was reported in newspapers across the country.

To explain the matter, Brother Rutherford gave a radio discourse on October 6 on the subject "Saluting a Flag," in which he said: "To many persons the saluting of the flag is merely a formalism and has little or no significance. To those who sincerely consider it from the Scriptural standpoint, it means much.

"The flag representatively stands for the visible ruling powers. To attempt by law to compel a citizen or child of a citizen to salute any object or thing, or to sing so-called 'patriotic songs', is entirely unfair and wrong. Laws are made and enforced to prevent the commission of overt acts that result in injury to another, and are not made for the purpose of compelling a person to violate his conscience, and particularly when that conscience is directed in harmony with Jehovah God's Word.

"The refusal to salute the flag, and to stand mute, as this boy did, could injure no one. If one sincerely believes that God's commandment is against the saluting of flags, then to compel that person to salute a flag contrary to the Word of God, and contrary to his conscience, works a great injury to that person. The State has no right by law or otherwise to work injury to the people."

Further explanation of the reasons for the position taken by Jehovah's Witnesses was provided in the booklet *Loyalty,* published also in 1935. Attention was directed to such scriptures as the following: *Exodus 20:3-7,* which commanded that worship go only to Jehovah and that God's servants were not to make or bow before any image or likeness of anything in heaven or on earth; *Luke 20:25,* where Jesus Christ directed that not only should Caesar's things be paid back to Caesar but what belongs to God must be rendered to Him; and *Acts 5:29,* where the apostles firmly stated, "We must obey God as ruler rather than men."

In the United States, the propriety of compelling anyone to salute a flag was submitted to the courts. On June 14, 1943, the U.S. Supreme Court reversed its own former decision and, in the case of *West Virginia State Board of Education v. Barnette,* ruled that compulsory flag saluting was inconsistent with the guarantee of freedom set out in the nation's own constitution.*

The issue involving nationalistic ceremonies has by no means been limited to Germany and the United States. In North and South America, Europe, Africa, and Asia, Jehovah's Witnesses have been cruelly persecuted because of their nonparticipation, even though they stand respectfully during flag-salute or similar ceremonies. Children have been beaten; many have been expelled from school. Numerous court cases have been fought.

Observers have felt impelled to acknowledge, however, that in this, as in other matters, Jehovah's Witnesses have proved to be like the early Christians. Yet, as stated in the book *The American Character:* "To the overwhelming majority . . . the objections of the Witnesses were as unintelligible as the objections of the

Carleton and Flora Nichols. When their son refrained from saluting the flag, this became national news

---
* For further details, see Chapter 30, "Defending and Legally Establishing the Good News."

Christians [in the Roman Empire] to making a formal sacrifice to the Divine Emperor were to Trajan and Pliny." This was to be expected, since Jehovah's Witnesses, like the early Christians, viewed matters not as the world does but according to Bible principles.

Their Position Clearly Stated

After Jehovah's Witnesses had endured grueling tests of their Christian neutrality for many years, *The Watchtower* of November 1, 1979, reaffirmed their position. It also explained what accounted for the action taken by individual Witnesses when it said: "As a result of diligent study of God's Word, these young Christians were able to make a decision. No one else made this decision for them. They were able to make it individually, on the basis of each one's Bible-trained conscience. Their decision was to refrain from acts of hatred and violence against their fellowmen of other nations. Yes, they believed in, and wanted to share in, the fulfillment of Isaiah's well-known prophecy: 'They will have to beat their swords into plowshares and their spears into pruning shears. Nation will not lift up sword against nation, neither will they learn war anymore.' (Isa. 2:4) These young men of all nations did just that."

During the years that their adherence to Christian neutrality was being put to the test, reexamination of what the Bible says, at Romans 13:1-7, about "the superior authorities" led to a clearer statement of the Witnesses' relationship to secular governments. This was published in the *Watchtower* issues of November 1, November 15, and December 1, 1962, and was reaffirmed in the issue of November 1, 1990. Those articles emphasized the position of Jehovah God as "the Supreme One," while also pointing out that secular rulers are "superior authorities" only in relation to other humans and in the sphere of activity in which God permits them to function in the present system of things. The articles showed the need for true Christians conscientiously to honor such secular rulers and to render obedience to them in all matters that do not conflict with God's law and their Bible-trained conscience.—Dan. 7:18; Matt. 22:21; Acts 5:29; Rom. 13:5.

Firm adherence to these Bible standards by Jehovah's Witnesses has earned them a reputation for separateness from the world that reminds people of the early Christians.

When the World Had Its Holidays

When Jehovah's Witnesses cast aside religious teachings that had pagan roots, they also quit sharing in many customs that were similarly tainted. But for a time, certain holidays were not given the careful scrutiny that they needed. One of these was Christmas.

'No one else made the decision for them'

This holiday was celebrated yearly even by members of the Watch Tower Society's headquarters staff at the Bethel Home in Brooklyn, New York. For many years they had been aware that December 25 was not the correct date, but they reasoned that the date had long been popularly associated with the birth of the Savior and that doing good for others was proper on any day. However, after further investigation of the subject, the members of the Society's headquarters staff, as well as the staffs at the Society's branch offices in England and in Switzerland, decided to stop sharing in Christmas festivities, so no Christmas celebration was held there after 1926.

R. H. Barber, a member of the headquarters staff who made a thorough investigation of the origin of Christmas customs and the fruitage that these were yielding, presented the results in a radio broadcast. That information was also published in *The Golden Age* of December 12, 1928. It was a thorough exposé of the God-dishonoring roots of Christmas. Since then, the pagan roots of Christmas customs have become general public knowledge, but few people make changes in their way of life as a result. On the other hand, Jehovah's Witnesses were willing to make needed changes in order to be more acceptable as servants of Jehovah.

When shown that celebrating the birth of Jesus had actually become of greater interest to people than the ransom provided by his death; that the revelry of the holiday and the spirit in which many gifts were given did not honor God; that the magi whose gift-giving was being imitated were actually demon-inspired astrologers; that parents set an example for their children in lying by what they told them about Santa Claus; that "St. Nicholas" (Santa Claus) was admittedly another name for the Devil himself; and that such festivals were, as acknowledged by Cardinal Newman in his *Essay on the Development of Christian Doctrine*, "the very instruments and appendages of demon-worship" the church had adopted —when made aware of these things, Jehovah's Witnesses promptly and permanently stopped having any part in Christmas celebrations.

Why they quit celebrating Christmas

Jehovah's Witnesses have good times with their families and friends. But they do not participate in holidays and celebrations that are linked with pagan gods (as is true of such holidays as Easter, New Year's Day, May Day, and Mother's Day). (2 Cor. 6:14-17) Like the early Christians,* they do not even celebrate birthdays. They also respectfully refrain from sharing in national holidays that memorialize political or military events and refrain from giving worshipful honor to national heroes. Why? Because Jehovah's Witnesses are no part of the world.

---

* *The History of the Christian Religion and Church, During the Three First Centuries,* by Augustus Neander, p. 190.

Helping Their Fellowman

Reverence toward the gods was at the heart of the social and cultural life of the Roman Empire. Since Christians abstained from sharing in anything tainted by the pagan gods, the people viewed Christianity as an affront to their way of life; and according to the historian Tacitus, Christians were said to be haters of mankind. Conveying a similar feeling, Minucius Felix, in his writings, quotes a Roman as saying to a Christian acquaintance: "You do not attend the shows; you take no part in the processions . . . abhor the sacred games." The populace of the ancient Roman world little understood the Christians.

Similarly today, Jehovah's Witnesses are not understood by many in the world. People may admire the high moral standards of the Witnesses but feel that the Witnesses should share with the world around them in its

Practices That Have Been Abandoned

This Christmas celebration at Brooklyn Bethel in 1926 was their last. The Bible Students gradually came to appreciate that neither the origin of this holiday nor the practices associated with it honored God

For years, Bible Students wore a cross and crown as a badge of identification, and this symbol was on the front cover of the "Watch Tower" from 1891 to 1931. But in 1928 it was emphasized that not a decorative symbol but one's activity as a witness showed he was a Christian. In 1936 it was pointed out that the evidence indicates that Christ died on a stake, not a two-beamed cross

"THEY ARE NO PART OF THE WORLD" 201

activities and get involved in helping to make the world a better place. However, those who get to know Jehovah's Witnesses firsthand learn that there is a Biblical reason for everything they do.

Far from shutting themselves off from the rest of mankind, Jehovah's Witnesses devote their lives to helping their fellowmen in the way that Jesus Christ set the example. They assist people to learn how to cope successfully with the problems of life now by acquainting them with the Creator and the guidelines for life that are set out in his inspired Word. They freely share with their neighbors Bible truths that can transform a person's entire outlook on life. At the core of their belief is the realization that "the world is passing away," that soon God will intervene to bring the present wicked system to an end, and that a glorious future awaits those who remain no part of the world and put their full faith in the Kingdom of God.—1 John 2:17.

In their "Daily Manna" book, Bible Students kept a list of birthdays. But after they quit celebrating Christmas and when they realized that birthday celebrations were giving undue honor to creatures (one reason that early Christians never celebrated birthdays), the Bible Students quit this practice too

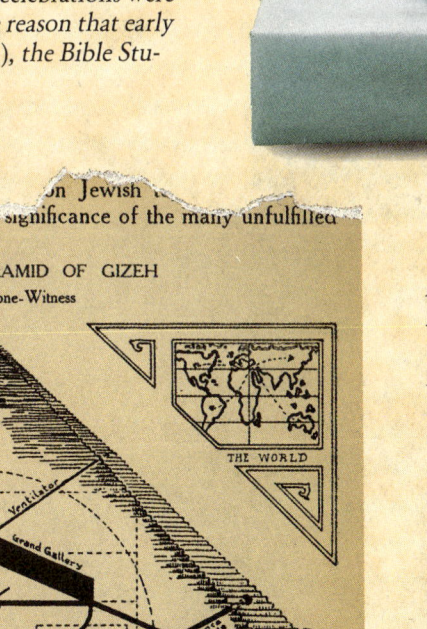

For some 35 years, Pastor Russell thought that the Great Pyramid of Gizeh was God's stone witness, corroborating Biblical time periods. (Isa. 19: 19) But Jehovah's Witnesses have abandoned the idea that an Egyptian pyramid has anything to do with true worship. (See "Watchtower" issues of November 15 and December 1, 1928)

WATCH TOWER BIBLE AND TRACT SOCIETY OF PENNSYLVANIA
A NONPROFIT CORPORATION
DEC. 15, 1884

SECTION 3

An Association of Brothers

Is it possible for millions of people out of all nations and languages to work together as a genuine association of brothers?

The record of Jehovah's modern-day Witnesses answers with a resounding Yes! This section (Chapters 15 to 21) tells how their organization functions. It conveys the zeal with which they proclaim God's Kingdom and the love that is manifest as they work together and as they care for one another in times of crisis.

CHAPTER 15

DEVELOPMENT OF THE ORGANIZATION STRUCTURE

THE operation of the organization of Jehovah's Witnesses has undergone significant changes since Charles Taze Russell and his associates first began to study the Bible together in 1870. When the early Bible Students were few in number, they had very little of what outsiders would view as characterizing an organization. Yet, today, as people observe the congregations of Jehovah's Witnesses, their conventions, and their preaching of the good news in over 200 lands, they marvel at how smoothly the organization operates. How has it developed?

A clergy class had no place among them

The Bible Students were keenly interested in understanding not only Bible doctrine but also the *manner in which God's service was to be performed,* as indicated by the Scriptures. They realized that the Bible made no provision for titled clergymen, with a laity to whom they would preach. Brother Russell was determined that there would be no clergy class among them.* Through the columns of the *Watch Tower,* its readers were frequently reminded that Jesus told his followers: "Your Leader is one, the Christ," but, "All you are brothers."—Matt. 23:8, 10.

Early Association of Bible Students

Readers of the *Watch Tower* and related publications soon saw that in order to please God, they had to sever ties with any church that proved itself unfaithful to God by putting creeds and traditions of men ahead of his written Word. (2 Cor. 6:14-18) But after withdrawing from the churches of Christendom, where did they go?

In an article entitled "The Ekklesia,"# Brother Russell pointed out that the true church, the Christian congregation, is not an organization with

---

* In 1894, Brother Russell arranged for Zion's Watch Tower Tract Society to send out qualified brothers as speakers. They were given signed certificates for use in introducing themselves to the local groups. These certificates did not confer authority to preach nor did they signify that what the bearer said was to be accepted without proper scrutiny in the light of God's Word. However, since some persons misconstrued their intent, within a year Brother Russell had the certificates recalled. He cautiously endeavored to avoid anything that observers might interpret to be even the appearance of a clergy class.

Zion's Watch Tower, October-November 1881, pp. 8-9.

members who have subscribed to some man-made creed and have their names written on a church register. Rather, he explained, it is made up of persons who have "consecrated" (or, dedicated) their time, talents, and life to God, and who have before them the prospect of sharing in the heavenly Kingdom with Christ. These, he said, are Christians who are united in bonds of Christian love and common interest, who respond to the direction of the spirit of God, and who submit to the headship of Christ. Brother Russell was not interested in setting up some other arrangement, and he was strongly against contributing in any way to the sectarianism that existed among professed Christians.

At the same time, he fully appreciated the need for the Lord's servants to assemble together, in harmony with the counsel at Hebrews 10:23-25. He personally traveled to visit and upbuild readers of the *Watch Tower* and to bring them together with others in their own area who were of like mind. Early in 1881 he requested that those who were holding regular meetings notify the Watch Tower office as to where these were being held. He saw the value of keeping them in touch with one another.

However, Brother Russell emphasized that they were not attempting to set up an "earthly organization." Rather, he said, "we adhere only to that *heavenly organization*—'whose names are written in heaven.' (Heb. 12:23; Luke 10:20.)" Because of Christendom's sordid history, reference to "church organization" usually reminded a person of sectarianism, clergy domination, and membership on the basis of adhering to a creed formulated by a religious council. So, when referring to themselves, Brother Russell felt that the term "association" was a better one.

Not attempting to set up an "earthly organization"

He was well aware that Christ's apostles had formed congregations and appointed elders in each. But he believed that Christ was again present, though invisibly so, and was himself personally directing the final harvest of those who would be heirs with him. In view of the circumstances, Brother Russell initially felt that during the time of harvest the arrangement for elders that had existed in the first-century Christian congregations was not needed.

Nevertheless, as the Bible Students grew in number, Brother Russell realized that the Lord was maneuvering matters in a manner different from what he himself had anticipated. An adjustment in viewpoint was needed. But on what basis?

Meeting the Early Needs of the Growing Association

The *Watch Tower* of November 15, 1895, was devoted almost entirely to the subject "Decently and in Order." Candidly, Brother Russell there acknowledged: "The apostles had much to say to the early Church concerning *order* in the assemblies of the saints; and apparently we have been rather negligent of this wise counsel, feeling it to be of rather minor importance, because the Church is so near the end of her course and the harvest is a time of separating." What moved them to take a fresh look at that counsel?

That article listed four circumstances: (1) It was evident that the spiritual development of individuals varied one from another. There were temptations, trials, difficulties, and dangers that not all were equally prepared to meet. Thus, there was a need for wise and discreet overseers, men of experience and ability, deeply interested in looking out for the spiritual welfare of all and capable of instructing them in the truth. (2) It had been seen that the flock needed to be defended against 'wolves in sheep's clothing.' (Matt. 7:15, *KJ*) They needed to be fortified by being helped to gain a thorough knowledge of the truth. (3) Experience had shown that if there was no arrangement for appointment of elders to safeguard the flock, some would *take* that position and come to view the flock as their own. (4) Without an orderly arrangement, individuals loyal to the truth might find their services unwanted because of the influence of a few who disagreed with them.

In the light of this, the *Watch Tower* stated: "We have no hesitation in commending to the Churches* in every place, whether their numbers be large or small, the Apostolic counsel, that, in every company, elders be chosen from among their number to 'feed' and 'take the oversight' of the flock." (Acts 14:21-23; 20:17, 28) The local congregations followed through on this sound Scriptural counsel. This was an important step in establishing a congregation structure in harmony with what existed in the days of the apostles.

How were elders chosen?

In accord with the way they understood matters then, however, the selection of elders, and of deacons to assist them, was made by congregation vote. Each year, or more often if necessary, the qualifications of those who might serve were considered, and a vote was taken. It was basically a democratic procedure, but one that was hedged about with limitations designed to act as a safeguard. All in the congregation were urged to review carefully the Biblical qualifications and to express by vote, not their own opinion, but what they believed to be the will of the Lord. Since only those "fully consecrated" were eligible to vote, their collective vote, when guided by the Word and spirit of the Lord, was viewed as expressing the Lord's will in the matter. Although Brother Russell may not have been completely

---

* At times the local groups were referred to as "churches," in harmony with the language used in the *King James Version*. They were also called ecclesias, in accord with the term used in the Greek Bible text. The expression "classes" was likewise employed, for they were in reality bodies of students meeting regularly to study. Later, when they were called companies, this was a reflection of their awareness that they were in a spiritual warfare. (See Psalm 68:11, *KJ*, margin.) After publication of the *New World Translation of the Christian Greek Scriptures* in 1950, the modern-language Bible term "congregation" came into regular use in most lands.

Why the Change?

When questioned on his change of view regarding selection of elders in the various groups of the Lord's people, C. T. Russell replied:

"First of all I hasten to assure you that I have never laid claim to infallibility. . . . We do not deny growing in knowledge, and that we now see in a slightly different light the will of the Lord respecting Elders or leaders in the various little groups of his people. Our error in judgment was in expecting too much of the dear brethren who, coming early into the Truth, became the natural leaders of these little companies. The ideal view of them which we fondly entertained was, that the knowledge of the Truth would have upon them a very humbling effect, causing them to appreciate their own insignificance, and that whatever they knew and were able to present to others was as mouthpieces of God and because used of him. Our ideal hopes were that these would in every sense of the word be examples to the flock; and that should the Lord's providence bring into the little company one or more equally competent, or more competent, to present the Truth, that the spirit of love would lead them in honor to prefer one another, and thus to help and urge one another to participation in the service of the Church, the body of Christ.

"With this thought in mind we concluded that the larger measures of grace and truth now due and appreciated by the Lord's consecrated people would make it unnecessary for them to follow the course outlined by the apostles in the early Church. Our mistake was in failing to realize that the arrangements outlined by the apostles under divine supervision are superior to anything that others could formulate, and that the Church as a whole will need to have the regulations instituted by the apostles until, by our change in the resurrection, we shall all be made complete and perfect and be directly in association with the Master.

"Our mistake gradually dawned upon us as we beheld amongst dear brethren to some extent the spirit of rivalry, and on the part of many a desire to hold the leadership of meetings as an office instead of as a service, and to exclude and hinder from developing as leaders other brethren of equal ability naturally and of equal knowledge of the Truth and competency in wielding the sword of the Spirit."—"*Zion's Watch Tower,*" March 15, 1906, p. 90.

aware of it, his recommendation of this arrangement was perhaps influenced to some extent not only by his determination to avoid any semblance of an exalted clergy class but also by his own background as a teenager in the Congregational Church.

When the *Millennial Dawn* volume entitled *The New Creation* (published in 1904) again discussed in detail the role of elders and the manner in which they were to be selected, special attention was directed to Acts

Facilities Used by the Society a Century Ago in the Pittsburgh Area

The Bible House, shown here, served as the headquarters for 19 years, from 1890 to 1909*

Brother Russell had his study here

* In 1879, the headquarters was at 101 Fifth Avenue, Pittsburgh, Pennsylvania. The offices were moved to 44 Federal Street, Allegheny (Pittsburgh's North Side), in 1884; and later in the same year, to 40 Federal Street. (In 1887, this was designated 151 Robinson Street.) When more space was needed, in 1889, Brother Russell built the Bible House, shown at the left, at 56-60 Arch Street, Allegheny. (This was later renumbered 610-614 Arch Street.) For a short period in 1918-19, they once again had their principal office in Pittsburgh, on the third floor at 119 Federal Street.

14:23. Concordances compiled by James Strong and Robert Young were cited as authorities for the view that the statement "they had ordained them elders" (*KJ*) should be translated "they had elected them elders by a show of hands."* Some Bible translations even say that the elders were 'appointed by vote.' (Young's *Literal Translation of the Holy Bible;* Rotherham's *Emphasised Bible*) But who was to do that voting?

Adopting the view that the voting was to be done by the congregation as a whole did not always yield the results that were hoped for. Those voting were to be persons who were "fully consecrated," and some who were elected truly met the Scriptural qualifications and humbly served their brothers. But the voting often reflected personal preference rather than the Word and spirit of God. Thus, in Halle, Germany, when certain ones who thought they should be elders did not get the positions they wanted, they caused severe dissension. In Barmen, Germany, among those who were candidates in 1927 were men who opposed the work of the Society, and there was considerable shouting during the showing of hands at election time. So it was necessary to switch over to a secret ballot.

Back in 1916, years before these incidents, Brother Russell, with deep

---

* The literal meaning of the word used in the Greek Bible text (*khei·ro·to·ne'o*) is "to extend, stretch out, or lift up the hand," and, by extension, it could also mean "to elect or choose to an office by lifting up of hands."—*A Greek and English Lexicon to the New Testament*, by John Parkhurst, 1845, p. 673.

Members of the Bible House family that served here in 1902

The building included this typesetting and composition department (top right), a shipping department (bottom right), literature storage, living quarters for the staff, and a chapel (assembly hall) that would seat about 300

concern, had written: "A horrible state of affairs prevails in some Classes when an election is to be held. The servants of the Church attempt to be rulers, dictators—sometimes even holding the chairmanship of the meeting with the apparent object of seeing that they and their special friends shall be elected as Elders and Deacons. . . . Some quietly try to take advantage of the Class by having the election at some time which is especially favorable to them and their friends. Others seek to pack the meeting with their friends, bringing in comparative strangers, who have no thought of being regular in attendance at the Class, but come merely as an act of friendship to vote for one of their friends."

Did they simply need to learn how to handle elections along democratic lines more smoothly, or was there something from God's Word that they had not yet discerned?

Organizing to Get the Good News Preached

At a very early point, Brother Russell recognized that one of the most important responsibilities of every member of the Christian congregation was the work of evangelizing. (1 Pet. 2:9) The *Watch Tower* explained that it was not to Jesus alone but to all his spirit-anointed followers that the prophetic words of Isaiah 61:1 applied, namely: "Jehovah has anointed me to tell good news," or, as the *King James Version* renders Jesus' quotation of this passage, "He hath anointed me to preach the gospel."—Luke 4:18.

As early as 1881, the *Watch Tower* carried the article "Wanted 1,000 Preachers." This was an appeal to every member of the congregation to use whatever time he could (a half hour, an hour, or two, or three) to share in spreading Bible truth. Men and women who did not have families that were dependent on them and who could give half or more of their time exclusively to the Lord's work were encouraged to undertake work as colporteur evangelists. The number varied considerably from year to year, but by 1885 there were already about 300 who were sharing in this work as colporteurs. Some others also had a part but on a more limited scale. Suggestions were given to the colporteurs as to how to go about their work. But the field was vast, and at least at the start, they selected their own territory and moved from one area to another largely as it seemed best to them. Then when they met at conventions, they would make needed adjustments to coordinate their efforts.

The same year that the colporteur service began, Brother Russell had a number of tracts (or booklets) printed for free distribution. Outstanding among these was *Food for Thinking Christians*, which was distributed to the number of 1,200,000 in the first four months. The work involved in arranging this printing and distribution gave rise to the formation of Zion's Watch Tower Tract Society in order to care for necessary details. To prevent disruption of the work in the event of his death, and to facilitate the handling of donations to be used in the work, Brother Russell filed for legal registration of the Society, and this was officially recorded on December 15, 1884. This brought into existence a needed legal instrumentality.

As the need arose, branch offices of the Watch Tower Society were established in other lands. The first was in London, England, on April 23, 1900. Another, in Elberfeld, Germany, in 1902. Two years later, on the other side of the earth, a branch was organized in Melbourne, Australia. At the time of this writing, there are 99 branches worldwide.

Although the organizational arrangements that were needed to provide quantities of Bible literature were taking form, at first it was left to the congregations to work out any local arrangements for public distribution of that material. In a letter dated March 16, 1900, Brother Russell stated how he viewed the matter. That letter, addressed to "Alexander M. Graham, and the Church at Boston, Mass.," said: "As you all know, it is my decided intention to leave with each company of the Lord's people the management of their own affairs, according to their own judgments, offering suggestions, not by way of interference, but by way merely of advice." This included not only their meetings but also the way they carried

To provide closer supervision, branch offices were established. The first one was in London, England, in this building

on their field ministry. Thus, after offering the brothers some practical counsel, he concluded with the comment: "This is merely a suggestion."

Some activities required more specific direction from the Society. In connection with the showing of the "Photo-Drama of Creation," it was left to each congregation to determine whether they were willing and able to rent a theater or other facility for a local presentation. However, it was necessary to move equipment from city to city, and schedules had to be met; so in these respects centralized direction was provided by the Society. Each congregation was encouraged to have a Drama Committee to care for local arrangements. But a superintendent sent out by the Society gave careful attention to details in order to make sure that everything went smoothly.

As the years 1914 and then 1915 passed, those spirit-anointed Christians waited eagerly for the fulfillment of their heavenly hope. At the same time, they were encouraged to keep busy in the Lord's service. Even though they viewed their remaining time in the flesh as very brief, it became evident that in order to carry on the preaching of the good news in an orderly manner, more direction was needed than when they had numbered just a few hundred. Shortly after J. F. Rutherford became the second president of the Watch Tower Society, that direction took on new aspects. The March 1, 1917, issue of *The Watch Tower* announced that, henceforth, all territory to be worked by colporteurs and by pastoral workers* in the congregations would be assigned by the Society's office. Where there were both local workers and colporteurs sharing in such field service in a city or a county, the territory was divided up among them by a locally appointed district committee. This arrangement contributed to a truly remarkable distribution of *The Finished Mystery* within just a few months in 1917-18. It was also valuable in achieving a lightning distribution of 10,000,000 copies of a powerful exposé of Christendom in a tract that featured the subject "The Fall of Babylon."

Shortly after this, members of the Society's administrative staff were arrested, and on June 21, 1918, they were sentenced to 20-year prison terms. The preaching of the good news came to a virtual standstill. Was this the time when they would at last be united with the Lord in heavenly glory?

A few months later, the war ended. The following

---

* For details, see Chapter 25, "Preaching Publicly and From House to House."

> **Whose Work Is It?**
>
> Toward the end of his earthly life, Charles Taze Russell wrote: "Too often do God's people forget that the Lord Himself is at the head of His work. Too often the thought is, We will do a work and get God to co-labor with us in our work. Let us get the right focus on the matter, and perceive that God has purposed and is carrying out a great work; and that it will succeed, entirely regardless of us and our effort; and that it is a great privilege granted to the people of God to co-labor with their Maker in the carrying out of His plans, His designs, His arrangements, in His way. Viewing matters from this standpoint, our prayer and our watching should be with a view to knowing and doing the will of the Lord, content whatever lot we see, since 'tis our God who leads us. This is the program which the Watch Tower Bible and Tract Society has sought to follow."
> —"*The Watch Tower,*" May 1, 1915.

year the officials of the Society were released. They were still in the flesh. It was not what they had expected, but they concluded that God must still have work for them to do here on earth.

They had just been through severe tests of their faith. However, in 1919, *The Watch Tower* strengthened them with stirring Scriptural studies on the theme "Blessed Are the Fearless." These were followed by the article "Opportunities for Service." But the brothers did not envision the extensive organizational developments that would take place during the decades that would follow.

Proper Example for the Flock

Brother Rutherford did appreciate that for the work to continue to move ahead in an orderly and unified way, no matter how short the time might be, proper example for the flock was vital. Jesus had described his followers as sheep, and sheep follow their shepherd. Of course, Jesus himself is the Fine Shepherd, but he also uses older men, or elders, as undershepherds of his people. (1 Pet. 5:1-3) Those elders must be men who themselves participate in the work that Jesus assigned and who encourage others to do so. They must genuinely have the evangelizing spirit. At the time of distribution of *The Finished Mystery*, however, some of the elders had held back; certain ones had even been quite vocal in discouraging others from sharing.

A director appointed by the Society

A highly significant step toward correcting this situation was taken in 1919 when the magazine *The Golden Age* began publication. This was to become a powerful instrument for publicizing the Kingdom of God as the only lasting solution to the problems of mankind. Each congregation that desired to share in this activity was invited to ask the Society to register it as a "service organization." Then a director, or service director as he came to be known, not subject to yearly election, was appointed by the Society.* As the local representative of the Society, he was to organize the work, assign territory, and encourage participation by the congregation in the field service. Thus, alongside the democratically elected elders and deacons, another type of organizational arrangement began to function, one that recognized appointive authority outside the local congregation and that gave greater emphasis to the preaching of the good news of God's Kingdom.#

During the years that followed, the work of Kingdom proclamation was given tremendous impetus, as by an irresistible force. The events in 1914 and thereafter had made it evident that the great prophecy in which the Lord

---

* Through the service director, the field service of those associated with the congregation, or class, was to be reported to the Society each week, starting in 1919.

As outlined in the folder *Organization Method*, each congregation was to elect an assistant director and a stockkeeper. These, along with the Society-appointed director, made up the local service committee.

Jesus Christ described the conclusion of the old system was undergoing fulfillment. In the light of this, in 1920, *The Watch Tower* pointed out that as foretold at Matthew 24:14, this was the time to proclaim the good news concerning "the end of the old order of things and the establishment of Messiah's kingdom."* (Matt. 24:3-14) After attending the Bible Students convention at Cedar Point, Ohio, in 1922, the delegates left with the slogan ringing in their ears: "Advertise, advertise, advertise, the King and his kingdom." The role of true Christians came even more prominently into focus in 1931 when the name Jehovah's Witnesses was adopted.

It was obvious that Jehovah had assigned his servants a work in which all of them could share. There was enthusiastic response. Many made major adjustments in their lives in order to devote their full time to this work. Even among those devoting just part time, a considerable number were spending full days in the field service on the weekends. Responding to encouragement contained in *The Watchtower* and the *Informant* in 1938 and 1939, many of Jehovah's Witnesses at that time conscientiously endeavored to devote 60 hours each month to the field service.

Among those zealous Witnesses were numerous humble, devoted servants of Jehovah who were elders in the congregations. However, in some places, during the 1920's and early in the 1930's, there was also considerable resistance to the idea of *everyone* participating in the field service. Democratically elected elders were often quite vocal in disagreeing with what *The Watch Tower* said about the responsibility to preach to people outside the congregation. Refusal to listen to what God's spirit, by means of the Holy Scriptures, had to say to the congregation on this matter hindered the flow of God's spirit in those groups.—Rev. 2:5, 7.

Measures were taken in 1932 to correct this situation. The point of principal concern was not whether some prominent elders might be offended or whether some of those associated with the congregations might withdraw. Rather, the desire of the brothers was to please Jehovah and to do his will. To that end, the August 15 and September 1 issues of *The Watchtower* that year featured the subject "Jehovah's Organization."

Some elders did not want to preach outside the congregation

Those articles showed pointedly that all who really were part of Jehovah's organization would be doing the work that his Word said must be done during this period of time. The articles advocated the view that Christian eldership was not *an office to which one could be elected* but was a condition attainable by spiritual growth. Special emphasis was given to Jesus' prayer that his followers might "all be one"—in union with God and Christ, and thus at unity with one another in doing God's will. (John 17:21) And with what result? The second article answered that "every one of the remnant must be a witness to the name and kingdom of Jehovah God."

---

* *The Watch Tower*, July 1, 1920, pp. 195-200.

Oversight was not to be entrusted to any who failed or refused to do what they reasonably could to share in public witnessing.

At the conclusion of the study of these articles, congregations were invited to pass a resolution indicating their agreement. Thus the annual congregational election of men to be elders and deacons was eliminated. In Belfast, Northern Ireland, as elsewhere, some of the former "elective elders" left; other individuals who shared their view went with them. This resulted in a thinning out of the ranks but a toning up of the entire organization. Those who remained were people who were willing to shoulder the Christian responsibility of witnessing. Instead of voting for elders, the congregations—still using democratic methods—selected a service committee* made up of spiritually mature men who actively shared in public witnessing. The members of the congregation also voted for a chairman to preside at their meetings as well as for a secretary and treasurer. All of these were men who were active witnesses of Jehovah.

With congregation oversight now entrusted to men who were interested not in personal position but in doing God's work—bearing witness to his name and Kingdom—and who were setting a good example by their own participation in it, the work moved ahead more smoothly. Although they did not then know it, there was much to be done, a more extensive witness than what had already been given, an ingathering that they had not expected. (Isa. 55:5) Jehovah was evidently preparing them for it.

A few with hope of eternal life on earth were beginning to associate with them.# However, the Bible foretold the gathering of a *great multitude* (or, great crowd) with a view to their preservation through the coming great tribulation. (Rev. 7:9-14) In 1935 the identity of this great multitude was made clear. Changes in selection of overseers during the 1930's equipped the organization better to care for the work of gathering, teaching, and training them.

For most of Jehovah's Witnesses, this expanded work was a thrilling development. Their field ministry took on fresh significance. However, some were not eager to preach. They held back, and they tried to justify their inactivity by arguing that no great multitude would be gathered until after Armageddon. But the majority perceived a fresh opportunity to demonstrate their loyalty to Jehovah and their love for their fellowman.

How did those of the great crowd fit into the organization structure? They were shown the role that God's Word assigned to the "little flock" of spirit-anointed ones, and they gladly worked in harmony with that

---

Thinning the ranks but toning up the organization

---

* The service committee at that time included not more than ten members. One of these was the service director, who was not elected locally but was appointed by the Society. The others worked with him to arrange and carry on the witness work.

For a number of years, from 1932 onward, these were referred to as Jonadabs.

V. D. M. QUESTIONS

V.D.M. Questions

The letters V.D.M. represent the Latin words "Verbi Dei Minister," or Minister of the Divine Word.

In 1916 a list of questions on Scriptural matters was prepared by the Society. Those who would represent the Society as speakers were asked to answer each of the questions in writing. This enabled the Society to know the thoughts, sentiments, and understanding of these brothers as respects fundamental Bible truths. The written answers were checked carefully by an examining board in the Society's offices. Those recognized to be qualified as speakers were to have a grade of 85 percent or better.

Later, many of the elders, deacons, and other Bible Students asked if they could have a list of the questions. In time, it was stated that it would be beneficial if the classes selected as their representatives only persons who had qualified as V.D.M.

When the Society conferred the degree of Minister of the Divine Word, this did not mean that the individual was being ordained. It simply implied that the examining board in the Society's offices had reviewed the doctrinal development of the person, and to a reasonable extent his reputation, and concluded that he was worthy of being called a Minister of the Divine Word.

The V.D.M. questions are as follows:

(1) What was the first creative act of God?
(2) What is the meaning of the word "Logos," as associated with the Son of God? and what is signified by the words Father and Son?
(3) When and how did sin enter the world?
(4) What is the Divine penalty for sin upon the sinners? and who are the sinners?
(5) Why was it necessary for the "Logos" to be made flesh? and was He "incarnated"?
(6) Of what nature was the Man Christ Jesus from infancy to death?
(7) Of what nature is Jesus since the resurrection; and what is His official relation to Jehovah?
(8) What is the work of Jesus during this Gospel Age—during the time from Pentecost until now?
(9) What has thus far been done for the world of mankind by Jehovah God? and what by Jesus?
(10) What is the Divine purpose in respect to the Church when completed?
(11) What is the Divine purpose in respect to the world of mankind?
(12) What will be the fate of the finally incorrigible?
(13) What will be the reward or blessings which will come to the world of mankind through obedience to Messiah's Kingdom?
(14) By what steps may a sinner come into vital relationship with Christ and with the Heavenly Father?
(15) After a Christian has been begotten of the Holy Spirit, what is his course, as directed in the Word of God?
(16) Have you turned from sin to serve the living God?
(17) Have you made a full consecration of your life and all your powers and talents to the Lord and His service?
(18) Have you symbolized this consecration by water immersion?
(19) Have you taken the I. B. S. A. [International Bible Students Association] Vow of holiness of life?
(20) Have you read thoroughly and carefully the six volumes of STUDIES IN THE SCRIPTURES?
(21) Have you derived much enlightenment and benefit therefrom?
(22) Do you believe you have a substantial and permanent knowledge of the Bible which will render you more efficient as a servant of the Lord throughout the remainder of your life?

Buildings Used During Early Days in Brooklyn

Bethel Home
122-124 Columbia Heights

Dining room in the Bethel Home

Tabernacle
Offices, literature storage, mailing department, typesetting equipment, and an 800-seat auditorium were located here, at 17 Hicks Street (used from 1909 to 1918)

The auditorium

arrangement. (Luke 12:32-44) They also learned that, like the spirit-anointed ones, they had the responsibility to share the good news with others. (Rev. 22:17) Since they wanted to be earthly subjects of God's Kingdom, that Kingdom should come first in their lives, and they should be zealous in telling others about it. To fit the Bible's description of those who would be preserved through the great tribulation into God's new world, they must be persons who "keep on crying with a loud voice, saying: 'Salvation we owe to our God, who is seated on the throne, and to the Lamb.'" (Rev. 7:10, 14) In 1937, as their numbers began to grow and their zeal for the Lord became manifest, they were also invited to help carry the load of responsibility in congregation oversight.

However, they were reminded that the organization is Jehovah's, not that of any man. There was to be no division between the remnant of the spirit-anointed ones and those of the great crowd of other sheep. They

Early Factories

Bethel family members who worked at the Myrtle Avenue factory in 1920 (right)

35 Myrtle Avenue (1920-22)

18 Concord Street (1922-27)

117 Adams Street (1927-   )

were to work together as brothers and sisters in Jehovah's service. As Jesus had said, "I have other sheep, which are not of this fold; those also I must bring, and they will listen to my voice, and they will become one flock, one shepherd." (John 10:16) The reality of this was becoming evident.

Amazing developments had taken place in the organization in a relatively short period of time. But was there more that needed to be done so that the affairs of the congregations would be conducted in full harmony with Jehovah's ways as set out in his inspired Word?

Theocratic Organization

"Theocracy" means "God-rule." Was that the kind of rule that governed the congregations? Did they not only worship Jehovah but also look to him to direct their congregational affairs? Did they conform fully to what he said about these matters in his inspired Word? The two-part article

"Organization" that appeared in *The Watchtower* of June 1 and 15, 1938, pointedly stated: "Jehovah's organization is in no wise democratic. Jehovah is supreme, and his government or organization is strictly theocratic." Yet, in the local congregations of Jehovah's Witnesses at that time, democratic procedures were still employed in selecting most of those charged with oversight of meetings and field service. Further changes were in order.

How were appointments to be made?

But did not Acts 14:23 indicate that elders in the congregations were to be designated to office by a 'stretching forth of the hand,' as in voting? The first of those *Watchtower* articles entitled "Organization" acknowledged that this text had in the past been misunderstood. It was not by a 'stretching forth of the hand' on the part of *all the members of the congregation* that appointments had been made among first-century Christians. Instead, it was shown, *the apostles and those authorized by them* were the ones that 'stretched forth their hands.' This was done not by participating in a congregation vote but by laying their hands on qualified individuals. This was a symbol of confirmation, approval, or appointment.* The early Christian congregations at times made recommendations of qualified men, but final selection or approval was given by the apostles, who had been directly commissioned by Christ, or by those authorized by the apostles. (Acts 6:1-6) *The Watchtower* drew attention to the fact that only in letters to responsible overseers (Timothy and Titus) did the apostle Paul, under the direction of holy spirit, give instructions to appoint overseers. (1 Tim. 3:1-13; 5:22; Titus 1:5) None of the inspired letters addressed to the congregations contained such instructions.

How, then, were current appointments to service in the congregations to be made? The *Watchtower* analysis of theocratic organization showed from the Scriptures that Jehovah appointed Jesus Christ "head of the . . . congregation"; that when Christ as the Master returned, he would entrust his "faithful and discreet slave" with responsibility "over all his belongings"; that this faithful and discreet slave was made up of all those on earth who had been anointed with holy spirit to be joint heirs with Christ and who were unitedly serving under his direction; and that Christ would use that slave class as his agency in providing needed oversight for the congregations. (Col. 1:18; Matt. 24:45-47; 28:18) It would be the duty of the

---

* When the Greek verb *khei·ro·to·ne′o* is defined as meaning only 'to elect by stretching out the hand,' this fails to take note of the later meaning of the word. Thus, *A Greek-English Lexicon,* by Liddell and Scott, edited by Jones and McKenzie and reprinted in 1968, defines the word as meaning *"stretch out the hand,* for the purpose of giving one's vote in the assembly . . . II. c. acc. pers. [with accusative of person], *elect,* prop[erly] *by show of hands* . . . b. later, generally, *appoint,* . . . *appoint to an office* in the Church, [*pre·sby·te′rous*] *Act. Ap.* [Acts of the Apostles] 14.23." That later usage was current in the days of the apostles; the term was used in that sense by the first-century Jewish historian Josephus in *Jewish Antiquities,* Book 6, chapter 4, paragraph 2, and chapter 13, paragraph 9. The grammatical structure itself of Acts 14:23 in the original Greek shows that Paul and Barnabas were the ones who did what was there described.

slave class to apply prayerfully the instructions clearly stated in God's inspired Word, using it to determine who qualified for positions of service.

Since the visible agency that would be used by Christ is the faithful and discreet slave (and the facts of modern-day history already considered show that this "slave" employs the Watch Tower Society as a legal instrument), *The Watchtower* explained that theocratic procedure would require that appointments of service be made through this agency. Even as the congregations in the first century recognized the governing body in Jerusalem, so today the congregations would not prosper spiritually without central supervision.—Acts 15:2-30; 16:4, 5.

To keep matters in proper perspective, however, it was pointed out that when *The Watchtower* referred to "The Society," this meant, not a mere legal instrumentality, but the body of anointed Christians that had formed that legal entity and used it. Thus the expression stood for the faithful and discreet slave with its Governing Body.

Even before the *Watchtower* articles entitled "Organization" were published in 1938, when the congregations in London, New York, Chicago, and Los Angeles had grown to the point that it was advisable to divide them into smaller groups, they had requested that the Society appoint all their servants. The June 15, 1938, issue of *The Watchtower* now invited all the other congregations to take similar action. To that end, the following resolution was suggested:

"We, the company of God's people taken out for his name, and now at . . . . , recognize that God's government is a pure theocracy and that Christ Jesus is at the temple and in full charge and control of the visible organization of Jehovah, as well as the invisible, and that 'THE SOCIETY' is the visible representative of the Lord on earth, and we therefore request 'The Society' to organize this company for service and to appoint the various servants thereof, so that all of us may work together in peace, righteousness, harmony and complete unity. We attach hereto a list of names of persons in this company that to us appear more fully mature and who therefore appear to be best suited to fill the respective positions designated for service."*

Practically all the congregations of Jehovah's Witnesses readily agreed to this. Those few that held back soon ceased to have any share at all in proclaiming the Kingdom and thus ceased to be Jehovah's Witnesses.

---

* Later in the same year, 1938, *Organization Instructions,* published as a four-page folder, gave further details. It explained that the local congregation was to appoint a committee to act on its behalf. That committee was to consider the brothers in the light of the qualifications set out in the Scriptures and make recommendations to the Society. When traveling representatives of the Society visited the congregations, they reviewed the qualifications of local brothers and their faithfulness in caring for their assignments. Their recommendations were also taken into account by the Society in its making of appointments.

Benefits of Theocratic Direction

It is obvious that if teachings, standards of conduct, and organizational or witnessing procedures could be decided on locally, the organization would soon lose its identity and unity. The brothers could easily be divided by social, cultural, and national differences. Theocratic direction, on the other hand, would assure that benefits from spiritual progress would reach out to all the congregations worldwide without hindrance. There would thus come to exist the genuine unity that Jesus prayed would prevail among his true followers, and the evangelizing work that he commanded could be fully accomplished.—John 17:20-22.

However, it has been claimed by some that by advocating this organizational change, J. F. Rutherford simply was endeavoring to gain greater control over the Witnesses and that he used this means to assert his own authority. Was that really the case? There is no doubt that Brother Rutherford was a man of strong convictions. He spoke out forcefully and without compromise for what he believed to be the truth. He could be quite brusque in handling situations when he perceived that people were more concerned about self than they were about the Lord's work. But Brother Rutherford was genuinely humble before God. As Karl Klein, who became a member of the Governing Body in 1974, later wrote: "Brother Rutherford's prayers at morning worship . . . endeared him to me. Though he had such a powerful voice, when addressing God he sounded just like a little boy talking to his daddy. What a fine relationship with Jehovah that revealed!" Brother Rutherford was fully convinced as to the identity of Jehovah's visible organization, and he endeavored to make sure that no man or group of men would be able to hinder brothers locally from receiving the full benefit of the spiritual food and direction that Jehovah was providing for His servants.

Was Rutherford simply trying to gain greater control?

Although Brother Rutherford served for 25 years as president of the Watch Tower Society and devoted all his energy to advancing the work of the organization, he was not the leader of Jehovah's Witnesses, and he did not want to be. At a convention in St. Louis, Missouri, in 1941, shortly before his death, he spoke about the matter of leadership, saying: "I want to let any strangers here know what you think about a man being your leader, so they won't be forgetting. Every time something rises up and starts to grow, they say there is some man a leader who has a great following. If there is any person in this audience who thinks that I, this man standing here, is the leader of Jehovah's witnesses, say Yes." The response was an impressive silence, broken only by an emphatic "No" from several in the audience. The speaker continued: "If you who are here believe that I am just one of the servants of the Lord, and we are working shoulder to shoulder in unity, serving God and serving Christ, say Yes." In unison the assembly roared out a decisive "Yes!" The following month an audience in England responded in exactly the same way.

In some areas the benefits of theocratic organization were felt quickly. Elsewhere, it took longer; those who did not prove to be mature, humble servants were in time removed, and others were appointed.

Nevertheless, as theocratic procedures took hold more fully, Jehovah's Witnesses rejoiced to be experiencing what was foretold at Isaiah 60:17. Using figurative terms to depict the improved conditions that would come to exist among God's servants, Jehovah there says: "Instead of the copper I shall bring in gold, and instead of the iron I shall bring in silver, and instead of the wood, copper, and instead of the stones, iron; and I will appoint peace as your overseers and righteousness as your task assigners." This is not describing what humans would do but, rather, what God himself would do and the benefits that his servants would receive as they submitted to it. Peace must prevail in their midst. Love of righteousness must be the force impelling them to serve.

From Brazil, Maud Yuille, wife of the branch overseer, wrote to Brother Rutherford: "The article 'Organization' in the June 1 and 15 [1938] *Towers* impels me to express in a few words to you, whose faithful service Jehovah is using, my gratitude to Jehovah for the marvelous arrangement that he has made for his visible organization, as outlined in these two *Watchtowers*. . . . What a relief it is to see the end of 'Home Rule for Happy Hollow', including 'women's rights' and other unscriptural procedure that subjected some souls to local opinions and individual judgment, instead of to [Jehovah God and Jesus Christ], thereby bringing reproach upon Jehovah's name. It is true that only 'in the recent past the Society has designated all in the organization as "servants"', yet I observe that for many years previous to that time you have in your correspondence with your brethren acknowledged yourself as 'your brother and servant, by His grace'."

J. F. Rutherford in 1941. The Witnesses knew that he was not their leader

Regarding this organizational adjustment, the branch in the British Isles reported: "The good effect of this was quite amazing. The poetic and prophetic description of this in Isaiah chapter sixty is full of beauty but not overdrawn. Everyone in the truth was talking about it. It was the main topic of conversation. A general sense of invigoration prevailed—a readiness to press a directed battle. As world tension increased, joy in theocratic rule abounded."

Traveling Overseers Strengthen the Congregations

Organizational ties were further fortified as a result of the service of traveling overseers. In the first century, the apostle Paul outstandingly engaged in such activity. At times, such men as Barnabas, Timothy, and Titus also shared. (Acts 15:36; Phil. 2:19, 20; Titus 1:4, 5) They were all zealous evangelizers. In addition, they encouraged the congregations by their discourses. When issues arose that could affect the unity of the congregations, these were submitted to the central governing body. Then, "as they traveled on through the cities," those entrusted with the responsibility "would deliver to those there for observance the decrees that had been decided upon by the apostles and older men who were in Jerusalem." The result? "The congregations continued to be made firm in the faith and to increase in number from day to day."—Acts 15:1–16:5; 2 Cor. 11:28.

Already in the 1870's, Brother Russell was visiting the groups of Bible Students—the twos and the threes as well as larger groups—to upbuild them spiritually. A few other brothers shared in the 1880's. Then, in 1894, arrangements were made for the Society to have well-qualified speakers travel more regularly to help the Bible Students to grow in knowledge and appreciation for the truth and to draw them closer together.

Keeping in touch with the twos and threes as well as larger groups

If possible, the speaker would spend a day or perhaps several days with a group, giving one or two public discourses and then visiting smaller groups and individuals for discussion of some of the deeper things of God's Word. An effort was made to have each group in the United States and Canada visited twice a year, though not usually by the same brother. In selecting these traveling speakers, emphasis was placed on meekness, humility, and clear understanding of the truth as well as loyal adherence to it and ability to teach it with clarity. Theirs was by no means a paid ministry. They were simply provided with food and lodging by the local brothers, and to the extent necessary, the Society helped them with travel expenses. They came to be known as pilgrims.

Many of these traveling representatives of the Society were dearly loved by those whom they served. A. H. Macmillan, a Canadian, is remembered as a brother to whom God's Word proved to be "like a burning fire." (Jer. 20:9) He just had to talk about it, and he did, speaking to audiences not only in Canada but also in many parts of the United States and in other lands. William Hersee, another pilgrim, is fondly remembered because of the special attention that he gave to young folks. His prayers also made a lasting impression because they reflected a depth of spirituality that touched the hearts of young and old alike.

Travel was not easy for the pilgrims in the early days. To serve the group near Klamath Falls, Oregon, for example, Edward Brenisen journeyed first by train, then overnight by stagecoach, and finally by bone-

Development of the Organization Structure

jarring buckboard wagon out into the mountains to the farm where they would be meeting. Early in the morning, the day after their meeting, a brother provided a horse for him to ride some 60 miles to the nearest railroad station so that he could travel to his next assignment. It was a strenuous life, but good results came from the efforts of the pilgrims. Jehovah's people were strengthened, unified in their understanding of God's Word, and drawn closer together even though widely dispersed geographically.

In 1926, Brother Rutherford began to implement arrangements that changed the work of the pilgrims from that of simply traveling speakers into that of traveling supervisors and promoters of field service by the congregations. To emphasize their new responsibilities, in 1928 they were called regional service directors. They worked right along with the local brothers, giving them personal instruction in the field service. At this time it was possible for them to reach each congregation in the United States and in some other lands about once a year, while also keeping in touch with individuals and small groups that had not yet been organized for service.

New responsibilities for traveling overseers

During the years that followed, the work of traveling overseers underwent various modifications.* It was greatly intensified in 1938 when all the servants in the congregations were appointed theocratically. Visits to the congregations at regular intervals during the next few years afforded opportunity to provide personal training to each of the appointed servants and increased help in the field service for everyone. In 1942, before traveling overseers were again sent out to the congregations, they were given some intensive schooling; as a result, their work was carried out with greater uniformity. Their visits were quite brief (one to three days, depending on the size of the congregation). During that time they checked the congregation records, met with all the servants to offer any needed counsel, gave one or more talks to the congregation, and took the lead in field service. In 1946 the visits were lengthened to one week for each congregation.

This arrangement for visits to the congregations was supplemented in 1938 by the service of the regional servant in a new role. He covered a larger area, periodically spending a week with each of the brothers who were traveling in a zone (circuit) to visit the congregations. During his visit he

---

* From 1894 to 1927, traveling speakers sent out by the Society were known first as Tower Tract Society representatives, then as pilgrims. From 1928 to 1936, with increased emphasis on field service, they were called regional *service directors*. Starting with July 1936, to emphasize their proper relationship to the local brothers, they became known as regional *servants*. From 1938 to 1941, zone servants were assigned to work with a limited number of congregations on a rotation basis, thus getting back to the same groups at regular intervals. After an interruption of about a year, this service was revived in 1942 with servants to the brethren. In 1948 the term circuit servant was adopted; now, circuit *overseer*.

From 1938 through 1941, regional servants, in a new role, regularly served local assemblies, where Witnesses from a limited area (a zone) met for a special program. When this work was revived in 1946, these traveling overseers were known as *district* servants; now, district *overseers*.

Traveling Overseers
A Few of the Thousands Who Have Served

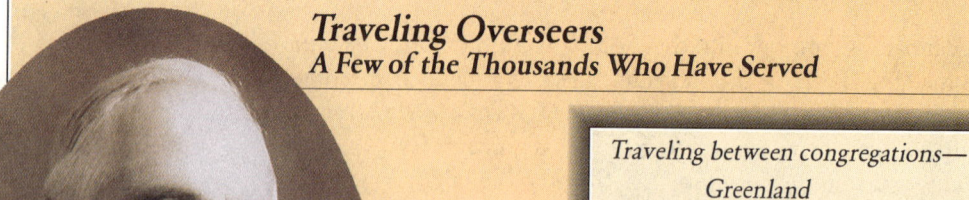

Canada, 1905-33

Traveling between congregations—
Greenland   Venezuela

England, 1920-32

Mobile accommodations in Namibia

Finland, 1921-26, 1947-70

United States, 1907-15

Lesotho

Mexico

Peru

Sierra Leone

Sharing with local Witnesses in field service in Japan

Providing practical counsel to pioneers in Hawaii

Meeting with local elders in Germany

Instructing a congregation in France

served on the program of an assembly that was attended by all the congregations in that zone.* This arrangement was a great stimulus to the brothers and provided regular opportunity for baptism of new disciples.

"Someone Who Loves the Service"

Among those who shared in this service starting in 1936 was John Booth, who, in 1974, became a member of the Governing Body. When being interviewed as a potential traveling supervisor, he was told: "Eloquent speakers are not what is needed, just someone who loves the service and will take the lead in it and will talk about service at the meetings." Brother Booth had that love for Jehovah's service, as evidenced by his zealous pioneer service since 1928, and he stirred up a zeal for evangelizing in others by both example and words of encouragement.

The first congregation that he visited, in March 1936, was in Easton, Pennsylvania. He later wrote: "I would usually arrive at a place in time for field service in the morning, have a meeting with the servants of the company in the early evening and afterward another with the whole company. Usually I would spend just two days with a company and only one day with a smaller group, at times visiting six such groups a week. I was continually on the move."

Two years later, in 1938, he was assigned, as a regional servant, to care for a zone assembly (now known as circuit assembly) every week. These helped to strengthen the brothers during a time when persecution was becoming intense in some areas. Recalling those days and his varied responsibilities, Brother Booth said: "The very week [in which I was a witness in a court case involving some 60 Witnesses in Indianapolis, Indiana] I was a defendant in another case in Joliet, Illinois, an attorney for a brother in yet another one in Madison, Indiana, and, in addition, had charge of a zone assembly each weekend."

Two years after these zone assemblies were revived in 1946 (now as circuit assemblies), Carey Barber was among those assigned as district servants. He had already been a member of the Bethel family in Brooklyn, New York, for 25 years. His first district covered the entire western part of the United States. At first, travel between assemblies was about 1,000 miles each week. As the number and the size of congregations multiplied, those distances shrank, and numerous circuit as-

John Booth, traveling overseer in the U.S.A. from 1936 to 1941

* This arrangement took effect on October 1, 1938. There was increasing difficulty in arranging for assemblies during the war years, so zone assemblies were suspended late in 1941. Once again, however, in 1946, the arrangement was renewed, and the occasions when a number of congregations met together for special instruction were called circuit assemblies.

Development of the Organization Structure

semblies were often held within a single metropolitan area. After 29 years of experience as a traveling overseer, Brother Barber was invited to return to the world headquarters in 1977 as a member of the Governing Body.

During times of war and of intense persecution, traveling overseers frequently risked their freedom and their lives to care for the spiritual well-being of their brothers. During the time of the Nazi occupation of Belgium, André Wozniak continued to visit the congregations and helped to supply them with literature. The Gestapo were frequently hot on his heels but never succeeded in seizing him.

In Rhodesia (now known as Zimbabwe) in the late 1970's, people lived in fear, and travel was curtailed during a period of internal war. But traveling overseers of Jehovah's Witnesses, as loving shepherds and overseers, proved to be "like a hiding place from the wind" to their brothers. (Isa. 32:2) Some would walk for days through bush country, traveling up and down mountains, crossing dangerous rivers, sleeping at night in the open—all in order to reach isolated congregations and publishers, to encourage them to remain firm in the faith. Among these was Isaiah Makore, who narrowly escaped when bullets whistled over his head during a battle between government soldiers and "freedom fighters."

Other traveling overseers have for many years served the organization on an international basis. The presidents of the Watch Tower Society have frequently traveled to other lands to give attention to organizational needs and to speak at conventions. Such visits have done much to keep Jehovah's Witnesses everywhere keenly aware of their international brotherhood. Brother Knorr especially pursued this activity on a regular basis, visiting each branch and missionary home. As the organization grew, the world was divided into ten international zones, and beginning on January 1, 1956, qualified brothers, under the direction of the president, started to assist with this service so that it could be given regular attention. Those zone visits, now carried on under the direction of the Service Committee of the Governing Body, continue to contribute to the global unity and forward movement of the entire organization.

Still other significant developments have contributed to the present organization structure.

Further Theocratic Alignment

In the midst of World War II, Joseph F. Rutherford died, on January 8, 1942, and Nathan H. Knorr became the third president of the Watch

Carey Barber, whose district included a vast part of the United States

Brother Knorr regularly visited each branch and missionary home

Tower Society. The organization was under heavy pressure because of bans imposed on its activity in many lands, mob violence under the guise of patriotism, and the arrest of Witnesses as they distributed Bible literature in their public ministry. Would a change of administration result in a slowing down of the work at such a critical time? The brothers caring for administrative matters looked to Jehovah for his direction and blessing. In harmony with their desire for divine guidance, they reexamined the organization structure itself to see whether there were any areas where there could be closer conformity to Jehovah's ways.

Then, in 1944, a service assembly was held in Pittsburgh, Pennsylvania, in connection with the Watch Tower Society's annual meeting. On September 30, prior to that annual meeting, a series of highly significant talks were given on what the Scriptures say as to the organization of Jehovah's servants.* Attention was focused on the Governing Body. On that occasion it was emphasized that theocratic principle must apply to all the agencies used by the faithful and discreet slave class. It was explained that the legal corporation did not have as members all the "consecrated" people of God. It merely represented them, acting as a legal agency on their behalf. However, inasmuch as the Society was the publishing agent used to provide Jehovah's Witnesses with literature that contained spiritual enlightenment, the Governing Body was logically and of necessity closely associated with the officers and directors of that legal Society. Were theocratic principles being fully applied in its affairs?

The Society's charter set out a shareholder arrangement in which each aggregate contribution of $10 (U.S.) entitled the contributor to a vote in connection with selection of members of the board of directors and officers of the Society. Perhaps it seemed that such contributions gave evidence of genuine interest in the work of the organization. However, this arrangement presented problems. Brother Knorr, the Society's president, explained: "From the provisions of the Society's charter, it would seem that the being a part of the governing body was dependent upon the contributions to the legal Society. But according to the will of God this could not be so among his true chosen people."

It was a fact that Charles Taze Russell, who for the Society's first 32

---

* The substance of these talks is found in the October 15 and November 1, 1944, issues of *The Watchtower*.

years was foremost in the governing body, was financially, physically, and mentally the greatest contributor to the Society. But it was not a monetary contribution that determined how the Lord used him. It was his complete dedication, his tireless zeal, his uncompromising stand for God's Kingdom, and his unbreakable loyalty and faithfulness that marked him in God's sight as suitable for the service. With respect to the theocratic organization, the rule applies: "God has set the members in the body, each one of them, just as he pleased." (1 Cor. 12:18) "However," Brother Knorr explained, "inasmuch as the charter of the Society provided for voting shares to be issued to contributors of funds to the Society's work, it tended to bedim or encroach upon this Theocratic principle with respect to the governing body; and it also tended to endanger it or create hindrances for it."

Hence, at the business meeting of all shareholder-voters of the Society on October 2, 1944, it was unanimously voted that the Society's charter be revised and be brought into closer harmony with theocratic principles. Membership would not now be unlimited as to number but would be between 300 and 500, all of whom would be men chosen by the board of directors, not on the basis of monetary contributions, but because they were mature, active, faithful Witnesses of Jehovah who were serving full-time in the work of the organization or were active ministers of congregations of Jehovah's Witnesses. These members would vote for the board of directors, and the board of directors would then select its officers. These new arrangements went into effect the following year, on October 1, 1945. What a protection this has proved to be in an era when hostile elements have frequently manipulated business affairs so as to take control of corporations and then restructure them to suit their own aims!

Jehovah's blessing on these forward strides in conforming to theocratic principles has been manifest. Despite the extreme pressure brought upon the organization during World War II, the number of Kingdom proclaimers continued to grow. Without letup, they vigorously continued to witness about God's Kingdom. From 1939 to 1946, there was an amazing increase of

---

Early Legal Corporations

Zion's Watch Tower Tract Society. First formed in 1881 and then legally incorporated in the state of Pennsylvania on December 15, 1884. In 1896 its name was changed to **Watch Tower Bible and Tract Society.** Since 1955 it has been known as **Watch Tower Bible and Tract Society of Pennsylvania.**

Peoples Pulpit Association. Formed in 1909 in connection with the Society's moving of its principal offices to Brooklyn, New York. In 1939 the name was changed to **Watchtower Bible and Tract Society, Inc.** Since 1956 it has been known as **Watchtower Bible and Tract Society of New York, Inc.**

International Bible Students Association. Incorporated in London, England, on June 30, 1914.

In order to meet legal requirements, other corporations have been formed by Jehovah's Witnesses in many communities and lands. However, Jehovah's Witnesses are not divided up into national or regional organizations. They are a united global brotherhood.

157 percent in the ranks of Jehovah's Witnesses, and they reached out to six more lands with the good news. During the next 25 years, the number of active Witnesses grew by nearly another 800 percent, and they reported regular activity in an additional 86 lands.

Specialized Training for Overseers

Some outside observers viewed it as inevitable that when the organization became larger, its standards would be relaxed. But, in contrast, the Bible foretold that righteousness and peace would prevail among Jehovah's servants. (Isa. 60:17) That would require careful and ongoing education of responsible overseers in God's Word, a clear understanding of his judicial standards, and a consistent application of those standards. Such education has been provided. A thorough study of God's righteous requirements has been progressively provided in *The Watchtower,* and this material has been systematically studied by every congregation of Jehovah's Witnesses worldwide. But, in addition to that, overseers of the flock have been given much added instruction.

Principal overseers of the Society's branches have been brought together for special training at the time of international conventions. From 1961 through 1965, specially designed school courses, eight to ten months in length, were conducted for them in New York. From 1977 into 1980, there was another series of special five-week courses for them. Their training included verse-by-verse study of all the books of the Bible as well as consideration of organizational details and ways in which to further the preaching of the good news. There are no nationalistic divisions among Je-

Principal overseers of the Society's branches have been brought together for special training (New York, 1958)

The Kingdom Ministry School has provided valuable instruction for overseers around the globe

hovah's Witnesses. No matter where they live, they adhere to the same high Bible standards and believe and teach the same things.

Circuit and district overseers have also been given special attention. Many of them have attended the Watchtower Bible School of Gilead or one of its Extension Schools. Periodically, they are also brought together at the Society's branch offices, or they meet at other convenient locations, for seminars of a few days or a week.

In 1959 another outstanding provision went into operation. This was the Kingdom Ministry School, attended by circuit and district overseers as well as by congregation overseers. It began as a full-month study course. After being used for a year in the United States, the material for the course was translated into other languages and was progressively used around the globe. Since it was not possible for all the overseers to arrange to be away from their secular work for a full month, a two-week version of the course was used starting in 1966.

This school was not a seminary in which men were being trained in preparation for ordination. Those who attended were already ordained ministers. Many of them had been overseers and shepherds of the flock for decades. Their course of study was an opportunity to discuss in detail the instructions from God's Word regarding their work. Great emphasis was laid on the importance of the field ministry and how to do it effectively. Because of changing moral standards in the world, considerable time was also devoted to discussion of upholding Bible standards of morality. This course has been followed up in recent times by seminars every two or three

Kingdom Ministry School at a refugee camp in Thailand, 1978; in the Philippines, 1966 (upper left)

Organization instructions have been progressively published (first in English, then in other languages) to coordinate the activity of the Witnesses and to inform all concerning the provisions made to assist them in their ministry

years, as well as by helpful meetings conducted by traveling overseers with local elders several times each year. These afford opportunity to give special attention to current needs. They are a safeguard against any drifting away from Bible standards, and they contribute toward uniform handling of situations in all the congregations.

Jehovah's Witnesses take to heart the admonition at 1 Corinthians 1:10: "I exhort you, brothers, through the name of our Lord Jesus Christ that you should all speak in agreement, and that there should not be divisions among you, but that you may be fitly united in the same mind and in the same line of thought." This is not a forced conformity; it results from education in God's ways as recorded in the Bible. Jehovah's Witnesses delight in God's ways and his purpose. If any cease to take pleasure in living according to Bible standards, they are free to leave the organization. But if any start to preach other beliefs or disregard Bible morality, overseers take action to safeguard the flock. The organization applies the Bible counsel: "Keep your eye on those who cause divisions and occasions for stumbling contrary to the teaching that you have learned, and avoid them."—Rom. 16:17; 1 Cor. 5:9-13.

The Bible foretold that God would cause just such a climate to exist among his servants, one in which righteousness would prevail and bear peaceful fruitage. (Isa. 32:1, 2, 17, 18) Those conditions strongly appeal to people who love what is right.

How many of such lovers of righteousness will be gathered before the end of the old system? Jehovah's Witnesses do not know. But Jehovah knows what his work will require, and in his own time and his own way he sees that his organization is equipped to care for it.

Gearing Up for Explosive Growth

When research was being done under the supervision of the Governing Body in preparation of the reference work *Aid to Bible Understanding,* attention was once more directed to the way in which the first-century Christian congregation was organized. A careful study was made of such Biblical terms as "older man," "overseer," and "minister." Could the modern-day organization of Jehovah's Witnesses conform more fully to the pattern that had been preserved in the Scriptures as a guide?

Jehovah's servants were determined to continue to yield to divine direction. At a series of conventions held in 1971, attention was directed to the governing arrangements of the early Christian congregation. It was pointed out that the expression *pre·sby'te·ros* (older man, elder), as used in the Bible, was not limited to elderly persons, nor did it apply to all in the congregations who were spiritually mature. It was especially used in an official sense with reference to overseers of the congregations. (Acts 11:30; 1 Tim. 5:17; 1 Pet. 5:1-3) These received their positions by appointment, in harmony with requirements that came to be part of the inspired Scriptures. (Acts 14:23; 1 Tim. 3:1-7; Titus 1:5-9) Where enough qualified men were available, there was more than one elder in the congregation. (Acts 20:17; Phil. 1:1) These made up "the body of older men," all of whom had the same official status, and not one of whom was the most prominent or powerful member in the congregation. (1 Tim. 4:14) To assist the elders, it was explained, there were also appointed "ministerial servants," in accord with the requirements set out by the apostle Paul. —1 Tim. 3:8-10, 12, 13.

Arrangements were promptly put into operation to bring the organization into closer conformity to this Biblical pattern. These began with the Governing Body itself. Its membership was enlarged beyond the seven who, as members of the board of directors of the Watch Tower Bible and Tract Society of Pennsylvania, had been serving as a governing body for Jehovah's Witnesses. No fixed number of members for the Governing Body was set. In 1971, there were 11; for a few years, there were as many as 18; in 1992, there were 12. All of them are men anointed of God as joint heirs with Jesus Christ. The 12 serving as members of the Governing Body in 1992 had among them at that time a record of over 728 years of full-time service as ministers of Jehovah God.

It was determined on September 6, 1971, that the chairmanship at meetings of the Governing Body should rotate annually according to the alphabetical arrangement of the family names of its members. This actually went

An enlarged Governing Body with rotating chairmanship

into effect on October 1. Governing Body members also took turns, on a weekly basis, in presiding at morning worship and the *Watchtower* Study for members of the headquarters staff.* This arrangement went into effect on September 13, 1971, when Frederick W. Franz led the program of morning worship at the Society's headquarters in Brooklyn, New York.

During the following year, preparation was made for adjustments in the oversight of the congregations. No longer would there be just one congregation servant assisted by a specified number of other servants. Men who were Scripturally qualified would be appointed to serve as elders. Others, who met the Bible's requirements, would be appointed to be ministerial servants. This opened the way for a greater number to share in congregation responsibilities and thus to gain valuable experience. None of Jehovah's Witnesses had any idea then that the number of congregations would increase by 156 percent during the next 21 years, reaching a total of 69,558 in 1992. But the Head of the congregation, the Lord Jesus Christ, evidently was making preparation for what was to come.

In the early 1970's, careful thought was given to further reorganization of the Governing Body. Ever since the incorporation of the Watch Tower Society in 1884, publishing of literature, supervision of the global evangelizing work, and arrangements for schools and conventions had been cared for under the direction of the office of the president of the Watch Tower Bible and Tract Society. But after careful analysis and discussion of details over a period of many months, a new arrangement was unanimously adopted on December 4, 1975. Six committees of the Governing Body were formed.

The *Chairman's Committee* (made up of the current chairman of the Governing Body, the preceding chairman, and the one next in line to be chairman) receives reports on major emergencies, disasters, and campaigns of persecution, and it sees that these are handled promptly with the Governing Body. The *Writing Committee* supervises the putting of spiritual food into written, recorded, and video form for Jehovah's Witnesses and for distribution to the public, and it oversees translation work into hundreds of languages. The *Teaching Committee's* responsibility is to supervise schools and assemblies, also district and international conventions, for Jehovah's people, as well as Bethel family instruction and the outlining of material to be used for such purposes. The *Service Committee* supervises all areas of the evangelizing work, including the activity of congregations

---

'Like the Primitive Christian Community'

The religious publication "Interpretation" stated in July 1956: "In their organization and witnessing work, they [Jehovah's Witnesses] come as close as any group to approximating the primitive Christian community.... Few other groups make as extensive a use of Scripture in their messages, both oral and written, as they do."

---

* Later on, they selected other members of the Bethel family to share in caring for those assignments.

and traveling overseers. The printing, publishing, and shipping of literature as well as the operation of factories and the handling of legal and business matters are all supervised by the *Publishing Committee*. And the *Personnel Committee* has oversight of arrangements for personal and spiritual assistance to members of Bethel families and is responsible for inviting new members to serve in the Bethel families around the world.

Additional helpful committees are assigned to oversee the factories, the Bethel homes, and the farms associated with the world headquarters. On these committees the Governing Body makes liberal use of the abilities of members of the "great crowd."—Rev. 7:9, 15.

Adjustments were also made in the oversight of the Society's branches. Since February 1, 1976, each branch has been supervised by a committee of three or more members, depending on needs and the size of the branch. These work under the direction of the Governing Body in caring for the Kingdom work in their area.

In 1992, further assistance was provided for the Governing Body when a number of helpers, mainly from among the great crowd, were assigned to share in the meetings and work of the Writing, Teaching, Service, Publishing, and Personnel committees.*

This spreading out of responsibility has proved to be very beneficial. Along with adjustments already made in the congregations, it has helped to move out of the way any obstacle that might sidetrack individuals from appreciating that Christ is the Head of the congregation. It has proved to be most advantageous to have a number of brothers taking counsel together on matters affecting the Kingdom work. Additionally, this reorganization has made it possible to provide needed supervision in the many areas where it has been urgently needed during an era that has seen organizational growth of truly explosive proportions. Long ago, Jehovah foretold through the prophet Isaiah: "The little one himself will become a thousand, and the small one a mighty nation. I myself, Jehovah, shall speed it up in its own time." (Isa. 60:22) Not only has he speeded it up but he has also provided the needed direction so that his visible organization would be able to care for it.

Needed supervision during an era of explosive growth

The immediate interest of Jehovah's Witnesses is in the work that God has given them to do during these final days of the old world, and they are well organized to accomplish it. Jehovah's Witnesses see unmistakable evidence that this organization is not of men but of God and that God's own Son, Jesus Christ, is directing it. As ruling King, Jesus will safeguard his faithful subjects through the coming great tribulation and make sure that they are effectively organized for accomplishing God's will during the Millennium to come.

---

* *The Watchtower*, April 15, 1992, pp. 7-17, 31.

CHAPTER 16

MEETINGS
FOR WORSHIP, INSTRUCTION, AND ENCOURAGEMENT

CONGREGATION meetings are an important part of the activity of Jehovah's Witnesses. Even when circumstances make it very difficult, they endeavor to attend their meetings regularly, in harmony with the Bible's exhortation: "Let us consider one another to incite to love and fine works, not forsaking the gathering of ourselves together, as some have the custom, but encouraging one another, and all the more so as you behold the day drawing near." (Heb. 10:24, 25) Where possible, each congregation holds meetings three times a week, for a total of 4 hours and 45 minutes. However, the nature of the meetings, as well as their frequency, has varied according to what has been needed at the time.

In the first century, manifestations of the miraculous gifts of the spirit were a prominent feature of Christian meetings. Why? Because by means of these gifts, God bore witness to the fact that he was no longer using the Jewish religious system but that his spirit was now on the newly formed Christian congregation. (Acts 2:1-21; Heb. 2:2-4) At the meetings of early Christians, prayers were offered, praises to God were sung, and emphasis was placed on prophesying (that is, conveying revelations of the divine will and purpose) and imparting instruction that would upbuild those who heard it. Those Christians lived at a time when there were marvelous developments in connection with God's purpose. They needed to understand these and know how to work in harmony with them. However, the way in which some of them handled matters at their meetings was not balanced, and as the Bible shows, counsel was needed so that things would be done in the most beneficial way.—1 Cor. 14:1-40.

Were the features that characterized the meetings of those early Christians also evident when the Bible Students met together in the 1870's and thereafter?

Filling Spiritual Needs of Early Bible Students

Charles Taze Russell and a small group of associates in and around Allegheny, Pennsylvania, formed a class for Bible study in 1870. As a result of their meetings, they gradually grew in love for God and his Word and progressively came to know what the Bible itself teaches. There was no miraculous speaking in tongues at these meetings. Why not? Such miraculous gifts had accomplished their objective in the first century, and as the Bible foretold, they had ceased. "The next step of progress," Brother Russell explained, "was the manifestation of the *fruits* of the Spirit, as St. Paul most clearly points out." (1 Cor. 13:4-10) Furthermore, as also in the first century, there was urgent evangelizing work to do, and for this they needed to be encouraged. (Heb. 10:24, 25) Before long, they were having two regular meetings each week.

Brother Russell realized that it was important for Jehovah's servants to be a unified people, no matter where they might be scattered around the globe. So, in 1879, shortly after the *Watch Tower* began to be published, its readers were invited to make request for Brother Russell or one of his associates to visit them. A clearly stated stipulation was "No charge made nor money taken." After a number of requests came in, Brother Russell set out on a month-long trip that took him as far as Lynn, Massachusetts, with meetings for four to six hours a day at each stop. The subject featured was "Things Pertaining to the Kingdom of God."

Early in 1881, Brother Russell urged *Watch Tower* readers who as yet had no regular meetings in their area: "Establish one in your own home with your own family, or even a few that may be interested. Read, study, praise and worship together, and where two or three are met in His name, the Lord will be in your midst—your teacher. Such was the character of some of the meetings of the church in the days of the Apostles. (See Philemon, 2)."

The program of meetings developed gradually. Suggestions were offered, but it was left up to each local group to decide what was best for their circumstances. A speaker might occasionally deliver a discourse, but greater emphasis was given to meetings in which everyone could freely participate. Some classes of Bible Students did not at first make much use of the Society's publications at their meetings, but traveling ministers, the pilgrims, helped them to see the value of doing so.

Meetings that called for personal participation

After some of the volumes of *Millennial Dawn* had been published, these began to be used as a basis for study. In 1895 the study groups came to be known as Dawn Circles for Bible Study.* Some in Norway later referred to them as "reading and conversation meetings," adding: "Extracts from Brother Russell's books were read aloud, and when

---

* Later these meetings were called Berean Circles for Bible Study, in imitation of the first-century Beroeans who were commended for "carefully examining the Scriptures."—Acts 17:11.

persons had comments or questions, they raised their hands." Brother Russell recommended that at such studies participants make use of a variety of translations of the Scriptures, marginal references in the Bible, and Bible concordances. The studies were often held with groups of moderate size, in a private home, on an evening convenient to the group. These were forerunners of the present-day Congregation Book Study.

Brother Russell realized that more was needed than just study of doctrinal matters. There must also be expressions of devotion so that people's hearts would be moved by appreciation of God's love and by a desire to honor and serve him. The classes were urged to arrange a special meeting for this purpose once a week. These were sometimes referred to as "Cottage Meetings" because they were held in private homes. The program included prayers, hymns of praise, and testimonies related by those in attendance.* These testimonies were sometimes encouraging experiences; included, too, were the trials, difficulties, and perplexities confronted during recent days. In some places these meetings fell considerably short of their objective because of excessive emphasis on self. Kindly suggestions for improvement were set out in *The Watch Tower*.

Recalling those meetings, Edith Brenisen, the wife of one of the early pilgrims in the United States, said: "It was an evening for meditation upon Jehovah's loving care and for close association with our brothers and sisters. As we listened to some of their experiences we grew to know them better. Observing their faithfulness, seeing how they overcame their difficulties, often helped us in solving some of our own perplexities." In time, however, it became apparent that meetings designed to equip each one to share in the evangelizing work were more beneficial.

The way in which the Sunday meeting was handled in some places was of concern to the brothers. Some classes tried to discuss the Bible verse by verse. But at times the differences of opinion as to meaning were not at all upbuilding. To improve the situation, certain ones in the congregation in Los Angeles, California, developed outlines for *topical* Bible study, with questions and references to be examined by all the class before coming to the meeting. In 1902 the Society made available a Bible containing "Berean Bible Study Helps," including a topical index.# To further simplify matters, starting with the March 1, 1905, *Watch Tower,* outlines for congregation discussion were published, with questions as well as references to the Bible and the Society's publications for research. These continued until

Not merely a mental philosophy but expressions that would move the heart

---

* Because of their content, these meetings were also called Prayer, Praise and Testimony Meetings. In view of the importance of prayer, it was in time recommended that once every three months the meeting be simply a prayer service, including hymns but no experiences.

In 1907 the Berean study helps were revised, greatly enlarged, and updated. About 300 more pages of helpful material were added in the 1908 printing.

Early Congregations

By 1916, there were some 1,200 groups of Bible Students worldwide

Durban, South Africa, 1915 (top right); British Guiana (Guyana), 1915 (middle right); Trondheim, Norway, 1915 (lower right); Hamilton, Ont., Canada, 1912 (bottom); Ceylon (Sri Lanka), 1915 (lower left); India, 1915 (upper left)

Praising Jehovah in Song

As the ancient Israelites and Jesus himself used songs in worship, so do Jehovah's Witnesses in modern times. (Neh. 12:46; Mark 14:26) While expressing praise to Jehovah and appreciation for his works, such singing has helped to impress Bible truths on both the mind and the heart.

Many collections of songs have been used by Jehovah's Witnesses over the years. Words have been updated in harmony with progressive understanding of God's Word.

1879: "Songs of the Bride"
(*144 hymns expressing the desires and hopes of Christ's bride*)

1890: "Poems and Hymns of Millennial Dawn"
(*151 poems and 333 hymns, published without music. Most were the works of well-known writers*)

1896: "Watch Tower" of February 1 was devoted to "Zion's Glad Songs of the Morning"
(*Words for 11 songs, with music; lyrics written by Bible Students*)

1900: "Zion's Glad Songs"
(*82 songs, many of them written by one Bible Student; to supplement the earlier collection*)

1905: "Hymns of the Millennial Dawn"
(*The 333 songs published in 1890, but with music*)

1925: "Kingdom Hymns"
(*80 songs, with music, especially for children*)

Karl Klein leading a convention orchestra in 1947

1914, by which time study questions on the volumes of *Studies in the Scriptures* were published for use as a basis for Berean Studies.

All the classes had the same material available, but the number of weekly meetings varied from one to four or more, according to what was arranged locally. In Colombo, Ceylon (now Sri Lanka), beginning in 1914, meetings were actually being held seven days a week.

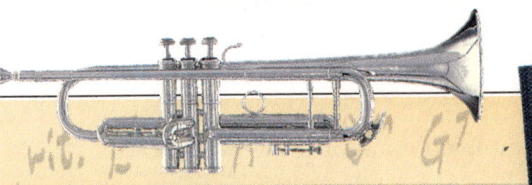

1928: "Songs of Praise to Jehovah"
(337 songs, a mixture of new ones written by the Bible Students and older hymns. In the lyrics, special effort was made to break away from sentiments of false religion and from creature worship)

1944: "Kingdom Service Song Book"
(62 songs. Adapted to Kingdom service needs of the times. No credits were given to authors or composers)

1950: "Songs to Jehovah's Praise"
(91 songs. This songbook had more up-to-date themes and dispensed with archaic language. It was translated into 18 languages)

1966: "Singing and Accompanying Yourselves With Music in Your Hearts"
(119 songs covering every aspect of Christian living and worship. Music known to have originated with secular or false-religious sources was deleted. Orchestral recordings of the entire book were made and were extensively used as accompaniment in congregation meetings. Some vocal selections were also recorded. Starting in 1980, recordings of orchestral arrangements of "Kingdom Melodies" were produced so that at home individuals could enjoy music that would be upbuilding)

1984: "Sing Praises to Jehovah"
(225 Kingdom songs, with words and melodies composed entirely by dedicated servants of Jehovah from all parts of the earth. Phonograph records and audiocassettes were produced to accompany singing)

At their early Cottage Meetings, the Bible Students included songs of praise. Singing also soon became a feature of their conventions. Some sang one of the songs before breakfast, in connection with their morning worship, as was done for many years at the Bible House. Although singing in local congregations was largely dispensed with in about 1938, it was revived again in 1944 and continues to be a significant feature of the congregation meetings and convention programs of Jehovah's Witnesses.

The Bible Students were encouraged to learn to do research, to "prove all things," to express thoughts in their own words. (1 Thess. 5:21, *KJ*) Brother Russell encouraged a full and free discussion of the study material. He also cautioned: "Never forget that the Bible is our Standard and that however God-given our helps may be they are 'helps' and not substitutes for the Bible."

Memorial of Christ's Death

■ *Active Witnesses*
■ *Attendance*

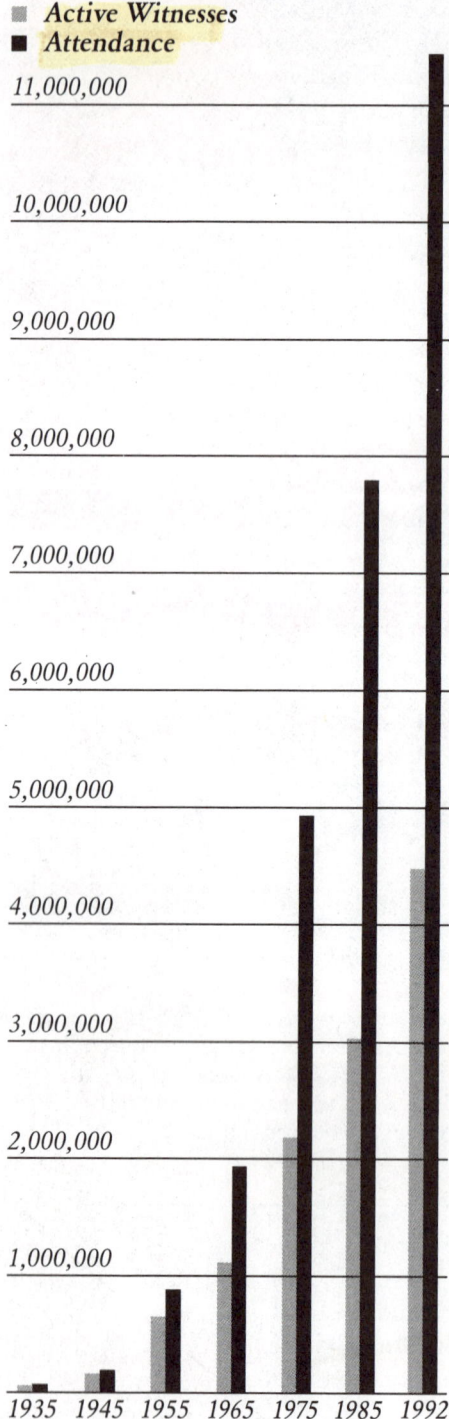

11,000,000
10,000,000
9,000,000
8,000,000
7,000,000
6,000,000
5,000,000
4,000,000
3,000,000
2,000,000
1,000,000

1935 1945 1955 1965 1975 1985 1992

Commemoration of the Lord's Death

Beginning in about 1876, arrangements were made each year by the Bible Students for commemoration of the Lord's death.* At first, the group in Pittsburgh, Pennsylvania, and vicinity met in the home of one of the friends. By 1883, attendance had grown to about a hundred there, and a hired hall was used. To accommodate the large audience expected in Pittsburgh in 1905, the brothers decided to secure the use of the spacious Carnegie Hall.

The Bible Students recognized this to be an annual observance, not something that was to be done every week. The date they kept the observance corresponded to Nisan 14 on the Jewish calendar, the time of Jesus' death. Over the years, there were some refinements in the way in which that date was calculated.# But the principal matter of concern was the significance of the event itself.

Although Bible Students met for this commemoration in groups of varying sizes in many places, any who could join the brothers in Pittsburgh were welcomed. From 1886 to 1893, readers of the *Watch Tower* were especially invited to come to Pittsburgh, if possible, and they did, from various parts of the United States and from Canada. This not only enabled them to celebrate the Memorial together but also helped them to cement ties of spiritual unity. However, as the number of classes grew, both in the United States and in other parts of the world, it was no longer practical to try to meet in one location, and they realized that more good would be accomplished by assembling with fellow believers in the area of one's home.

As the *Watch Tower* pointed out, there were many who professed to be believers in the ransom, and none

---

* This was, at times, referred to as the antitypical Passover, that is, the commemoration of the death of Jesus Christ, who was foreshadowed by the Passover lamb and was thus called "Christ our passover," at 1 Corinthians 5:7. In harmony with 1 Corinthians 11:20 (*KJ*), it was also called the Lord's Supper. It was sometimes termed "Anniversary Supper," thus drawing attention to the fact that it was an annual commemoration.

Compare *Watchtower* issues of March 1891, pages 33-4; March 15, 1907, page 88; February 1, 1935, page 46; and February 1, 1948, pages 41-3.

of these were turned away from the annual commemoration. But the occasion had special significance to those who truly belonged to Christ's "little flock." These are the ones who would share in the heavenly Kingdom. On the night before Jesus' death, when he instituted the Memorial, it was to individuals to whom such a hope was being extended that Christ said: "Keep doing this in remembrance of me."—Luke 12:32; 22:19, 20, 28-30.

Particularly beginning in the 1930's, prospective members of the "great multitude," or "great crowd" of other sheep, began to manifest themselves. (Rev. 7:9, 10, *KJ;* John 10:16) These were at that time referred to as Jonadabs. For the first time, in its issue of February 15, 1938, *The Watchtower* specifically invited them to be present at the Memorial, saying: "After six p.m. on April 15 let each company of the anointed assemble and celebrate the Memorial, their companions the Jonadabs also being present." They did attend, not as partakers, but as observers. Their presence began to swell the number of those on hand at the time of the Memorial of Christ's death. In 1938 the total attendance was 73,420, while those who partook of the emblematic bread and wine numbered 39,225. In the years that followed, those present as observers also began to include large numbers of newly interested persons and others who had not yet become active Witnesses of Jehovah. Thus, in 1992, when the peak number of those sharing in the field ministry was 4,472,787, attendance at the Memorial was 11,431,171, and the number of partakers of the emblems was just 8,683. In some lands the attendance has been as many as five or six times the number of active Witnesses.

Because of their deep regard for the significance of Christ's death, Jehovah's Witnesses commemorate the Memorial even when they are confronted by very difficult circumstances. During the 1970's, when wartime curfews in Rhodesia (now known as Zimbabwe) made it impossible to go out in the evening, the brothers in some areas would all gather in the home of one of Jehovah's Witnesses during the day and then celebrate the Memorial in the evening. Of course, they could not return home after the meeting, so they would stay overnight. The remaining evening hours were used to sing Kingdom songs and relate experiences, which was a source of added refreshment.

In concentration camps during World War II, the Memorial was celebrated, even though doing that could have resulted in severe punishment if the guards found out. When isolated in prison in Communist China from 1958 to 1963 because of his Christian faith, Harold King celebrated the Memorial the best way he could under the circumstances. He later said: "From my prison window I watched the moon

Though isolated in a Chinese prison, Harold King continued to celebrate the Memorial

grow full near the start of spring. I calculated as carefully as I could the date for the celebration." He improvised the needed emblems, making a little wine from black currants and using rice, which is unleavened, for the bread. He also said: "I sang and prayed and gave a regular talk for the occasion, just as would be done in any congregation of Jehovah's people. So I felt that each year I was united with my brothers all over the world on this most important occasion."

Where Young Ones Fit In

During the early years, the publications and the meetings of the Bible Students were not particularly geared to young people. They could attend the meetings, and some of them did so and listened eagerly. But there was no special effort to involve them in what took place. Why not?

The understanding of the brothers at that time was that only a very short time was left until all the members of Christ's bride would be united with him in heavenly glory. The *Watch Tower,* in 1883, explained: "We who are in training for the high calling cannot turn aside from the *special work of this age*—the work of preparing 'the Bride, the Lamb's wife.' The Bride is to make herself ready; and just at the present moment, when the last touches of adornment are being put on preparatory to the wedding, every member's service is required in this all-important, present work."

Parents were strongly urged to shoulder their own God-given responsibility to care for the spiritual instruction of their children. Separate Sunday schools for youths were not encouraged. It was obvious that Christendom's use of Sunday schools had done much harm. Parents who sent their

Juvenile Bible class in Germany, in the early 1930's

In Switzerland, in the mid-1930's, Witness youths published this magazine (below) and staged Bible dramas (as shown below in the center) for large audiences

children to such schools often took the view that this arrangement relieved them of the responsibility to give religious instruction to their children. The children, in turn, because they were not looking to their parents as a primary source of instruction about God, were not motivated to honor their parents and obey them as they should.

However, from 1892 to 1927, the *Watch Tower* did set aside space for comment on the text featured in the "International Sunday School Lessons," which were then popular in many Protestant churches. These texts were for many years selected by F. N. Peloubet, a Congregational clergyman, and his assistants. The *Watch Tower* discussed these texts from the standpoint of the Bible Students' advanced understanding of the Scriptures, free from the creeds of Christendom. It was hoped that in this way the *Watch Tower* would find its way into some of the churches, that the truth would thus be presented, and that some church members would accept it. Of course, the difference was evident, and this angered the Protestant clergy.

The year 1918 came, and the remnant, or remaining ones of the anointed, were still on the earthly scene. The number of children at their meetings had also greatly increased. Often the youngsters had simply been allowed to play while their parents studied. Yet, young people, too, needed to learn to "seek righteousness, seek meekness," if they would be "hid in the day of the LORD's anger." (Zeph. 2:3, *KJ*) So, in 1918 the Society encouraged the congregations to arrange for a juvenile class for children from 8 to 15 years of age. In some places there were even primary classes for those too young to attend the juvenile class. At the same time, parental responsibility toward the children was again emphasized.

This led to other developments. *The Golden Age,* in 1920, carried a feature entitled "Juvenile Bible Study," with questions accompanied by Scripture citations in which the answers could be found. That same year, *The Golden Age ABC* was published; it was an illustrated booklet for use by parents in teaching basic Bible truths and Christian qualities to their youngsters. A book entitled *The Way to Paradise,* written by W. E. Van Amburgh, followed in 1924. It was adapted to "intermediate students of the Bible." For a time it was used at the meetings for younger ones. Additionally, in America, "Junior Witnesses" had their own arrangements for field service. In Switzerland a youth group formed an association called "Jehovah's Youth," for those between 13 and 25 years of age. They had their own secretary's office in Berne, and a special magazine, *Jehovah's Youth,* was edited and printed on the Society's presses there. These youths had their own meetings and even put on Bible dramas, as they did in the Volkshaus in Zurich for an audience of 1,500.

What was taking place, however, was that an organization was developing within the organization of Jehovah's servants. This would not contribute to unity, and it was discontinued in 1936. In April 1938, during a visit to Australia, J. F. Rutherford, the Society's president, found that a class for children was being held apart from the convention for adults. He immediately arranged for all the children to be brought into the main convention, which was greatly to their benefit.

In that same year, *The Watchtower* reviewed the entire matter of separate classes for young folks in the congregation. That study again emphasized the fact that parents are responsible to instruct their own children. (Eph. 6:4; compare Deuteronomy 4:9, 10; Jeremiah 35:6-10.) It also showed that the Bible provides no precedent for segregating young ones by means of junior classes. Instead, they were to be present with their parents to hear God's Word. (Deut. 31:12, 13; Josh. 8:34, 35) When further explanation of study material was needed, this could be given by the parents at home. Furthermore, the articles pointed out that arrangements for such separate classes were actually detracting from the house-to-house preaching of the good news. How so? Because the teachers were staying out of the field service to prepare for these classes and to conduct them. So, all separate classes for youths were discontinued.

All in the family are encouraged to attend meetings together

Right down to the present, it remains the custom among Jehovah's Witnesses for the entire family to attend congregation meetings together. Children are helped by their parents to prepare so that they can participate in appropriate ways. Additionally, a fine array of publications has been provided for parents to use in giving young folks instruction at home. Among these have been the books *Children*, in 1941; *Listening to the Great Teacher*, in 1971; *Your Youth—Getting the Best Out Of It*, in 1976; *My Book of Bible Stories*, in 1978; and *Questions Young People Ask—Answers That Work*, in 1989.

Equipping All to Be Active Evangelizers

Ever since the first issues of the *Watch Tower* were published, its readers have been regularly reminded of the privilege and responsibility of all true Christians to proclaim the good news about God's purpose. The congregation meetings have helped to prepare their hearts and minds for this activity by building up their love for Jehovah and their knowledge of his purpose. Especially, however, following the convention at Cedar Point, Ohio, in 1922, greatly increased emphasis was placed on what was being accomplished in the field service and how to share in it effectively.

The *Bulletin*,* a folder containing information directly related to the

---

* Even before 1900 a pamphlet entitled *Suggestive Hints to Colporteurs* was sent to those who enrolled for this special service. Starting in 1919 the *Bulletin* was published to provide stimulus for the field service, first in distributing *The Golden Age* and later with regard to all the various types of evangelizing activity.

field service, contained a brief testimony, then called a canvass, that was to be memorized and used when witnessing to people. During the greater part of 1923, at the first of each month, as a stimulus to united efforts to advertise the Kingdom, half of the Wednesday-night Prayer, Praise and Testimony Meeting was set aside for testimonies regarding the field service.

At least by 1926, monthly meetings where field service was discussed were called Workers' Meetings. Those who actually participated in such service were usually the ones that attended. At these meetings, methods being used to witness to others were discussed, and plans for future activity were made. By 1928 the Society was urging the congregations to have such meetings each week. In another four years, congregations were beginning to replace the Testimony (or, Declaration) Meeting with what had come to be called the Service Meeting, and the Society encouraged everyone to attend. For over 60 years, this weekly meeting has been held by the congregations. By means of discourses, discussions involving audience participation, demonstrations, and interviews, specific help is provided in connection with all aspects of the Christian ministry.

This type of meeting certainly did not originate in the 20th century. Jesus himself gave detailed instructions to his disciples before sending them out to preach. (Matt. 10:5–11:1; Luke 10: 1-16) Later, they built one another up by gathering to relate experiences they had while engaging in the ministry.—Acts 4: 21-31; 15:3.

As for training in public speaking, in the early years this was not done at the regular congregation meetings. However, at least by 1916, it was suggested that those who felt that they had some potential as public speakers might hold classes *by themselves,* with perhaps an elder present as a moderator to hear them and to offer counsel for improvement in content and delivery of their talks. These gatherings, attended only by males in the congregation, later came to be known as Schools of the Prophets. When reviewing the events of those days, Grant Suiter recalled: "The constructive criticism that I got at the school was nothing compared with that which I received from my father personally after he had attended one of the sessions to hear me try to make a speech." To help those who were trying to make progress, brothers privately compiled and printed a textbook of instructions on speaking, along with outlines for a variety of discourses. In time, however, these Schools of the Prophets were discontinued. To fill the special

"Bulletin" (1919-35), "Director" (1935-36), "Informant" (1936-56), and now "Our Kingdom Ministry" in 100 languages—all have provided regular instructions for united field ministry by Jehovah's Witnesses

Demonstrations at Service Meetings help Witnesses to improve their personal field ministry (Sweden)

need that existed at that time, full attention was being focused on equipping every member of the congregation to share to the full in house-to-house evangelizing.

Was it possible to equip each member of this growing international organization not only to give a brief witness and to offer Bible literature but also to speak effectively and to be a teacher of God's Word? That was the objective of a special school established in each congregation of Jehovah's Witnesses, beginning in 1943. It had already been in operation at the world headquarters of Jehovah's Witnesses since February 1942. Every week, instruction was given, and students delivered talks and were counseled on them. At first, only males gave talks in the school, though the entire congregation was encouraged to attend, to prepare the lessons, and to participate in reviews. In 1959 the sisters were also privileged to enroll, for training in discussing Bible subjects in a one-on-one setting.

Regarding the effect of this school, the Watch Tower Society's branch in South Africa reported: "This very fine arrangement succeeded in a short while in helping many brothers who had imagined they would never be public speakers to become very efficient on the platform and more effective in the field. In all parts of South Africa the brothers welcomed this new provision of Jehovah and put it into operation with enthusiasm. This was done despite great obstacles of language and lack of education on the part of some."

The Theocratic Ministry School continues to be an important meeting in the congregations of Jehovah's Witnesses. Nearly all who are able to do so are enrolled. Young and old, new Witnesses and those with much experience participate. It is an ongoing program of education.

The Public Invited to See and Hear

Jehovah's Witnesses are in no sense a secret society. Their Bible-based beliefs are fully explained in publications that are available to anyone. Additionally, they put forth special effort to invite the public to attend meetings to see and hear for themselves what takes place.

Jesus Christ gave personal instruction to his disciples, but he also spoke in public—along the seashore, on a mountainside, in synagogues, in the temple area in Jerusalem—where the crowds could hear. (Matt. 5:1, 2; 13:1-9; John 18:20) In imitation of this, as early as the 1870's, the Bible Students began to arrange meetings where friends and neighbors and others who might be interested could hear a discourse about God's purpose for humankind.

Special effort was put forth to have these discourses at places that would be convenient for the public. This was known as class extension work. In 1911, congregations that had sufficient talented speakers were encouraged to arrange for some of these to go to surrounding towns and villages to put on meetings in public halls. Where possible, they arranged for a series of six discourses. Following the final one, the speaker inquired as to how many in the audience felt sufficient interest in Bible study to come together regularly. Over 3,000 of such discourses were held the first year.

Young Witness in Kenya gains experience by giving a talk to his father in the Theocratic Ministry School

Starting in 1914, the "Photo-Drama of Creation" was also taken to the public. The brothers charged no admission. Since then, they have used other motion pictures and slide showings. Beginning in the 1920's, extensive use of the radio by the Watch Tower Society enabled people to hear Bible discourses in their own homes. Then, in the 1930's, lectures delivered by J. F. Rutherford were recorded and played at thousands of public gatherings.

By 1945, there was a large number of public speakers who had been trained in the Theocratic Ministry School. In January of that year, a well-coordinated campaign of public meetings was launched. The Society provided outlines for a series of eight timely discourses. Handbills, and sometimes placards, were used for advertising. In addition to using the congregations' regular meeting places, the brothers made special efforts to arrange for these public meetings in territories where no congregation existed. All in the congregations could share—by advertising the meetings, by personally supporting them, as well as by welcoming newcomers and answering their questions. During the first year of this special activity, 18,646 public meetings were put on in the United States, with a total attendance of 917,352. The following year the number of public meetings rose to 28,703 for the American field. And in Canada, where 2,552 of such meetings were arranged in 1945, there were 4,645 the following year.

In the majority of congregations of Jehovah's Witnesses, Public Meetings are now part of the regular schedule of weekly meetings. They are in the form of a discourse during which everyone is encouraged to look up

As of 1992, Bible study material for congregations of Jehovah's Witnesses was being published simultaneously in 66 languages, and more continue to be added

key Scripture texts as these are read and discussed. These meetings are a rich source of spiritual instruction for the congregation and newcomers alike.

People who attend the meetings of Jehovah's Witnesses for the first time are often pleasantly surprised. A prominent politician in Zimbabwe went to a Kingdom Hall to find out what was going on there. He was a man with a violent disposition, and he deliberately went unshaved and with hair uncombed. He expected that the Witnesses would chase him away. Instead, they showed genuine interest in him and encouraged him to have a home Bible study. Now he is a humble and peaceable Christian Witness.

There are millions of persons who, having attended the meetings of Jehovah's Witnesses, have felt moved to say: "God is really among you." —1 Cor. 14:25.

Suitable Places in Which to Meet

In the days of the apostles of Jesus Christ, Christians frequently held their meetings in private homes. In some places they were able to speak in Jewish synagogues. In Ephesus the apostle Paul gave discourses for two years in a school auditorium. (Acts 19:8-10; 1 Cor. 16:19; Philem. 1, 2) Similarly, in the latter part of the 19th century, the Bible Students met in private homes, sometimes spoke in church chapels, and used other halls that could be rented. In a few instances, they later purchased buildings that had formerly been used by other religious groups and made use of these on a regular basis. That was the case with the Brooklyn Tabernacle and the London Tabernacle.

But they neither needed nor wanted ornate buildings for their meetings. A few congregations purchased and renovated suitable structures; others built new halls. After 1935 the name Kingdom Hall gradually came into use to designate these places for congregation meetings. These are usually attractive in appearance but not pretentious. The architecture may vary from place to place, but the purpose of the building is functional.

A Unified Program of Instruction

During the latter part of the 19th century and the early part of the 20th century, spiritual growth and activity varied considerably from one congregation to another. They shared in common certain basic beliefs that set them apart from Christendom. Yet, while some of the brothers deeply appreciated the means by which Jehovah was feeding his people, others were easily swayed by the opinions of individuals who had strong personal views on matters.

Before his death Jesus prayed that his followers would "all be one"—at unity with God and Christ and with one another. (John 17:20, 21) This was not to be a forced unity. It would result from a unified program of education that found response in receptive hearts. As had long ago been foretold: "All your sons will be persons taught by Jehovah, and the peace of your sons will be abundant." (Isa. 54:13) To enjoy that peace in full measure, all needed opportunity to benefit from the progressive instruction that Jehovah was providing through his visible channel of communication.

For many years the Bible Students used the various volumes of *Studies in the Scriptures,* along with the Bible, as a basis for discussion. What they contained was, indeed, spiritual "food at the proper time." (Matt. 24:45) However, continued examination of the Scriptures under the direction of God's spirit made it evident that there was more to learn and that much spiritual cleansing was still needed by Jehovah's servants. (Mal. 3:1-3; Isa. 6:1-8) Furthermore, after the establishment of the Kingdom in 1914, many prophecies were being fulfilled in rapid succession, and these pointed to urgent work in which all true Christians should be engaged. This timely Scriptural information was regularly provided through the columns of *The Watch Tower.*

Realizing that not everyone in the congregations was benefiting from these articles, some of the traveling representatives of the Society recommended to the headquarters office that at regular weekly meetings the congregations all study *The Watch Tower.* That recommendation was passed along to the congregations, and "Berean Questions" for use in study of principal *Watch Tower* articles became a regular feature of the magazine, beginning with the issue of May 15, 1922. Most congregations had such a study one or more times each week, but the extent to which they really studied what was in the magazine varied. In some places, because the conductor had much to say, this study ran for two hours or more.

Unifying the program of spiritual feeding

During the 1930's, however, theocratic organization replaced democratic procedures. This greatly influenced how study of *The Watchtower** was viewed. Greater attention was directed to understanding what was in the study material provided by the Society. Those who had used the meetings as opportunities to air personal views and who resisted the responsibility to share in the field ministry gradually withdrew. With patient help the brothers learned how to confine the study to an hour. As a result, there was greater participation; meetings were more lively. A spirit of genuine unity also came to pervade the congregations, based on a unified spiritual feeding program in which God's Word was the standard for truth.

In 1938, *The Watchtower* was being published in about 20 languages. Everything appeared first in English. It usually was not available in other languages for several months, or perhaps even a year, because of the time

---

* The name *Zion's Watch Tower and Herald of Christ's Presence* was changed, on January 1, 1909, to *The Watch Tower and Herald of Christ's Presence.* As of October 15, 1931, the name became *The Watchtower and Herald of Christ's Presence.*

MEETINGS—FOR WORSHIP, INSTRUCTION, AND ENCOURAGEMENT

required to translate and print it. However, with a change in printing methods, during the 1980's, simultaneous publication of *The Watchtower* was achieved in many languages. By 1992, congregations understanding any of 66 languages were able to study the same material at the same time. Thus the vast majority of Jehovah's Witnesses worldwide partake of the same spiritual food week by week. In all of North and South America, in most of Europe, in a number of lands in the Orient, in many places in Africa, and on a large number of islands around the globe, Jehovah's people enjoy a simultaneous arrangement for spiritual feeding. Together, they are being "fitly united in the same mind and in the same line of thought."—1 Cor. 1:10.

Attendance figures for their congregation meetings indicate that Jehovah's Witnesses take their meetings seriously. In Italy, where there were about 172,000 active Witnesses in 1989, weekly attendance at Kingdom Hall meetings was 220,458. In contrast, a Catholic press agency says that 80 percent of Italians say they are Catholic but that only about 30 percent attend church services with any degree of regularity. Viewed proportionately, the picture is similar in Brazil. In Denmark, as of 1989, the National Church claimed 89.7 percent of the population as members, but only 2 percent were attending church once a week! Among Jehovah's Witnesses in Denmark, weekly attendance figures at that time ran 94.7 percent. In Germany, a poll by the Allensbach Opinion Research Institute in 1989 indicated that 5 percent of Lutherans and 25 percent of Catholics in the Federal Republic attended church regularly. However, at the Kingdom Halls of Jehovah's Witnesses, weekly attendance exceeded the number of Witnesses.

Those in attendance have often put forth great effort to be on hand. In the 1980's, a 70-year-old woman in Kenya was regularly walking six miles and wading through a river to get to the meetings each week. To attend meetings in her own language, a Korean Witness in the United States regularly traveled three hours each way, riding a bus, a train, and a boat, as well as walking. In Suriname, one family with little income spent a full day's wages for bus fare each week in order to get to the meetings. In Argentina, a family regularly traveled 30 miles and spent one fourth of the family's income to attend meetings for Bible study. Where illness completely prevents some from attending congregation meetings, arrangements are often made for them to be tied in by telephone or to hear a tape recording of the program.

Jehovah's Witnesses take seriously the Bible's counsel not to forsake gathering together for spiritual upbuilding. (Heb. 10:24, 25) And it is not only for meetings in their local congregations that they are present. Attendance at conventions is also a highlight of their annual program of events.

The Witnesses take their meetings seriously

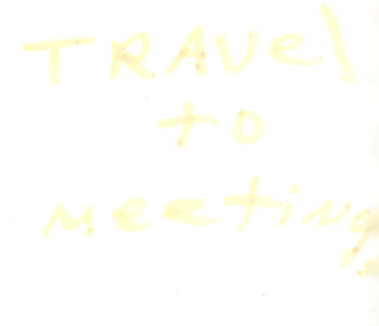

CHAPTER 17

CONVENTIONS
PROOF OF
OUR BROTHERHOOD

CONVENTIONS have become a regular feature of the modern-day organization of Jehovah's Witnesses. But national and international gatherings of worshipers of Jehovah took place long before the 20th century.

Jehovah required all the males in ancient Israel to assemble at Jerusalem for three seasonal festivals each year. Some of the men brought their entire family along. In fact, the Mosaic Law required that every family member —men, women, and little ones—be present on certain occasions. (Ex. 23: 14-17; Deut. 31:10-13; Luke 2:41-43) At first, the attenders were people who lived within the boundaries of Israel. Later, when the Jews became widely dispersed, those in attendance came from many nations. (Acts 2:1, 5-11) They were drawn together not merely because Israel and Abraham were their forefathers but because they recognized Jehovah as their grand heavenly Father. (Isa. 63:16) These festivals were happy occasions. They also helped all who were present to keep their minds on the word of God and not to become so involved in the daily affairs of life that they might forget the more important spiritual matters.

In like manner, the conventions of Jehovah's Witnesses in modern times center on spiritual interests. To sincere observers these conventions give undeniable evidence that the Witnesses are united by strong ties of Christian brotherhood.

Early Conventions of Bible Students

Arrangements for gatherings of Bible Students from various cities and lands developed gradually. Unlike traditional church groups, the Bible Students, by means of their conventions, quickly got to know fellow believers in other places. At first, these conventions were held at Allegheny, Pennsylvania, in connection with the annual commemoration of the Lord's death. In 1891 notice was specifically given that there would be a "convention for Bible study and for celebrating the Lord's Memorial Supper." The following year, the *Watch Tower* carried a prominent heading announcing "BELIEVERS' CONVENTION, AT ALLEGHENY, PA., . . . APRIL 7TH TO 14TH, INCLUSIVE, 1892."

CONVENTIONS—PROOF OF OUR BROTHERHOOD   255

The public in general was not invited to those early conventions. But, in 1892, some 400 persons who had given evidence of faith in the ransom and sincere interest in the Lord's work were present. The program included five days of intensive Bible study and another two days of helpful counsel for the colporteurs.

Said one who was present for the first time for one of these gatherings: "I have been at many Conventions, but never before at one like this, where the will and plan of God are the only and the incessant topic from rising until retiring; in the house, on the street, at meeting, at lunch and everywhere." Regarding the spirit displayed by the delegates, one from Wisconsin, U.S.A., wrote: "I was much impressed by the spirit of love and brotherly kindness manifested on all occasions."

A change in arrangements for the annual convention took place in 1893. In order to take advantage of favorable railroad fares in connection with the Columbian Exposition that summer, the Bible Students gathered in Chicago, Illinois, from August 20 to 24. This was their first convention outside the Pittsburgh area. However, with a view to making the best possible use of time and money for the Lord's work, no further general conventions were held for a few years.

Then, starting in 1898, the Bible Students in various places began to take the initiative locally to arrange for assemblies, to be attended by people in a limited area. In 1900 there were 3 general conventions organized by the Society; but there were also 13 local assemblies in the United States and Canada, most of which were for just one day and were often held in connection with the visit of one of the pilgrims. The number kept growing.

"I was much impressed by the spirit of love and brotherly kindness"

Delegates to the IBSA convention in Winnipeg, Man., Canada, in 1917

Convention trains —all aboard!

By 1909 there were at least 45 local assemblies in North America, in addition to conventions served by Brother Russell on special tours that took him to various parts of the continent. A main portion of the program at one-day assemblies was designed especially to stir interest on the part of the public. Attendance ranged from perhaps a hundred up to several thousand.

On the other hand, general conventions, attended mainly by the Bible Students, emphasized instruction for those fairly well established in the way of the truth. For these conventions, special trains filled with delegates would come from principal cities. Attendance was, on occasion, as high as 4,000, even including a few delegates from Europe. These were times of genuine spiritual refreshment that resulted in increased zeal and love on the part of Jehovah's people. Said one brother at the close of such a convention in 1903: "I would not take a thousand dollars for the good I have received from this Convention;—and I am only a poor man, too."

Pilgrim brothers who might be in the area spoke at the assemblies. Brother Russell also endeavored to attend and serve on the program at local assemblies as well as at larger conventions in the United States and often in Canada. That involved much travel. Most of it was done on weekend trips. But, in 1909, a brother in Chicago hired several railroad cars to transport delegates who traveled with Brother Russell from one convention to another on a tour. In 1911 and 1913, entire trains were chartered by the same brother to take hundreds of delegates on convention tours lasting a month or more and covering the western United States and Canada.

Travel on such a convention train was a memorable experience. In 1913, Malinda Keefer boarded one at Chicago, Illinois. Years later, she said: "It didn't take long to realize we were one big family . . . and the train was our home for a month." As the train pulled out of the station, those who came to see them off sang "God Be With You Till We Meet Again," all the while waving hats and handkerchiefs till the train was out of sight. Sister Keefer added: "At every stop on the trip there were conventions being held

—most were for three days, and we stayed one day with each convention. During these stops Brother Russell gave two talks, one to the friends in the afternoon, and another to the public in the evening on the subject 'Beyond the Grave.'"

In other lands too, the number of assemblies was growing. They were often quite small. About 15 were present for the first one in Norway, in 1905; but it was a beginning. Six years later, when Brother Russell visited Norway, special effort was put forth to invite the public, and the attendance on that occasion was estimated at 1,200. During 1909, when he attended conventions in Scotland, he spoke to about 2,000 in Glasgow and another 2,500 in Edinburgh on the intriguing subject "The Thief in Paradise, the Rich Man in Hell, and Lazarus in Abraham's Bosom."

At the conclusion of the early conventions, the brothers had what they called a love feast, reflecting their feeling of Christian brotherhood. What did this "love feast" include? As an example, the speakers would line up with plates of diced bread, and then the audience would file past, partaking of the bread, shaking hands, and singing "Blest Be the Tie That Binds Our Hearts in Christian Love." Tears of joy often ran down their cheeks as they sang. Later, as their numbers grew, they dispensed with the handshaking and breaking of bread but would conclude with song and prayer and, often, prolonged applause to express their appreciation.

Launching a Global Campaign of Kingdom Proclamation

The first major convention after World War I took place at Cedar Point, Ohio (on Lake Erie, 60 miles west of Cleveland), from September 1 to 8 in 1919. Following Brother Russell's death, some who had been prominently associated with the organization fell away. The brothers underwent severe testing. Earlier in 1919, the Society's president and his associates had been released from their unjust imprisonment. So there was keen anticipation. Although first-day attendance was rather low, later in the day more delegates arrived on special trains. Then the hotels that had offered to accommodate the delegates were swamped. R. J. Martin and A. H. Macmillan (both of whom were included in the group recently released from prison) volunteered to help. They worked at assigning rooms till past midnight, and Brother Rutherford and many of the others had a good time serving as bellhops, carrying luggage and escorting the friends to their rooms. There was an infectious spirit of enthusiasm among them all.

Some 2,500 were expected to attend. However, in every way the convention proved to be more than anticipated. By the second day, the auditorium was already overcrowded and additional halls were put to use. When that did not prove adequate, the sessions were moved outdoors into an area where there was a pleasant grove of trees. About 6,000 Bible Students from the United States and Canada were present.

J. F. Rutherford speaking at Cedar Point, Ohio, in 1919. He urged all to share zealously in announcing God's Kingdom, using "The Golden Age"

For the principal talk on Sunday, at least 1,000 of the public also came, swelling the audience to fully 7,000, whom the speaker addressed in the open air without the aid of any microphone or amplifying system. In that discourse, "The Hope for Distressed Humanity," J. F. Rutherford made it clear that the Messianic Kingdom of God is the solution to mankind's problems, and he also showed that the League of Nations (which was then being brought to birth and which had already been endorsed by the clergy) was in no way a political expression of God's Kingdom. The Sandusky *Register* (a local newspaper) carried an extensive report on that public discourse, as well as a résumé of the activity of the Bible Students. Copies of that paper were sent to newspapers throughout the United States and Canada. But there was much more to the publicity that emanated from this convention.

The real climax of the entire convention was Brother Rutherford's "Address to Co-laborers," which was later published under the title "Announcing the Kingdom." This was directed to the Bible Students themselves. During that speech the significance of the letters GA that had appeared on the convention program and in various locations at the convention site became clear. Announcement was made concerning the coming publication of a new magazine, *The Golden Age,* for use in directing the attention of people to the Messianic Kingdom. After outlining the work to be done, Brother Rutherford said to the audience: "The door of opportunity is opening before you. Enter it quickly. Remember as you go forth in this work you are not soliciting merely as the agent of a magazine, but you are an ambassador of the King of kings and Lord of lords, announcing to the people in this dignified manner the incoming of the Golden Age, the glorious kingdom of our Lord and Master, for which true Christians have hoped and prayed for many centuries." (See Revelation 3:8.) When the speaker asked how many desired to share in the work, the enthusiastic response was inspiring to behold. As one man, the audience of 6,000 rose to their feet. By the following year, more than 10,000 were sharing in the field service. The entire convention had a unifying and invigorating effect on those in attendance.

Three years later, in 1922, another memorable convention was held at Cedar Point. It was a nine-day program, from September 5 to 13. In addition to the delegates from the United States and Canada, some came from Europe. Meetings were conducted in ten languages. The average daily attendance was about 10,000; and for the talk "Millions Now Living Will Never Die," so many of the public were in the audience that the attendance nearly doubled.

The Bible Students did not gather at this convention with the thought that they were planning for work here on earth that would extend for

Convention at Cedar Point in 1922. The call went out: "Advertise the King and Kingdom"

decades into the future. In fact, they said that it might well be their last general convention before "the deliverance of the church . . . into the heavenly phase of the kingdom of God, and indeed into the actual and very presence of our Lord and our God." But however short the time might be, the doing of God's will was their foremost concern. With that in mind, on Friday, September 8, Brother Rutherford delivered the memorable discourse "The Kingdom."

Prior to this, large banners containing the letters ADV had been hung in various parts of the grounds. During the discourse the significance of those letters became evident when the speaker urged: "Be faithful and true witnesses for the Lord. Go forward in the fight until every vestige of Babylon lies desolate. Herald the message far and wide. The world must know that Jehovah is God and that Jesus Christ is King of kings and Lord of lords. This is the day of all days. Behold, the King reigns! You are his publicity agents. Therefore *advertise, advertise, advertise,* the King and his kingdom." At that moment a large banner, 36 feet long, unfolded before the audience. On it was the rousing slogan "Advertise the King and Kingdom." It was a dramatic moment. The audience applauded enthusiastically. Elderly Brother Pfannebecker, in the assembly orchestra, waved his violin above his head and said loudly with his heavy German accent: "Ach, Ya! Und now ve do it, no?" And they did.

Four days later, while the convention was still in session, Brother Rutherford personally shared with other conventioners as they engaged in the work of Kingdom proclamation from house to house in the area within 45 miles of the convention site. It did not end with that. The work of Kingdom proclamation had been given a powerful impetus that would reach around the globe. That year more than 17,000 zealous workers in 58 lands shared in giving the witness. Decades later, George Gangas, who was at that convention and who later became a member of the Governing Body, said regarding that program at Cedar Point: "It was something that was written indelibly in my mind and heart, that will never be forgotten as long as I live."

Milestones in Spiritual Growth

All the conventions have been times of refreshment and instruction in God's Word. But some of them have been remembered for decades as spiritual milestones.

Seven of these occurred, one year after another, from 1922 through 1928, in the United States, Canada, and Britain. One reason for the significance of these conventions was the powerful resolutions that were adopted, all seven of which are listed in the box on the next page. Although the Witnesses were relatively few in number, they distributed as many as 45 million copies of one resolution, and 50 million of several others, in many

George Gangas was at Cedar Point in 1922. For some 70 years since then he has zealously proclaimed God's Kingdom

languages worldwide. Some were broadcast on international radio hookups. Thus an extraordinary witness was given.

Yet another historic convention was held in Columbus, Ohio, in 1931. On Sunday, July 26, after hearing Scriptural argument, the Bible Students adopted a new name—Jehovah's Witnesses. How appropriate! Here is a name that directs primary attention to the Creator himself and that clearly identifies the responsibility of those who worship him. (Isa. 43:10-12) The adoption of that name infused the brothers with greater zeal than ever before as proclaimers of God's name and Kingdom. As a letter written that year by a Danish Witness expressed it: "Oh, what a magnificent name, Jehovah's Witnesses, yes, may all of us indeed be such."

In 1935 another memorable convention was held, in Washington, D.C. On the second day of that convention, Friday, May 31, Brother Rutherford discussed the great multitude, or great crowd, referred to at Revelation 7:9-17. For over half a century, the Bible Students had tried in vain to identify that group correctly. Now, at Jehovah's due time, in the light of events already under way, it was pointed out that these are persons who have the prospect of living forever right here on earth. This understanding gave fresh significance to the evangelizing work and explained Scripturally a major change that was then just beginning to take place in the makeup of the modern-day organization of Jehovah's Witnesses.

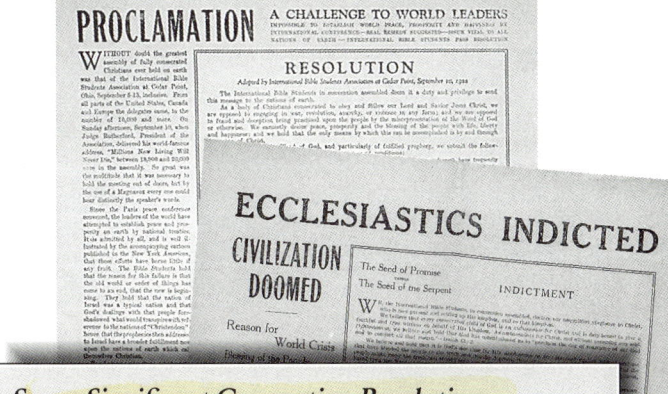

Seven Significant Convention Resolutions

In 1922, the resolution entitled *"A Challenge to World Leaders"* called on them to prove that humans have the wisdom to rule this earth or else to admit that peace, life, liberty, and endless happiness can come only from Jehovah through Jesus Christ.

In 1923, there was *"A Warning to All Christians"* of the urgent necessity to flee from organizations that fraudulently claim to represent God and Christ.

In 1924, *"Ecclesiastics Indicted"* laid bare the unscriptural doctrines and practices of Christendom's clergy.

In 1925, *"Message of Hope"* showed why those that claim to be the guiding lights of the world have failed to satisfy man's greatest needs and how only God's Kingdom can do so.

In 1926, *"A Testimony to the Rulers of the World"* put them on notice that Jehovah is the only true God and that Jesus Christ now rules as earth's rightful King. It urged the rulers to use their influence to turn the minds of the people to the true God so that disaster might not befall them.

In 1927, the *"Resolution to the Peoples of Christendom"* exposed the financial-political-religious combine that oppresses mankind. It urged the people to abandon Christendom and put their confidence in Jehovah and his Kingdom in the hands of Christ.

In 1928, the *"Declaration Against Satan and for Jehovah"* made clear that Jehovah's anointed King, Jesus Christ, will soon restrain Satan and destroy his evil organization, and it urged all who love righteousness to take their stand on Jehovah's side.

Delegates to the 1931 convention in Columbus, Ohio, who enthusiastically embraced the name Jehovah's Witnesses

The convention in St. Louis, Missouri, in 1941 is remembered by many who were present for an opening-day talk entitled "Integrity," in which Brother Rutherford focused attention on the great issue that confronts all intelligent creation. Ever since the talk "Ruler for the People," in 1928, the issues raised by Satan's rebellion had been given repeated attention. But now it was pointed out that "the primary issue raised by Satan's defiant challenge was and is that of UNIVERSAL DOMINATION." Appreciation for that issue and for the importance of maintaining integrity to Jehovah as Universal Sovereign has been a powerful motivating factor in the lives of Jehovah's servants.

In the midst of World War II, in 1942, when some wondered whether the preaching work was perhaps just about finished, the convention public talk delivered by N. H. Knorr, the newly designated president of the Watch Tower Society, was "Peace—Can It Last?" The explanation in that discourse of the symbolic "scarlet-colored wild beast" of Revelation chapter 17 opened up to the view of Jehovah's Witnesses a period following World War II in which there would be opportunity to direct yet more people to God's Kingdom. This gave impetus to a global campaign that over the years has reached into more than 235 lands and is not yet finished.

Another milestone was reached during a convention at New York's Yankee Stadium on August 2, 1950. On that occasion it was an amazed and highly delighted audience that first received the *New World Translation of the Christian Greek Scriptures*. The rest of the *New World Translation* was released in installments during the following decade. This modern-language rendering of the Sacred Scriptures restored the personal name of God to its rightful place in his Word. Its fidelity to what is in the original Bible languages has made it a tremendous asset to Jehovah's Witnesses in their own study of the Scriptures as well as in their evangelizing work.

On the next-to-last day of that convention, F. W. Franz, then vice president of the Watch Tower Society, addressed the audience on "New Systems of Things." For many years Jehovah's Witnesses had believed that even before Armageddon some of Jehovah's pre-Christian servants would be raised from the dead to be princes of the new world, in fulfillment of Psalm 45:16. You can imagine, then, the effect on the vast audience when the speaker asked: "Would this international assembly be happy to know that *here, tonight,* in our midst, there are a number of prospective *princes of the new earth?*" There was tremendous and sustained applause along with shouts of joy. Then the speaker showed that the Biblical use of the term translated "prince" along with the record of faithfulness of many of the "other sheep" in modern times allowed for the belief that some now living might well be selected by Jesus Christ for princely service. He also pointed out, however, that there would be no bestowing of titles on those entrusted with such service. Concluding his discourse, he urged: "Onward, then, steadily, all of us together, as a New World society!"

There have been many other highly significant discourses delivered at conventions of Jehovah's Witnesses: In 1953, "New World Society Attacked From the Far North" was a gripping explanation of the significance of the attack by Gog of Magog as described in Ezekiel chapters 38 and 39. That same year, the discourse "Filling the House With Glory" thrilled those who heard it as they saw before their very eyes tangible evidence of the fulfillment of Jehovah's promise, at Haggai 2:7, to bring the precious things, the desirable things, out of all nations into Jehovah's house.

JEHOVAH'S WITNESSES—PROCLAIMERS OF GOD'S KINGDOM

The most outstanding convention of modern times, however, was held in New York in 1958, when over a quarter of a million people overflowed the largest facilities available to hear the discourse "God's Kingdom Rules—Is the World's End Near?" Delegates were on hand from 123 lands, and their reports to the convention audience helped to strengthen the bonds of international brotherhood. To contribute to the spiritual growth of those present and for their use in teaching others, publications were released in 54 languages during that extraordinary convention.

In 1962, a series of talks on the theme "Subjection to Superior Authorities" corrected the understanding that the Witnesses had as to the meaning of Romans 13:1-7. In 1964, "Passing Over From Death to Life" and "Out of the Tombs to a Resurrection" broadened their appreciation of Jehovah's great mercy as manifest in the provision of the resurrection. And many, many more of such convention highlights could be cited.

Each year there are tens of thousands, yes, hundreds of thousands, of new ones in attendance at the conventions. Although information presented is not always new to the organization as a whole, it often opens up to new attenders an understanding of the divine will that truly thrills them. They may see and be moved to take hold of opportunities for service that change the entire course of their life.

At many conventions attention has been focused on the meaning of certain books of the Bible. For example, in 1958 and again in 1977, bound books were released that were devoted to discussion of the prophecies recorded by the prophet Daniel regarding God's purpose to have one world government with Christ as King. In 1971, it was the book of Ezekiel that was given attention, with its emphasis on the divine declaration, "The nations will have to know that I am Jehovah." (Ezek. 36:23) In 1972, prophecies recorded by Zechariah and Haggai were given detailed consideration. In 1963, 1969, and 1988, there were extensive discussions of thrilling prophecies of Revelation, which vividly foretell the fall of Babylon the Great and the incoming of God's glorious new heavens and new earth.

The conventions have highlighted varied themes —Theocracy's Increase, Clean Worship, United Worshipers, Courageous Ministers, Fruitage of the Spirit,

"New World Translation of the Christian Greek Scriptures" being released by N. H. Knorr in 1950

Discourses by F. W. Franz on fulfillment of Bible prophecy were a convention highlight (New York, 1958)

CONVENTIONS—PROOF OF OUR BROTHERHOOD 265

Disciple-Making, Good News for All Nations, Divine Name, Divine Sovereignty, Sacred Service, Victorious Faith, Kingdom Loyalty, Integrity Keepers, Trust in Jehovah, Godly Devotion, Light Bearers, and many more. Each of these has contributed to the spiritual growth of the organization and those associated with it.

Stimulus to the Evangelizing Work

Large conventions, as well as smaller assemblies, have been a source of great encouragement in connection with the preaching of the good news. Discourses and demonstrations have provided practical instruction. Experiences enjoyed in the field ministry as well as those related by people who have recently been helped to learn Bible truth are always on the program. In addition, the actual field service that was scheduled during conventions for many years was very beneficial. It gave a fine witness in the convention city and was a source of great encouragement to the Witnesses themselves.

Field service became part of the scheduled convention activity in Winnipeg, Manitoba, Canada, in January 1922. It was also featured during the general convention held at Cedar Point, Ohio, later that year. Thereafter, it became a regular practice to set aside a day, or part of a day or parts of several days, for delegates to share together in preaching activity right in and around the convention city. In large metropolitan areas, this gave people who might seldom be contacted by the Witnesses an opportunity to hear the good news about God's purpose to give eternal life to lovers of righteousness.

In Denmark the first of such service days at a convention was arranged in 1925, when 400 to 500 met at Nørrevold. For many of the 275 who shared in field service at that convention, it was their first time. Some were apprehensive. But after they had a taste of it, they became enthusiastic evangelizers in their home territories as well. Following that

For many years field service was a prominent part of every convention. Los Angeles, U.S.A., 1939 (bottom); Stockholm, Sweden, 1963 (inset)

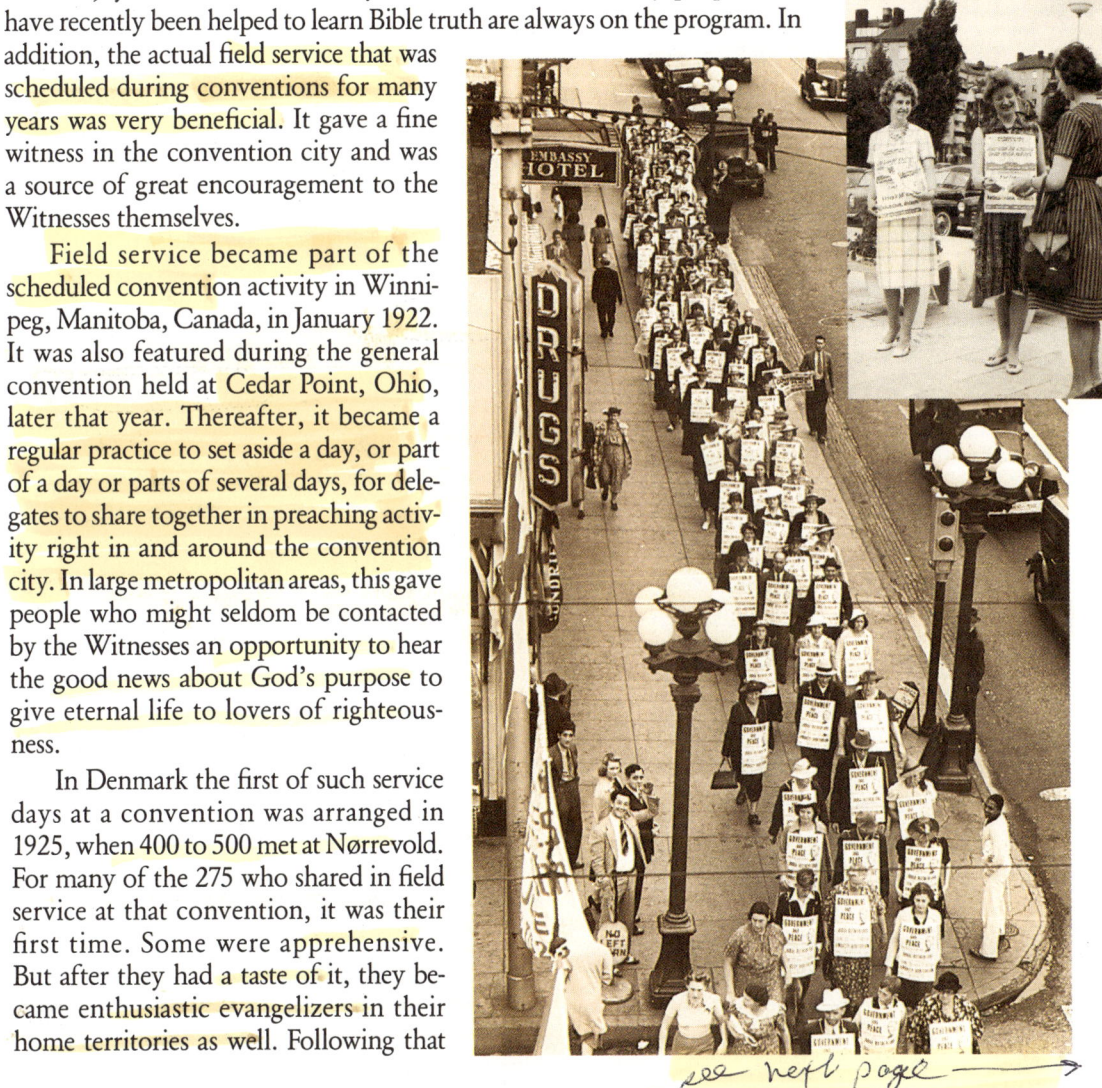

When J. F. Rutherford spoke from Washington, D.C., in 1935, the message was carried by radio and telephone lines to six continents

convention and until the end of World War II, there were many one-day service assemblies held in Denmark, and the brothers were invited from surrounding towns. Increased zeal was evident as they shared unitedly in the ministry and then met to hear talks. Similar service assemblies—but two days in length—were held in Britain and the United States.

At bigger conventions the field activity of the delegates often took on large proportions. Beginning in 1936, the convention public talk was advertised by orderly parades of Witnesses who wore placards and distributed handbills. (Those placards were initially referred to as "sandwich signs" because they were worn one in front and one in back.) At times, a thousand or more Witnesses participated in such parades at a given convention. Others shared in regular house-to-house calls, inviting all to come and hear the program. It was most encouraging to individual Witnesses to work with others and to see hundreds, even thousands, of other Witnesses sharing in the ministry along with them. At the same time, the public within a considerable radius came to know that Jehovah's Witnesses were in town; people had opportunity to hear for themselves what the Witnesses teach and to observe their conduct firsthand.

The talks given at the conventions often were heard by far more than the visible audience. When Brother Rutherford, at a convention in Toronto, Canada, in 1927, delivered the lecture "Freedom for the Peoples," it was carried by a history-making chain of 53 broadcasting stations to a vast international radio audience. The next year, from Detroit, Michigan (U.S.A.), the speech "Ruler for the People" was broadcast by twice as many stations, and shortwave radio carried it to listeners as far away as Australia, New Zealand, and South Africa.

In 1931, major radio networks refused to cooperate with plans to broadcast a convention discourse by Brother Rutherford; so the Watch Tower Society, working with the American Telephone and Telegraph Company, forged its own network of 163 stations, including the largest wire-connected network that had ever been on the air, to carry the message "The Kingdom, the Hope of the World." Additionally, over 300 other stations in many parts of the world broadcast the program by transcription.

During the convention at Washington, D.C., in 1935, Brother Rutherford spoke on the subject "Government," forcefully drawing attention to the fact that Jehovah's Kingdom under Christ will soon replace all human governments. Over 20,000 in the Washington Auditorium heard it. The speech was also carried by radio and telephone lines around the globe, reaching Central and South America, Europe, South Africa, islands of the Pacific, and lands of the Orient. Those who heard the talk in this way may well have numbered in the millions. Two leading Washington newspapers broke their contracts to publish the discourse. But sound cars were deployed by the brothers to 3 points in the city and 40 other places surrounding Washington, and from these the speech was rebroadcast to further audiences estimated at 120,000.

Then, in 1938, from Royal Albert Hall, in London, England, the straightforward discourse "Face the Facts" was carried to some 50 convention cities around the globe, with a total attendance of about 200,000. In addition, a vast radio audience heard that speech.

Thus, although Jehovah's Witnesses were relatively few in number, their conventions played an important role in the public proclamation of the Kingdom message.

Postwar Conventions in Europe

For those who were present, certain conventions stand out above all others. This was true of the ones in Europe immediately after World War II.

One such convention was in Amsterdam, the Netherlands, on August 5, 1945, less than four months after the Witnesses had been released from the German concentration camps. Some 2,500 delegates were expected; 2,000 of these would need rooming accommodations. To fill the need for places to sleep, local Witnesses spread straw on the floor of their homes. From all directions the delegates came by every means possible—by boat, in trucks, on bicycles, and some hitchhiking.

At that convention they laughed and wept, they sang, and they thanked Jehovah for his goodness. As one who attended said: "Theirs was the unspeakable joy of a theocratic organization just freed from fetters!" Before the war, there had been fewer than 500 Witnesses in the Netherlands. A total of 426 were arrested and imprisoned; of these, 117 died as a direct result of persecution. What joy when at the assembly some found loved ones that they thought were dead! Others shed tears as they searched in vain. That evening 4,000 listened with rapt attention to the public talk that explained why Jehovah's Witnesses had been the objects of such intense persecution. In spite of what they had suffered, they were getting organized to press ahead with their God-given work.

The following year, 1946, the brothers in Germany arranged for a convention in Nuremberg. They were granted the use of the Zeppelinwiese, Hitler's former parade grounds. On the second day of the convention, Erich Frost, who had personally experienced the brutality of the Gestapo and had spent years in a Nazi concentration camp, delivered the public talk "Christians in the Crucible." The 6,000 Witnesses in attendance were joined by 3,000 of the public from Nuremberg for the occasion.

The final day of that convention proved to be one when sentences were to be announced at the war-crimes trials there in Nuremberg. Military authorities declared a curfew for that day, but after prolonged negotiations they agreed that in view of the stand that Jehovah's Witnesses had taken in the face of Nazi opposition, it would be inappropriate to hinder them from concluding their convention in peace. Thus, on that final day, the brothers assembled to hear the stirring talk "Fearless Despite World Conspiracy."

They saw the hand of Jehovah in what was taking place. At the very time that men representing a regime that had tried to exterminate them were being sentenced, Jehovah's Witnesses were meeting to worship Jehovah at the place where Hitler had put on some of his most spectacular displays of Nazi power. Said the convention chairman: "Just being able to experience this day, which is just a preview of the triumph of God's people over their enemies at the battle of Armageddon, was worth nine years in concentration camp."

In Nuremberg, Germany, in 1946, Erich Frost gave the fiery discourse "Christians in the Crucible"

Other Memorable Conventions

As the activity of Jehovah's Witnesses has expanded, conventions have been held around the earth. All of them have had outstanding features for those who were present.

At Kitwe, Northern Rhodesia (now Zambia), in the hub of the Copperbelt, a convention was scheduled to be held during the visit of the president of the Watch Tower Society in 1952. The site was a large area on the outskirts of one of the mining camps, in a place now known as Chamboli. The top of an abandoned anthill was leveled, and a thatched shelter was built on it to serve as a platform. Other thatched shelters for sleeping, with double decks, extended out 200 yards from the main seating area like the spokes of a wheel. Men and boys slept in some; women and girls in others. Some of the delegates had traveled two weeks by bicycle to be present. Others had walked for days and then finished the trip on a primitive bus.

During sessions those in the audience were very attentive, though seating was on hard bamboo benches in the open. They had come to hear, and they did not want to miss a word. The singing of that audience of 20,000 brought tears to the eyes—it was so beautiful. There was no accompaniment by musical instruments, but the harmony of the voices was exquisite. Not just in their singing but in every way, unity was manifest among these Witnesses, though they were from many backgrounds and tribes.

Open-air convention in Kitwe, Northern Rhodesia, during visit of N. H. Knorr in 1952

And can you imagine the feelings of Jehovah's Witnesses in Portugal when, after a struggle for freedom of worship that had gone on for nearly 50 years, the Witnesses there gained legal recognition on December 18, 1974. At that time they numbered only about 14,000. Within a few days, 7,586 of them packed out a sports pavilion in Porto. The following day, another 39,284 overflowed a football stadium in Lisbon. Brothers Knorr and Franz were with them for that happy occasion, one that many will never forget.

Organizing International Gatherings

For well over half a century, Jehovah's Witnesses have held large, multicity conventions simultaneously in many lands. Their feeling of international brotherhood has been heightened on these occasions when they have all been able to hear principal discourses originating in a key city.

In 1958 an audience of 253,922, overflowing two large stadiums in New York, heard the message "God's Kingdom Rules—Is the World's End Near?"

Polo Grounds

It was not until 1946, however, that a large international convention drew together in one city delegates from many parts of the earth. This was at Cleveland, Ohio. Although travel in the postwar era was still difficult, attendance reached 80,000, including 302 delegates from 32 countries outside the United States. Sessions were held in 20 languages. Much practical instruction was given with a view to expanding the work of evangelizing. One of the convention highlights was Brother Knorr's talk about problems of reconstruction and expansion. The audience applauded enthusiastically as they heard plans for enlargement of the Society's headquarters printing and office

Yankee Stadium

facilities, as well as its radio broadcasting facilities, for establishment of branch offices in principal countries of the world, and for expansion of missionary work. Immediately after that convention, details were worked out so that Brothers Knorr and Henschel could make an around-the-world trip to implement what had been discussed.

In the years that followed, truly history-making conventions were held in New York City's Yankee Stadium. At the first of these, from July 30 to August 6, 1950, delegates were present from 67 lands. Included on the program were brief reports by branch servants, missionaries, and other

Features of Some of the Big Conventions

Hundreds of enthusiastic delegates arrived by ship, thousands by plane, tens of thousands by automobile and bus

Good organization and lots of willing workers were required to locate and assign sufficient rooming accommodations

During these eight-day conventions, hot meals—tens of thousands of them—were regularly served to delegates

In 1953, a trailer and tent city accommodated more than 45,000 delegates

In New York, in 1958, 7,136 got baptized—more than at any one time since Pentecost of 33 C.E.

Greeting signs from many lands were displayed, and sessions were held in 21 languages, in New York in 1953

JEHOVAH'S WITNESSES—PROCLAIMERS OF GOD'S KINGDOM

delegates. These gave the convention thrilling glimpses of the intense evangelizing work being done in all the lands from which they had come. The final day, attendance rose to 123,707 for the discourse "Can You Live Forever in Happiness on Earth?" The theme of the convention was "Theocracy's Increase." Attention was directed to the great increase in numbers. Yet, as the chairman, Grant Suiter, emphatically pointed out, this was not done to laud any brilliant minds within the visible organization. Rather, he declared: "The new strength of numbers is dedicated to Jehovah's honor. That is the way it should be, and we would not have it any other way."

In 1953, another convention was held at Yankee Stadium in New York. This time the attendance peaked at 165,829. As was true of the first convention there, the program was packed with discussions of thrilling Bible prophecies, practical counsel on how to accomplish the preaching of the good news, and reports from many lands. Although sessions began at about 9:30 a.m., they usually did not conclude until 9:00 or 9:30 p.m. The convention provided eight full days of joyful spiritual feasting.

For their largest convention, in New York in 1958, it was necessary to use not only Yankee Stadium but also the nearby Polo Grounds as well as overflow areas outside the stadiums to accommodate the convention crowds. On the final day, when every seat was filled, special permission was granted to use even the playing field of Yankee Stadium, and what a thrilling sight it was as thousands streamed in, removed their shoes, and sat on the grass! The count showed 253,922 in attendance to hear the public discourse. A further evidence of Jehovah's blessing on the ministry of his servants was seen when 7,136 at this convention symbolized their dedication by water immersion—well over twice the number that were baptized on the historic occasion of Pentecost 33 C.E., as reported in the Bible!—Acts 2:41.

Grant Suiter, convention chairman at Yankee Stadium in 1950

John Groh (seated), discussing convention organization with George Couch in 1958

The entire operation of these conventions gave evidence of something much more than efficient organization. It was a manifestation of God's spirit at work among his people. Brotherly love that has as its basis love for God was evident everywhere. There were no high-salaried organizers. Every department was manned by unpaid volunteers. Christian brothers and sisters, often family groups, cared for the refreshment stands. They also prepared hot meals, and in huge tents outside the stadium, they served the delegates at a rate of up to a thousand per minute. Tens of thousands —all of them glad to have a share in the work—served as attendants and cared for all the needed construction, cooking and serving of meals, cleanup, and much more.

Not high-salaried convention organizers, but unpaid volunteers

More volunteers devoted hundreds of thousands of hours in order to fill the housing needs of delegates. In some years, to care for at least some of the conventioners, trailer and tent cities were organized. In 1953 the Witnesses harvested 40 acres of grain, free of charge, for a farmer in New Jersey who leased them his land for their trailer city. Sanitary facilities, lighting, showers, laundry rooms, cafeteria, and grocery stores were all installed to care for a population that exceeded 45,000. As they moved in, a city sprang up overnight. Scores of thousands more were housed in hotels and private homes in and around New York. It was a mammoth undertaking. With Jehovah's blessing, it was carried out successfully.

Conventions on the Move

The members of this international brotherhood are keenly interested in fellow Witnesses in other lands. As a result, they have seized opportunities to attend conventions outside their home countries.

When the first of the Clean Worship Assembly series convened at Wembley Stadium in London, England, in 1951, Witnesses from 40 lands were present. The program emphasized the practical side of true worship and the making of the ministry one's life career. From England, many Witnesses traveled to the Continent, where nine more conventions were to be held during the next two months. The largest of these was in Frankfurt am Main, Germany, where 47,432 were present from 24 lands. The warmth of the brothers was demonstrated at the close of the program when the orchestra began to play and the German brothers broke out in a spontaneous farewell song commending to God their fellow Witnesses who had come from abroad to join them. Handkerchiefs were waved, and hundreds flocked across the field to express personal appreciation for this grand theocratic festival.

In 1955, more of the Witnesses arranged to visit their Christian brothers abroad at convention time. By means of two chartered ships (each with 700 passengers) and 42 chartered planes, delegates from the United States and

Canada went to Europe. The European edition of the paper *The Stars and Stripes,* published in Germany, described the influx of Witnesses as "probably the biggest mass movement of Americans through Europe since the Allied invasion during World War II." Other delegates came from Central and South America, Asia, Africa, and Australia. In spite of efforts of Christendom's clergy to prevent the Witnesses from holding their conventions in Rome and Nuremberg, these two and six more were held in Europe during the summer. Attendance ranged from 4,351 in Rome to 107,423 in Nuremberg. Another group of 17,729 assembled at the Waldbühne in what was then called West Berlin, which could be reached with somewhat less risk by brothers from the Eastern zone of that era. Many of these had been in prison for their faith or had family members who were then in prison, but they were still firm in faith. How appropriate the convention theme—"Triumphant Kingdom"!

Though there had already been many international conventions, what took place in 1963 was the first of its kind. It was an around-the-world convention. Beginning in Milwaukee, Wisconsin, in the United States, it moved to New York; next, to four major cities in Europe; through the Middle East; on to India, Burma (now Myanmar), Thailand, Hong Kong, Singapore, the Philippines, Indonesia, Australia, Taiwan, Japan, New Zealand, Fiji, the Republic of Korea, and Hawaii; and then back to the North American mainland. In all, delegates from 161 lands were present. Total attendance exceeded 580,000. There were 583, from some 20 lands, that moved with the convention, attending in one country after another, clear around the globe. Special tours enabled them to see places of religious interest, and they also shared with their local brothers and sisters in the house-to-house ministry. These travelers cared for their own expenses.

Latin American delegates had been well represented at most of the international conventions. But in 1966-67, it was their turn to host the conventions. Those who attended will never forget the drama that brought to life the Bible account regarding Jeremiah and that helped everyone to appreciate its meaning for our day.* Bonds of Christian love were strengthened as visitors saw firsthand the background against which a vast campaign of Bible education is being carried on in Latin America. They were deeply moved by the strong faith of fellow believers, many of whom had overcome seemingly insurmountable obstacles—family opposition, floods, loss of possessions—to be in attendance. They were greatly encouraged by experiences such as that of a frail Uruguayan special pioneer sister who was interviewed and who had with her on the platform many of the 80 persons she had already helped to progress to the point of Christian baptism! (As of 1992, she had helped 105 persons to the point of baptism. She was still frail and still a special pioneer!) How heartwarming, too, to meet missionaries from the very earliest

---

* Seventy more of such dramas were presented at conventions during the next 25 years.

CONVENTIONS—PROOF OF OUR BROTHERHOOD　　　　　　　　　　277

Gilead classes still on the job in their assignments! Those conventions were a fine stimulus to the work being done in that part of the world. In many of those lands, there are now 10, 15, or even 20 times as many praisers of Jehovah as there were then.

A few years later, in 1970-71, it was possible for Witnesses from abroad to fellowship with their brothers at international conventions held in Africa. The largest of these conventions was in Lagos, Nigeria, where all the facilities had to be built from the ground up. To protect delegates from the hot sun, a bamboo city was built—seating areas, dormitories, cafeteria, and other departments. This required 100,000 bamboo poles and 36,000 large, woven reed mats—all of them prepared by the brothers and sisters. The program was put on in 17 languages simultaneously. Attendance reached 121,128, and 3,775 new Witnesses were baptized. Numerous tribal groups were represented, and many of those present were people who used to war against

In 1963 an around-the-world convention was held, with delegates from some 20 lands traveling with it right around the globe

Kyoto, Japan (lower left), was one of 27 convention cities. Delegates in the Republic of Korea got acquainted (center). A Maori greeting in New Zealand (lower right)

Unity between black and white

one another. But now, what a joy to see them united in the bonds of genuine Christian brotherhood!

After the convention, some of the foreign delegates traveled by bus into Igboland to see the area most seriously affected by the recent civil war. A great sensation was caused in town after town as the visitors were greeted and embraced by local Witnesses. People rushed into the streets to watch. Such a demonstration of love and unity between black and white was something they had never seen before.

In certain lands the number of Jehovah's Witnesses makes it impossible for them all to come together in one place. However, on occasion, several large conventions have been held at the same time, followed by more, week after week. In 1969, the unity felt at conventions arranged in this way was enhanced by the fact that some of the principal speakers shuttled back and forth by air between the conventions, thus serving them all. In 1983 and 1988, a similar oneness was felt when a number of large conventions using the same language were tied together, even internationally, by telephone transmission of key discourses given by members of the Governing Body. The real foundation of the unity among Jehovah's Witnesses, however, is the fact that they all worship Jehovah as the only true God, they all hold to the Bible as their guide, they all benefit from the same spiritual feeding program, they all look to Jesus Christ as their Leader, they all seek to manifest the fruits of God's spirit in their lives, they all put their trust in God's Kingdom, and they all share in taking the good news of that Kingdom to others.

Organized for International Praise to Jehovah

Jehovah's Witnesses have increased in number to the point that they outnumber the population of scores of individual nations. In order for their conventions to accomplish the greatest good, much careful planning is required. However, simple published requests as to where Witnesses from various areas should attend are usually all that is needed to assure that there will be ample room for everyone. When international conventions are planned, it is now often necessary for the Governing Body to consider not only the number of Witnesses from other countries who would like to go and are in position to do so but also the size of available convention facilities, the number of local Witnesses who will be attending, and the amount of housing available for delegates; then a maximum figure can be allotted for each country. That was true in connection with the three "Godly Devotion" Conventions held in Poland in 1989.

For those conventions some 90,000 of Jehovah's Witnesses were expected from Poland, in addition to thousands of newly interested persons. Many were also invited to attend from Britain, Canada, and the United

A convention that served 17 language groups simultaneously, in a bamboo city built for the occasion (Lagos, Nigeria, 1970)

States. Large delegations were welcomed from Italy, France, and Japan. Others came from Scandinavia and Greece. At least 37 lands were represented. For certain portions of the program, it was necessary to interpret Polish or English talks into as many as 16 other languages. Total attendance was 166,518.

Large groups of Witnesses at these conventions had come from what was then the Soviet Union and from Czechoslovakia; sizable groups were also present from other Eastern European countries. Hotels and school dormitories could not house everyone. Hospitably, the Polish Witnesses opened their hearts and their homes, gladly sharing what they had. One congregation of 146 provided sleeping places for over 1,200 delegates. For some who attended these conventions, it was the first time they had ever been at a large gathering of more than 15 or 20 of Jehovah's people. Their hearts welled up with appreciation as they looked out at the tens of thousands in the stadiums, joined with them in prayer, and united their voices in songs of praise to Jehovah. When they mingled together between sessions, there were warm embraces, even though difference of language often kept them from saying in words what was in their hearts.

As the convention came to an end, their hearts were filled with gratitude to Jehovah, who made it all possible. In Warsaw, after the farewell comments by the chairman, the audience burst into applause that did not abate for at least ten minutes. After the final song and prayer, the applause resumed, and the audience lingered in the stands for a long time. They had waited many years for this occasion, and they did not want it to end.

The following year, 1990, less than five months after the lifting of a 40-year-long ban on Jehovah's Witnesses in what was then East Germany, another thrilling international convention was held, this one in Berlin. Among the 44,532 present were delegates from 65 different countries. From some lands, just a few had come; from Poland, some 4,500. Words could not express the deep feelings of those who had never before had the freedom to attend such a convention, and when the entire audience joined in songs of praise to Jehovah, they could not hold back their tears of joy.

Three large conventions were held in Poland in 1989, with delegates on hand from 37 lands

Thousands were baptized in Chorzów

The audience applauded at great length in Warsaw

T. Jaracz (on the right) spoke to delegates in Poznan

Delegates from what was then the U.S.S.R. (below)

Portions of the program in Chorzów were translated into 15 languages

Later that year, when a similar convention was held in São Paulo, Brazil, two large stadiums were needed to accommodate the international audience of 134,406. This was followed by a convention in Argentina, where again two stadiums were used simultaneously to accommodate the international audience. As 1991 began, further international conventions were getting under way in the Philippines, Taiwan, and Thailand. Large audiences from many nations were also on hand that year for conventions in Eastern Europe—in Hungary, Czechoslovakia, and what is now Croatia. And in 1992, delegates from 28 lands counted it a special privilege to be among the 46,214 in St. Petersburg for the first truly international convention of Jehovah's Witnesses in Russia.

Opportunities for Regular Spiritual Refreshment

Not all the conventions held by Jehovah's Witnesses are international gatherings. However, the Governing Body arranges for major conventions once a year, and the same program is enjoyed worldwide in many languages. These conventions may be quite large, providing opportunity for fellowship with other Witnesses from many places, or they may be smaller and held in many cities, making it easier for new ones to attend and enabling the public in hundreds of smaller cities to get a good closeup view of a large cross section of Jehovah's Witnesses.

In addition, once a year each circuit (made up of perhaps 20 congregations) assembles for a two-day program of spiritual counsel and encouragement.* Also, since September 1987, a special assembly day, an upbuilding one-day program, is arranged for each circuit once a year. Where possible, a member of the Society's headquarters staff or someone from the local branch office is sent out to share in the program. These programs are greatly appreciated by Jehovah's Witnesses. In many areas the assembly sites are not distant or hard to reach. But that is not always the case. A traveling overseer recalls an elderly couple who walked 47 miles with suitcases and blankets to attend a circuit assembly in Zimbabwe.

Field service during the convention is no longer a feature at all these assemblies, but that is not because the Witnesses in any way view it as less important. In most cases people who live near the assembly sites are now being visited regularly by the local Witnesses—in some instances, every few weeks. The assembly delegates keep alert to opportunities for informal witnessing, and their Christian conduct gives a powerful witness in another way.

Evidence of True Brotherhood

The brotherhood manifest among the Witnesses at their conventions is

---

* From 1947 to 1987, these had been held twice each year. Down till 1972, they were three-day assemblies; then a two-day program was instituted.

readily evident to observers. They can see that there is no partiality among them and that genuine warmth is evident even among those who may be meeting one another for the first time. At the time of the Divine Will International Assembly in New York in 1958, the New York *Amsterdam News* (August 2) reported: "Everywhere Negroes, whites and Orientals, from all stations in life and all parts of the world, mingled joyously and freely. . . . The worshiping Witnesses from 120 lands have lived and worshiped together peacefully showing Americans how easily it can be done. . . . The Assembly is a shining example of how people can work and live together."

More recently, when Jehovah's Witnesses held simultaneous conventions in Durban and in Johannesburg, South Africa, in 1985, the delegates included all the major racial and language groups in South Africa, as well as representatives from 23 other lands. The warm fellowship among the 77,830 in attendance was readily evident. "This is beautiful," said a young Indian woman. "To see Coloureds, Indians, whites, and blacks all mixing together has changed my whole outlook on life."

This feeling of brotherhood goes beyond smiles, handshakes, and calling one another "brother" and "sister." As an example, when arrangements were being made for the "Everlasting Good News" Assembly worldwide in 1963, Jehovah's Witnesses were notified that if they would like to help others financially to attend a convention, the Society would be glad to see that the funds benefited brothers in all parts of the earth. There was no solicitation, and nothing was taken for administrative expenses. The funds all went for the stated purpose. In this way, 8,179 were assisted to attend the convention. Delegates from every country in Central and South America were given help, as were thousands from Africa and many in the Middle East and the Far East. A large proportion of those assisted were brothers and sisters who had devoted many years to the full-time ministry.

Toward the end of 1978, a convention was scheduled to be held in Auckland, New Zealand. Witnesses in the Cook Islands knew about it and longed to be present. But the economy in the islands was such that it would have cost each one a small fortune to make the trip. However, loving spiritual brothers and sisters in New Zealand contributed the round-trip fares for some 60 of the islanders. How happy they were to be present to share the spiritual feast with their Maori, Samoan, Niuean, and Caucasian brothers!

Typical of the spirit among Jehovah's Witnesses was what took place at the conclusion of the "Divine Justice" District Convention in Montreal, Canada, in 1988. For four days Arabic, English, French, Greek, Italian, Portuguese, and Spanish delegates had been enjoying the same program but in their own languages. However, at the end of the final session, all 45,000 of them joined together in the Olympic Stadium in a moving display of brotherhood and unity of purpose. Together they sang, each group in its own tongue, "Come sing with us . . . 'Jehovah reigns; let earth rejoice.'"

CHAPTER 18

"SEEKING FIRST THE KINGDOM"

THE principal theme of the Bible is the sanctification of Jehovah's name by means of the Kingdom. Jesus Christ taught his followers to seek first the Kingdom, putting it ahead of other interests in life. Why?

The Watchtower has frequently explained that by reason of the fact that he is the Creator, Jehovah is the Universal Sovereign. He deserves to be held in highest esteem by his creatures. (Rev. 4:11) However, very early in human history, a spirit son of God who made himself Satan the Devil defiantly challenged Jehovah's sovereignty. (Gen. 3:1-5) Furthermore, Satan imputed selfish motives to all who served Jehovah. (Job 1:9-11; 2:4, 5; Rev. 12:10) Thus the peace of the universe was disrupted.

For decades now, Watch Tower publications have pointed out that Jehovah has made provision for settling these issues in a manner that magnifies not only his almighty power but also the greatness of his wisdom, his justice, and his love. A central part of that provision is the Messianic Kingdom of God. By means of that Kingdom, mankind is given ample opportunity to learn the ways of righteousness. By means of it, the wicked will be destroyed, Jehovah's sovereignty will be vindicated, and his purpose will be accomplished to make the earth a paradise populated with people who truly love God and one another and who are blessed with perfection of life.

Because of its importance, Jesus counseled his followers: "Keep on, then, seeking first the kingdom." (Matt. 6:10, 33) Jehovah's Witnesses in modern times have given abundant evidence that they endeavor to heed that counsel.

Forsaking All for the Kingdom

At an early date, the Bible Students gave consideration to what was meant by seeking first the Kingdom. They discussed Jesus' parable in which he compared the Kingdom to a pearl of such high value that a man "sold all the things he had and bought it." (Matt. 13:45, 46) They pondered the significance of Jesus' counsel to a rich young ruler to sell everything, distribute to poor people, and follow him. (Mark 10:17-30)* They realized that if they were going to prove worthy of having a share in God's

---
* *Watch Tower*, August 15, 1906, pp. 267-71.

Kingdom, they must make the Kingdom their first interest, gladly using their lives, their abilities, their resources, in its service. Everything else in life had to take second place.

Charles Taze Russell personally took that counsel to heart. He sold his prospering haberdashery business, gradually reduced other business interests, and then used all his earthly possessions to help people in a spiritual way. (Compare Matthew 6:19-21.) It was not something that he did for merely a few years. Right down till his death, he used all his resources—his mental ability, his physical health, his material possessions—to teach others the great message of Messiah's Kingdom. At Russell's funeral an associate, Joseph F. Rutherford, stated: "Charles Taze Russell was loyal to God, loyal to Christ Jesus, loyal to the cause of Messiah's Kingdom."

In April 1881 (when only a few hundred persons were attending meetings of the Bible Students), the *Watch Tower* published an article entitled "Wanted 1,000 Preachers." This included an invitation to men and women who did not have dependent families to take up work as colporteur evangelists. Employing the language of Jesus' parable at Matthew 20:1-16, the *Watch Tower* asked: "Who has a burning desire to go and labor in the Vineyard, and has been praying that the Lord would open the way"? Those who could give at least half of their time exclusively to the Lord's work were encouraged to apply. To assist them with expenses of travel, food, clothing, and shelter, Zion's Watch Tower Tract Society provided the early colporteurs with Bible literature for distribution, stated the modest contribution that could be asked for the literature, and invited the colporteurs to keep a portion of the funds thus received. Who responded to these arrangements and took up the colporteur service?

By 1885 there were around 300 colporteurs associated with the Society. In 1914 the number finally exceeded 1,000. It was not an easy work. After calling at the homes in four small towns and finding only three or four persons who were interested to any extent, one of the colporteurs wrote: "I must say that I felt rather lonely traveling so far, meeting so many, and finding so little concern expressed about God's plan and Church. Assist me with your prayers, that I may properly and fearlessly present the truth, and not become weary in well doing."

They Offered Themselves Willingly

Those colporteurs were real trailblazers. They penetrated the most inaccessible corners of the land at a time when transportation was very primitive and the roads were, for the most part, little more than wagon tracks. Sister Early, in New Zealand, was one who did that. Starting out well before World War I, she devoted 34 years to such service full-time before she died in 1943. She covered much of the country on a bicycle. Even when she became crippled with arthritis and could not ride, she used the bicycle to lean

Sister Early traveled throughout much of New Zealand on a bicycle to share the Kingdom message

"SEEKING FIRST THE KINGDOM"

on and to carry her books around the business territory of Christchurch. She could climb stairs, but she had to descend them backwards because of her crippling disability. Nevertheless, as long as she had any strength, she used it in Jehovah's service.

These folks did not take up this work because they felt confident in themselves. Some were by nature very timid, but they loved Jehovah. Before witnessing in business territory, one such sister asked each of the Bible Students in her area to pray for her. In time, as she gained experience, she became very enthusiastic about the activity.

When Malinda Keefer talked to Brother Russell in 1907 about her desire to enter the full-time service, she said that she felt the need to gain more knowledge first. In fact, it was just the preceding year that she had first come in contact with the literature of the Bible Students. Brother Russell's reply was: "If you want to wait until you know it all you will never get started, but you will learn as you go along." Without holding back, she quickly began in Ohio, in the United States. She often called to mind Psalm 110:3, which says: "Your people will offer themselves willingly." For the next 76 years, she kept on doing just that.* She started out single. For 15 years she enjoyed serving in the married state. But after her husband died, she kept right on going, with Jehovah's help. Looking back over the years, she said: "How thankful I am that I offered myself willingly as a pioneer when a young woman and always put Kingdom interests first!"

When general conventions were held in the early days, arrangements were often made for special sessions with the colporteurs. Questions were answered, training was provided for newer ones, and encouragement was given.

From 1919 onward, there were many more of Jehovah's servants who prized God's Kingdom so highly that they too truly built their lives around it. Some of them were able to set aside secular pursuits and devote themselves fully to the ministry.

Caring for Material Needs

How did they care for their material needs? Anna Petersen (later Rømer), a full-time evangelizer in Denmark, recalled: "We got help from literature placements for the daily expenses, and our needs were not great. If there were bigger expenses, these were always met in one way or another. Sisters used to give us some clothes, dresses or coats, and we could put these right on and wear them, so we were well dressed. And some winters I took some office work for a couple of months. . . . By buying when there were

For 76 years—single, married, and then as a widow—Malinda Keefer devoted herself to the full-time ministry

---
* See *The Watchtower*, February 1, 1967, pages 92-5.

sales on, I could buy what clothing I needed for a whole year. Things went fine. We were never in need." Material things were not their principal concern. Their love for Jehovah and his ways was like a fire burning within them, and they simply had to express it.

For lodging they might rent a modest room while they called on people in the area. Some of them used a trailer—nothing elaborate, just a place to sleep and eat. Others slept in tents as they moved from place to place. In some places brothers arranged for "pioneer camps." Witnesses in the area might furnish a home, and one person would be assigned to supervise it. Pioneers serving in that area could use the accommodations, and they would share the expenses involved.

These full-time workers did not allow lack of money to prevent sheeplike people from obtaining Bible literature. Pioneers often traded for produce such as potatoes, butter, eggs, fresh and canned fruit, chickens, soap, and almost anything else. They were not getting rich; rather, this was a means of helping sincere people to have the Kingdom message, while at the same time obtaining physical necessities of life so the pioneers could continue their ministry. They had confidence in Jesus' promise that if they would "keep on . . . seeking first the kingdom and [God's] righteousness," then necessary food and covering would be provided.—Matt. 6:33.

Willing to Serve Wherever There Was Need

Their earnest desire to do the work that Jesus had assigned to his disciples led the full-time workers to new territories, even to new lands. When Frank Rice was invited to leave Australia to open up the preaching of the good news on Java (now part of Indonesia) in 1931, he had ten years of experience in the full-time ministry behind him. But now there were new customs, as well as new languages to learn. He could use English to witness to some in the shops and offices, but he wanted to witness to others also. He

Canada

Simple house-cars provided lodging for some early pioneers as they moved from place to place

India

"SEEKING FIRST THE KINGDOM"

studied hard, and in three months he knew enough Dutch to start going from house to house. Then he studied Malay.

Frank was just 26 years old when he went to Java, and for most of the six years he was there and on Sumatra, he worked alone. (Toward the end of 1931, Clem Deschamp and Bill Hunter came from Australia to help with the work. As a team, they made a preaching tour inland, while Frank worked in and around the capital of Java. Later, Clem and Bill also received assignments that took them to separate areas.) There were no congregation meetings that Frank could attend. Sometimes it was very lonely, and more than once he struggled with thoughts of giving up and going back to Australia. But he kept going. How? The spiritual food contained in *The Watch Tower* helped to strengthen him. In 1937 he moved on to an assignment in Indochina, where he narrowly escaped with his life during the violent upheavals that followed World War II. That spirit of willingness to serve was still alive in the 1970's when he wrote to express his joy over the fact that his entire family was serving Jehovah and to say that he and his wife were once again preparing to move to a place in Australia where there was greater need.

Frank Rice (standing at the right), Clem Deschamp (seated in front of Frank, with Clem's wife, Jean, next to them), and a group on Java including fellow Witnesses and newly interested ones

'Trusting in Jehovah With All Their Heart'

Claude Goodman determined to 'trust in Jehovah with all his heart and not to lean on his own understanding,' so he chose colporteur service as a Christian evangelizer instead of a secular business opportunity. (Prov. 3: 5, 6) Along with Ronald Tippin, who had helped him to learn the truth, he served as a colporteur in England for over a year. Then, in 1929, the two made themselves available to go to India.* What a challenge that presented!

In the years that followed, they traveled not only on foot and by passenger train and bus but also by freight train, oxcart, camel, sampan, ricksha, and even plane and private train. Sometimes they spread their bedrolls in railway waiting rooms, in a cattle shed, on jungle grass, or on cow-dung flooring in a cottage, but there were also times when they slept in lush hotels and in a raja's palace. Like the apostle Paul, they learned the secret of contentment whether they were low on provisions or had an abundance. (Phil. 4:12, 13) Usually they had very little that was of material value, but they never were without what they really needed. They personally experienced the fulfillment of Jesus' promise that if they would seek first the

---

* See *The Watchtower,* December 15, 1973, pages 760-5.

JEHOVAH'S WITNESSES—PROCLAIMERS OF GOD'S KINGDOM

Kingdom and God's righteousness, the material necessities of life would be provided.

There were serious bouts with dengue fever, malaria, and typhoid, but loving care was provided by fellow Witnesses. There was service to be carried out amid the squalor of cities such as Calcutta, and there was witnessing to be done on the tea plantations in the mountains of Ceylon (now known as Sri Lanka). To fill the spiritual needs of the people, literature was offered, recordings were played in the local languages, and talks were given. As the work increased, Claude also learned how to operate a printing press and to care for work in the Society's branch offices.

In his 87th year, he could look back on a life rich with experiences in Jehovah's service in England, India, Pakistan, Ceylon, Burma (now Myanmar), Malaya, Thailand, and Australia. Both as a single young man and as a husband and father, he kept the Kingdom first in his life. It was less than two years after his baptism that he entered the full-time service, and he viewed that as his career for the rest of his life.

Claude Goodman's life of full-time ministry led him to service in India and seven other lands

God's Power Made Perfect in Weakness

Ben Brickell was another one of those zealous Witnesses—much like other people, in that he shared their needs and infirmities. He was outstanding in faith. In 1930 he entered the colporteur work in New Zealand, where he witnessed in territories that were not covered again for decades. Two years later, in Australia, he undertook a five-month preaching trip through desert country where no witness had previously been given. His bicycle was heavily laden with blankets, clothing, food, and bound books to place. Though other men had perished when trying to travel through this area, he pressed on, with confidence in Jehovah. Next, he served in Malaysia, where serious cardiac problems developed. He did not quit. After a period of recuperation, he resumed full-time preaching activity in Australia. About a decade later, serious illness put him in the hospital, and when discharged he was told by the doctor that he was "85 percent incapacitated for work." He could not even walk down the street to do shopping without intermittent rest.

But Ben Brickell was determined to get going again, and he did, stopping to rest as necessary. Soon

---

"Where Are the Nine?"

At the Memorial of Christ's death, in 1928, a tract given to all in attendance was entitled "Where Are the Nine?" Its discussion of Luke 17:11-19 touched Claude Goodman's heart and moved him to get into the colporteur, or pioneer, work and to persevere in that service.

"SEEKING FIRST THE KINGDOM"   289

he was back witnessing in the rugged Australian outback. He did what he could to care for his health, but his service to Jehovah was the main thing in his life until his death 30 years later in his mid-60's.* He recognized that the lack that existed as a result of his weakness could be filled by Jehovah's power. At a convention in Melbourne in 1969, he served at a pioneer desk with a large badge on his lapel, reading: "If you want to know about pioneering, ask me."—Compare 2 Corinthians 12:7-10.

When Ben Brickell had good health, he enjoyed using it in Jehovah's service; serious health problems in later years did not make him quit

Reaching Jungle Villages and Mountain Mining Camps

Zeal for Jehovah's service moved not only men but also women to take up work in untouched fields. Freida Johnson was one of the anointed, rather small and in her 50's when she worked alone through parts of Central America, covering such areas as the north coast of Honduras on horseback. It required faith to work by herself in this area, visiting the scattered banana plantations, the towns of La Ceiba, Tela, and Trujillo, and even the lonely Carib villages beyond. She witnessed there in 1930 and 1931, again in 1934, and in 1940 and 1941, placing thousands of pieces of literature containing Bible truth.

During those years another zealous worker started her career in the full-time ministry. This was Kathe Palm, who was born in Germany. What moved her to action was attending the convention in Columbus, Ohio, in 1931, at which the Bible Students embraced the name Jehovah's Witnesses. It was then that she determined to seek first the Kingdom, and in 1992, at 89 years of age, she was still doing it.

Her pioneer service began in New York City. Later, in South Dakota, she had a partner for a few months but then carried on alone, traveling on horseback. When invited to serve in Colombia, South America, she readily accepted, arriving there late in 1934. Once again, she had a partner for a while but then was alone. This did not make her feel that she had to quit.

A couple invited her to join them in Chile. Here was another vast territory, one that stretched 2,650 miles along the west coast of the South American continent. After preaching in the office buildings of the capital, she struck out for the remote north. In every mining camp, every company

---

* See *The Watchtower,* September 1, 1972, pages 533-6.

Kathe Palm witnessed in all sorts of territory, from big-city office buildings to the most remote mining camp and sheep ranch in Chile

town, large or small, she witnessed from door to door. Workers high up in the Andes were surprised to have a lone woman call on them, but she was determined to miss no one in the area assigned to her. Later, she moved to the south, where some *estancias* (sheep ranches) covered as much as a quarter of a million acres. The people there were friendly and hospitable and welcomed her to their table at mealtime. In this and other ways, Jehovah cared for her, so that she had the physical necessities of life.

Preaching the good news of God's Kingdom has filled her life.* Looking back on her years of service, she said: "I feel that I have had a very rich life. Each year when I attend an assembly of Jehovah's people, I get a warm, satisfied feeling as I see so many persons with whom I have had Bible studies publishing the good news, helping others to come to the water of life." She has had the joy of seeing the number of praisers of Jehovah in Chile grow from about 50 to over 44,000.

"Here I Am! Send Me"

After hearing a lecture based on Jehovah's invitation to service as recorded at Isaiah 6:8 and the prophet's positive response, "Here I am! Send me," Martin Poetzinger, in Germany, was baptized. Two years later, in 1930, he entered the full-time ministry in Bavaria.# Before long, officials there prohibited preaching by the Witnesses, meeting places were closed, and literature was confiscated. The Gestapo threatened. But those developments in 1933 did not bring Brother Poetzinger's ministry to an end.

He was invited to serve in Bulgaria. Testimony cards in Bulgarian were used to introduce the Bible literature. But many people were illiterate. So, Brother Poetzinger took lessons to learn their language, which used the Cyrillic alphabet. When literature was left with a family, it was often necessary for young children to read it to their parents.

For most of the first year, Brother Poetzinger was alone, and he wrote: "At the Memorial, I delivered the talk myself, prayed myself, and closed the meeting all by myself." During 1934, foreigners were deported, so he went to Hungary. Here another new language had to be learned so that he could share the good news. From Hungary he went to the countries then known as Czechoslovakia and Yugoslavia.

Many were the happy experiences he had—finding lovers of truth as he walked through the countryside and villages, with literature packed on his back; experiencing Jehovah's care as hospitable people offered food and

---
* *The Watchtower,* December 15, 1963, pp. 764-6.
# See *The Watchtower,* December 1, 1969, pages 729-32; September 15, 1988, page 31.

"SEEKING FIRST THE KINGDOM"   291

even a bed for the night; talking far into the evening to those who came to his lodging to hear more of the comforting message of the Kingdom.

There were also severe tests of faith. When serving outside his native land, and without funds, he experienced a serious illness. No doctor was willing to see him. But Jehovah provided. How? Finally, the senior consultant of the local hospital was contacted. This man, a firm believer in the Bible, cared for Brother Poetzinger as he would have for a son, doing so free of charge. The doctor was impressed with the self-sacrificing spirit of this young man, which was evident in the work he was doing, and he accepted a set of the Society's books as a gift.

Another severe test came four months after marriage. Brother Poetzinger was arrested in December 1936 and was confined first in one concentration camp and then in another, while his wife was held in yet another such camp. They did not see each other for nine years. Jehovah did not prevent such cruel persecution, but he did strengthen Martin, his wife Gertrud, and thousands of others to endure it.

After he and his wife were released, Brother Poetzinger enjoyed many years of service as a traveling overseer in Germany. He was present for thrilling conventions held in the postwar era on Hitler's former parade grounds in Nuremberg. But now those grounds were filled with a vast crowd of loyal supporters of God's Kingdom. He attended unforgettable conventions in New York's Yankee Stadium. He enjoyed to the full his training at the Watchtower Bible School of Gilead. And in 1977 he became a member of the Governing Body of Jehovah's Witnesses. His outlook, right down till he finished his earthly course in 1988, can best be expressed with the words: 'This one thing I do—seek first the Kingdom.'

The determination of both Martin and Gertrud Poetzinger is expressed in the words: 'This one thing I do—seek first the Kingdom'

Learning What It Really Means

The spirit of self-sacrifice clearly is not something new among Jehovah's Witnesses. When the very first volume of *Millennial Dawn* was published back in 1886, the matter of consecration (or, as we would say today, dedication) was frankly discussed. It was pointed out on the basis of the Scriptures that true Christians "consecrate" everything to God; that includes their abilities, their material possessions, their very lives. Christians thus become stewards of what has been "consecrated" to God, and as stewards, they must render an account—not to men but to God.

A growing number of the Bible Students truly gave of themselves in the service of God. They used to the full their abilities, their possessions, their vital energy, in doing his will. On the other hand, there were those who felt that what was most important was to cultivate what they called Christian character so that they might qualify to share in the Kingdom with Christ.

Although the responsibility of each true Christian to witness to others about God's Kingdom had often been stated by Brother Russell, this received even greater emphasis after World War I. The article "Character or Covenant—Which?" in *The Watch Tower* of May 1, 1926, is a striking example. It frankly considered the harmful effects from what was called character development and then stressed the importance of fulfilling one's obligations to God by *actions*.

Earlier, *The Watch Tower* of July 1, 1920, had examined Jesus' great prophecy about 'the sign of his presence and the end of the world.' (Matt. 24:3, *KJ*) It focused attention on the preaching work that must be done in fulfillment of Matthew 24:14 and identified the message to be proclaimed, saying: "The good news here is concerning the end of the old order of things and the establishment of Messiah's kingdom." *The Watch Tower* explained that on the basis of where Jesus stated this in relation to other features of the sign, this work would have to be accomplished "between the time of the great world war [World War I] and the time of the 'great tribulation' mentioned by the Master in Matthew 24:21, 22." That work was urgent. Who would do it?

This responsibility clearly rested on the members of "the church," the true Christian congregation. However, in 1932, by means of the August 1 issue of *The Watchtower*, these were counseled to encourage the "Jehonadab class" to share with them in the work, in harmony with the spirit of Revelation 22:17. The Jehonadab class—whose hope is everlasting life in the Paradise earth—responded, and many of them zealously so.

The vital importance of this work has been strongly emphasized: "It is just as essential to participate in the service of the Lord as it is to attend a meeting," said *The Watch Tower* in 1921. "Each one must be a preacher of the gospel," it pointed out in 1922. "Jehovah has made preaching the most important work any of us could do in this world," it stated in 1949. The apostle Paul's declaration at 1 Corinthians 9:16 has been quoted frequently: "Necessity is laid upon me. Really, woe is me if I did not declare the good news!" This scripture has been applied to each one of Jehovah's Witnesses.

How Many Do the Preaching? To What Extent? Why?

Were any being compelled to engage in this work contrary to their will? "No," *The Watch Tower* answered, in its issue of August 1, 1919, "no one is compelled to do anything. It is all purely voluntary service, performed by

Increased emphasis on the responsibility to witness

love for the Lord and his cause of righteousness. Jehovah never drafts anyone." Regarding the motivation behind such service, *The Watch Tower* of September 1, 1922, further stated: "One who really has gratitude in his heart and appreciates what God has done for him will want to do something in return; and the more his appreciation of God's kindness to him increases, the greater will be his love; and the greater his love, the greater will be the desire to serve him." Love for God, it was explained, is shown by keeping his commandments, and one of those commandments is to preach the glad tidings of the Kingdom of God.—Isa. 61:1, 2; 1 John 5:3.

Those who have undertaken this activity have not been enticed by any idea of worldly ambition. They have been frankly told that when they go from house to house or offer literature on a street corner, they will be viewed as "foolish, weak, lowly," that they will be "despised, persecuted," and that they will be classed as "not of much account from a worldly standpoint." But they know that Jesus and his early disciples were treated in the same way.—John 15:18-20; 1 Cor. 1:18-31.

Do Jehovah's Witnesses think that somehow they are earning salvation by their preaching activity? Not at all! The book *United in Worship of the Only True God*, which has been used since 1983 to help students to advance to Christian maturity, discusses this matter. It states: "Jesus' sacrifice has also opened to us the opportunity for eternal life . . . This is not a reward that we earn. No matter how much we do in Jehovah's service, we can never build up such merit that God will owe us life. Eternal life is 'the gift God gives . . . by Christ Jesus our Lord.' (Rom. 6:23; Eph. 2:8-10) Nevertheless, if we have faith in that gift and appreciation for the manner in which it was made possible, we will make this manifest. Discerning how marvelously Jehovah has used Jesus in accomplishing His will and how vital it is that all of us follow Jesus' steps closely, we will make the Christian ministry one of the most important things in our life."

Can it be said that *all* of Jehovah's Witnesses are proclaimers of God's Kingdom? Yes! That is what being one of Jehovah's Witnesses means. Over half a century ago, there were some who felt that it was not necessary for them to have a part in the field service, going out in public and from house to house. But today none of Jehovah's Witnesses claim exemption from such service because of position in the local congregation or in the worldwide organization. Male and female as well as young and old participate. They view it as a precious privilege, a sacred service. Not a few do it in spite of serious infirmities. And as for any who simply are physically unable to go from house to house, they find other ways to reach people and give them a personal witness.

In the past, there was at times a tendency to allow newer ones to participate in the field service too soon. But in recent decades, greater

They view house-to-house witnessing as a precious privilege

emphasis has been placed on their qualifying before being invited. What does that mean? It does not mean that they have to be able to explain everything in the Bible. But, as the book *Organized to Accomplish Our Ministry* explains, they must know and believe the Bible's basic teachings. They must also be living clean lives, in harmony with Bible standards. Each one must truly want to be one of Jehovah's Witnesses.

Understanding what whole-souled service is

It is not expected that all of Jehovah's Witnesses will do the same amount of preaching. The circumstances of individuals vary. Age, health, family responsibilities, and depth of appreciation are all factors. This has always been recognized. It was emphasized by *The Watchtower* in its issue of December 1, 1950, when discussing "the good soil" in Jesus' parable of the sower, at Luke 8:4-15. The *Kingdom Ministry School Course,* prepared for elders in 1972, analyzed the requirement of 'loving Jehovah with one's whole soul' and explained that "what is vital is not the quantity one does in relation to what someone else does, but doing what one can." (Mark 14: 6-8) Encouraging sober self-analysis, however, it also showed that such love means "that every fiber of one's existence is involved in lovingly serving God; no function, capacity or desire in life is excepted." All our faculties, our whole soul, must be mobilized to do God's will. That textbook emphasized that "God requires, not merely participation, but whole-souled service."—Mark 12:30.

Unfortunately, the tendency of imperfect humans is to go to an extreme, emphasizing one thing while neglecting another. So, back in 1906, Brother Russell found it necessary to caution that self-sacrifice does not mean sacrificing others. It does not mean failing to make reasonable provision for one's wife, dependent children, or elderly parents so that one can be free to preach to others. From time to time since then, similar reminders have appeared in the Watch Tower publications.

Gradually, with the help of God's Word, the entire organization has sought to achieve Christian balance—manifesting zeal for the service of God, while giving proper attention to all aspects of being a real Christian. Although "character development" was built on a wrong understanding, *The Watchtower* has shown that the fruits of the spirit and Christian conduct are not to be minimized. In 1942, *The Watchtower* said quite pointedly: "Some have unwisely concluded that if they were engaged in the house-to-house witness work they could pursue with freedom from punishment any course their appetites might call for. One should remember that merely engaging in the witness work is not all that is required."—1 Cor. 9:27.

Getting Priorities Straight

Jehovah's Witnesses have come to appreciate that 'seeking first the Kingdom and God's righteousness' is a matter of getting their priorities straight. It includes giving a proper place in one's life to personal study of God's Word and regular attendance at congregation meetings and not allowing other pursuits to take priority. It involves making decisions that reflect a genuine desire to conform to the requirements of God's Kingdom, as set out in the Bible. That includes using Bible principles as the basis for decisions involving family life, recreation, secular education, employment, business practices, and relations with one's fellowmen.

Seeking first the Kingdom is more than just having some share each month in talking to others about God's purpose. It means giving Kingdom interests first place in one's entire life, while caring properly for other Scriptural obligations.

There are many ways in which devoted Witnesses of Jehovah promote Kingdom interests.

What "seeking first the kingdom" really means

The Privilege of Bethel Service

Some serve as members of the global Bethel family. This is a staff of full-time ministers who have volunteered to do whatever they may be assigned in preparing and publishing Bible literature, in caring for necessary office work, and in providing support services for such operations. This is not work in which they gain personal prominence or material possessions. Their desire is to honor Jehovah, and they are satisfied with the provisions made for them in the way of food, lodging, and a modest reimbursement for personal expenses. Because of the way of life of the Bethel family, secular authorities in the United States, for example, view them as members of a religious order who have taken a vow of poverty. Those who are at Bethel find joy in being able to use their lives to the full in Jehovah's service and in doing work that benefits large numbers of their Christian brothers and newly interested persons, sometimes internationally. Like others of Jehovah's Witnesses, they also share regularly in the field ministry.

The first Bethel family (or, Bible House family, as they were then known) was located in Allegheny, Pennsylvania. As of 1896, the staff numbered 12. In 1992, there were upwards of 12,900 Bethel family members, serving in 99 lands. In addition, when there has not been enough housing on the Society's premises, hundreds of other volunteers have commuted to Bethel homes and factories every day in order to share in the work. They have counted it a privilege to have a part in the work being done. As there is need, thousands of other Witnesses offer to leave behind secular work and other activity for varying periods of time to assist with construction of facilities needed by the Society for use in connection with the global preaching of the good news of God's Kingdom.

Many of the members of the global Bethel family have made it their life's work. Frederick W. Franz, who in 1977 became the Watch Tower

Bethel Service

Personal study is important to Bethel family members

Spain

At each Bethel Home, the day begins with discussion of a Bible text

Finland

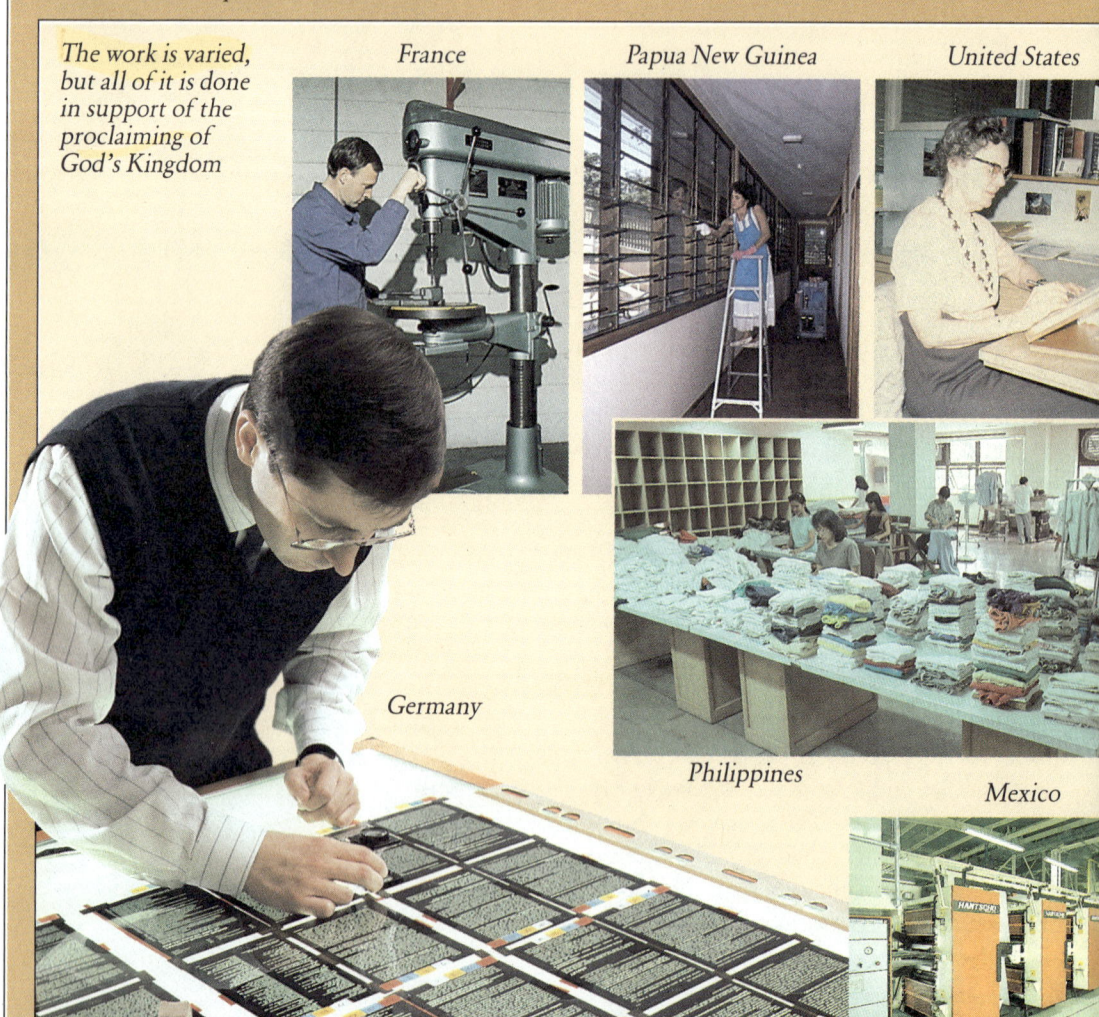

The work is varied, but all of it is done in support of the proclaiming of God's Kingdom

France

Papua New Guinea

United States

Germany

Philippines

Mexico

As is true of Jehovah's Witnesses everywhere, Bethel family members share in the field service

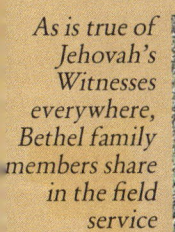

Switzerland

Each Monday evening the Bethel family studies "The Watchtower" together

Italy

Britain

Nigeria

Netherlands

Brazil

South Africa

Japan

As of 1992, there were 12,974 sharing in Bethel service in 99 lands

Society's fourth president, had by that time already been a member of the Bethel family in New York for 57 years, and he continued in Bethel service for another 15 years, until he died in 1992. Heinrich Dwenger began his Bethel service in Germany in 1911, thereafter modestly serving wherever he was assigned; and in 1983, the year of his death, he was still enjoying his service as a member of the Bethel family in Thun, Switzerland. George Phillips, from Scotland, accepted an assignment to the branch office in South Africa in 1924 (when it supervised preaching activity from Cape Town to Kenya) and continued to serve in South Africa until his death in 1982 (at which time seven branch offices of the Society and some 160,000 Witnesses were active in that area). Christian sisters, such as Kathryn Bogard, Grace DeCecca, Irma Friend, Alice Berner, and Mary Hannan, also devoted their adult lives to Bethel service, doing so right to the finish. Many other Bethel family members have likewise been serving for 10, 30, 50, 70, and more years.*

A Few With Long Records of Bethel Service

Heinrich Dwenger —Germany (about 15 years of 1911-33), Hungary (1933-35), Czechoslovakia (1936-39), then Switzerland (1939-83)

George Phillips —South Africa (1924-66, 1976-82)

Fleshly sisters (Kathryn Bogard and Grace DeCecca) who devoted a combined total of 136 years to Bethel service —United States

F. W. Franz —United States (1920-92)

Self-Sacrificing Traveling Overseers

Worldwide, there are some 3,900 circuit and district overseers who, along with their wives, also care for assignments wherever they are needed, usually in their home country. Many of these have left behind homes and now move every week or every few weeks to serve the congregations assigned. They receive no salary but are grateful for food and lodging where they serve, along with modest provision for personal expenses. In the United States, where 499 circuit and district overseers were serving in 1992, these traveling elders average 54 years in age, and some of them have been serving in this capacity for 30, 40, or more years. In a number of

---

* See *The Watchtower*, May 1, 1987, pages 22-30; April 1, 1964, pages 212-15; December 1, 1956, pages 712-19; August 15, 1970, pages 507-10; October 1, 1960, pages 601-5; June 15, 1968, pages 378-81; April 1, 1968, pages 217-21; April 1, 1959, pages 220-3.

lands, these overseers travel by automobile. Territory in the Pacific area often requires the use of commercial planes and boats. In many places circuit overseers reach remote congregations by horseback or on foot.

Pioneers Fill an Important Need

In order to get the preaching of the good news started in places where there are no Witnesses, or to provide help that may be especially needed in an area, the Governing Body may arrange to send in special pioneers. These are full-time evangelizers who devote at least 140 hours each month to the field ministry. They make themselves available to serve anywhere they are needed in their own country or, in some cases, in nearby lands. Since their service requirements leave them little or no time for secular work to provide for material needs, they are given a modest expense reimbursement for housing and other necessities. In 1992, there were over 14,500 special pioneers in various parts of the earth.

When the first special pioneers were sent out in 1937, they spearheaded the work of playing recorded Bible talks for householders right at their doorsteps and using recordings as the basis for Bible discussions on return visits. This was done in large cities where there already were congregations. After a few years, the special pioneers began to be directed particularly into areas where no congregations existed or where congregations were in great need of help. As a result of their effective work, hundreds of new congregations were formed.

Instead of covering a territory and moving on, they would work a given area repeatedly, following up on all interest and conducting Bible studies. Meetings were arranged for interested ones. Thus, in Lesotho, southern Africa, on his first week in a new assignment, a special pioneer invited everyone he met to come and see how Jehovah's Witnesses conduct the Theocratic Ministry School. He and his family put on the full program. Then he invited all to the *Watchtower* Study. After initial curiosity was satisfied, 30 continued to attend the *Watchtower* Study, and average attendance at the school was 20. In lands where Gilead-trained missionaries did much to get the preaching of the good news under way, faster growth sometimes took place when native-born Witnesses began to qualify for special pioneer service, for these could often work even more effectively among the local people.

In addition to these zealous workers, there are hundreds of thousands more of Jehovah's Witnesses who also energetically promote Kingdom interests. These include young and old, male and female, married and single persons. Regular pioneers devote a minimum of 90 hours each month to the field ministry; auxiliary pioneers, at least 60 hours. They decide where they would like to preach. Most of them work with established congregations; some move to isolated areas. They care for their own physical needs by doing some secular work, or their family members may help to make provision for them. During 1992, over 914,500 shared in such service as regular or auxiliary pioneers for at least part of the year.

Schools With Special Objectives

To equip volunteers for certain types of service, special schooling is provided. Since 1943, for example, Gilead School has trained thousands of experienced ministers for missionary work, and graduates have been sent to all parts of the earth. In 1987 the Ministerial Training School went into operation to help fill special needs, including care for congregations as well as other responsibilities. The arrangement for this school to convene in various places minimizes travel of students to a central location as well as the need to learn another language in order to benefit from the schooling. All who are invited to attend this school are elders or ministerial servants who have given evidence that they truly seek first the Kingdom. Many have made themselves available to serve in other lands. Their spirit is like that of the prophet Isaiah, who said: "Here I am! Send me."—Isa. 6:8.

In order to improve the effectiveness of those already serving as regular and special pioneers, the Pioneer Service School was put into operation starting in 1977. Where possible, the school was arranged in each circuit around the world. All pioneers were invited to benefit from this two-week course. Progressively since then, pioneers who have completed their first year of service have been given the same training. Down till 1992, over 100,000 pioneers had been trained in this school in the United States alone; upwards of 10,000 were being trained each year. Another 55,000 had been trained in Japan, 38,000 in Mexico, 25,000 in Brazil, and 25,000 in Italy. In addition to this course, pioneers regularly enjoy a special meeting with the circuit overseer during his semiannual visits with each congregation and a special training session with both the circuit overseer and the district overseer at the time of the annual circuit assembly. Thus, those making up the large army of Kingdom proclaimers who serve as pioneers are not only willing workers but also well-trained ministers.

Pioneer Service School (as shown here in Japan) has provided special training for tens of thousands of zealous workers

Serving Where the Need Is Greater

Many thousands of Jehovah's Witnesses—some of whom are pioneers, and others not—have made themselves available to serve not only in their home community but also in other areas where there is a great need for proclaimers of the good news. Each year thousands spend a period of weeks or months, according to what they personally can arrange, in areas often quite distant from their homes in order to witness to people who are not regularly visited by Jehovah's Witnesses. Thousands more have pulled up stakes and relocated in order to provide such help over an extended period. Many of these are married couples or families with children. Their moves have often involved going a relatively short distance, but some have made such moves repeatedly over the years. Many of these zealous Witnesses have even taken up service in foreign lands —some for a few years, others on a permanent basis. They do whatever secular work is required in order to care for their needs, and the moves are made at their own expense. Their one desire is to share as fully as their circumstances permit in spreading the Kingdom message.

When the family head is not a Witness, he may move his family because of employment. But family members who are Witnesses may see this as an opportunity to spread the Kingdom message. That was true of two Witnesses from the United States who found themselves at a construction camp in the jungle in Suriname in the late 1970's. Twice a week they got up at 4:00 a.m., caught a company bus for a rough one-hour trip to a village, and spent the day preaching. Before long they were conducting 30 Bible studies each week with truth-hungry people. Today, there is a congregation in that formerly unreached part of the rain forest.

Seizing Every Appropriate Opportunity to Witness

Of course, not all of Jehovah's Witnesses move to other countries, or even to other towns, to carry on their ministry. Their circumstances may not permit them to pioneer. Nevertheless, they are well aware of the Bible admonition to put forth "all earnest effort" and to have "plenty to do in the work of the Lord." (2 Pet. 1:5-8; 1 Cor. 15:58) They show that they seek first the Kingdom when they put its interests ahead of secular work and recreation. Those whose hearts are filled with appreciation for the Kingdom share regularly in the field ministry to the extent that their circumstances permit, and many of them change their circumstances so they can share more fully. They are also constantly on the lookout to seize appropriate opportunities to witness to others about the Kingdom.

As an example, John Furgala, who owned a hardware business in Guayaquil, Ecuador, set up an attractive display of Bible literature in his store. While his helper would fill an order, John would witness to the customer.

In Nigeria a zealous Witness who supported his family by working as an electrical contractor was also determined to use well his contacts so as to give a witness. Since he owned the business, he determined the schedule of activity. Each morning, before the day's work, he gathered his wife, children, employees, and apprentices for a discussion of the day's Bible text, along with

Zealous Witnesses put Kingdom interests ahead of secular work and recreation

experiences from the *Yearbook of Jehovah's Witnesses*. At the beginning of each year, he would also give his customers a copy of the Watch Tower Society's calendar, along with two magazines. As a result, some of his employees and some customers have joined him in the worship of Jehovah.

There are many of Jehovah's Witnesses who share that same spirit. Regardless of what they are doing, they are constantly looking for opportunities to share the good news with others.

A Large Army of Happy Full-Time Evangelizers

With the passing of years, the zeal of Jehovah's Witnesses for the preaching of the good news has not abated. Even though many householders have told them quite firmly that they are not interested, there are large numbers who are grateful that the Witnesses help them to understand the Bible. The determination of Jehovah's Witnesses is to continue preaching until Jehovah himself gives clear indication that this work is completed.

Instead of slacking off, the worldwide association of Jehovah's Witnesses has actually intensified its preaching activity. In 1982 the annual global report showed that 384,856,662 hours had been devoted to the field ministry. Ten years later (in 1992) 1,024,910,434 hours were devoted to this work. What accounted for that great increase in activity?

It is true that the number of Jehovah's Witnesses had grown. But not to that extent. During that period, while the number of Witnesses increased by 80 percent, the number of pioneers soared 250 percent. On an average each month, 1 out of every 7 of Jehovah's Witnesses worldwide was in some branch of the full-time preaching work.

Who were the ones sharing in such pioneer service? As an example, in the Republic of Korea, many Witnesses are housewives. Family responsibilities may not permit them all to pioneer on a regular basis, but large numbers have used the long winter school vacations as opportunities for auxiliary pioneer service. As a result, 53 percent of the total Witnesses in the Republic of Korea were in some branch of full-time service in January 1990.

In the early years, it was a zealous pioneer spirit on the part of Filipino Witnesses that enabled them to reach the hundreds of inhabited islands in the Philippines with the Kingdom message. That zeal has been even more evident since then. In 1992, on an average each month, 22,205 publishers were sharing in the field ministry as pioneers in the Philippines. Included among them were many youths who had chosen to 'remember their Creator' and use their youthful vigor in his service. (Eccl. 12:1) After a decade of pioneer service, one of such youths said: "I have learned to be patient, to lead a simple life, to rely on Jehovah, and to be humble. It is true that I have also experienced hardships and discouragements, but all of these are nothing compared with the blessings that pioneering has brought."

"SEEKING FIRST THE KINGDOM"

During April and May of 1989, *The Watchtower* featured an exposé of Babylon the Great, which is false religion in its many forms worldwide. The articles were published simultaneously in 39 languages and given intensive distribution. In Japan, where the number of Witnesses who are pioneering has often been over 40 percent, a new peak of 41,055 auxiliary pioneers enrolled to help in the work that April. In the Osaka Prefecture, Takatsuki City, Otsuka Congregation, 73 of the 77 baptized publishers were in some form of pioneer service that month. On April 8, when all the publishers in Japan were urged to have some part in distributing this vital message, hundreds of congregations, such as the Ushioda Congregation, in Yokohama City, arranged for day-long street and house-to-house service, from 7:00 a.m. till 8:00 p.m., in order to reach everyone possible in the area.

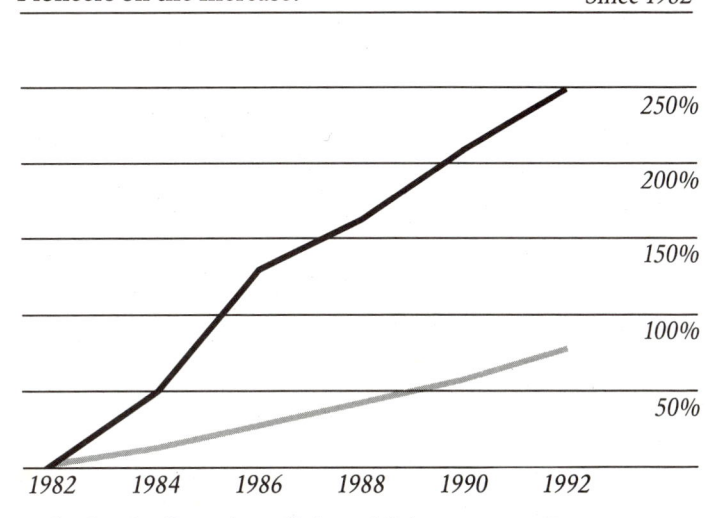

Pioneers on the Increase!

Percent Increase Since 1982

— Pioneers
— Publishers

As is true everywhere, Jehovah's Witnesses in Mexico work to care for their material needs. Nevertheless, each month during 1992, on an average 50,095 of Jehovah's Witnesses there also made room in their lives for the pioneer service in order to help truth-hungry people learn about God's Kingdom. In some families all in the household cooperated in order to enable the entire group, or at least some of them, to pioneer. They enjoy a fruitful ministry. During 1992, Jehovah's Witnesses in Mexico were regularly conducting 502,017 home Bible studies with individuals and family groups.

The elders who serve the needs of the congregations of Jehovah's Witnesses have heavy responsibilities. Most of the elders in Nigeria are men with families, and that is true of elders in many other places too. Yet, in addition to preparing to conduct or to share in congregation meetings, as well as to do needed shepherding of the flock of God, some of these men also pioneer. How is it possible? Careful scheduling of time and good family cooperation are often important factors.

It is obvious that, worldwide, Jehovah's Witnesses have taken to heart Jesus' admonition to 'keep on seeking first the kingdom.' (Matt. 6:33) What they are doing is a heartfelt expression of their love for Jehovah and their appreciation for his sovereignty. Like the psalmist David, they say: "I will exalt you, O my God the King, and I will bless your name to time indefinite, even forever."—Ps. 145:1.

CHAPTER 19

GROWING TOGETHER IN LOVE

WHEN writing to fellow Christians, the apostles of Jesus Christ pointed out the need for individuals to grow not only in accurate knowledge but also in love. The basis for this was the love shown by God himself and the self-sacrificing love of Christ, in whose footsteps they endeavored to walk. (John 13:34, 35; Eph. 4:15, 16; 5:1, 2; Phil. 1:9; 1 John 4:7-10) They were a brotherhood, and when they helped one another, the bonds of love became even stronger.

When famine gave rise to economic hardship for the brothers in Judea, Christians in Syria and in Greece shared their possessions in order to assist them. (Acts 11:27-30; Rom. 15:26) When some were persecuted, the suffering experienced was keenly felt by other Christians, and these sought to render aid.—1 Cor. 12:26; Heb. 13:3.

Of course, all humans have the capacity to love, and others besides Christians engage in acts of humanitarian kindness. But people in the Roman world recognized that the love shown by Christians was different. Tertullian, who had been a jurist in Rome, quoted the remarks of people of the Roman world regarding Christians, saying: "'Look,' they say, 'how they love one another . . . and how they are ready to die for each other.'" (*Apology*, XXXIX, 7) John Hurst, in his *History of the Christian Church* (Volume I, page 146), relates that people in ancient Carthage and Alexandria, during periods of pestilence, drove away from their presence those who were afflicted and stripped from the bodies of the dying anything that might be of value. In contrast, he reports, Christians in these places shared their possessions, nursed the sick, and buried the dead.

Do Jehovah's Witnesses in modern times engage in works that demonstrate such concern for the well-being of others? If so, are these performed by only a few scattered individuals, or does the organization as a whole encourage and support such efforts?

Loving Help in Local Congregations

Among Jehovah's Witnesses, care for orphans and widows in the congregation, as well as for any faithful ones who experience severe adversity, is viewed as part of their worship. (Jas. 1:27; 2:15-17; 1 John 3:17, 18) Secular governments generally make provision for hospitals, housing for the elderly, and welfare arrangements for unemployed people in the community at large, and Jehovah's Witnesses support those arrangements by conscientiously paying their taxes. However, recognizing that only God's Kingdom can lastingly solve the problems of humankind, Jehovah's Witnesses devote themselves and their resources primarily to teaching others about that. This is a vital service that no human government provides.

In the more than 69,000 congregations of Jehovah's Witnesses worldwide, special needs that arise because of advanced age and infirmity of individuals are usually cared for on a personal basis. As shown at 1 Timothy 5:4, 8, the responsibility rests primarily upon each Christian to care for his own household. Children, grandchildren, or other close relatives display Christian love by providing assistance to elderly and infirm ones according to their needs. Congregations of Jehovah's Witnesses do not weaken this sense of responsibility by taking over family obligations. However, if there are no close family members, or if those who have the responsibility simply cannot carry the load by themselves, others in the congregation lovingly come to their aid. Where necessary, the congregation as a whole may make provision for some assistance to a needy brother or sister who has a long record of faithful service.—1 Tim. 5:3-10.

Attention to these needs is not left to chance. At sessions of the Kingdom Ministry School, which the elders have attended repeatedly since 1959, their obligation before God in this regard as shepherds of the flock has frequently been given special consideration. (Heb. 13:1, 16) It is not that they were unaware of this need before then. In 1911, for example, material relief was provided by the Oldham Congregation in Lancashire, England, to those among them who were facing severe economic problems. However, since then the global organization has grown, the number experiencing severe problems has increased, and Jehovah's Witnesses have become increasingly aware of what the Bible shows they should do in such situations. Especially in recent years, the responsibilities of each Christian toward those among them with special needs—the elderly, the infirm, single-parent families, and those in economic difficulty—have been discussed by all the congregations at their meetings.*

Attention to cases of special need not left to chance

The concern that individual Witnesses show for others goes far beyond saying, "Keep warm and well fed." They demonstrate loving personal interest. (Jas. 2:15, 16) Consider a few examples.

When a young Swedish woman, one of Jehovah's Witnesses, contracted meningitis while visiting Greece in 1986, she also experienced what it

---

* See *The Watchtower,* September 15, 1980, pages 21-6; October 15, 1986, pages 10-21; June 1, 1987, pages 4-18; July 15, 1988, pages 21-3; March 1, 1990, pages 20-2.

means to have Christian brothers and sisters in many lands. Her father in Sweden was notified. He immediately got in touch with an elder in the local congregation of Jehovah's Witnesses in Sweden and, through him, with a Witness in Greece. Until she was able to return to Sweden three weeks later, the young Witness's new friends in Greece never left her unattended.

Likewise, when an elderly Witness, a widower, in Wallaceburg, Ontario, Canada, needed assistance, a family that he had aided spiritually showed their appreciation by making him part of the family. A few years later when they moved to Barry's Bay, he went with them. He lived with them and was lovingly cared for by them for 19 years, until he died in 1990.

In New York City, a Witness couple cared for an elderly man who was attending meetings at their Kingdom Hall, doing so for some 15 years, until he died in 1986. When he had a stroke, they looked after his shopping, cleaning, cooking, and laundry. They treated him as though he were their own father.

Needs of other kinds also are given loving attention. A Witness couple in the United States had sold their home and moved to Montana to help a congregation there. In time, however, serious health problems developed, the brother was laid off from work, and their finances were depleted. How would they manage? The brother prayed to Jehovah for help. As he finished praying, a fellow Witness knocked on the door. Together they went

United States

After World War II, they shipped food and clothing to fellow Witnesses in need in 18 lands

Switzerland

out for a cup of coffee. When the brother returned, he found the kitchen counter stacked with groceries. With the groceries was an envelope containing funds and a note that read: "From your brothers and sisters, who love you very much." The congregation had realized their need, and they had all shared in filling it. Deeply moved by their love, he and his wife could not help giving way to tears and thanking Jehovah, whose example of love motivates his servants.

Help that results from loving personal concern

The generous concern that Jehovah's Witnesses show for those among them who fall into need has come to be widely known. At times, impostors have taken advantage of it. So the Witnesses have had to learn to be cautious, while not stifling their desire to help worthy ones.

When War Leaves People Destitute

In many parts of the earth, people have been left destitute as a result of war. Relief organizations endeavor to provide help, but this machinery often works slowly. Jehovah's Witnesses do not take the view that the work done by such agencies relieves them of responsibility toward their Christian brothers in these areas. When they know that their brothers are in need, they do not 'shut the door of their tender compassions' upon such ones but promptly do what they can to bring relief to them.—1 John 3: 17, 18.

During World War II, even within countries hard-pressed by shortages, Witnesses in the countryside who still had food supplies shared these with less fortunate brothers in the cities. In the Netherlands this was done at great risk because of harsh restrictions imposed by the Nazis. When on such a relief mission on one occasion, Gerrit Böhmermann was leading a group of brothers on transport bikes that were loaded with food covered with tarpaulins. Suddenly they came upon a checkpoint in the city of Alkmaar. "There was no choice but to trust fully in Jehovah," said Gerrit. Without slowing down much, he called out loudly to the officer: *"Wo ist Amsterdam?"* (Which way to Amsterdam?) The officer stepped aside and pointed ahead as he yelled: *"Geradeaus!"* (Straight ahead!) *"Danke schön!"* (Thank you!) was Gerrit's response as the entire fleet of transport bikes went through at full speed while an astonished crowd watched. On another occasion, Witnesses succeeded in bringing a whole boatload of potatoes to their brothers in Amsterdam.

Right within the concentration camps in Europe, this spirit was shown by Jehovah's Witnesses. While incarcerated in a camp near Amersfoort, in the Netherlands, a 17-year-old lost weight until he became a walking skeleton. But in later years, he never forgot that after they had been forced to exercise in the pouring rain till midnight and then were deprived of food, a Witness from another part of the camp managed to get to him and press a piece of bread into his hand. And in the Mauthausen concentration camp in Austria, a Witness whose assignment required that he go from one section of the camp to another often risked his life by taking food that Witnesses had saved from their meager rations to other Witnesses who were being more severely deprived.

Following the war Jehovah's Witnesses who emerged from German prisons and concentration camps had nothing but the prison garb on their backs. The property of many not in prison had been devastated. Food, clothing, and fuel were in short supply throughout much of Europe. Jehovah's Witnesses in these lands quickly organized congregation meetings and began to help others spiritually by sharing with them the good news of God's Kingdom. But they themselves needed help in other ways. Many of them were so weak from hunger that they often fainted during the meetings.

Coming to grips with massive needs for relief

Here was a situation that the Witnesses had not faced before on such a large scale. However, the very month that the war officially ended in the Pacific area, Jehovah's Witnesses held a special convention in Cleveland, Ohio, at which they discussed what needed to be done to provide relief for their Christian brothers in war-torn lands and how to go about it. The heartwarming discourse "His Unspeakable Gift," delivered by F. W. Franz, presented Scriptural counsel that fully met the needs of the situation.*

Within a few weeks, as soon as any travel in the area was permitted, N. H. Knorr, president of the Watch Tower Society, and M. G. Henschel were on their way to Europe to see the conditions firsthand. Even before they departed on that trip, relief arrangements were being put into operation.

Early shipments went out from Switzerland and Sweden. More followed from Canada, the United States, and other lands. Although the number of Witnesses in the lands that were in a position to provide such help then numbered only about 85,000, they undertook to send clothing and food to fellow Witnesses in Austria, Belgium, Bulgaria, China, Czechoslovakia, Denmark, England, Finland, France, Germany, Greece, Hungary, Italy, the Netherlands, Norway, the Philippines, Poland, and Romania. That was not a onetime effort. Relief shipments continued for two and a half years. Between January 1946 and August 1948, they dispatched 1,056,247 pounds of clothing, 124,110 pairs of shoes, and 718,873 pounds of food as gifts to fellow Witnesses. None of the funds were siphoned off for administrative expenses. The sorting and packing was done by unpaid volunteers. Funds contributed were *all* used to help the people for whom they were intended.

* See *The Watchtower*, December 1, 1945, pages 355-63.

Of course, the need for relief to refugees and to others left destitute by war did not end back there in the 1940's. There have been hundreds of wars since 1945. And the same loving concern has continued to be shown by Jehovah's Witnesses. This was done during and after the Biafran war in Nigeria, from 1967 to 1970. Similar aid was provided in Mozambique during the 1980's.

In Liberia too, there was famine as a result of the war that began in 1989. As people fled, the Watch Tower compound in Monrovia was packed with hundreds of refugees. Whatever food was available there, as well as water from the well, was shared with both Witnesses and non-Witness neighbors. Then, as soon as circumstances permitted, further relief supplies came from Witnesses in Sierra Leone and Côte d'Ivoire in West Africa, the Netherlands and Italy in Europe, and the United States.

Again, in 1990, after war in Lebanon had left sections of Beirut looking as if an earthquake had struck, elders among Jehovah's Witnesses organized an emergency relief committee to give needed help to the brothers. They did not have to call for volunteers; each day many offered their help.

During a period of great political and economic upheaval in Europe, Jehovah's Witnesses in Austria, Czechoslovakia, Hungary, and Yugoslavia sent more than 70 tons of needed items to their Christian brothers in Romania in 1990.

This was followed by more relief missions into Eastern Europe. The Governing Body asked the Watch Tower Society's branch office in Denmark to organize relief for needy Witnesses in Ukraine. Congregations were notified and were eager to share. On December 18, 1991, five trucks and two vans driven by Witness volunteers arrived at Lviv with 22 tons of supplies—an expression of loving concern for their Christian brothers. Continuing into 1992, shipments also arrived from the Witnesses in Austria—over 100 tons of food and clothing. More supplies were dispatched from the Witnesses in the Netherlands—first 26 tons of food, next a convoy of 11 trucks containing clothing, then more food to cope with the ongoing need. The recipients were grateful to God and looked to him for wisdom in using what had been provided. They united in prayer before unloading the trucks and again when the job was done. Other large relief shipments were sent by Witnesses in Italy, Finland, Sweden, and Switzerland. At the time that all of this was going on, turbulent conditions among the republics that formerly made up Yugoslavia gave rise to need there. Supplies of food, clothing, and medication were also dispatched to that area.

"You Really Love One Another"

After watching Witness volunteers in war-torn Lebanon completely restore the badly damaged home of one of their Christian sisters, her neighbors felt impelled to ask: "Where does this love come from? What kind of people are you?" And a Muslim woman, watching as the home of a Witness was being cleaned and repaired, declared: "You really love one another. Yours is the right religion."

In 1990, Witnesses in nearby lands united their efforts to help fellow believers in Romania

Meanwhile, Witnesses in the cities there opened their homes to care for those whose dwellings had been destroyed.

Sometimes those who desperately need help are in remote places, and their situation is not widely known. That was true of 35 families of Jehovah's Witnesses in Guatemala. Their villages had been invaded by warring factions. When they were finally able to return in 1989, they needed help to rebuild. To supplement assistance made available by the government to repatriates, the Watch Tower Society's branch office formed an emergency committee to assist these Witness families, and some 500 other Witnesses from 50 congregations volunteered to help with the rebuilding.

There are other situations that also bring people into dire need through no fault of their own. Earthquakes, hurricanes, and floods are frequent occurrences. On an average, it is said, the world is hit by more than 25 major disasters each year.

When Natural Forces Go on a Rampage

When major emergencies affecting Jehovah's Witnesses arise because of disasters, immediate steps are taken to provide needed assistance. Local elders have learned that when confronted with such situations, they should put forth earnest effort to get in touch with each one in the congregation. The branch office of the Watch Tower Society that supervises the Kingdom work in that area promptly checks on the situation and then reports to the world headquarters. Where more help is needed than can be provided locally, carefully coordinated arrangements are made, at times even on an international scale. The objective is not to try to raise the living standard of those affected but to help them to have the necessities of life to which they were accustomed.

Simply a report of the disaster on television is enough to move many Witnesses to phone responsible elders in the area to offer their services or to provide money or materials. Others may send funds to the branch office or to the world headquarters to be used for relief purposes. They know that help is needed, and they want to share. Where there is greater need, the Watch Tower Society may notify the brothers in a limited area so that they can help as they are able. A relief committee is formed in order to coordinate the handling of matters in the disaster area.

GROWING TOGETHER IN LOVE   311

Thus, when most of Managua, Nicaragua, was devastated by a powerful earthquake in December 1972, overseers of the congregations of Jehovah's Witnesses in that area met within hours to coordinate their efforts. An immediate check was made as to the welfare of each Witness in the city. That same day relief supplies began to arrive from nearby congregations; then they quickly came from Costa Rica, Honduras, and El Salvador. Fourteen relief distribution points were set up around the outskirts of Managua. Money and supplies from Witnesses in many parts of the world were channeled into Nicaragua through the Watch Tower Society's international headquarters. Food and other supplies (including candles, matches, and soap) were dispensed according to the size of each household, a seven-day supply being given to each family. At the peak of operations, some 5,000 persons—Witnesses, their families, and relatives with whom they were staying—were being fed. The relief operations continued for ten months. Upon seeing what was being done, government agencies and the Red Cross also made food, tents, and other supplies available.

In 1986, when volcanic eruptions forced the evacuation of 10,000 people from the island of Izu-Oshima, near the coast of Japan, boats carrying the refugees were met by Jehovah's Witnesses who searched diligently to locate their spiritual brothers. Said one of the evacuees: "When we left Oshima, we ourselves did not know where we were going." Everything had happened so quickly. "As we got off the ship, however, we spotted a sign saying, 'Jehovah's Witnesses.' . . . Tears welled up in my wife's eyes as she

Witnesses who survived an earthquake in Peru built their own refuge city and helped one another

Relief supplies brought by other Witnesses (below) were among the first to reach the area

was overcome by relief at finding our brothers there to meet us at the pier." After observing how the evacuee Witnesses were cared for, not only at their arrival but also thereafter, even people who had formerly ostracized them said: "You did a good thing in sticking with that religion."

Every effort is made by the Witnesses to get help into disaster areas just as quickly as possible. In 1970, when Peru was struck by one of the most devastating earthquakes in its history, emergency relief funds were promptly dispatched from the world headquarters in New York, and 15 tons of clothing followed. Even before that shipment arrived, however, Witnesses had driven a caravan of vehicles with relief supplies into the area where cities and villages had been destroyed, doing so within hours after the roads were opened. Progressively in the days and weeks that followed, they provided needed help, both material and spiritual, to the various groups high in the Andes. And, in 1980, when parts of Italy were rocked by a severe earthquake during the evening of November 23, the first truckload of supplies dispatched by the Witnesses arrived in the stricken area the very next day. They immediately set up their own kitchen, from which food cooked by the sisters was distributed each day. An observer of relief efforts on one Caribbean island remarked: "The Witnesses worked faster than the government." Perhaps this is true at times, but Jehovah's Witnesses definitely appreciate the help of officials who facilitate their efforts to reach such disaster areas quickly.

During a period of famine in Angola in 1990, it was learned that Witnesses there were in dire need of food and clothing. Reaching them could be a problem, however, because there had been a ban on Jehovah's Witnesses in that country for many years. Nevertheless, their Christian brothers in South Africa loaded a truck with 25 tons of relief supplies. En route, they visited the consulate of Angola and were granted permission to cross the border. In order to reach the brothers, they had to pass through 30 military roadblocks, and where a bridge had been blown up, they had to cross a river at flood stage on the temporary structure that had been erected in its place. In spite of all of this, the entire shipment was delivered safely.

In times of disaster, more is done than simply shipping relief supplies to the area. When explosions and fire devastated an area in a suburb of Mexico City in 1984, Witnesses quickly arrived to provide help. But many of the Witnesses in the area could not be accounted for, so the elders organized a systematic search to locate each one. Some had dispersed to other localities. Nevertheless, the elders persisted until they located all of them. Assistance was given according to what was needed. In the case of a sister who had lost her husband and a son, that involved caring for funeral arrangements and then providing full support, materially and spiritually, for the sister and her remaining children.

A systematic search to locate each Witness in the disaster area

Panama

Mexico

Guatemala

Frequently, much more is needed than medical supplies, a few meals, and some clothing. In 1989 a storm destroyed the homes of 117 Witnesses in Guadeloupe and severely damaged the homes of 300 others. Jehovah's Witnesses in Martinique quickly came to their aid; then the Witnesses in France shipped over 100 tons of building materials as a gift to help them. On the island of St. Croix, when a Witness who had lost her home told workmates that fellow Witnesses were coming from Puerto Rico to help, they said: "They will not do anything for you. You are black, not Spanish like them." What a surprise for those workmates when she soon had a completely new house! Following an earthquake in Costa Rica in 1991, local Witnesses and international volunteers joined forces to help fellow Witnesses in the disaster area. Expecting nothing in return, they rebuilt 31 homes and 5 Kingdom Halls and repaired others. Observers stated: 'Other groups talk love; you show it.'

The efficiency with which relief efforts have been carried out by Jehovah's Witnesses has often amazed onlookers. In California, U.S.A., in 1986, a levee on the Yuba River broke and floodwaters forced tens of thousands of people to leave their homes. Christian elders in the area got in touch with the headquarters in New York, and a relief committee was formed. As soon as the water began to subside, hundreds of volunteers were ready to work. Before secular relief agencies had been able to get under way, homes of the Witnesses were already being refurbished. Why were they able to move so quickly?

A principal factor was the willingness of the Witnesses to volunteer immediately without pay, as well as their donating the materials needed.

Relief efforts often include providing materials and volunteers to help fellow Witnesses rebuild their homes

Another factor was that they were experienced in organizing and working together, since they do this regularly in order to operate their conventions and to build new Kingdom Halls. Yet another vital factor is that they have given much thought to what the Bible means when it says, "Have intense love for one another."—1 Pet. 4:8.

The contributions that are made to meet such needs frequently come from individuals who have very little themselves. As their accompanying letters often say: 'The gift is small, but our whole heart goes out to our sisters and brothers.' 'I wish I could send more, but what Jehovah has allowed me to have I wish to share.' Like the first-century Christians in Macedonia, they earnestly beg for the privilege of having a share in providing essentials of life for those who have come into need. (2 Cor. 8:1-4) When over 200,000 Koreans were left homeless as a result of flooding in 1984, Jehovah's Witnesses in the Republic of Korea responded so generously that the branch office had to make it known that no more help was needed.

Observers can readily see that something more than a feeling of responsibility or general humanitarianism motivates the Witnesses. They truly love their Christian brothers and sisters.

In addition to caring for physical needs, Jehovah's Witnesses give special attention to the spiritual needs of their brothers in disaster areas. Arrangements are made just as quickly as possible for congregation meetings to resume. In Greece, in 1986, this required setting up a large tent outside the city of Kalamata to use as a Kingdom Hall, and smaller ones at various locations for midweek Congregation Book Studies. Similarly, after the physical needs of survivors of the devastating mud slide at Armero, Colombia, in 1985, had been cared for, the remaining funds were used to construct new Kingdom Halls for three congregations in the area.

Even while such reconstruction work is under way, Jehovah's Witnesses continue to comfort others with the satisfying answers that God's Word gives to their questions about the purpose of life, the reason for disasters and death, and the hope for the future.

Witness relief efforts include spiritual upbuilding. Both in Kalamata, Greece, and outside the city, tents were quickly set up for meetings

GROWING TOGETHER IN LOVE   315

The relief efforts of the Witnesses are not meant to care for the physical needs of everyone in the disaster area. In accord with Galatians 6:10, these are intended primarily for 'those related to them in the faith.' At the same time, they gladly assist others as they are able. They have done this, for example, when providing food for earthquake victims in Italy. In the United States, when helping flood and storm victims, they have also cleaned and repaired the homes of distraught neighbors of Witnesses. When asked why they would perform such acts of kindness for a stranger, they simply reply that they love their neighbors. (Matt. 22:39) Following a devastating hurricane in southern Florida, U.S.A., in 1992, the well-organized relief program of the Witnesses was so well-known that some business establishments and individuals who were not Witnesses and who wanted to make significant donations of relief supplies turned these over to the Witnesses. They knew that their gift would not be simply left in a stockpile, nor would it be used for profit, but it would truly benefit the hurricane victims, both Witnesses and non-Witnesses. Their willingness to help non-Witnesses in time of disaster was so greatly appreciated in Davao del Norte, in the Philippines, that town officials passed a resolution saying so.

Doing good to non-Witnesses too

However, not everyone loves true Christians. Frequently, they are the objects of vicious persecution. This situation, too, brings a generous outpouring of loving support for fellow Christians.

In the Face of Vicious Persecution

The apostle Paul compared the Christian congregation to the human body and said: "Its members should have the same care for one another. And if one member suffers, all the other members suffer with it." (1 Cor. 12:25, 26) That is how Jehovah's Witnesses react when they hear reports about the persecution of their Christian brothers.

In Germany during the Nazi era, the government took harsh repressive measures against Jehovah's Witnesses. There were only some 20,000 Witnesses in Germany at the time, a relatively small band despised by Hitler. United action was needed. On October 7, 1934, every congregation of Jehovah's Witnesses throughout Germany met secretly, prayed together, and sent a letter to the government stating their determination to continue to serve Jehovah. Then many of those in attendance fearlessly went out to witness to their neighbors about Jehovah's name and Kingdom. On the same day, Jehovah's Witnesses throughout the rest of the earth also met in their congregations and, after united prayer, sent cablegrams to the Hitler government in support of their Christian brothers.

In 1948, after the clergy-inspired persecution of Jehovah's Witnesses in Greece was laid bare, the president of Greece and various ministers of

> **True Brothers and Sisters**
>
> Regarding Cuban Witness refugees in Fort Chaffee, Arkansas, the "Arkansas Gazette" said: "They were the very first to be relocated into new homes because their American 'brothers and sisters' —fellow Jehovah's Witnesses—sought them out. . . . When Witnesses call their spiritual counterparts in any land 'brothers and sisters,' they really mean it."—Issue of April 19, 1981.

government received thousands of letters from Jehovah's Witnesses in behalf of their Christian brothers. These came from the Philippines, Australia, North and South America, and other areas.

When *Awake!* magazine exposed the inquisitional methods being employed against the Witnesses in Spain in 1961, letters of protest deluged the authorities there. Officials were shocked to find that people around the world knew exactly what they were doing, and as a result, even though the persecution continued, some of the police began to deal with the Witnesses with greater restraint. In various African lands too, officials have heard from Witnesses in many other parts of the world when they learned of cruel treatment being meted out to their Christian brothers and sisters there.

If no favorable response is forthcoming from the government, the persecuted Witnesses are not forgotten. Because of persisting in religious persecution for many years, some governments have repeatedly been deluged with letters of appeal and protest. That was true of Argentina. On one occasion in 1959, the secretary of the Ministry of Foreign Affairs and Cults took one of our brothers to a room where there were several bookcases filled with letters that had poured in from all over the world. He was amazed that someone as far away as Fiji would write appealing for freedom of worship in Argentina.

In certain instances increased freedom has been granted when rulers realized that people worldwide knew what they were doing and that there were many who really cared. That was true in Liberia in 1963. Outrageous treatment had been meted out by government soldiers to convention delegates at Gbarnga. The president of Liberia was deluged with letters of protest from around the world, and the U.S. State Department intervened because a U.S. citizen was involved. Finally, President Tubman wired the Watch Tower Society's headquarters expressing willingness to receive a delegation of Jehovah's Witnesses to discuss matters. Two of the delegates —Milton Henschel and John Charuk—had been at Gbarnga. Mr. Tubman acknowledged that what had occurred was "an outrage" and said: "I am sorry this thing happened."

Following that interview, an Executive Order was issued notifying "all people throughout the country, that Jehovah's Witnesses shall have the right and privilege of free access to any part of the country to carry on their missionary work and religious worship without molestation from anyone. They shall have the protection of the law both of their person and their property and the right to freely worship God according to the dictates of their consciences, observing in the meantime the laws of the Republic by showing respect to the national flag when it is being hoisted or lowered at ceremonies by standing at attention." But it was not required that they salute, in violation of their Christian conscience.

However, as of 1992, no such official pronouncement had yet been forthcoming in Malawi, though violence against the Witnesses there had subsided to a considerable extent. Jehovah's Witnesses there have been the victims of some of the most vicious religious persecution in African history. One wave of such persecution swept the country in 1967; another began early in the 1970's. Tens of thousands of letters were written in their behalf from all parts of the world. Phone calls were made. Cablegrams were sent. On humanitarian grounds many prominent people of the world were moved to speak out.

So extreme was the brutality that some 19,000 of Jehovah's Witnesses and their children fled across the border to Zambia in 1972. The nearby Witness congregations in Zambia quickly gathered food and blankets for their brothers. Money and supplies donated by Jehovah's Witnesses all over the world poured into Watch Tower branch offices and were channeled to the refugees by the headquarters office in New York. More than enough came in to care for all the needs of the refugees in the camp at Sinda Misale. As news spread through the camp of the arrival of trucks bearing food, clothing, and tarpaulins to provide covering, the Malawian brothers could not help giving way to tears of joy because of this evidence of the love of their Christian brothers.

Tears of joy because of the love shown by their Christian brothers

When any of their number are held in detention, fellow Witnesses do not forsake them, not even when personal risk is involved. During the ban in Argentina, when a group of Witnesses were detained for 45 hours, four other Witnesses brought food and clothing for them, only to be imprisoned themselves. In 1989 the wife of a circuit overseer in Burundi, upon learning of the plight of her Christian brothers, tried to take food to the prison for them. But she herself was arrested and held hostage for two weeks, because the police were trying to get their hands on her husband.

Along with whatever they can do in all these ways, love for their Christian brothers moves Jehovah's Witnesses to raise their voices in prayer to God in their behalf. They do not pray that God put an immediate stop to wars and food shortages, because Jesus Christ foretold such things for our time. (Matt. 24:7) Nor do they pray for God to prevent all persecution, because the Bible clearly states that true Christians will be persecuted. (John 15:20; 2 Tim. 3:12) But they do earnestly petition that their Christian brothers and sisters be strengthened to stand firm in faith in the face of whatever hardship comes upon them. (Compare Colossians 4:12.) The record testifying to their spiritual strength gives abundant evidence that such prayers have been answered.

CHAPTER 20

BUILDING TOGETHER ON A GLOBAL SCALE

THE feeling of genuine brotherhood among Jehovah's Witnesses is manifest in many ways. Those who attend their meetings see evidence of it. At their conventions it is demonstrated on an enlarged scale. It is also clearly evident as they work together to provide suitable places of assembly for their congregations.

As the decade of the 1990's began, there were upwards of 60,000 congregations of Jehovah's Witnesses worldwide. During the preceding decade, 1,759 new congregations had been added, on an average, each year. By the early 1990's, that rate had increased to over 3,000 per year. Providing suitable places for them all to meet has been a monumental task.

Kingdom Halls

As was true of the first-century Christians, many congregations of Jehovah's Witnesses initially used private homes for most of their meetings. In Stockholm, Sweden, the few who first held regular meetings there used a carpentry shop, which they rented for use after the day's work in the shop was done. Because of persecution, a small group in the province of La Coruña, Spain, held their first meetings in a small storehouse, or granary.

When more space was needed, in lands where there was freedom to do so, the local congregations of Jehovah's Witnesses would rent a meeting place. However, if this was a hall that was also used by other organizations, equipment had to be hauled in or set up for each meeting, and there was frequently the lingering smell of tobacco smoke. Where possible, the brothers would rent an unused store or upstairs room that would be used exclusively by the congregation. But, in time, in many places high rents and unavailability of suitable places made it necessary to work out other

The first building that was called Kingdom Hall, in Hawaii

arrangements. In some instances buildings were purchased and renovated.

Before World War II, there were a few congregations that built meeting places specially designed for their use. Even as early as 1890, a group of Bible Students in the United States at Mount Lookout, West Virginia, built their own meeting place.* Widespread building of Kingdom Halls, however, did not get under way until the 1950's.

The name Kingdom Hall was suggested in 1935 by J. F. Rutherford, who was then president of the Watch Tower Society. In connection with the Society's branch facilities in Honolulu, Hawaii, he arranged for the brothers to construct a hall where meetings could be held. When James Harrub asked what Brother Rutherford was going to call the building, he replied: "Don't you think we should call it 'Kingdom Hall,' since that is what we are doing, preaching the good news of the Kingdom?" Thereafter, where possible, halls regularly being used by the Witnesses gradually began to be identified by signs that said "Kingdom Hall." Thus, when the London Tabernacle was renovated in 1937-38, it was renamed Kingdom Hall. In time, the principal local meeting place of congregations worldwide came to be known as the Kingdom Hall of Jehovah's Witnesses.

Many early Kingdom Halls were rented buildings or were simply rooms above stores; a few were built by the Witnesses

More Than One Way to Do It

Decisions about whether to rent or to build Kingdom Halls are made locally by the individual congregations. They also shoulder any construction and maintenance expenses. In order to conserve funds, the vast majority of congregations have endeavored to do as much of the building work as possible without resorting to commercial contractors.

The halls themselves may be built of brick, stone, wood, or other materials, depending upon cost as well as what is available in the area.

---

* It was known as the "New Light" Church because those who associated there felt that as a result of reading Watch Tower publications, they had new light on the Bible.

Working Together to Build Kingdom Halls Quickly

Thousands of new congregations are formed each year. In most instances, new Kingdom Halls are built by the Witnesses themselves. These pictures were taken during the building of a Kingdom Hall in Connecticut, U.S.A., in 1991

Friday, 7:40 a.m.

Friday, 12 noon

All unpaid volunteers, glad to work side by side

They look to Jehovah for his blessing, and they take time out to discuss counsel from his Word

Major work completed, Sunday, 6:10 p.m.

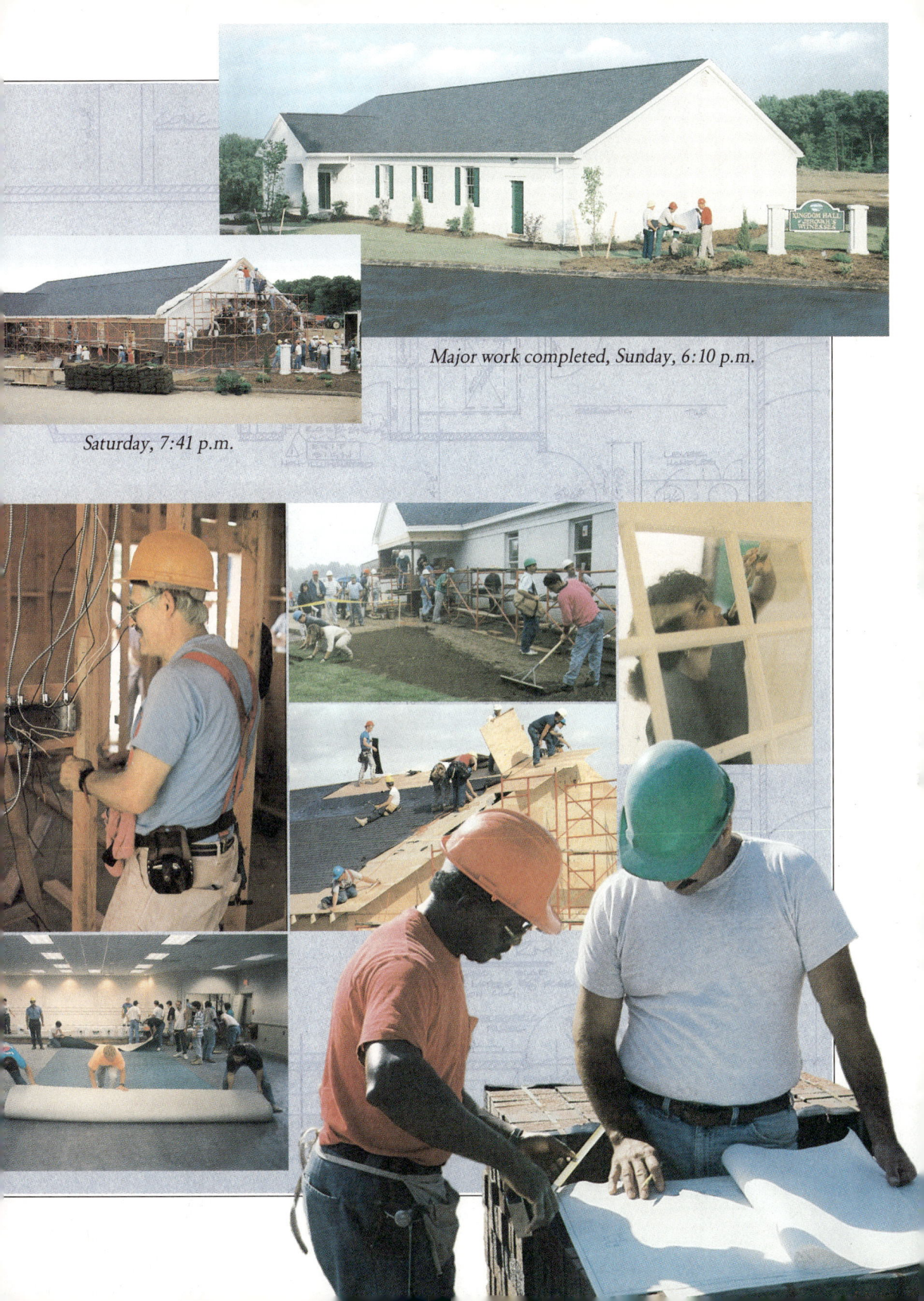

Saturday, 7:41 p.m.

In Katima Mulilo, Namibia, long grass was used for a thatched roof, and mud from anthills (which sets very hard) was molded for walls and floor. Witnesses in Segovia, Colombia, made their own cement building blocks. Unhewn lava from Mount Lassen was used in Colfax, California.

With meeting attendance often exceeding 200 in 1972, the congregation at Maseru, Lesotho, knew that they needed to build a suitable Kingdom Hall. Everyone helped with the project. Elderly brothers walked up to 20 miles in order to have a share. Children rolled drums of water to the site. The sisters provided meals. They also used their feet to pound the ground, compacting it in preparation for the pouring of the concrete floor slab, all the while singing Kingdom songs and stamping to the rhythm of the music. Sandstone, available from nearby mountains at the cost of fetching it, was used for the walls. The result was a Kingdom Hall that could seat about 250.

At times, Witnesses from nearby congregations assisted with the building work. Thus, in 1985, when Jehovah's Witnesses at Imbali, a black township in South Africa, built a hall that would comfortably seat 400, fellow Witnesses from nearby Pietermaritzburg and Durban came to help. Can you imagine how amazed the neighbors were when, during those days of racial unrest in South Africa, they saw scores of white, Colored, and Indian Witnesses pouring into the township and working shoulder to shoulder with their black African brothers? As the local mayor declared: "It can only be done with love."

No matter how willing the spirit, congregations found that local circumstances limited what the brothers could do. Men in the congregations had families to support and could ordinarily work on such a project only on weekends and perhaps a little in the evenings. Many congregations had few, if any, who were skilled in the building trades. Nevertheless, a relatively simple, somewhat open structure suitable to the tropics might be put up in a few days or perhaps a few weeks. With the help of Witnesses in surrounding congregations, more substantial buildings might be completed in five or six months. In other cases it might require a year or two.

Yet, as they moved into the 1970's, Jehovah's Witnesses worldwide were increasing at a rate of two to three new congregations per day. By the early 1990's, the rate of increase was up to nine congregations per day. Could their compelling need for new Kingdom Halls be met?

Developing Quick-Construction Techniques

Early in the 1970's, in the United States, over 50 Witnesses from nearby congregations pitched in to help construct a new Kingdom Hall in Carterville, Missouri, for the group that had been meeting in Webb City. On one weekend they erected the main framework and did considerable

Witnesses from nearby congregations helped with the work

work on the roof. There was still much to be done, and it took months to complete the job; but an important part of it had been completed in a very short period.

During the next decade, as the brothers worked together on about 60 halls, obstacles were overcome, and more efficient methods were developed. In time, they realized that after work on the foundation was done, they might almost be able to complete an entire Kingdom Hall in a single weekend.

Several congregation overseers—all from the midwestern United States—began to work toward that goal. When congregations asked for help with their Kingdom Hall construction, one or more of these brothers would discuss the project with them and provide details concerning the preparation that had to be cared for locally before the job could be done. Among other things, construction permits had to be obtained, the foundation and the concrete floor slab had to be poured, electrical service had to be operational, underground plumbing had to be in place, and dependable arrangements had to be made for delivery of building materials. Then a date could be set for putting up the Kingdom Hall itself. The building was not going to be prefabricated; it would be built from the ground up right on the site.

Who would do the actual construction work? To the extent possible, it was done with voluntary, unpaid labor. Entire families often shared. Those organizing the project would contact Witnesses who were tradesmen and who had expressed a willingness to participate in these projects. Many of them eagerly looked forward to each new building project. Other Witnesses who learned about the projects wanted to have a part; hundreds from the surrounding area—and from more distant places—flocked to the building sites, anxious to offer their services in whatever way they could. Most of them were not professional builders, but they certainly gave evidence that they fit the description of those who would be supporters of Jehovah's Messianic King as set out at Psalm 110:3, which says: "Your people will offer themselves willingly."

On Thursday evening before the big push was to begin, those supervising the project met to work out final details. The next evening, workers were shown a slide presentation on procedure so that they would understand how the work was going to be done. Emphasis was placed on the importance of godly qualities. The brothers were encouraged to work together in love, to be kind, to show patience and consideration. Everyone was encouraged to work at a steady pace but not to rush and not to hesitate to take a few minutes to share an upbuilding experience with someone. Early the next morning, construction began.

Construction work was done with voluntary, unpaid labor

Emphasis was placed on spiritual qualities

At an appointed time early on Saturday morning, everyone would stop what he was doing to listen to a discussion of the Scripture text for the day. Prayer was offered, for it was well appreciated that success of the entire undertaking depended on Jehovah's blessing.—Ps. 127:1.

When the work began, it moved swiftly. In an hour the walls were up. Roof trusses followed. Sheeting for the walls was nailed into place. The electricians began running wires. Air-conditioning and heating ducts were installed. Cabinets were built and put into position. Sometimes it rained all weekend, or the weather turned bitterly cold or was excessively hot, but the work went on. There was no competition, no rivalry among the tradesmen.

Frequently, before sundown on the second day, the Kingdom Hall was completed—nicely decorated inside, perhaps even landscaped on the outside. When it was more practical, jobs were scheduled to extend over three days, or perhaps two weekends. At the end of the project, many of the workers would remain, tired but very happy, to enjoy the first regular congregation meeting, a study of *The Watchtower*.

Doubtful that quality work could be done so fast, several people in Guymon, Oklahoma, U.S.A., called the city inspector. "I told them that if they wanted to see something done right, they ought to visit the hall!" said the inspector when later relating the incident to the Witnesses. "You people are even doing correctly what will be *hidden and not seen!*"

As the need for Kingdom Halls increased, the brothers who had developed many of the quick-construction methods trained others. Reports of what was being done spread to other lands. Could such construction methods be employed there too?

Quick Construction Goes International

Kingdom Hall building in Canada was lagging far behind the needs of the congregations. The Witnesses in Canada invited those who were organizing quick-construction projects in the United States to explain how they handled it. At first, the Canadians were rather doubtful that it could be done in Canada, but they decided to try. The first Kingdom Hall built in this manner in Canada went up at Elmira, Ontario, in 1982. By 1992, there were 306 Kingdom Halls in Canada that had been put up in this way.

The Witnesses in Northampton, England, thought they could do it too. Their project, in 1983, was the first in Europe. Brothers experienced in this type of construction traveled from the United States and Canada to oversee the project and to help local Witnesses learn how to do it. Other volunteers were on hand from as far afield as Japan, India, France, and Germany. They were there as volunteers, not for pay. How was it all possible? As the overseer of a team of Irish Witnesses that worked on such a project said, 'It is successful because all the brothers and sisters pull together under the influence of Jehovah's spirit.'

Even when local building regulations seem to make such projects impossible, the Witnesses have found that, frequently, when details are outlined for city officials, they are glad to cooperate.

After a quick-construction project in Norway, north of the Arctic Circle, the newspaper *Finnmarken* exclaimed: "Just fantastic. That is the only expression we can find that describes what Jehovah's Witnesses did last weekend." Similarly, when Witnesses on New Zealand's North Island put up an attractive Kingdom Hall in two and a half days, the front-page headline on the local newspaper declared: "Project Close to a Miracle." The article added: "Perhaps the most mind-boggling aspect of the exercise was the organisation and sheer quiet of the operation."

The remoteness of location where the Kingdom Hall is needed does not prove to be an insurmountable barrier. In Belize a quick-construction project was done, even though it meant transporting every piece of material to an island 36 miles from Belize City. When an air-conditioned Kingdom Hall was put up in Port Hedland, Western Australia, one weekend, it was with materials and a work force that practically all came from 1,000 miles or more away. Travel expenses came out of the workers' own pockets. Most of those who had a part in the project did not personally know the Witnesses in the Port Hedland Congregation, and very few of them would ever attend meetings there. But that did not deter them from expressing their love in this way.

Even where the number of Witnesses is small, this has not prevented the use of such methods for building halls. Some 800 Witnesses from Trinidad volunteered to travel to Tobago to help their 84 Christian brothers and sisters there to build a hall in Scarborough in 1985. The 17 Witnesses (most of them women and children) in Goose Bay, Labrador, definitely needed help if they were ever going to have a Kingdom Hall of their own. In 1985, Witnesses from other parts of Canada chartered three planes to take 450 of them to Goose Bay to do the job. After two days of hard work, they had a dedication program in the completed hall on Sunday evening.

This does not mean that all Kingdom Halls are now being put up with quick-construction methods, but ever-growing numbers of them are.

Regional Building Committees

By mid-1986 the rate at which new Kingdom Halls were needed had greatly accelerated. During the preceding year, 2,461 new congregations had been formed worldwide; 207 of these were in the United States. Some Kingdom Halls were being used by three, four, or even five congregations. As the Scriptures had foretold, Jehovah was truly speeding up the work of ingathering.—Isa. 60:22.

To assure the best possible use of personnel and to enable all who were building Kingdom Halls to benefit from experience that had been gained, the Society began to coordinate their activity. As a start, in 1987 the United States was divided up among 60 Regional Building Committees. There was plenty for all of them to do; some of them soon had projects lined up for a year or more. Those appointed to serve on these committees were men who, first of all, were spiritually qualified, elders in the congregations, exemplary in their exercise of the fruitage of God's spirit. (Gal. 5:22, 23) Many of them also had experience in real estate, engineering, construction, business management, safety, and related fields.

Congregations were encouraged to consult with the Regional Building Committee before choosing a site for a new Kingdom Hall. Where there was more than one congregation in a city, they were also urged to consult with the circuit overseer(s), the city overseer, and elders from nearby congregations. Congregations that were planning major renovation or the building of a new Kingdom Hall were advised to benefit from the experience of the brothers on the Regional Building Committee for their area and from the guidelines that the Society had furnished them. Through that committee, arrangements would be coordinated for assembling the needed skilled personnel from among brothers and sisters in some 65 trades who had already volunteered to help on such projects.

As procedures were refined, it was possible to reduce the number of workers involved in any one project. Instead of having thousands at the construction site either watching or offering their services, there were seldom more than 200 on site at any given time. Instead of spending an entire weekend there, workers were on hand only when their particular skills were needed. Thus they had more time to spend with their families and for activity with their home congregations. When local brothers could do certain types of work in a reasonable time, it was often found to be more practical to bring in the quick-construction group only for those aspects of the work for which they were more urgently needed.

Quality construction, safety, minimum cost, speed

Although the entire operation moved at amazing speed, this was not the primary consideration. Of greater importance was the providing of quality construction of modest Kingdom Halls designed to meet local needs. Careful planning was done so as to accomplish this while keeping expenses to a minimum. Measures were taken to see that safety was given high priority—the safety of workers, neighbors, passersby, and future occupants of the Kingdom Hall.

As reports concerning this arrangement for building Kingdom Halls reached other lands, the branch offices of the Society that believed it would be advantageous in their areas were provided with needed details. By 1992, Regional Building Committees appointed by the Society were helping with Kingdom Hall construction in such countries as Argentina, Australia,

Kingdom Halls in Various Lands

The meeting places used by Jehovah's Witnesses are usually modest. They are clean, comfortable, attractive in their surroundings

Peru

Philippines

France

Republic of Korea

Japan

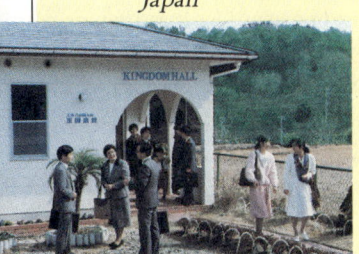

Papua New Guinea

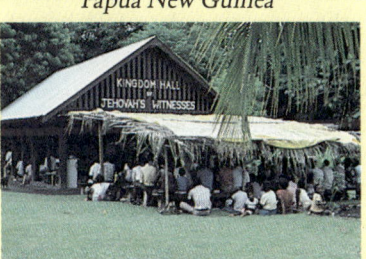

Ireland

Colombia

Norway

Lesotho

Britain, Canada, France, Germany, Japan, Mexico, South Africa, and Spain. Building methods were adapted to local circumstances. When assistance from another branch was needed for Kingdom Hall construction, this was arranged through the Society's headquarters office. In some parts of the world, new halls were being put up in days; elsewhere, in weeks or perhaps in a few months. With careful planning and coordinated effort, the time required to provide a new Kingdom Hall was definitely being reduced.

The building activities of Jehovah's Witnesses have not been limited to Kingdom Halls. Larger facilities are needed when groups of congregations meet for annual circuit assemblies and special assembly days.

Filling the Need for Assembly Halls

Over the years, facilities of many kinds have been used for circuit assemblies. Jehovah's Witnesses have rented such places as civic auditoriums, schools, theaters, armories, sports arenas, and fairgrounds. In a few localities, very fine facilities were available at a reasonable price. More often, much time and effort was required to clean the place, set up sound equipment, erect a platform, and truck in chairs. Sometimes there were last-minute cancellations. As the number of congregations grew, it became more and more difficult to find enough suitable places. What could be done?

Once again, the solution was for Jehovah's Witnesses to have places of their own. This would involve renovating suitable structures and building new ones. The first of such Assembly Halls in the United States was a theater in Long Island City, New York, renovated and put to use by Jehovah's Witnesses late in 1965.

At about the same time, Witnesses on the Caribbean island of Guadeloupe were designing an Assembly Hall to meet their needs. They felt that it would be advantageous if they could have their circuit assemblies in many different locations. But most of the towns did not have facilities that were large enough. So the Witnesses built a portable structure made of steel pipes and aluminum roofing, something that would be adequate for 700 people and that could be erected wherever there was an available plot of land that was relatively flat. They had to enlarge the hall again and again, until it reached a capacity of 5,000. Just imagine moving, setting up, and dismantling 30 tons of material for every assembly! That Assembly Hall was built and taken down several times a year for 13 years, until land for the portable hall became hard to find and it was necessary to purchase land and erect a permanent Assembly Hall, which now serves for circuit assemblies and district conventions.

In quite a few places, Assembly Hall projects made use of existing buildings. In England, at Hays Bridge, Surrey, a 50-year-old school com-

A portable Assembly Hall!

plex was purchased and renovated. It is nestled in 28 acres of beautiful countryside. Former movie theaters and an industrial warehouse were remodeled and put to use in Spain; an unused textile factory in Australia; a dance hall in Quebec, Canada; a bowling alley in Japan; a warehouse in the Republic of Korea. All of these were made over into attractive Assembly Halls that could serve well as large centers for Bible education.

Other Assembly Halls were completely new, having been constructed from the ground up. The unique octagonal design of the hall at Hellaby, South Yorkshire, England, along with the fact that much of the work was done with volunteer labor gave rise to an article in the journal of the Institution of Structural Engineers. The Assembly Hall at Saskatoon, Saskatchewan, in Canada, was designed to seat 1,200; but when interior walls are pulled into place, the structure can be used as four side-by-side Kingdom Halls. Haiti's Assembly Hall (prefabricated and shipped from the United States) was open on two sides so that those seated inside would constantly be cooled by the prevailing winds—a welcome relief from the hot Haitian sun. The hall in Port Moresby, Papua New Guinea, was designed in such a way that sections of the walls could be opened like doors in order to accommodate crowds larger than would fit inside.

The decision to build an Assembly Hall is not made by a small group of overseers who then expect everyone else to support it. Before any new Assembly Hall is built, the Society sees to it that a careful analysis is made as to the need for it and the amount of use that it will have. Consideration is given not just to local enthusiasm for the project but also to the overall needs of the field. It is discussed with all the congregations that will be involved, in order to ascertain the desire and ability of the brothers to support it.

New York City

Two of the first Assembly Halls

Guadeloupe

Assembly Halls of Jehovah's Witnesses

In order to accommodate their periodic assemblies, Jehovah's Witnesses in some areas have found it practical to build their own Assembly Halls. Much of the construction work is done by local Witnesses. Here are just a few of these halls in use in the early 1990's

Britain

Venezuela

Italy

Germany

Canada

Japan

Thus, when the work gets under way, Jehovah's Witnesses in the area are wholeheartedly behind it. Each project is financed by the Witnesses themselves. The financial needs are explained, but contributions are voluntary and anonymous. Careful planning is done in advance, and the project benefits from experience already gained in building Kingdom Halls and, frequently, from Assembly Hall projects in other places. Where necessary, some aspects of the work may be let out to commercial contractors, but most of it is usually done by enthusiastic Witnesses. This may cut the cost in half.

With a work force made up of skilled professionals and others who volunteer their time and talents, the entire project usually moves along quickly. Some projects may require more than a year. But on Vancouver Island in Canada, in 1985, some 4,500 volunteers completed a 25,000-square-foot Assembly Hall in just nine days. The structure also includes a 200-seat Kingdom Hall for use by local congregations. In New Caledonia, a curfew was imposed by the government in 1984 because of political unrest, yet up to 400 volunteers worked on the Assembly Hall at a time, and it was completed in just four months. Near Stockholm, Sweden, a beautiful, practical Assembly Hall, with 900 padded oak chairs, was built in seven months.

Sometimes persistent efforts in the courts have been necessary in order to obtain permits to build these Assembly Halls. That was true in Canada at Surrey, British Columbia. When the land was purchased, the zoning requirements allowed for the building of such a place of worship. But after building plans were submitted, in 1974, the Council for the District of Surrey passed a bylaw stipulating that churches and assembly halls could be built only in Zone P-3—a zone that did not exist! Yet, 79 churches had previously been built in the municipality without any trouble. The matter was taken to court. Repeated rulings were given in favor of Jehovah's Witnesses. When hindrance of prejudiced officials was at last cleared aside, the volunteer workers pursued the project with such enthusiasm that they completed it in about seven months. As was true of Nehemiah in his efforts to rebuild the walls of ancient Jerusalem, they felt that the 'hand of God was upon them' to accomplish the work.—Neh. 2:18.

Resorting to the courts

When Jehovah's Witnesses in the United States purchased the Stanley Theater in Jersey City, New Jersey, the building was on the state's register of historic places. Although the theater was in a deplorable state of disrepair, it had excellent potential for use as an Assembly Hall. Yet, when the Witnesses wanted to do needed repair work, city officials refused permits. The mayor did not want Jehovah's Witnesses in that area; he had other plans for the property. Court action was needed in order to restrain officials from the unlawful use of their authority. The court ruled in favor of the Witnesses. Soon after that, local residents voted the mayor out of office. Work on the hall moved ahead quickly. The result was a beautiful

Assembly Hall that seated over 4,000. It is a place that businessmen and residents of the city alike are proud of.

During the past 27 years, in many parts of the globe, attractive and practical Assembly Halls have been built by Jehovah's Witnesses to serve as centers for Bible education. Such halls are now found in ever-increasing numbers in North and South America, Europe, Africa, and the Orient, as well as on many islands. In some lands—for example, Nigeria, Italy, and Denmark—Jehovah's Witnesses have even built larger, permanent, open-air facilities that can be used for their district conventions.

Yet, Assembly Halls and Kingdom Halls are not the only building projects in which Jehovah's Witnesses are involved in order to further the proclamation of God's Kingdom.

Offices, Printeries, and Bethel Homes Worldwide

Around the globe in 1992, there were 99 branch offices of the Watch Tower Society, each of which served to coordinate the activities of Jehovah's Witnesses in its part of the world field. Over one half of these branches were doing printing of various kinds to further the work of Bible education. Those who work at the branches are housed, for the most part, as a large family in homes called Bethel, meaning "House of God." Because of expansion in the number of Jehovah's Witnesses and their preaching activity, it has been necessary to enlarge these facilities and to build new ones.

So rapid has been the growth of the organization that there have frequently been 20 to 40 of such branch-expansion programs in progress at a time. This has required a vast international construction program.

Because of the enormous amount of construction work being done worldwide, the Watch Tower Society has its own Engineering and Drafting Department at its New York headquarters. Engineers with many years of experience have left their secular work and volunteered to assist full-time with building projects that are directly connected with Kingdom activity. Additionally, those who have experience have trained other men and women in the work of engineering, design, and drafting. By coordinating work through this department, experience gained in branch construction in any part of the world can benefit those working on projects in other lands.

In time, the great amount of work being done made it beneficial to open a Regional Engineering Office in Japan to assist with construction blueprints for projects in the Orient. Other Regional Engineering Offices operate in Europe and Australia, with personnel drawn from a variety of lands. These work in close cooperation with the headquarters office, and their services, along with use of computer technology, cut down on the drafting personnel needed at any given construction site.

Large-scale international expansion

Some projects are relatively modest in size. That was true of the branch office built in Tahiti in 1983. This included office space, storerooms, and accommodations for eight volunteer workers. It was also true of the four-story branch building erected on the Caribbean island of Martinique during the years 1982 to 1984. These structures might not seem extraordinary to big-city dwellers in other lands, but they attracted public attention. The newspaper *France-Antilles* declared that the branch building in Martinique was "an architectural masterpiece" that reflected a "great love for work well done."

In contrast from the standpoint of size, the buildings that were finished in Canada in 1981 included a printery, or factory, with upwards of 100,000 square feet of floor space and a residence building for 250 volunteers. At Cesario Lange, in Brazil, the Watch Tower complex completed that same year included eight buildings, with nearly 500,000 square feet of floor space. It required 10,000 truckloads of cement, stone, and sand, as well as enough concrete pilings to reach twice the height of Mount Everest! In 1991, when a large new printery was completed in the Philippines, it was also necessary to provide an 11-story residence building.

To meet the needs of the growing number of Kingdom proclaimers in Nigeria, a large building project got under way in Igieduma in 1984. This was to include a factory, a spacious office building, four connected residence buildings, and other needed facilities. Plans were laid to have the factory completely prefabricated and then shipped from the United States. But then the brothers were confronted with seemingly impossible import deadlines. When these deadlines were met and everything arrived safely at the construction site, the Witnesses did not take the credit but gave thanks to Jehovah for his blessing.

Workers gave credit to Jehovah, not to themselves

Rapid Expansion Around the Globe

So rapid has been the growth of the work of Kingdom proclamation, however, that even after major expansion of branch facilities in a country, it has often been necessary to start building again within a relatively short time. Consider a few examples.

In Peru a fine new branch—with office space, 22 bedrooms as well as other basic facilities for Bethel family members, and a Kingdom Hall—was completed at the end of 1984. But response to the Kingdom message in that South American land was much greater than anticipated. Four years later it was necessary to duplicate the existing complex, this time using an antiseismic design.

A spacious new branch complex was completed in Colombia in 1979. It appeared that it would provide ample space for many years to come. However, within seven years the number of Witnesses in Colombia had

Growth at a rate that no human could have predicted

nearly doubled, and the branch was now printing the magazines *La Atalaya* and *¡Despertad!* not only for Colombia but also for four neighboring countries. They had to start building again in 1987—this time where there was more land for expansion.

During 1980, Jehovah's Witnesses in Brazil devoted some 14,000,000 hours to public preaching of the Kingdom message. The figure soared to nearly 50,000,000 in 1989. More people were showing a desire to have their spiritual hunger satisfied. The extensive branch facilities dedicated in 1981 were no longer sufficient. Already by September 1988, excavation for a new factory was in progress. This one would provide 80 percent more floor space than there was in the existing factory, and of course, residence facilities to care for the enlarged Bethel family would also be needed.

At Selters/Taunus, Germany, the Watch Tower Society's second-largest printing complex was dedicated in 1984. Five years later, because of increases in Germany as well as opportunities to expand the witness work in lands for which the branch there prints literature, plans were under way to enlarge the factory by over 85 percent and to add other support facilities.

The Japan branch had moved from Tokyo to large new facilities in Numazu in 1972. There was further major expansion in 1975. By 1978 another property had been obtained, at Ebina; and work on a factory more than three times as large as that at Numazu quickly got started. This was completed in 1982. It was still not enough; more buildings were added by 1989. Would it not have been possible to build just once and make it large enough? No. The number of Kingdom proclaimers in Japan had doubled *again and again* in a way that no human could have anticipated. From 14,199 in 1972, their ranks had soared to 137,941 in 1989, and a large proportion of them were devoting full time to the ministry.

A similar pattern is seen in other parts of the globe. Within a decade —and sometimes within a few years—after the building of large branches equipped for printing, it was necessary to undertake major expansion. That was true in Mexico, Canada, South Africa, and the Republic of Korea, among others.

Who does the actual construction work? How is it all accomplished?

Many Thousands Eager to Help

In Sweden, out of the 17,000 Witnesses in the country at the time of building their branch at Arboga, some 5,000 volunteered to help with the work. Most were simply willing helpers, but there were also enough highly skilled professionals to see that the work was done right. Their motivation? Love for Jehovah.

When an official at a surveyor's office in Denmark heard that all the work on a new branch at Holbæk was going to be done by Jehovah's Witnesses, he expressed misgivings. Nevertheless, among the Witnesses who volunteered to help, all the needed know-how was found. Yet, would they have been better off if commercial contractors had been hired to do the job? After the project was completed, experts from the town's building department toured the premises and commented on the fine workmanship —something they rarely see on commercial jobs nowadays. As for the official who had earlier expressed misgivings, he smiled and said: "You see, at that time I didn't know the kind of organization you people have."

Population centers in Australia are widely scattered; so, most of the 3,000 who volunteered to work on the branch facilities at Ingleburn between 1978 and 1983 had to travel at least 1,000 miles. However, bus travel for groups of volunteers was coordinated, and congregations en route hospitably offered to supply meals and association for the brothers at rest stops. Some of the brothers sold homes, closed businesses, took vacations, and made other sacrifices in order to share in the project. Teams of experienced tradesmen came in—some of them more than once—to pour concrete, hang ceilings, put up fences. Others donated materials.

The majority of volunteers on these projects were unskilled, but with a little training, some of them took on big responsibilities and did excellent work. They learned how to fabricate windows, operate tractors, mix concrete, and lay bricks. They enjoyed a definite advantage over non-Witnesses who do the same kind of work commercially. In what way? Those who were experienced were willing to share their knowledge. No one was afraid that someone else would take his job; there was plenty for everyone to do. And there was strong motivation to do high-quality work, because it was being done as an expression of love for God.

At all the construction sites, some Witnesses form the nucleus of the construction "family." During work at Selters/Taunus, Germany, from 1979 to 1984, several hundred generally made up that nucleus of workers. Thousands of others joined them for varying periods of time, many on weekends. There was careful planning so that when volunteers arrived, there was plenty for them to do.

As long as people are imperfect, there will be problems, but those who work on these projects try to resolve these on the basis of Bible principles. They know that doing things in a Christian manner is more important than efficiency. As a reminder, at the construction site in Ebina, Japan, there were large signs with pictures of workers in hard hats, and on each of the hard hats was inscribed in Japanese characters one of the fruits of God's spirit: love, joy, peace, long-suffering, kindness, goodness, faith, mildness, self-control. (Gal. 5:22, 23) Those who visit the job sites can see and hear the difference. Expressing his own observations, a news reporter who toured the branch construction site in Brazil said: "There are no disorders or lack of cooperation . . . This Christian atmosphere makes it different here from that customarily seen in Brazilian civil construction."

Constant Growth at World Headquarters

While the Watch Tower Society's branches have been growing, it has also been necessary to expand the facilities of the world headquarters. There have been major additions to its factory and office quarters in Brooklyn and in other locations in New York State more than ten times since World War II. To house personnel, it has been necessary to build or purchase and renovate numerous buildings, both large and small. Further major expansion in Brooklyn was announced in August 1990 and in January 1991—even while north of New York City construction begun in 1989 was continuing on the extensive Watchtower Educational Center, designed to accommodate 1,200 persons, including resident staff and students.

Since 1972, there has been no letup in construction work at the world headquarters in Brooklyn and its closely associated facilities in other parts of New York and in New Jersey. In time, it became obvious that even though they numbered in the hundreds, the regular construction workers were unable to keep up with the work. So, in 1984 an ongoing temporary-worker program was instituted. Letters were sent out to the then 8,000 congregations in the United States to invite qualified brothers to come for a week or more to help out. (A similar program had already worked well in some of the branches, including Australia, where those able to stay two weeks were invited to volunteer.) Workers would be provided lodging and meals but would pay their own travel expenses and would receive no wages. Who would respond?

They counted it a privilege to help with construction at headquarters

By 1992, well over 24,000 applications had been processed! At least 3,900 of these were for persons who were coming back for a 2nd or 3rd, even a 10th or 20th, time. Most of them were elders, ministerial servants, or pioneers—persons with fine spiritual qualifications. All of them were volunteering to do whatever was needed, whether it called for them to use their trade or not. The work was often heavy and dirty. But they counted it a privilege to contribute in this way to the advancement of Kingdom interests. Some felt that it helped them to better appreciate the spirit of self-sacrifice that characterizes the work done at the world headquarters. All of them felt richly rewarded as a result of being present for the Bethel family's program of morning worship and weekly family *Watchtower* study.

International Volunteers

As the need for rapid expansion grew, an arrangement for international volunteers was initiated in 1985. It was by no means the start of interna-

Each group is reminded that being a spiritual person and doing quality work take priority over doing the job fast

Newly arrived temporary construction workers at the world headquarters in New York

tional cooperation in building, but the arrangement was now carefully coordinated from headquarters. All who share are Witnesses who volunteer to help with construction work outside their own country. They are skilled workers, as well as marriage mates who go with their husbands to help in whatever way they can. Most of them pay for their own travel expenses; none get wages for what they do. Some of them go on a short-term basis, usually staying from two weeks to three months. Others are long-term volunteers, remaining for a year or more, perhaps until the project is completed. Over 3,000 of Jehovah's Witnesses from 30 different countries had part in this during the first five years, and more were eager to share as their skills were needed. They count it a privilege to give of themselves and their means to advance the interests of God's Kingdom in this way.

The international volunteers are provided with a place to stay and meals to eat. Comforts are often minimal. The local Witnesses greatly appreciate what their visiting brothers are doing, and where possible, they welcome them to share their homes, however humble these may be. Meals are most often eaten at the work site.

The brothers from abroad are not there to do the whole job. Their aim is to work along with the local construction team. And hundreds, even thousands, of others in the country may also come to help on weekends or for a week or more at a time. In Argentina, 259 volunteers from other countries worked along with several thousand local brothers, some of whom were on the job every day, others for a few weeks, and many more on weekends. In Colombia, over 830 international volunteers helped for varying periods of time. There were also upwards of 200 local volunteers

International Construction Program Fills Urgent Needs

Rapid growth of the organization has required ongoing expansion of offices, factories, and Bethel homes around the globe

International volunteers give assistance to local Witnesses

Spain

Construction methods used make it possible for many volunteers with limited experience to do valuable work

Puerto Rico

New Zealand

Skilled workers gladly make their services available

Greece

Brazil

Use of durable materials helps to keep long-term maintenance costs down

Britain

High-quality work results from personal interest on the part of those who do it; this is an expression of their love for Jehovah

Canada

These projects are enjoyable occasions; many lasting friendships are made

Colombia

Sign in Japan reminded workers of safety measures, also of the need to show the fruits of God's spirit

who shared in the project full-time and, each weekend, another 250 or more who helped. A total of more than 3,600 different individuals took part.

Difference of language can present problems, but it does not prevent the international groups from working together. Sign language, facial expressions, a good sense of humor, and a desire to accomplish a job that will honor Jehovah help to get the work done.

Outstanding growth in the organization—consequently the need for larger branch facilities—is sometimes experienced in lands where the number of people who are skilled in the building trades is limited. But this is no hindrance among Jehovah's Witnesses, who gladly help one another. They work together as part of a global family that is not divided by nationality, skin color, or language.

In Papua New Guinea, the volunteers who came from Australia and New Zealand each trained a Papua New Guinean in his trade, in harmony with the request of the Government Labour Department. In this way, while giving of themselves, local Witnesses learned trades that could help them to care for the needs of themselves and their families.

When a new branch was needed in El Salvador, the local brothers were joined by 326 volunteers from abroad. For the project in Ecuador, 270 Witnesses from 14 lands worked alongside their Ecuadoran brothers and sisters. Some international volunteers helped on several projects that were under way at the same time. They rotated between construction sites in Europe and Africa, according to the need for their trade skills.

By 1992, international volunteers had been sent out to 49 branch locations to assist the local building crews. In some instances those who received help from this program were able, in turn, to provide assistance to others. Thus, having benefited from the labors of about 60 long-term international servants who helped with the branch building project in the Philippines, as well as over 230 volunteers from abroad who helped for shorter periods, some of the Filipinos made themselves available to help build facilities in other parts of Southeast Asia.

Building work is being done by Jehovah's Witnesses because of needs that exist now in connection with preaching the good news. With the help of Jehovah's spirit, they want to give the greatest witness possible during the time that remains before Armageddon. They are convinced that God's new world is very close at hand, and they have faith that they will survive as an organized people into that new world, under the rule of God's Messianic Kingdom. It is also their hope that perhaps many of the fine facilities that they have built and dedicated to Jehovah will continue to be used after Armageddon as centers from which knowledge of the only true God can be diffused until it truly fills the earth.—Isa. 11:9.

They work as a global family, not divided by nationality, skin color, or language

CHAPTER 21

HOW IS IT ALL FINANCED?

IT IS obvious that the work carried on by Jehovah's Witnesses requires money. Building Kingdom Halls, Assembly Halls, branch offices, factories, and Bethel homes involves money, and more is needed to maintain them. Expenses are also incurred in publishing and distributing literature for Bible study. How is all of this financed?

Unfounded speculations regarding this have been publicized by persons who oppose the work of Jehovah's Witnesses. But a review of the evidence supports the answer that the Witnesses themselves give. What is that? Most of the work is done by volunteers, who neither expect nor desire financial return for their services, and organizational expenses are met by voluntary donations.

"Seats Free. No Collections"

As early as the second issue of the *Watch Tower*, in August 1879, Brother Russell stated: "'Zion's Watch Tower' has, we believe, JEHOVAH for its backer, and while this is the case it will never *beg* nor *petition* men for support. When He who says: 'All the gold and silver of the mountains are mine,' fails to provide necessary funds, we will understand it to be time to suspend the publication." Consistent with that, there is no begging for money in the literature of Jehovah's Witnesses.

What is true of their literature is also true of their meetings. There are no emotional appeals for funds in their congregations or at their conventions. No collection plates are passed; no envelopes in which to put money are distributed; no letters of solicitation are sent to congregation members. Congregations never resort to bingo or raffles to raise funds. As early as 1894, when the Watch Tower Society sent out traveling speakers, it published this notice for the benefit of everyone: "Let it be understood from the first that collections or other solicitations of money are neither authorized nor approved by this Society."

Thus, since very early in their modern-day history, handbills and other printed invitations to the public to attend the meetings of Jehovah's Witnesses have carried the slogan "Seats Free. No Collections."

Beginning early in 1914, the Bible Students rented theaters as well as other auditoriums and invited the public to these to see the "Photo-Drama of

"Solicitations of money are neither authorized nor approved by this Society"

Creation." This was a four-part presentation, eight hours in all, made up of slides and motion pictures synchronized with sound. During the first year alone, millions of persons saw it in North America, Europe, Australia, and New Zealand. Although some theater owners charged for *reserved* seats, the Bible Students never requested an admission fee. And no collections were taken.

Later, for over 30 years, the Watch Tower Society operated radio station WBBR in New York City. Jehovah's Witnesses also used the services of hundreds of other stations to broadcast programs of Bible education. But never did they use such broadcasts to beg for money.

How, then, are the donations that finance their activity obtained?

Supported by Voluntary Donations

The Bible sets the pattern. Under the Mosaic Law, there were certain contributions that were voluntary. Others were required of the people. The giving of a tithe, or tenth part, was one of the latter. (Ex. 25:2; 30: 11-16; Num. 15:17-21; 18:25-32) But the Bible also shows that Christ fulfilled the Law, and God brought it to an end; so Christians are not bound by its regulations. They do not tithe, nor are they under obligation to give any other contribution of a specified amount or at a particular time. —Matt. 5:17; Rom. 7:6; Col. 2:13, 14.

Instead, they are encouraged to cultivate a spirit of generosity and liberality in imitation of the marvelous example set by Jehovah himself and by his Son, Jesus Christ. (2 Cor. 8:7, 9; 9:8-15; 1 John 3:16-18) Thus, with reference to giving, the apostle Paul wrote to the Christian congregation in Corinth: "Let each one do just as he has resolved in his heart, not grudgingly or under compulsion, for God loves a cheerful giver." When informed of a need, this presented them with 'a test of the genuineness of their love,' as Paul explained. He also said: "If the readiness is there first, it is especially acceptable according to what a person has, not according to what a person does not have."—2 Cor. 8:8, 12; 9:7.

In the light of this, the comment by Tertullian regarding meetings held by people who were endeavoring to practice Christianity in his day (c.155– after 220 C.E.) is interesting. He wrote: "Even if there is a chest of a sort, it is not made up of money paid in entrance-fees, as if religion were a matter of contract. Every man once a month brings some modest coin—or whenever he wishes, and only if he does wish, and if he can; for nobody is compelled; it is a

> ### God Does Not Beg
>
> "He who said, 'If I were hungry I would not tell thee, for the world is mine and the fullness thereof.... I will take no bullock out of thy house, nor he goats out of thy folds; for every beast of the forest is mine, and the cattle upon a thousand hills' (Psa. 50:12, 9, 10), is able to carry on his great work without begging for funds either from the world or from his children. Neither will he compel his children to sacrifice anything in his service, nor will he accept anything from them short of a cheerful, free-will offering."—*Zion's Watch Tower,* September 1886, p. 6.

voluntary offering." (*Apology*, XXXIX, 5) During the centuries since then, however, the churches of Christendom have engaged in every conceivable money-raising scheme to finance their activities.

Charles Taze Russell refused to imitate the churches. He wrote: "It is our judgment that money raised by the various begging devices in the name of our Lord is offensive, unacceptable to him, and does not bring his blessing either upon the givers or the work accomplished."

Principal emphasis is on the value of sharing the truth with others

Rather than attempt to curry favor with those who had wealth, Brother Russell clearly stated, in harmony with the Scriptures, that the majority of the Lord's people would be poor in this world's goods but rich in faith. (Matt. 19:23, 24; 1 Cor. 1:26-29; Jas. 2:5) Instead of emphasizing the need for money in order to spread Bible truth, he focused attention on the importance of cultivating the spirit of love, the desire to give, and the desire to assist others, especially by sharing the truth with them. To those who had ability in making money and who suggested that by devoting themselves principally to business affairs they would have more to contribute financially, he said that it would be better to limit such activity and to *give of themselves and of their time* in spreading the truth. That is still the position taken by the Governing Body of Jehovah's Witnesses.*

In actual practice, how much do people give? What they do is a personal decision. However, in the matter of giving, it should be noted that Jehovah's Witnesses do not think merely in terms of material possessions. At their district conventions in 1985-86, they discussed the subject "Honoring Jehovah With Our Valuable Things." (Prov. 3:9) It was emphasized that these valuable things include not only material possessions but also physical, mental, and spiritual assets.

Back in 1904, Brother Russell pointed out that a person who has made a full consecration (or, dedication, as we now say) to God "has already *given* all that he has to the Lord." Thus, he should now "consider himself as appointed by the Lord the *steward* of his own time, influence, money, etc., and each is to seek to use these talents to the best of his ability, to the Master's glory." He added that, guided by the wisdom from above, "in proportion as his love and zeal for the Lord grow day by day through a knowledge of the Truth and the attainment of its spirit, he will find himself giving more and more of time, more and more of his influence, and more and more of such means as are at his command, for the service of the Truth." —*Studies in the Scriptures*, "The New Creation," pp. 344-5.

During those early years, the Watch Tower Society had what it called the Tower Tract Fund. What was that? The following interesting details were set out on the back of stationery sometimes used by Brother Russell:

---

* See *The Watchtower*, September 1, 1944, page 269; December 15, 1987, pages 19-20.

"This fund consists of the *free-will offerings* of those who have been fed and strengthened by the 'meat in due season' which the above publications [made available by the Watch Tower Society], as God's instrumentalities, are now laying before the consecrated saints, the world over.

"This fund is constantly employed in sending out, *gratis,* thousands of copies of Zion's Watch Tower and Old Theology Tracts most suitable to new readers. It also assists in the spread of the paper-bound editions of the Dawn series, by aiding those disposed to circulate them—colporteurs and others. It also provides a 'poor fund' by which any of the Lord's children who, through age, or sickness, or from other cause, are unable to subscribe for the Watch Tower are supplied *free,* upon condition of their sending a letter or card at the beginning of each year, stating their desire and inability.

"No one is ever *asked* to contribute to this fund: all donations must be voluntary. We remind our readers of the Apostle's words (1 Cor. 16:1, 2) and corroborate them by saying that those who can give and do give to spread the truth are sure to be repaid in spiritual favors."

The global activity of Jehovah's Witnesses in proclaiming the good news of God's Kingdom continues to be supported by voluntary donations. In addition to the Witnesses themselves, many appreciative interested persons count it a privilege to support this Christian work with their voluntary contributions.

Financing Local Places of Meeting

Each congregation of Jehovah's Witnesses has suitable contribution boxes where people can put whatever donations they desire—when they wish to do so and if they can. It is handled in a private manner so that others are not usually aware of what a person may do. It is between him and God.

There are no salaries to be paid, but it does cost money to maintain a meeting place. In order to fill that need, members of the congregation have to be informed. However, over 70 years ago, *The Watch Tower* made clear that with regard to contributions, there should be no pleading or urging —simply a plain, honest statement of the facts. In line with this viewpoint, congregation meetings do not include frequent discussions of financial matters.

Sometimes, however, there are special needs. It may be that plans are being made to refurbish or enlarge a Kingdom Hall or perhaps to build a new one. In order to ascertain what funds will be available, the elders may ask those in the congregation to write on slips of paper what they individually expect to be able to donate to the project or, possibly, to make

A plain, honest statement of the facts

available for a number of years. Additionally, the elders may ask that individuals or families write on slips what they feel able to contribute on a weekly or monthly basis, with Jehovah's blessing. No names are signed. These are not promissory notes, but they do provide a basis for intelligent planning.—Luke 14:28-30.

In Tarma, Liberia, the congregation obtained needed funds in a somewhat different way. Some in the congregation raised rice for a Witness in his field while he devoted a full year to cutting trees and hand-sawing planks, which were then sold to obtain money for their building project. In Paramaribo, Suriname, although materials had to be purchased, a congregation needed no money for land, because a Witness donated her land for the Kingdom Hall and only asked that her home be moved to the back of the property. The extremely high real-estate prices in Tokyo, Japan, made it difficult for congregations there to obtain land on which to build Kingdom Halls. In order to help solve this problem, several families offered the use of the land on which their own homes were built. They simply requested that after their home was replaced by a new Kingdom Hall, they be provided with an apartment upstairs.

As congregations grew and divided, those located within a given area often tried to assist one another in order to provide suitable Kingdom Halls. In spite of that generous spirit, something else was needed. Property values and building costs skyrocketed, and individual congregations often found it impossible to handle these. What could be done?

Congregations help one another to obtain needed Kingdom Halls

At the "Kingdom Unity" District Conventions in 1983, the Governing Body outlined an arrangement that called for application of the principle set out at 2 Corinthians 8:14, 15, which encourages letting the surplus of those who have it offset the deficiency of others so that "an equalizing might take place." Thus those who have little will not have so little that they are hindered in their efforts to serve Jehovah.

Each congregation was invited to arrange for a box marked "Contributions for Society Kingdom Hall Fund." Everything put into that box would be used only for that purpose. Money contributed throughout the country would thus be made available to offset the deficiency of congregations that badly needed a Kingdom Hall but could not arrange for it on the terms that local banks required. After a careful survey to ascertain where the need was really the most pressing, the Society began to make that money available to congregations that needed to build or otherwise acquire new Kingdom Halls. As more contributions were received and (in lands where it could be done) loans were repaid, still more congregations could be assisted.

This arrangement went into operation first in the United States and Canada, and since then it has spread to over 30 lands in Europe, Africa,

Latin America, and the Far East. By 1992, in just eight of these lands, money had already been made available to assist in providing 2,737 Kingdom Halls, accommodating 3,840 congregations.

Even in lands where this arrangement was not in operation, but where there was urgent need for Kingdom Halls that could not be financed locally, the Governing Body endeavored to make other arrangements to see that help was provided. Thus an equalizing took place, so that those who had little did not have too little.

Caring for Expansion of the World Headquarters

Operation of the world headquarters has also required funds. Following World War I, when the Watch Tower Bible and Tract Society found it advantageous to print and bind its own books, an arrangement was worked out by which the needed machinery was bought in the name of private parties—fellow servants of Jehovah. Instead of paying a profit to a commercial company for manufacturing the books, the Society applied this amount each month to reducing the debt for the equipment. As the benefits of this were realized, the cost of much of the literature to the public was cut to about half. What was being done was to further the preaching of the good news, not to enrich the Watch Tower Society.

In a few years, it was evident that larger facilities were needed at the world headquarters in order to care for the global work of Kingdom preaching. Again and again, as the organization has grown and the preaching activity has been intensified, it has become necessary to add to these facilities. Rather than go to the banks for needed funds to enlarge and equip the headquarters offices and factories as well as the support facilities in and around New York, the Society has explained the need to the brothers. This has been done, not frequently, but only 12 times over a period of 65 years.

There has never been solicitation. Any who wanted to make donations were invited to do so. Those who chose to lend funds were assured that if an unexpected and urgent need arose, their loan would be repaid upon receipt of their request for it. Thus in its handling of matters, the Society endeavored to avoid working any hardship on individuals and congregations that kindly made funds available. The support given by Jehovah's Witnesses by means of their contributions has always enabled the Society to repay all loans. Such contributions sent to the Society are not taken for granted. To the extent possible, these are acknowledged by letters and other statements of appreciation.

The work of the organization is not maintained by donations of a group of wealthy donors. Most of the contributions are from individuals who have only moderate means—many of them, very little of this world's

Most of the contributions are from individuals who have only moderate means

goods. Included are young children who want to share in this way in supporting the Kingdom work. The hearts of all these donors are moved by deep appreciation for Jehovah's goodness and a desire to help others to learn of his gracious provisions.—Compare Mark 12:42-44.

Financing Expansion of Branch Facilities

As the Kingdom-preaching work has taken on greater proportions in various parts of the world, it has been necessary to enlarge the organization's branch facilities. This is done under the direction of the Governing Body.

Thus, after reviewing recommendations from the branch in Germany, directions were given in 1978 to locate suitable property and then to build an entirely new complex. Could the German Witnesses care for the expenses involved? The opportunity was extended to them. At the completion of that project in 1984, at Selters, at the western edge of the Taunus Mountains, the branch office reported: "Tens of thousands of Jehovah's Witnesses—rich and poor, young and old—contributed millions of dollars to help pay for the new facilities. Due to their generosity, the entire project could be completed without the necessity of borrowing money from worldly agencies or of having to go into debt." Additionally, about 1 out of every 7 Witnesses in the Federal Republic of Germany had shared in the actual construction work at Selters/Taunus.

In some other lands, the local economy or the financial condition of Jehovah's Witnesses has made it very difficult, even impossible, for them to build needed branch offices to supervise the work or factories in which to publish Bible literature in the local languages. The Witnesses within the country have been given opportunity to do what they can. (2 Cor. 8: 11, 12) But lack of funds in a country is not allowed to hinder the spread of the Kingdom message there if needed finances are available elsewhere.

Thus, while local Witnesses do what they can, in a large part of the world a considerable portion of the money needed for branch buildings is provided by donations made by Jehovah's Witnesses in other lands. That was true in connection with the building of the large complexes completed in South Africa in 1987, Nigeria in 1990, and the Philippines in 1991. It was also true of Zambia, where potential printing facilities were still under construction in 1992. It has likewise been true of many projects of smaller proportions, such as those completed in India in 1985; Chile in 1986; Costa Rica, Ecuador, Guyana, Haiti, and Papua New Guinea in 1987; Ghana in 1988; and Honduras in 1989.

In some lands, however, the brothers have been surprised at what they could accomplish locally with Jehovah's blessing on their united efforts. In the early 1980's, for example, the branch in Spain was making moves toward major enlargement of its facilities. The branch asked the Governing

Body to provide the needed finances. But because of heavy expenditures in other directions at that time, such help was not then available. If given the opportunity, could the Spanish Witnesses, with their relatively low wages, provide sufficient funds for such an enterprise?

The situation was explained to them. Gladly they came forward with their jewels, rings, and bracelets so that these could be turned into cash. When one elderly Witness was asked whether she was sure she really wanted to donate the heavy gold bracelet that she had handed in, she replied: "Brother, it is going to do far more good paying for a new Bethel than it will on my wrist!" An older sister dug out a pile of musty bank notes that she had stashed away under the floor of her home over the years. Couples contributed the money they had saved for trips. Children sent their savings. A youngster who was planning to buy a guitar donated the money toward the branch project instead. Like the Israelites at the time that the tabernacle was built in the wilderness, the Spanish Witnesses proved to be generous and willinghearted contributors of all that was needed in a material way. (Ex. 35:4-9, 21, 22) Then they offered themselves—full-time, during vacations, on weekends—to do the work itself. From all over Spain they came—thousands of them. Other Witnesses from Germany, Sweden, Great Britain, Greece, and the United States, to mention a few, joined with them to complete what had at first seemed like an impossible task.

Is There a Profit From the Literature?

As of 1992, Bible literature was being published at the world headquarters and at 32 branches worldwide. Vast

---

Donations Were Not Always in the Form of Money

Witnesses in the far north of Queensland prepared and sent to the Watch Tower construction site in Sydney, Australia, four semitrailer loads of prime timber that then had an estimated value of between A$60,000 and A$70,000.

When the Watch Tower factory at Elandsfontein, South Africa, was being enlarged, an Indian brother phoned and asked that they please pick up a donation of 500 bags (110 pounds each) of cement—at a time when there was a scarcity of it in the country. Others offered their trucks for use by the Society. An African sister paid a firm to deliver 20 cubic yards of building sand.

In the Netherlands when new branch facilities were being put up at Emmen, huge quantities of tools and work clothing were donated. One sister, though very ill, knitted a pair of woolen stockings for each of the workers during the winter period.

To build a new branch office and potential printery at Lusaka, Zambia, construction materials were purchased with funds provided by Witnesses in other lands. Materials and equipment that were not available locally were trucked into Zambia as donations to the work there.

A Witness in Ecuador, in 1977, donated an 84-acre piece of land. Here an Assembly Hall and a new branch complex were constructed.

Local Witnesses in Panama opened their homes to accommodate volunteer workers; some who owned buses provided transportation; others shared in providing 30,000 meals that were served at the construction site.

For workers at the project in Arboga, Sweden, one congregation baked and sent 4,500 buns. Others sent honey, fruit, and jam. A farmer near the building site, though not a Witness, provided two tons of carrots.

amounts of it were being provided for distribution by Jehovah's Witnesses. But none of this was done for commercial gain. Decisions as to the languages in which literature would be printed and the countries to which it would be shipped were made not for any commercial advantage but solely with a view to accomplishing the work that Jesus Christ assigned to his followers.

As early as July 1879, when the very first issue of the *Watch Tower* was published, it carried a notice saying that those too poor to pay for a subscription (then only 50¢, U.S., per year) could have it free if they would simply write to make request. The principal objective was to help people learn about Jehovah's grand purpose.

To that end, since 1879 tremendous amounts of Bible literature have been distributed to the public without charge. In 1881 and thereafter, approximately 1,200,000 copies of *Food for Thinking Christians* were distributed gratis. Many of these were in the form of a 162-page book; others, in newspaper format. Scores of tracts of varying sizes were published during the years that followed. The vast majority of these (literally hundreds of millions of copies) were distributed without charge. The number of tracts and other publications given out kept growing. In 1915 alone, the report showed that 50,000,000 copies of tracts in some 30 languages were supplied for worldwide distribution without charge. Where was the money for all of this coming from? Largely from voluntary donations to the Society's Tract Fund.

There was also literature that was offered for a contribution during the early decades of the Society's history, but the suggested contribution was kept as low as possible. This literature included bound books of 350 to 744 pages. When the Society's colporteurs (as full-time preachers were then known) offered these to the public, they stated the amount suggested as a contribution. Their objective, however, was not to make money but to get vital Bible truths into the hands of the people. They wanted people to read the literature and benefit from it.

They were more than willing to give a person literature (making a contribution for it themselves) if the householder was destitute. But it had been observed that many people were more inclined to read a publication if they gave something for it, and what they contributed could, of course, be used to print more literature. Yet, emphasizing the fact that the Bible Students were not seeking financial gain, the Society's service instruction sheet, the *Bulletin*, of October 1, 1920, said: "Ten days after having delivered the booklet [one that consisted of 128 pages], call again upon the parties and ascertain whether they have read it. If they have not, ask that they return the book and refund their money. Tell them that you are not a book agent, but that you are interested in giving this message of comfort and cheer to everybody, and that if they are not sufficiently interested in a fact

Much literature distributed without charge—who pays for it?

that so closely concerns them . . . , you wish to put the book into the hands of someone who will be interested." Jehovah's Witnesses have not continued to use that method, for they have found that other family members sometimes pick up the literature and benefit from it; but what was done back then does highlight the real objective of the Witnesses.

For many years they referred to their distribution of literature as "selling." But this terminology caused some confusion, and so beginning in 1929, it was gradually dropped. The term did not really fit their activity, for their work was not commercial. Their objective was not money-making. Their entire motivation was to preach the good news of God's Kingdom. Because of this, in 1943 the Supreme Court of the United States held that Jehovah's Witnesses could not be required to obtain a commercial peddling license before distributing their literature. And the Canadian judiciary thereafter quoted with approval the reasoning set out by the U.S. Supreme Court in that decision.*

In many lands Jehovah's Witnesses have regularly offered their literature on a contribution basis. The suggested contribution has been so low, compared to other books and magazines, that many people have offered to contribute more. But great effort has been made on the part of the organization to keep the suggested contribution down so that it will be within the means of the many millions of people who have very little of this world's goods but who are grateful to receive a Bible or Bible literature. The objective in suggesting a contribution, however, has not been the enrichment of the organization of Jehovah's Witnesses.

Where the law construes any distribution of Bible literature as commercial if the distributor suggests a contribution for the literature, Jehovah's Witnesses gladly leave it with anyone who shows sincere interest and promises to read it. Those who want to donate something to further the work of Bible education may give whatever they like. That is done, for example, in Japan. In Switzerland, until recently, contributions for literature were accepted, but only up to a stated sum; so if householders wanted to give more, the Witnesses simply returned it or provided the householder with additional literature. Their desire was, not to collect money, but to preach the good news of God's Kingdom.

In 1990, because of highly publicized financial scandals in some of Christendom's religions, coupled with an increasing tendency by governments to classify religious activity as a commercial enterprise, Jehovah's Witnesses made some adjustments in their activity in order to avoid any misunderstanding. The Governing Body directed that in the United States, all

Murdock v. Commonwealth of Pennsylvania, 319 U.S. 105 (1943); *Odell v. Trepanier*, 95 C.C.C. 241 (1949).

They gladly leave literature with anyone who shows sincere interest and promises to read it

literature that the Witnesses distribute—Bibles, as well as tracts, booklets, magazines, and bound books explaining the Bible—be provided to people on the sole precondition that they read it, no contribution being suggested. The activity of Jehovah's Witnesses is in no way commercial, and this arrangement served to further differentiate them from religious groups that commercialize religion. Of course, most people are aware that it costs money to print such literature, and those who appreciate the service being performed by the Witnesses may want to donate something to help with the work. It is explained to such persons that the worldwide work of Bible education conducted by Jehovah's Witnesses is supported by voluntary donations. Donations are gladly accepted, but they are not solicited.

Those who share in the field ministry are not doing it for financial gain. They donate their time, and they pay for their own transportation. If someone shows interest, they arrange to return each week, absolutely free of charge, to give personal instruction in the Bible. Only love for God and for their fellowman could motivate them to continue to engage in such activity, often in the face of indifference and outright opposition.

What is done with money that is donated?

Funds received at the world headquarters of Jehovah's Witnesses or at its branch offices are used, not for the enrichment of the organization or any individual, but to further the preaching of the good news. Back in 1922, *The Watch Tower* reported that because of the economic situation in Europe, books printed there for the Society were being paid for chiefly by the American office and were often being left with the people at less than cost. Although Jehovah's Witnesses now operate printing establishments in many lands, some countries to which the literature is shipped are not able to send any funds out of the country to cover the cost. The generous voluntary donations of Jehovah's Witnesses in lands where they have sufficient resources help to offset the lack in countries where they have little.

The Watch Tower Society has always endeavored to use all the resources at its disposal to further the preaching of the good news. In 1915, as president of the Society, Charles Taze Russell said: "Our Society has not sought to lay up earthly riches, but has been, rather, a spending institution. Whatever God's providence sent in to us without solicitation we have sought to spend as wisely as possible in harmony with the Word and Spirit of the Lord. Long ago we announced that when the funds would cease, the activities of the Society would cease proportionately; and that as the funds increased, the Society's activities would be enlarged." The Society has continued to do exactly that.

Right down to the present, the organization uses available funds to send out traveling overseers to fortify the congregations and to encourage them in their public ministry. It continues to send missionaries and graduates of the Ministerial Training School to lands where there is special need. It also uses whatever funds are available to send special pioneers into areas where little or no preaching of the Kingdom message has yet been done. As reported in the *1993 Yearbook of Jehovah's Witnesses,* during the previous service year, $45,218,257.56 (U.S.) was expended in these ways.

Not Serving for Personal Gain

No financial profit is made by any members of the Governing Body, officers of its legal agencies, or other prominent persons associated with the organization as a result of the work of Jehovah's Witnesses.

Regarding C. T. Russell, who served as president of the Watch Tower Society for over 30 years, one of his associates wrote: "As a means of determining whether his course was in harmony with the Scriptures, and also as a means of demonstrating his own sincerity, he decided to test the Lord's approval as follows: (1) Devote his life to the cause; (2) Invest his fortune in the promulgation of the work; (3) Prohibit collections at all meetings; (4) Depend on unsolicited contributions (wholly voluntary) to continue the work after his fortune was exhausted."

Instead of using religious activity to acquire material wealth for himself, Brother Russell spent all his resources in the Lord's work. After his death it was reported in *The Watch Tower:* "He devoted his private fortune entirely to the cause to which he gave his life. He received the nominal sum of $11.00 per month for his personal expenses. He died, leaving no estate whatsoever."

With regard to those who would carry on the work of the Society, Brother Russell stipulated in his will: "As for compensation, I think it wise to maintain the Society's course of the past in respect to salaries—that none be paid; that merely reasonable expenses be allowed to those who serve the Society or its work in any manner." Those who would serve at the Society's Bethel homes, offices, and factories, as well as its traveling representatives, were to be provided merely food, shelter, and a moderate amount for expenses—enough for immediate needs but "no provision . . . for the laying up of money." That same standard applies today.

Those who are accepted for special full-time service at the world headquarters of Jehovah's Witnesses all subscribe to a vow of poverty, as have all the members of the Governing Body and all the other members of the Bethel family there. This does not mean that they live a drab life, without any comforts. But it does mean that they share, without partiality, the modest provisions of food, shelter, and expense reimbursement that are made for all in such service.

Thus the organization carries on its work with complete dependence on the help that God gives. Without compulsion but as a real spiritual brotherhood that reaches into all parts of the earth, Jehovah's Witnesses gladly use their resources to accomplish the work that Jehovah, their grand heavenly Father, has given them to do.

"He devoted his private fortune entirely to the cause to which he gave his life"

WORLD HEADQUARTERS OF JEHOVAH'S WITNESSES

The global activity of Jehovah's Witnesses has been directed from Brooklyn, New York, U.S.A., since 1909. These buildings have housed headquarters offices since 1980

Watchtower Educational Center, at Patterson, New York (under construction in 1992

Some of the residence buildings for the thousands who serve at the world headquarters

354

Former hotels in Brooklyn renovated to provide room for 1,476 more volunteer workers

Housing for Bethel family at Wallkill, New York

... these factory buildings (in Brooklyn, ...w York), Bibles, books, and brochures ... 180 languages are produced ... global distribution

Millions of audiocassettes of Biblical material are produced in this factory in Brooklyn each year. From here, shipping is also coordinated. Upwards of 15,000 tons of Bible literature and other material per year is shipped to all parts of the world

In this factory at Watchtower Farms, near Wallkill, New York, hundreds of millions of copies of "The Watchtower" and "Awake!," in 14 languages, are printed each year

Jehovah's Witnesses and the legal corporations that they use have offices and printeries in many parts of the world. Pictures on the following pages show many, though not all, of these facilities. Where new buildings were being constructed in 1992, architectural renderings are shown. Statistics given apply as of 1992.

North America and the West Indies

Alaska

Visitors to the Society's branch office receive a warm welcome. Here in Alaska, as elsewhere, Jehovah's Witnesses preach from house to house, though temperatures sometimes drop to -60° F.

Airplane used to carry Kingdom proclaimers to remote parts of the territory

Bahamas

Watch Tower publications reached the Bahamas by 1901. Regular witnessing was first done here in 1926. Since then well over 4,600,000 pieces of Bible literature have been distributed in the islands now supervised from this office.

Barbados

Over 140 religious groups in Barbados claim to be Christian. Since 1905, Jehovah's Witnesses have been helping people here to see for themselves what the Bible says.

Belize

About half the population of Belize live in rural areas. To reach certain interior villages, Jehovah's Witnesses make annual trips on foot with backpacks and briefcases.

Costa Rica

The Society first established a branch office in Costa Rica in 1944. Since the 1950's, Costa Ricans sharing in true worship have numbered in the thousands.

DOMINICAN REPUBLIC

Watch Tower literature was distributed here as early as 1932. But personal instruction of interested people began in 1945, when the missionaries shown at the left arrived. In recent years, when tens of thousands of people became eager to study the Bible with the Witnesses, these branch facilities became necessary.

EL SALVADOR

Some witnessing was done here in 1916. However, it was first in 1945 that at least one person in El Salvador was ready to undergo Christian water immersion (shown here). Since then, thousands more have become servants of Jehovah.

GUADELOUPE

The publisher-to-population ratio in territory served by this branch office is one of the best in the world. Many people in Guadeloupe appreciatively receive the good news.

CANADA

The Society's office in Canada supervises the preaching of the good news in the second-largest country in the world. Well over 100,000 Kingdom proclaimers are busy in this land.

Administrative building (overlapping photo of present branch complex)

Northwest Territories

Logging camps of British Columbia

Cattle ranches of A[...]

GUATEMALA

Although Spanish is the official language of Guatemala, a variety of complex Indian languages are spoken here. The Society's office endeavors to see that everyone has opportunity to hear about God's Kingdom.

ASOCIACION DE LOS TESTIGOS DE JEHOVA

361

French Quebec

Maritime Provinces

HAITI

Serving Jehovah brings great joy to Jehovah's Witnesses in Haiti, in spite of the often difficult conditions that surround them.

HONDURAS

Since 1916, well over 23,000,000 hours have been devoted to teaching the Bible to inhabitants of this land. At times, Jehovah's Witnesses have also had to teach people how to read and write (as you see here) to enable them to study God's Word themselves.

JAMAICA

Hundreds in Jamaica became devoted servants of Jehovah during the time when prospective heirs of the heavenly Kingdom were being gathered. Since 1935, thousands more have joined in preaching the Kingdom message. This branch office is being built to help care for their spiritual needs.

LEEWARD ISLANDS (ANTIGUA)

As early as 1914, the good news was being preached in the islands now cared for by this office. Again and again since then, people in this part of the earth have been invited to "take life's water free."—Rev. 22:17.

MEXICO

New center for Bible education being erected by Jehovah's Witnesses in Mexico

Office facilities being used in 1992

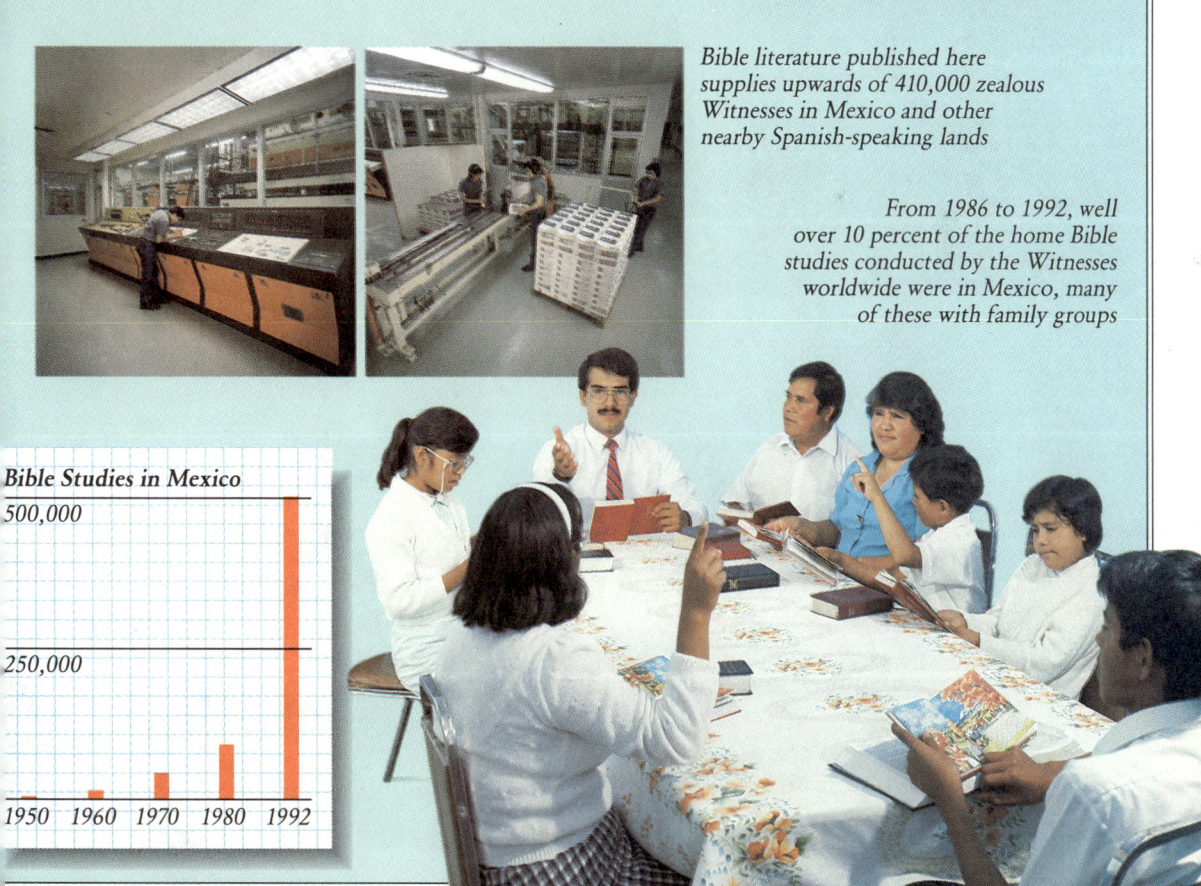

Bible literature published here supplies upwards of 410,000 zealous Witnesses in Mexico and other nearby Spanish-speaking lands

From 1986 to 1992, well over 10 percent of the home Bible studies conducted by the Witnesses worldwide were in Mexico, many of these with family groups

Bible Studies in Mexico

500,000

250,000

1950 1960 1970 1980 1992

MARTINIQUE

Seeds of truth were sown here as early as 1946. But when Xavier and Sara Noll (shown here) came from France in 1954, they were able to remain and cultivate the interest found. By 1992, over 3,200 persons were sharing with them in proclaiming the Kingdom message.

NETHERLANDS ANTILLES (CURAÇAO)

Twenty-three missionaries have served in the territory of this branch office. Two of the original group (shown here) who arrived in 1946 were still on the job in 1992.

NICARAGUA

Starting in 1945, when missionaries arrived, Jehovah's Witnesses in Nicaragua began to increase. By 1992 they numbered over 9,700. The people who want the Witnesses to teach them the Bible now far outnumber the local Witnesses.

Panama

...nce the end of the 19th century, people
...Panama have been receiving
...lp in learning God's
...quirements for
...ernal life.

Puerto Rico

...nce 1930, over 83,000,000 pieces of Bible literature have been distributed in Puerto Rico, and 25,000,000 return
...sits have been made to provide further help to interested persons. Translation work done here helps
...make Bible literature available to some 350,000,000 worldwide who speak Spanish.

Trinidad

The good news was already being intensely proclaimed in Trinidad as early as 1912. Many Witnesses, including these three trained at Gilead School, have devoted their full time to this work.

SOUTH AMERICA

ARGENTINA

A Kingdom proclaimer was first sent to this country in 1924. Much help was later given by Gilead-trained missionaries, including Charles Eisenhower (shown here), who arrived with his wife in 1948. By 1992, general supervision, as well as Bible literature, was being provided from these facilities for upwards of 96,000 of Jehovah's Witnesses in Argentina. Literature was also being sent from here to supply the more than 44,000 Witnesses in Chile.

Bolivia

Bolivians have been hearing the Kingdom message since 1924. Thousands receive Bible literature appreciatively and benefit from regular home Bible studies.

Chile

By 1919, Watch Tower literature had reached Chile. The preaching supervised by this office now extends from windblown sheep ranches in the south to remote mining camps in the north, from the Andes Mountains to the ocean.

Ecuador

A major contribution to the preaching of the good news in Ecuador was made by upwards of 870 Witnesses (such as the two shown here) who left their homelands to serve where the need was greater. This branch now provides help for more than 22,000 zealous praisers of Jehovah.

BRAZIL

In 1992, when the Society's branch office, printery, and Bethel Home were being enlarged to this size, Jehovah's Witnesses in Brazil numbered upwards of 335,000 and were baptizing more than 27,000 disciples each year. The printery here also provides literature for distribution in Bolivia, Paraguay, and Uruguay

GUYANA

The Society has had a branch office in Guyana since 1914. The Witnesses have reached deep into the interior and endeavored to give everyone opportunity to hear the good news. Although the country's population even now is less than a million, the Witnesses have devoted more than 10,000,000 hours to preaching and teaching in this land.

Two large stadiums used for an international convention of Jehovah's Witnesses in São Paulo in 1990; more than 100 additional conventions were also scheduled

Kingdom Proclaimers in Brazil

1950	
1960	
1970	
1980	
1992	

(300,000 / 200,000 / 100,000)

PARAGUAY

Preaching of the good news was under way in Paraguay by the mid-1920's. Since 1946, 112 Gilead-trained missionaries have helped to give the witness. To reach language groups apart from the local Spanish and Guarani, other Witnesses have also volunteered to move in from various lands.

From Germany

From Korea

From Japan

COLOMBIA

PERU

Pioneers preaching high in the Andes

Bible literature was distributed in Peru by a visiting Bible Student as early as 1924. The first congregation was formed here 21 years later. Now there are in Peru over 43,000 active proclaimers of God's Kingdom.

371

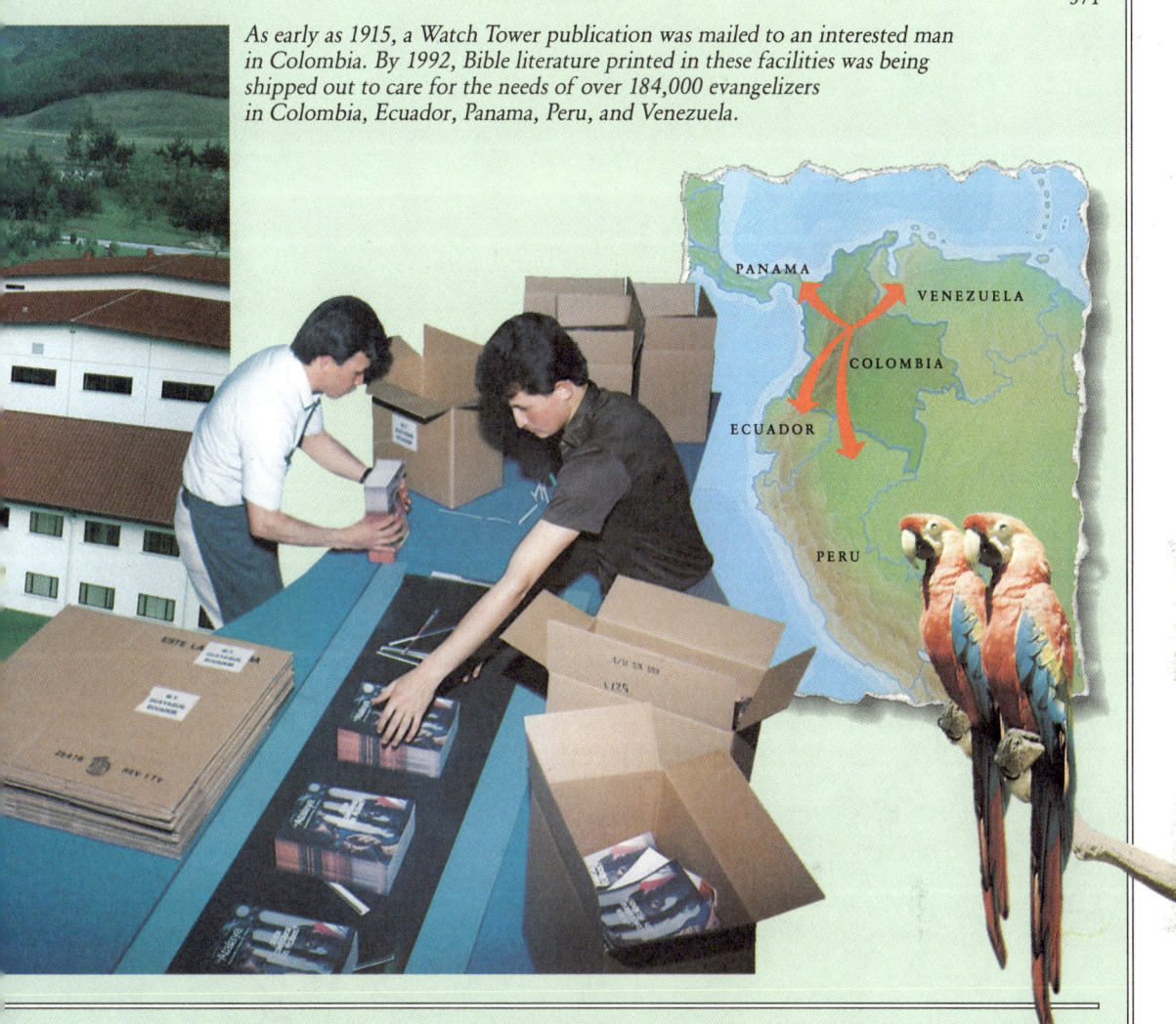

As early as 1915, a Watch Tower publication was mailed to an interested man in Colombia. By 1992, Bible literature printed in these facilities was being shipped out to care for the needs of over 184,000 evangelizers in Colombia, Ecuador, Panama, Peru, and Venezuela.

SURINAME

In about 1903 the first study group was formed here. Today these branch facilities are needed to supervise congregations throughout the country—in primitive areas, the districts, and the city.

URUGUAY

Since 1945, over 80 missionaries have contributed to the Kingdom proclamation in Uruguay. The ones shown here have been serving in Uruguay since the 1950's. By 1992, more than 8,600 local Witnesses were serving along with them.

VENEZUELA

Some Watch Tower literature was distributed in Venezuela in the mid-1920's. A decade later a mother-and-daughter pioneer team from the United States began a zealous period of preaching here, covering the capital repeatedly and making excursions to towns throughout the country. Now there are more than 60,000 active Witnesses in Venezuela.

Bullring in Valencia with crowd of 74,600 for special assembly in 1988

EUROPE AND THE MEDITERRANEAN

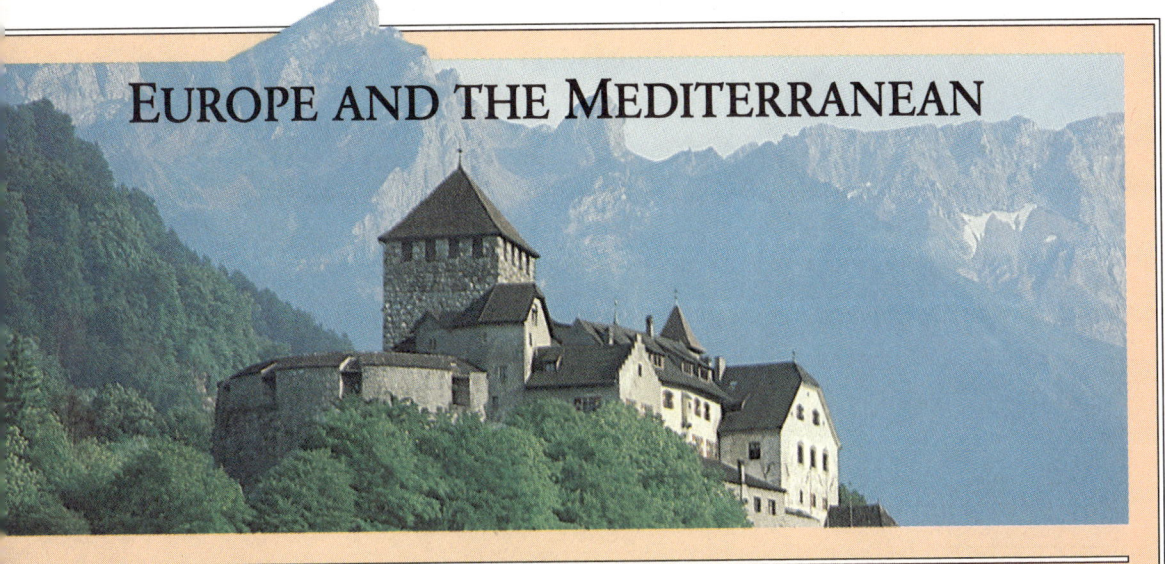

AUSTRIA

Upwards of 270 congregations meet in Kingdom Halls throughout Austria

As early as the 1890's, some people in Austria were being given opportunity to benefit from the good news. Since the 1920's, there has been moderate but steady growth in the number of praisers of Jehovah in this land.

BELGIUM

Belgium has become one of the crossroads of the world. To care for the diverse population found here, this branch distributes Bible literature in more than 100 languages.

BRITAIN

The activity of over 125,000 of Jehovah's Witnesses in Britain is supervised from this branch office. Witnesses from Britain have also taken up assignments to spread the Kingdom message in other European countries as well as in Africa, South America, Australia, the Orient, and islands of the sea.

IBSA House

Watch Tower House

Bible literature is printed here in English, Maltese, Gujarati, and Swahili

The Service Department cares for more than 1,300 congregations in Britain

Literature supplies are sent to all parts of England, Scotland, Wales, Ireland, and Malta, as well as to places in Africa and the Caribbean

FRANCE

Printery/office in Louviers

Translation and photocomposition of all Watch Tower publications printed worldwide for French-speaking people are done at the branch in France. (Upwards of 120,000,000 people speak French.) Literature is regularly printed here in a variety of languages and is shipped out to lands in Europe, Africa, the Middle East, the Indian Ocean, and the Pacific Ocean.

Translation

Photocomposition

Office/residence in Boulogne-Billancourt

Residence in Incarville to house Bethel family

GERMANY

Despite ruthless efforts to annihilate them in Germany during the Nazi era, Jehovah's Witnesses did not abandon their faith. Since 1946, they have devoted upwards of 646,000,000 hours to spreading Bible truth throughout the country.

In addition to translating Bible literature into German, this branch at Selters/Taunus does printing in more than 40 languages

CYPRUS

Shortly after the death of Jesus Christ, the good news was being preached to the people of Cyprus. (Acts 4: 32-37; 11:19; 13:1-12) In modern times, that preaching has been renewed, and a thorough witness continues to be given under the direction of this branch office.

Enlarged facilities at Selters/Taunus

Large quantities of literature produced here are regularly shipped to more than 20 lands; magazines are printed in many languages and sent to upwards of 30 countries

The Society's own trucks are used to ship literature throughout Germany

DENMARK

Since the 1890's, there has been extensive witnessing in Denmark. Printing of Bible literature has been done here not only in Danish but also in Faeroese, Greenlandic, and Icelandic.

Aerial view of the branch (entrance shown in inset)

ITALY

Italian Bible literature is both translated and printed here. This branch prints and binds books for use especially in Italy and other nearby countries.

Various views of branch facilities near Rome

FINLAND

Bible truth reached Finland from Sweden in 1906. Since then, it has been carried to every corner of the country, even far above the Arctic Circle. Scores from here have attended Gilead School to be trained for service wherever they were needed in the world field. Others have moved out on their own to serve in lands where the need was greater.

of thousands, on seeing what the Bible really
have begun to assemble with Jehovah's Witnesses

In the face of constant hostility from the Roman Catholic Church, Jehovah's Witnesses in Italy have devoted more than 550,000,000 hours since 1946 to personal calls on their neighbors to discuss the Bible with them. As a result, 194,000 people in Italy are now active worshipers of Jehovah

ICELAND

Iceland, which has population of only bout 260,000, over ,620,000 pieces of ible literature have een distributed in rder to help people to hoose life. Now over 60 persons here erve Jehovah, the rue God.

Georg Lindal, who pioneered here from 1929 to 1953; during most of that time, he was the only Witness in the country

GREECE

The apostle Paul was one of the first to declare the good news in Greece. (Acts 16:9-14; 17:15; 18:1; 20:2) Although the Greek Orthodox Church has intensely persecuted Jehovah's Witnesses for many years, there are now upwards of 24,000 faithful servants of Jehovah in this land. The branch shown here is some 40 miles north of Athens.

Photo taken in 1990 during clergy-led demonstration against the Witnesses

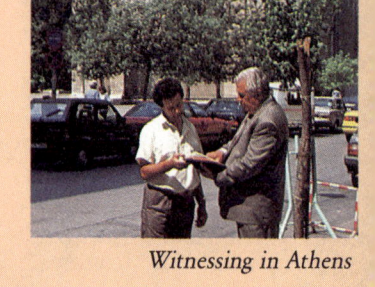

Witnessing in Athens

IRELAND

Response to the Bible's message was slow for many years in Ireland. Much clergy opposition was encountered. But after 100 years of persistent witnessing, there is now an abundant spiritual harvest.

Branch office in Dublin

Two longtime pioneers in field service

POLAND

...hese facilities are being used to provide assistance to the more than 100,000 Witnesses in Poland. From ...939 to 1945, their worship was banned, but their numbers increased from 1,039 in 1939 to 6,994 ...1946. When banned again in 1950, they numbered 18,116; but shortly after that ...an was lifted in 1989, reports showed that there were over 91,000.

For years they held small assemblies out in the woods; now their conventions fill the country's largest stadiums —and more than one stadium at a time

Poznan (1985)

LUXEMBOURG

Luxembourg is one of the very small nations of Europe. But for some 70 years, the Kingdom message has been preached here too. Especially before World War II, help was given by Witnesses who came in from France, Germany, and Switzerland.

NETHERLANDS

From this branch in Emmen, supervision is provided for the activity of over 32,000 zealous Witnesses in the Netherlands. Translation of all publications into Dutch is done in these facilities. Much of the reproduction of Bible-based videocassettes in European languages is also handled from here.

NORWAY

A hundred years ago, a Norwegian who had moved to America and learned Bible truths there brought that good news back to his hometown. Since then, Jehovah's Witnesses have visited every part of Norway again and again to talk to the people about God's Kingdom.

PORTUGAL

For decades after the government signed a concordat with the Vatican, the police arrested Witnesses and deported their missionaries. But the remaining Witnesses continued to meet for worship, to preach to others, and to multiply. At last, in 1974 they were granted legal recognition.

This office supervises the activity of more than 40,000 Witnesses in Portugal. It has also given much help to African lands that had strong ties with Portugal

International convention held in Lisbon in 1978

SWEDEN

For over 100 years, Jehovah's Witnesses have been preaching in Sweden. Within the past ten years, they have devoted over 38,000,000 hours to this activity. Many congregations in Sweden now speak any of a dozen languages other than Swedish.

To help people of all sorts in Sweden, publications are stocked here in 70 languages

SPAIN

This branch cares for upwards of 92,000 Witnesses in Spain. It prints "The Watchtower" and "Awake!" for both Spain and Portugal. In spite of unrelenting efforts of the Catholic clergy to use the State to stop Jehovah's Witnesses, the Witnesses have shared Bible truths with the Spanish people since 1916. Finally, in 1970, when Jehovah's Witnesses in Spain numbered over 11,000, they were granted legal recognition. Since then, their numbers have increased some eightfold.

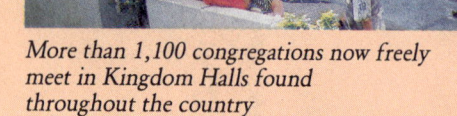

More than 1,100 congregations now freely meet in Kingdom Halls found throughout the country

SWITZERLAND

Since 1903 the Watch Tower Society has had an office in Switzerland. One of the Society's earliest European printeries was located in this country. For many years the branch here in Thun printed magazines for use in scores of other lands.

Africa

Benin

Benin is made up of some 60 ethnic groups speaking 50 dialects. When thousands of these people broke free from their former religions, fetish priests and the clergy of Christendom alike became infuriated. But repeated waves of persecution did not stop the growth of true worship in this land.

Convention held in 1990

Central African Republic

As early as 1947, the Kingdom message began to reach people here. A man who had attended some Witness meetings elsewhere shared with others what he had learned. Soon there was a study group, the ones attending quickly began to witness, and those worshiping Jehovah increased in numbers.

CÔTE D'IVOIRE

Gilead-trained missionaries helped to introduce true worship in this West African land in 1949. More than a hundred of such missionaries have served here. Each year, well over a million hours are now being devoted to searching out truth-hungry people in the area cared for by this branch office.

GHANA

The preaching of the good news in Ghana got under way in 1924. Now this office in Accra supervises more than 640 congregations in Ghana. It has also cared for translating Bible literature into Ewe, Ga, and Twi and printing it in these languages.

KENYA

In 1931, two of Jehovah's Witnesses traveled from South Africa to preach in Kenya. Since 1963 the Society's office in Kenya has, at various times, provided supervision for evangelizing in many other countries in East Africa (as shown below). International conventions in Kenya in 1973, 1978, and 1985 have contributed to the witness given.

Nairobi convention (1973)

Meeting in Kingdom Hall adjoining the branch office

NIGERIA

The good news has been preached in this count[ry] since early in the 1920's. Evangelizers have also been sent from Nigeria to other parts of West Africa, and Bible literature printed here contin[ues] to fill needs in nearby lands. In Nigeria itself, Jehovah's Witnesses have put into the hands of people more than 28,000,000 pieces of literatu[re] to help them to understand God's Word.

From the Service Department, supervision is provided for well over 160,000 Kingdom proclaimers in Nigeria

LIBERIA

Those who have become Jehovah's Witnesses here have faced numerous tests of their faith —when breaking away from local superstitions, when forsaking polygamy, when persecuted by officials to whom they had been misrepresented, and when surrounded by political and ethnic groups at war. Yet, true worship continues to unite people of all sorts in this land.

Convention in Calabar, Nigeria (1990)

MAURITIUS

As early as 1933, zealous Witnesses from South Africa visited this island in the Indian Ocean. There are now upwards of a thousand Witnesses in Mauritius who urge their neighbors to seek Jehovah so that they might be viewed by him with favor when he destroys the present wicked system.—Zeph. 2:3.

SOUTH AFRICA

For over 80 years, the Watch Tower Society has had a branch office in South Africa. Zealous evangelizers from here have done much to spread the Kingdom message into other countries in southern and eastern Africa. In the territory that was formerly under this branch (where there were 14,674 Kingdom proclaimers in 1945), there are now more than 300,000 active Witnesses of Jehovah.

SENEGAL

Though the number of Witnesses here is small, the branch office has endeavored to see to it that each city, each ethnic group, and the people of every religion, not only in Senegal but also in surrounding countries, have opportunity to hear the Bible's heartwarming message.

391

More than 110 translators work under the direction of this branch to prepare Bible literature in 16 African languages

Printing is done here in upwards of 40 languages

SIERRA LEONE

Preaching of the good news in Sierra Leone got started in 1915. Growth has at times been slow. But when those who did not hold to Jehovah's high standards were removed and those who did not serve with right motives withdrew, the ones loyal to Jehovah prospered spiritually.

ZAMBIA

This branch office supervises the activity of more than 110,000 Witnesses in south-central Africa. The Society's first office here was established in 1936. Since then, Jehovah's Witnesses in Zambia have made upwards of 186,000,000 return visits to give added help to interested ones. They have also taught many to read so they could study the Bible personally and share it with others.

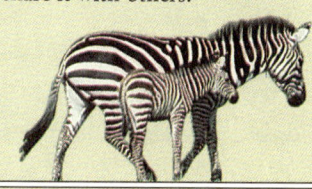

A series of conventions in Zambia in 1992 was attended by 289,643

ZIMBABWE

Jehovah's Witnesses have been active in Zimbabwe since the 1920's. During the following years, they were confronted with bans on their literature, prohibitions of assemblies, and denial of permission for missionaries to preach to the African population. Gradually, obstacles were overcome, and this office now looks after upwards of 20,000 Witnesses.

THE ORIENT

HONG KONG

Watch Tower publications are translated here into Chinese, which, in its many dialects, is spoken by more than a billion people. In Hong Kong itself, the preaching of the good news began when C. T. Russell lectured at city hall in 1912.

INDIA

Witnesses who preach in Malayalam

. . . in Nepali

. . . in Gujarati

This branch supervises the proclamation of the Kingdom message to over one sixth of the earth's population. At present, this office directs translation into 18 languages and printing in 19. Among these is Hindi (spoken by 367 million people) also Assamese, Bengali, Gujarati, Kannada, Malayalam, Marathi, Nepali, Oriya, Punjabi, Tamil, Telugu, and Urdu (each spoken by tens of millions).

JAPAN

Jehovah's Witnesses in Japan, as elsewhere, are zealous proclaimers of God's Kingdom. In 1992 alone, they devoted upwards of 85,000,000 hours to preaching the good news. On an average, about 45 percent of the Japanese Witnesses share in the pioneer service each month.

Bible literature is published here in many languages, including Japanese, Chinese, and languages of the Philippines

A Regional Engineering Office assists with work on branch facilities in various lands

Pioneers in Japan

1975	
1980	
1985	
1992	

(75,000 / 50,000 / 25,000)

REPUBLIC OF KOREA

Some 16 million pieces of Bible literature, in addition to tracts, are produced here annually to supply the more than 70,000 Witnesses in the Republic of Korea. About 40 percent of the Korean Witnesses are in the pioneer service.

MYANMAR

When the Watch Tower Society established a branch office here in 1947, there were only 24 of Jehovah's Witnesses in the country. The more than 2,000 Witnesses now active in Myanmar endeavor to reach not only inhabitants of the cities but also the more numerous rural population.

PHILIPPINES

In 1912, C. T. Russell spoke in Manila's Grand Opera House on the subject "Where Are the Dead?" Since that time Jehovah's Witnesses here have devoted upwards of 483,000,000 hours in witnessing to the people found on the approximately 900 inhabited islands of the Philippines. General supervision of more than 110,000 Witnesses in 3,200 congregations is provided from this branch. Printing is done here in eight languages to fill local needs.

Witnesses from some of the major language groups in the Philippines

Sri Lanka

Before World War I, the good news was being preached in Ceylon (now Sri Lanka), to the south of India. A study group was quickly organized. Since 1953 the Society has had a branch office in the capital city, to give the Sinhalese, the Tamils, and the other ethnic groups in this country opportunity to hear the Kingdom message.

Taiwan

Congregation in Taipei

Some witnessing was done here in the 1920's. But it got under way on a more consistent basis in the 1950's. Now these new branch facilities are being constructed to provide a center for increased activity in this part of the earth.

Thailand

1963 convention

Delegates from abroad in 1991

During the 1930's, pioneer Witnesses came from Britain, Germany, Australia, and New Zealand to share Bible truth with the people of Thailand (then known as Siam). Delegates from many lands attended international conventions here in 1963, 1978, 1985, and 1991 to encourage local Witnesses and to stimulate spread of the Kingdom message.

ISLANDS OF THE PACIFIC

FIJI

The office in Fiji was established in 1958. For a time it supervised the work of Kingdom proclamation in 12 countries and 13 languages. Now the Fiji branch focuses its attention on the approximately one hundred inhabited islands of the Fijian group.

International conventions here in 1963, 1969, 1973, and 1978 helped to draw local Witnesses closer to those in other lands

GUAM

The office in Guam directs preaching of the good news on islands spread over some 3,000,000 square miles of the Pacific Ocean. Translation of Bible literature into nine languages comes under its supervision.

Circuit overseer often travels by airplane between islands

Local Witnesses (as shown here in Micronesia) may use boats to reach their territory

HAWAII

The Watch Tower Society has had a branch office in Honolulu since 1934. Some from Hawaii have shared in evangelizing work not only on the Hawaiian islands but also in Japan, Taiwan, Guam, and islands of Micronesia.

NEW CALEDONIA

In spite of hindrance from religious opposers, Jehovah's Witnesses brought the message of God's Kingdom to New Caledonia. Many people listened appreciatively. In 1956 the first congregation was formed. Now there are upwards of 1,300 praisers of Jehovah here.

NEW ZEALAND

In 1947 the Watch Tower Society established a branch office in New Zealand to provide closer supervision for the preaching of the good news here.

Translating done at this branch enables the inhabitants of Samoa, Rarotonga, and Niue to receive regular spiritual upbuilding.

Translators and proofreaders cooperate to provide publications of high quality

AUSTRALIA

The Watch Tower Society has had a branch office in Australia since 1904. In the past this branch supervised the work of Kingdom proclamation over nearly a quarter of the globe's surface, including China, Southeast Asia, and islands of the South Pacific.

At present, this branch prints Bible literature in more than 25 languages. The printery here helps to supply literature needed by some 78,000 Witnesses located in areas supervised by eight branches in the South Pacific.

Regional Engineering Office assists with branch construction in the South Pacific and Southeast Asia.

Lands supplied with literature from the Australia branch

PAPUA NEW GUINEA

A special challenge faces Jehovah's Witnesses in this land—the people speak some 700 distinct languages. Witnesses from at least ten other lands have moved here to share in the work. They have worked hard to learn local languages. Interested ones translate for those who speak another tongue. Pictures are also effectively used as aids in teaching.

Solomon Islands

A Bible study conducted internationally by mail brought the Kingdom message to the Solomon Islands by the early 1950's. In spite of severe obstacles, Bible truth spread. This branch office and the spacious Assembly Hall are results of local ingenuity, international cooperation, and an abundance of Jehovah's spirit.

Tahiti

By the early 1930's, Jehovah's Witnesses had reached Tahiti with the Kingdom message. Here, in the midst of the Pacific Ocean, a thorough witness is being given. During just the past four years, the witnessing done amounts to more than five hours of talking, on an average, to every man, woman, and child on the island.

Western Samoa

Western Samoa is one of the smallest nations of the world, but Jehovah's Witnesses have a branch office here too. This facility was being built in 1992 to care for activity on these and other nearby islands, including American Samoa.

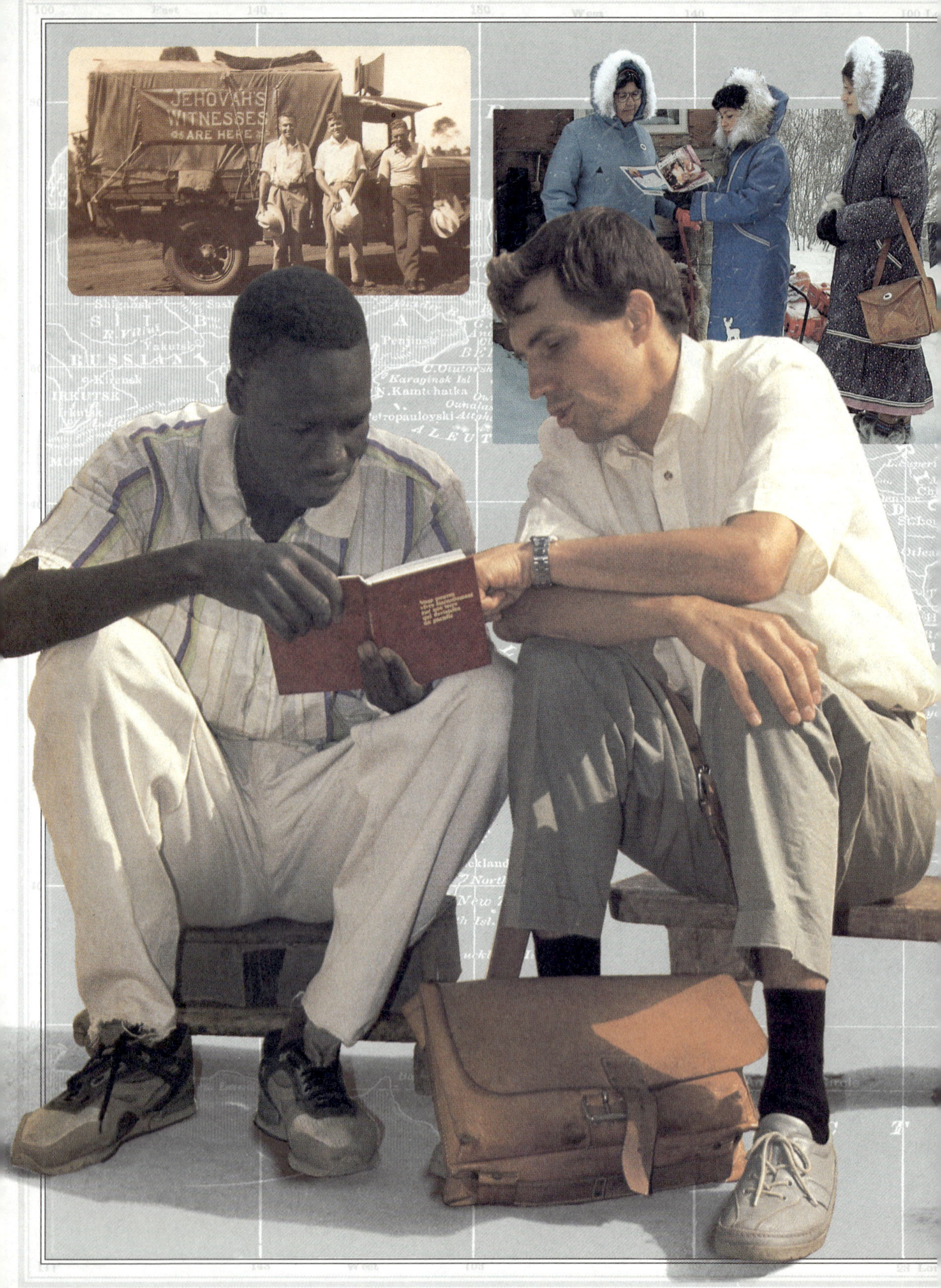
JEHOVAH'S
WITNESSES
ARE HERE

SECTION 4

Proclaiming the Good News in All the Inhabited Earth

How has the proclamation of God's Kingdom as mankind's only hope reached out into all parts of the globe? Here, in Chapters 22 to 24, is the thrilling report, along with heartwarming experiences of those who have shared in it.

CHAPTER 22

WITNESSES TO THE MOST DISTANT PART OF THE EARTH

PART 1
This is the first of five parts in a chapter that reports how the activity of Jehovah's Witnesses has reached around the earth. Part 1, which covers the era from the 1870's through 1914, is on pages 404 to 422. Human society has never recovered from the convulsions caused by World War I, which began in 1914. That was the year that the Bible Students had long identified as marking the end of the Gentile Times.

BEFORE he ascended to heaven, Jesus Christ commissioned his apostles, saying: "You will be witnesses of me . . . to the most distant part of the earth." (Acts 1:8) He had also foretold that "this good news of the kingdom will be preached in all the inhabited earth for a witness to all the nations." (Matt. 24:14) That work was not completed in the first century. A major part of it has been done in modern times. And the record of its accomplishment from the 1870's to the present is truly thrilling.

Although Charles Taze Russell came to be widely known for his well-advertised discourses on the Bible, his interest was not merely in large audiences but in people. Thus, shortly after he began to publish the *Watch Tower* in 1879, he undertook extensive traveling to visit small groups of readers of the magazine to discuss the Scriptures with them.

C. T. Russell urged those who believed the precious promises of God's Word to have a part in sharing them with other people. Those whose hearts were deeply touched by what they were learning showed real zeal in doing just that. To assist in the work, printed material was provided. Early in 1881, a number of tracts appeared. Material from these was then combined with additional information to form the more comprehensive *Food for Thinking Christians,* and 1,200,000 copies of this were prepared for distribution. But how could the small band of Bible Students (perhaps 100 at that time) put out all of these?

WITNESSES TO THE MOST DISTANT PART OF THE EARTH   405

Reaching Church Attenders

Some were given to relatives and friends. A number of newspapers agreed to send a copy to each of their subscribers. (Special emphasis was put on weekly and monthly papers so that *Food for Thinking Christians* would reach many people who lived in rural areas.) But much of the distribution was accomplished on several consecutive Sundays in front of churches in the United States and Britain. There were not enough Bible Students to do it all personally, so they hired others to help.

Brother Russell dispatched two associates, J. C. Sunderlin and J. J. Bender, to Britain to supervise the distribution of 300,000 copies there. Brother Sunderlin went to London, while Brother Bender traveled north into Scotland and then worked his way south. Principal attention was given to larger cities. By means of newspaper ads, capable men were located, and contracts were made with them to arrange for enough helpers to distribute their allotment of copies. Nearly 500 distributors were recruited in London alone. The work was done quickly, on two consecutive Sundays.

That same year, arrangements were made for Bible Students who could spend half or more of their time exclusively in the Lord's work to be colporteurs, distributing literature for Bible study. These forerunners of the

C. T. Russell personally gave Bible discourses in over 300 cities (in areas indicated by the dots) in North America and the Caribbean—in many of them 10 or 15 times

ones known today as pioneers achieved a truly remarkable distribution of the good news.

During the following decade, Brother Russell prepared a variety of tracts that could easily be used to disseminate some of the outstanding Bible truths that had been learned. He also wrote several volumes of *Millennial Dawn* (later known as *Studies in the Scriptures*). Then he began to make personal evangelizing trips to other lands.

Russell Travels Abroad

In 1891 he visited Canada, where enough interest had been generated since 1880 that an assembly attended by 700 could now be held in Toronto. He also traveled to Europe in 1891 to see what could be done to forward the spread of the truth there. This trip took him to Ireland, Scotland, England, many of the countries on the European continent, Russia (the area now known as Moldova), and the Middle East.

What did he conclude from his contacts on that trip? "We saw no opening or readiness for the truth in Russia . . . We saw nothing to encourage us to hope for any harvest in Italy or Turkey or Austria or Germany," he reported. "But Norway, Sweden, Denmark, Switzerland, and especially England, Ireland and Scotland, are fields ready and waiting to be harvested. These fields seem to be crying out, Come over and help us!" This was an era when the Catholic Church still forbade Bible reading, when many Protestants were forsaking their churches, and when not a few, disillusioned by the churches, were rejecting the Bible altogether.

In order to help those people who were spiritually hungry, after Brother Russell's trip in 1891 intensified efforts were put forth to translate literature into the languages of Europe. Also, arrangements were made to print and stock literature supplies in London so that these would be more readily available for use in Britain. The British field did, indeed, prove to be ready for harvesting. By 1900, there were already nine congregations and a total of 138 Bible Students—among them some zealous colporteurs. When Brother Russell again visited Britain in 1903, a thousand gathered in Glasgow to hear him speak on "Millennial Hopes and Prospects," 800 attended in London, and audiences of 500 to 600 in other towns.

In confirmation of Brother Russell's observations, however, after his visit 17 years passed before the first congregation of Bible Students was formed in Italy, at Pinerolo. And what about Turkey? During the late 1880's, Basil Stephanoff had preached in Macedonia, in what was then European Turkey. Although some had seemed to show interest, certain ones who professed to be brothers made false reports, leading to his imprisonment. Not until 1909 did a letter from a Greek in Smyrna (now Izmir), Turkey, report that a group there was appreciatively studying the Watch

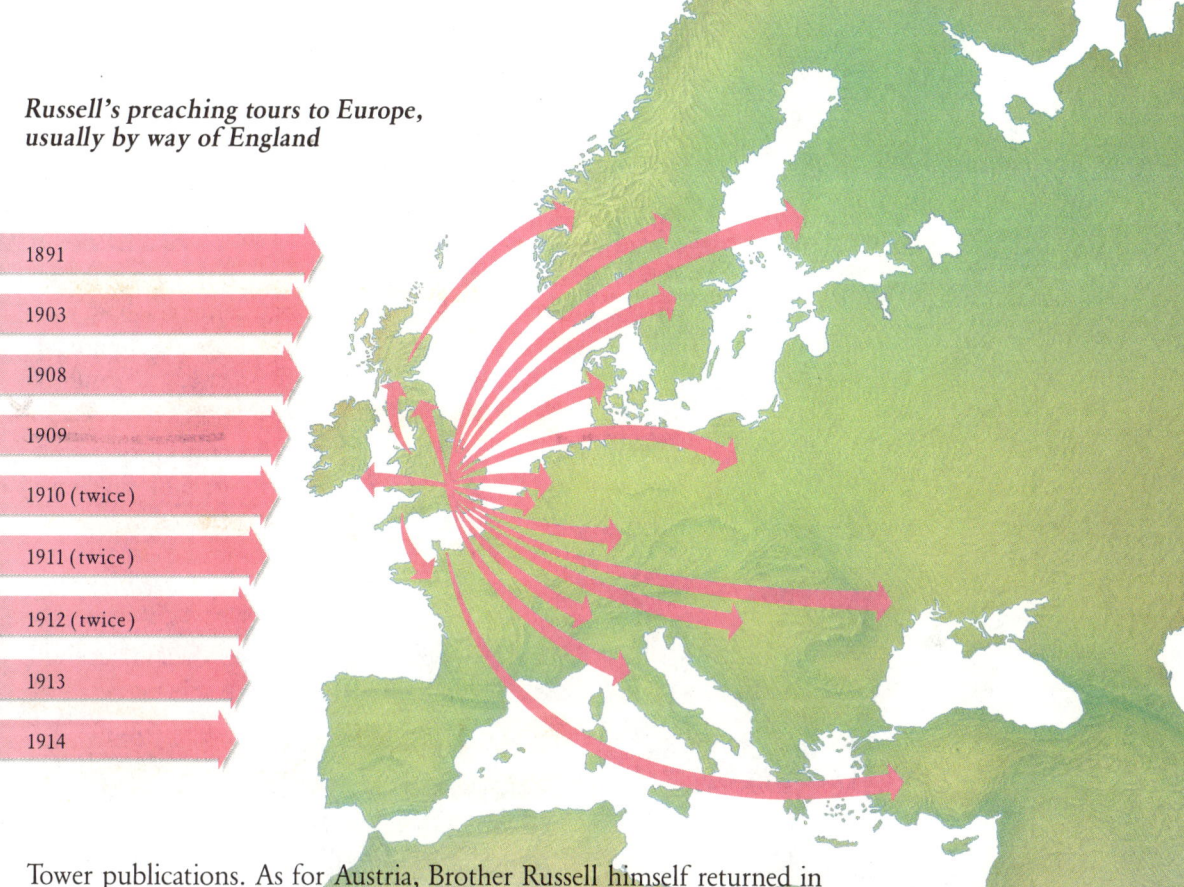

Russell's preaching tours to Europe, usually by way of England

1891
1903
1908
1909
1910 (twice)
1911 (twice)
1912 (twice)
1913
1914

Tower publications. As for Austria, Brother Russell himself returned in 1911 to speak in Vienna, only to have the meeting broken up by a mob. In Germany too, appreciative response was slow in coming. But the Scandinavians showed greater awareness of their spiritual need.

Scandinavians Share With One Another

Many Swedes were living in America. In 1883 a sample copy of the *Watch Tower* translated into Swedish was made available for distribution among them. These soon found their way by mail to friends and relatives in Sweden. No Norwegian literature had yet been produced. Nevertheless, in 1892, the year after Brother Russell's trip to Europe, Knud Pederson Hammer, a Norwegian who had learned the truth in America, personally returned to Norway to witness to his relatives.

Then, in 1894, when literature began to be published in Dano-Norwegian, Sophus Winter, a 25-year-old Danish-American, was sent to Denmark with a supply to distribute. By the next spring, he had placed 500 volumes of *Millennial Dawn*. Within a short time, a few others who read those publications were sharing in the work with him. Sadly, he later lost sight of the value of the precious privilege that was his; but others continued to let the light shine.

NORWAY

Arctic Circle

When convinced that he had found the truth, Andreas Øiseth zealously distributed Bible literature in nearly every part of Norway

JEHOVAH'S WITNESSES—PROCLAIMERS OF GOD'S KINGDOM

Before he abandoned the service, however, Winter did some colporteuring in Sweden. Shortly after that, at the home of a friend on the island of Sturkö, August Lundborg, a young Salvation Army captain, saw two volumes of *Millennial Dawn.* He borrowed them, read them eagerly, resigned from the church, and started to share with others what he had learned. Another young man, P. J. Johansson, had his eyes opened as a result of reading a tract that he picked up on a park bench.

As the Swedish group began to grow, some went over to Norway to distribute Bible literature. Even before that, literature had arrived in Norway by mail from relatives in America. It was in this way that Rasmus Blindheim got started in Jehovah's service. Among others in Norway, Theodor Simonsen, a preacher of the Free Mission, received the truth during those early years. He started to refute the hellfire teaching in his speeches at the Free Mission. His audience jumped to their feet in excitement over this wonderful news; but when it was learned that he had been in touch with the "Millennial Dawn," he was dismissed from the church. Nevertheless, he kept right on talking about the good things that he had learned. Another young man who received some literature was Andreas Øiseth. Once convinced that he had the truth, he left the family farm and undertook colporteur work. Systematically he worked his way north, then south along the fjords, not bypassing any community. In the winter he carried his supplies—food, clothing, and literature—on a kick-sled, and hospitable people provided places for him to sleep. In an eight-year trip, he covered nearly the entire country with the good news.

August Lundborg's wife, Ebba, went from Sweden into Finland to do colporteur work in 1906. At about the same time, men returning from the United States brought some Watch Tower literature with them and began to share what they were learning. Thus within a few years, Emil Österman, who was looking for something better than what the churches offered, came into possession of *The Divine Plan of the Ages.* He shared it with his friend Kaarlo Harteva, who was also searching. Recognizing the value of what they had, Harteva translated it into Finnish and, with Österman's help in financing, arranged for it to be published. Together they set out to distribute it. Displaying a genuine evangelizing spirit, they talked to people in public places, made calls from house to house, and gave discourses in large auditoriums that were packed to capacity. In Helsinki, after exposing Christendom's false doctrines, Brother Harteva invited the audience to use the Bible to defend belief in immortality of the soul, if they could. All eyes turned toward the clergymen present. No one spoke up; none could answer the clear statement found at Ezekiel 18:4. Some in the audience said they could hardly sleep that night after what they had heard.

Humble Gardener Becomes Evangelizer in Europe

Meanwhile, Adolf Weber, at the encouragement of an elderly Anabaptist friend, left Switzerland for the United States in search of a fuller understanding of the Scriptures. There, in response to an ad, he became a gardener for Brother Russell. With the help of *The Divine Plan of the Ages* (then available in German) and meetings conducted by Brother Russell, Adolf gained the Bible knowledge that he was seeking, and he was baptized in 1890. The 'eyes of his heart were enlightened,' so that he truly appreciated what a grand opportunity had opened up to him. (Eph. 1:18) After witnessing zealously for a time in the United States, he returned to the land of his birth to take up work "in the Lord's vineyard" there. Thus, by the mid-1890's, he was back in Switzerland sharing Bible truth with those who had receptive hearts.

Adolf earned his livelihood as a gardener and forester, but his prime interest was evangelizing. He witnessed to those with whom he worked, as well as to people in nearby Swiss towns and villages. He knew several languages, and he used this knowledge to translate the Society's publications into French. When winter came he would load his knapsack with Bible literature and go on foot into France, and at times he traveled northwest into Belgium and south into Italy.

To reach people that he might not contact personally, he placed ads in newspapers and magazines, drawing attention to literature available for Bible study. Elie Thérond, in central France, responded to one of the ads, recognized the ring of truth in what he read, and soon began spreading the message himself. In Belgium, Jean-Baptiste Tilmant, Sr., also

Adolf Weber, a humble gardener, spread the good news from Switzerland to other countries in Europe

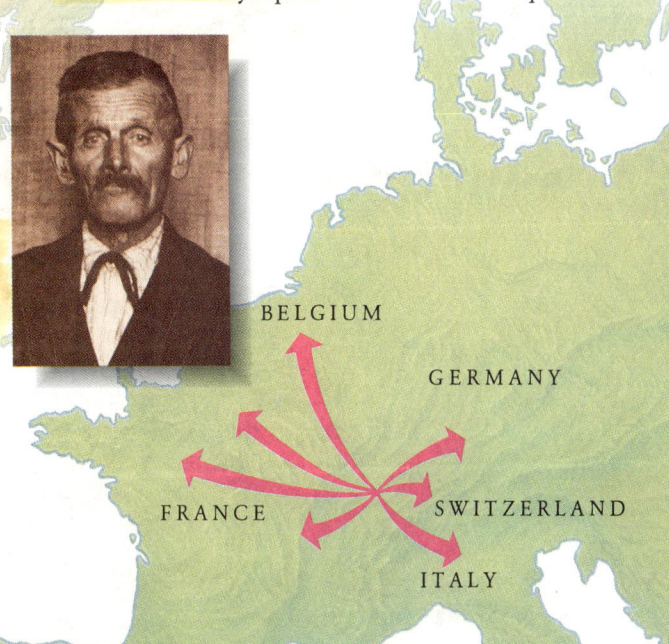

saw one of the ads in 1901 and obtained two volumes of *Millennial Dawn*. What a thrill for him to see Bible truth presented so clearly! How could he possibly refrain from telling his friends! By the following year, a study group was meeting regularly in his home. Soon afterward the activity of that little group was yielding fruit even in northern France. Brother Weber kept in touch with them, periodically visiting the various groups that developed, building them up spiritually and giving them instructions on how to share the good news with others.

When the Good News Reached Germany

A short time after some of the publications began to appear in German, in the mid-1880's, German-Americans who appreciated them began to send copies to relatives in the land of their birth. A nurse working at a hospital in Hamburg shared copies of *Millennial Dawn* with others at the hospital. In 1896, Adolf Weber, in Switzerland, was placing ads in German-language newspapers and mailing tracts to Germany. The following year a literature depot was opened in Germany to facilitate distribution of the German edition of the *Watch Tower,* but results were slow in coming. However, in 1902, Margarethe Demut, who had learned the truth in Switzerland, moved to Tailfingen, east of the Black Forest. Her zealous personal witnessing helped to lay the foundation for one of the early groups of Bible Students in Germany. Samuel Lauper, from Switzerland, moved to the Bergisches Land, northeast of Cologne, to spread the good news in that area. By 1904, meetings were being held there in Wermelskirchen. Among those present was an 80-year-old man, Gottlieb Paas, who had been looking for the truth. On his deathbed, not long after those meetings began, Paas held up the *Watch Tower* and said: "This is the truth; hold on to it."

The number interested in these Bible truths gradually increased. Although it was expensive, arrangements were made to insert free sample copies of the *Watch Tower* into newspapers in Germany. A report published in 1905 says that more than 1,500,000 copies of these *Watch Tower* samples had been distributed. That was a great accomplishment for a very small group.

The Bible Students did not all feel that by reaching people close to home they had done what was necessary. As early as 1907, Brother Erler, from Germany, made trips into Bohemia in what was then Austria-Hungary (later part of Czechoslovakia). He distributed literature warning of Armageddon and telling of the blessings that would come to mankind thereafter. By 1912 another Bible Student had distributed Bible literature in the Memel area, in what is now Lithuania. Many responded enthusiastically to the message, and several fairly large groups of Bible Students were quickly formed there. However, when they learned that true Christians must also be witnesses, their numbers began to dwindle. Nevertheless, a few proved themselves to be genuine imitators of Christ, "the faithful and true witness."—Rev. 3:14.

When Nikolaus von Tornow, a German baron with large estates in Russia, was in Switzerland in about 1907, he was handed one of the Watch Tower Society's tracts. Two years later he appeared at the Berlin Congregation, in Germany, decked out in his best attire and accompanied by his personal servant. It took a while for him to appreciate why God would entrust priceless truths to such unassuming people, but what he read at 1 Corinthians 1:26-29 helped: "You behold his calling of you, brothers, that not many wise in a fleshly way were called, not many powerful, not many of noble birth . . . , in order that no flesh might boast in the sight of God." Convinced that he had found the truth, von Tornow sold his estates in Russia and devoted himself and his resources to furthering the interests of pure worship.

In 1911, when a young German couple, the Herkendells, got married, the bride requested of her father, as a dowry, money for an unusual honeymoon. She and her husband had in mind making a strenuous trip that would take many months. Their honeymoon was a preaching trip into Russia to reach German-speaking people there. Thus in many ways people of all sorts were sharing with others what they had learned about God's loving purpose.

Hermann Herkendell, along with his bride, took a honeymoon trip of many months to preach to German-speaking people in Russia

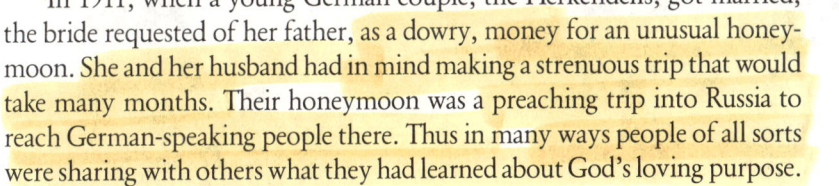

Growth in the British Field

After the intensive distribution of literature in Britain in 1881, some churchgoers saw the need to act on what they had learned. Tom Hart of Islington, London, was one of those impressed by the *Watch Tower's* Scriptural counsel, "Get out of her, my people"—that is, get out of Christendom's Babylonish churches and follow Bible teaching. (Rev. 18:4) He resigned from the chapel in 1884, followed by a number of others.

Many who associated with the study groups developed into effective evangelizers. Some offered Bible literature in the parks of London and other places where people were relaxing. Others concentrated on business houses. The more usual way, however, was to make house-to-house visits.

Sarah Ferrie, a subscriber for the *Watch Tower,* wrote to Brother Russell saying that she and a few friends in Glasgow would like to volunteer to share in tract distribution. What a surprise when a truck pulled up at her door with 30,000 pamphlets, all to be distributed free! They moved into action. Minnie Greenlees, along with her three young sons, with a "pony and trap" for transportation, pressed the distribution of Bible literature into the Scottish countryside. Later on, Alfred Greenlees and Alexander

Colporteurs in England and Scotland endeavored to give everyone opportunity to receive a witness; even their children helped with the distribution of tracts

MacGillivray, traveling on bicycles, distributed tracts throughout much of Scotland. Instead of paying others to distribute the literature, dedicated volunteers were now doing the work themselves.

Their Hearts Impelled Them

In one of his parables, Jesus had said that people who 'heard the word of God with a fine and good heart' would bear fruit. Sincere appreciation for God's loving provisions would move them to share the good news about God's Kingdom with others. (Luke 8:8, 11, 15) Regardless of their circumstances, they would find some way to do it.

Thus it was from an Italian sailor that an Argentine traveler obtained a portion of the tract *Food for Thinking Christians*. While in port in Peru, the traveler wrote for more, and with heightened interest he wrote again, from Argentina in 1885, to the editor of the *Watch Tower* to request literature. That same year a member of the British Navy, who was sent with his battery to Singapore, took the *Watch Tower* with him. He was delighted with what he learned from the magazine and freely used it there to make known the Bible's view on topics that were matters of public discussion. In 1910 a ship on which two Christian women were traveling stopped over at the port in Colombo, Ceylon (now Sri Lanka). They seized the opportunity to witness to Mr. Van Twest, the shipping master of the port. They spoke earnestly to him about the good things they had learned from the book *The Divine Plan of the Ages*. As a result, Mr. Van Twest became a Bible Student, and the preaching of the good news got under way in Sri Lanka.

WITNESSES TO THE MOST DISTANT PART OF THE EARTH   413

Even those who could not travel sought ways to share heartwarming Bible truths with people in other countries. As revealed by a letter of appreciation published in 1905, someone in the United States had sent *The Divine Plan of the Ages* to a man in St. Thomas, in what was then the Danish West Indies. After reading it, the recipient had got down on his knees and expressed his earnest desire to be used by God in the doing of his will. In 1911, Bellona Ferguson in Brazil cited her case as "a positive, living proof that there are none too far away to be reached" by the waters of truth. She had evidently been receiving the Society's publications by mail since 1899. Sometime before World War I, a German immigrant in Paraguay found one of the Society's tracts in his mailbox. He ordered more literature and soon broke off his ties with Christendom's churches. There was no one else in the country to do it, so he and his brother-in-law decided to baptize each other. Indeed, a witness was being given in distant parts of the earth, and it was bearing fruit.

Yet others of the Bible Students felt impelled to travel to the place where they or their parents were born to tell friends and relatives about Jehovah's wonderful purpose and how they could share in it. Thus, in 1895, Brother Oleszynski returned to Poland with good news about the "ransom, restitution and the high calling"; though, sadly, he did not endure in that service. In 1898 a former professor, a Hungarian, left Canada to spread the Bible's urgent message in his homeland. In 1905 a man who had become a Bible Student in America returned to Greece to witness. And in 1913 a young man carried seeds of Bible truth from New York back to his family's hometown, Ramallah, not far from Jerusalem.

Bellona Ferguson, in Brazil—"none too far away to be reached"

Opening Up the Caribbean Area

While the number of evangelizers was growing in the United States, Canada, and Europe, Bible truth was also beginning to take hold in Panama, Costa Rica, Dutch Guiana (now Suriname), and British Guiana (now Guyana). Joseph Brathwaite, who was in British Guiana when he was helped to understand God's purpose, left for Barbados in 1905 to devote his full time to teaching it to people there. Louis Facey and H. P. Clarke, who heard the good news when working in Costa Rica, returned to Jamaica in 1897 to share their newfound faith among their own people. Those who embraced the truth there were zealous workers. In 1906 alone, the group in Jamaica distributed about

E. J. Coward zealously spread Bible truth in the Caribbean area

1,200,000 tracts and other pieces of literature. Another migrant worker, who learned the truth in Panama, carried the Bible's message of hope back to Grenada.

Revolution in Mexico in 1910-11 was another factor in bringing truth-hungry persons the message of God's Kingdom. Many people fled north into the United States. There some of them came in touch with the Bible Students, learned about Jehovah's purpose to bring lasting peace to mankind, and sent literature back into Mexico. However, this was not the first time that Mexico had been reached with this message. As early as 1893, the *Watch Tower* published a letter from F. de P. Stephenson, of Mexico, who had read some of the Watch Tower Society's publications and wanted to have more to share with his friends both in Mexico and in Europe.

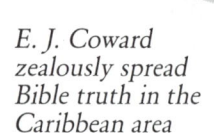

To open more of the Caribbean lands to the preaching of Bible truth and to organize regular meetings for study, Brother Russell sent E. J. Coward to Panama in 1911 and then to the islands. Brother Coward was an emphatic and colorful speaker, and audiences frequently numbering in the hundreds flocked to hear his discourses refuting the doctrines of hellfire and immortality of the human soul, also telling of the glorious future for the earth. He moved from one town to the next, and from one island to another—St. Lucia, Dominica, St. Kitts, Barbados, Grenada, and Trinidad—reaching as many people as possible. He also spoke in British Guiana. While in Panama, he met W. R. Brown, a zealous young Jamaican brother, who thereafter served along with Brother Coward on a number of the Caribbean islands. Later on, Brother Brown helped to open up yet other fields.

In 1913, Brother Russell himself spoke in Panama, Cuba, and Jamaica. For a public discourse that he gave in Kingston, Jamaica, two auditoriums were packed, and still some 2,000 persons had to be turned away. When the speaker said nothing about money and when no collection was taken, the press took note.

Light of Truth Reaches Africa

Africa too was being penetrated by the light of truth during this period. A letter sent from Liberia in 1884 revealed that a Bible reader there had come into possession of a copy of *Food for Thinking Christians* and wanted more to share with others. A few years after that, it was reported that a clergyman in Liberia had left his pulpit in order to be free to teach Bible truths that he was learning with the aid of the *Watch Tower* and that regular meetings were being held there by a group of Bible Students.

ALASKA

GREENLAND

CANADA

PACIFIC OCEAN

UNITED STATES OF AMERICA

ATLANTIC OCEAN

ST. PIERRE & MIQUELON

BERMUDA

CAYMAN ISLANDS

MEXICO

BELIZE

GUATEMALA
EL SALVADOR
HONDURAS
PANAMA
COSTA RICA
NICARAGUA

GUYANA
SURINAME
FRENCH GUIANA

VENEZUELA
COLOMBIA
ECUADOR
PERU
BRAZIL
BOLIVIA
PARAGUAY
CHILE
URUGUAY
ARGENTINA
FALKLAND ISLANDS

BAHAMAS
CUBA
TURKS & CAICOS ISLANDS
JAMAICA
HAITI
DOMINICAN REPUBLIC
PUERTO RICO
VIRGIN ISLANDS (U.S.)
VIRGIN ISLANDS (BRITISH)
ANGUILLA
SABA
ST. MAARTEN
ST. EUSTATIUS
ST. KITTS
NEVIS
MONTSERRAT
ANTIGUA
GUADELOUPE
DOMINICA
MARTINIQUE
ST. LUCIA
ST. VINCENT
BARBADOS
GRENADA
ARUBA
CURAÇAO
BONAIRE
TRINIDAD

CARIBBEAN SEA

GREENLAND
ICELAND
FAEROE ISLANDS
SWEDEN
NORWAY
FINLAND
RUSSIA
ESTONIA
LATVIA
DENMARK
LITHUANIA
NETHERLANDS
IRELAND
BRITAIN
BELARUS
POLAND
GERMANY
BELGIUM
CZECHOSLOVAKIA
UKRAINE
LUXEMBOURG
FRANCE
AUSTRIA
MOLDOVA
KAZAKHSTAN
HUNGARY
ROMANIA
SWITZERLAND
ITALY
BOSNIA & HERZEGOVINA
LIECHTENSTEIN
SLOVENIA
CROATIA
BULGARIA
GEORGIA
UZBEKISTAN
KYRGYZSTAN
PORTUGAL
SPAIN
ALBANIA
ARMENIA
YUGOSLAVIA
GREECE
TURKEY
TURKMENISTAN
TAJIKISTAN
GIBRALTAR
MADEIRA
MALTA
CYPRUS
SYRIA
AZERBAIJAN
TUNISIA
LEBANON
IRAQ
AFGHANISTAN
MOROCCO
ISRAEL
IRAN
ALGERIA
JORDAN
KUWAIT
BAHRAIN
PAKISTAN
MYAN
LIBYA
EGYPT
NEPAL
WESTERN SAHARA
BHUTAN
SAUDI ARABIA
UNITED ARAB EMIRATES
INDIA
QATAR
MAURITANIA
MALI
NIGER
OMAN
SENEGAL
GUINEA-BISSAU
CHAD
SUDAN
YEMEN
BANGLA
DJIBOUTI
GAMBIA
BURKINA FASO
GUINEA
SIERRA LEONE
NIGERIA
CENTRAL AFRICAN REPUBLIC
ETHIOPIA
LIBERIA
SRI LANKA
BENIN
CAMEROON
TOGO
SOMALIA
GHANA
UGANDA
CÔTE D'IVOIRE
CONGO
KENYA
GABON
ZAIRE
SÃO TOMÉ
SEYCHELLES
RWANDA
BURUNDI
TANZANIA
EQUATORIAL GUINEA
MALAWI
COMOROS
INDIAN OCEAN
MAYOTTE
ANGOLA
ST. HELENA
ZAMBIA
MOZAMBIQUE
ZIMBABWE
MAURITIUS
MADAGASCAR
RODRIGUES
NAMIBIA
BOTSWANA
RÉUNION
ATLANTIC OCEAN
SWAZILAND
SOUTH AFRICA
LESOTHO

PACIFIC OCEAN

ALASKA

MONGOLIA
DEMOCRATIC PEOPLE'S REPUBLIC OF KOREA
REPUBLIC OF KOREA
JAPAN
CHINA
MACAO
TAIWAN
HONG KONG
VIETNAM
THAILAND
CAMBODIA
MALAYSIA
BRUNEI
SINGAPORE
PHILIPPINES
SAIPAN
ROTA
YAP
GUAM
BELAU
POHNPEI
MARSHALL ISLANDS
CHUUK
KOSRAE
NAURU
KIRIBATI
HAWAII
INDONESIA
PAPUA NEW GUINEA
SOLOMON ISLANDS
TUVALU
TOKELAU
WALLIS & FUTUNA ISLANDS
WESTERN SAMOA
AMERICAN SAMOA
VANUATU
FIJI
AUSTRALIA
NEW CALEDONIA
TONGA
NIUE
COOK ISLANDS
TAHITI
NORFOLK ISLAND
NEW ZEALAND

A Dutch Reformed minister from Holland took some of the publications of C. T. Russell with him when he was sent to South Africa in 1902. Although he did not lastingly benefit from them, Frans Ebersohn and Stoffel Fourie, who saw the literature in his library, did. A few years later, the ranks in that part of the field were fortified when two zealous Bible Students emigrated from Scotland to Durban, South Africa.

Sadly, among those who obtained literature written by Brother Russell and then taught some of it to others, there were a few, such as Joseph Booth and Elliott Kamwana, who mixed in their own ideas, which were designed to agitate for social change. To some observers in South Africa and Nyasaland (later Malawi), this tended to confuse the identity of the genuine Bible Students. Nevertheless, many were hearing and showing appreciation for the message that directed attention to God's Kingdom as the solution to mankind's problems.

As for widespread preaching in Africa, however, this was yet future.

To the Orient and Islands of the Pacific

Shortly after Bible publications prepared by C. T. Russell were first distributed in Britain, they also reached the Orient. In 1883, Miss C. B. Downing, a Presbyterian missionary in Chefoo (Yantai), China, received a copy of the *Watch Tower*. She appreciated what she learned about restitution and shared the literature with other missionaries, including Horace Randle, associated with the Baptist Mission Board. Later, he had his interest further stimulated by an advertisement for *Millennial Dawn* that appeared in the London *Times*, and this was followed up by copies of the book itself—one from Miss Downing and another sent by his mother in England. At first, he was shocked by what he read. But once convinced that the Trinity is not a Bible teaching, he resigned from the Baptist Church and proceeded to share with other missionaries what he had learned. In 1900 he reported that he had sent out 2,324 letters and some 5,000 tracts to missionaries in China, Japan, Korea, and Siam (Thailand). At that time it was mainly to Christendom's missionaries that the witness was being given in the Orient.

During that same time period, seeds of truth were also sown in Australia and New Zealand. The first of these "seeds" to arrive in Australia may have been taken there in 1884 or shortly there-

Frank Grove (left) and Ed Nelson (here seen with their wives) each devoted more than 50 years to spreading the Kingdom message full-time throughout New Zealand

after by a man who was first approached by a Bible Student in a park in England. Other "seeds" came by mail from friends and relatives overseas.

Within a few years after the Commonwealth of Australia was formed in 1901, hundreds of persons there were subscribers for the *Watch Tower*. As a result of the activity of those who saw the privilege of sharing the truth with others, thousands of tracts were sent to people whose names were on the electoral rolls. More were distributed on the streets, and bundles of them were tossed from train windows to workers and lone cottagers in remote areas along the railroad lines. The people were being notified of the approaching end of the Gentile Times in 1914. Arthur Williams, Sr., talked about this to all the customers in his store in Western Australia and invited interested ones to his home for further discussions.

Who reached New Zealand first with Bible truth is not now known. But by 1898, Andrew Anderson, a resident of New Zealand, had read enough of the Watch Tower publications to be moved to spread the truth there as a colporteur. His efforts were reinforced in 1904 by other colporteurs who came from America and from the Society's branch office that was established in that same year in Australia. Mrs. Thomas Barry, in Christchurch, accepted six volumes of *Studies in the Scriptures* from one of the colporteurs. Her son Bill read them in 1909 during a six-week boat trip to England and recognized the truthfulness of what they contained. Years later his son Lloyd became a member of the Governing Body of Jehovah's Witnesses.

Among the zealous workers in those early days was Ed Nelson, who, though not overly endowed with tact, devoted his full time for 50 years to spreading the Kingdom message from the north tip of New Zealand to the south. After a few years, he was joined by Frank Grove, who cultivated his memory to compensate for poor eyesight and who also pioneered for more than 50 years until his death.

A World Tour to Further the Preaching of the Good News

A further major effort was put forth in 1911-12 to help people of the Orient. The International Bible Students Association sent a committee of seven men, headed by C. T. Russell, to examine firsthand the conditions there. Wherever they went they spoke about God's purpose to bring blessings to mankind by means of the Messianic Kingdom. Sometimes their audience was small, but in the Philippines and in India, there were thousands. They did not endorse the campaign then popular in Christendom to collect funds for world conversion. Their observation was that most of the efforts of Christendom's missionaries were being expended to promote secular education. But Brother Russell was convinced that what the people needed was "the Gospel of God's loving provision of Messiah's coming Kingdom." Instead of expecting to convert the world, the Bible Students understood from the Scriptures that what was to be done then was to give

C. T. Russell and six associates made a trip around the world in 1911-12 to further the preaching of the good news

a *witness* and that this would serve toward the gathering of "an elect few from *all* nations, peoples, kindreds and tongues for membership in [Christ's] Bride class—to sit with Him in His throne during the thousand years, cooperating in the work of uplifting the race as a whole."*—Rev. 5: 9, 10; 14:1-5.

After spending time in Japan, China, the Philippines, and other locations, the members of the committee logged an additional 4,000 miles of travel in India. Some individuals living in India had read the Society's literature and had written letters to express their appreciation for it as early as 1887. Active witnessing had also been done among the Tamil-speaking people since 1905 by a young man who, as a student in America, had met Brother Russell and learned the truth. This young man helped to establish some 40 Bible study groups in the south of India. But, after preaching to others, he himself became disapproved by forsaking Christian standards. —Compare 1 Corinthians 9:26, 27.

At about the same time, however, A. J. Joseph, of Travancore (Kerala), in response to an inquiry that he mailed to a prominent Adventist, was sent

---

* A full report on this world tour appears in *The Watch Tower* of April 15, 1912.

a volume of *Studies in the Scriptures*. Here he found satisfying Scriptural answers to his questions about the Trinity. Soon he and other family members were out in the rice paddies and coconut plantations of southern India sharing their newfound beliefs. After Brother Russell's visit in 1912, Brother Joseph undertook full-time service. By rail, bullock cart, barge, and foot, he traveled to distribute Bible literature. When he gave public discourses, these were often disrupted by the clergy and their followers. At Kundara, when a "Christian" clergyman was using his followers to disrupt such a meeting and to throw dung on Brother Joseph, a Hindu gentleman of influence came to see what the noise was all about. He asked the clergyman: 'Is that the example set by Christ for Christians to follow, or is what you are doing like the conduct of the Pharisees of Jesus' time?' The clergyman retreated.

Before the four-month world tour by the IBSA committee was completed, Brother Russell had arranged for R. R. Hollister to be the Society's representative in the Orient and to follow through in spreading to peoples there the message of God's loving provision of the Messianic Kingdom. Special tracts were prepared in ten languages, and millions of these were circulated throughout India, China, Japan, and Korea by native distributors. Then books were translated into four of these languages to provide further spiritual food for those who showed interest. Here was a vast field, and much remained to be done. Yet, what had been accomplished thus far was truly amazing.

A. J. Joseph, of India, with his daughter Gracie, who served as a Gilead-trained missionary

An Impressive Witness Was Given

Before the devastation of the first world war was unleashed, an extensive witness had been given worldwide. Brother Russell had made speaking trips to hundreds of cities in the United States and Canada, had undertaken repeated trips to Europe, had spoken in Panama, Jamaica, and Cuba, as well as in principal cities of the Orient. Tens of thousands of persons had personally heard his stirring Bible discourses and had observed as he publicly answered from the Scriptures questions raised by both friends and foes. Much interest was thus aroused, and thousands of newspapers in America, Europe, South Africa, and Australia regularly published Brother Russell's sermons. Millions of books, as well as hundreds of millions of tracts and other pieces of literature in 35 languages, had been distributed by the Bible Students.

INDIA

Outstanding though his role was, it was not only Brother Russell who was preaching. Others too, scattered around the globe, were uniting their voices as witnesses of Jehovah and of his Son, Jesus Christ. Those who shared were not all public speakers. They came from all walks of life, and they used every appropriate means at their disposal to spread the good news.

In January 1914, with the end of the Gentile Times less than a year away, yet another intensive witness was launched. This was the "Photo-Drama of Creation," which emphasized in a fresh manner God's purpose for the earth. It did this by means of beautifully hand-painted color slides and motion pictures, synchronized with sound. The public press in the United States reported that across the country audiences totaling hundreds of thousands were viewing it weekly. By the end of the first year, total attendance in the United States and Canada had reached nearly eight million. In London, England, there were overflow crowds at the Opera House and the Royal Albert Hall to see this presentation that consisted of four 2-hour parts. Within half a year, over 1,226,000 had attended in 98 cities in the British Isles. Crowds in Germany and Switzerland packed out available halls. It was also seen by large audiences in Scandinavia and the South Pacific.

What a remarkable, intensive, global witness was given during those early decades of the modern-day history of Jehovah's Witnesses! But, really, the work was just beginning.

Only a few hundred had actively shared in spreading Bible truth during the early 1880's. By 1914, according to available reports, there were about 5,100 that participated in the work. Others may occasionally have distributed some tracts. The workers were relatively few.

This small band of evangelizers had, in various ways, already spread their proclamation of God's Kingdom into 68 lands by the latter part of 1914. And their work as preachers and teachers of God's Word was established on a fairly consistent basis in 30 of these lands.

Millions of books and hundreds of millions of tracts had been distributed before the Gentile Times ended. In addition to that, by 1913 as many as 2,000 newspapers were regularly publishing sermons prepared by C. T. Russell, and in the year 1914 audiences totaling over 9,000,000 persons on three continents saw the "Photo-Drama of Creation."

Truly, an amazing witness had been given! But there was much more to come.

PART 2

The work of Kingdom proclamation from 1914 through 1935 is covered on pages 423 to 443. Jehovah's Witnesses point to 1914 as the time when Jesus Christ was enthroned as heavenly King with authority over the nations. When on earth, Jesus foretold that a global preaching of the Kingdom message in the face of intense persecution would be part of the sign of his presence in Kingdom power. What actually occurred during the years following 1914?

THE first world war quickly engulfed Europe in 1914. Then it reached out to involve countries comprising an estimated 90 percent of the world's population. How did events associated with that war affect the preaching activity of Jehovah's servants?

The Dark Years of World War I

During the early years of the war, there was little hindrance except in Germany and France. Tracts were freely distributed in many places, and there was continued use of the "Photo-Drama," though on a much more limited scale after 1914. As the war fever intensified, the clergy in the British West Indies had it rumored that E. J. Coward, who represented the Watch Tower Society, was a German spy, so he was ordered to leave. When distribution of the book *The Finished Mystery* got under way in 1917, opposition became widespread.

The public was eager to obtain that book. The Society's initial order with the printers had to be increased over tenfold in just a few months. But the clergy of Christendom were furious over the exposure of their false doctrines. They seized on wartime hysteria to denounce the Bible Students to government officials. Across the United States, men and women identified with distribution of literature of the Bible Students were mobbed, also tarred

While the world was embroiled in war, R. R. Hollister and Fanny Mackenzie were busy taking a message of peace to the people of China, Japan, and Korea

KOREA

JAPAN

CHINA

PACIFIC OCEAN

and feathered. In Canada, homes were searched, and persons found with certain publications of the International Bible Students Association were subject to a heavy fine or imprisonment. However, Thomas J. Sullivan, who was then in Port Arthur, Ontario, reported that on one occasion, when he was put into jail for a night, the police in that city took home copies of the banned literature for themselves and their friends, thus distributing the entire available stock—some 500 or 600 copies.

The headquarters of the Watch Tower Society itself came under attack, and members of the administrative staff were sentenced to long prison terms. It appeared to their enemies that the Bible Students had been dealt a deathblow. Their witnessing in a manner that attracted widespread public attention virtually came to a stop.

Though confined in prison, they found opportunities to preach

Nevertheless, even Bible Students who were confined in prison found opportunities to talk to fellow prisoners about God's purpose. When the officers of the Society and their close associates arrived at the prison in Atlanta, Georgia, they were at first forbidden to preach. But they discussed the Bible among themselves, and others were attracted to them by their deportment, their manner of life. After a few months, the deputy warden assigned them to give religious instruction to other prisoners. The number increased until about 90 attended the classes.

Other loyal Christians also found ways to witness during those war years. This at times resulted in spreading the Kingdom message into lands where the good news had not yet been preached. Thus, in 1915 a Bible Student in New York, a Colombian, mailed the Spanish edition of *The Divine Plan of the Ages* to a man in Bogotá, Colombia. After about six months, a reply arrived from Ramón Salgar. He had studied the book carefully, was delighted with it, and wanted 200 copies to distribute to others. Brother J. L. Mayer, from Brooklyn, New York, also mailed out many copies of the Spanish-language *Bible Students Monthly*. A considerable number of these went to Spain. And when Alfred Joseph, who was then in Barbados, took a work contract in Sierra Leone, West Africa, he seized opportunities to witness there about the Bible truths he had recently learned.

For the colporteurs, whose ministry involved calling at homes and places of business, it was often more difficult. But several who went into El Salvador, Honduras, and Guatemala were busy there in 1916 sharing life-giving truths with the people. During this period Fanny Mackenzie, a colporteur of British nationality, made two trips to the Orient by boat, stopping in China, Japan, and Korea to distribute Bible literature, and then she followed up interest by writing letters.

Nevertheless, according to available records, the number of Bible Students reported as having some share in preaching the good news to others during 1918 decreased by 20 percent worldwide when compared with the report for 1914. After the harsh treatment meted out to them during the war years, would they persist in their ministry?

Infused With Renewed Life

On March 26, 1919, the president of the Watch Tower Society and his associates were released from their unjust imprisonment. Plans quickly took shape to push ahead with worldwide proclamation of the good news of God's Kingdom.

At a general convention at Cedar Point, Ohio, in September of that year, J. F. Rutherford, then president of the Society, gave a discourse that highlighted the announcing of the glorious incoming of God's Messianic Kingdom as the truly important work for Jehovah's servants.

The actual number who were then sharing in that work, however, was small. Some who had fearfully held back during 1918 became active again, and a few more joined their ranks. But the records that are available show that in 1919 there were only some 5,700 who were actively witnessing, in 43 lands. Yet Jesus had foretold: "This good news of the kingdom will be preached in *all the inhabited earth* for a witness to *all the nations.*" (Matt. 24:14) How could that be accomplished? They did not know, nor did they know how long the witnessing would continue. Nevertheless, those who were loyal servants of God were willing and eager to get on with the work. They had confidence that Jehovah would direct matters in harmony with his will.

Infused with zeal for what they saw laid out in God's Word, they went to work. Within three years the number having a part in publicly proclaiming God's Kingdom nearly tripled, according to available reports, and during 1922 they were busy preaching in 15 lands more than in 1919.

An Intriguing Subject

What an exciting message they proclaimed—"Millions now living will never die!" Brother Rutherford had given a discourse on this subject in 1918. It was also the title of a 128-page booklet published in 1920. From 1920 through 1925, that same subject was featured again and again around the world in public meetings in all areas where speakers were available and in upwards of 30 languages. Instead of saying, as Christendom does, that all good people would go to heaven, this discourse focused attention on the Bible-based hope of eternal life on a paradise earth for obedient mankind. (Isa. 45:18; Rev. 21:1-5) And it expressed the conviction that the time for the realization of that hope was very near.

Newspaper notices and billboards were used to advertise the lectures. The subject was intriguing. On February 26, 1922, upwards of 70,000 attended at 121 locations in Germany alone. It was not unusual for a single

Willing and eager to get on with the work!

audience to number into the thousands. In Cape Town, South Africa, for example, 2,000 were present when the lecture was given at the Opera House. At the university auditorium in the capital city of Norway, not only was every seat filled but so many were turned away that the program had to be repeated an hour and a half later—again to a packed house.

In Klagenfurt, Austria, Richard Heide told his father: "I am going to hear that talk whatever anyone might say. I want to know whether this is just bluff or if there is any truth in it!" He was deeply moved by what he heard, and soon he and his sister, as well as their parents, were telling others about it.

But the Bible's message was not just for people who would attend a public lecture. Others too needed to be made aware of it. Not only the public at large but also political and religious leaders needed to hear it. How would that be accomplished?

Distribution of Powerful Declarations

The printed page was used to reach millions of people who previously had only hearsay acquaintance with the Bible Students and the message that they proclaimed. From 1922 through 1928, an effective witness was given by means of seven powerful declarations, resolutions adopted at the annual conventions of the Bible Students. The number of printed copies of most of the individual resolutions distributed following those conventions totaled 45 to 50 million—a truly amazing accomplishment for the small band of Kingdom proclaimers then serving!

The 1922 resolution was entitled "A Challenge to World Leaders" —yes, a challenge to justify their claim that they could establish peace, prosperity, and happiness for humankind or, failing that, to acknowledge that only God's Kingdom by his Messiah can accomplish these things. In Germany, that resolution was sent by registered mail to the exiled German

In many lands the lecture "Millions Now Living Will Never Die" attracted large audiences

Witnesses to the Most Distant Part of the Earth

kaiser, to the president, and to all the members of the Imperial Diet; and some four and a half million copies went to the public. In South Africa, Edwin Scott, carrying the literature in a bag on his back and with a stick in one hand to ward off fierce dogs, covered 64 towns, personally distributing 50,000 copies. Thereafter, when the Dutch clergy in South Africa called at the homes of parishioners to take up collections, many of the parishioners shook the resolution in their clergyman's face and said: "You ought to read this and you would not come around again to get money from us."

In 1924 the resolution entitled "Ecclesiastics Indicted" laid bare the unscriptural teachings and practices of the clergy, exposed their role during the world war, and urged people to study the Bible to learn for themselves about the marvelous provisions made by God for the blessing of humankind. In Italy at that time, printers were required to put their name on anything they printed, and they were held responsible for the contents. The Bible Student supervising the work in Italy submitted a copy of the resolution to the government authorities, who inspected it and readily gave permission to have it printed and distributed. The printers too agreed to publish it. The brothers in Italy distributed 100,000 copies. They particularly saw to it that the pope and other high officials of the Vatican each received a copy.

In France, distribution of this resolution brought a vehement and often violent reaction from the clergy. In desperation a clergyman in Pomerania, Germany, filed legal charges against the Society and its manager, but the clergyman lost the case when the court heard the contents of the entire resolution. In order to avoid interference with their work on the part of those who did not want people to know the truth, the Bible Students in the province of Quebec, in Canada, left resolutions at homes during the early morning hours, starting at 3:00 a.m. Those were exciting times!

Showing Gratitude for Satisfying Answers

During World War I, many Armenians were ruthlessly driven from their homes and the land of their birth. Only two decades earlier, hundreds

Edwin Scott, in South Africa, personally distributed 50,000 copies of "A Challenge to World Leaders"

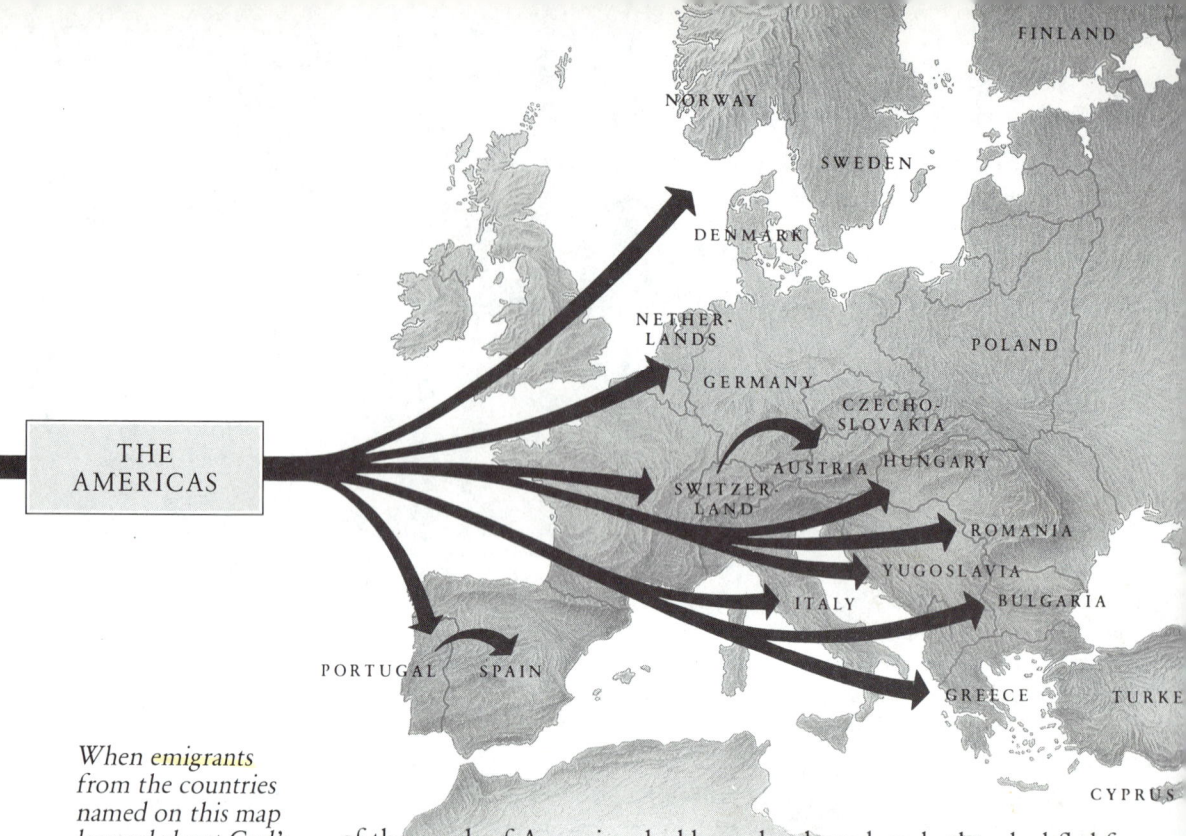

When emigrants from the countries named on this map learned about God's marvelous purpose to bless humankind, they felt impelled to take that news back to their homelands

of thousands of Armenians had been slaughtered, and others had fled for their lives. A few of these people had read the Watch Tower Society's publications in their homeland. But far more of them were given a witness in the lands to which they traveled as refugees.

After the harsh experiences that they had endured, many had serious questions as to why God permitted evil. How long would it continue? When would it end? Some of them were grateful to learn the satisfying answers found in the Bible. Groups of Armenian Bible Students quickly developed in various cities in the Middle East. Their zeal for Bible truth touched the lives of others. In Ethiopia, Argentina, and the United States, fellow Armenians embraced the good news and gladly accepted the responsibility of sharing it with others. One of such was Krikor Hatzakortzian, who as a lone pioneer spread the Kingdom message in Ethiopia in the mid-1930's. On one occasion, when falsely charged by opposers, he even had opportunity to witness to the emperor, Haile Selassie.

Taking Precious Truths Back to Their Native Lands

A burning desire to share vital Bible truths impelled many people to return to the land of their birth to engage in evangelizing. Their response was similar to that of the people from many lands who were in Jerusalem in 33 C.E. and who became believers when holy spirit moved the apostles and their associates to speak in many tongues "about the magnificent things of God." (Acts 2:1-11) Just as those first-century believers carried the truth back to their homelands, so did these modern-day disciples.

Both men and women who had learned the truth abroad returned to Italy. They came from America, Belgium, and France and zealously proclaimed the Kingdom message where they settled. Colporteurs from the Italian-speaking Swiss canton of Ticino also moved into Italy to carry on their work. Although their numbers were few, as a result of their united activity they soon reached nearly all the principal cities and many of the villages of Italy. They were not counting the hours that they spent in this work. Convinced that they were preaching truths that God wanted people to know, they often worked from morning till night to reach as many people as possible.

Greeks who had become Bible Students in nearby Albania and as far away as America also gave attention to their homeland. They were thrilled when they learned that worship of icons is unscriptural (Ex. 20:4, 5; 1 John 5:21), that sinners are not roasted in hellfire (Eccl. 9:5, 10; Ezek. 18:4; Rev. 21:8), and that God's Kingdom is mankind's real and only hope (Dan. 2:44; Matt. 6:9, 10). They were eager to share these truths with their fellow countrymen—personally or by mail. As a result, groups of Jehovah's Witnesses began to develop in Greece and on the Greek isles.

Following World War I, thousands of people from Poland moved into France to work in the coal mines. The French congregations did not pass them by because they spoke a different tongue. They found ways to share Bible truths with these miners and their families, and the number who responded favorably soon outnumbered the French Witnesses. When, as a result of a government deportation order, 280 had to return to Poland in 1935, this only served to reinforce the spread of the Kingdom message there. Thus, in 1935, there were 1,090 Kingdom proclaimers who shared in giving a witness in Poland.

Others responded to invitations to leave their homeland to take up service in foreign fields.

Zealous European Evangelizers Help in Foreign Fields

With international cooperation, the Baltic States (Estonia, Latvia, and Lithuania) heard the heartwarming truths about God's Kingdom. During the 1920's and 1930's, zealous brothers and sisters from Denmark, England, Finland, and Germany did extensive witnessing in this area. Much literature was placed, and thousands heard the Bible discourses that were given. From Estonia regular radio broadcasts of Bible programs in several languages reached even into what was then the Soviet Union.

Responding to the call for evangelizers, Willy Unglaube served in Europe, Africa, and the Orient

From Germany willing workers during the 1920's and 1930's took up assignments in such places as Austria, Belgium, Bulgaria, Czechoslovakia, France, Luxembourg, the Netherlands, Spain, and Yugoslavia. Willy Unglaube was among them. After serving for a time at the Magdeburg Bethel, in Germany, he went on to care for assignments as a full-time evangelizer in France, Algeria, Spain, Singapore, Malaysia, and Thailand.

When a call went out from France for help during the 1930's, colporteurs from Britain gave evidence that they were aware that the Christian commission to preach required evangelizing not only in their own land but also in other parts of the earth. (Mark 13:10) John Cooke was one of the zealous workers who answered the Macedonian call. (Compare Acts 16: 9, 10.) During the next six decades, he cared for service assignments in France, Spain, Ireland, Portugal, Angola, Mozambique, and South Africa. His brother Eric left his job at Barclay's Bank and joined John in the full-time ministry in France; thereafter, he too served in Spain and Ireland and shared in missionary work in Southern Rhodesia (now Zimbabwe) and South Africa.

In May 1926, George Wright and Edwin Skinner, in England, accepted an invitation to help to broaden out the Kingdom work in India. Their assignment was huge! It included all of Afghanistan, Burma (now Myanmar), Ceylon (now Sri Lanka), India, and Persia (now Iran). On arrival in Bombay, they were greeted by the monsoon rains. However, not being overly concerned about personal comfort or convenience, they were soon traveling to the far corners of the country to locate known Bible Students to encourage them. They also placed large quantities of literature to stimulate interest among others. The work was done with intensity. Thus, during 1928 the 54 Kingdom proclaimers in Travancore (Kerala), in southern India, arranged for 550 public meetings attended by about 40,000 persons. In 1929 four more pioneers from the British field moved to India to help with the work. And in 1931 another three from England arrived in Bombay. Again and again they reached out to various parts of this vast country, distributing literature not only in English but also in the Indian tongues.

Meanwhile, what was happening in Eastern Europe?

A Spiritual Harvest

Before the first world war, seeds of Bible truth had been scattered in Eastern Europe, and some had taken root. In 1908, Andrásné Benedek, a humble Hungarian woman, had returned to Austria-Hungary to share with others the good things that

By 1992, Eric Cooke and his brother John (seated) had each been in full-time service for over 60 years, enjoying thrilling experiences in Europe and Africa

she had learned. Two years later, Károly Szabó and József Kiss had also come back to that land and were spreading Bible truth especially in areas that later came to be known as Romania and Czechoslovakia. Despite violent opposition by irate clergy, study groups were formed, and extensive witnessing was done. Others joined them in making public declaration of their faith, and by 1935 the ranks of Kingdom proclaimers in Hungary had grown to 348.

Romania nearly doubled its size when the map of Europe was reshaped by the victors following World War I. It was reported that within this enlarged country, in 1920, there were about 150 groups of Bible Students, with which 1,700 persons were associated. The following year, at the celebration of the Lord's Evening Meal, nearly 2,000 partook of the Memorial emblems, indicating that they professed to be spirit-anointed brothers of Christ. That number increased dramatically during the next four years. In 1925, there were 4,185 in attendance at the Memorial, and as was customary then, most of them undoubtedly partook of the emblems. However, the faith of all of these would be put to the test. Would they prove to be genuine "wheat" or only an imitation? (Matt. 13:24-30, 36-43) Would they really do the work of witnessing that Jesus had assigned to his followers? Would they persevere in it in the face of intense opposition? Would they be faithful even when others displayed a spirit like that of Judas Iscariot?

The report for 1935 indicates that not all had the sort of faith that enabled them to endure. In that year, there were just 1,188 who had some share in giving a witness in Romania, though more than twice that number were at that time partaking of the Memorial emblems. Nevertheless, the faithful ones kept busy in the Master's service. They shared with other humble people the Bible truths that brought such joy to their own hearts. One outstanding way that they did this was by literature distribution. Between 1924 and 1935, they had already placed with interested ones upwards of 800,000 books and booklets, in addition to tracts.

What about Czechoslovakia, which had become a nation in 1918 after the collapse of the Austro-Hungarian Empire? Here an even more intense witness was contributing to the spiritual harvest. Earlier preaching had been done in Hungarian, Russian, Romanian, and German. Then, in 1922, several Bible Students returned from America to direct attention to the Slovak-speaking population, and the following year a couple from Germany began to concentrate on the Czech territory. Regular assemblies, though small, helped to

When he went to India in 1926, Edwin Skinner had an assignment that included five countries; faithfully he kept on preaching there for 64 years

encourage and unify the brothers. After the congregations became better organized for house-to-house evangelizing in 1927, growth became more evident. In 1932 a powerful stimulus to the work was given by an international convention in Prague, attended by about 1,500 from Czechoslovakia and neighboring countries. In addition to this, large crowds viewed a four-hour version of the "Photo-Drama of Creation" that was shown from one end of the country to the other. In a period of just a decade, upwards of 2,700,000 pieces of Bible literature were distributed to the various language groups in this land. All this spiritual planting, cultivating, and watering contributed to a harvest in which 1,198 Kingdom proclaimers shared in the year 1935.

Yugoslavia (known first as the Kingdom of the Serbs, Croats, and Slovenes) had come into existence as a result of the reshaping of the map of Europe following the first world war. As early as 1923, it was reported that a group of Bible Students were witnessing in Belgrade. Later the "Photo-Drama of Creation" was shown to large crowds throughout the country. When Jehovah's Witnesses came under severe persecution in Germany, the ranks in Yugoslavia were fortified with German pioneers. Without concern for personal comfort, they reached out into the most remote parts of this mountainous country to preach. Others of those pioneers went into Bulgaria. Efforts were also being made to preach the good news in Albania. In all these places, seeds of Kingdom truth were sown. Some of the seeds bore

During the 1920's and 1930's, evangelizers moved out from Germany to many lands to give a witness

fruit. But it would not be until later years that there would be a larger harvest in these places.

Farther south, on the continent of Africa, the good news was also being spread by those who deeply appreciated the privilege of being witnesses for the Most High.

Spiritual Light Shines in West Africa

About seven years after a Bible Student from Barbados first went to West Africa under a work contract, he wrote to the Watch Tower Society's office in New York to inform them that quite a few people were showing interest in the Bible. A few months later, on April 14, 1923, at Brother Rutherford's invitation, W. R. Brown, who had been serving in Trinidad, arrived in Freetown, Sierra Leone, with his family.

Promptly, arrangements were made for Brother Brown to give a discourse in the Wilberforce Memorial Hall. On April 19, there was an audience of some 500 in attendance, including most of the clergy of Freetown. The following Sunday he spoke again. His subject was one that C. T. Russell had often used—"To Hell and Back. Who Are There?" Brother Brown's discourses were regularly punctuated with Scripture quotations made visible to the audience by means of lantern slides. As he spoke, he would repeatedly say: "Not Brown says, but the Bible says." Because of this, he came to be known as "Bible Brown." And as a result of his logical, Scriptural presentation, some prominent church members resigned and took up Jehovah's service.

He traveled extensively to get the Kingdom work started in additional areas. To that end he delivered numerous Bible lectures and distributed large amounts of literature, and he encouraged others to do the same. His evangelizing took him into Gold Coast (now Ghana), Liberia, The Gambia, and Nigeria. From Nigeria others carried the Kingdom message into Benin (then known as Dahomey) and Cameroon. Brother Brown knew that the public had little regard for what they called "the white man's religion," so at the Glover Memorial Hall in Lagos, he spoke on the failure of Christendom's religion. After the meeting the enthusiastic audience obtained 3,900 books to read and to share with others.

When Brother Brown first went to West Africa, only a handful of persons there had heard the Kingdom message. When he left 27 years later, well over 11,000 were active Witnesses of Jehovah in that area. Religious falsehoods were being laid bare; true worship had taken root and was spreading rapidly.

Alfred and Frieda Tuček, equipped with necessities of life and literature for witnessing, served as pioneers in Old Yugoslavia

Up the East Coast of Africa

Quite early in the 20th century, some of the publications of C. T. Russell had been circulated in the southeast part of Africa by individuals who had adopted a few of the ideas set out in those books but had then mixed them with their own philosophy. The result was a number of so-called Watchtower movements that had no connection whatever with Jehovah's Witnesses. Some of them were politically oriented, stirring up unrest among the native Africans. For many years the bad reputation made by those groups presented obstacles to the work of Jehovah's Witnesses.

Nevertheless, a number of Africans discerned the difference between the true and the false. Itinerant workers carried the good news of God's Kingdom to nearby lands and shared it with people who spoke the African languages. The English-speaking population in southeast Africa received the message, for the most part, by means of contacts with South Africa. In some countries, however, strong official opposition, fueled by Christendom's clergy, hindered preaching on the part of European Witnesses among the African-language groups. Nevertheless, the truth spread, though many people who showed interest in the Bible's message needed more help to make sound practical application of what they were learning.

Some fair-minded government officials did not accept without question the vicious charges made against the Witnesses by Christendom's clergy. That was true of a police commissioner in Nyasaland (now Malawi) who disguised himself and went to the meetings of the native Witnesses to find out for himself what sort of people they were. He was favorably impressed. When approval was given by the government to have a resident European representative, Bert McLuckie and later his brother Bill were sent there in the mid-1930's. They kept in touch with the police and the district commissioners so that these officials would have a clear understanding of their activity and would not confuse Jehovah's Witnesses with any movements falsely called Watchtower. At the same time, they worked patiently, along with Gresham Kwazizirah, a mature local Witness, to help the hundreds who wanted

Throughout West Africa, "Bible Brown" vigorously shared in exposing false worship

to associate with the congregations to appreciate that sexual immorality, abuse of alcoholic drinks, and superstition could have no place in the lives of Jehovah's Witnesses.—1 Cor. 5:9-13; 2 Cor. 7:1; Rev. 22:15.

In 1930, there were only about a hundred of Jehovah's Witnesses in the whole of southern Africa. Yet, they had an assignment that included, roughly, all of Africa south of the equator and some territories that extended north of that. Covering such a vast expanse of territory with the Kingdom message called for real pioneers. Frank and Gray Smith were of that sort.

They sailed 3,000 miles east and north from Cape Town and then continued for four days over rough roads by automobile to reach Nairobi, Kenya (in British East Africa). In less than a month, they placed 40 cartons of Bible literature. But, sadly, on the return trip, Frank died of malaria. Despite this, a short while later, Robert Nisbet and David Norman started out —this time with 200 cartons of literature—to preach in Kenya and Uganda, also Tanganyika and Zanzibar (both now Tanzania), reaching as many people as possible. Other similar expeditions spread the Kingdom message to the islands of Mauritius and Madagascar in the Indian Ocean and to St. Helena in the Atlantic Ocean. Seeds of truth were sown, but they did not immediately sprout and grow everywhere.

From South Africa the preaching of the good news also spread into Basutoland (now Lesotho), Bechuanaland (now Botswana), and Swaziland, as early as 1925. About eight years later, when pioneers were again preaching in Swaziland, King Sobhuza II gave them a royal welcome. He assembled his personal bodyguard of a hundred warriors, listened to a thorough witness, and then obtained all the publications of the Society that the brothers had with them.

Gradually the number of Jehovah's Witnesses grew in this part of the world field. Others joined with the few who had pioneered the work in Africa early in this 20th century, and by 1935 there were 1,407 on the continent of Africa who reported having a share in the work of witnessing about God's Kingdom. Substantial numbers of these were in South Africa and Nigeria.

Zealous pioneers such as Frank Smith and his brother Gray (shown in the upper picture) spread the good news up the east coast of Africa

Other large groups that identified themselves as Jehovah's Witnesses were located in Nyasaland (now Malawi), Northern Rhodesia (now Zambia), and Southern Rhodesia (now Zimbabwe).

During this same period, attention was being directed also to Spanish- and Portuguese-speaking lands.

Cultivating Spanish and Portuguese Fields

While World War I was still in progress, *The Watch Tower* was first published in Spanish. It bore the address of an office in Los Angeles, California, which had been set up to give special attention to the Spanish-speaking field. Brothers from that office gave much personal help to interested ones both in the United States and in lands to the south.

Juan Muñiz, who had become one of Jehovah's servants in 1917, was encouraged by Brother Rutherford in 1920 to leave the United States and return to Spain, his native land, to get the Kingdom-preaching work organized there. The results were limited, however, not because of any lack of zeal on his part, but because he was constantly followed by the police; so after a few years, he was transferred to Argentina.

In Brazil a few worshipers of Jehovah were already preaching. Eight humble sailors had learned the truth while on leave from their ship in New York. Back in Brazil early in 1920, they were busy sharing the Bible's message with others.

George Young, a Canadian, was sent to Brazil in 1923. He certainly helped to stimulate the work. Delivering numerous public lectures through interpreters, he showed what the Bible says about the condition of the dead, exposed spiritism as demonism, and explained God's purpose for the blessing of all the families of the earth. His lectures were all the more persuasive because at times he showed on a screen the Bible texts being discussed so that the audience could see these in their own language. While he was in Brazil, Bellona Ferguson, of São Paulo, was finally able to get baptized, along with four of her children. She had waited 25 years for this opportunity. Among those who embraced the truth were some who then made themselves available to help with translation of literature into Portuguese. Soon there was a good supply of publications in that language.

From Brazil, Brother Young went on to Argentina in 1924 and arranged for free distribution of 300,000 pieces of literature in Spanish in 25 of the principal towns and cities. That same year he also personally traveled to Chile, Peru, and Bolivia to distribute tracts.

George Young was soon on his way to care for a new assignment. This time it was Spain and Portugal. After being introduced by the British ambassador to local government officials, he was able to arrange for Brother

George Young shared in widespread proclamation of God's Kingdom in South America, Spain, and Portugal

Rutherford to speak to audiences in Barcelona and Madrid, as well as in the capital of Portugal. Following these discourses, a total of more than 2,350 persons turned in their names and addresses with requests for further information. Thereafter, the speech was published in one of Spain's large newspapers, and in tract form it was sent by mail to people throughout the country. It also appeared in the Portuguese press.

By these means the message reached far beyond the borders of Spain and Portugal. By the end of 1925, the good news had penetrated into the Cape Verde Islands (now Republic of Cape Verde), Madeira, Portuguese East Africa (now Mozambique), Portuguese West Africa (now Angola), and islands in the Indian Ocean.

The following year arrangements were made to print the powerful resolution "A Testimony to the Rulers of the World" in the Spanish paper *La Libertad*. Radio broadcasts and the distribution of books, booklets, and tracts, as well as showings of the "Photo-Drama of Creation," helped to intensify the witness. In 1932 several English pioneers responded to the invitation to help out in this field, and they systematically covered large sections of the country with Bible literature until the Spanish Civil War made it necessary for them to leave.

Meanwhile, upon arriving in Argentina, Brother Muñiz had quickly started preaching, while supporting himself by repairing clocks. In addition to his work in Argentina, he gave attention to Chile, Paraguay, and Uruguay. At his request some brothers came from Europe to witness to the German-speaking population. Many years later Carlos Ott related that they began their day's service at 4:00 a.m. by leaving tracts under every door in a territory. Later in the day, they would call to give a further witness and to offer more Bible literature to interested householders. From Buenos Aires those who shared in the full-time ministry spread throughout the country, first following the railroad lines that radiated for hundreds of miles from the capital like spread fingers on your hand, then using every other means of transport they could find. They had very little materially and endured much hardship, but they were rich spiritually.

One of those zealous workers in Argentina was Nicolás Argyrós, a Greek. Early in 1930, when he obtained some literature published by the Watch Tower Society, he was especially impressed by a booklet entitled *Hell*, with subtitles that asked "What Is It? Who Are There? Can They Get Out?" He was amazed to find that this booklet did not depict sinners as roasting on a grill. What a surprise when he realized that hellfire was a religious lie invented to frighten people, just as it had frightened him! He promptly set out to share the truth—first with Greeks; then, as his Spanish improved, with others. Each month he devoted between 200 and 300

Juan Muñiz (left), who had been preaching in South America since 1924, was on hand to welcome N. H. Knorr when he first visited Argentina over 20 years later

Nicolás Argyrós spread the Bible's liberating truth into 14 of Argentina's provinces

hours to sharing the good news with others. Using his feet and any other available means of transport, he spread Bible truths into 14 of the 22 provinces of Argentina. As he moved from place to place, he slept in beds when these were offered by hospitable folks, often out in the open, and even in a barn with a burro for an alarm clock!

Another who had the spirit of a real pioneer was Richard Traub, who had learned the truth in Buenos Aires. He was eager to share the good news with people across the Andes, in Chile. In 1930, five years after he was baptized, he arrived in Chile —the only Witness in a country of 4,000,000 people. At first, he had only the Bible with which to work, but he began to call from house to house. There were no congregation meetings that he could attend, so on Sundays, at the usual meeting time, he would walk to Mount San Cristóbal, sit in the shade of a tree, and immerse himself in personal study and prayer. After he rented an apartment, he began to invite people to meetings there. The only other person to turn up for the first meeting was Juan Flores, who asked: "And the others, when will they come?" Brother Traub simply replied: "They will come." And they did. In less than a year, 13 became baptized servants of Jehovah.

Four years later, two Witnesses who had never met before teamed up to preach the good news in Colombia. After a productive year there, Hilma Sjoberg had to return to the United States. But Kathe Palm boarded a ship to Chile, using the 17 days at sea to witness to both crew and passengers. During the next decade, she worked from Chile's northernmost seaport, Arica, to its southernmost possession, Tierra del Fuego. She called at business houses and witnessed to government officials. Using a saddlebag across her shoulders to carry literature, and toting such necessities as a blanket in which to sleep, she reached the most distant mining camps and sheep ranches. It was the life of a true pioneer. And there were others who shared that same spirit—some single, some married, young and old.

During the year 1932, a special effort was made to spread the Kingdom message in Latin American lands where little preaching had yet been done. In that year the booklet *The Kingdom, the Hope of the World* was given a remarkable distribution. This booklet contained a discourse that had already been heard on an international radio broadcast. Now some 40,000 copies of the speech in printed form were distributed in Chile, 25,000 copies in Bolivia, 25,000 in Peru, 15,000 in Ecuador, 20,000 in Colombia, 10,000 in Santo Domingo (now the Dominican Republic),

WITNESSES TO THE MOST DISTANT PART OF THE EARTH

and another 10,000 in Puerto Rico. Indeed, the Kingdom message was being proclaimed, and with great intensity.

By 1935, there were in South America itself just 247 who had joined their voices to proclaim that only God's Kingdom will bring true happiness to humankind. But what a witness they were giving!

Reaching People Even in More Remote Areas

Jehovah's Witnesses were by no means taking the view that their responsibility before God was fulfilled if they simply talked to a few who happened to be their neighbors. They endeavored to reach everyone with the good news.

People who lived in places to which the Witnesses could not then travel personally could be reached in other ways. Thus, in the late 1920's, the Witnesses in Cape Town, South Africa, mailed out 50,000 booklets to all farmers, lighthouse keepers, forest rangers, and others living off the beaten track. An up-to-date postal directory was also obtained for all of South-West Africa (now known as Namibia), and a copy of the booklet *The Peoples Friend* was mailed to everyone whose name appeared in that directory.

In 1929, F. J. Franske was put in charge of the Watch Tower Society's schooner *Morton* and was assigned, along with Jimmy James, to reach people in Labrador and all the outports of Newfoundland. In the winter Brother Franske traveled the coast with a dog team. To cover the cost of the Bible literature he left with them, the Eskimos and Newfoundlanders gave him such items as leather goods and fish. A few years later, he sought out the miners, loggers, trappers, ranchers, and Indians in the rough Cariboo country of British Columbia. As he traveled, he hunted in order to have meat, picked wild berries, and baked his bread in a frying pan over an open campfire. Then, at another time, he and a partner used a salmon-trolling boat for transport as they carried the Kingdom message to every island, inlet, logging camp, lighthouse, and settlement along the west coast of

Throughout South-West Africa (now Namibia) people received this booklet by mail in 1928

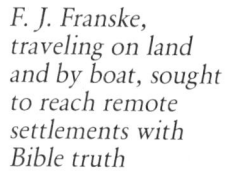

F. J. Franske, traveling on land and by boat, sought to reach remote settlements with Bible truth

Canada. He was only one of many who were putting forth special efforts to reach people living in remote areas of the earth.

Starting in the late 1920's, Frank Day worked his way north through the villages of Alaska, preaching, placing literature, and selling eyeglasses in order to care for his physical needs. Though hobbling on an artificial leg, he covered an area that stretched from Ketchikan to Nome, a distance of about 1,200 miles. As early as 1897, a gold miner had obtained copies of *Millennial Dawn* and the *Watch Tower* while in California and was making plans to take these back to Alaska with him. And in 1910, Captain Beams, the skipper of a whaling ship, had placed literature at his Alaskan ports of call. But the preaching activity began to widen out as Brother Day made his summertime trips into Alaska again and again for more than 12 years.

Two other Witnesses, using a 40-foot motorboat named *Esther,* worked their way up the Norwegian coast far into the Arctic. They witnessed on the islands, at lighthouses, in the coastal villages, and in isolated places far back in the mountains. Many people welcomed them, and in a year's time, they were able to place 10,000 to 15,000 books and booklets explaining God's purpose for humankind.

The Islands Hear Jehovah's Praises

It was not only those islands that were close to mainland shores that were given a witness. Out in the middle of the Pacific Ocean, in the early 1930's, Sydney Shepherd spent two years traveling by boat to preach in the Cook Islands and Tahiti. Farther west, George Winton was visiting the New Hebrides (now Vanuatu) with the good news.

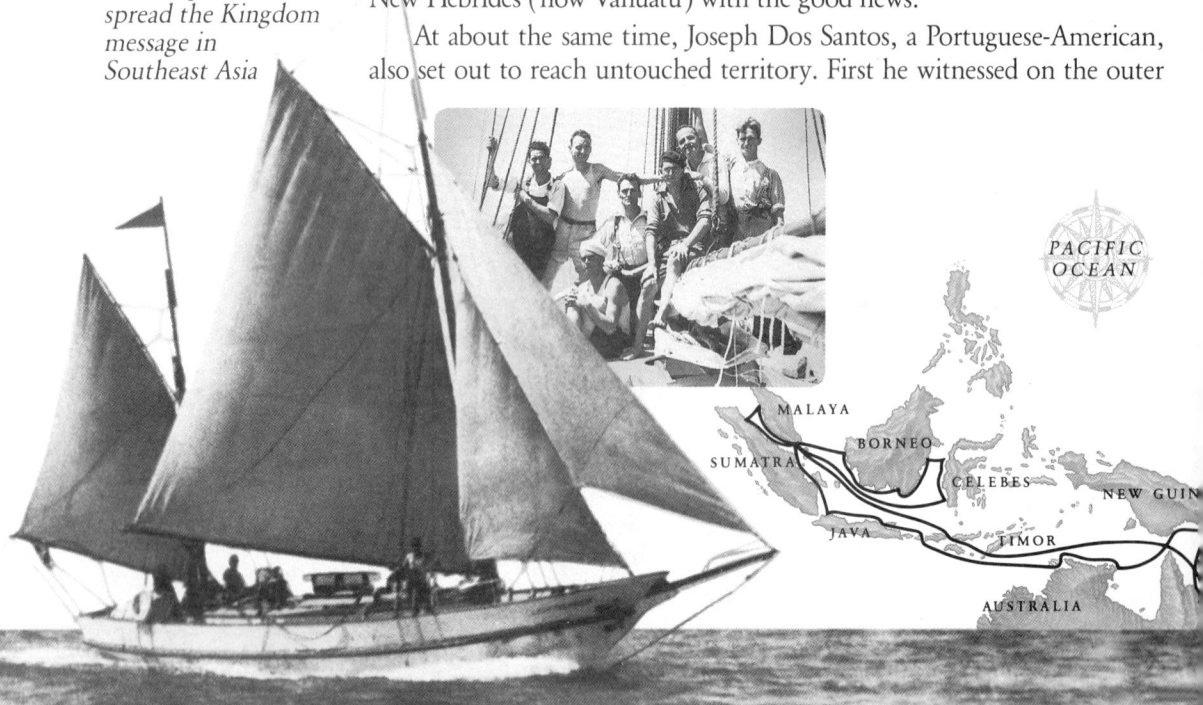

At about the same time, Joseph Dos Santos, a Portuguese-American, also set out to reach untouched territory. First he witnessed on the outer

Aboard the "Lightbearer," zealous pioneers spread the Kingdom message in Southeast Asia

islands of Hawaii; then he undertook an around-the-globe preaching tour. When he reached the Philippines, however, he received a letter from Brother Rutherford asking him to stay there to build up and organize the Kingdom-preaching activity. He did, for 15 years.

At this time the Society's branch in Australia was directing attention to the work in and around the South Pacific. Two pioneers sent out from there gave an extensive witness in Fiji in 1930-31. Samoa received a witness in 1931. New Caledonia was reached in 1932. A pioneer couple from Australia even took up service in China in 1933 and witnessed in 13 of its principal cities during the next few years.

The brothers in Australia realized that more could be accomplished if they had a boat at their disposal. In time they outfitted a 52-foot ketch that they called *Lightbearer* and, starting early in 1935, used it as a base of operations for several years for a group of zealous brothers as they witnessed in the Netherlands East Indies (now Indonesia), Singapore, and Malaya. Arrival of the boat always attracted much attention, and this often opened the way for the brothers to preach and place much literature.

Meanwhile, on the other side of the earth, two pioneer sisters from Denmark decided to make a vacation trip to the Faeroe Islands in the North Atlantic Ocean in 1935. But they had in mind more than a scenic trip. They went equipped with thousands of pieces of literature, and they used them well. Defying wind and rain and the hostility of the clergy, they covered as much of the inhabited islands as they could during their stay.

They defied wind, rain, and the hostility of the clergy

Farther to the west, Georg Lindal, an Icelandic-Canadian, undertook an assignment that lasted much longer. At the suggestion of Brother Rutherford, he moved to Iceland to pioneer in 1929. What endurance he showed! For most of the next 18 years, he served there alone. He visited the towns and villages again and again. Tens of thousands of pieces of literature were placed, but at that time no Icelanders joined him in Jehovah's service. With the exception of just one year, there were no Witnesses with whom he could associate in Iceland until 1947, when two Gilead-trained missionaries arrived.

When Men Forbid What God Commands

While sharing in their public ministry, it was not at all unusual, especially from the 1920's through the 1940's, for the Witnesses to encounter opposition, usually stirred up by local clergymen and sometimes by government officials.

In a rural area north of Vienna, Austria, the Witnesses found themselves confronted by a hostile crowd of villagers agitated by the local priest, who was backed by the constabulary. The priests were determined that there would be no preaching by Jehovah's Witnesses in their villages. But the Witnesses, determined to carry out their God-given assignment, changed their approach and returned another day, entering the villages in roundabout ways.

Regardless of threats and demands on the part of men, Jehovah's Witnesses realized that they had an obligation to God to proclaim his Kingdom. They chose to obey God as ruler rather than men. (Acts 5:29) Where local officials tried to deny religious freedom to Jehovah's Witnesses, the Witnesses simply brought in reinforcements.

After repeated arrests in one section of Bavaria, in Germany, in 1929, they hired two special trains—one to start in Berlin and the other in Dresden. These were joined together at Reichenbach, and at 2:00 a.m. the one train entered the Regensburg area with 1,200 passengers that were eager to have a part in giving a witness. Travel was expensive, and everyone had paid his own fare. At each railroad station, some were dropped off. A number of them had brought bicycles so that they could reach out into the countryside. The entire district was covered in a single day. As they saw the results of their united efforts, they could not help but call to mind God's promise to his servants: "Any weapon whatever that will be formed against you will have no success." —Isa. 54:17.

A witness of extraordinary proportions was given in Germany before the "Ernste Bibelforscher" were banned there

So zealous were the Witnesses in Germany that between 1919 and 1933, they distributed, it is estimated, at least 125,000,000 books, booklets, and magazines, as well as millions of tracts. Yet, there were only about 15,000,000 families in Germany at that time. During that period Germany received a witness as thorough as that given in any country on earth. In that part of the earth was found one of the largest concentrations of persons who professed to be spirit-anointed followers of Christ. But during the following years, they also experienced some of the most grueling tests of integrity.—Rev. 14:12.

In the year 1933, official opposition to the work of Jehovah's Witnesses in Germany greatly intensified. The homes of Witnesses and the Society's branch office were searched repeatedly by the Gestapo. Bans were imposed on the activity of the Witnesses in most of the German states, and some were arrested. Many tons of their Bibles and Bible literature were publicly burned. On April 1, 1935, a *national* law was passed banning the *Ernste Bibelforscher* (the Earnest Bible Students, or Jehovah's Witnesses), and systematic efforts were made to deprive them of their livelihood. In turn, the Witnesses shifted all their meetings to small groups, arranged to reproduce their material for Bible study in forms that the Gestapo would not readily recognize, and adopted preaching methods that were not so conspicuous.

Even before this, since 1925, the brothers in Italy had been living under a Fascist dictatorship, and in 1929 a concordat had been signed between the Catholic Church and the Fascist State. True Christians were hunted down without mercy. Some met in barns and haylofts in order to avoid being arrested. Jehovah's Witnesses in Italy at that time were very few in number;

however, their efforts to spread the Kingdom message were reinforced in 1932 when 20 Witnesses from Switzerland crossed into Italy and carried out a lightning distribution of 300,000 copies of the booklet *The Kingdom, the Hope of the World*.

In the Far East too, pressure was building up. There were arrests of Jehovah's Witnesses in Japan. Large quantities of their Bible literature were destroyed by officials in Seoul (in what is now the Republic of Korea) and Pyongyang (in what is now the Democratic People's Republic of Korea).

In the midst of this mounting pressure, in 1935, Jehovah's Witnesses gained a clear understanding from the Bible of the identity of the "great multitude," or "great crowd," of Revelation 7:9-17. (*KJ, NW*) This understanding opened up to them an awareness of an unanticipated and urgent work. (Isa. 55:5) No longer did they hold the view that all who were not of the "little flock" of heirs of the heavenly Kingdom would at some future time have opportunity to bring their lives into line with Jehovah's requirements. (Luke 12:32) They realized that the time had come to make disciples of such people now with a view to their survival into God's new world. How long the gathering of this great crowd out of all nations would continue they did not know, though they felt that the end of the wicked system must be very near. Exactly how the work would be accomplished in the face of persecution that was spreading and becoming more vicious, they were not sure. However, of this they were confident—since 'the hand of Jehovah is not too short,' he would open the way for them to carry out his will.—Isa. 59:1.

In the year 1935, Jehovah's Witnesses were relatively few in number —just 56,153 worldwide.

They were preaching in 115 lands during that year; but in nearly one half of those lands, there were fewer than ten Witnesses. Only two countries had 10,000 or more active Witnesses of Jehovah (the United States, with 23,808; Germany, with an estimated 10,000 out of the 19,268 who had been able to report two years earlier). Seven other lands (Australia, Britain, Canada, Czechoslovakia, France, Poland, and Romania) each reported more than 1,000 but fewer than 6,000 Witnesses. The record of activity in 21 other countries shows between 100 and 1,000 Witnesses each. Yet, during that one year, this zealous band of Witnesses worldwide devoted 8,161,424 hours to proclaiming God's Kingdom as mankind's only hope.

In addition to the lands in which they were busy during 1935, they had already spread the good news to other places, so that 149 lands and island groups had thus far been reached with the Kingdom message.

PART 3
A global report of the preaching of the Kingdom message from 1935 through 1945 is set out on pages 444 to 461. The year 1935 is highly significant because at that time the great multitude, or great crowd, of Revelation 7:9 was identified. In connection with the gathering of that group, Jehovah's Witnesses began to discern that the Bible set before them a work of greater proportions than any that had preceded it. How did they go about it when the nations became embroiled in World War II and a majority of lands imposed bans on them or their Bible literature?

AS Jehovah's Witnesses shared in their ministry during the 1930's, their aim was to reach as many people as possible with the Kingdom message. If they discerned exceptional interest, some of them might stay up much of the night explaining Bible truths and answering questions to satisfy spiritually hungry ones. But in most cases, the Witnesses simply used brief presentations that were designed to stir up the interest of householders, and then they let the literature or public Bible lectures do the rest. Theirs was a work of informing people, sowing seeds of Kingdom truth.

Intense Effort to Reach Many People With the Good News

The work was done with a sense of urgency. As an example, early in the 1930's, when Armando Menazzi, in Córdoba, Argentina, read the clear exposition of Bible truth in the booklets *Hell* and *Where Are the Dead?*, he acted decisively. (Ps. 145:20; Eccl. 9:5; Acts 24:15) Moved by what he learned, and inspired by the zeal being shown by Nicolás Argyrós, he sold his auto-repair shop to devote himself to preaching the truth as a pioneer. Then, in the early 1940's, with his encouragement the Witnesses in Córdoba bought an old bus, installed beds, and used this vehicle to take ten or more publishers on preaching expeditions that lasted a week, two weeks, or even three months. As these trips were planned, different brothers and sisters from the congregation were given opportunity to go along. Each one in the group had his assigned work—cleaning, cooking,

Some colporteurs placed many cartons of literature; householders received numerous Bible sermons in each book

or fishing and hunting for food. In at least ten Argentine provinces, this zealous group preached from house to house, covering cities as well as villages and reaching out to scattered farms.

A similar spirit was manifested in the Australian field. Much witnessing was done in the heavily populated coastal cities. But the Witnesses there also sought to reach people who lived in remote areas. Thus, on March 31, 1936, in order to reach people on the sheep and cattle stations scattered across the outback, Arthur Willis and Bill Newlands struck out on a trip that took them a total of 12,250 miles. For much of their journey, there were no roads—only bush tracks through the treeless desert with its oppressive heat and howling dust storms. But they pressed on. Wherever interest was found, they played recorded Bible discourses and left literature. On other occasions, John E. (Ted) Sewell went with them; and then he volunteered to serve in Southeast Asia.

The territory supervised by the Society's branch in Australia reached far beyond Australia itself. It included China and island groups and nations stretching from Tahiti on the east to Burma (now Myanmar) on the west, a distance of 8,500 miles. Within that area were such places as Hong Kong, Indochina (now Cambodia, Laos, and Vietnam), the Netherlands East Indies (including such islands as Sumatra, Java, and Borneo), New Zealand, Siam (now Thailand), and Malaya. It was not unusual for the branch overseer, Alexander MacGillivray, a Scotsman, to invite a zealous young pioneer into his office, show him a map of the branch territory, and ask: 'Would you like to be a missionary?' Then, pointing to an area in which little or no preaching had been done, he would ask: 'How would you like to open up the work in this territory?'

During the early 1930's, some of these pioneers had already done

Armando Menazzi (center front) and a happy group that traveled with him on a preaching expedition in their "pioneer home on wheels"

Arthur Willis, Ted Sewell, and Bill Newlands—three who took the Kingdom message to the Australian outback

much work in the Netherlands East Indies (now Indonesia) and Singapore. In 1935, Frank Dewar, a New Zealander, traveled with a group of these pioneers aboard the *Lightbearer* as far as Singapore. Then just before the boat went on to the northwest coast of Malaya, Captain Eric Ewins said: "Well, Frank, here we are. This is as far as we can take you. You chose to go to Siam. Now, off you go!" But Frank had nearly forgotten about Siam. He had been enjoying his service with the group on the boat. Now he was on his own.

He made a stopover in Kuala Lumpur until he could get together enough money for the rest of the trip, but, while there, he was in a traffic accident—a truck knocked him off his bicycle. After recuperating, with just five dollars in his pocket, he boarded the train bound from Singapore to Bangkok. But with faith in Jehovah's ability to provide, he got on with the work. Claude Goodman had preached there briefly in 1931; but when Frank arrived in July 1936, there were no Witnesses on hand to welcome him. During the next few years, however, others had a part in the work—Willy Unglaube, Hans Thomas, and Kurt Gruber from Germany and Ted Sewell from Australia. They distributed much literature, but most of it was in English, Chinese, and Japanese.

When a letter was sent to the Society's headquarters saying that the brothers needed literature in the Thai language but had no translator,

Alexander MacGillivray, as overseer of the Australia branch, helped to plan preaching expeditions to many countries and islands

Place Names Are Ones That Were in Use During the 1930's

WITNESSES TO THE MOST DISTANT PART OF THE EARTH

Brother Rutherford replied: "I am not in Thailand; you are there. Have faith in Jehovah and work diligently, and you will find a translator." And they did. Chomchai Inthaphan, a former headmistress of the Presbyterian Girls' School in Chiang Mai, embraced the truth, and by 1941 she was translating Bible literature into Thai.

One week after Frank Dewar took up preaching in Bangkok, Frank Rice, who had pioneered the Kingdom work on Java (now part of Indonesia), came through on his way to a new assignment in what was then French Indochina. As he had done in his earlier territory, he preached to those who spoke English while he learned the local language. After covering Saigon (now Ho Chi Minh City), he taught some English lessons in order to buy an old car that he could use to reach the northern part of the country. His concern was not material comforts but Kingdom interests. (Heb. 13:5) Using the car he purchased, he witnessed in towns and villages and at isolated homes all the way to Hanoi.

Frank Dewar (shown here with his wife and their two daughters) went to Thailand as a lone pioneer in 1936 and was still a special pioneer in 1992

Bold Publicity

To arouse interest in the Kingdom message and to alert people to the need to take decisive action, eye-catching means were used by the Witnesses in many lands. Starting in 1936 in Glasgow, Scotland, the Witnesses advertised convention discourses by wearing placards and distributing handbills in shopping areas. Two years later, in 1938, in connection with a convention in London, England, another striking feature was added. Nathan H. Knorr and Albert D. Schroeder, who later served together on the Governing Body, led a parade of nearly a thousand Witnesses through the central business district of London. Every other one of the marchers wore a placard advertising the public talk "Face the Facts," to be delivered by J. F. Rutherford at the Royal Albert Hall. Those in between carried signs that read "Religion Is a Snare and a Racket." (At that time they understood religion to be all worship that was not in harmony with God's Word, the Bible.) Later in the week, to neutralize the hostile reaction of some of the public, signs reading "Serve God and Christ the King" were interspersed with the earlier ones. This activity was not easy for many of Jehovah's Witnesses, but they looked at it as another way to serve Jehovah, another test of their loyalty to him.

Not everyone was pleased with the bold publicity that Jehovah's Witnesses gave to their message. The clergy in Australia and New Zealand put pressure on the managers of radio stations to suppress all broadcasts sponsored by Jehovah's Witnesses. In April 1938, when Brother Rutherford was en route to Australia

Chomchai Inthaphan used her ability as a translator to reach the Thai people with the good news found in the Bible

to deliver a radio address, public officials allowed themselves to be influenced to cancel arrangements that had been made for him to use the Sydney Town Hall and radio facilities. Quickly the Sydney Sports Grounds were hired, and as a result of the extensive news publicity surrounding the opposition to Brother Rutherford's visit, an even larger crowd came to hear his discourse. On other occasions, when the Witnesses were denied the use of radio facilities, they responded by giving intense publicity to meetings at which Brother Rutherford's lectures were reproduced with transcription equipment.

The clergy in Belgium sent out children to throw stones at the Witnesses, and priests would personally go around to the homes to collect literature that had been distributed. But some of the villagers liked what they were learning from Jehovah's Witnesses. They would often say: "Give me several of your booklets; when the priest comes, I can give him one to satisfy him and keep the rest to read!"

The following years, however, led to even stronger opposition to Jehovah's Witnesses and the Kingdom message that they proclaimed.

Preaching in Europe in the Face of Wartime Persecution

Because they would not abandon their faith and desist from preaching, thousands of Jehovah's Witnesses in Austria, Belgium, France, Germany, and the Netherlands were imprisoned or sent to Nazi concentration camps. There brutal treatment was the order of the day. Those not yet in prison carried on their ministry cautiously. They often worked with just the Bible and offered other literature only when making return visits on interested persons. To avoid arrest, Witnesses would call at one door in an apartment house and then perhaps go to another building, or after calling at just one house they would go to another street before approaching another house. But they were by no means timid about giving a witness.

On December 12, 1936, just a few months after the Gestapo had arrested thousands of the Witnesses and other interested persons in a nationwide effort to stop their work, the Witnesses themselves conducted a campaign. With lightning speed they put tens of thousands of copies of a printed resolution in mailboxes and under the doors of people throughout Germany. These protested the cruel treatment being meted out to their Christian brothers and sisters. Within an hour after the distribution began, the police were racing around trying to catch the distributors, but they laid their hands on only about a dozen in the entire country.

In Germany, Jehovah's Witnesses gave this open letter extensive public distribution in 1937, even though their worship was under government ban

Officials were shocked that such a campaign could be carried out after all that the Nazi government had done to suppress the work. Furthermore, they became afraid of the populace. Why? Because when the police and other uniformed officials went to the homes and asked whether the inhabitants had received such a leaflet, most of the people denied it. In fact, by far the majority of them had not. Copies had been delivered to only two or three households in each building. But the police did not know that. They assumed that one had been left at each door.

During the months that followed, Nazi officials loudly denied the charges made in that printed resolution. So, on June 20, 1937, the Witnesses who were still free distributed another message, an open letter that was unsparing in its detail about the persecution, a document that named officials and cited dates and places. Great was the consternation among the Gestapo over this exposure and over the ability of the Witnesses to achieve such a distribution.

Numerous experiences of the Kusserow family, from Bad Lippspringe, Germany, manifested that same determination to give a witness. An example involves what occurred after Wilhelm Kusserow had been executed publicly in Münster by the Nazi regime because of his refusal to compromise his faith. Wilhelm's mother, Hilda, immediately went to the prison and urgently requested the body for burial. She said to her family: "We will give a great witness to the people who knew him." At the funeral Wilhelm's father, Franz, offered a prayer that expressed faith in Jehovah's loving provisions. At the grave Wilhelm's brother Karl-Heinz spoke words of comfort from the Bible. For this they did not go unpunished, but to them the important thing was honoring Jehovah by giving a witness concerning his name and his Kingdom.

As wartime pressures mounted in the Netherlands, the Witnesses there wisely adjusted their meeting arrangements. These were now held only in groups of ten or less in private homes. Meeting places were frequently changed. Each Witness attended only with his own group, and none would divulge the address of the study, not even to a trusted friend. At that time

Family of Franz and Hilda Kusserow—every one of them a faithful Witness of Jehovah, though all in the family (except a son who had died in an accident) were put into concentration camps, prisons, or reform schools because of their faith

Some in Austria and Germany who risked their lives to duplicate or distribute precious material for Bible study, such as that shown in the background

Therese Schreiber *Peter Gölles*
Elfriede Löhr *Albert Wandres*
August Kraft *Ilse Unterdörfer*

in history, when entire populations were being driven from their homes as a result of the war, Jehovah's Witnesses knew that people urgently needed the comforting message that is found only in God's Word, and they fearlessly shared it with them. But a letter from the branch office reminded the brothers of the caution that Jesus had demonstrated on various occasions when confronted by opposers. (Matt. 10:16; 22:15-22) As a result, when they encountered a person who showed hostility, they made careful note of the address so that special precautions could be taken when working that territory in the future.

In Greece widespread suffering was experienced by the populace during the German occupation. The most severe treatment meted out to Jehovah's Witnesses, however, came as a result of vicious misrepresentation by the clergy of the Greek Orthodox Church, who insisted that the police and the courts take action against them. Many of the Witnesses were imprisoned or were banished from their hometowns and sent to obscure villages or were confined under harsh conditions on barren islands. Nevertheless, they kept on witnessing. (Compare Acts 8:1, 4.) Often this was done by talking to people in parks and public gardens, by sitting on the benches with them and telling them about God's Kingdom. When genuine interest was found, a precious piece of Bible literature was lent to the person. Such literature was later returned and used again and again. Many lovers of truth gratefully accepted the help offered by the Witnesses and even joined with them in sharing the good news with others, though this brought bitter persecution upon them.

An important factor in the courage and perseverance of the Witnesses was their being built up by spiritual food. Though supplies

They Refused to Stop Witnessing Even Though Imprisoned

Shown here are only a few of the thousands who suffered for their faith in prisons and concentration camps during World War II

1. Adrian Thompson, New Zealand. Imprisoned in 1941 in Australia; his application for exemption from conscription was rejected when Australia banned Jehovah's Witnesses. After his release, as traveling overseer, he strengthened the congregations in their public ministry. Served as a missionary and the first traveling overseer in postwar Japan; continued to preach zealously until his death in 1976.

2. Alois Moser, Austria. In seven prisons and concentration camps. Still an active Witness in 1992 at 92 years of age.

3. Franz Wohlfahrt, Austria. Execution of his father and his brother did not deter Franz. Held in Rollwald Camp in Germany for five years. Still witnessing in 1992 at 70 years of age.

4. Thomas Jones, Canada. Imprisoned in 1944, then held in two work camps. After 34 years of full-time service, he was appointed in 1977 to be a member of the Branch Committee supervising the preaching work in all of Canada.

5. Maria Hombach, Germany. Repeatedly arrested; in solitary confinement for three and a half years. As a courier, she risked her life to take Bible literature to fellow Witnesses. In 1992, a faithful member of the Bethel family at 90 years of age.

6. Max and Konrad Franke, Germany. Father and son, both imprisoned repeatedly, and for many years. (Konrad's wife, Gertrud, was also in prison.) All remained loyal, zealous servants of Jehovah, and Konrad was in the forefront of rebuilding the preaching work of the Witnesses in postwar Germany.

7. A. Pryce Hughes, England. Sentenced to two terms at Wormwood Scrubs, London; had also been imprisoned because of his faith during World War I. In the forefront of the work of Kingdom preaching in Britain down till his death in 1978.

8. Adolphe and Emma Arnold with daughter Simone, France. After Adolphe was imprisoned, Emma and Simone continued to witness, also to distribute literature to other Witnesses. Emma, when in prison, was put in solitary confinement for persistently witnessing to other prisoners. Simone was sent to a reform school. All continued to be zealous Witnesses.

9. Ernst and Hildegard Seliger, Germany. Between them, more than 40 years in prisons and concentration camps for their faith. Even in prison they persisted in sharing Bible truths with others. When free they devoted their full time to preaching the good news. Brother Seliger died a loyal servant of God in 1985; Sister Seliger, in 1992.

10. Carl Johnson, United States. Two years after baptism, imprisoned with hundreds of other Witnesses at Ashland, Kentucky. Has served as a pioneer and as a circuit overseer; in 1992, still taking the lead in the field ministry as an elder.

11. August Peters, Germany. Torn away from his wife and four children, he was imprisoned 1936-37, also 1937-45. After release, instead of doing less preaching, he did more, in full-time service. In 1992, at 99 years of age, he was still serving as a member of the Bethel family and had seen the number of Jehovah's Witnesses in Germany grow to 163,095.

12. Gertrud Ott, Germany. Imprisoned at Lodz, Poland, then Auschwitz concentration camp; next in Gross-Rosen and Bergen-Belsen in Germany. After the war she served zealously as a missionary in Indonesia, Iran, and Luxembourg.

13. Katsuo Miura, Japan. Seven years after his arrest and imprisonment in Hiroshima, much of the prison where he was confined was destroyed by the atom bomb that desolated the city. However, doctors found no evidence that he suffered injury fro. the radiation. He used the final years of his life as a pioneer.

14. Martin and Gertrud Poetzinger, Germany. A few mont. after marriage, they were arrested and forcibly separated for nir years. Martin was sent to Dachau and Mauthausen; Gertrud, to Ravensbrück. In spite of brutal treatment, their faith did not wa ver. After release they devoted all their efforts to Jehovah's service. For 29 years he served as a traveling overseer throughout C many; then, as a member of the Governing Body until his death 1988. In 1992, Gertrud continued to be a zealous evangelizer.

15. Jizo and Matsue Ishii, Japan. After distributing Bible lit ature throughout Japan for a decade, they were imprisoned. Though the work of Jehovah's Witnesses in Japan was crushed d ing the war, Brother and Sister Ishii witnessed zealously again a ter the war. By 1992, Matsue Ishii had seen the number of activ Witnesses in Japan increase to over 171,000.

16. Victor Bruch, Luxembourg. Imprisoned in Buchenwald, Lublin, Auschwitz, and Ravensbrück. At 90 years of age, still ac tive as an elder of Jehovah's Witnesses.

17. Karl Schurstein, Germany. A traveling overseer before F ler came to power. Incarcerated for eight years, then killed by t SS in Dachau in 1944. Even within the camp, he continued to build others up spiritually.

18. Kim Bong-nyu, Korea. Confined for six years. At 72 years age, still telling others about the Kingdom of God.

19. Pamfil Albu, Romania. After being brutally mistreated, he [was] sent to a labor camp in Yugoslavia for two and a half years. [Aft]er the war he was imprisoned two more times, for another [ ] years. He did not stop speaking about God's purpose. Before his [dea]th he helped thousands in Romania to serve with the global or[gan]ization of Jehovah's Witnesses.

20. Wilhelm Scheider, Poland. In Nazi concentration camps [19]39-45. In Communist prisons 1950-56, also 1960-64. Until his [dea]th in 1971, he unwaveringly devoted his energies to the pro[cla]iming of God's Kingdom.

21. Harald and Elsa Abt, Poland. During and after the war, [Har]ald spent 14 years in prison and concentration camps because [of h]is faith but continued to preach even there. Elsa was torn away [fro]m their infant daughter and then held in six camps in Poland, [Ger]many, and Austria. In spite of a 40-year ban on Jehovah's Wit[nes]ses in Poland even after the war, all of them continued to be [zea]lous servants of Jehovah.

22. Ádám Szinger, Hungary. During six court trials, sentenced [to] 23 years, of which he served 8 1/2 years in prison and labor [cam]ps. When free, served as a traveling overseer for a total of 30 [yea]rs. At 69 years of age, still a loyal congregation elder.

23. Joseph Dos Santos, the Philippines. Had devoted 12 years as full-time proclaimer of Kingdom message before imprisonment in 1942. Revitalized the activity of Jehovah's Witnesses in the Philippines after the war and personally continued in pioneer service until his death in 1983.

24. Rudolph Sunal, United States. Imprisoned at Mill Point, West Virginia. After release he devoted full time to spreading the knowledge of God's Kingdom—as a pioneer, a member of the Bethel family, and a circuit overseer. Still pioneering in 1992, at 78 years of age.

25. Martin Magyarosi, Romania. From prison, 1942-44, continued to give direction for the preaching of the good news in Transylvania. When released he traveled extensively to encourage fellow Witnesses in their preaching and was himself a fearless Witness. Imprisoned again in 1950, he died in a labor camp in 1953, a loyal servant of Jehovah.

26. R. Arthur Winkler, Germany and the Netherlands. First sent to Esterwegen concentration camp; kept preaching in the camp. Later, in the Netherlands, he was beaten by the Gestapo until unrecognizable. Finally he was sent to Sachsenhausen. A loyal, zealous Witness until his death in 1972.

27. Park Ock-hi, Korea. Three years in Sodaemun Prison, Seoul; subjected to indescribable torture. At 91 years of age, in 1992, still zealously witnessing, as a special pioneer.

of literature for distribution to others eventually became quite depleted in some parts of Europe during the war, they managed to circulate among themselves faith-strengthening material that had been prepared by the Society for study by Jehovah's Witnesses worldwide. At the risk of their lives, August Kraft, Peter Gölles, Ludwig Cyranek, Therese Schreiber, and many others shared in reproducing and distributing study material that was smuggled into Austria from Czechoslovakia, Italy, and Switzerland. In the Netherlands, it was a kindly prison guard who helped by procuring a Bible for Arthur Winkler. In spite of all the precautions taken by the enemy, refreshing waters of Bible truth from *The Watchtower* reached even into the German concentration camps and circulated among the Witnesses there.

Confinement in prisons and concentration camps did not stop Jehovah's Witnesses from being witnesses. When the apostle Paul was in prison in Rome, he wrote: "I am suffering evil to the point of prison bonds . . . Nevertheless, the word of God is not bound." (2 Tim. 2:9) The same proved to be true in the case of Jehovah's Witnesses in Europe during World War II. Guards observed their conduct; some asked questions, and a few became fellow believers, even though it meant the loss of their own freedom. Many prisoners who were confined with the Witnesses had come from such lands as Russia, where very little preaching of the good news had been done. After the war some of these returned to their homeland as Jehovah's Witnesses, eager to spread the Kingdom message there.

Brutal persecution and the effects of total war could not prevent the

Witnesses at convention in Shanghai, China, in 1936; nine of this group got baptized on that occasion

foretold gathering of people to Jehovah's great spiritual house for worship. (Isa. 2:2-4) From 1938 to 1945, most of the lands of Europe showed substantial increases in the number sharing publicly in such worship by proclaiming God's Kingdom. In Britain, Finland, France, and Switzerland, the Witnesses experienced increases of approximately 100 percent. In Greece, there was nearly a sevenfold increase. In the Netherlands, twelvefold. But by the end of 1945, details had not yet come from Germany or Romania, and only sketchy reports had come in from a number of other lands.

Outside Of Europe During Those War Years

In the Orient too, the world war gave rise to extreme hardship for Jehovah's Witnesses. In Japan and Korea, they were arrested and subjected to beatings and torture because they advocated God's Kingdom and would not worship the Japanese emperor. Eventually they were cut off from all contact with Witnesses in other lands. For many of them, the only opportunities to give a witness were when being interrogated or when on trial in court. By the end of the war, the public ministry of Jehovah's Witnesses in these lands had virtually come to a halt.

When the war reached the Philippines, the Witnesses were mistreated by both sides because they would not support either the Japanese or the resistance forces. To avoid being seized, many Witnesses abandoned their homes. But as they moved from place to place, they preached—lending literature when there was some available, and later using only the Bible. As the war front receded, they even outfitted several boats to carry large groups of Witnesses to islands where little or no witnessing had been done.

Though wartime conditions forced them to flee, they kept on preaching

In Burma (now Myanmar), it was not Japanese invasion but pressure from Anglican, Methodist, Roman Catholic, and American Baptist clergymen exerted on colonial officials that led to a ban on the literature of Jehovah's Witnesses in May 1941. Two Witnesses working in the cable office saw a telegram that alerted them to what was coming, so the brothers quickly moved literature out of the Society's depot in order to avert its being confiscated. Efforts were then made to send much of the literature overland into China.

At that time the U.S. government was trucking vast amounts of war material over the Burma Road to support the Chinese Nationalist government. The brothers tried to secure space on one of those trucks but were rebuffed. Efforts to obtain a vehicle from Singapore also failed. However, when Mick Engel, who was in charge of the Society's Rangoon (now Yangon) depot, approached a high U.S. official, he was granted permission to transport the literature on army trucks.

Nevertheless, after that when Fred Paton and Hector Oates approached the officer controlling the convoy into China and asked for space, he nearly had a fit! "What?" he shouted. "How can I give you precious space in

In spite of a ban on their worship, these Witnesses held a convention at Hargrave Park, near Sydney, Australia, in 1941

my trucks for your miserable tracts when I have absolutely no room for urgently needed military and medical supplies rotting here in the open?" Fred paused, reached into his briefcase, showed him the letter of authorization, and pointed out that it would be a very serious matter if he ignored the direction given by officials in Rangoon. Not only did the road controller arrange to transport two tons of books but he placed a light truck, with driver and supplies, at the disposal of the brothers. They headed northeast over the dangerous mountain road into China with their precious cargo. After witnessing in Pao-shan, they pressed on to Chungking (Pahsien). Thousands of pieces of literature telling about Jehovah's Kingdom were distributed during the year that they spent in China. Among others to whom they personally witnessed was Chiang Kai-shek, the president of the Chinese Nationalist government.

Meanwhile, as bombing intensified in Burma, all but three of the Witnesses there left the country, most of them for India. The activity of the three who remained was, of necessity, limited. Yet they continued to witness informally, and their efforts bore fruit after the war.

In North America too, Jehovah's Witnesses were confronted by severe obstacles during the war. Widespread mob violence and unconstitutional application of local laws brought great pressure on the preaching work. Thousands were imprisoned because of taking their stand as Christian neutrals. Yet, this did not slow down the house-to-house ministry of the Witnesses. Furthermore, beginning in February 1940, it became common to see them on the streets in business districts offering *The Watchtower* and

Consolation (now *Awake!*). Their zeal became even stronger. Though undergoing some of the most intense persecution ever experienced in that part of the world, the Witnesses more than doubled in numbers in both the United States and Canada from 1938 to 1945, and the time they devoted to their public ministry tripled.

In many lands identified with the British Commonwealth (in North America, Africa, Asia, and islands of the Caribbean and of the Pacific) either Jehovah's Witnesses or their literature was put under government ban. One of such lands was Australia. An official notice published there on January 17, 1941, at the direction of the governor-general, made it illegal for Jehovah's Witnesses to meet for worship, to circulate any of their literature, or even to have it in their possession. Under the law it was possible to challenge the ban in court, and this was promptly done. But it was over two years before Mr. Justice Starke of the High Court declared that the regulations on which the ban was based were "arbitrary, capricious and oppressive." The full High Court removed the ban. What did Jehovah's Witnesses do in the meantime?

In imitation of the apostles of Jesus Christ, they 'obeyed God as ruler rather than men.' (Acts 4:19, 20; 5:29) They continued to preach. In spite of numerous obstacles, they even arranged for a convention at Hargrave Park, near Sydney, December 25-29, 1941. When the government refused rail transportation to some of the delegates, a group from Western Australia equipped their vehicles with gas-producing units operating on charcoal and struck out on a 14-day cross-country trek, which included spending one week traversing the pitiless Nullarbor Plain. They arrived safely and enjoyed the program along with the other six thousand delegates. The following year another assembly was held, but this time it was divided up into 150 smaller groups in seven major cities across the country, with speakers shuttling from one location to the next.

As conditions in Europe deteriorated in 1939, some pioneer ministers of Jehovah's Witnesses volunteered to serve in other fields. (Compare Matthew 10:23; Acts 8:4.) Three German pioneers were sent from Switzerland to Shanghai, China. A number went to South America. Among those transferred to Brazil were Otto Estelmann, who had been visiting and helping congregations in Czechoslovakia, and Erich Kattner, who had served at the Watch Tower Society's office in Prague. Their new assignment was not an easy one. They found that in some farm areas, the Witnesses would get up early and preach until 7:00 a.m. and then do further field service late into the evening. Brother Kattner recalls that as he moved from place to place, he often slept in the open, using his literature bag as a pillow. —Compare Matthew 8:20.

Both Brother Estelmann and Brother Kattner had been hounded by the Nazi secret police in Europe. Did their move to Brazil free them from persecution? On the contrary, after just a year, they found themselves under prolonged house arrest and imprisonment at the instigation of officials who were apparently Nazi sympathizers! Opposition from the Catholic clergy was also common, but the Witnesses persisted in their God-given work. They constantly reached out to cities and towns in Brazil where the Kingdom message had not yet been preached.

A review of the global situation shows that in the majority of lands where Jehovah's Witnesses were located during World War II, they were confronted with government bans either on their organization or their literature. Though they had been preaching in 117 lands in 1938, the war years (1939-45) saw bans on their organization or literature, or deportation of their ministers, in over 60 of those lands. Even where there were no bans, they faced mob violence and were frequently arrested. In spite of all of this, the preaching of the good news did not stop.

The Great Crowd Begins to Manifest Itself in Latin America

Right in the midst of the war years, in February 1943, with an eye on work to be done in the postwar era, the Watch Tower Society inaugurated Gilead School in New York State to train missionaries for foreign service. Before the end of the year, 12 of those missionaries had already begun to serve in Cuba. The field there proved to be very productive.

As early as 1910, some seeds of Bible truth had reached Cuba. C. T. Russell had given a discourse there in 1913. J. F. Rutherford had spoken on the radio in Havana in 1932, and there was a rebroadcast of the material in Spanish. But growth was slow. There was widespread illiteracy at

Cuban Witnesses at a convention in Cienfuegos in 1939

that time and much religious prejudice. Interest shown was at first largely among the English-speaking population that had come from Jamaica and other places. By 1936 there were just 40 Kingdom proclaimers in Cuba. But the planting and watering of seeds of Kingdom truth then began to yield more fruit.

In 1934 the first Cubans had been baptized; others followed. Starting in 1940, daily radio broadcasts coupled with bold street witnessing reinforced the house-to-house ministry there. Even before Gilead-trained missionaries arrived in 1943, there were 950 in Cuba who had embraced the good news and were preaching it to others, though not all of them were sharing regularly. During the two years following the arrival of the missionaries, the numbers increased even more rapidly. By 1945, Jehovah's Witnesses in Cuba numbered 1,894. Although most of them had come from a religion that taught that all faithful supporters of the church would go to heaven, the vast majority of those who became Jehovah's Witnesses eagerly embraced the prospect of eternal life on earth in a restored paradise. (Gen. 1:28; 2:15; Ps. 37:9, 29; Rev. 21:3, 4) Only 1.4 percent of them professed to be spirit-anointed brothers of Christ.

N. H. Knorr (left) at São Paulo convention in 1945, with Erich Kattner as interpreter

In yet another way, help was provided for the Latin American field by the Society's world headquarters. Early in 1944, N. H. Knorr, F. W. Franz, W. E. Van Amburgh, and M. G. Henschel spent ten days in Cuba to strengthen the brothers there spiritually. During that time a convention was held in Havana, and arrangements for better coordination of the preaching work were outlined. This trip also took Brother Knorr and Brother Henschel to Costa Rica, Guatemala, and Mexico to assist Jehovah's Witnesses in those lands.

In 1945 and 1946, N. H. Knorr and F. W. Franz made tours that enabled them to speak and work with the Witnesses in 24 lands in the area from Mexico to the southern tip of South America as well as in the Caribbean. They personally spent five months in that part of the world, providing loving help and direction. In some places they met with just a handful of interested persons. So that there would be regular arrangements for meetings and field service, they personally assisted with the organizing of the first congregations in Lima, Peru, and Caracas, Venezuela. Wherever

By late 1945, missionaries from Gilead School had already taken up service in 18 lands in this part of the world

Charles and Lorene Eisenhower
Cuba

John and Adda Parker
Guatemala

Emil Van Daalen
Puerto Rico

Olaf Olson
Colombia

Don Burt
Costa Rica

Gladys Wilson
El Salvador

Hazel Burford
Panama

Louise Stubbs
Chile

congregation meetings were already being held, they attended these and, on occasion, provided counsel on how to improve their practical value in connection with the evangelizing work. Where possible, arrangements were made for public Bible talks during these visits. The talks were given intensive publicity through the use of placards worn by Witnesses and through handbills distributed on the streets. As a result, the 394 Witnesses in Brazil were pleased to have 765 at their convention in São Paulo. In Chile, where there were 83 Kingdom proclaimers, 340 came to hear the specially advertised discourse. In Costa Rica the 253 local Witnesses were delighted to have a total of 849 at their two assemblies. These were occasions of warm fellowship among the brothers.

The objective, however, was not merely to have memorable conventions. During these tours the representatives from headquarters placed special emphasis on the importance of making return visits on interested people and conducting home Bible studies with them. If people were going to become real disciples, they needed regular instruction from God's Word. As a result, the number of home Bible studies grew rapidly in this part of the world.

While Brother Knorr and Brother Franz were making these service tours, more Gilead-trained missionaries were arriving in their assignments. By the end of 1944, some were serving in Costa Rica, Mexico, and Puerto Rico. In 1945, other missionaries were helping to get the preaching work better organized in Barbados, Brazil, British Honduras (now Belize), Chile, Colombia, El Salvador, Guatemala, Haiti, Jamaica, Nicaragua, Panama, and Uruguay. When the first two missionaries arrived in the Dominican Republic in 1945, they were the only Witnesses in the country. The effect of the ministry of the early missionaries was quickly felt. Said Trinidad Paniagua about the first missionaries sent to Guatemala: "This was exactly what we needed—teachers of the Word of God who would help us understand how to go about doing the work."

So the groundwork was being laid for expansion in this part of the world field. On the Caribbean islands, there were 3,394 Kingdom proclaimers by the end of 1945. In Mexico, there were 3,276, and another 404 in Central America. In South America, 1,042. For this part of the world, that represents an increase of 386 percent during the previous seven years, a very turbulent period of human history. But it was just a beginning. Growth of truly explosive proportions was yet ahead! The Bible had foretold that "a great crowd . . . out of all nations and tribes and peoples and tongues" would be gathered as worshipers of Jehovah before the great tribulation.—Rev. 7:9, 10, 14.

When World War II began in 1939, there were just 72,475 of Jehovah's Witnesses preaching in 115 lands (if counted according to the national divisions of the early 1990's). In spite of the intense persecution that they experienced on a global scale, they more than doubled in number by the end of the war. Thus, the report for 1945 showed 156,299 Witnesses active in the 107 lands for which it has been possible to compile reports. By that time, however, 163 lands had actually been reached with the Kingdom message.

The witness given during the years from 1936 to 1945 was truly amazing. During that decade of world turmoil, these zealous Witnesses of Jehovah devoted a total of 212,069,285 hours to proclaiming to the world that God's Kingdom is the only hope for humankind. They also distributed 343,054,579 books, booklets, and magazines to help people to understand the Scriptural basis for that confidence. To help sincerely interested ones, in 1945 they were conducting, on an average, 104,814 free home Bible studies.

PART 4

While World War II was still in progress, Jehovah's Witnesses were laying plans for intensified activity in the postwar era. The report on pages 462 to 501 sets out fascinating details of what actually occurred from 1945 through 1975 as they increased in numbers, reached out to many more lands, and engaged in preaching and teaching God's Word in a more thorough manner than ever before.

MOST of the islands of the West Indies had been reached in some way with the Kingdom message by 1945. But a more thorough witness needed to be given. Missionaries trained at Gilead School would play an important role.

Missionaries Intensify the Witness in the West Indies

By 1960 these missionaries had served on 27 islands or island groups in the Caribbean. Half of these places had no congregation of Jehovah's Witnesses when the missionaries arrived. The missionaries proceeded to conduct home Bible studies with interested persons, and they organized regular meetings. Where there were congregations already, they gave valuable training to local publishers. As a result, the quality of the meetings and effectiveness in the ministry improved.

The early Bible Students had been witnessing in Trinidad since before World War I, but following the arrival of missionaries from Gilead

The "Sibia" served as a floating missionary home in the West Indies

S. Carter

G. Maki

R. Parkin

A. Worsley

BAHAMAS

VIRGIN ISLANDS (BRITISH)
VIRGIN ISLANDS (U.S.)
LEEWARD ISLANDS
WINDWARD ISLANDS

in 1946, the conducting of home Bible studies with interested persons was given strong impetus. In Jamaica the preaching of the good news had been under way for almost half a century, and there were a thousand local Witnesses by the time the first missionary arrived; but they were glad to have help in reaching the more educated people, especially in the suburban area around the capital city. On the other hand, in Aruba much witnessing had already been done in the English-speaking community, so the missionaries directed attention to the native population. Everyone needed to hear the good news.

To make sure that people on all the islands in this part of the earth had opportunity to hear about God's Kingdom, in 1948 the Watch Tower Society outfitted the 59-foot schooner *Sibia* as a floating missionary home. The crew was assigned to take the Kingdom message to every island of the West Indies where no one was active in preaching the good news. Gust Maki was the captain, and with him were Stanley Carter, Ronald Parkin, and Arthur Worsley. They started with the Out Islands of the Bahamas group, then worked their way to the southeast through the Leeward Islands and the Windward Islands. What effect did their visits have? At St. Maarten a businessman told them: "The people never used to talk about the Bible, but since you've been here everybody is talking about the Bible." Later, the *Sibia* was replaced by a larger boat, the *Light*. There were also changes in the crew. Within a decade the special work being done with the use of these boats had been accomplished, and land-based proclaimers of the good news were following through.

"Since you've been here everybody is talking about the Bible"

Witnessing First in the Larger Cities

As was true in the West Indies, so also in Central and South America, there were already people in many areas who had some of the Watch Tower Society's publications before missionaries from Gilead School arrived. However, in order to reach everyone with the good news and to help sincere ones to become genuine disciples, improved organization was needed.

By the time the second world war ended in 1945, there were hundreds of Jehovah's Witnesses in Argentina and Brazil; some three thousand in Mexico; a few very small congregations in British Guiana (now Guyana), Chile, Dutch Guiana (now Suriname), Paraguay, and Uruguay; and a handful of publishers in Colombia, Guatemala, and Venezuela. But as for Bolivia, Ecuador, El Salvador, Honduras, and Nicaragua, activity of Jehovah's Witnesses was not established on any permanent basis until the arrival of missionaries that had been trained at Gilead School.

The missionaries directed special attention initially to principal centers of population. It is noteworthy that in the first century, the apostle Paul did

As missionaries in Bolivia, Edward Michalec (left) and Harold Morris (right) preached first here in La Paz

much of his preaching in cities along the main routes of travel in Asia Minor and in Greece. In Corinth, one of the most prominent cities of ancient Greece, Paul devoted 18 months to teaching the Word of God. (Acts 18:1-11) In Ephesus, a crossroads for travel and commerce in the ancient world, he proclaimed the Kingdom of God for over two years.—Acts 19:8-10; 20:31.

In a similar manner, when Edward Michalec and Harold Morris, missionary graduates of Gilead School, arrived in Bolivia in 1945, they did not seek out a location with the most agreeable climate. Instead, they gave first attention to La Paz, the capital, which is located in the Andes at an elevation of nearly 12,000 feet. It is a struggle for newcomers to climb the steep streets at this altitude; their hearts often pound like trip-hammers. But the missionaries found many people who were interested in the message of the Bible. There in the capital, it was not unusual for them to be told: "I'm an apostolic Roman Catholic, but I don't like the priests." In just two months, the two missionaries were conducting 41 home Bible studies.

During the following decade, as more missionaries arrived and the number of local Witnesses grew, attention was given to other Bolivian cities: Cochabamba, Oruro, Santa Cruz, Sucre, Potosí, and Tarija. Thereafter, more attention could be directed to smaller cities and towns and the rural areas too.

Similarly, in Colombia the missionaries began organized preaching in the capital, Bogotá, in 1945, and in the coastal city of Barranquilla the following year. After that, attention was progressively directed to Cartagena, Santa Marta, Cali, and Medellín. More people could be reached in a short period by working the larger cities first. With the help of those who learned the truth there, the message would soon be carried to surrounding areas.

If very little interest was manifest in a city, the missionaries were moved to other places. Thus, in Ecuador, when three years of work in the mid-1950's had not produced one person who had the courage to take a stand for the truth in fanatically religious Cuenca, Carl Dochow was transferred to Machala, a city populated by easygoing, open-minded people. About a decade later, however, the people of Cuenca were given another opportunity. A different spirit was found, obstacles were overcome, and by 1992 in and around Cuenca, more than 1,200 people had become Jehovah's Witnesses and were organized into 25 congregations!

Searching Patiently for the Sheeplike Ones

Much patience has been required in order to search out truly sheeplike persons. To locate them in Suriname, Jehovah's Witnesses have preached to Amerindians, Chinese, Indonesians, Jews, Lebanese, descendants of Dutch settlers, and jungle tribes made up of Bush Negroes, whose forebears were runaway slaves. Among them have been found hundreds who were truly hungering for the truth. Some have had to break away from deep involvement in animism and spiritistic practices. One such was Paitu, a witch doctor, who took to heart the message of the Bible and then dumped his idols, amulets, and potions into the river. (Compare Deuteronomy 7:25; 18:9-14; Acts 19:19, 20.) In 1975 he dedicated himself to Jehovah, the true God.

A considerable number of the inhabitants of Peru live in small villages scattered up in the Andes and in the jungle surrounding the headwaters of the Amazon. How could they be reached? In 1971 a family of Witnesses from the United States traveled to Peru to visit their missionary son, Joe Leydig. When they became aware of the vast number of villages tucked here and there in the mountain valleys, their concern for these people moved them to do something. They helped to provide one house car at first, and then two more, as well as trail bikes for use on extensive preaching expeditions into these remote areas.

In spite of the effort put forth, in many places it seemed that only very few showed interest in the Bible's message. You can well imagine how the group of six young missionaries in Barquisimeto, Venezuela, felt in the early 1950's when, after a full year of diligent preaching, they saw hardly any progress. Although the people were quite friendly, most of them were steeped in superstition and viewed it as a sin for them even to read a text from the Bible. Any who did show interest were soon discouraged by family members or neighbors. (Matt. 13:19-21) But, with confidence that there must be some sheeplike ones in Barquisimeto and that Jehovah would gather them in his due time, the missionaries kept on calling from house to house. So, how heartwarming it was for Penny Gavette one day when a gray-haired woman listened to her and then said:

The boat "El Refugio," built by Witnesses in Peru, was used to take the Kingdom message to people along rivers in the upper Amazon region

"What you have just told me is what I read in that Bible so many years ago"

"Senorita, ever since I was a young girl, I have waited for someone to come to my door and explain the things you have just told me. You see, when I was a girl, I used to clean the home of the priest, and he had a Bible in his library. I knew that we were forbidden to read it, but I was so curious to know why that, one day when no one was looking, I took it home with me and read it secretly. What I read made me realize that the Catholic Church had not taught us the truth and so was not the true religion. I was afraid to say anything to anyone, but I was sure that some day the ones teaching the true religion would come to our town. When the Protestant religion came, I thought at first that they must be the ones, but I soon discovered that they taught many of the same falsehoods that the Catholic Church taught. Now, what you have just told me is what I read in that Bible so many years ago." Eagerly she agreed to study the Bible and became one of Jehovah's Witnesses. In spite of family opposition, she served Jehovah faithfully until her death.

Considerable effort was required in order to gather such sheeplike ones into congregations and train them to share in Jehovah's service. As an example, in Argentina, Rosendo Ojeda regularly traveled about 40 miles from General San Martín, Chaco, to conduct a meeting in the home of Alejandro Sozoñiuk, an interested person. The trip frequently took ten hours, some of it on a bicycle, some on foot, at times wading through water up to the armpits. Once a month for five years he made the trip, staying a week each time to witness in the area. Was it worth it? He has no doubt about it because the result was a happy congregation of praisers of Jehovah.

Promoting Education for Life

In Mexico, Jehovah's Witnesses carried on their work in line with the laws governing cultural organizations there. The objective of the Witnesses was to do more than simply hold meetings where discourses were given. They wanted people to be like those Beroeans in the apostle Paul's day who were able to 'carefully examine the Scriptures to see whether the things taught them were really so.' (Acts 17:11) In Mexico, as in many other lands, this has often involved providing special help to people who have had no schooling but who want to be able to read God's inspired Word themselves.

Literacy classes conducted by Jehovah's Witnesses in Mexico have helped tens of thousands of people there to learn to read and write. This work is appreciated by Mexico's Department of Public Education, and in 1974 a director in their General Office for Adult Education wrote a letter to La Torre del Vigía de México, a civil association used by Jehovah's Witnesses, saying: "I take this opportunity to warmly congratulate you . . .

for the praiseworthy cooperation that your association has been extending year after year in benefit of our people."

While preparing people for eternal life as subjects of God's Kingdom, the education provided by the Witnesses also elevates their family life now. After a judge in El Salto, Durango State, had performed marriage ceremonies on various occasions for Jehovah's Witnesses, he stated in 1952: "We claim to be such good patriots and citizens but we are put to shame by Jehovah's Witnesses. They are an example to us because they do not permit a single person in their organization who is living consensually and has not legalized his relationship. And, you Catholics, almost all of you are living immoral lives and have not legalized your marriages."

This educational program also helps people to learn to live together in peace, to love one another instead of hating and killing. When a Witness began to preach in Venado, Guanajuato State, he found that the people were all armed with rifles and pistols. Feuds led to the wiping out of families. But Bible instruction brought major changes. Rifles were sold in order to buy Bibles. Over 150 in the area soon became Jehovah's Witnesses. Figuratively, they 'beat their swords into plowshares' and began to pursue the ways of peace.—Mic. 4:3.

Many God-fearing Mexicans have taken to heart what Jehovah's Witnesses have taught them from God's Word. As a result, the few thousand publishers in Mexico following World War II soon became 10,000, then 20,000, 40,000, 80,000, and more as the Witnesses showed others how to apply the counsel of God's Word and how to teach it to others.

Literacy classes conducted by the Witnesses in Mexico have enabled tens of thousands of people to read God's Word

Assembling Together Under Adversity

As the number of Jehovah's Witnesses increased, however, they found that in one land after another, they had to overcome difficult obstacles in order to hold assemblies for Christian instruction. In Argentina they were placed under government ban in 1950. Nevertheless, out of obedience to God, they did not stop preaching, nor did they forsake assembling together. Arrangements were somewhat more complicated, but assemblies were held.

Brother Knorr (front right) met with Witnesses in small assemblies on farms and in the mountains in Argentina when they were denied freedom to assemble more openly

For example, late in 1953, Brother Knorr and Brother Henschel visited Argentina to serve a nationwide assembly. Brother Knorr entered the country from the west, and Brother Henschel began his visits in the south. They spoke to groups gathered on farms, in a fruit orchard, at a picnic by a mountain stream, and in private homes. Often they had to travel long distances from one group to the next. Arriving in Buenos Aires, they each served on programs in nine locations one day, and in eleven homes the next day. All together, they addressed 56 groups, with a combined attendance of 2,505. It was a strenuous schedule, but they were happy to serve their brothers in that way.

When preparing for an assembly in Colombia in 1955, the Witnesses contracted for the use of a hall in Barranquilla. But, under pressure from the bishop, the mayor and the governor intervened, and the contract was canceled. With just one day's notice, the brothers relocated the assembly, arranging to hold it on the premises of the Society's branch office. Nevertheless, as the first evening session was getting under way, armed police arrived with orders to disband the assembly. The brothers persisted. An appeal to the mayor the next morning brought an apology from his secretary, and nearly 1,000 persons squeezed onto the Society's property for the final day of the program of that "Triumphant Kingdom" Assembly. In spite of the circumstances that then existed, the brothers were thus fortified with needed spiritual counsel.

Serving Where the Need Is Greater

The field was large, and the need for workers was great in Latin America, as it was in many other places. In 1957, at conventions worldwide, individuals and families who were mature Witnesses of Jehovah were encouraged to consider actually moving to areas of greater need to take up residence and carry on their ministry there. Similar encouragement was given in various ways thereafter. The invitation was much like the one presented by God to the apostle Paul, who saw in vision a man who entreated him: "Step over into Macedonia and help us." (Acts 16:9, 10) What was the response to the modern-day invitation? Jehovah's servants offered themselves willingly.—Ps. 110:3.

For a family with small children, it takes a great deal of faith to uproot themselves, leave relatives and home and secular employment, and travel to a completely new environment. The move may require accepting a very different standard of living and, in some instances, learning a new language. Yet, thousands of individual Witnesses and families have made such moves in order to help others to learn of Jehovah's loving provisions for eternal life.

Responding quickly, a number of Jehovah's Witnesses made the move in the late 1950's; others in the 1960's; more in the 1970's. And the movement of Witnesses to areas of greater need continues down to the present.

From where have they come? Large numbers from Australia, Canada, New Zealand, and the United States. Many from Britain, France, and Germany. Also from Austria, Belgium, Denmark, Finland, Italy, Japan, the Republic of Korea, Norway, Spain, Sweden, and Switzerland, among others. As the number of Jehovah's Witnesses has increased in Argentina, Brazil, Mexico, and other Latin American lands, these too have provided workers who are willing to serve in other countries where there is great need. Similarly, in Africa zealous workers have moved from one country to another to help give a witness.

To what areas have they moved? Lands such as Afghanistan, Malaysia, and Senegal, and islands such as Réunion and St. Lucia. About 1,000 moved into Ireland, where they served for varying lengths of time. A considerable number went to Iceland, despite its long, dark winters, and some stayed, becoming pillars in the congregations and providing loving help to newer ones. Especially has much good been done in Central and South America. Over 1,000 Witnesses moved to Colombia, upwards of 870 to Ecuador, more than 110 to El Salvador.

Harold and Anne Zimmerman were among those who made the move. They had already served as missionary teachers in Ethiopia. However, in 1959, when they were finalizing arrangements to move from the United States to Colombia to share in spreading the Kingdom message there, they were rearing four children, who ranged in age from five months to five years. Harold went ahead to look for work. When he arrived in the country, local news reports disturbed him. An undeclared civil war was in progress, and there were mass killings in the interior of the country. 'Do I really want to bring my family down to live in conditions like these?' he asked himself. He searched his memory for some guiding example or principle in the Bible. What came to mind was the Bible account of the fearful spies who took back to the Israelite camp a bad report about the Promised Land. (Num. 13: 25–14:4, 11) That settled it; he did not want to be

Among the thousands of Witnesses who moved to other countries to serve where the need was greater were families, such as Harold and Anne Zimmerman with their four young children (Colombia)

like them! He promptly arranged for his family to come. Not until their funds had dwindled to just three dollars did he find the needed secular work, but they had what was really necessary. The amount of such work that he had to do to support his family varied over the years, but he has always endeavored to keep Kingdom interests in first place. When they first went to Colombia, there were about 1,400 Witnesses in the country. What amazing growth they have seen since then!

Serving where the need for Witnesses is greater does not always require that a person go to another country. Thousands of individual Witnesses and families have moved to other areas within their own country. A family in Bahia State, Brazil, moved to the town of Prado, where there were no Witnesses. Despite objections from the clergy, they lived and worked in that town and the surrounding area for three years. An abandoned church building was purchased and transformed into a Kingdom Hall. Before long, there were over a hundred active Witnesses in the area. And that was only the beginning.

Thousands moved to areas within their own country where the need for Witnesses was greater

In ever-increasing numbers, lovers of righteousness in Latin America are responding to the invitation recorded in Psalm 148: 'Praise Jah, you people! Praise Jehovah from the earth, all you national groups.' (Vss. 1, 7-11) Indeed, by 1975 there were praisers of Jehovah in every country in Latin America. The report for that year showed that 80,481, organized into 2,998 congregations, were serving in Mexico. Another 24,703, in 462 congregations, were talking about Jehovah's kingship in Central America. And in South America, there were 206,457 public praisers of Jehovah in 3,620 congregations.

Reaching Out to the Pacific Islands

While rapid expansion was taking place in South America, Jehovah's Witnesses were also directing attention to the islands of the Pacific. There are hundreds of these islands scattered between Australia and the Americas, many of them scarcely pushing their heads above the ocean surface. Some of them are populated by only a few families; others, by tens of thousands of people. Early in the 1950's, official prejudice made it impossible for the Watch Tower Society to send missionaries to many of these islands. But the people there too needed to hear about Jehovah and his Kingdom. This is in harmony with the prophecy recorded at Isaiah 42: 10-12, which says: "Sing to Jehovah a new song, his praise from the extremity of the earth . . . In the islands let them tell forth even his praise." Thus, in 1951, at a convention in Sydney, Australia, pioneers and circuit overseers who were interested in having a part in spreading the Kingdom message to the islands were invited to meet with Brother Knorr. At that time about 30 volunteered to undertake preaching in the tropical islands.

Among them were Tom and Rowena Kitto, who soon found themselves in Papua, where there were at that time no Witnesses. They started their work among the Europeans in Port Moresby. Before long, they were spending evenings in Hanuabada, the "Big Village," with a group of 30 to 40 Papuans who were hungry for spiritual truth. From them, word spread to other villages. In a short time, the Kerema people sent a delegation asking that a Bible study be conducted with them. Then a headman from Haima came, pleading: "Please come and teach my people about the truth!" And so it spread.

Another couple, John and Ellen Hubler, went to New Caledonia to establish the work there. When they arrived in 1954, they had only one-month tourist visas. But John obtained secular work, and this helped them to obtain an extension. In time, other Witnesses—31 in all—made similar moves. At first, they carried on their ministry in outlying areas so as not to attract too much attention. Later, they began preaching in the capital, Nouméa. A congregation was formed. Then, in 1959, a member of Catholic Action got into a key government position. There were no more visa renewals for Witnesses. The Hublers had to leave. Watch Tower publications were banned. Yet, the Kingdom good news had a foothold, and the number of Witnesses continued to grow.

In Tahiti many people had shown interest in the work of Jehovah's Witnesses when brothers made brief visits there. But in 1957, there were no local Witnesses, their work was banned, and Watch Tower missionaries were denied entry. However, Agnes Schenck, a citizen of Tahiti then living in the United States, had become one of Jehovah's Witnesses. Upon learning of the need for Kingdom proclaimers in Tahiti, she, her husband, and their son sailed from California in May 1958. Shortly after that, two other families joined them, though they could obtain only three-month tourist visas. By the next year, a congregation was formed in Papeete. And in 1960 the government granted recognition to a locally organized association of Jehovah's Witnesses.

In response to a call for volunteers, Tom and Rowena Kitto moved to Papua to teach Bible truth

John and Ellen Hubler, followed by 31 other Witnesses, moved to New Caledonia. Before they had to leave, a congregation was firmly established there

In order to spread the Kingdom message, two missionary sisters en route back to their assignment stopped to visit a relative on the island of Niue. The month they spent there was very fruitful; much interest was found. But when the next interisland boat arrived, they had to leave. Soon, however, Seremaia Raibe, a Fijian, obtained an employment contract with the Public Works Department in Niue and then used all his free time to preach. However, as a result of clergy pressure, Brother Raibe's residence permit was canceled after a few months, and in September 1961 the Legislative Assembly decided not to allow any more of Jehovah's Witnesses into the country. Nevertheless, the preaching of the good news there continued. How? The local Witnesses, though quite new, persevered in serving Jehovah. Furthermore, the local government had already accepted in its employ William Lovini, a native Niuean who had been living in New Zealand. Why was he eager to return to Niue? Because he had become one of Jehovah's Witnesses and wanted to serve where the need was greater. By 1964 the number of Witnesses there rose to 34.

In 1973, David Wolfgramm, a citizen of Tonga, with his wife and eight children, was living in a comfortable home in New Zealand. But they left that behind and moved to Tonga to advance Kingdom interests. From there they shared in pushing the work farther afield in the islands of Tonga, about 30 of which are inhabited.

Much time, effort, and expense have been required to reach the islands. But Jehovah's Witnesses view the lives of their fellowmen as precious and spare nothing in their efforts to help them to benefit from Jehovah's loving provision for eternal life in his new world.

"A priceless reward"

A family that sold their farm in Australia and moved to one of the Pacific islands summed up their feelings in this way: "To hear these islanders say that they have come to know Jehovah, to hear them call our children their children, this because they love them so for the truth, to watch both Kingdom interest and attendance grow, to hear these lovely people say: 'My children will marry only in the Lord,' and this after being associated with many centuries of tradition and Eastern-type marriages, to watch them straighten and clean up marital tangles, . . . to see them studying as they mind the cattle by the roadside, after backbreaking work in the rice field, to know that they are discussing the wrongness of idolatry, the beauty of Jehovah's name at the local store and other places, to have an elderly Indian mother call you brother and sister and ask to go with you to tell the folk about the true God . . . All this adds up to a priceless reward for having taken the step that we did in answer to the call from the South Pacific."

More than these Pacific islanders were receiving attention, however. Starting in 1964, experienced pioneers from the Philippines were assigned to reinforce zealous missionaries who were already at work in Hong Kong, Indonesia, the Republic of Korea, Laos, Malaysia, Taiwan, Thailand, and Vietnam.

In the Face of Family and Community Pressure

When a person becomes one of Jehovah's Witnesses, this is not always accepted by his family and the community as being simply a matter for personal decision.—Matt. 10:34-36; 1 Pet. 4:4.

Most of those who have become Jehovah's Witnesses in Hong Kong have been young folk. But these young people have been under tremendous pressure in a system that makes higher education and better-paying jobs a priority. Parents view their children as an investment that will ensure their living comfortably in their later years. Thus, when the parents of a young man in Kwun Tong realized that the Bible study, meeting attendance, and field service of their son were going to interfere with his making money, their opposition became intense. His father chased him with a meat cleaver; his mother spit on him in public. Verbal abuse continued almost nonstop for months. Once he asked his parents: "Didn't you raise me for love?" And they replied: "No, for money!" Nevertheless, the young man continued to put his worship of Jehovah first; but when he left home, he also continued to assist his parents financially to the best of his ability, for he knew that this would be pleasing to Jehovah. —Matt. 15:3-9; 19:19.

In close-knit communities, severe pressure often comes from more than the immediate family. One who experienced this was Fuaiupolu Pele in Western Samoa. It was viewed as unthinkable among the people for a Samoan to reject the customs and religion of his forefathers, and Pele knew that he would be called to account. He studied hard and prayed earnestly to Jehovah. When summoned by the high chief of the family to a meeting at Faleasiu, he was confronted by six chiefs, three orators, ten pastors, two theological teachers, the high chief who was presiding, and older men and women of the family. They cursed and condemned both him and another family member who was showing interest in Jehovah's Witnesses. A debate ensued; it lasted until four in the morning. Pele's use of the Bible irritated some who were present, and they yelled: "Take that Bible away! Leave off that Bible!" But at last the high chief in a weak voice said: "You won, Pele." But Pele replied: "Pardon me,

As a young man in Western Samoa, Fuaiupolu Pele faced intense family and community pressure when he decided to become one of Jehovah's Witnesses

Sir, I did not win. This night you heard the message of the Kingdom. It is my sincere hope you will heed it."

When There Is Intense Clergy Opposition

Christendom's missionaries had arrived in the Pacific islands in the 1800's. Their arrival, in many places, had been peaceful; elsewhere it had been backed by military force. In some areas they had apportioned the islands among themselves by a "gentleman's agreement." But there had also been religious wars, in which Catholics and Protestants had fought one another for control. These religious "shepherds," the clergy, now used every means at their disposal to keep Jehovah's Witnesses out of what they viewed as their own domain. Sometimes they pressured officials to expel Witnesses from certain islands. Other times they took the law into their own hands.

On the island of New Britain, in the village of Vunabal, a group from the Sulka tribe showed keen interest in Bible truth. But one Sunday in 1959, while John Davison was conducting a Bible study with them, a mob of Catholics, under the direction of the Catholic catechist, pushed their way into the house and brought the study to a halt by their shouting and abuse. This was reported to the police at Kokopo.

Rather than abandon the sheep, the Witnesses returned the following week to continue providing spiritual help for appreciative ones in Vunabal. The Catholic priest was there too, though uninvited by the villagers, and he brought along several hundred Catholics of another tribe. After being agitated by the priest, those from his church swore at the Witnesses, spit on them, shook their fists, and ripped up the Bibles of the villagers, while the priest stood with folded arms and smiled. The police who endeavored to control the situation were visibly shaken. Many of the villagers became frightened too. But at least one of the villagers proved to be courageous and took his stand for what he knew to be the truth. Now, hundreds of others on that island have done likewise.

However, not all religious teachers showed an antagonistic spirit toward Jehovah's Witnesses. Shem Irofa'alu, in the Solomon Islands, felt a sincere responsibility toward those who looked to him as their religious leader. After reading the Watch Tower Society's book *From Paradise Lost to Paradise Regained*, he realized that someone had lied to him. He and the religious teachers under his jurisdiction listened to discussions with the Witnesses, asked questions, and looked up the scriptures in the Bible. Then they agreed that they wanted to become Jehovah's Witnesses, so they proceeded to convert the churches in their 28 villages into Kingdom Halls.

After Shem Irofa'alu and his associates became convinced that what Jehovah's Witnesses teach is really the truth, churches in 28 villages in the Solomon Islands were converted into Kingdom Halls

An Onrushing Torrent of Truth in Africa

Particularly beginning in the early 1920's, much effort was put forth so that people in all parts of Africa would have opportunity to come to know Jehovah, the true God, and to benefit from his loving provisions. When the second world war ended, there were active Witnesses of Jehovah in 14 lands on the African continent. Another 14 African countries had been reached with the Kingdom message, but no Witnesses were reporting activity in these in 1945. During the next 30 years, through 1975, the preaching of the good news penetrated 19 more countries in Africa. In nearly all these lands, as well as on surrounding islands, congregations began to be formed—a few in some lands, over a thousand in Zambia, nearly two thousand in Nigeria. How did all of that come about?

The spreading of the Kingdom message was like an onrushing torrent of water. For the most part, water courses through river channels, although some overflows onto adjoining land; and if an obstruction blocks the way, the water finds an alternate path or builds up volume and pressure until it bursts over the top.

Using its regular organizational channels, the Watch Tower Society assigned full-time ministers—pioneers, special pioneers, and missionaries—to lands where little or no preaching had been done. Wherever they went, they invited people to "take life's water free." (Rev. 22:17) By way of example, in northern Africa, four special pioneers from France extended that invitation to the people of Algeria in 1952. Soon a fortune-teller there accepted the truth, recognized that she must abandon her profession in order to please Jehovah, and began to witness to her former clients. (Deut. 18: 10-12) The pioneers made effective use of the book *"Let God Be True"* to help sincere individuals to see the difference between the Holy Bible and religious tradition. So powerful was it in liberating people from false religious practices that a clergyman displayed the book in his pulpit and pronounced a curse upon it, upon those who were distributing it, and upon those who were reading it.

Qualified Witnesses were sent into lands where there was a special need

In 1954 a missionary was expelled from Catholic Spain because of teaching the Bible without approval of the clergy; so the following year, he and his pioneer companion took up preaching in Morocco. Soon they were joined by a family of five of Jehovah's Witnesses who had been deported from Tunisia, where considerable agitation had been caused when a Jewish couple accepted Jesus as the Messiah and quickly began to share their new faith with others. Farther to the south, pioneers from Ghana were directed into Mali in 1962. Later, French pioneers serving in Algeria were also asked to help in Mali. In turn, a considerable number of those who later became Witnesses there entered the ranks of full-time service. In

1966 eight special pioneers from Nigeria took up assignments in Niger, a sparsely populated country that includes part of the Sahara Desert. Burundi was given opportunity to hear the Kingdom message when two special pioneers were sent there from Northern Rhodesia (now Zambia) in 1963, followed by four missionaries trained at Gilead School.

There were also missionaries in Ethiopia in the early 1950's. The Ethiopian government required that they establish a regular mission and teach school, which they did. But, in addition to that, they were busy teaching the Bible, and soon there was a constant flow of people coming to the missionary home, new ones arriving every day to request that someone help them to understand the Bible. During the three decades following World War II, 39 countries on the African continent benefited from the help of such Gilead-trained missionaries.

At the same time, the waters of truth were overflowing into spiritually parched areas by means of Jehovah's Witnesses whose secular work brought them into contact with other people. Thus, Witnesses from Egypt whose work required that they move to Libya in 1950 preached zealously during their free hours. That same year a Witness who was a wool merchant, along with his family, moved from Egypt to Khartoum, Sudan. He made it a practice to witness to customers before doing business with them. One of the first Witnesses in Senegal (then part of French West Africa) went there, in 1951, as a representative of a commercial firm. He also appreciated his responsibilities as a Witness of the Most High. In 1959, in connection with secular work, a Witness went to Fort-Lamy (now N'Djamena), in what later became Chad, and he used the opportunity to spread the Kingdom message in that land. In countries adjoining Niger were traders who were Jehovah's Witnesses; so, while special pioneers were busy in Niger from 1966 on, these traders were also preaching to people from Niger with whom they did business. And two Witnesses whose husbands went to Mauritania to work in 1966 seized the opportunity to witness in that area.

People who were refreshed by 'the water of life' shared it with others. For example, in 1947 an individual who had attended some meetings but was not himself one of Jehovah's Witnesses moved from Cameroon to Ubangi-Shari (now

To preach in Ethiopia in the early 1950's, the Witnesses were required to establish a mission and teach school

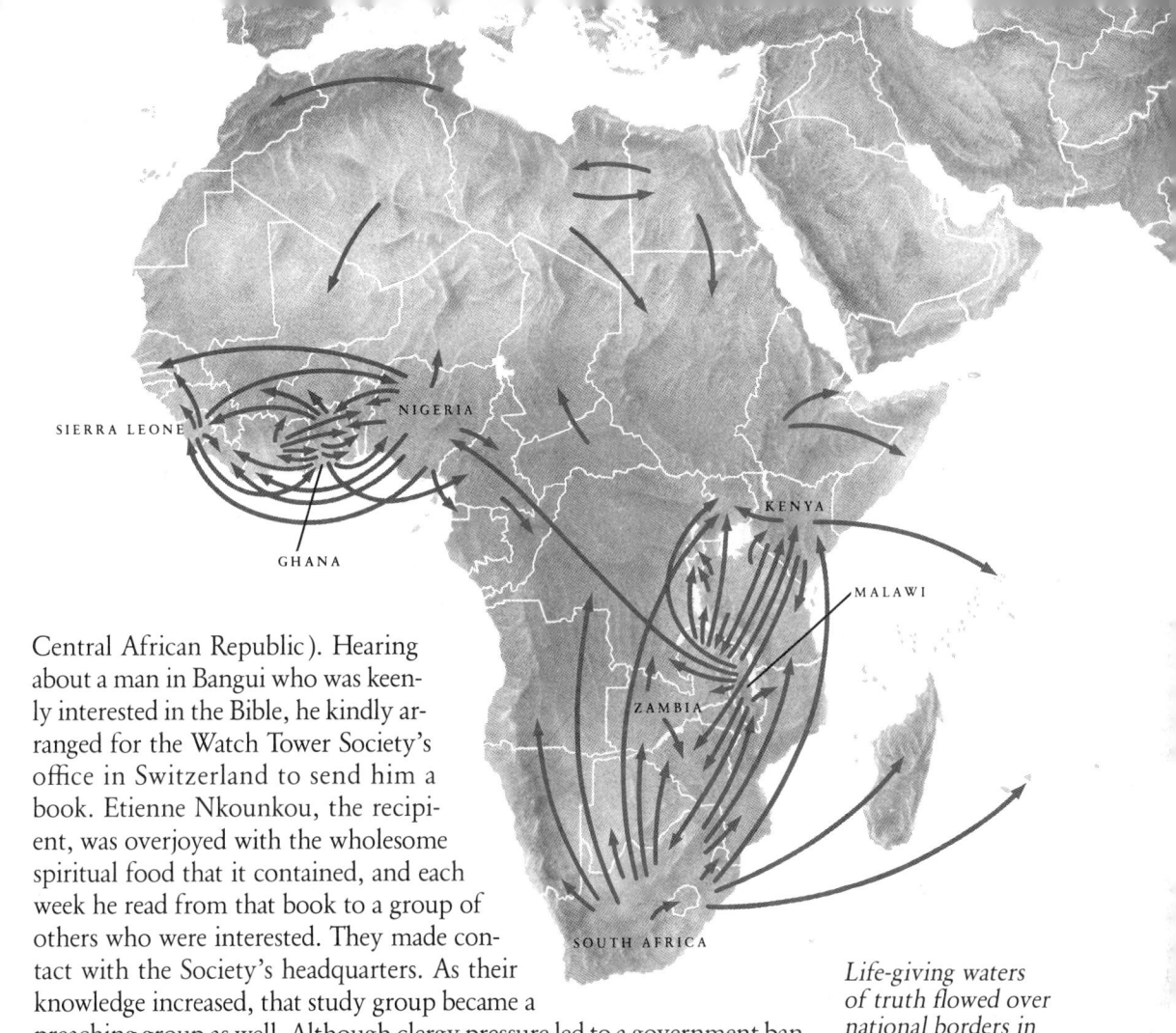

Central African Republic). Hearing about a man in Bangui who was keenly interested in the Bible, he kindly arranged for the Watch Tower Society's office in Switzerland to send him a book. Etienne Nkounkou, the recipient, was overjoyed with the wholesome spiritual food that it contained, and each week he read from that book to a group of others who were interested. They made contact with the Society's headquarters. As their knowledge increased, that study group became a preaching group as well. Although clergy pressure led to a government ban on Watch Tower literature, these new Witnesses continued to preach with just the Bible. People in that land love to hear Bible discussions, so by the time the ban on some of the Society's publications was lifted in 1957, the Witnesses there already numbered upwards of 500.

Life-giving waters of truth flowed over national borders in many directions in Africa

When Obstacles Were Raised Up

When obstacles hindered the flow of life-giving water, it soon got through in some other way. Ayité Sessi, a pioneer from Dahomey (now Benin), had preached in French Togo (now Togo) for only a short time in 1949 when the government forced him to leave. But the following year Akakpo Agbetor, a former boxer, originally from Togo, returned to his homeland along with his brother. Because this was the land of his birth, he was able to witness quite freely, even holding meetings. Although pioneers who had taken up assignments in Fernando Po (now part of Equatorial Guinea) in about 1950 were deported after a short time as a result of religious intolerance, other Witnesses later secured work contracts that enabled them to live in that area. And, of course, in harmony with Jesus' command, they preached.—Mark 13:10.

Emmanuel Mama, a circuit overseer from Ghana, was sent to Upper Volta (now called Burkina Faso) for a few weeks in 1959 and was able to do much witnessing in Ouagadougou, the capital. But there were no Witnesses living in the country. Four years later, seven Witnesses, originally from Togo, Dahomey (now Benin), and Congo, moved to Ouagadougou and sought employment so that they could serve in this area. A few months later, they were joined by several special pioneers from Ghana. However, as a result of clergy pressure on the officials, in 1964, after the Witnesses had been there for less than a year, they were arrested, held for 13 days, and then expelled from the country. Had their efforts been worthwhile? Emmanuel Johnson, a resident of the country, had learned where Bible truth could be found. He continued to study with Jehovah's Witnesses by mail, and he got baptized in 1969. Yes, the Kingdom work had a foothold in another country.

When application was made for visas that would enable Gilead-trained missionaries to serve in the Ivory Coast (now called Côte d'Ivoire), French officials withheld approval. So, in 1950, Alfred Shooter, from the Gold Coast (now Ghana), was sent to the capital of the Ivory Coast as a pioneer. Once he was established, his wife joined him; and a few months later, a missionary couple, Gabriel and Florence Paterson, came. Problems arose. One day, their literature was seized because it had not been approved by the government, and the brothers were fined. But they later found their books on sale in the marketplace, so they bought them back and made good use of them.

Meanwhile, these brothers visited numerous government offices in an endeavor to obtain permanent visas. Mr. Houphouët-Boigny, who later became president of the Ivory Coast, offered to help. "The truth," he remarked, "has no barrier whatsoever. It is like a mighty river; dam it and it will overflow the dam." When a Catholic priest and a Methodist minister tried to interfere, Ouezzin Coulibaly, a government deputy, said: "I represent the people of this country. We are the people, and we like Jehovah's Witnesses and so we want them to stay here in this country."

Disciples Who Truly Understand

When giving instructions to "make disciples of people of all the nations," Jesus also directed that those who would become disciples—those who believed Christ's teachings and applied them—should be baptized. (Matt. 28:19, 20) In harmony with this, there is provision for baptism of new disciples at the periodic assemblies and conventions of Jehovah's Wit-

When threatened with deportation, Gabriel Paterson (shown here) was reassured by a prominent official: 'The truth is like a mighty river; dam it and it will overflow the dam'

In 1970 at a convention in Nigeria, 3,775 new Witnesses were immersed; care was taken to be sure that each one really qualified

nesses. The number baptized on any given occasion may be relatively few. However, at a convention in Nigeria in 1970, there were 3,775 new Witnesses immersed. Large numbers are not the objective, though.

When it was realized, in 1956, that some in the Gold Coast who were getting baptized had not built their faith on an adequate foundation, an arrangement was instituted there to screen baptismal candidates. Responsibility was placed on local congregation overseers in the Gold Coast to examine personally each immersion candidate to make sure that he had a sound knowledge of basic Bible truths, that he was living in harmony with Bible standards, and that he clearly understood the obligations that go with being a dedicated, baptized Witness of Jehovah. In time, a similar procedure was put into effect worldwide. A detailed outline for use in reviewing basic Bible teachings with baptismal candidates was provided in 1967 in the book *"Your Word Is a Lamp to My Foot."* After years of experience, a further refinement of that outline was published in 1983 in the book *Organized to Accomplish Our Ministry*.

With such an arrangement, were the needs of people who have had little or no formal schooling taken into account?

Coping With the Problem of Illiteracy

In 1957 the United Nations Educational, Scientific, and Cultural Organization estimated that approximately 44 percent of the world's population 15 years of age or older could not read or write. It was reported that in 42 countries in Africa, 2 in the Americas, 28 in Asia, and 4 in Oceania, 75 percent of the adults were illiterate. Yet, they too needed opportunity to learn the law of God so that they could prepare to be subjects of his Kingdom. Many who could not read had keen minds and could remember much of what they heard, but they still could not read the precious Word of God themselves and make use of printed Bible study aids.

For years individual Witnesses had been giving personal help to people who wanted to learn to read. However, in 1949 and 1950, literacy classes were inaugurated by Jehovah's Witnesses in each of their congregations in many African lands. The classes were usually held in Kingdom Halls, and in some places the entire village was invited to benefit from the program.

Where the government was sponsoring a literacy program, Jehovah's Witnesses gladly cooperated with it. In many areas, however, the Witnesses had to develop and use their own instruction manuals. Tens of thousands of persons, including thousands of women and elderly folks, have been helped to become literate by means of these classes conducted by Jehovah's Witnesses. As a result of the way the course was designed, not only have they learned to read and write but at the same time they have become acquainted with basic truths from God's Holy Word. This has helped to qualify them to share in the disciple-making work that Jesus commanded. The desire to do this effectively has motivated many to put forth earnest effort to learn to read.

When a new Witness in Dahomey (now Benin), West Africa, was turned away by a householder because the Witness could not read, the Witness made up his mind to overcome that problem. In addition to attending the literacy classes, he applied himself personally. Six weeks later he called on the same householder; the man was so amazed to hear this person, who such a short time ago had been illiterate, reading to him from God's Word that he also showed interest in what the Witness was teaching. Some who have been instructed in these literacy classes have, in time, even become traveling overseers, with a number of congregations to teach. That was true of Ezekiel Ovbiagele in Nigeria.

Educating by Means of Motion Pictures and Slide Showings

To assist those demonstrating interest in the Bible to appreciate the magnitude of Jehovah's visible organization, a motion picture was released in 1954. This film, *The New World Society in Action*, also helped to break down community prejudice.

In what is now Zambia, a portable generator was often needed in order to show the film. A white canvas stretched between two trees served as a screen. In Barotse Province the paramount chief viewed the film with his royal family, and then he wanted it shown to the public. As a result, the next evening 2,500 persons saw it. Total attendance for the film showings in Zambia over a 17-year period exceeded one million. Those in attendance were delighted with what they saw. From nearby Tanganyika (now part of Tanzania), it was reported that after the showing of the film, the air was filled with cries of the crowd saying, *"Ndaka, ndaka"* (Thank you, thank you).

WITNESSES TO THE MOST DISTANT PART OF THE EARTH 481

After the motion picture *The New World Society in Action,* other films followed: *The Happiness of the New World Society, Proclaiming "Everlasting Good News" Around the World, God Cannot Lie,* and *Heritage.* There have also been slide showings, with commentary, on the practicality of the Bible in our time, the pagan roots of doctrines and practices of Christendom, and the meaning of world conditions in the light of Bible prophecy, as well as slide showings about Jehovah's Witnesses as an organization, featuring a visit to their world headquarters, thrilling conventions in lands where they were formerly banned, and a review of their modern-day history. All of these have helped people to realize that Jehovah does indeed have a people on the earth and that the Bible is His inspired Word.

Film showings (in Africa and around the world) gave audiences a glimpse of the magnitude of Jehovah's visible organization

Identifying the Real Sheep

In certain countries, people who simply had in their possession some Watch Tower publications claimed to be Jehovah's Witnesses or used the name Watch Tower. But had they changed their beliefs and way of life to conform to Bible standards? When given needed instruction, would they prove to be truly sheeplike persons who heed the voice of the Master, Jesus Christ?—John 10:4, 5.

A startling letter was received at the Watch Tower Society's branch office in South Africa, in 1954, from a group of Africans at Baía dos Tigres, a penal settlement in the south of Angola. The writer, João Mancoca, said: "The group of Jehovah's Witnesses in Angola is composed of 1,000 members. These have as their leader Simão Gonçalves Toco." Who was Toco? Were his followers really Jehovah's Witnesses?

Arrangements were made for John Cooke, a missionary who could speak Portuguese, to visit Angola. After a long interview with a colonial official, Brother Cooke was permitted to visit Mancoca. Brother Cooke learned that in the 1940's, when Toco was associated with a Baptist mission in the Belgian Congo (now Zaire), he had obtained some Watch Tower literature and had shared with close associates what he learned. But then, spiritists influenced the group, and in time Toco completely stopped using the Watch Tower literature and the Bible. Instead, he sought direction through spirit mediums.

His followers were repatriated to Angola by the government and then were dispersed to various parts of the country.

Mancoca had been one of Toco's associates, but Mancoca tried to persuade others to stop practicing spiritism and to adhere to the Bible. Some of Toco's followers did not like this and, making false charges, denounced Mancoca to the Portuguese authorities. As a result, Mancoca and those who shared his views were deported to a penal colony. From there he got in touch with the Watch Tower Society and obtained more Bible literature. He was humble, spiritually minded, and keenly interested in working closely with the organization through which he had learned the truth. After Brother Cooke had spent many hours discussing Bible truths with this group, there was no question in his mind that João Mancoca was truly one of the Lord's sheep. Under the most difficult circumstances, Brother Mancoca has proved that for many years now.

Interviews were also held with Toco and some of his followers. With some few exceptions, however, they did not give evidence of the sheeplike qualities of Christ's followers. So, at that time, there were not 1,000 Witnesses of Jehovah in Angola but only about 25.

Meanwhile, in the Belgian Congo (now Zaire), another confusion of identity had developed. There was a religiopolitical movement known as Kitawala, which at times also made use of the name Watch Tower. In the homes of some of its members were found publications of Jehovah's Witnesses, which they had obtained by mail. But the beliefs and practices of the Kitawala (including racism, subversion of authority in order to bring about political or social change, and gross sexual immorality in the name of worship) in no way represented those of Jehovah's Witnesses. Yet, certain published reports endeavored to implicate the Watch Tower Society of Jehovah's Witnesses with the Kitawala.

Repeated efforts of Jehovah's Witnesses to send trained supervisors into the country were rebuffed by Belgian officials. Catholic and Protestant groups were delighted. Particularly from 1949 on, cruel repressive measures were taken against those in the Belgian Congo who endeavored to study the Bible with the aid of Watch Tower literature. But it was as one of the faithful Witnesses there said: "We are like a bag of African corn. Wherever they shall take us, the Word will drop, one by one, until the time when the rain will come, and they shall see us raised up everywhere." And so it was that in spite of difficult conditions, from 1949 to 1960, the number who reported activity as Jehovah's Witnesses increased from 48 to 1,528.

João Mancoca (shown here with his wife, Mary) has loyally served Jehovah for decades in the face of very difficult conditions

Gradually the officials came to appreciate that Jehovah's Witnesses are very different from the Kitawala. When the Witnesses were granted some freedom to assemble, government observers often remarked about their good conduct and orderliness. When there were violent demonstrations to demand political independence, people knew that Jehovah's Witnesses were not involved. In 1961 a qualified Witness supervisor, Ernest Heuse, Jr., from Belgium, was finally able to enter the country. With much diligent effort, it was possible to help the brothers gradually to bring their congregations and their personal lives into fuller harmony with God's Word. There was much to be learned, and it required great patience.

In 1961, Ernest Heuse, Jr., with his family, was able to enter Zaire (then called Congo) to help provide spiritual instruction for those who truly wanted to serve Jehovah

Thinking that it would enhance their position, the Kitawala from some areas sent long lists of their people who wanted to be recognized as Jehovah's Witnesses. Wisely, Brother Heuse dispatched qualified brothers to these areas to find out what kind of people they were. Instead of accepting large groups, they conducted Bible studies with individuals.

In time, the real sheep, those who truly looked to Jesus Christ as their Shepherd, became manifest. And there were many of these. They, in turn, taught others. Over the years, scores of Watch Tower missionaries from abroad came to work along with them, to help them to gain a more accurate knowledge of God's Word and to provide needed training. By 1975, there were 17,477 of Jehovah's Witnesses in Zaire, organized in 526 congregations, busy preaching and teaching God's Word to others.

Breaking the Power of the Fetish

To the west of Nigeria lies the country of Benin (formerly known as Dahomey), with a population divided into 60 ethnic groups speaking some 50 languages and dialects. As is true in much of Africa, animism is the traditional religion, and this is coupled with ancestor worship. Such a religious environment clouds the lives of people with superstition and fear. Many who profess to be Christians also practice animism.

From the late 1920's into the 1940's, Jehovah's Witnesses from Nigeria scattered many seeds of Bible truth in Dahomey by occasional visits to distribute Bible literature. Many of those seeds simply needed a little watering in order to become fruitful. That care was provided in 1948 when Nouru

Akintoundé, a native of Dahomey who had been living in Nigeria, returned to Dahomey to pioneer. Within four months, 300 persons quickly responded to the truth and shared with him in the field ministry. This response surpassed all reasonable expectations.

As a result of this activity, agitation was quickly aroused not only among Christendom's clergy but also among the animists. When the secretary of the fetish convent in Porto-Novo showed interest in the truth, the fetish chief proclaimed that the secretary would die in seven days. But this former convent secretary firmly stated: "If it is the fetish that made Jehovah, I will die; but if Jehovah is the supreme God, then he will vanquish the fetish." (Compare Deuteronomy 4:35; John 17:3.) To make his prediction come true, on the night of the sixth day, the fetish chief indulged in all sorts of witchcraft and then proclaimed that this former convent secretary was dead. However, there was great consternation among the fetish worshipers the next day when she came to the market in Cotonou very much alive. Later, one of the brothers hired a car and drove her through Porto-Novo so that all could see for themselves that she was alive. Following this, many other fetish worshipers took a firm stand for the truth. —Compare Jeremiah 10:5.

Soon, as a result of intense religious pressure, Watch Tower publications were banned in Dahomey. But, in obedience to Jehovah God, the Witnesses continued to preach, often with just the Bible. Sometimes they would engage in door-to-door work as "traders," with all sorts of goods. If the conversation went well, they would turn attention to the Bible, and they might even produce from within a large interior pocket of their garment a precious piece of Bible literature.

When the police gave them much difficulty in the cities, then they would preach in the rural areas. (Compare Matthew 10:23.) And when they were thrown into prison, they preached there. In 1955, Witnesses in prison found at least 18 interested persons among prisoners and prison officials at Abomey.

Within just a decade after the Dahoman pioneer brother returned to his homeland to preach, there were 1,426 sharing in the ministry—and that even though their work was under government ban!

More Workers Share in the Harvest

It was obvious that there were many people throughout Africa who were hungering for the truth. The harvest was great, but the workers were few. Therefore, it was encouraging to the brothers as they saw how the Master of the harvest, Jesus Christ, answered their prayers for more workers to help with the spiritual ingathering.—Matt. 9:37, 38.

Much literature had been placed in Kenya in the 1930's by traveling pioneers, but there had been little follow-up work. However, in 1949, Mary Whittington, with her three young children, emigrated from Britain to live in Nairobi with her husband, who was employed there. Sister Whittington had been baptized for scarcely a year, but she had the spirit of a pioneer. Though she knew of no other Witnesses in Kenya, she set out to help others in this large territory to learn the truth. Despite obstacles, she did not back down. Other Witnesses also came—from Australia, Britain, Canada, South Africa, Sweden, the United States, and Zambia—personally arranging to move there to share the Kingdom hope with the people.

Though she had been baptized only a year and knew of no other Witnesses in Kenya, Mary Whittington set out to help others learn the truth

In addition, missionary couples were sent to help with the harvest. At first the men were obligated to do secular work in order to remain in the country, and so they were limited in the time they had available for the ministry. But their wives were free to serve as pioneers. In time, well over a hundred Gilead-trained missionaries came to Kenya. When independence neared, with an end to the segregation that British colonial rule had enforced, the European Witnesses studied Swahili and quickly broadened out their activity to reach the native Africans. The number of Witnesses in this part of the global field grew rapidly.

In 1972, Botswana too received help with the spiritual harvest when Witnesses from Britain, Kenya, and South Africa moved into its larger cities. Three years later, Gilead-trained missionaries also came. To a large extent, however, the population is scattered in rural villages. In order to reach them, Witnesses from South Africa have traveled across the desert region known as the Kalahari. In isolated communities they have witnessed to village headmen, to schoolteachers, and often to groups of 10 or 20 appreciative listeners. Said one elderly man: "You came all this way to talk to us about these things? That is kind, very kind."

"Bible Brown" had given powerful Bible discourses in Liberia during the 1920's, but there was considerable opposition. The spiritual harvest work there did not really progress until the arrival of missionaries trained at Gilead School. Harry Behannan, who came in 1946, was the first. Many more shared in the following years. Native Liberians gradually joined them in the work, and by 1975 the number of praisers of Jehovah exceeded a thousand.

Even more preaching had been done by "Bible Brown" in Nigeria. This was a nation divided up into numerous kingdoms, city states, and social systems, with people speaking upwards of 250 languages and dialects. Religion was a further divisive factor. With little tact but with powerful Scriptural arguments, the early Witnesses there exposed the clergy and their false teachings. When their literature was banned during World War II, the brothers preached with the Bible alone. People who loved truth responded appreciatively. They quit the churches, then abandoned polygamy and forsook their jujus, which the churches had tolerated. By 1950 the number of Jehovah's Witnesses sharing in proclaiming the Kingdom message in Nigeria was 8,370. By 1970, there were more than ten times that number.

Persistent legal obstacles had to be overcome in order to provide spiritual help to interested ones in Southern Rhodesia (now known as Zimbabwe). Efforts to obtain legal recognition had begun in the mid-1920's. In 1932, pioneers from South Africa were ordered to leave the country and were arbitrarily told that no appeal could be made. But they appealed anyway. Charges that Watch Tower literature was seditious had to be dealt with in the courts. In the early 1940's, brothers spent time in jail because of distributing publications that explained the Bible. Not until 1966 were Jehovah's Witnesses given full legal recognition as a religious organization in Zimbabwe. For over 40 years, the spiritual harvesting work had been carried on under considerable difficulty, but during that time courageous workers had helped over 11,000 to become servants of Jehovah God.

Witnessing to Governors and Kings

Jesus knew that his disciples would encounter opposition in their ministry. He told them that they would be delivered up before "local courts," even before "governors and kings," and that this would be "for a witness to them and the nations." (Matt. 10:17, 18) Jehovah's Witnesses have experienced exactly what Jesus foretold, and in harmony with what he said, they have endeavored to use the opportunity to give a witness.

Some officials have allowed fear to hold them back from doing good to Christ's followers. (John 12:42, 43) Llewelyn Phillips saw evidence of this in 1948 when he had private interviews with a number of government officials in the Belgian Congo, with a view to bringing relief to persecuted Witnesses there. He explained the beliefs and activities of Jehovah's Witnesses to these men. But during the interview, the governor-general wistfully asked: "And if I help you, what will happen to me?" He knew that

With powerful Scriptural arguments, early Witnesses in Nigeria exposed the clergy and their false teachings

the Roman Catholic Church exercised great influence in that land.

However, the paramount chief of the Swazi nation, King Sobhuza II, was not too concerned about the opinion of the clergy. He had often spoken with Jehovah's Witnesses, had much of their literature, and was kindly disposed toward them. On "Good Friday" each year, he would invite the African clergymen to his royal kraal. He would let them talk, but he would also call on one of Jehovah's Witnesses to speak. In 1956 the Witness spoke about the doctrine of immortality of the soul and honorary titles of religious leaders. When he was finished, the paramount chief asked the clergymen: "Are these things said here by Jehovah's witnesses true or false? If false, state how." They could not refute them. On one occasion the paramount chief even burst out in laughter at the consternation of the clergy over what a Witness said.

The police were often the ones delegated to demand from the Witnesses reasons for what they were doing. From the congregation in Tangier, Morocco, Witnesses made regular trips to Ceuta, a seaport under Spanish control but on the Moroccan coast. Stopped by the police on one occasion in 1967, the Witnesses were interrogated for two hours, during which time an excellent witness was given. At one point, two police inspectors asked whether the Witnesses believed in the "Virgin Mary." When told that the Gospel accounts show that Mary had other children after the virgin birth of Jesus, and that these were Jesus' half brothers and sisters, the officers let out a gasp of surprise and said that such a thing could never be found in the Bible. When shown John 7:3-5, one of the officers looked at it at length without saying a word; so the other said: "Give me that Bible. *I'll* explain the text!" The first officer replied: "Don't bother. This text is too clear." Many other questions were asked and answered in a relaxed atmosphere. After that, there was very little interference from the authorities as the Witnesses preached in that area.

Men prominent in government have become well acquainted with Jehovah's Witnesses and their ministry. Some of them appreciate that the work done by the Witnesses is truly beneficial for the people. Late in 1959,

Mary Nisbet (front center), flanked by her sons Robert and George, who pioneered in East Africa in the 1930's, and (in the rear) her son William and his wife Muriel, who served in East Africa from 1956 to 1973

when preparations were being made for the independence of Nigeria, the governor-general, Dr. Nnamdi Azikiwe, requested that W. R. Brown be present as a representative of Jehovah's Witnesses. He said to his Council of Ministers: "If all the religious denominations were like Jehovah's witnesses, we would have no murders, burglaries, delinquencies, prisoners and atomic bombs. Doors would not be locked day in and day out."

A truly great spiritual harvest was being gathered in Africa. By 1975, there were 312,754 Witnesses preaching the good news in 44 countries on the African continent. In nine of those countries, there were fewer than 50 who were taking a stand for Bible truth and sharing in the evangelizing work. But the Witnesses view the life of each one as precious. In 19 of these lands, those who shared in the house-to-house ministry as Jehovah's Witnesses numbered in the thousands. Dramatic increases were reported in some areas. In Angola, for example, from 1970 to 1975, the number of Witnesses increased from 355 to 3,055. In Nigeria, in 1975, there were 112,164 of Jehovah's Witnesses. These were not merely people who enjoyed reading Watch Tower literature, nor were they merely those who occasionally might attend meetings at a Kingdom Hall. All of them were active proclaimers of God's Kingdom.

The Orient Produces Praisers of Jehovah

As was true in many other places, the activity of Jehovah's Witnesses in the Philippines expanded rapidly following World War II. As soon as possible after his release from prison on March 13, 1945, Joseph Dos Santos got in touch with the Watch Tower Society's office in New York. He wanted to obtain all the Bible study material and organization instructions that the brothers in the Philippines had missed during the war. Then he visited congregations personally to unify and strengthen them. That

At a convention in the Philippines in 1945, instructions were given on how to teach by means of home Bible studies

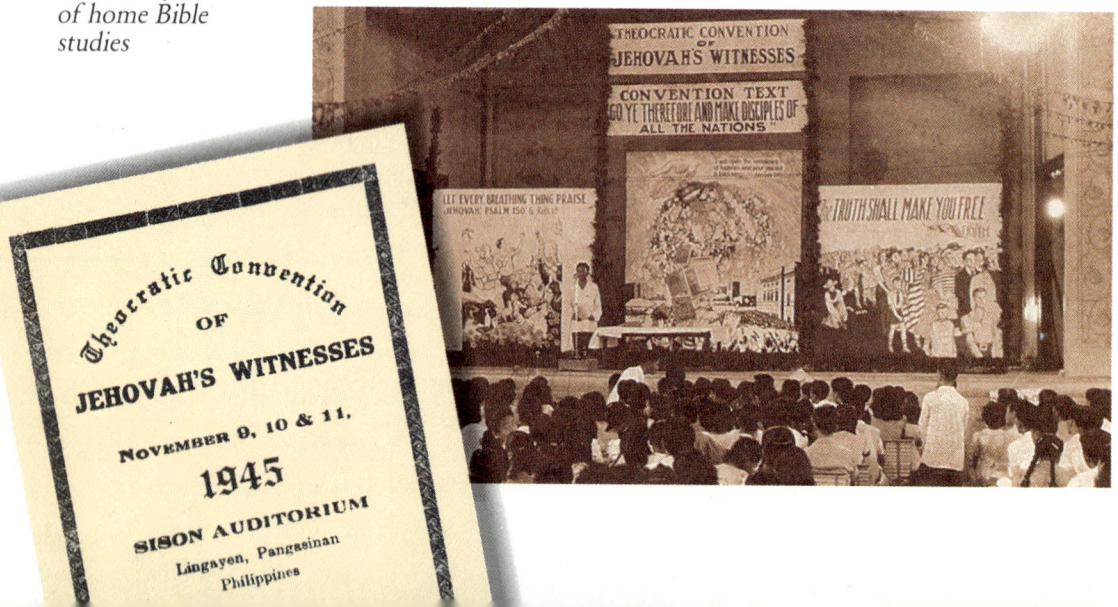

Gilead-trained missionaries, such as Stanley Jones (left) and Harold King (right), served here from 1947 to 1958, along with families of zealous local Witnesses

From Chefoo, thousands of letters, tracts, and books were sent out between 1891 and 1900

C. T. Russell spoke in Shanghai and visited 15 cities and villages, 1912

Colporteurs distributed much literature up and down the China coast, with trips to the interior, 1912-18

Japanese colporteurs served here, 1930-31

Pioneers from Australia and Europe witnessed in Shanghai, Peking, Tientsin, Tsingtao, Pei-tai-ho, Chefoo, Weihaiwei, Canton, Swatow, Amoy, Foochow, Hankow, and Nanking during the 1930's and 1940's. Others came in over the Burma Road and witnessed in Pao-shan, Chungking, Ch'eng-tu. Local pioneers served in Shensi and Ningpo

Radio broadcasts were made in Chinese from Shanghai, Peking, and Tientsin during the 1930's; as a result, letters requesting literature came from many parts of China

Much effort was put forth to reach the people of China with the good news of Jehovah's Kingdom

same year a national convention was held in Lingayen, Pangasinan, where instructions were given on how to teach truth-hungry people by means of home Bible studies. The following years saw a concerted effort to translate and publish more material in the local languages—Tagalog, Iloko, and Cebuano. The foundation was being laid for expansion, and it came quickly.

Within a decade after the war ended, the number of Witnesses in the Philippines increased from about 2,000 to more than 24,000. In another 20 years, there were well over 78,000 praisers of Jehovah there.

Among the first countries of the Orient to which missionaries trained at Gilead School were sent was China. Harold King and Stanley Jones arrived in Shanghai in 1947; Lew Ti Himm, in 1949. The three German pioneers who had begun work there in 1939 were on hand to greet them. This was a land where the majority of people were Buddhists and did not quickly respond to discussion of the Bible. Inside their homes were shrines and altars. With mirrors over doorways, they tried to frighten away evil spirits. Red tags with 'good luck' sayings and fearsome pictures of Buddhist gods adorned gateways. But those were times of great change in China. Under Communist rule everyone was required to study 'the thoughts of Mao Tse-tung.' After their secular work, they were to attend lengthy sessions at which Communism was expounded. In the midst of all of this, our brothers kept busy preaching the good news of God's Kingdom.

Many of those who were willing to study with Jehovah's Witnesses had previously had some contact with the Bible through the churches of Christendom. That was true of Nancy Yuen, a church worker and housewife who was grateful for what the Witnesses showed her in the Bible. Soon she was sharing zealously in the house-to-house work and conducting Bible studies herself. Others to whom they preached were of typical Chinese and Buddhist background and had no previous knowledge of the Bible. In 1956 a peak of 57 publishers was reached. However, that same year, after being arrested six times for preaching, Nancy Yuen was kept in prison. Others were either arrested or forced to leave the country. Stanley Jones and Harold King were placed under arrest on October 14, 1958. Before being brought to trial, they were detained for two years. During that time they were interrogated constantly. When finally taken to court in 1960, they were sentenced to long prison terms. Thus, in October 1958 the public activity of Jehovah's Witnesses in China was forcibly brought to a halt. But their preaching never completely stopped. Even in prison and in labor camps, there were ways to witness. In the future would more be done in this vast country? This would be known in due time.

Don and Mabel Haslett, the first postwar missionaries in Japan, engaging in street witnessing

Meanwhile, what was taking place in Japan? Only about a hundred of Jehovah's Witnesses had been preaching there before the second world war. When faced with brutal repressive measures during the war years, many of these compromised. Although a few maintained their integrity, organized public preaching came to a halt. However, the proclaiming of Jehovah's Kingdom was given a new start in that part of the world when Don Haslett, a Gilead-trained missionary, arrived in Tokyo in January 1949. Two months later, his wife, Mabel, was able to join him there. This was a field where many people were hungry for the truth. The emperor had renounced his claim to godship. Shinto, Buddhism, Catholicism, and *Kyodan* (made up of various Protestant groups in Japan) had all lost face with the people because of going along with Japan's war effort, which had ended in defeat.

By the end of 1949, 13 missionaries from Gilead School

were busy in Japan. More followed—upwards of 160 in all. There was very little literature with which to work. Some of the missionaries had spoken old-style Japanese in Hawaii, but they had to learn the up-to-date language. The others had learned a few basics but had to resort frequently to their Japanese-English dictionaries until they became better acquainted with their new language. Before long, the Ishii and Miura families, who had not forsaken their faith during the war years, made contact with the organization and once again began to participate in the public ministry.

Missionary homes were progressively opened in Kobe, Nagoya, Osaka, Yokohama, Kyoto, and Sendai. From 1949 to 1957, the main endeavor was to establish the Kingdom work in the large cities on Japan's main island. Then the workers began to move out to other cities. The field was vast. It was obvious that if all Japan was to receive a thorough witness, many pioneer ministers would be needed. This was stressed, many volunteered, and there was marvelous response to the united efforts of these hardworking ministers! The first decade yielded 1,390 praisers of Jehovah. By the mid-1970's, there were 33,480 zealous praisers of Jehovah spread throughout Japan. And the pace of ingathering was speeding up.

For 25 years Lloyd Barry (right) served in Japan, first as a missionary and then as branch overseer

In the same year that Don Haslett arrived in Japan, 1949, the Kingdom work in the Republic of Korea was also given great impetus. Korea had been under Japanese domination during the world war, and the Witnesses had been ruthlessly persecuted. Although a small group met together for study after the war, there was no contact with the international organization until after Choi Young-won saw a report about Jehovah's Witnesses in 1948 in the American Army newspaper *Stars and Stripes*. The next year a congregation of 12 publishers was formed in Seoul. Later that year Don and Earlene Steele, the first missionaries from Gilead School, arrived. Seven months later, six more missionaries followed.

They were having excellent results—an average of 20 Bible studies each and meeting attendance of as many as 336. Then the Korean War broke out. Hardly more than three months after that last group of missionaries had arrived, they were all evacuated to Japan. It was more than a year before Don Steele was able to return to Seoul, and another year before Earlene could join him. In the meantime the Korean brothers had remained firm and had been zealous in preaching, in spite of the fact that homes had been lost and many of them were refugees. But now, with the fighting past, attention was given

Don and Earlene Steele, the first of many missionaries who served in the Republic of Korea

In years past, mobs sometimes chased Fred Metcalfe when he tried to preach from the Bible in Ireland; but later when people stopped to listen, thousands became Jehovah's Witnesses

to providing more literature in Korean. Conventions and an influx of more missionaries gave stimulus to the work. By 1975, there were 32,693 of Jehovah's Witnesses in the Republic of Korea—almost as many as in Japan—and there was potential for excellent growth, because over 32,000 home Bible studies were being conducted.

What Was the Situation in Europe?

The end of World War II in Europe did not result in full freedom for Jehovah's Witnesses there to carry on their work of Bible education without opposition. In some places officials respected them because of their firm stand during the war. But elsewhere powerful tides of nationalism and religious animosity led to further persecution.

Among the Witnesses in Belgium were some who had come from Germany to share in preaching the good news. Because they would not support the Nazi regime, the Gestapo had tracked them down like wild beasts. But now Belgian officials accused some of these same Witnesses of being Nazis and had them imprisoned and then deported. Despite all of this, the number of Witnesses sharing in the field ministry in Belgium more than tripled within five years after the war.

What was behind much of the persecution? The Roman Catholic Church. Wherever it had the power to do so, it was unrelenting in its war to stamp out Jehovah's Witnesses.

Knowing that many people in the West feared Communism, the Catholic clergy in the Irish city of Cork, in 1948, whipped up opposition to Jehovah's Witnesses by constantly referring to them as "Communist devils." As a result, when Fred Metcalfe was sharing in the field ministry, he was confronted by a mob that punched and kicked him and scattered his Bible literature on the street. Happily, a policeman came along just then and dispersed the mobsters. In the face of all of this, the Witnesses persevered. Not all the Irish people agreed with the violence. Later, even some who shared in it wished that they had not. Most of the Catholic people in Ireland had never seen a Bible. But, with loving patience, some of them were helped to take hold of the truth that sets men free.—John 8:32.

Though the Witnesses in Italy numbered only about a hundred in 1946, three years later they had 64 *congregations*—small but hardworking. The clergy were worried. Unable to refute the Bible truths preached by Jehovah's Witnesses, the Catholic clergy pressured government authorities to try to get rid of them. Thus, in 1949, Witness missionaries were ordered out of the country.

Repeatedly the Roman Catholic clergy sought to disrupt or prevent assemblies of the Witnesses in Italy. They used hecklers to try to disrupt an assembly in Sulmona in 1948. In Milan they put pressure on the chief of police to cancel the permit for a convention at Teatro dell'Arte in 1950. Again, in 1951, they got the police to cancel permission for an assembly in Cerignola. But in 1957, when the police ordered a Witness convention in Milan to be closed down, the Italian press objected, and questions were raised in parliament. The Rome weekly *Il Mondo,* of July 30, 1957, did not hesitate to state that the action had been taken "to satisfy the archbishop," Giovanni Battista Montini, who later became Pope Paul VI. It was well-known that for centuries the Catholic Church had forbidden circulation of the Bible in languages used by the general public. But Jehovah's Witnesses persisted in letting sincere Catholics see for themselves what the Bible says. The contrast between the Bible and church dogma was obvious. Despite the intense efforts of the Catholic Church to prevent it, thousands were leaving the church, and by 1975 there were 51,248

In spite of clergy opposition, thousands flocked to Witness conventions in Italy (Rome, 1969)

During bans, congregation meetings were often held in the countryside, picnic-style, as here in Portugal

of Jehovah's Witnesses in Italy. All of these were active evangelizers, and their numbers were multiplying rapidly.

In Catholic Spain when organized activity of Jehovah's Witnesses was gradually revived after 1946, it came as no surprise that the clergy there also pressured secular officials to try to stop them. Congregation meetings of Jehovah's Witnesses were disrupted. Missionaries were forced out of the country. Witnesses were arrested for simply having the Bible or Bible literature in their possession. They were often detained in filthy jails up to three days, then released—only to be arrested, interrogated, and put in prison again. Many served sentences of a month or more. The priests urged secular authorities to track down anyone who studied the Bible with Jehovah's Witnesses. Even after the Religious Liberty Law was passed in 1967, changes came slowly. Nevertheless, by the time Jehovah's Witnesses were finally given legal recognition in 1970, there were already over 11,000 of them in Spain. And five years later, they numbered upwards of 30,000, each one an active evangelizer.

And what about Portugal? Here too, missionaries were ordered out of the country. Egged on by the Catholic clergy, the police searched the homes of Jehovah's Witnesses, confiscated their literature, and disrupted their meetings. In January 1963 the commander of the Public Security Police of Caldas da Rainha even issued a written order forbidding them to 'exercise their activities of Bible reading.' But the Witnesses did not forsake their service to God. There were over 13,000 of them by the time they gained legal recognition in Portugal in 1974.

In other parts of Europe, secular authorities raised obstacles to the preaching of the good news by classifying the distribution of Bible literature as a commercial activity, subject to laws on commerce. In a number of the cantons of Switzerland, peddling ordinances were applied to the distribution of literature by Jehovah's Witnesses on a voluntary contribution. As the Witnesses carried on their activity, they were subjected to numerous arrests and court actions. When the cases came to trial, however, some courts, including the High Court of the canton of Vaud, in 1953, ruled that the activity of Jehovah's Witnesses could not properly be viewed as peddling. Meanwhile, in Denmark an effort was made to limit the hours during which Witnesses could offer literature, restricting their activity to times authorized by law for the operation of commercial shops. This too had to be fought in the courts. Despite the obstacles, Jehovah's Witnesses continued to proclaim God's Kingdom as the only hope for mankind.

Another issue affecting Jehovah's Witnesses in Europe, as well as in other parts of the earth, was Christian neutrality. Because their Christian consciences would not permit them to get involved in conflicts between factions of the world, they were sentenced to prison in one country after another. (Isa. 2:2-4) This took young men away from their regular house-to-house ministry. But one beneficial result was an intensive witness to lawyers, judges, military officers, and prison guards. Even in prison the Witnesses found some way to preach. Although the treatment in some prisons was brutal, Witnesses confined at the Santa Catalina prison in Cádiz, Spain, were able to use some of their time to witness through the mail. And in Sweden much publicity was given to the way cases involving the neutrality of Jehovah's Witnesses were handled. Thus, in many ways people were made aware of the fact that Jehovah does have witnesses on the earth and that they adhere firmly to Bible principles.

There was something else that kept the Witnesses before the public eye. It also had a powerful, invigorating effect on their evangelizing work.

Conventions Contributed to the Witness

When Jehovah's Witnesses held an international convention in Paris, France, in 1955, television news reports gave the entire nation glimpses of what took place. In 1969 another convention was held near Paris, and it was evident that the ministry of the Witnesses had been fruitful. Those baptized at the convention numbered 3,619, or about 10 percent of the average attendance. Regarding this, the popular Paris evening newspaper *France-Soir* of August 6, 1969, said: "What worries the clergy of other religions is not the means of spectacular distribution of publications used by Jehovah's witnesses, but, rather, their making converts. Each of Jehovah's witnesses has the obligation to witness or proclaim his faith by using the Bible from house to house."

During a three-week period that same summer of 1969, four other large international conventions were held in Europe—in London,

Witnesses in prison in Cádiz, Spain, continued to preach by writing letters

Large conventions gave the public opportunity to see and hear for themselves what sort of people the Witnesses are

Paris, France (1955)

Nuremberg, Germany (1955)

Copenhagen, Rome, and Nuremberg. The Nuremberg convention was attended by 150,645 from 78 countries. Besides airplanes and ships, some 20,000 cars, 250 buses, and 40 special trains were needed to transport the delegates to that convention.

The conventions not only fortified and equipped Jehovah's Witnesses for their ministry but also gave the public opportunity to see for themselves what sort of people Jehovah's Witnesses are. When an international convention was scheduled for Dublin, Ireland, in 1965, intense religious pressure was used to force cancellation of the arrangements. But the convention was held, and many householders in Dublin provided accommodations for delegates. With what result? "We have not been told the truth about you," commented some of the landladies after the convention. "The priests lied to us, but now that we know you, we will always be happy to have you again."

When People Speak Another Language

In recent decades Jehovah's Witnesses in Europe have found that communicating with people of other nationalities has presented a special challenge. Large numbers have moved from one country to another to take advantage of employment opportunities. Some European cities have become the seats of major international institutions, with personnel who do not all speak the local language.

Of course, multilingual territory has been a fact of life for centuries in some places. In India, for example, there are 14 principal languages and perhaps 1,000 minor languages and dialects. Papua New Guinea claims more than 700 languages. But it was particularly during the 1960's and 1970's that the Witnesses in Luxembourg found that their territory had become one that included people from over 30 different nations—and after that at least another 70 nationalities arrived. Sweden reports that it has changed from a country with one language used by nearly everyone to a society that speaks 100 different tongues. How have Jehovah's Witnesses dealt with this?

At first, they often simply endeavored to find out the language of the householder and then tried to obtain some literature that he could read. In Denmark, tape recordings were made in order to let sincere Turkish people hear the message in their own language. Switzerland had a large contingent of guest workers from Italy and Spain. The experience of Rudolf Wiederkehr in helping some of these is typical of how things started. He tried to witness to an Italian man, but neither of them knew much of the other's language. What could be done? Our brother left an Italian *Watchtower* with him. Despite the language problem, Brother Wiederkehr returned. A Bible study was started with the man, his wife, and their 12-year-old son. Brother Wiederkehr's study book was in German, but he supplied Italian copies for the family. Where words were lacking, gestures were used. Sometimes the young boy, who was learning German in school, served as interpreter. That entire family embraced the truth and quickly began to share it with others.

But literally millions of workers from Greece, Italy, Portugal, Spain, Turkey, and Yugoslavia were moving into Germany and other countries. Spiritual help could be given to them more effectively in their own languages. Soon some of the local Witnesses began to learn the languages of the guest workers. In Germany, language classes in Turkish were even arranged by the branch office. Witnesses in other countries who knew the needed language were invited to move to places where there was a special need for help.

Some of the workers from abroad had never met Jehovah's Witnesses before and truly had a hunger for spiritual things. They were grateful for the effort being put forth to help them. Many foreign-language congregations were formed. In time, some of these guest workers returned to their homelands to carry on the ministry in areas that previously had not had a thorough witness regarding God's Kingdom.

Where words were lacking, gestures were used

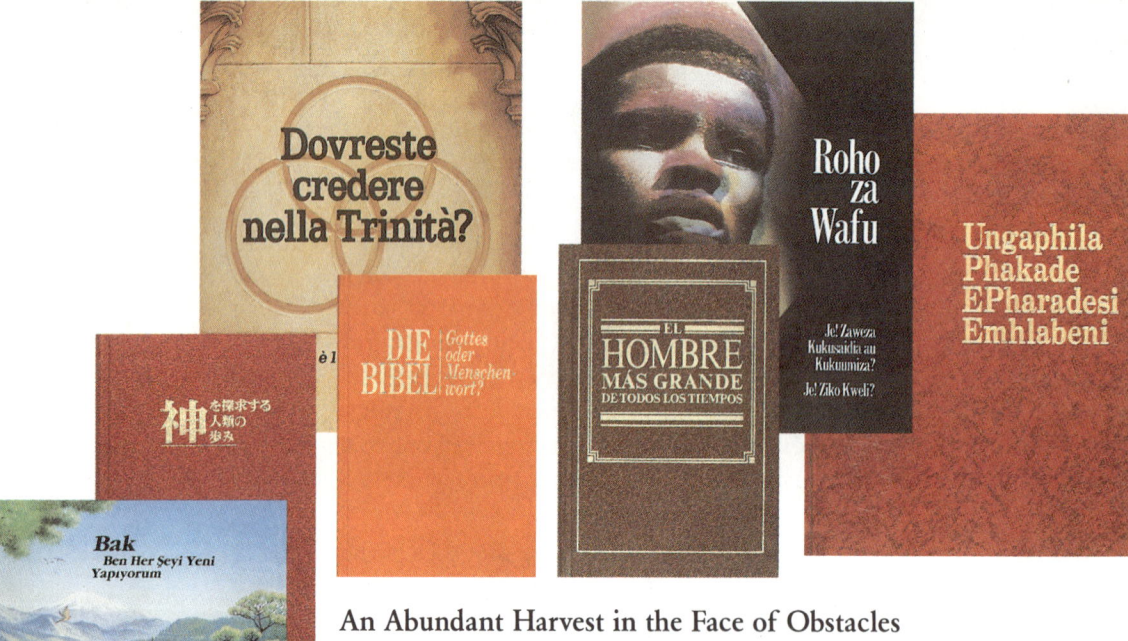

To reach everyone in Luxembourg with the good news, Jehovah's Witnesses have had to use literature in at least a hundred languages

An Abundant Harvest in the Face of Obstacles

Jehovah's Witnesses employ the same methods of preaching throughout the earth. In North America they have been actively evangelizing for over a century. It is not surprising, then, that there has been an abundant spiritual harvest there. By 1975, there were 624,097 active Witnesses of Jehovah within the U.S. mainland and Canada. However, this was not because their preaching in North America was being done without opposition.

Although the Canadian government had lifted its ban on Jehovah's Witnesses and their legal corporations by 1945, benefits from that decision were not immediately felt in the province of Quebec. In September 1945, Catholic mobs attacked Jehovah's Witnesses in Châteauguay and Lachine. Witnesses were arrested and charged with sedition because literature they distributed criticized the Roman Catholic Church. Others were put into jail because they distributed Bible literature that had not been approved by the chief of police. By 1947, there were 1,700 cases against the Witnesses pending in the courts of Quebec.

While test cases were being pushed through the courts, Witnesses were instructed to preach the gospel by word of mouth, using just the Bible—the Catholic *Douay Version* where possible. Full-time ministers from other parts of Canada volunteered to learn French and moved to Quebec in order to share in the spread of true worship there.

Many sincere Catholic people invited the Witnesses into their homes and asked questions, though they often said: 'I'm a Roman Catholic and will never change.' But when they saw for themselves what the Bible says, tens of thousands of them, because of love for the truth and a desire to please God, did change.

In the United States too, it was necessary to argue before the courts to establish the right of Jehovah's Witnesses to preach publicly and from house to house. From 1937 to 1953, there were 59 such cases involving the Witnesses that were taken all the way up to the Supreme Court in Washington, D.C.

Attention to Unassigned Territories

The objective of Jehovah's Witnesses is not merely to do *something* in the preaching of the good news but to reach *everyone possible* with the Kingdom message. To that end, the Governing Body of Jehovah's Witnesses has assigned each branch office responsibility for a specific part of the world field. As congregations are formed within the branch territory, each congregation is given a part of that territory in which to preach. The congregation then divides up the area into sections that can be assigned to groups and to individual ministers in the congregation. These endeavor to reach each household on a regular basis. But what about areas not yet assigned to congregations?

In 1951 a tabulation was made of all the counties in the United States to determine which were not receiving regular visits from Jehovah's Witnesses. At that time, nearly 50 percent were not being worked or were being only partially covered. Arrangements were made for Witnesses to carry on their ministry in these areas during the summer months or at other appropriate times, with a view to developing congregations. When people were not at home, a printed message was sometimes left, along with a piece of Bible literature. Bible studies were conducted by mail. Later, special pioneers were sent to such territories to follow up on interest located.

This activity was not limited to the 1950's. Around the world, in lands where the principal cities are receiving a witness but unassigned territory exists, an earnest effort continues to be made to reach the people who are not contacted regularly. In Alaska in the 1970's, about 20 percent of the population lived in remote villages. Many of these people could best be found in the winter when fishing nearly comes to a standstill. But that is the time when severe icing and whiteouts make flying hazardous. Nevertheless, the Eskimo, Indian, and Aleut population needed the opportunity to learn of the provision for everlasting life under God's Kingdom. To reach them, a group of 11 Witnesses using small planes flew to some 200 villages scattered over an area of 326,000 square miles during a two-year period. All of this was financed by voluntary contributions provided by local Witnesses.

In addition to such preaching expeditions, mature Witnesses have been encouraged to consider actually moving into areas within their own

The objective? Reach everyone possible with the Kingdom message

country where the need for Kingdom proclaimers is greater. Thousands have responded. Among those in the United States who have done so are Eugene and Delia Shuster, who left Illinois in 1958 to serve in Hope, Arkansas. They have stayed for over three decades to locate interested persons, organize them into a congregation, and help them to grow to Christian maturity.

At the encouragement of their circuit overseer, in 1957, Alexander B. Green and his wife left Dayton, Ohio, to serve in Mississippi. First they were assigned to Jackson and two years later to Clarksdale. In time, Brother Green served in five other locations. All of these had small congregations that were in need of assistance. He supported himself by doing janitorial work, gardening, furniture refinishing, automobile repair work, and so forth. But his principal efforts were directed toward preaching the good news. He helped the local Witnesses to grow spiritually, worked with them to reach the people in their territory, and often assisted them in building a Kingdom Hall before he moved on.

In 1967, when Gerald Cain became a Witness in the western United States, he and his family strongly felt the urgency of the evangelizing work. Even before any of them were baptized, they were making arrangements to serve where the need was greater. For four years they worked with the congregation in Needles, California. It had responsibility for a territory that included parts of three states in the western United States. When health considerations required a move, they again selected a place where there was special need for help, and they converted part of their home there into a Kingdom Hall. Other moves have followed, but always a major consideration has been getting located in a place where they could be of the greatest help in witnessing.

As the number of congregations has multiplied, in some areas the need for qualified elders has been keenly felt. To meet this need, thousands of elders have volunteered to commute regularly (and at their own expense) to congregations outside their community. They make the trip three, four, five, or more times a week—to share in the meetings of the congregation and in the field ministry and also to shepherd the flock. This has been done not only in the United States but in El Salvador, Japan, the Netherlands, Spain, and many other lands. In some instances the elders and their families have moved, in order to fill this need.

What have been the results? Consider one country. Back in 1951, when arrangements to work unassigned territory were first announced, there were about 3,000 congregations in the United States, with an average of 45 publishers per congregation. By 1975, there were 7,117 congregations, and the average number of active Witnesses associated with each congregation had risen to nearly 80.

The witness given to Jehovah's name and Kingdom from 1945 to 1975 was far greater than all that had been accomplished up till then.

The number of Witnesses had grown from 156,299 in 1945 to 2,179,256 around the globe in 1975. Each one of these had a personal share in publicly preaching about the Kingdom of God.

In 1975, Jehovah's Witnesses were busy in 212 lands (counted according to the way the map was divided in the early 1990's). Within the U.S. mainland and Canada, 624,097 of them were carrying out their ministry. In Europe, outside what was then the Soviet Union, there were another 614,826. Africa was hearing the Bible's message of truth from the 312,754 Witnesses who were sharing in the work there. Mexico, Central America, and South America were being served by 311,641 Witnesses; Asia, by 161,598; Australia and the many islands earth wide, by 131,707.

During the 30 years down to 1975, Jehovah's Witnesses devoted 4,635,265,939 hours to public preaching and teaching. They also placed 3,914,971,158 books, booklets, and magazines with interested people to help them to appreciate how they could benefit from Jehovah's loving purpose. In harmony with Jesus' command to make disciples, they made 1,788,147,329 return visits on interested persons, and in 1975 they were conducting an average of 1,411,256 free home Bible studies with individuals and families.

By 1975 the preaching of the good news had actually reached into 225 lands. In more than 80 lands that the good news had reached by 1945 but where there were no congregations that year, congregations of zealous Witnesses were thriving by 1975. Among these places were the Republic of Korea with 470 congregations, Spain with 513, Zaire with 526, Japan with 787, and Italy with 1,031.

During the period from 1945 to 1975, the vast majority of persons who became Jehovah's Witnesses did not profess to be anointed with God's spirit with heavenly life in view. In the spring of 1935, the number who partook of the emblems at the Lord's Evening Meal totaled fully 93 percent of the those who were sharing in the field ministry. (Later in that same year, the "great multitude" of Revelation 7:9 was identified as being made up of persons who would live forever on earth.) By 1945 the number of Witnesses who looked forward to life on a paradise earth had increased to the point that they made up 86 percent of those who shared in preaching the good news. By 1975 those who professed to be spirit-anointed Christians were less than one half of 1 percent of the total worldwide organization of Jehovah's Witnesses. Though scattered in about 115 lands at that time, these anointed ones continued to serve as a unified body under Jesus Christ.

PART 5

In 1975 important decisions were made regarding the way that the activity of Jehovah's Witnesses would be supervised from their world headquarters. They did not then know what fields might yet open up for an extensive witness before the end of the present world system or how much preaching would still be done in lands where they had openly preached for many years. But they wanted to make the best possible use of every opportunity. Pages 502 to 520 relate some of the exciting developments.

THERE have been big changes in South America. It was not many years ago that Jehovah's Witnesses in Ecuador faced Catholic mobs, Catholic priests in Mexico ruled as virtual kings in many villages, and government bans were imposed on Jehovah's Witnesses in Argentina and Brazil. But circumstances have changed significantly. Now many of those who were taught to fear or to hate the Witnesses are themselves Jehovah's Witnesses. Others gladly listen when the Witnesses call on them to share the Bible's message of peace. Jehovah's Witnesses are well-known and widely respected.

Large conventions and Christian conduct of the delegates attracted attention

The size of their conventions and the Christian conduct of those attending have attracted attention. Two of such conventions, held simultaneously in São Paulo and Rio de Janeiro, Brazil, in 1985, had a peak attendance of 249,351. Later, 23 additional conventions, held to accommodate interested persons in the rest of Brazil, raised the total attendance to 389,387. Results of the work Jehovah's Witnesses in Brazil had been doing as teachers of God's Word were clearly in evidence when 4,825 persons symbolized their dedication to Jehovah by water immersion at that round of conventions. Just five years later, in 1990, it was necessary to hold 110 conventions throughout Brazil to accommodate the 548,517 who attended. This time 13,448 presented themselves for water immersion. Across the country hundreds of thousands of individuals and families were welcoming Jehovah's Witnesses to instruct them in God's Word.

And what about Argentina? After decades of government restrictions, Jehovah's Witnesses there were again able to assemble freely in 1985. What a joy it was for 97,167 to be present at their first series of conventions! Under the heading "A Kingdom That Is Growing—That of Jehovah's Witnesses," the local news publication *Ahora* marveled at the orderliness of the convention crowd in Buenos Aires, their total lack of racial and social prejudice, their peaceableness, and the love they manifested. Then it concluded: "Whether or not we share their ideas and doctrines, this entire multitude deserves our greatest respect." However, many Argentines went beyond that. They began to study the Bible with Jehovah's Witnesses, and they attended Kingdom Hall meetings to observe how the Witnesses apply Bible principles in their lives. Then these observers made a decision. During the next seven years, tens of thousands of them dedicated their lives to Jehovah, and the number of Witnesses in Argentina increased by 71 percent!

Response to the good news of God's Kingdom was even more extraordinary in Mexico. In years past, Jehovah's Witnesses there had been frequently assaulted by mobs instigated by priests. But the fact that the Witnesses did not retaliate or seek revenge greatly impressed honesthearted persons. (Rom. 12:17-19) They also observed that the Witnesses based all their beliefs on the Bible, God's inspired Word, instead of on human traditions. (Matt. 15:7-9; 2 Tim. 3:16, 17) They could see that the Witnesses had faith that truly sustained them in the face of adversity. More and more families welcomed Jehovah's Witnesses when they offered to conduct free home Bible studies with them. In fact, during 1992, 12 percent of the Bible studies being conducted by the Witnesses worldwide were in Mexico, and a considerable number of these were with large families. As a result, the number of Jehovah's Witnesses in Mexico—not merely those who were attending their meetings but the ones who were active public proclaimers of God's Kingdom—soared from 80,481 in 1975 to 354,023 in 1992!

In Europe too, extraordinary events contributed to the spread of the Kingdom message.

Amazing Developments in Poland

Although the work of Jehovah's Witnesses had been banned in Poland from 1939 to 1945 (during the period of Nazi and Soviet domination) and again starting in July 1950 (under Soviet control), Jehovah's Witnesses had not ceased preaching there. Though they numbered only 1,039 in 1939, in 1950 there were 18,116 Kingdom proclaimers, and these continued to be zealous (though cautious) evangelizers. (Matt. 10:16) As for assemblies, however, these had been held out of public view—in the countryside, in barns, in forests. But, beginning in 1982, the Polish government permitted them to hold one-day assemblies of modest size in rented facilities.

Then, in 1985 the largest stadiums in Poland were made available to Jehovah's

Morumbi Stadium, in São Paulo, Brazil (shown below), and Maracanã Stadium, in Rio de Janeiro, were needed simultaneously in 1985 to accommodate crowds for the convention of Jehovah's Witnesses

Witnesses for four large conventions during the month of August. When a delegate from Austria arrived by airplane, he was surprised to hear an announcement over the loudspeaker welcoming Jehovah's Witnesses to Poland for their convention. Aware of the change in government attitude that this indicated, an elderly Polish Witness who was there to welcome the visitor could not help giving way to tears of joy. In attendance at these conventions were 94,134 delegates, including groups from 16 lands. Did the general public know what was taking place? Yes, indeed! During and after these conventions, they read reports in their major newspapers, saw the convention crowds on television, and heard portions of the program on national radio. Many of them liked what they saw and heard.

Plans for even larger conventions in Poland were under way when, on May 12, 1989, the government granted legal recognition to Jehovah's Witnesses as a religious association. Within three months, three international conventions were in session—in Chorzów, Poznan, and Warsaw—with a combined attendance of 166,518. Amazingly, thousands of Witnesses from what were then the Soviet Union (U.S.S.R.) and Czechoslovakia were able to secure needed permission to travel and were in attendance. Was the disciple-making work of Jehovah's Witnesses yielding results in these lands where atheism had been strongly advocated by the State for decades? The answer was evident when 6,093, including many youths, presented themselves for water immersion at those conventions.

Some of the baptism candidates in Chorzów, Poland, in 1989

The public could not help but see that the Witnesses were different —in a very wholesome way. In the public press, they read statements like the following: "Those who worship Jehovah God—as they themselves say—greatly value their gatherings, which are certainly a manifestation of unity among them. . . . As regards orderliness, peacefulness, and cleanliness, convention participants are examples to imitate." (*Życie Warszawy*) Some of the Polish people decided to do more than just observe the conventioners. They wanted Jehovah's Witnesses to study the Bible with them. As a result of such instruction in God's Word, the number of Jehovah's Witnesses in Poland increased from 72,887 in 1985 to 107,876 in 1992; and during that latter year, they devoted upwards of 16,800,000 hours to telling yet others about the marvelous hope set out in the Scriptures.

"As regards orderliness, peacefulness, and cleanliness, convention participants are examples to imitate"

However, it was not only in Poland that exciting changes were taking place.

More of Eastern Europe Opens Its Doors

Hungary granted legal status to Jehovah's Witnesses in 1989. What was then the German Democratic Republic (GDR) removed its 40-year ban on the Witnesses in 1990, just four months after demolition of the Berlin Wall began. The following month the Christian Association of Jehovah's Witnesses in Romania was officially recognized by the new Romanian government. In 1991 the Ministry of Justice in Moscow declared that the Charter of the "Religious Organization of Jehovah's Witnesses in the U.S.S.R." was officially registered. That same year legal recognition was granted to the work of Jehovah's Witnesses in Bulgaria. During 1992, Jehovah's Witnesses in Albania were granted legal status.

What did Jehovah's Witnesses do with the freedom granted them? A journalist asked Helmut Martin, coordinator of the work of Jehovah's Witnesses in the GDR: "Are you going to get involved in politics?" After all, that was what many of Christendom's clergy were doing. "No," replied Brother Martin, "Jesus gave his disciples a Scriptural assignment, and we see that as our main job."—Matt. 24:14; 28:19, 20.

Jehovah's Witnesses were certainly not just beginning to care for that responsibility in this part of the world. Although it had been necessary for them to carry out their activity under very difficult circumstances for many years, in most of these lands congregations (meeting in small groups) had been functioning, and witnessing had been done. But now a new opportunity was opening up. They could hold meetings to which they could freely invite the public. They could openly preach from house to house, without fear of being imprisoned. Here were lands with a combined population of more than 390,000,000, where there was much work

Some Historic Conventions in 1991

Prague, Czechoslovakia

Zagreb, Croatia (right)

Tallinn, Estonia (right)

Budapest, Hungary (above)

Baia-Mare, Romania (right)

Usolye-Sibirskoye, Russia (below)

Alma-Ata, Kazakhstan (above)

Kiev, Ukraine (left)

to be done. With a keen awareness that we live in the last days of the present world system of things, Jehovah's Witnesses acted quickly.

Even before legal recognition was granted, members of the Governing Body had visited a number of lands to see what could be done to help their Christian brothers. After bans were lifted, they traveled into more of these areas to help organize the work. Within a few years, they had personally met and spoken with Witnesses in Poland, Hungary, Romania, Czechoslovakia, Russia, Ukraine, Estonia, and Belarus.

Conventions were arranged to fortify Witnesses living in these lands and to thrust prominently before the public the message of God's Kingdom. Less than five months after the ban was lifted by what was then the GDR, such a convention was held at Berlin's Olympia Stadium. Witnesses from 64 other lands readily responded to an invitation to attend. They counted it a privilege to enjoy that occasion with Christian brothers and sisters who had for decades demonstrated loyalty to Jehovah in the face of intense persecution.

Both in 1990 and in 1991, other conventions were held throughout Eastern Europe. After four local assemblies had been held in Hungary in 1990, arrangements were made for an international gathering at the Népstadion in Budapest in 1991. In attendance were 40,601 from 35 countries. For the first time in more than 40 years, Jehovah's Witnesses were able to hold public conventions in Romania in 1990. A series of assemblies throughout the nation, and later two larger conventions, were held that year. There were eight more conventions in 1991, with an attendance of 34,808. In 1990, in what was then Yugoslavia, conventions were held in *each one* of the republics that made up the country. The following year, although the country was threatened by civil war, 14,684 of Jehovah's Witnesses enjoyed an international convention in Zagreb, the capital of Croatia. The police were astonished as they saw Croats, Montenegrins, Serbians, Slovenians, and others gathered in peace to listen to the program.

In what was then Czechoslovakia too, conventions were quickly arranged. A national convention in Prague in 1990 was attended by 23,876. Those who managed the stadium were so pleased with what they saw that they made available to the Witnesses the largest facilities in the country for their next convention. On that historic occasion, in 1991, there were 74,587 enthusiastic conventioners that filled the Strahov Stadium in Prague. Czech and Slovak delegates were delighted and enthusiastically applauded when announcement was made of the release of the complete *New World Translation of the Holy Scriptures* in their own languages, for use in the public ministry as well as in personal and congregational study.

It was also during 1991 that, for the first time in history, Jehovah's Witnesses were able to hold conventions openly in places that were then within the Soviet Union. After a convention in Tallinn, Estonia, there was one in Siberia. Four were held in major cities in Ukraine, and one in Kazakhstan. Attendance totaled 74,252. And as recent fruitage of the disciple-making work of Jehovah's Witnesses in these areas, 7,820 presented themselves for water immersion. This was no emotional decision made because they felt excited about the convention. The baptismal candidates had been carefully prepared in advance over a period of months—and in some cases, years.

From where did all these people come? It was obvious that the work of Jehovah's Witnesses was not just beginning in that part of the earth. Watch Tower publications had been mailed to an interested person in Russia as far back as 1887. The first president of the Watch Tower Society had

Historic conventions were held in places where Witnesses had for decades been under ban

himself visited Kishinev (now in Moldova) in 1891. Some Bible Students had gone into Russia to preach during the 1920's; but there had been strong official resistance, and the few groups that showed interest in the Bible's message were small. However, the situation changed during and after World War II. National borders were reshaped, and large segments of population were relocated. As a result, more than a thousand Ukrainian-speaking Witnesses from what had been eastern Poland found themselves within the Soviet Union. Other Witnesses who lived in Romania and Czechoslovakia found that the places where they lived had become part of the Soviet Union. In addition, Russians who had become Jehovah's Witnesses while in German concentration camps returned to their homeland, and they took with them the good news of God's Kingdom. By 1946, there were 4,797 Witnesses active in the Soviet Union. Many of these were moved from place to place by the government over the years. Some were consigned to prison camps. Wherever they went they witnessed. Their numbers grew. Even before the government granted them legal recognition, groups of them were active all the way from Lviv in the west to Vladivostok on the Soviet Union's eastern border, across the sea from Japan.

Many Now Willing to Listen

When the Witnesses held conventions in what was then the U.S.S.R. in 1991, the public had opportunity to take a closer look at them. How did they react? In Lviv, Ukraine, a police official told one of the conventioners: "You excel in teaching others what is good, you talk about God, and you do not engage in violence. We were discussing why we used to persecute you, and we concluded that we had not listened to you and had not known anything about you." But now many were listening, and Jehovah's Witnesses wanted to help them.

To carry on their work most effectively in these lands, Bible literature was needed. Great effort was put forth to provide it quickly. At Selters/Taunus, Germany, Jehovah's Witnesses nearly doubled their printing facilities. Although this expansion was not yet completed, about two weeks after the ban was lifted in what was then East Germany, 25 tons of literature was dispatched to this area from the printing plant at Selters. From the time of the lifting of bans in Eastern European lands until 1992, nearly 10,000 tons of literature in 14 main languages was shipped into these various countries from Germany, another 698 tons from Italy, and more from Finland.

Having been largely isolated for many years, the Witnesses in some countries also needed help with matters of congregation oversight and organization administration. To fill this urgent need, experienced elders —those who could speak the language of the country, where possible—

Thousands of tons of Bible literature was shipped into Eastern European lands were contacted in Germany, the United States, Canada, and elsewhere. Would they be willing to move to one of these lands in Eastern Europe to help fill the need? The response was gratifying indeed! Where advantageous, elders who had been trained at Gilead School or in the Ministerial Training School were also sent.

Then, in 1992 a remarkable international convention was held in St. Petersburg, the second-largest city in Russia. About 17,000 of the delegates were from 27 lands outside Russia. Extensive advertising of the convention was done. Among those who came were people who had never before heard of Jehovah's Witnesses. Attendance reached a peak of 46,214. Delegates were present from all parts of Russia, some from as far east as Sakhalin Island, near Japan. Large groups came from Ukraine, Moldova, and other countries that had formerly been part of the U.S.S.R. They brought good news with them. Reports showed that individual congregations in cities such as Kiev, Moscow, and St. Petersburg were having average attendances at their meetings that were double or more the number of Witnesses. Many people who wanted Jehovah's Witnesses to study the Bible with them had to be put on waiting lists. From Latvia, some 600 delegates had come and even more from Estonia. A congregation in St. Petersburg had over a hundred ready for baptism at the convention. Many of those who show interest are younger people or individuals who are well educated. Truly, a great work of spiritual harvest is under way in this vast territory that was long viewed by the world as a stronghold of atheism!

Qualified elders volunteered to move to lands where there was special need

Fields White for Harvesting

As attitudes regarding religious freedom changed, other countries, too, lifted restrictions on Jehovah's Witnesses or granted them legal recognition that had long been denied. In many of these places, an abundant spiritual harvest was ready to be gathered. Conditions were like those Jesus described to his disciples when he said: "Lift up your eyes and view the fields, that they are white for harvesting." (John 4:35) Consider just a few places where this was true in Africa.

A ban had been imposed on the house-to-house ministry of Jehovah's Witnesses in Zambia in 1969. As a result, Witnesses there devoted more time to conducting home Bible studies with interested ones. Others too began searching out the Witnesses so they could receive instruction. Gradually government restrictions were eased, and meeting attendance increased. In 1992, there were 365,828 who attended the Lord's Evening Meal in Zambia, 1 in every 23 of the population!

To the north of Zambia, in Zaire, thousands more wanted to learn what Jehovah's Witnesses teach about Christian living and about God's purpose for mankind. In 1990 when circumstances permitted the

Witnesses to reopen their Kingdom Halls, in some areas as many as 500 people flocked to their meetings. Within two years the 67,917 Witnesses in Zaire were conducting 141,859 home Bible studies with such persons.

The number of lands that were opening up was astounding. In 1990, Watch Tower missionaries who had been expelled from Benin 14 years earlier were now officially given the opportunity to return, and the door was opened for others to come. That same year the Minister of Justice in Cape Verde Republic signed a decree that approved the statutes of the local Association of Jehovah's Witnesses, thus giving them legal recognition. Then, in 1991 official relief came to Jehovah's Witnesses in Mozambique (where former rulers had severely persecuted them), Ghana (where their activity had been under an official freeze), and Ethiopia (where it had not been possible to preach openly or to hold assemblies for 34 years). Before year's end Niger and Congo had also granted them legal recognition. Early in 1992, bans were lifted or legal recognition was granted to Jehovah's Witnesses in Chad, Kenya, Rwanda, Togo, and Angola.

Here were fields ready for spiritual harvesting. In Angola, for example, the Witnesses quickly experienced a 31-percent increase; furthermore, the nearly 19,000 Kingdom proclaimers there were conducting almost 53,000 home Bible studies. To provide needed administrative help for this vast program of Bible education in Angola as well as in Mozambique (where many speak Portuguese), qualified elders from Portugal and Brazil were invited to move to Africa to carry on their ministry. Portuguese-speaking missionaries were assigned to the newly opened territory of Guinea-Bissau. And capable Witnesses in France and other lands were invited to help accomplish the urgent work of preaching and disciple making in Benin, Chad, and Togo, where French is spoken by many people.

Among those areas that have yielded especially abundant crops of praisers of Jehovah are the ones that formerly were Roman Catholic strongholds. In addition to Latin America, this proved to be true of France (where the 1992 report showed 119,674 Witness evangelizers), Spain (where there were 92,282), the Philippines (with 114,335), Ireland (with a Witness growth rate of 8 to 10 percent per year), and Portugal.

When 37,567 attended a Witness convention in Lisbon, Portugal, in 1978, the newsmagazine *Opção* stated: "For anyone who has been at Fátima during pilgrimage time, this in reality is very different. . . . Here [at the convention of Jehovah's Witnesses] the mysticism disappears, giving way to the holding of a meeting where believers in common accord discuss their problems, their faith and their spiritual outlook. Their conduct toward one another gives the distinctive mark of a caring relationship." During the following decade, the number of Witnesses in Portugal increased by nearly 70 percent.

International convention of Jehovah's Witnesses, in St. Petersburg, Russia, in 1992

A warm international spirit

From Russia

From Moldova

From Ukraine

Many younger folks were present

M. G. Henschel (left) discusses program with Stepan Kozhemba (center), with aid of interpreter

Foreign delegates brought Russian Bibles for use by Witnesses throughout Russia

And what about Italy? A severe shortage of candidates for the Catholic priesthood has forced some seminaries to close their doors. Numerous churches no longer have a parish priest. In many cases former church buildings now house shops or offices. Despite all of this, the church has fought hard to stop Jehovah's Witnesses. In years past they pressured officials to deport Witness missionaries and demanded that the police shut down their meetings. In some areas during the 1980's, parish priests had stickers put on the doors of everyone (including some who happened to be Jehovah's Witnesses), saying: "Do Not Knock. We Are Catholic." Newspapers carried the headlines: "Church's Cry of Alarm Against the Jehovah's Witnesses" and "'Holy War' Against Jehovah's Witnesses."

When the first-century Jewish priesthood tried to silence the apostles, Gamaliel, a teacher of the Law, wisely counseled: "If this scheme or this work is from men, it will be overthrown; but if it is from God, you will not be able to overthrow them." (Acts 5:38, 39) What was the outcome when the 20th-century Roman Catholic priesthood tried to silence Jehovah's Witnesses? The work of the 120 Witnesses in Italy in 1946 was not overthrown. Instead, by 1992, there were 194,013 active Witnesses associated with 2,462 congregations throughout the country. They have virtually filled Italy with their teaching of God's Word. Since 1946 they have devoted over 550 million hours to talking to their fellow Italians about God's Kingdom. While doing this, they have put into their hands millions of copies of the Bible itself as well as upwards of 400 million books, booklets, and magazines explaining the Scriptures. They want to make sure that the people of Italy have full opportunity to take their stand on Jehovah's side before Armageddon comes. While doing so, they keep in mind what the apostle Paul wrote at 2 Corinthians 10:4, 5, namely: "The weapons of our warfare are not fleshly, but powerful by God for overturning strongly entrenched things. For we are overturning reasonings and every lofty thing raised up against the knowledge of God."

In the 1980's the Catholic Church declared war on the Witnesses, according to these Italian news clippings

It is not only to former Catholic strongholds that Jehovah's Witnesses direct attention. They know that Jesus Christ said: "In all the nations the good news has to be preached." (Mark 13:10) And this is the work that the Witnesses are doing. By 1992, there were 12,168 of them busy telling people in India about God's Kingdom. Another 71,428 of them were preaching in the Republic of Korea. In Japan, there were 171,438, and their numbers were growing every month. They also continued to reach out to lands where little or no preaching had yet been done.

Thus, during the latter part of the 1970's, they were able, for the first time, to carry the Kingdom message to people living on the Marquesas Islands and on Kosrae—both in the Pacific Ocean. They also reached Bhutan, which adjoins the southern border of China, and Comoros, off the east coast of Africa. During the 1980's the first preaching work by Jehovah's Witnesses was reported from the Wallis and Futuna Islands, as well as from the islands of Nauru and Rota, all in the southwest Pacific. Some of these are relatively small places; but people live there, and lives are precious. Jehovah's Witnesses are keenly aware of Jesus' prophecy that before the end would come, the Kingdom message would be preached "in all the inhabited earth." —Matt. 24:14.

Contacting People Wherever and Whenever Possible

While house-to-house preaching continues to be the principal method employed by Jehovah's Witnesses to reach people, they realize that not even by this systematic method do they come in touch with everyone. With a feeling of urgency, they continue to search out people wherever they can be found.—Compare John 4:5-42; Acts 16:13, 14.

When boats dock at the ports of Germany and the Netherlands, even for a brief stop, Jehovah's Witnesses endeavor to visit them, witnessing first to the captain and then to the crew. They carry Bible literature in many languages for the men. In the native markets of Chad, in central Africa, it is not unusual to see a group of 15 or 20 persons gathered around one of Jehovah's Witnesses who is talking to them about the hope of God's Kingdom. Working in shifts, the Witnesses talk to stall holders and the thousands of Saturday-morning shoppers at the flea markets in Auckland, New Zealand. People who pass through the bus terminals in Guayaquil, Ecuador—many of them from distant parts of the

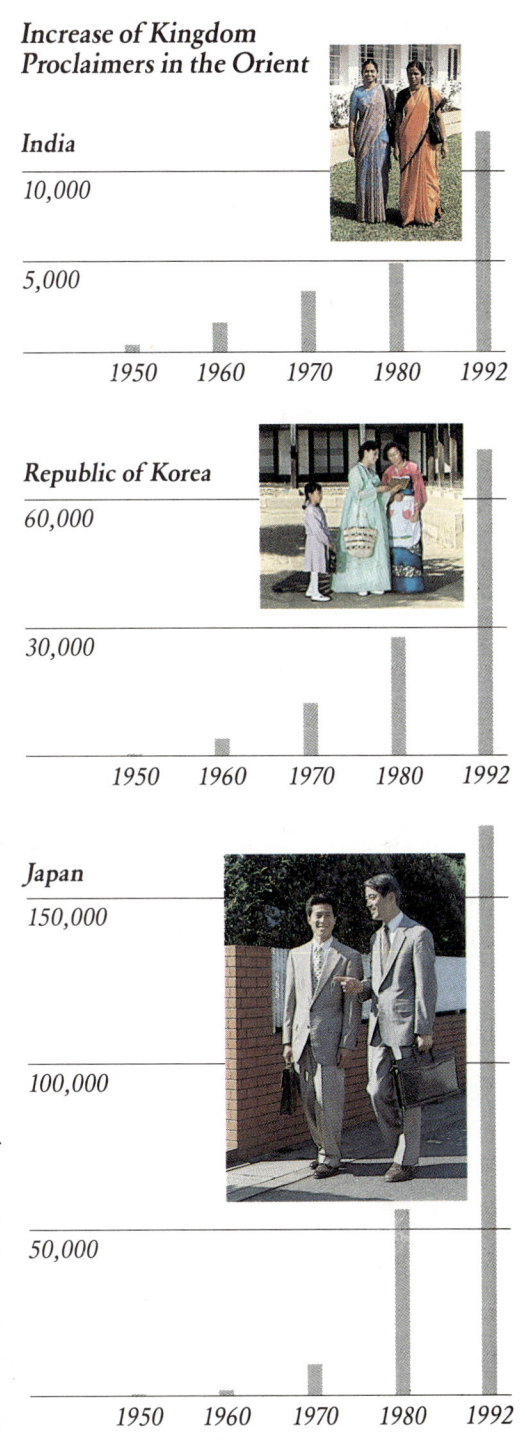

Increase of Kingdom Proclaimers in the Orient

India

When ships dock at Rotterdam, the Netherlands, Witnesses are there to talk to the men about God's Kingdom

country—are approached there by Witnesses who offer them a timely brochure or *La Atalaya* and *¡Despertad!* Those who work the night shift in round-the-clock food markets in New York City are visited on the job by Witnesses so that they too can have the opportunity to hear the good news.

When traveling on planes, trains, buses, and subways, many of Jehovah's Witnesses share precious Bible truths with fellow passengers. During lunch breaks at their secular work and at school, also when people come to their door for business reasons, they seize opportunities to witness. They know that many of these people may not be at home when the Witnesses make their regular calls.

While witnessing to others, they do not forget close family members and other relatives. But when Maria Caamano, a Witness in Argentina, tried to tell her family how deeply moved she was by what she learned from the Bible, they poked fun at her or were indifferent. She did not give up but made a trip of 1,200 miles to witness to others of her relatives. Some responded favorably. Little by little, others listened. As a result, there are now among her relatives over 80 adults and upwards of 40 children who have embraced the Bible's truths and are sharing these with others.

To aid his relatives, Michael Regan moved back to his hometown, Boyle, County Roscommon, in Ireland. He witnessed to all of them. His niece was impressed by the happy spirit and wholesome way of life of Michael's children. Soon she and her husband agreed to a Bible study. When they got baptized, her father banned her from the family home. Gradually, however, his attitude softened, and he accepted some literature—intending to expose the "error" of the Witnesses. But he soon realized that what he was reading was the truth, and in time he got baptized. Upwards of 20 members of the family are now associated with the congregation, most of whom have already been baptized.

What about people in prison? Could they benefit from the message of God's Kingdom? Jehovah's Witnesses do not ignore them. At a penitentiary in North America, arrangements for personal Bible studies with inmates, coupled with attendance at regular meetings conducted in the prison by Jehovah's Witnesses, produced such good results that the prison administration made it possible to hold assemblies there. These were attended not only by prisoners but also by thousands of Witnesses from outside. In other lands too, earnest efforts are being made to witness to men and women in prison.

Jehovah's Witnesses do not believe that Bible study will reform all prison inmates. But they know from experience that some can be helped, and they want to give them the opportunity to embrace the hope of God's Kingdom.

Repeated Efforts to Reach Hearts

Again and again Jehovah's Witnesses call on people. As Jesus' early disciples did, they "go continually" to the people in their assigned territories to endeavor to stir up their interest in the Kingdom of God. (Matt. 10: 6, 7) In some places they are able to visit all the households in their area just once a year; elsewhere, they call every few months. In Portugal, in the greater Lisbon area, where there is a ratio of 1 Witness to every 160 of the population, people are visited by the Witnesses every week or so. In Venezuela, there are cities where territories are regularly covered more than once a week.

When Jehovah's Witnesses make repeated calls, they are not trying to force the Bible's message on people. They are simply endeavoring to give them opportunity to make an intelligent decision. Today, some people may say they are not interested; but drastic changes in their lives or in world conditions may make them more receptive at another time. Because of prejudice or because of simply being too busy to listen, many people have never really heard what the Witnesses teach. But repeated friendly calls may make them take notice. People are often impressed by the honesty and moral integrity of Witnesses who live in their neighborhood or are their workmates. As a result, in time, some become interested enough to find out what their message is all about. Said one such woman in Venezuela, after she gladly accepted literature and the offer of a free home Bible study: "Never before had anyone explained these things to me."

In a kindly way, the Witnesses endeavor to reach the hearts of those to whom they talk. In Guadeloupe, where there was 1 Witness for every 57 of the population in 1992, it is not uncommon for householders to say, "I'm not interested." To that, Eric Dodote

Even where territory is covered often, as here in Guadeloupe, the Witnesses continue to try to reach the hearts of their neighbors with the good news

would reply: "I understand you, and I put myself in your place." Then he would add: "But I ask you, Would you like to live in better conditions than those existing today?" After listening to what the householder said, he would use the Bible to show how God will bring about such conditions in His new world.

Covering Territory Even More Thoroughly

In recent years it has become increasingly difficult in some lands to find people at home. Frequently, both husband and wife are secularly employed, and on weekends they may pursue recreation away from home. To cope with this situation, in many lands Jehovah's Witnesses are doing an increasing amount of their door-to-door witnessing in the evening. In Britain, not only do some Witnesses follow up on not-at-home calls between six and eight in the evening but others, in an effort to contact people before they leave for work, make such calls before eight in the morning.

Even where people are at home, it may be very difficult to reach them without a previous invitation, on account of high-security measures taken because of the prevalence of crime. But in Brazil when some who are hard to contact go for an early-morning stroll on the boardwalk at Copacabana Beach, they may be approached by a zealous Witness who is out there just as early engaging others in conversation about how God's Kingdom will solve mankind's problems. In Paris, France, when people return to their apartments late in the afternoon, they may find a friendly Witness couple near the entrance of the building, waiting to talk to individual residents who are willing to spend a few minutes to hear about the means that God will use to bring true security. In Honolulu, New York City, and many other places, efforts are also made to reach occupants of high-security buildings by telephone.

If they manage to contact someone in each home, the Witnesses still do not feel that their task is accomplished. Their desire is to reach as many individuals as possible in each house. Sometimes this is accomplished by calling on different days or at different times. In Puerto Rico when a householder said she was not interested, a Witness asked if there was anyone else in the house to whom she might talk. This led to a conversation with the man of the house, who had been ill for 14 years and was largely confined to his bed. His heart was warmed by the hope set out in God's Word. With renewed interest in life, he was soon out of bed, attending meetings at the Kingdom Hall, and sharing his newfound hope with others.

Intensifying the Witness as the End Draws Near

Another factor has contributed greatly to the intensifying of the witness in recent years. This is the upsurge in the number of Witnesses who

Their desire is to reach as many individuals as possible in each house

are serving as pioneers. Keenly desiring to devote as much of their time as possible to the service of God, and with loving concern for their fellowmen, they arrange their affairs to spend 60, 90, 140 or more hours each month in the field ministry. As was true of the apostle Paul when preaching in Corinth, Greece, those who take up pioneer service become "intensely occupied with the word," seeking to witness to just as many people as possible about the Messianic Kingdom.—Acts 18:5.

In 1975 there were 130,225 pioneers worldwide. By 1992 there were 605,610 on an average each month (including regular, auxiliary, and special pioneers). Thus, during a period when the number of Witnesses worldwide grew by 105 percent, those who made room to share in the full-time ministry increased 365 percent! As a result, the amount of time actually being devoted to witnessing soared from about 382 million to over a billion hours a year!

'The Little One Has Become a Thousand'

Jesus Christ commissioned his followers to be witnesses of him to the most distant part of the earth. (Acts 1:8) Through the prophet Isaiah, Jehovah had foretold: "The little one himself will become a thousand, and the small one a mighty nation. I myself, Jehovah, shall speed it up in its own time." (Isa. 60:22) The record clearly shows that Jehovah's Witnesses are doing the work that Jesus foretold, and they have experienced the kind of growth that God himself promised.

At the close of World War II, they were found principally in North America and Europe; there were some in Africa; and others, in smaller groups, were scattered around the globe. By no means had they reached every country with the Kingdom message, nor had they reached every part of those lands where they were preaching. With amazing speed, however, that picture has been changing.

Consider North America. The mainland extends from Canada in the north to Panama, with nine lands in between. By 1945 there were 81,410 Witnesses in this vast area. Four of the lands reported fewer than 20 Witnesses each, and one country had no organized preaching work at all. Since then, an intensive and sustained witness has been given in all these lands. As of 1992, there were 1,440,165 of Jehovah's Witnesses in this part of the earth. In most of these lands, each Witness, on an average, now has only a few hundred persons to whom to witness. A large proportion of the population is visited by the Witnesses every few months; many are called on every week. Over 1,240,000 home Bible studies are regularly being conducted with interested individuals and groups.

What about Europe? This part of the globe extends from Scandinavia south to the Mediterranean. Outside most of the area formerly known as the Soviet Union, an extensive witness had already been given in Europe before World War II. Since then, new generations have grown up, and they too are being shown from the Scriptures that God's Kingdom will soon replace all human governments. (Dan. 2:44) From the few thousand Witnesses who carried on their preaching activity under severe restrictions during the war, the number of Kingdom proclaimers in the 47 lands on which reports were published in 1992 had risen to 1,176,259, including those in places that previously were part of the U.S.S.R., in both Europe and Asia. In each of five countries—Britain, France, Germany, Italy, and Poland—there were well over 100,000 zealous Witnesses. And what were all these Witnesses doing? Their report for 1992 shows that during that year, they devoted more than 230,000,000 hours to preaching publicly, making house-to-house calls, and conducting home Bible studies. In their evangelizing, these Witnesses did not bypass even the small republic of San Marino, principalities such as Andorra and Liechtenstein, or Gibraltar. Truly, the foretold witness was being given.

Amazing growth and the potential for further expansion

Africa too is receiving an extensive witness. The records show that up till 1945, the good news had reached into 28 countries on that continent, but very little actual witnessing had been done in most of these countries. Since that time, however, much has been accomplished there. By 1992, there were 545,044 zealous Witnesses on the African continent, preaching the good news in 45 countries. At the commemoration of the Lord's Evening Meal that year, there were 1,834,863 present. So, not only has the growth been amazing but the potential for further expansion is extraordinary!

The report for South America is no less remarkable. Although all but one of the 13 countries had been reached with the Bible's message before World War II, at that time there were only 29 congregations on the entire continent, and there was as yet no organized preaching activity in some of the countries. Most of the Kingdom-preaching work was then in the future. Since that time the Witnesses there have worked vigorously. Those who have been refreshed by the water of life gladly invite others, saying: 'Come, and take life's water free.' (Rev. 22:17) In 1992, there were 683,782 of Jehovah's servants in 10,399 congregations in South America happily sharing in this work. Some of them were reaching out into areas that had not had a thorough witness. Others were calling again and again where a witness had already been given, to encourage people to "taste and see that Jehovah is good." (Ps. 34:8) Regularly they were conducting 905,132 home Bible studies to help interested ones to make Jehovah's ways their own way of life.

Consider also Asia and the many islands and island groups around the globe. What has been accomplished there? Up till the postwar era, many of these places had scarcely been touched with the proclamation of the Kingdom. But Jesus Christ foretold that this good news of the Kingdom would be preached "in all the inhabited earth for a witness to all the nations." (Matt. 24:14) In harmony with that, during the decades since World War II, the preaching of the good news that had previously reached 76 of these countries, islands, and island groups spread out to another 40 and was intensified in places reached earlier. In this vast territory, in 1992 there were 627,537 devoted Witnesses who took great delight in making known Jehovah's "mighty acts and the glory of the splendor of his kingship." (Ps. 145:11, 12) Their ministry was not easy. In some places they had to travel for hours by boat or plane to reach remote islands in their territory. But during 1992 they devoted upwards of 200,-000,000 hours to the evangelizing work and conducted 685,211 regular home Bible studies.

Fulfillment of the promise that 'the little one would become a thousand' has surely come to pass, and abundantly so! In each of more than 50 lands where there was not even a 'little one'—where there were none of Jehovah's Witnesses back in 1919, where they had done no preaching at all—there are today more than a thousand praisers of Jehovah. In some of these lands, there are now *tens of thousands,* yes, even *more than a hundred thousand,* of Jehovah's Witnesses who are zealous proclaimers of the Kingdom of God! Worldwide, Jehovah's Witnesses have become "a mighty nation"—more in number as a united global congregation than the individual population of any one of at least 80 self-governing nations of the world.

How Much of a Witness in "Other Countries"?

Included in all the above, as of 1992, there were still 24 "other countries"—the ones where Jehovah's Witnesses were under severe government restrictions and for which no detailed reports are published. Much witnessing has been done in some of these countries. Yet, in certain lands the number of Witnesses is quite limited. There are still people who have not heard the Kingdom message. But Jehovah's Witnesses are confident that the needed witness will be given. Why?

Because the Scriptures show that Jesus Christ, from his heavenly throne, is himself supervising the work. (Matt. 25:31-33) Under his direction an "angel flying in midheaven" is entrusted with the responsibility to declare everlasting good news and to urge "every nation and tribe and tongue and people" to "fear God and give him glory." (Rev. 14:6, 7) There is no power in heaven or on earth that can stop Jehovah from drawing to himself those who are "rightly disposed for everlasting life."—Acts 13:48; John 6:44.

No part of the earth is so isolated that the Kingdom message cannot reach it. Relatives visit. Telephones and mail carry news. Businessmen, laborers, students, and tourists come in contact with people of other nations. As in the past, so now, the vital news that Jehovah has enthroned his heavenly King with authority over the nations continues to be made known by these means. The angels can see to it that those who are hungering and thirsting for truth and righteousness are reached.

If it is the Lord's will for more direct preaching of the Kingdom message to be done in some areas where governments have hindered it until now, God can bring about conditions that cause those governments to change their policies. (Prov. 21:1) And where doors of opportunity may yet open, Jehovah's Witnesses will gladly give of themselves to see that people in those lands receive as much assistance as possible to learn of Jehovah's loving purpose. They are determined to continue to serve without letup until Jehovah by means of Jesus Christ says the work is done!

In 1992, Jehovah's Witnesses were busy preaching in 229 lands. By that year the good news of God's Kingdom had in various ways reached into 235 lands. Ten of these were first reached following 1975.

How intense a witness was given? Well, during the first 30 years after World War II, Jehovah's Witnesses devoted 4,635,265,939 hours to preaching and teaching about Jehovah's name and Kingdom. However, with more Witnesses and a larger proportion of them in full-time service, during the next 15 years (just half as many years), 7,858,677,940 hours were devoted to witnessing publicly and from house to house as well as to conducting home Bible studies. And the intensity of the work continued to grow, as they reported another 951,870,021 hours in this activity during 1990/91 and over a billion hours the next year.

The amount of Bible literature distributed by the Witnesses to publicize the Kingdom, along with the diversity of languages in which it has been made available, finds no equal in any human field of endeavor. The records are incomplete; but the reports that are still available show that in 294 languages, 10,107,565,269 books, booklets, brochures, and magazines, as well as uncounted billions of tracts, were put into the hands of interested people between the years 1920 and 1992.

At the time of this writing, the global witness is not yet completed. But the work that has been accomplished and the circumstances under which it has been done give convincing evidence of the operation of the spirit of God.

CHAPTER 23

MISSIONARIES PUSH WORLDWIDE EXPANSION

ZEALOUS activity of missionaries who are willing to serve wherever they are needed has been an important factor in the global proclamation of God's Kingdom.

Long before the Watch Tower Bible and Tract Society established a school for the purpose, missionaries were being sent to other lands. The Society's first president, C. T. Russell, recognized the need for qualified people to initiate and take the lead in preaching the good news in foreign fields. He sent out men for that purpose—Adolf Weber to Europe, E. J. Coward to the Caribbean area, Robert Hollister to the Orient, and Joseph Booth to southern Africa. Sadly, Booth proved to be more interested in his own schemes; so, in 1910, William Johnston was sent from Scotland to Nyasaland (now Malawi), where Booth's adverse influence had been especially felt. Thereafter, Brother Johnston was assigned to set up a branch office for the Watch Tower Society in Durban, South Africa, and later he served as branch overseer in Australia.

After the first world war, J. F. Rutherford sent out even more missionaries—for example, Thomas Walder and George Phillips from Britain to South Africa, W. R. Brown from an assignment in Trinidad to West Africa, George Young from Canada to South America and to Europe, Juan Muñiz first to Spain and then to Argentina, George Wright and Edwin Skinner to India, followed by Claude Goodman, Ron Tippin, and more. They were real pioneers, reaching out to areas where little or no preaching of the good news had been done and laying a solid foundation for future organizational growth.

There were others, too, whose missionary spirit moved them to undertake preaching outside their own country. Among them were Kate Goas and her daughter Marion, who devoted years to zealous service in Colombia and Venezuela. Another was Joseph Dos Santos, who left Hawaii on a preaching trip that led to 15 years of ministry in the Philippines. There was also Frank Rice, who traveled by cargo ship from Australia to open up the preaching of the good news on the island of Java (now in Indonesia).

However, in 1942 plans took shape for a school with a course specially designed to train both men and women who were willing to undertake such missionary service wherever they were needed in the global field.

Gilead School

In the midst of world war, it may have seemed impractical from a human standpoint to plan for expansion of Kingdom-preaching activities in foreign fields. Yet, in September 1942, with reliance on Jehovah, the directors of two of the principal legal corporations used by Jehovah's Witnesses approved the proposal by N. H. Knorr for establishment of a school designed to train missionaries and others for specialized service. It was to be called the Watchtower Bible College of Gilead. Later that name was changed to the Watchtower Bible School of Gilead. No tuition was to be charged, and students would be housed and fed at the expense of the Society for the period of their training.

Among those who were invited to help outline the course of study was Albert D. Schroeder, who had already gained much experience in the Service Department at the Society's headquarters in Brooklyn and as the Society's branch overseer in Britain. His positive outlook, the way in which he gave of himself, and his warm interest in the students endeared him to those he taught during the 17 years that he served as registrar and as an instructor in the school. In 1974 he became a member of the Governing Body, and the following year he was assigned to serve on its Teaching Committee.

Students of the first class of Gilead School

Brother Schroeder and his fellow instructors (Maxwell Friend, Eduardo Keller, and Victor Blackwell) outlined a five-month study course that emphasized study of the Bible itself and theocratic organization, also Bible doctrines, public speaking, field ministry, missionary service, religious history, divine law, how to deal with government officials, international law, keeping records, and a foreign language. Modifications in the curriculum have taken place over the years, but study of the Bible itself and the importance of the evangelizing work have always held first place. The aim of the course is to strengthen the faith of the students, to help them to develop the spiritual qualities needed to meet successfully the challenges of missionary service. Emphasis has been placed on the importance of total reliance on Jehovah and loyalty to him. (Ps. 146:1-6; Prov. 3:5, 6; Eph. 4:24) Students are not given pat answers to everything but are trained in research and are helped to appreciate *why* Jehovah's Witnesses believe as they do and why they adhere to certain ways of doing things. They learn to discern *principles* with which they can work. Thus a foundation is laid for further growth.

Emphasis on the importance of total reliance on Jehovah and loyalty to him

Invitations to prospective students for the first class were sent out on December 14, 1942. It was mid-winter when the 100 students making up that class enrolled at the school facilities located in upstate New York, at South Lansing. They were willing, eager, and somewhat nervous. Although class studies were the immediate concern, they could not help but wonder where in the world field they would be sent after graduation.

In a discourse to that first class on February 1, 1943, the opening day of school, Brother Knorr said: "You are being given further preparation for work similar to that of the apostle Paul, Mark, Timothy, and others who traveled to all parts of the Roman Empire proclaiming the message of the Kingdom. They had to be fortified with the Word of God. They had to have a clear knowledge of His purposes. In many places they had to stand alone against the high and mighty of this world. Your portion may be the same; and God will be your strength thereunto.

"There are many places where the witness concerning the Kingdom has not been given to a great extent. The people living in these places are in darkness, held there by religion. In some of these countries where there are a few Witnesses it is noted that the people of good-will hear readily and would associate themselves with the Lord's organization, if instructed properly. There must be hundreds and thousands more that could be reached if there were more laborers in the field. By the Lord's grace, there will be more.

"It is NOT the purpose of this college to equip you to be ordained ministers. You are ministers already and have been active in the ministry for years. . . . The course of study at the college is for the exclusive purpose of

Albert Schroeder discussing features of the tabernacle with Gilead students

preparing you to be more able ministers in the territories to which you go. . . .

"Your principal work is that of preaching the gospel of the Kingdom from house to house as did Jesus and the apostles. When you shall have found a hearing ear, arrange for a back-call, start a home study, and organize a company [congregation] of all suchlike ones in a city or town. Not only will it be your good pleasure to organize a company, but you must help them to understand the Word, strengthen them, address them from time to time, aid them in their service meetings and their organization. When they are strong and can go on their own and take over the territory, you can depart to some other city to proclaim the Kingdom. From time to time it may be necessary for you to return to build them up in the most holy faith and straighten them out in the doctrine; so your work will be that of looking after the Lord's 'other sheep', and not forsaking them. (John 10:16) Your real work is to help the people of good-will. You will have to use initiative, but looking to God's guidance."*

Five months later the members of that first class completed their specialized training. Visas were obtained, travel arrangements were made, and they began to move out to nine Latin-American lands. Three months after their graduation, the first Gilead-trained missionaries to leave the United States were on their way to Cuba. By 1992, over 6,500 students from more than 110 countries had been trained and had thereafter served in well over 200 lands and island groups.

Right down to the time of his death 34 years after the inauguration of Gilead School, Brother Knorr demonstrated keen personal interest in the work of the missionaries. Each school term, he would visit the current class a number of times if at all possible, giving lectures and taking along with him other members of the headquarters staff to speak to the students. After the graduates of Gilead began their service abroad, he personally visited the missionary groups, helped them to work out problems, and gave them needed encouragement. As the number of missionary groups multiplied,

---

* *The Watchtower*, February 15, 1943, pp. 60-4.

he arranged for other well-qualified brothers to make such visits too, so that all the missionaries, no matter where they were serving, would receive regular personal attention.

These Missionaries Were Different

Christendom's missionaries have established hospitals, refugee centers, and orphanages to care for people's material needs. Casting themselves in the role of champions of poor people, they have also stirred up revolution and participated in guerrilla warfare. In contrast, missionary graduates of Gilead School *teach people the Bible*. Instead of setting up churches and expecting people to come to them, they call from house to house to find and teach those who are hungering and thirsting for righteousness.

Maxwell Friend lecturing in the Gilead School amphitheater

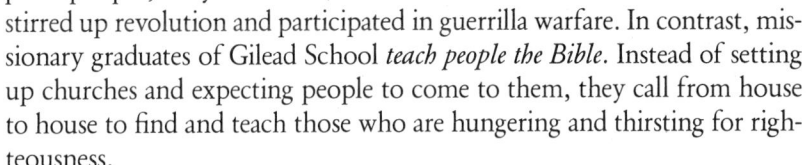

Adhering closely to God's Word, Witness missionaries show people why the true and lasting solution to mankind's problems is God's Kingdom. (Matt. 24:14; Luke 4:43) The contrast between this work and that of Christendom's missionaries was emphasized to Peter Vanderhaegen in 1951 when en route to his assignment in Indonesia. The only other passenger aboard the cargo ship was a Baptist missionary. Although Brother Vanderhaegen tried to talk to him about the good news of God's Kingdom, the Baptist made it clear that his consuming interest was in supporting the efforts of Chiang Kai-shek in Taiwan to return to power on the mainland.

Nevertheless, many other people have come to appreciate the value of what is stated in God's Word. In Barranquilla, Colombia, when Olaf Olson witnessed to Antonio Carvajalino, who had been a strong supporter of a particular political movement, Brother Olson did not take sides with him, nor did he advocate some other political ideology. Instead, he offered to study the Bible free of charge with Antonio and his sisters. Soon Antonio realized that God's Kingdom really is the only hope for the poor people of Colombia and the rest of the world. (Ps. 72:1-4, 12-14; Dan. 2:44) Antonio and his sisters became zealous servants of God.

The fact that Witness missionaries are separate and distinct from Christendom's religious system was highlighted in another way in an incident in

Rhodesia (now Zimbabwe). When Donald Morrison called at the home of one of Christendom's missionaries there, the missionary complained that the Witnesses were not respecting boundaries that had been set. What boundaries? Well, the religions of Christendom had divided up the country into areas in which each would operate without interference from the others. Jehovah's Witnesses could not go along with such an arrangement. Jesus had said that the Kingdom message was to be preached in *all the inhabited earth*. Christendom definitely was not doing it. The Gilead-trained missionaries were determined to do a thorough job of it, in obedience to Christ.

These missionaries were sent out, not to be served, but to serve. It was evident in many ways that this really is what they endeavored to do. It is not wrong to accept material provisions that are offered freely (and not as a result of solicitation) in appreciation for spiritual help. But to reach the hearts of the people in Alaska, John Errichetti and Hermon Woodard found that it was beneficial to take at least some time to work with their hands to provide for their physical needs, as the apostle Paul had done. (1 Cor. 9:11, 12; 2 Thess. 3:7, 8) Their primary activity was preaching the good news. But when they received hospitality, they also helped with jobs that needed to be done—for example, tarring a man's roof because they realized that he needed help. And when they traveled from place to place by boat, they gave a hand with the unloading of freight. People quickly realized that these missionaries were not at all like the clergy of Christendom.

Gilead graduations were spiritual highlights

. . . some at large conventions (New York, 1950)

. . . some on the school campus (where N. H. Knorr is shown speaking in front of the school library, in 1956)

Gilead School campus at South Lansing, New York, as it appeared during the 1950's

In some places it was necessary for Witness missionaries to take up secular work for a time just to get established in a country so that they could carry on their ministry there. Thus, when Jesse Cantwell went to Colombia, he taught English in the medical department of a university until the political situation changed and religious restrictions ended. After that he was able to use his experience full-time in the ministry as a traveling overseer for Jehovah's Witnesses.

In many places, the missionaries had to start off with tourist visas that allowed them to be in a country for a month or perhaps several months. Then they had to leave and enter again. But they persisted, repeating the process over and over until needed residence papers could be obtained. Their hearts were set on helping people in the countries to which they had been assigned.

These missionaries did not view themselves as superior to the local people. As a traveling overseer, John Cutforth, who was originally a schoolteacher in Canada, visited congregations as well as isolated Witnesses in Papua New Guinea. He sat on the floor with them, ate with them, and accepted invitations to sleep on a mat on the floor in their homes. He enjoyed

Hermon Woodard (left) and John Errichetti (right) serving in Alaska

fellowship with them as they walked together in the field ministry. But this was amazing to non-Witnesses who observed it, for European pastors of Christendom's missions had a reputation of keeping aloof from the local people, mixing with their parishioners only briefly at some of their meetings, but never eating with them.

The people among whom these Witnesses served sensed the loving interest of the missionaries and of the organization that had sent them out. In response to a letter from João Mancoca, a humble African confined in a penal colony in Portuguese West Africa (now Angola), a Watch Tower missionary was sent to provide spiritual help. Looking back on that visit, Mancoca later said: "I had no more doubt that this was the true organization which has God's support. I had never thought or believed that any other religious organization would do such a thing: without payment, send a missionary from far to visit an insignificant person just because he wrote a letter."

Living Conditions and Customs

Frequently the living conditions in lands to which missionaries were sent were not as materially advanced as those in the places from which they had come. When Robert Kirk landed in Burma (now Myanmar) early in 1947, the effects of war were still in evidence, and few homes had electric lights. In many lands, the missionaries found that laundry was done piece by piece with a washboard or on rocks at a river instead of with an electric washing machine. But they had come to teach people Bible truth, so they adjusted to local conditions and got busy in the ministry.

In the early days, it was often the case that no one was waiting to welcome the missionaries. It was up to them to find a place to live. When Charles Eisenhower, along with 11 others, arrived in Cuba in 1943, they slept on the floor the first night. The next day they bought beds and made closets and dressers from apple boxes. Using whatever contributions they received from literature placements, along with the modest allowance that was provided by the Watch Tower Society for special pioneers, each group of missionaries looked to Jehovah to bless their efforts to pay the rent, obtain food, and meet other necessary expenses.

Preparation of meals sometimes required a change in thinking. Where there was no refrigeration, daily trips to the market were necessary. In many lands cooking was done over charcoal or wood fires instead of on a gas or an electric stove. George and Willa Mae Watkins, assigned to Liberia, found that their stove consisted of nothing more than three rocks used to support an iron kettle.

What about water? Looking at her new home in India, Ruth McKay said: 'Here is a home like none I've ever seen. The kitchen has no sink, just a tap in the corner wall with a raised strip of concrete to prevent the water from running all over the floor. It is not a 24-hour flow of water, but water has to be stored for times when the supply is cut off.'

Because they were not accustomed to local conditions, some of the missionaries were plagued with illness during the early months in their assignment. Russell Yeatts had one spell of dysentery after another when he arrived in Curaçao in 1946. But a local brother had offered such a fervent prayer of thanks to Jehovah for the missionaries that they just could not think of leaving. Upon arriving in Upper Volta (now Burkina Faso), Brian and Elke Wise found themselves in a harsh climate that takes its toll on one's health. They had to learn to cope with daytime temperatures of 109° F. During their first year, the intense heat along with malaria caused Elke to be sick for weeks at a time. The next year, Brian was confined to bed for five months with a severe case of hepatitis. But they soon found that they had as many good Bible studies as they could handle—and then some. Love for those people helped them to persevere; so did the fact that they viewed their assignment as a privilege and as good training for whatever Jehovah had in store for them in the future.

John Cutforth using visual aids to teach in Papua New Guinea

As the years passed, more of the missionaries were welcomed to their assignments by those who had gone before them or by local Witnesses. Some were assigned to lands where the principal cities were quite modern. Starting in 1946, the Watch Tower Society also endeavored to provide a suitable home and basic furniture for each missionary group as well as funds for food, thus freeing them of this concern and enabling them to direct more of their attention to the preaching work.

In a number of places, travel was an experience that tested their endurance. After it rained, more than one missionary sister in Papua New Guinea found herself carrying supplies in a backpack while walking through the bush on a slippery footpath that was so muddy that it sometimes pulled off her shoes. In South America, not a few missionaries have had hair-raising

WATCHTOWER BIBLE SCHOOL OF GILEAD

Missionaries in Ireland, with district overseer, in 1950

Graduates en route to missionary assignments in the Orient in 1947

Some missionaries and fellow workers in Japan in 1969

Missionaries in Brazil in 1956

. . . in Uruguay in 1954

. . . in Italy in 1950

First four Gilead-trained missionaries sent to Jamaica

First missionary home in Salisbury (now Harare, Zimbabwe), in 1950

Malcolm Vigo (Gilead, 1956-57) with his wife Linda Louise; together they have served in Malawi, Kenya, and Nigeria

Robert Tracy (left) and Jesse Cantwell (right) with their wives—missionaries in traveling work in Colombia in 1960

bus rides on narrow roads high in the Andes Mountains. It is an experience not soon forgotten when your bus, on the outer edge of the road, passes another large vehicle going in the opposite direction on a curve without a guardrail and you feel the bus start to tip over the precipice!

Political revolutions seemed to be a regular part of life in certain places, but the Witness missionaries kept in mind Jesus' statement that his disciples would be "no part of the world"; so they were neutral as to such conflicts. (John 15:19) They learned to suppress any curiosity that would expose them to needless danger. Frequently, the best thing was simply to stay off the streets until the situation had cooled down. Nine missionaries in Vietnam were living right in the heart of Saigon (now Ho Chi Minh City) when war engulfed that city. They could see bombs being dropped, fires throughout the city, and thousands of people fleeing for their lives. But appreciating that Jehovah had sent them to extend life-giving knowledge to truth-hungry people, they looked to him for protection.

Even when there was relative peace, it was difficult for the missionaries to carry on their ministry in some sections of Asian cities. Just the appearance of a foreigner in the narrow streets of a poor section of Lahore, Pakistan, was enough to attract a crowd of unwashed, unkempt children of all ages. Shouting and jostling one another, they would follow the missionary from house to house, often barging into the homes in the wake of the publisher. Soon the whole street had been told the price of the magazines and that the stranger was 'making Christians.' Under such circumstances, it was usually necessary to leave the area. The departure was frequently made to the accompaniment of screaming, hand-clapping, and, at times, a shower of stones.

Local customs frequently required some adjustments on the part of the missionaries. In Japan they learned to leave their shoes on the porch when entering a house. And they had to become accustomed, if possible, to sitting on the floor before a low table at Bible studies. In some parts of Africa, they learned that using the left hand to offer something to another person was viewed as an insult. And they found that in that part of the world, it was bad manners to try to explain the reason for their visit before engaging in some light conversation—inquiring mutually about health and answering questions as to where one is from, how many children one has, and so forth. In Brazil missionaries found that instead of knocking on doors, they usually needed to clap their hands at the front gate in order to summon the householder.

However, in Lebanon the missionaries were confronted with customs of another sort. Few brothers brought their wives and daughters to meetings. The women who did attend always sat in the back, never in among the men. The missionaries, unaware of the custom, caused no little disturbance at their first meeting. A married couple sat toward the front, and the single missionary girls sat wherever there was an empty seat. But after the meeting a discussion of Christian principles helped to clear the air. (Compare Deuteronomy 31:12; Galatians 3:28.) The segregation stopped. More wives and daughters attended the meetings. They also joined the missionary sisters in the house-to-house ministry.

The Challenge of a New Language

The small group of missionaries that arrived in Martinique in 1949 had very little knowledge of French, but they knew that the people needed the Kingdom message. With real faith they started out from door to door, trying to read a few verses from the Bible or an excerpt from a publication they were offering. With patience their French gradually improved.

Although it was their desire to help the local Witnesses and other interested ones, the missionaries themselves were often the ones that needed help first—with the language. Those who were sent to Togo found that the grammar of Ewe, the principal native tongue, was quite different from that of European languages, also that the voice pitch in which a word is stated may change the meaning. Thus, the two-letter word *to,* when spoken in a raised pitch, can mean ear, mountain, father-in-law, or tribe; with a low pitch, it means buffalo. Missionaries taking up service in Vietnam were confronted with a language that employed six variations of tone on any given word, each tone resulting in a different meaning.

Edna Waterfall, assigned to Peru, did not soon forget the first house at which she tried to witness in Spanish. In a cold sweat, she stumbled through her memorized presentation, offered literature, and arranged for a Bible study with an elderly lady. Then the woman said in perfect English: "All right, that is all very fine. I will study with you and we will do it all in Spanish to help you learn Spanish." Shocked, Edna replied: "You know English? And you let me do all of that in my wobbly Spanish?" "It was good for you," the woman answered. And, indeed, it was! As Edna soon came to appreciate, actually speaking a language is an important part of learning it.

Language class in missionary home in Côte d'Ivoire

In Italy, when George Fredianelli tried to speak the language, he found that what he thought were Italian expressions (but were actually Italianized English words) were not being understood. To cope with the problem, he decided to write out his talks for congregations in full and deliver them from a manuscript. But many in his audience would fall asleep. So he discarded the manuscript, spoke extemporaneously, and asked the audience to help him when he got stuck. This kept them awake, and it helped him to progress.

To give the missionaries a start with their new language, the Gilead study course for the early classes included such languages as Spanish, French, Italian, Portuguese, Japanese, Arabic, and Urdu. Over the years, upwards of 30 languages were taught. But since the graduates of a given class did not all go to places where the same language was spoken, these language classes were later replaced with arrangements for an intensive period of supervised language study on arrival in their assignments. For the first month, newcomers totally immersed themselves in language study for 11 hours a day; and the following month, half their time was spent in language study at home, and the other half was devoted to using that knowledge in the field ministry.

It was observed, however, that actual use of the language in the field ministry was a principal key to progress; so an adjustment was made. During the first three months in their assignment, new missionaries who did not know the local language would spend four hours a day with a qualified teacher, and right from the start, by witnessing to local people about God's Kingdom, they would apply what they were learning.

Gilead Classes

1943-60: School at South Lansing, New York. In 35 classes, 3,639 students from 95 lands graduated, most being assigned to missionary service. Circuit and district overseers serving in the United States were also included in the classes.

1961-65: School in Brooklyn, New York. In 5 classes, 514 students graduated and were sent to lands where the Watch Tower Society had branch offices; most of the graduates were entrusted with administrative assignments. Four of these classes had 10-month courses; one, an 8-month course.

1965-88: School in Brooklyn, New York. In 45 classes, each with a 20-week course, another 2,198 students were trained, most of these for missionary service.

1977-80: School in Brooklyn, New York. Five-week Gilead course for Branch Committee members. Fourteen classes were held.

1980-81: Gilead Cultural School of Mexico; 10-week course; three classes; 72 Spanish-speaking graduates prepared for service in Latin America.

1981-82, 1984, 1992: Gilead Extension School in Germany; 10-week course; four classes; 98 German-speaking students from European lands.

1983: Classes in India; 10-week course, conducted in English; 3 groups; 70 students.

1987-   : Ministerial Training School, with an 8-week course, held in key locations in various parts of the world. As of 1992, graduates had already been serving in more than 35 lands outside the country of their origin.

1988-   : School at Wallkill, New York. Twenty-week course in preparation for missionary service is currently conducted there. It is planned that the school will be moved to the Watchtower Educational Center at Patterson, New York, when this is completed.

Many missionary groups worked as teams to improve their grasp of the language. They would discuss a few, or as many as 20, new words each day at breakfast and then endeavor to use these in their field ministry.

Learning the local language has been an important factor in their winning the confidence of people. In some places, there is a measure of distrust of foreigners. Hugh and Carol Cormican have served singly or as a married couple in five African countries. They are well aware of the distrust that often exists between Africans and Europeans. But they say: "Speaking in the local language quickly dispels this feeling. Further, others who are not inclined to listen to the good news from their fellow countrymen will readily listen to us, take literature, and study, because we have made the effort to speak to them in their own language." In order to do that, Brother Cormican learned five languages, apart from English, and Sister Cormican learned six.

Of course, there can be problems when trying to learn a new language. In Puerto Rico a brother who was offering to play a recorded Bible message for householders would close up his phonograph and go to the next door when the person replied, *"¡Como no!"* To him, that sounded like "No," and it took a while before he learned that the expression means "Why not!" On the other hand, missionaries sometimes did not understand when the householder said he was not interested, so they kept right on witnessing. A few sympathetic householders benefited as a result.

A good sense of humor helped!

There were humorous situations too. Leslie Franks, in Singapore, learned that he had to be careful not to talk about a coconut (*kelapa*) when he meant a head (*kepala*), and grass (*rumput*) when he meant hair (*rambut*). A missionary in Samoa, because of mispronunciation, asked a native, "How is your beard?" (he did not have one), when what was intended was a polite inquiry about the man's wife. In Ecuador, when a bus driver started abruptly, Zola Hoffman, who was standing up in the bus, was thrown off balance and landed in a man's lap. Embarrassed, she tried to apologize. But what came out was, *"Con su permiso"* (With your permission). When the man good-naturedly replied, "Go right ahead, Lady," the other passengers burst into laughter.

Nevertheless, good results in the ministry were forthcoming because the missionaries tried. Lois Dyer, who arrived in Japan in 1950, recalls the advice given by Brother Knorr: "Do the best you can, and, even though you make mistakes, *do something!*" She did, and so did many others. During the next 42 years, the missionaries sent to Japan saw the number of Kingdom proclaimers there increase from just a handful to over 170,000, and the growth has kept right on. What a rich reward because, after having looked to Jehovah for direction, they were willing to try!

Opening New Fields, Developing Others

In scores of lands and island groups, it was the Gilead-trained missionaries who either began the work of Kingdom preaching or gave it needed impetus after a limited amount of witnessing had been done by others. They were evidently the first of Jehovah's Witnesses to preach the good news in Somalia, Sudan, Laos, and numerous island groups around the globe.

Some earlier preaching had been done in such places as Bolivia, Dominican Republic, Ecuador, El Salvador, Honduras, Nicaragua, Ethiopia, The Gambia, Liberia, Cambodia, Hong Kong, Japan, and Vietnam. But there were none of Jehovah's Witnesses reporting activity in these countries when the first missionary graduates of Gilead School arrived. Where possible, the missionaries undertook a systematic coverage of the country, concentrating first on the larger cities. They did not simply place literature and move on, as had the colporteurs of the past. They patiently called back on interested ones, conducted Bible studies with them, and trained them in the field ministry.

Other lands had only about ten Kingdom proclaimers (and, in many instances, fewer) before the arrival of the missionary graduates of Gilead School. Included among these were Colombia, Guatemala, Haiti, Puerto Rico, Venezuela, Burundi, Ivory Coast (now Côte d'Ivoire), Kenya, Mauritius, Senegal, South-West Africa (now Namibia), Ceylon (now Sri Lanka), China, and Singapore, along with many island groups. The missionaries set a zealous example in the ministry, helped local Witnesses to improve their abilities, organized congregations, and assisted brothers to qualify to take the lead. In many instances they also opened up the preaching work in areas that had not been touched before.

With this help the number of Witnesses began to grow. In most of these countries, there are now thousands of active Witnesses of Jehovah. In some of them, there are tens of thousands, or even more than a hundred thousand, praisers of Jehovah.

Some People Were Eager to Hear

In some areas missionaries found many people who were willing and eager to learn. When Ted and Doris Klein, graduates of Gilead's first class, arrived in the Virgin Islands in 1947, there were so many people who wanted to study the Bible that they frequently did not conclude their day of service until midnight. For the first public lecture that Brother Klein gave in the Market Square of Charlotte Amalie, there were a thousand in attendance.

Ted and Doris Klein, who found many people eager to hear Bible truth in the U.S. Virgin Islands in 1947

Harvey Logan (center front) with Amis Witnesses in front of Kingdom Hall, in the 1960's

Joseph McGrath and Cyril Charles were sent to the Amis territory in Taiwan in 1949. They found themselves living in houses with thatched roofs and dirt floors. But they were there to help people. Some of the Amis tribesmen had obtained Watch Tower literature, had been delighted by what they read, and had shared the good news with others. Now the missionaries were there to help them to grow spiritually. They were told that 600 persons were interested in the truth, but a total of 1,600 attended the meetings they held as they moved from village to village. These humble people were willing to learn, but they lacked accurate knowledge of many things. Patiently the brothers began to teach them, taking one subject at a time, often devoting eight or more hours to a question-and-answer discussion of a subject at each village. Training was also provided for the 140 who expressed a desire to share in witnessing from house to house. What a joyful experience that was for the missionaries! But much still needed to be done if there was to be solid spiritual growth.

About 12 years later, Harvey and Kathleen Logan, Gilead-trained missionaries who had been serving in Japan, were assigned to provide further assistance to the Amis brothers. Brother Logan spent much time helping them to understand basic Bible doctrine and principles as well as organizational matters. Sister Logan worked with the Amis sisters in the field service each day, after which she endeavored to study basic Bible truths with them. Then, in 1963, the Watch Tower Society arranged for delegates from 28 lands to assemble with the local Witnesses there in the village of Shou Feng, in connection with an around-the-world convention. All this began to lay a solid foundation for further growth.

In 1948, two missionaries, Harry Arnott and Ian Fergusson, arrived in Northern Rhodesia (now Zambia). There were already 252 congregations of native African Witnesses at that time, but now attention was also given to the Europeans who had moved there in connection with copper-mining operations. The response was exciting. Much literature was placed; those with whom Bible studies were conducted progressed rapidly. That year saw a 61-percent increase in the number of Witnesses active in the field ministry.

In many places it was not unusual for the missionaries to have waiting lists of people who wanted Bible studies. Sometimes relatives, neighbors, and other friends would also be present when studies were conducted. Even before people were able to have their own personal Bible study, they might be regularly attending meetings at the Kingdom Hall.

However, in other lands, though great effort was put forth by the missionaries, the harvest was very limited. As early as 1953, Watch Tower missionaries were sent to East Pakistan (now Bangladesh), where the population, which now exceeds 115,000,000, is predominantly Muslim and Hindu. Much effort was put forth to help the people. Yet, by 1992, there were only 42 worshipers of Jehovah in that land. However, in the eyes of the missionaries who serve in such areas, each one who takes up true worship is especially precious—because they are so rare.

Loving Help to Fellow Witnesses

The basic work of the missionaries is evangelizing, preaching the good news of God's Kingdom. But as they have personally engaged in this activity, they have also been able to provide much help to local Witnesses. The missionaries have invited them along in the field ministry and have shared with them suggestions on how to deal with difficult situations. By observing the missionaries, local Witnesses have often learned how to carry on their ministry in a more organized manner and how to be more effective teachers. In turn, the missionaries have been helped by local Witnesses to adjust to local customs.

On his arrival in Portugal in 1948, John Cooke took steps to organize systematic house-to-house work. Though they were willing, many of the local Witnesses needed training. He later said: "I shall never forget one of my very first outings in the ministry with the sisters in Almada. Yes, six of them went to the same house together. You can just imagine a group of six women standing around a door while one of them gave a sermon! But bit by bit things began to take shape and started to move."

The courageous example of missionaries helped Witnesses in the Leeward Islands to be bold, not intimidated by opposers who tried to interfere with the work. The faith shown by a missionary helped brothers in Spain to get started in the house-to-house ministry, in spite of the Catholic Fascist dictatorship under which they lived at the time. Missionaries serving in Japan after World War II set an example in tactfulness—not harping on the failure of the national religion, after the Japanese emperor had renounced his divinity, but rather presenting persuasive evidence for belief in the Creator.

Local Witnesses observed the missionaries and were often deeply affected in ways that the missionaries may not have realized at the time. In Trinidad, incidents that showed the humility of the missionaries, their willingness to put up with difficult conditions, and their hard work in Jehovah's service despite the hot weather are still talked about many years later. Witnesses in Korea were deeply impressed by the self-sacrificing spirit of missionaries who for ten years did not leave the country to visit their families because the government would not issue reentry permits except in a few emergency "humanitarian" cases.

During and after their initial Gilead schooling, most of the missionaries had a closeup view of the operation of the headquarters of Jehovah's visible organization. They often had considerable opportunity to associate with members of the Governing Body. Later, in their missionary assignments, they were able to convey to local Witnesses and newly interested persons eyewitness reports as to the way the organization functions as well as the appreciation that they themselves had for it. The depth of appreciation that they imparted regarding the theocratic operation of the organization was often an important factor in the growth that was experienced.

In many of the places to which the missionaries were sent, there were no congregation meetings when they arrived. So they made the needed arrangements, conducted the meetings, and handled most of the meeting parts until others qualified to share in these privileges. Constantly they were training other brothers so that they could qualify to take over the responsibility. (2 Tim. 2:2) The first meeting place was usually the missionary home. Later on, arrangements were made for Kingdom Halls.

Where congregations already existed, the missionaries contributed toward making the meetings more interesting and instructive. Their well-prepared comments were appreciated and soon set a pattern that others tried to imitate. Using their Gilead training, the brothers set a fine example in public speaking and

International Student Body

Students who have attended Gilead School have represented scores of nationalities and have come to the school from over 110 lands.

The first international group was the sixth class, in 1945-46.

Application was made to the U.S. government for foreign students to be admitted under nonimmigration student visa provisions. In response, the U.S. Office of Education gave recognition to Gilead School as offering education comparable to professional colleges and educational institutions. Thus, since 1953, U.S. consuls throughout the world have had the Watchtower Bible School of Gilead on their list of approved educational institutions. As of April 30, 1954, this school appeared in the publication entitled "Educational Institutions Approved by the Attorney General."

teaching, and they gladly spent time with local brothers to help them to learn the art. In lands where people were traditionally easygoing and not particularly time conscious, the missionaries also patiently helped them to appreciate the value of starting meetings on time and encouraged everyone to be there on time.

Conditions that they found in some places indicated that help was needed in order to build up appreciation for the importance of adhering to Jehovah's righteous standards. In Botswana, for example, they found that some of the sisters still put strings or beads on their babies as protection against harm, not fully appreciating that this custom was rooted in superstition and witchcraft. In Portugal they found circumstances that were causing disunity. With patience, loving help, and firmness when necessary, improved spiritual health became evident.

Patience, loving help, and firmness when necessary

Missionaries assigned to positions of oversight in Finland devoted much time and effort to training local brothers to reason on problems in the light of Bible principles and thus to come to a conclusion that is in agreement with God's own thinking. In Argentina they also helped the brothers to learn the value of a schedule, how to keep records, the importance of files. In Germany they helped loyal brothers who were in some respects quite rigid in their views, as a result of their fight for survival in the concentration camps, to imitate more fully the mild-tempered ways of Jesus Christ as they shepherded the flock of God.—Matt. 11:28-30; Acts 20:28.

The work of some of the missionaries involved dealing with government officials, answering their questions, and making application for legal recognition of the work of Jehovah's Witnesses. For example, over a period of nearly four years, Brother Joly, who was assigned to Cameroon with his wife, made repeated efforts to obtain legal recognition. He spoke to French and African officials often. Finally, after a change of government, legal recognition was granted. By this time the Witnesses had been active in Cameroon for 27 years and already numbered more than 6,000.

Meeting the Challenges of Traveling Service

Some of the missionaries have been assigned to serve as traveling overseers. There was a special need in Australia, where some of the efforts of the brothers had been unwisely diverted from Kingdom interests to secular pursuits during World War II. In time, this was set straight, and during a visit by Brother Knorr in 1947, emphasis was given to the importance of keeping the work of Kingdom preaching to the fore. Thereafter, the enthusiasm, fine example, and teaching methods of Gilead graduates who served as circuit and district overseers further helped to cultivate a genuine spiritual atmosphere among the Witnesses there.

Victor White, Gilead-trained district overseer, speaking in the Philippines in 1949

Sharing in such traveling service has often required a willingness to expend great effort and face danger. Wallace Liverance found that the only way to reach a family of isolated publishers in Volcán, Bolivia, was to walk 55 miles round-trip across rocky, barren terrain in the scorching sun at a height of about 11,000 feet, while carrying his sleeping bag, food, and water, as well as literature. To serve congregations in the Philippines, Neal Callaway frequently rode on overcrowded rural buses on which space was shared not only with people but also with animals and produce. Richard Cotterill began his work as a traveling overseer in India at a time when thousands of people were being killed because of religious hatred. When he was scheduled to serve the brothers in a riot area, the railroad booking clerk tried to dissuade him. It proved to be a nightmare journey for most of the passengers, but Brother Cotterill had deep love for his brothers, regardless of where they lived or what language they spoke. With confidence in Jehovah, he reasoned: "If Jehovah wills, I shall try to get there."—Jas. 4:15.

Encouraging Others to Share in Full-Time Service

As a result of the zealous spirit displayed by the missionaries, many whom they have taught have imitated their example by getting into the full-time service. In Japan, where 168 missionaries have served, there were 75,956 pioneers in 1992; over 40 percent of the publishers in Japan were in some branch of full-time service. In the Republic of Korea, the ratio was similar.

From lands where the ratio of Witnesses to the population is quite favorable, many full-time ministers have been invited to receive training at Gilead School and have then been sent out to serve in other places. Large numbers of the missionaries have come from the United States and Canada; about 400 from Britain; over 240 from Germany; upwards of 150 from Australia; more than 100 from Sweden; in addition to sizable numbers from Denmark, Finland, Hawaii, the Netherlands, New Zealand, and others. Some countries that were themselves helped by missionaries later also provided prospective missionaries for service in other lands.

Filling Needs in a Growing Organization

As the organization has grown, the missionaries themselves have taken on further responsibilities. A considerable number of them have served as elders or ministerial servants in congregations that they helped to develop. In many lands they were the first circuit and district overseers. As further development has made it advantageous for the Society to establish new branch offices, a number of missionaries have been entrusted with responsibility in connection with branch operation. In some cases those who have come to know the language well have been asked to help with translating and proofreading Bible literature.

They have especially felt rewarded, however, when those with whom they had studied God's Word, or brothers to whose spiritual growth they had made some contribution, became qualified to take on such responsibilities. Thus a couple in Peru were delighted to see some with whom they had studied serve as special pioneers, helping to strengthen new congregations and open up new territory. From a study conducted by a missionary with a family in Sri Lanka came one of the members of the Branch Committee for that country. Many others of the missionaries have had similar joys.

They have also faced opposition.

In the Face of Opposition

Jesus told his followers that they would be persecuted, even as he had been. (John 15:20) Since the missionaries usually came from abroad, often when intense persecution broke out in a country, this meant deportation.

In 1967, Sona Haidostian and her parents were arrested in Aleppo, Syria. They were held in prison for five months and were then expelled from the country without their belongings. Margarita Königer, from Germany, was assigned to Madagascar; but deportations, one after another, led to new assignments, in Kenya, Dahomey (Benin), and Upper Volta (Burkina Faso). Domenick Piccone and his wife, Elsa, were expelled from Spain in 1957 because of their preaching, then from Portugal in 1962, and from

Morocco in 1969. However, in each country while seeking to forestall expulsion orders, good was accomplished. A witness was given to officials. In Morocco, for example, they had opportunity to witness to officials in the Sécurité Nationale, a Supreme Court judge, the police chief of Tangier, and the U.S. consuls in Tangier and Rabat.

Expulsion of the missionaries has not resulted in putting an end to the work of Jehovah's Witnesses, as some officials expected. Seeds of truth already sown often continue to grow. For example, four missionaries carried on their ministry for only a few months in Burundi before the government forced them to leave in 1964. But one of them kept up correspondence with an interested person, who wrote to say that he was studying the Bible with 26 persons. A Tanzanian Witness who had recently moved to Burundi also kept busy preaching. Gradually their numbers grew until hundreds were sharing the Kingdom message with still others.

Elsewhere, before ordering deportation, officials resorted to brute force to try to make everyone submit to their demands. At Gbarnga, Liberia, in 1963, soldiers rounded up 400 men, women, and children who were attending a Christian convention there. The soldiers marched them to the army compound, threatened them, beat them, and demanded that everyone—regardless of nationality or religious belief—salute the Liberian flag. Among those in the group was Milton Henschel, from the United States. There were also some missionaries, including John Charuk from Canada. One of the Gilead graduates compromised, as he had done on an earlier occasion (though he had not made that known), and this no doubt contributed to compromise on the part of others who were at that assembly. It became evident who truly feared God and who were ensnared by fear of man. (Prov. 29:25) Following this, the government ordered all the Witness missionaries from abroad to leave the country, although later that same year an executive order from the president permitted them to return.

Margarita Königer, in Burkina Faso, conducting a home Bible study

Frequently, the action taken against the missionaries by government officials has been as a result of clergy pressure. Sometimes that pressure was exerted in a clandestine manner. At other times, everyone knew who was whipping up the opposition. George Koivisto will never forget his first morning in field service in Medellín, Co-

MISSIONARIES PUSH WORLDWIDE EXPANSION

lombia. Suddenly a howling mob of schoolchildren appeared, hurling stones and clumps of clay. The householder, who had never seen him before, hustled him inside and closed the wooden shutters, all the time apologizing for the behavior of the mob outside. When the police arrived, some blamed the schoolteacher for letting out the students. But another voice cried out: "Not so! It was the priest! He announced over the loudspeakers to let the students out to 'throw stones at the *Protestantes.*'"

Godly courage coupled with love for the sheep was needed. Elfriede Löhr and Ilse Unterdörfer were assigned to the valley of Gastein in Austria. In a short time, much Bible literature was placed with people who were hungry for spiritual food. But then the clergy reacted. They urged schoolchildren to shout at the missionaries in the streets and to run ahead of them to warn householders not to listen. The people grew afraid. But with loving perseverance, a few good studies were started. When a public Bible lecture was arranged, the curate stood challengingly right in front of the meeting place. But when the missionaries went out into the street to welcome the people, the curate disappeared. He summoned a policeman and then returned, hoping to disrupt the meeting. But his efforts failed. In time a fine congregation was formed there.

In towns near Ibarra, Ecuador, Unn Raunholm and Julia Parsons faced priest-inspired mobs again and again. Because the priest caused an uproar every time the missionaries showed up in San Antonio, the sisters decided to concentrate on another town, called Atuntaqui. But one day the local sheriff there excitedly urged Sister Raunholm to leave town quickly. "The priest is organizing a demonstration against you, and I do not have enough men to defend you," he declared. She vividly recalls: "The crowd was coming after us! The Vatican flag of white and yellow was waved before the group while the priest shouted slogans like 'Long live the Catholic Church!' 'Down with the Protestants!' 'Long live the virginity of the Virgin!' 'Long live the confession!' Each time, the crowd would echo the slogans word for word after the priest." Just then a couple of men invited the Witnesses into the local Workers' House for safety. There the missionaries busily witnessed to curious people who came in to see what was going on. They placed every bit of literature they had.

Unn Raunholm, a missionary since 1958, had to face priest-led mobs in Ecuador

Courses Designed to Fill Special Needs

During the years since the first missionaries were sent out from Gilead School, the organization of Jehovah's Witnesses has experienced growth at an astounding rate. In 1943, when the school opened, there were only 129,070 Witnesses in 54 lands (but 103 lands according to the way the map was divided in the early 1990's). By 1992, there were 4,472,787 Witnesses in 229 countries and island groups worldwide. As this growth has taken place, the needs of the organization have changed. Branch offices that at one time cared for less than a hundred Witnesses grouped in a few congregations are now supervising the activity of tens of thousands of Witnesses, and many of these branches have found it necessary to print literature locally in order to equip those sharing in the evangelizing work.

To meet the changing needs, 18 years after the opening of Gilead School, a ten-month course of training at the Society's world headquarters was provided especially for brothers who were carrying heavy loads of responsibility in the branch offices of the Watch Tower Society. Some of them had previously attended the five-month missionary course at Gilead; others had not. All of them could benefit from specialized training for their work. Discussions of how to handle various situations and meet organizational needs in harmony with Bible principles had a unifying effect. Their course featured a verse-by-verse analytical study of the entire Bible. It also provided a review of the history of religion; training in the details involved in operating a branch office, a Bethel Home, and a printery; and instructions on supervising field ministry, organizing new congregations, and opening up new fields. These courses (including a final one that was reduced to eight months) were conducted at the world headquarters, in Brooklyn, New York, from 1961 to 1965. Many of the graduates were sent back to the countries where they had been serving; some were assigned to other lands where they could make valuable contributions to the work.

As of February 1, 1976, a new arrangement was put into operation in the branch offices of the Society in order to gear up for further expansion anticipated in harmony with Bible prophecy. (Isa. 60:8, 22) Instead of having just one branch overseer, along with his assistant, to provide supervision for each branch, the Governing Body appointed three or more qualified brothers to serve on each Branch Committee. Larger branches might have as many as seven on the committee. To provide training for all these brothers, a special five-week Gilead course in Brooklyn, New York, was arranged. Fourteen classes made up of Branch Committee members from all parts of the world were given this specialized training at the world headquarters from late 1977 to 1980. It was an excellent opportunity to unify and refine operations.

Gilead School continued to train those who had years of experience in the full-time ministry and were willing and able to be sent abroad, but more could be used. To expedite the training, schools were put into operation in

MISSIONARIES PUSH WORLDWIDE EXPANSION   545

other countries as an extension of Gilead so that students would not have to learn English before qualifying to attend. In 1980-81, the Gilead Cultural School of Mexico provided training for Spanish-speaking students who helped to fill an immediate need for qualified workers in Central and South America. In 1981-82, 1984, and again in 1992, classes of a Gilead Extension School were also conducted in Germany. From there the graduates were sent to Africa, Eastern Europe, South America, and various island nations. Further classes were held in India in 1983.

As zealous local Witnesses have joined with the missionaries in expanding the Kingdom witness, the number of Jehovah's Witnesses has increased rapidly, and this has led to the formation of more congregations. Between 1980 and 1987, the number of congregations worldwide increased by 27 percent, to a total of 54,911. In some areas, though many were attending meetings and sharing in the field ministry, most of the brothers were quite new. There was an urgent need for experienced Christian men to serve as spiritual shepherds and teachers, as well as to take the lead in the evangelizing work. To help meet this need, in 1987 the Governing Body put into operation the Ministerial Training School as a segment of the Gilead School program of Bible education. The eight-week course includes an intense study of the Bible as well as personal attention to each student's spiritual development. Organizational and judicial matters, along with the responsibilities of elders and ministerial servants, are considered, and specialized training is provided in public speaking. Without interfering with the

Ministerial Training School

First class, Coraopolis, Pa., U.S.A., in 1987 (above)
Third class in Britain, at Manchester, in 1991 (right)

regular classes for training missionaries, this school has used other facilities, convening in various lands. Graduates are now filling vital needs in many countries.

Thus the expanded training provided by the Watchtower Bible School of Gilead has kept pace with the changing needs of the rapidly growing international organization.

"Here I Am! Send Me"

The spirit shown by the missionaries is like that of the prophet Isaiah. When Jehovah alerted him to an opportunity for special service, he responded: "Here I am! Send me." (Isa. 6:8) This willingness of spirit has moved thousands of young men and women to leave behind familiar surroundings and relatives to serve for the furtherance of God's will wherever they are needed.

Family circumstances have brought changes to the lives of many missionaries. A number who had children after becoming missionaries were able to stay in the land to which they were assigned, doing needed secular work and working with the congregations. Some, after years of service, had to return to their homeland in order to care for aging parents, or for other reasons. But they counted it a privilege to share in missionary service as long as they could.

Others have been able to make missionary service their life's work. To do it, they have all had to come to grips with challenging circumstances. Olaf Olson, who has enjoyed a long missionary career in Colombia, acknowledged: "The first year was the hardest." That was largely because of inability to express himself adequately in his new language. He added: "If I had kept thinking about the country I had left, I would not have been happy, but I made up my mind to live both bodily and mentally in Colombia, to make friends with the brothers and sisters in the truth there, to keep my life filled with the ministry, and my assignment soon became home to me."

Their persevering in their assignments was not because they necessarily found their physical surroundings to be ideal. Norman Barber, who served in Burma (now Myanmar) and India, from 1947 until his death in 1986, expressed himself in this way: "If a person rejoices to be used by Jehovah, then one place is as good as another. . . . Frankly speaking, tropical weather is not my idea of the ideal weather in which to live. Neither is the way tropical people live the way I would personally choose to live. But there are more important things to take into consideration than such trivial matters. Being able to render aid to people who are really spiritually poor is a privilege beyond human powers to express."

Many more share that view, and this self-sacrificing spirit has contributed greatly to fulfillment of Jesus' prophecy that this good news of the Kingdom will be preached in all the inhabited earth, for a witness to all nations, before the end comes.—Matt. 24:14.

'Rendering aid to people who are really spiritually poor is a privilege beyond human powers to express'

CHAPTER 24

BY HUMAN POWER? OR BY GOD'S SPIRIT?

THE assignment that Jesus Christ set before his followers was one of seemingly impossible proportions. Although few in number, they were to proclaim the good news of God's Kingdom in all the inhabited earth. (Matt. 24:14; Acts 1:8) Not only was the task gigantic in size but it was to be done in the face of apparently overwhelming odds because, as Jesus frankly told his disciples, they would be hated and persecuted in all nations.—Matt. 24:9; John 15:19, 20.

In the face of global opposition, Jehovah's Witnesses have vigorously applied themselves to accomplish the work that Jesus foretold. The extent to which the witness has already been given is a matter of record, and a truly spectacular one. But what has made it possible? Has it been human power or ingenuity? Or has it been the operation of the spirit of God?

The Bible record concerning the restoration of true worship in Jerusalem in the sixth century B.C.E. reminds us that God's own role in the accomplishment of his will should never be overlooked. Secular commentators may search for some other explanation for what takes place. However, when explaining how his purpose would be accomplished, God caused his prophet Zechariah to declare: "'Not by a military force, nor by power, but by my spirit,' Jehovah of armies has said." (Zech. 4:6) Jehovah's Witnesses do not hesitate to say that this is how the preaching of the Kingdom message is being accomplished today—not by resorting to military force, nor by reason of the personal power or influence of any prominent group of men, but as a result of the operation of Jehovah's spirit. Does the evidence support their conviction?

"'By my spirit,' Jehovah of armies has said"

"Not Many Wise in a Fleshly Way"

When writing to early Christians in Greece, the apostle Paul acknowledged: "You behold his calling of you, brothers, that not many wise in a fleshly way were called, not many powerful, not many of noble birth; but God chose the foolish things of the world, that he might put the wise men to shame; and God chose the weak things of the world, that he might put the strong things to shame; and God chose the ignoble things of the world and the things looked down upon, the things that are not, that he might bring to nothing the things that are, in order that no flesh might boast in the sight of God."—1 Cor. 1:26-29.

Jesus' own apostles were from the working class. Four were fishermen by trade. One had been a tax collector, a profession despised by the Jews. These apostles were men who were viewed by the Jewish clergy as "unlettered and ordinary," indicating that their education was not from the schools of higher learning. (Acts 4:13) This does not mean that none who had more secular or religious education became Christians. The apostle Paul had studied at the feet of the learned Gamaliel, a member of the Jewish Sanhedrin. (Acts 22:3) But, as the scripture says, there were "not many" of such.

History testifies that Celsus, a Roman philosopher of the second century C.E., makes it a matter of mockery that "labourers, shoemakers, farmers, the most uninformed and clownish of men, should be zealous preachers of the Gospel." (*The History of the Christian Religion and Church, During the Three First Centuries,* by Augustus Neander) In the face of the scorn and violent persecution heaped upon them in the Roman Empire, what fortified true Christians to continue to be proclaimers of the good news? Jesus had said that it would be God's holy spirit.—Acts 1:8.

In more recent times, Jehovah's Witnesses have likewise been reproached because they are, for the most part, common people, not ones whose station in life causes the world to look up to them. Among the first of Jehovah's modern-day servants to introduce the Kingdom message to people in Denmark was a shoemaker. In Switzerland and France, it was a gardener. In many parts of Africa, the message was carried by itinerant workers. In Brazil, sailors had a share. Quite a few of the Polish Witnesses in northern France were coal miners.

Having been deeply moved by what they had learned from God's Word with the help of Watch Tower publications, they wanted to demonstrate their love for Jehovah by obeying him, so they undertook the work that God's Word says true Christians would do. Since then, millions more from all walks of life have joined in this work. All of them are evangelizers.

Jehovah's Witnesses form the only religious organization in the world in which every member personally witnesses to nonbelievers, endeavors to answer their questions from the Bible, and urges them to put faith in God's Word. Other religious organizations acknowledge that this is what all Christians should do. Some have tried to encourage their church members to do it. But only Jehovah's Witnesses consistently do it. Whose direction, whose counsel, whose assurance of loving support, and whose promises motivate them to do this work that others shun? Ask them your-

What fortified them to continue preaching in spite of ridicule and violent persecution?

self. No matter what the nation in which they live, they will reply: "Jehovah's." To whom, then, should credit be given?

A Role Foretold for the Angels of God

In describing the events that would take place during the conclusion of this system of things, Jesus showed that it would not only be his followers on earth who would share in the gathering of lovers of righteousness. At Matthew chapter 13, when discussing the gathering of the final ones who would share with him in the heavenly Kingdom, Jesus said: "The reapers are angels." And from how large a field would they gather these "sons of the kingdom"? "The field is the world," Jesus explained. Thus, those gathered would come from the far-flung corners of the globe. Has this actually occurred?—Matt. 13:24-30, 36-43.

Indeed it has! Although the Bible Students numbered only a few thousand as the world entered its last days in 1914, the Kingdom message that they preached quickly encircled the globe. In the Orient, in countries of Europe, Africa, and the Americas, and in the islands, individuals embraced the opportunity to serve the interests of God's Kingdom and were gathered into one united organization.

In Western Australia, for example, the Kingdom message reached Bert Horton. Religion as he knew it did not interest him; he had been involved in politics and trade-union activities. But when his mother gave him the Watch Tower publication *The Divine Plan of the Ages* and he began to read it along with the Bible, he knew that he had found the truth. Spontaneously he shared it with his workmates. When he was able to locate the Bible Students, he gladly associated with them, got baptized in 1922, took up the full-time ministry, and offered to serve in whatever area Jehovah's organization directed.

On the other side of the earth, W. R. Brown, who had already been preaching in the Caribbean islands, left for Africa in 1923 to spread the Kingdom message there. He was not an independent preacher on some personal mission. He too was working with Jehovah's organized people. He had offered to serve where he was needed, and he took up the assignment in West Africa in response to direction from the headquarters office. Those who personally benefited from his ministry were also helped to appreciate the importance of working closely with Jehovah's organization.

The Kingdom proclamation also reached into South America. Hermán Seegelken in Mendoza, Argentina, had long been aware of the hypocrisy in both the Catholic and the Protestant churches. But in 1929 he too heard the message of the Kingdom, eagerly accepted it, and began to share it with others, in unity with Jehovah's servants worldwide. Similar experiences took place around the globe. People "out of every tribe and

Evidence of angelic direction

tongue and people and nation," though scattered geographically and pursuing diverse ways of life, not only listened but offered themselves in God's service. They were gathered into a unified organization to do the work that Jesus had foretold for this time. (Rev. 5:9, 10) What accounts for this?

The Bible says that the angels of God would have a vital role in it. Because of this, the proclamation of the Kingdom would reverberate around the globe like the sound of a trumpet from a superhuman source. In fact, by 1935 it had penetrated 149 lands—to the north, the south, the east, and the west, from one end of the earth to the other.

At first, only a "little flock" showed genuine appreciation for God's Kingdom and were willing to serve its interests. That is what the Bible had foretold. Now a rapidly growing "great crowd," numbering into the millions out of all nations, have come to be associated with them. That, too, was foretold in God's Word. (Luke 12:32; John 10:16; Rev. 7:9, 10) These are not people who simply profess to share the same religion but who, in reality, are divided among themselves by all the attitudes and philosophies that fragment the world around them. Jehovah's Witnesses do not merely talk about God's Kingdom while actually putting their trust in the rulership of men. Even at risk to their lives, they obey God as ruler. The Bible clearly states that the gathering together of such people who "fear God and give him glory" would be done under the direction of the angels. (Rev. 14:6, 7; Matt. 25:31-46) The Witnesses are firmly convinced that this is what has actually taken place.

On countless occasions, as they have shared in their ministry, they have seen convincing evidence of heavenly direction. For example, in Rio de Janeiro, Brazil, a group of Witnesses were completing their house-to-house calls one Sunday when one of the group said: "I want to continue working a while. For some reason I want to go to that house." The one in charge of the group suggested that they leave it for another day, but the publisher insisted. At that door the Witness found a woman who, with tears streaming down her face, said that she had just been praying for help. She had previously been contacted by the Witnesses but had not shown interest in the Bible's message. However, the sudden death of her husband had made her realize her need for spiritual help. She had looked for the Kingdom Hall, but in vain. Earnestly she had been praying to God for help, and now it was at her door. Not long thereafter she was baptized. She was convinced that God had heard her prayer and had taken the needed action to provide an answer.—Ps. 65:2.

A German Witness of Jehovah who used to live in New York made it a regular practice to pray to God for direction as she engaged in her ministry. There was an interested woman that she had been looking for, week after week, on the street because she did not know where the woman lived. Then, one day in 1987, as the Witness started out in the ministry, she prayed: "Jehovah, you know where she is. Please help me to find her." A few minutes later, she saw the woman sitting in a restaurant.

Was it just an accident? The Bible says that true Christians are "God's fellow workers" and that the angels are sent "to minister for those who are going to inherit salvation." (1 Cor. 3:9; Heb. 1:14) After the Witness told the woman how she had found her, the woman accepted an invitation to sit down and examine the Bible further that very day.

Reaching 'Inaccessible Territories' With the Good News

Jehovah's Witnesses have been persistent in their efforts to reach all lands with the Kingdom message. But this does not fully explain what has been accomplished. They have seen the Kingdom message spread out into areas where all their carefully planned efforts had been repulsed.

For example, on more than one occasion during the 1920's and 1930's, earnest representations were made to government officials in what was then the Soviet Union to obtain permission to ship Bible literature into that land or to print it there. The replies at that time were negative. There were a few of Jehovah's Witnesses in the Soviet Union, but much more help was needed to accomplish the preaching work that God's Word said must be done. Could anything be done to provide that help?

Interestingly, at the end of World War II, along with many other people, more than a thousand of Jehovah's Witnesses from what had been eastern Poland found themselves within the Soviet Union. In the Ravensbrück concentration camp, hundreds of young Russian women had come to know fellow prisoners who were Jehovah's Witnesses. Some of these women dedicated themselves to Jehovah during that time, and later they were returned to various parts of the Soviet Union. Hundreds of others also found themselves inhabitants of the Soviet Union as national borders changed during the war. The outcome was not what the Soviet government had in mind. The Governing Body of Jehovah's Witnesses did not arrange it. But it did serve toward the accomplishment of what God's inspired Word had foretold. Commenting on these developments, *The Watchtower* said: "Thus it can be seen how, in the Lord's providence, he can raise up witnesses in any land, there to hold high the banner of truth and make known the name of Jehovah."—Issue of February 1, 1946.

It has not been just one country that has said to Jehovah's Witnesses: 'You can't come in here!' or, 'You can't preach here.' It has occurred again and again around the earth, in literally scores of lands, frequently as a

'The Lord can raise up witnesses in any land'

result of clergy pressure on government officials. Some of these countries later granted legal status to Jehovah's Witnesses. But even before that took place, the worship of Jehovah, the Creator of heaven and earth, had been embraced by thousands of people within their borders. How was that accomplished?

The simple explanation is found in the Bible, namely, that angels of God have a prominent role in carrying to people of every nation the urgent appeal: "Fear God and give him glory, because the hour of the judgment by him has arrived, and so worship the One who made the heaven and the earth and sea and fountains of waters."—Rev. 14:6, 7.

Success Against Overwhelming Odds

What Jehovah's Witnesses have faced in some lands are not merely prohibitions imposed on their public ministry but efforts to stamp them out completely.

During World War I, a concerted effort was made by the clergy in the United States and Canada to put an end to the work of the Bible Students, as Jehovah's Witnesses were then known. This is a matter of public record. In spite of legal guarantees of freedom of speech and of religion, the clergy pressured government officials to ban literature of the Bible Students. Many were arrested and held without bail; others were viciously beaten. Officials of the Watch Tower Society and their close associates were given long prison terms in court proceedings that were later shown to be invalid. Said Ray Abrams in his book *Preachers Present Arms:* "An analysis of the whole case leads to the conclusion that the churches and the clergy were originally behind the movement to stamp out the Russellites," as the clergy disparagingly called the Bible Students. But following the war, those Bible Students emerged with greater vigor than ever to advertise Jehovah's King, Jesus Christ, and his Kingdom. From where did that renewed vigor come? The Bible had foretold such an occurrence and had said that it would be as a result of "spirit of life from God."—Rev. 11:7-11.

Following the rise of the Nazis to power in Germany, persecution of Jehovah's Witnesses intensified in lands that came under Nazi control. There were arrests and brutal treatment. Bans were imposed. Finally, in October 1934, congregations of Jehovah's Witnesses throughout Germany sent registered letters to the government stating clearly that they had no political objectives but that they were determined to obey God as ruler. At the same time, congregations of Witnesses worldwide sent cablegrams in support of their Christian brothers in Germany.

On that same day, October 7, 1934, in the office of Dr. Wilhelm Frick, in Berlin, Adolf Hitler with clenched fists declared regarding Jehovah's Witnesses: "This brood will be exterminated in Germany!" It was no idle threat. Widespread arrests occurred. According to a confidential notification of the Prussian Secret State Police dated June 24, 1936, a "special Gestapo Command" was formed to fight against the Witnesses. After extensive preparation the Gestapo launched their campaign to capture all of Jehovah's Witnesses and everyone suspected of being a Witness. During that offensive the entire police net was involved, leaving criminal elements unmolested.

Reports indicate that eventually some 6,262 German Witnesses were arrested. Karl Wittig, a former German government officer who was himself detained in several concentration camps, later wrote: "No other group of prisoners . . . was exposed to the sadism of the SS-soldiery in such a fashion as the Bible Students were. It was a sadism marked by an unending chain of physical and mental tortures, the likes of which no language in the world can express."

What was the result? In a book published in 1982, Christine King concludes: "Only against the Witnesses [in contrast to other religious groups] was the government unsuccessful." Hitler had vowed to exterminate them, and hundreds were killed. Nevertheless, Dr. King notes: "The work [of preaching about God's Kingdom] went on and in May 1945 the Jehovah's Witness movement was still alive, whilst National Socialism was not." She also points out: "No compromises had been made." (*The Nazi State and the New Religions: Five Case Studies in Non-Conformity*) Why was Hitler, with his well-equipped army, highly trained police, and numerous extermination camps, unable to carry out his threat to destroy this relatively small and unarmed group of what the world views as ordinary people? Why have other nations been unable to put a stop to their activity? Why is it that, not merely a few isolated individuals, but Jehovah's Witnesses as a whole have remained firm in the face of brutal persecution?

A united people who have proved firm in faith in the face of apparently overwhelming odds

The answer lies in some wise advice given by Gamaliel, a Law teacher, to fellow members of the Jewish Sanhedrin when they were dealing with a similar case involving the apostles of Jesus Christ. He said: "Do not meddle with these men, but let them alone; (because, if this scheme or this work is from men, it will be overthrown; but if it is from God, you will not be able to overthrow them;) otherwise, you may perhaps be found fighters actually against God."—Acts 5:38, 39.

Thus the historical facts show that the seemingly impossible task assigned by Jesus to his followers to perform in the face of apparently overwhelming odds is being accomplished not by human power but by God's spirit. As Jesus himself said in prayer to God: "Father, all things are possible to you."—Mark 14:36.

"Sia Dio Riconosciuto Verace"
الحق الذي يقود إلى الحياة الأبدية
Usted puede vivir para siempre en el paraíso en la Tierra
BAZAR LOURDES
MIUDEZAS EM GERAL
KOLBUS

SECTION 5

Kingdom Preaching Furthered by Production of Bible Literature

Preaching in all the inhabited earth—how could it be accomplished? As this section (Chapters 25 to 27) shows, the means used have involved the development of international facilities for publishing Bibles and Bible literature to reach people of all nations.

CHAPTER 25

PREACHING PUBLICLY AND FROM HOUSE TO HOUSE

WHEN Jesus Christ sent out his disciples, he instructed them: "As you go, *preach,* saying, 'The kingdom of the heavens has drawn near.'" (Matt. 10:7) And in his prophetic command to true Christians who would be living during the conclusion of the system of things, he said: "This good news of the kingdom *will be preached* in all the inhabited earth for a witness." (Matt. 24:14) What did that mean?

It did not mean that they were to build churches, ring a bell, and wait for a congregation to assemble to hear them give a sermon once a week. The Greek verb here rendered "preach" (*ke·rys'so*) means, basically, "make proclamation as a herald." The idea is not delivering sermons to a closed group of disciples but, rather, making open, public declaration.

Jesus himself set the example as to how it was to be done. He went to places where he could find people. In the first century, people regularly gathered in the synagogues to hear the Scriptures read. Jesus seized opportunities to preach to them there, not merely in one city but in cities and villages throughout Galilee and Judea. (Matt. 4:23; Luke 4:43, 44; John 18:20) Even more often, the Gospel records show, he preached by the seashore, on the mountainside, along the road, in villages, and in the homes of those who welcomed him. Wherever he found people, he talked about God's purpose for humankind. (Luke 5:3; 6:17-49; 7:36-50; 9:11, 57-62; 10:38-42; John 4:4-26, 39-42) And when he sent out his disciples, he instructed them to go to the homes of people to search out deserving ones and to witness to them about the Kingdom of God.—Matt. 10:7, 11-13.

Jehovah's Witnesses in modern times have endeavored to follow the pattern set by Jesus and his first-century disciples.

Heralding News of Christ's Presence

As Charles Taze Russell and his associates began to grasp the harmonious pattern of truth set out in God's Word, they were deeply moved by what they learned about the object and manner of Christ's return. Brother

Wherever he found people, Jesus talked about God's purpose for humankind

Russell felt both the need to make it known and a great urgency about doing it. He arranged his affairs to travel to places where there were people to whom he could speak about these Bible truths. He attended religious camp meetings and availed himself of opportunities to speak to them, as Jesus had preached in the synagogues. But he soon realized that more could be accomplished in other ways. His study of the Scriptures showed that Jesus and his apostles did the greater part of their preaching while speaking privately with individuals and when they were calling from house to house. He recognized, too, the value of following up a conversation by putting into the hands of people something in printed form.

Already in 1877 he had published the booklet *The Object and Manner of Our Lord's Return*. Two years later he undertook regular publication of the magazine *Zion's Watch Tower and Herald of Christ's Presence*. Yes, the objective was to *preach*, or to *herald*, vital news concerning Christ's presence.

As early as 1881, literature of the Bible Students was being handed out free of charge near the churches—not right at the church doors but nearby so that people who were religiously inclined would receive it. Many of the Bible Students gave such literature to acquaintances or sent it out by mail. By 1903 the *Watch Tower* recommended that they endeavor to reach *everyone* by house-to-house distribution of the tracts, instead of concentrating on church attenders. Not all Bible Students did this, but many responded with real zeal. It was reported, for example, that in a number of the large cities in the United States, as well as in their suburbs for ten miles or more in every direction, practically every house was visited. Millions upon

Tens of millions of these tracts were distributed, free of charge, near the churches, from house to house, and by mail

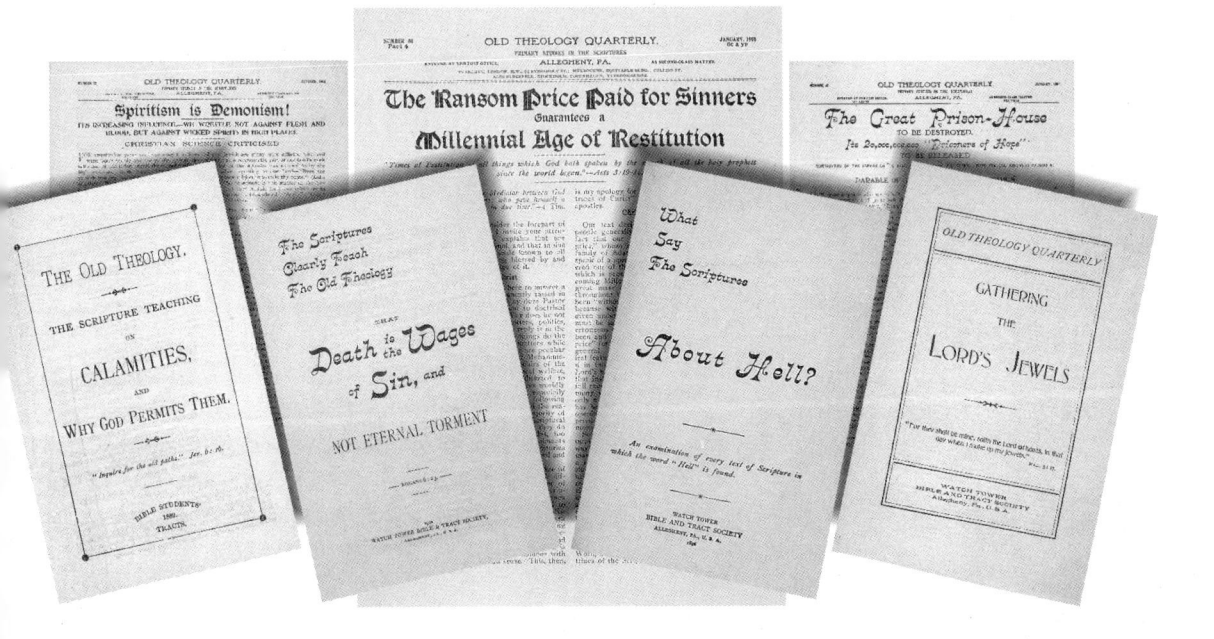

Colporteur evangelists distributed books explaining the Bible

millions of tracts, or booklets, were put out in this way. At that time most Bible Students who had a share in spreading the good news did it by some kind of free distribution of tracts and other literature.

Others of the Bible Students—more limited in number—served as colporteur evangelists, using a considerable portion of their time exclusively for this work.

Zealous Colporteurs Take the Lead

The first call for dedicated men and women who could use a substantial amount of their time in this service went out in April 1881. They would offer householders and businessmen a small book explaining Bible truths and a subscription for the *Watch Tower*. Their objective was to search out those who were truth-hungry and share enlightenment with them. For a time they tried saying just enough to stimulate interest, leaving at each home a packet containing literature for the householder to examine, and then returning in a few days. Some householders would return the literature; others might want to purchase it; frequently there would be opportunities for conversation. Regarding their objective, the *Watch Tower* stated: "It is not the selling of the packets, nor the taking of subscriptions, but the spread of the truth, by getting people to read."

The number who shared in this colporteur evangelism was relatively small. During the first 30 years, their ranks varied from a few up to 600 or so. These colporteurs were pioneers in the true sense of the word, opening up new territory. Anna Andersen was one who persevered in this service for decades, usually traveling on a bicycle, and she personally reached nearly every town in Norway with the good news. Other colporteurs traveled abroad and were the first to take the message to such lands as Finland, Barbados, El Salvador, Guatemala, Honduras, and Burma (now Myanmar). There were also some who were not free to move to other areas but who served as colporteur evangelists in their home territory.

The work by the colporteurs was outstanding. One who was serving on the west coast of the United States wrote in 1898 that during the previous 33 months, he had traveled 8,000 miles with his horse and rig, witnessed in 72 towns, made 18,000 calls, placed 4,500 books, taken 125 subscriptions, given away 40,000 tracts, and seen 40 people not only accept the message but also start sharing it with others. A husband-and-wife team serving in Australia succeeded in placing 20,000 books in the hands of interested persons during a period of just two and a half years.

Anna Andersen reached nearly every town in Norway with Bible literature

Were numerous placements the exception rather than the rule? Well, the report for 1909 shows that about 625 colporteurs (the total on the list at that time) received from the Society 626,981 bound books to place with the public (an average of more than a thousand for each colporteur), in addition to a large amount of free literature. They often could not carry enough books from house to house, so they would take orders and then return later to make deliveries.

Nevertheless, some objected: "This is not preaching!" But, in fact, as Brother Russell explained, it was preaching of a most effective sort. Instead of hearing just one sermon, people were receiving many sermons in printed form and thus could enjoy them again and again and could check their contents in their own Bible. This was evangelism that took into account the fact that general education had equipped people to read. The book *The New Creation* pointed out: "The fact that these evangelists are working on lines adapted to our day instead of upon the lines adapted to the past, is no more an argument against this work than is the fact that they travel by steam and electric power instead of on foot or on camels. The evangelization is through the presentation of the Truth . . . , the Word of God."

The genuine interest of the Bible Students in helping people was manifest in the thoroughness that in time became characteristic of their preaching work. *The Watch Tower* of March 1, 1917, outlined the program as follows: First, the colporteurs would call on the homes in an area, offering volumes of *Studies in the*

Special Blessing on Door-to-Door Work

"As at the first advent, work from door to door, instead of pulpit preaching, seems to be receiving the Lord's special blessing."—"Watch Tower," July 15, 1892.

Scriptures. Then, following up on names noted by the colporteurs or turned in at public meetings, pastoral workers* would call. They endeavored to stimulate a desire to read the literature, encouraged interested ones to attend specially arranged talks, and made an effort to arrange classes for Berean Bible study. When possible, the colporteurs would cover the same area again, and then the pastoral workers would follow through in order to keep in touch with those who showed interest. Later, other class workers would visit the same homes with volunteer matter, as they called the tracts and the other free literature that they offered. This made it possible for everyone to receive at least something that might stimulate a desire to learn more about God's purpose.

When only one or two colporteurs served in an area, and there was no congregation, the colporteurs often did the follow-up work themselves. Thus, when Hermann Herkendell and his partner went to Bielefeld, Germany, as colporteurs in 1908, they were specifically instructed to acquaint the interested ones in the area with one another and to form a congregation. A few years later, *The Watch Tower* mentioned other colporteurs who were giving personal attention to interested ones to the point that they were leaving a class of Bible Students in every town or city where they served.

A valuable aid in this work was provided in 1921 in the book *The Harp of God*. Especially designed to benefit beginners, the book eventually had a circulation of 5,819,037 in 22 languages. To assist those who obtained this book, the Society arranged a correspondence course in topical Bible study. This consisted of 12 questionnaires, sent out over a period of 12 weeks. With the use of this book, arrangements were also made for group Bible discussions in the homes of interested persons. A number of Bible Students would usually attend such a study.

The Witnesses were keenly aware, however, that the field was large and their numbers were few.—Luke 10:2.

Newspaper ads helped to reach people who were not being contacted in other ways

---

* The pastoral work was first organized during 1915-16 in the 500 or so congregations that had elected Brother Russell to be their pastor. As pastor, he had written a letter to them outlining the work, which was at first limited to the sisters. The following year brothers too were included in this activity. This pastoral work, carried on by a select group, continued until 1921.

PREACHING PUBLICLY AND FROM HOUSE TO HOUSE   561

Reaching Many When Numbers Were Few

The *Watch Tower* pointed out that those who were truly spirit-anointed Christians had the God-given responsibility to locate and assist all who were earnest Christians, whether they were churchgoers or not. (Isa. 61:1, 2) How could it be done?

The two Bible Students (J. C. Sunderlin and J. J. Bender) who were sent to England in 1881 could have accomplished relatively little by themselves; but with the assistance of hundreds of young men who were paid for their services, they managed to have 300,000 copies of *Food for Thinking Christians* distributed in just a short time. Adolf Weber, who returned to Switzerland with the good news in the mid-1890's, had a vast territory extending into several countries in which to preach. How could he cover it all? He personally traveled far as a colporteur, but he also placed advertisements in newspapers and made arrangements for booksellers to include Watch Tower publications in their collections. The small group of Bible Students in Germany in 1907 arranged to have 4,850,000 four-page tracts mailed out with newspapers. Shortly after the first world war, a Latvian brother who was a member of the Society's headquarters staff in New York paid for ads in newspapers in the land of his birth. A man who responded to one of those ads became the first Bible Student in Latvia. Use of such means of publicity, however, did not take the place of personal witnessing and the house-to-house search for deserving ones. Rather, it was used to amplify the proclamation.

More than ads were published in the newspapers, however. During the years leading up to World War I, under Brother Russell's supervision, his sermons were regularly published. In a short period, this picked up amazing momentum. More than 2,000 newspapers, with a combined readership of 15,000,000, were carrying these sermons concurrently in the United States, Canada, Britain, Australia, and South Africa. Could more be done? Brother Russell thought so.

After two years of preparation, the first exhibition of the "Photo-Drama of Creation" was given in January 1914. The "Photo-Drama" was presented in four parts. The eight-hour program included motion pictures and slides, coordinated with voice recordings. It was truly an extraordinary production that was designed to build up appreciation for the Bible and God's purpose as set out in it. Showings were organized so that 80 cities could be served each day. Advance advertising was done by means of newspapers, a generous number of window signs, and the distribution of large amounts of free printed matter designed to stimulate interest in the "Photo-Drama." Wherever it was

More than 2,000 newspapers on four continents carried Brother Russell's sermons concurrently

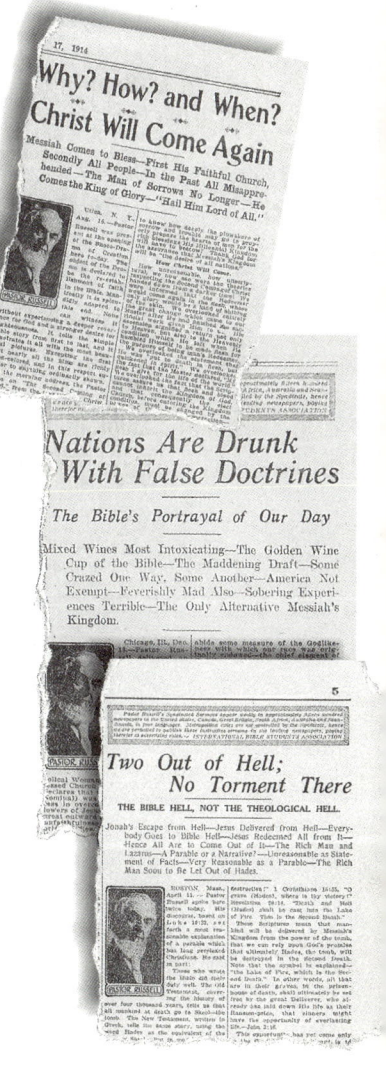

JEHOVAH'S WITNESSES—PROCLAIMERS OF GOD'S KINGDOM

shown, crowds turned out to see it. Within a year the "Photo-Drama" had reached audiences totaling upwards of 8,000,000 persons in the United States and Canada, and further capacity crowds were being reported from Britain and the European continent as well as Australia and New Zealand. The "Photo-Drama" was followed by a somewhat shorter version (without the motion pictures) for use in smaller towns and country areas. In various languages the Drama continued in use for at least two decades. Much interest was stirred up, names of interested ones were turned in, and follow-up calls were made.

Then, in the 1920's, another instrument became available to give wide publicity to the Kingdom message. Brother Rutherford felt strongly that the hand of the Lord was manifest in its development. What was it? Radio. Less than two years after the world's first commercial radio station began regular broadcasts (in 1920), J. F. Rutherford, president of the Watch Tower Society, went on the air to broadcast Bible truth. Here was an instrument that could reach millions of people simultaneously. Within two more years, in 1924, the Society had its own radio station, WBBR, in operation in New York. By 1933, the peak year, 408 stations were being used to carry the message to six continents. In addition to live broadcasts, programs on scores of subjects were prerecorded. Intense local advertising by distribution of printed announcements was done so that people would know about the broadcasts and could benefit from them. These broadcasts broke down much prejudice and opened the eyes of honesthearted ones. Many people, out of fear of their neighbors and the clergy, held back from attending meetings sponsored by the Bible Students, but this did not stop them from listening to the radio in the privacy of their own home. The broadcasts did not replace the need for house-to-house witnessing; but they did carry Bible truth to places that were hard to reach, and they provided excellent openings for conversations when the Witnesses personally visited the homes.

The "Photo-Drama of Creation" gave a powerful witness to millions of people in many lands

Responsibility of Each One to Witness

The responsibility to have a *personal* share in witnessing had been pointed out in the *Watch Tower* for decades. But from 1919 on, it was a topic of constant discussion in print and on convention programs. Yet, for many people it was not easy to approach strangers at their doors, and at first only a limited number of the Bible Students shared regularly in house-to-house witnessing.

Heartwarming Scriptural encouragement was given. "Blessed Are the Fearless" was the subject featured in the *Watch Tower* issues of August 1 and 15, 1919. It warned against fear of man, drew attention to Gideon's courageous 300 warriors who were alert and willing to serve in whatever way the Lord directed and against seemingly overwhelming odds, and commended Elisha's fearless reliance on Jehovah. (Judg. 7:1-25; 2 Ki. 6: 11-19; Prov. 29:25) In 1921 the article "Be of Good Courage" highlighted not merely the duty but *the privilege* that it is to serve on the Lord's side against satanic forces of darkness by having a share in doing the work foretold at Matthew 24:14. Those whose circumstances imposed limitations on them were urged not to be discouraged and at the same time not to hold back from doing what they could.

By frank Scriptural discussions, *The Watch Tower* made all who professed to be anointed servants of God aware of their responsibility to be proclaimers of God's Kingdom. The issue of August 15, 1922, had a concise, pointed article entitled "Service Essential"—that is, service in imitation of Christ, service that would take one to the homes of others to tell them about God's Kingdom. Later that same year, it was shown that such service, to be of value in the sight of God, must be motivated by love. (1 John 5:3) An article in the issue of June 15, 1926, stated that God is not at all impressed by formalistic worship; what he wants is obedience, and that includes appreciation for whatever means he is using to accomplish his purpose. (1 Sam. 15:22) The following year, when considering "Christians' Mission on Earth," attention was directed to Jesus' role as "the faithful and true witness" and to the fact that the apostle Paul preached "publicly and from house to house."—Rev. 3:14; Acts 20:20.

By means of radio, J. F. Rutherford was able to witness to millions of people worldwide right in their homes

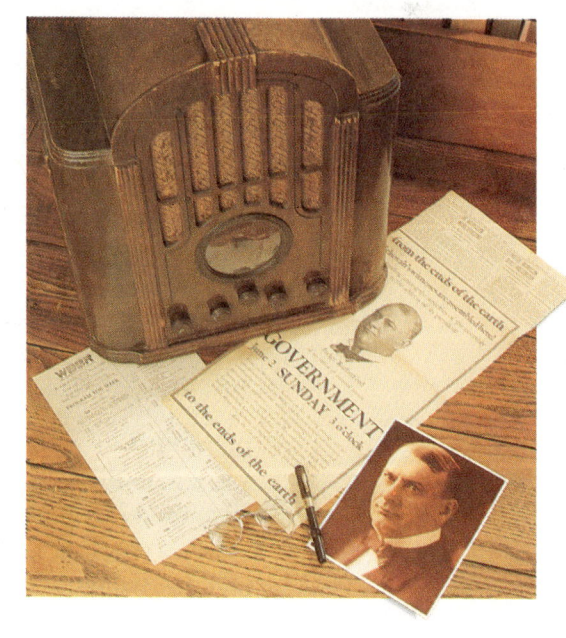

Detailed presentations for publishers to memorize were provided in the *Bulletin*, their monthly service instruction sheet. Encouragement was given to share in the field service regularly each week. But the number who actually witnessed by making house-to-house calls was small at first, and some who started out did not continue in the work. In the United States, for example, the average weekly number reported as sharing in the field service in 1922 was 2,712. But by 1924 the figure had dropped to 2,034.

Prepared to leave by bicycle for group witnessing in England

In 1926 the average rose to 2,261, with a peak of 5,937 sharing during one week of special activity.

Then, late in 1926, the Society began to encourage congregations to include a portion of Sunday as a time for group witnessing and to offer at that time not only tracts but also books for Bible study. In 1927, *The Watch Tower* urged loyal ones in the congregations to remove from positions of eldership any whose speech or actions showed that they did not accept the responsibility of witnessing publicly and from house to house. Thus, branches that were not bearing fruit were taken away, as it were, and the ones that remained were pruned so that they might bear more fruit to God's praise. (Compare Jesus' illustration at John 15:1-10.) Did this actually result in an increase in public praise to Jehovah? The year 1928 saw a 53-percent increase in the average weekly number of participants in witnessing in the United States!

No longer did the Witnesses simply hand people a free tract and move on. More of them spoke briefly to householders, endeavoring to stir up interest in the Bible's message, and then offered them books to read.

Those early Witnesses certainly were courageous, although not all of them were tactful. Nevertheless, they stood out as distinct from other religious groups. They did not just *say* that each one should bear witness to his faith. In ever-increasing numbers, they were actually doing it.

Testimony Cards and Phonographs

Late in 1933 a different method of preaching was begun. By way of introduction, the Witnesses handed people a testimony card that had a brief message for the householder to read. This was especially of great help to new publishers, who did not receive much training in those days. Generally, they made only a few brief remarks to the householder after the card had been read; some spoke at greater length, using the Bible. The use of testimony cards continued well into the 1940's. It allowed for rapid coverage of territory, and it enabled Witnesses to reach more people, get much valuable Bible literature into their hands, give a uniform witness, and even present the message to people whose language they could not speak. It also resulted in some awkward moments when householders kept the card and shut their door, making it necessary for the Witness to knock again to retrieve it!

Recorded Bible discourses too had a prominent role during the 1930's and early in the 1940's. In 1934 some of the Witnesses began to take a portable phonograph with them when they went witnessing. The machine was rather heavy, so they might keep it in their automobile or leave it at a convenient place until they found people who were willing to listen to a recorded Bible discourse. Then, in 1937, use of a portable phonograph right on the doorstep was inaugurated. The procedure was simple: After stating that he had an important Bible message, the Witness would put the needle on the record and let it do the talking. Kasper Keim, a German pioneer serving in the Netherlands, was most grateful for his "Aaron," as he called the phonograph, because he found it difficult to witness in Dutch. (Compare Exodus 4:14-16.) Out of curiosity entire families would sometimes listen to the records.

As of 1940, more than 40,000 phonographs were being used. That year a new vertical model designed and built by the Witnesses was introduced, and it was put to use especially in the Americas. It stirred up even greater curiosity because householders could not see the record as it was being played. Each record was 78 rpm and was four and a half minutes in length. The titles were short and to the point: "Kingdom," "Prayer," "Way to Life," "Trinity," "Purgatory," "Why Clergy Oppose Truth." Upwards of 90 different discourses were recorded; over a million records were put to use. The presentations were clear and easy to follow. Many householders listened appreciatively; a few reacted violently. But an effective and consistent witness was being given.

Boldly Heralding the Good News in Public Places

Although testimony cards and phonograph records were doing much of the "talking," great courage was required to be a Witness during those years. The very nature of the work thrust the individual Witnesses before the public.

Following the 1931 convention in Columbus, Ohio, Jehovah's Witnesses distributed the booklet *The Kingdom, the Hope of the World,* which included a resolution entitled "Warning From Jehovah" that was addressed "To the Rulers and to the People." They recognized that as Witnesses for Jehovah, a serious obligation rested on them to deliver the warning set out in his Word. (Ezek. 3:17-21) They did not simply put those booklets in the mail or slip them under doors. They delivered them personally. They called on all the clergy and, to the extent possible, politicians, military officers, and the executives of large corporations. Additionally,

Starting in 1933, printed testimony cards were used

Recorded Bible discourses gave a powerful witness during the 1930's and 1940's

they called on the public in general in the approximately one hundred lands where Jehovah's Witnesses were then carrying on organized witnessing.

By 1933 they were making use of powerful transcription machines to play recordings of straightforward Bible discourses in public places. Brothers Smets and Poelmans mounted their equipment on a tricycle and stood by it as it boomed out the message in the marketplaces and near the churches in Liège, Belgium. They were often out there ten hours a day. People in Jamaica would readily gather when they heard music, so the brothers there played music first. When crowds would pour out of the bush areas to the main roads to see what was happening, they would find Jehovah's Witnesses delivering the Kingdom message.

Some of that transcription equipment was installed in automobiles and on boats, with loudspeakers on the roof to make the sound carry farther. Bert and Vi Horton, in Australia, operated a van with a large sound horn mounted on top that was inscribed with the words "Kingdom Message." One year they made almost every street in Melbourne resound with stirring exposures of false religion and heartwarming descriptions of the blessings of God's Kingdom. During those years Claude Goodman was pioneering in India. Use of the sound car, with records in the local languages, enabled him to reach large crowds in bazaars, in parks, along the road —wherever people could be found.

When the brothers in Lebanon parked their sound car on a hill and broadcast lectures, the sound carried down into the valleys. People in the villages, not seeing the source of the voice, were sometimes frightened, thinking that God was speaking to them out of the heavens!

There were a few tense moments for the brothers, however. On one occasion, in Syria, a village priest left his dinner on the table, grabbed his big walking stick, and ran out into the crowd that was gathering to hear a Bible discourse broadcast from a sound car. Waving his stick angrily and shouting, he demanded: "Stop! I command you to stop!" But the brothers realized that not everyone agreed with him; there were those who wanted to hear. Soon, some of the crowd bodily picked up the priest and carried him back to his house, where they deposited him again at the dinner table! Despite clergy opposition, the Witnesses courageously saw to it that people had the opportunity to hear.

This era also saw extensive use of advertising placards worn by Witnesses in business areas as they distributed invitations to special lectures. It began in 1936 in Glasgow, Scotland. That year the same method of advertising was used in London, England, and then in the United States. Two years later such advertising was augmented by the carrying of signs held aloft on sticks. These signs proclaimed, "Religion Is a Snare and a Racket"* and, "Serve God and Christ the King." At the time of a convention, the line of marchers bearing these signs might be miles long. As they quietly marched, single file, along heavily traveled streets, the effect was like that of the army of ancient Israel going around Jericho before its walls fell. (Josh. 6:10, 15-21) From London, England, to Manila, in the Philippines, such bold public witnessing was done.

Yet another method of public witnessing was undertaken in 1940. In line with the scripture that refers to 'true wisdom calling aloud in the streets,' in February of that year Jehovah's Witnesses began street-corner distribution of *The Watchtower* and *Consolation* (now known as *Awake!*).# (Prov. 1:20) They would call out slogans drawing attention to the magazines and the message these contained. In large cities and small towns in all parts of the world, Jehovah's Witnesses offering their magazines have become a familiar sight. But doing that work requires courage, and especially

---

* That wording was based on the understanding that the term religion embraced all worship built on the traditions of men, instead of on God's Word, the Bible. However, in 1950, when the *New World Translation of the Christian Greek Scriptures* was published, footnotes at Acts 26:5, Colossians 2:18, and James 1:26, 27 indicated that the term religion could properly be used to refer to true worship or false. This was further clarified in *The Watchtower* of March 15, 1951, page 191, and the book *What Has Religion Done for Mankind?*, pages 8-10.

Some street witnessing with the magazines had been done on a trial basis the preceding year, in California, U.S.A. Even as far back as 1926, the Bible Students had engaged in general street distribution of booklets containing important messages. Much earlier, in 1881, they had distributed literature near the churches on Sundays.

Sound cars, sometimes many of them (as here in Australia), were used to broadcast Bible truth in public places

JEHOVAH'S WITNESSES—PROCLAIMERS OF GOD'S KINGDOM

was such courage needed when this work began, for it was an era when there was much persecution coupled with the fever of wartime nationalism.

When called on to share in such public witnessing, the Witnesses responded in faith. The number having a personal share in the work continued to increase. They counted it a privilege to demonstrate their integrity to Jehovah in this way. But there was more for them to learn.

Each One Able to Explain His Faith

An extraordinary program of education got under way in 1942. It started at the world headquarters of Jehovah's Witnesses, and by the next year, it began to be inaugurated in congregations of the Witnesses earth wide. With confidence that God's spirit was upon them and that he had put his word in their mouths, they were determined to preach that word even if persecutors were to deprive them of Watch Tower publications or the Bible itself. (Isa. 59:21) There were already lands, such as Nigeria, where the Witnesses had only the Bible to use when preaching, since the government had banned all Watch Tower literature and had even seized the publications many of the brothers had in their private libraries.

It was on February 16, 1942, that Brother Knorr inaugurated an advanced course in theocratic ministry at the Bethel Home in Brooklyn, New York. The course provided instruction in such matters as research, expressing oneself clearly and correctly, outlining material for presentation in discourses, delivering speeches effectively, presenting ideas persuasively, and being tactful. Both brothers and sisters were welcome to attend, but only males were invited to enroll and give student talks on which they would be counseled. The benefits quickly became evident not only in platform speaking but also in greater effectiveness in house-to-house preaching.

The following year this schooling began to be extended to the local congregations of Jehovah's Witnesses worldwide. First it was in English, then in other languages. The stated purpose of the school was to help each one of Jehovah's Witnesses to be able to teach others when calling on people from house to house, making return visits, and conducting Bible stud-

Illuminated signs in the windows of homes of Jehovah's Witnesses gave a round-the-clock witness

Advertising placards and signs contributed to a bold public witness (as here in Scotland)

Preaching Publicly and From House to House

ies. Each Witness was going to be helped to become a qualified minister. (2 Tim. 2:2) In 1959, sisters were also given opportunity to enroll in the school and present talks in field-service settings—not addressing themselves to the entire audience but, rather, to the one assigned to take the role of householder. And that was not all.

Since 1926, traveling representatives of the Society had been working along with individual Witnesses in the field service, in order to help them to improve their abilities. However, at an international convention in New York in 1953, with circuit and district overseers seated in front of the platform, Brother Knorr declared that the *principal work* of all servants, or overseers, should be to help every Witness to be a regular house-to-house minister. "Everyone," he said, "should be able to preach the good news from house to house." A global campaign was launched to achieve this.

Why such emphasis on the matter? Consider the United States as an example: At that time 28 percent of the Witnesses were limiting their activity to distributing handbills or standing on the streets with magazines. And over 40 percent of the Witnesses were sharing in the field service only irregularly, allowing months to go by without doing any witnessing at all. There was a need for loving assistance in the form of personal training. Plans were laid that would make it possible for all of Jehovah's Witnesses who were not already house-to-house Witnesses to be given help in approaching people at their doors, talking to them from the Bible, and answering their questions. They would learn to prepare Scriptural sermons that they could give in perhaps three minutes for people who were busy, or about eight minutes for others. The objective was to assist each Witness to become a mature Christian evangelizer.

It was not only the traveling overseers who gave this instruction. Local servants, or overseers, did too; and in the following years, other well-qualified Witnesses were assigned to train certain ones. For years, demonstrations of how to do the work had been provided on the congregation's weekly Service Meeting. But this was now coupled with increased emphasis on personal training in the field.

The results were outstanding. The number of Witnesses preaching

Street distribution of "The Watchtower" and "Consolation" (as shown here in U.S.A.) began in 1940

Starting in 1943, brothers in the congregations were given training in public speaking

from house to house increased, as did the number who regularly participated in the field ministry. Within a decade the total number of Witnesses worldwide rose 100 percent. They were also making 126 percent more return visits to answer Bible questions for interested people, and they were conducting 150 percent more regular home Bible studies with those who showed hunger for Bible truth. They were truly proving themselves to be qualified ministers.

In view of the varied educational and cultural backgrounds from which these Witnesses came, and the fact that they were scattered in small groups all over the earth, it is obvious why the Witnesses give credit, not to any man, but to Jehovah God for the way in which they have been equipped and trained to proclaim the good news. —John 14:15-17.

House-to-House Preaching —An Identifying Mark

At various times other religious groups have encouraged their members to call on the homes of people in their community to talk about religion. Some individuals have tried it. Certain ones may even do it as missionaries for a couple of years, but that is the end of it. However, it is only among Jehovah's Witnesses that virtually all, young and old, male and female, participate year in, year out, in the house-to-house ministry. It is only Jehovah's Witnesses who truly endeavor to reach all the inhabited earth with the Kingdom message, in obedience to the prophetic command at Matthew 24:14.

It is not that all of Jehovah's Witnesses find this work easy.* On the contrary, many of them, when they first started to study the Bible, said: 'There is one thing I will never do, and that is go from house to house!' Yet, it is an activity in which nearly all of Jehovah's Witnesses share if they are physically

---

Why the Witnesses Call Again and Again

Explaining why Jehovah's Witnesses make repeated calls at every home, "The Watchtower" of July 1, 1962, said: "Circumstances keep changing. Today a man may not be at home, next time he may be. Today he may be too busy to listen, but the next time he may not be. Today one member of the family answers the door, the next time another member does; and the Witnesses are concerned with reaching not only every home in their assignments but also, if possible, each mature person in each home. Often families are divided as to religion, so it is not always possible for one member to speak for the entire family. Besides, people keep moving and so the Witnesses never can be certain as to just whom they will meet at a certain door.

"Not only do the circumstances change, but the people themselves change.... For just some trifle a man may have been out of sorts and not at all willing to discuss religion or anything else no matter who came to his door, but it does not at all follow that he will be of that mental attitude at another time. Or, just because a man was not at all interested in discussing religion last month does not mean he might not be this month. Since the last time a Witness called this man may have had a soul-harrowing experience or in some other way learned something that made him humble instead of proud, hungry and conscious of his spiritual need instead of self-satisfied.

"Besides, the message the Witnesses bring sounds strange to many persons and they fail to grasp its urgency. Only by hearing it again and again do they gradually get the point."

---

* *The Watchtower,* May 15, 1981, pp. 12-16.

Home Bible studies are conducted with interested people. Below are publications specially designed for that—published first in English, then in many other languages

able to do so. And many who are not physically able do it anyway—in wheelchairs, with canes, and so forth. Others—completely unable to leave their home, or temporarily confined, or in order to reach otherwise inaccessible people—witness by telephone or by writing letters. Why this determined effort?

As they come to know Jehovah, their love for him changes their whole outlook on life. They want to talk about him. The wonderful things that he has in store for those who love him are just too good to keep to themselves. And they feel a responsibility before God to warn people about the great tribulation just ahead. (Matt. 24:21; compare Ezekiel 3:17-19.) But why do it by going from house to house?

They know that Jesus taught his disciples to go to the homes of people to preach and to teach. (Matt. 10:11-14) They are aware that after holy spirit was poured out at Pentecost 33 C.E., the apostles continued without letup to declare the good news "in the temple [in Jerusalem] and from house to house." (Acts 5:42) Every Witness knows Acts 20:20, which says that the apostle Paul taught "publicly and from house to house." And they see abundant evidence of Jehovah's blessing on this work in modern times. Thus, as they gain experience in the house-to-house ministry, the activity that they at one time dreaded often becomes something that they eagerly anticipate.

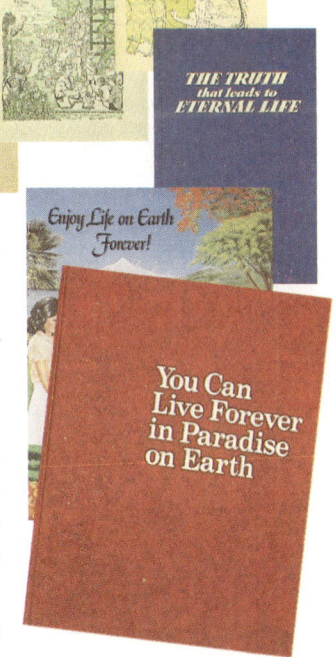

Young and old, male and female, Witnesses around the globe share in house-to-house witnessing

Romania

Bolivia

Zimbabwe

Hong Kong

And they are thorough about it. They keep careful records so that they can call back to talk to any who were not at home. Not only that, but they make repeated calls at every home.

Because of the effectiveness of the house-to-house ministry, opposers in many lands have tried to stop it. In order to gain official respect for their right to preach from door to door, Jehovah's Witnesses have appealed to government officials. Where necessary, they have gone to court in order to legally establish the right to spread the good news in this manner. (Phil. 1:7) And where repressive governments have persisted in forbidding such activity, Jehovah's Witnesses have at times simply done it in a less conspicuous manner or, if necessary, used other means to reach people with the Kingdom message.

Although radio and television broadcasts have been used to spread the Kingdom message, Jehovah's Witnesses recognize that the personal contact made possible by house-to-house calls is far more effective. It affords better opportunity to answer the questions of individual householders and to search out deserving ones. (Matt. 10:11) That is one of the reasons why, in 1957, the Watch Tower Society sold radio station WBBR in New York.

Having given a personal witness, however, Jehovah's Witnesses do not feel that their job is done. It is just a beginning.

"Make Disciples . . . Teaching Them"

Jesus commanded his followers to do more than preach. In imitation of him, they are also to *teach*. (Matt. 11:1) Before his ascension to heaven, he instructed them: "Go therefore and make disciples of people of all the nations, . . . teaching them to observe all the things I have commanded you." (Matt. 28:19, 20) Teaching (Greek, *di·da'sko*) differs from preaching in that the teacher does more than proclaim; he instructs, explains, offers proofs.

The *Watch Tower,* as early as April 1881, offered some brief suggestions on how to teach. Some of

Preaching Publicly and From House to House

the early colporteurs made it a point to call again on those who showed interest, to encourage them to read the Society's books and meet with others for regular study of God's Word. The book *The Harp of God* (published in 1921) was often used for that purpose. Later on, however, even more was done in the way of giving personal attention to interested ones. Recorded Bible lectures along with printed study guides were prominently used in this activity. How did that come about?

Since early 1933, the Society had supplemented its radio broadcasts with recordings played on portable transcription equipment in meeting halls, in parks, at factory gates, and so forth. Within a short time, Witnesses who located interested persons when calling from house to house were making arrangements to return to play some of these recordings for them in their homes. When the book *Riches* became available in 1936, discussions from it were used, after the recordings, to establish studies that could be attended by interested ones in the area. This work was emphasized especially with a view to helping prospective members of the "great multitude" to learn the truth.—Rev. 7:9, *KJ*.

At about that time, the Catholic hierarchy stepped up its pressure on owners and managers of radio stations as well as government agencies in a determined effort to stop the broadcasting of Watch Tower programs. A petition signed by 2,630,000 persons in the United States requested a public debate between J. F. Rutherford and a high official of the Roman Catholic Church. None of the Catholic clergy were willing to accept the challenge. So, in 1937, Brother Rutherford made recordings entitled "Exposed" and "Religion and Christianity," which presented basic Bible teachings, particularly in refutation of unscriptural Catholic doctrines. The same material was published in the booklets *Protection* and *Uncovered,* and a copy of *Uncovered* was personally delivered to everyone who had signed the petition so that the

Belgium

Uruguay

Fiji

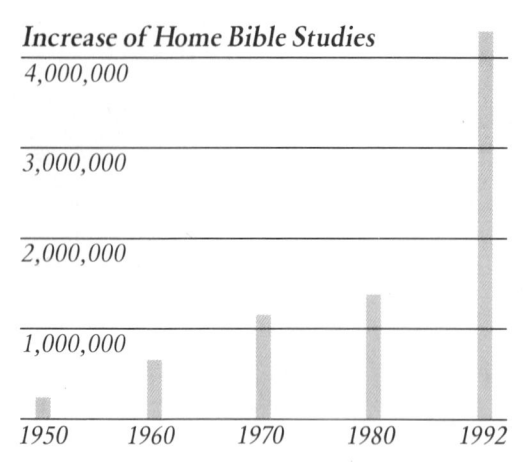

Increase of Home Bible Studies

4,000,000

3,000,000

2,000,000

1,000,000

1950   1960   1970   1980   1992

Melvin Sargent

Using "Every Way Possible"

"Those of us inside the Lord's organization have tried, in every way possible, to turn [the world's] attention to the message of life. We have used slogans, full-page advertisements, radio, sound cars, portable phonographs, gigantic conventions, parades of information-walkers carrying signs, and a growing army of house-to-house ministers. This activity has served to divide people—those in favor of God's established Kingdom on the one side, those against it on the other. This was the work foretold by Jesus for my generation."—Written in 1987 by Melvin Sargent, at 91 years of age.

people could read for themselves the Bible truths that the Catholic hierarchy was seeking to suppress.

In order to help people to see the issues clearly and to examine the Scriptural basis for these, the booklet *Model Study* No. 1 was printed for use at meetings arranged for interested people. The booklet contained questions, answers, and scriptures in support of the answers given. First, the conductor would have one or more discs of the aforementioned recorded lectures played so that everyone could hear the overall argument. Then, discussion would follow, using the material provided in the *Model Study* booklet and examining the scriptures themselves. *Model Study* No. 1 was followed by Nos. 2 and 3, coordinated with other recorded discourses. Such studies were organized first at locations where *groups* of interested people could be gathered, but soon they were also being held with *individuals* and *families*.

Since that time many excellent books have been provided especially for use by Jehovah's Witnesses in conducting home Bible studies. Those having the greatest circulation were *"Let God Be True," The Truth That Leads to Eternal Life,* and *You Can Live Forever in Paradise on Earth*. There were also 32-page booklets—*"This Good News of the Kingdom," God's Way Is Love, "Look! I Am Making All Things New,"* and many others. These were followed by brochures such as *Enjoy Life on Earth Forever!*, which contains a very simple and easy-to-understand presentation of basic Bible teachings.

The use of these instruments, coupled with extensive congregational and personal training, has resulted in a dramatic increase in the number of home Bible studies being conducted. In 1950, home Bible studies, often conducted each week, averaged 234,952. Studies that did not make sufficient progress were dropped. Many students progressed to the point that they, in turn, became teachers. In spite of the constant turnover, the number has continued to rise, often quite rapidly. As of 1992, the Witnesses were conducting 4,278,127 home Bible studies worldwide.

In order to accomplish this vast work of preaching and teaching, in the languages of all the earth, Jehovah's Witnesses have made extensive use of the printed page. This has required publishing operations of gigantic proportions.

CHAPTER 26

PRODUCING BIBLE LITERATURE FOR USE IN THE MINISTRY

THE written word has played a vital role in true worship. Jehovah gave the Ten Commandments to Israel, first orally and then in written form. (Ex. 20:1-17; 31:18; Gal. 3:19) To ensure that his Word would be transmitted accurately, God commanded Moses and a long line of prophets and apostles after him to write.—Ex. 34:27; Jer. 30:2; Hab. 2:2; Rev. 1:11.

Most of that early writing was done on scrolls. By the second century C.E., however, the codex, or leaf-book, was developed. This was more economical and easier to use. And the Christians were in the forefront of its use, as they saw its value in spreading the good news about the Messianic Kingdom of God. Professor E. J. Goodspeed, in his book *Christianity Goes to Press*, states regarding those early Christians as book publishers: "They were not only abreast of their times in such matters, they were in advance of them, and the publishers of the subsequent centuries have followed them."—1940, p. 78.

It comes as no surprise, therefore, that Jehovah's Witnesses today, as proclaimers of God's Kingdom, have in some respects been among those in the forefront of the printing industry.

Providing Literature for Early Bible Students

One of the first articles written by C. T. Russell was published, in 1876, in the *Bible Examiner*, edited by George Storrs of Brooklyn, New York. After Brother Russell became associated with N. H. Barbour of Rochester, New York, Russell provided funds for publication of the book *Three Worlds* and the paper known as *Herald of the Morning*. He served as a coeditor of that paper and, in 1877, used the facilities of the *Herald* to publish the booklet *The Object and Manner of Our Lord's Return*. Brother Russell had a keen mind for spiritual matters as well as business affairs, but it was Barbour who was experienced in typesetting and composition.

However, when Barbour repudiated the sin-atoning value of the ransom sacrifice of Jesus Christ, Brother Russell severed relations with him.

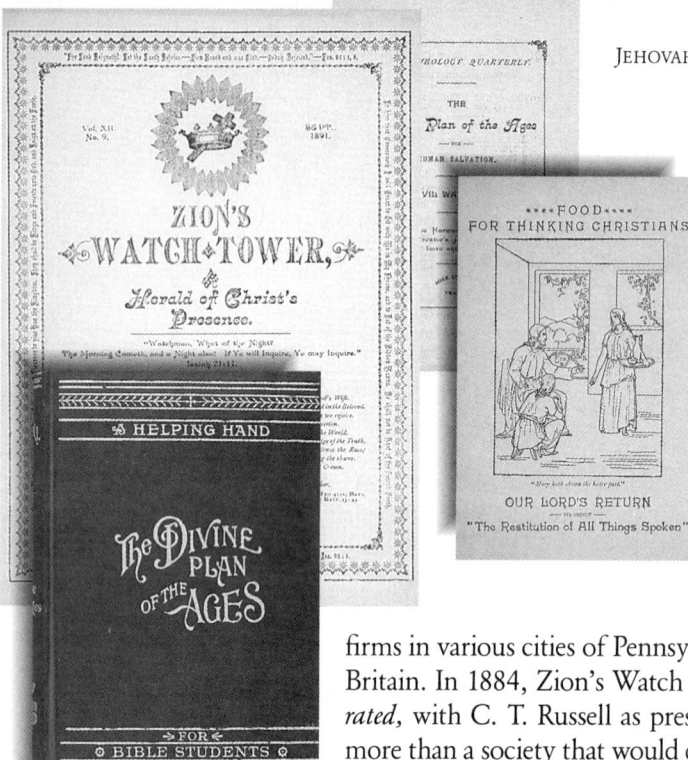

So, in 1879 when Russell undertook publication of *Zion's Watch Tower and Herald of Christ's Presence,* he had to rely on commercial printers.

The following year the first of an extensive series of tracts designed to interest people in Bible truths was prepared for publication. This work quickly took on immense proportions. In order to handle it, Zion's Watch Tower Tract Society was formed on February 16, 1881, with W. H. Conley as president and C. T. Russell as secretary and treasurer. Arrangements were made for the printing to be done by commercial firms in various cities of Pennsylvania, New York, and Ohio, as well as in Britain. In 1884, Zion's Watch Tower Tract Society* was *legally incorporated,* with C. T. Russell as president, and its charter showed that it was more than a society that would direct publishing. Its real objective was religious; it was chartered for "the dissemination of Bible Truths in various languages."

With what zeal that objective was pursued! In 1881, within a period of four months, 1,200,000 tracts totaling some 200,000,000 pages were published. (Many of these "tracts" were actually in the form of small books.) Thereafter, production of Bible tracts for free distribution soared to the tens of millions year after year. These tracts were printed in some 30 languages and were distributed not only in America but also in Europe, South Africa, Australia, and other lands.

Another aspect of the work opened up in 1886, when Brother Russell completed writing *The Divine Plan of the Ages,* the first of a series of six volumes that he personally penned. In connection with the publishing of the first four volumes in that series (1886-97), as well as tracts and the *Watch Tower* from 1887 to 1898, he made use of the Tower Publishing Company.# In time, typesetting and composition were done by the brothers at the Bible House in Pittsburgh. To keep expenses down, they also purchased the paper for printing. As for the actual printing and binding, Brother Russell often placed orders with more than one firm. He

Actual printing of these early publications was done by commercial firms

---

* In 1896 the name of the corporation was officially changed to Watch Tower Bible and Tract Society.

\# This was a firm owned by Charles Taze Russell. In 1898 he transferred assets of the Tower Publishing Company by donation to the Watch Tower Bible and Tract Society.

planned carefully, ordering far enough in advance to get favorable rates. From the time of the publication of the first book written by C. T. Russell down through 1916, a total of 9,384,000 of those six volumes were produced and distributed.

The publishing of Bible literature did not stop at Brother Russell's death. The following year the seventh volume of *Studies in the Scriptures* was printed. It was released to the Bethel family on July 17, 1917. So great was the demand for it that by the end of that year, the Society had placed orders for 850,000 copies in English with commercial printers and bookbinders. Editions in other languages were being produced in Europe. In addition, that year some 38 million tracts were printed.

But then, during a period of intense persecution in 1918, while officials of the Society were unjustly imprisoned, their headquarters (located in Brooklyn, New York) was dismantled. The plates for printing were destroyed. The greatly reduced staff moved the office back to Pittsburgh to the third floor of a building at 119 Federal Street. Would this bring to an end their producing of Bible literature?

Should They Do Their Own Printing?

After the release of the Society's president, J. F. Rutherford, and his associates from prison, the Bible Students assembled at Cedar Point, Ohio, in 1919. They considered what God had permitted to occur during the preceding year and what his Word indicated that they should be doing during the days ahead. Announcement was made that a new magazine, *The Golden Age,* was to be published as an instrument to use in pointing people to God's Kingdom as mankind's only hope.

As it had done in the past, the Society arranged for a commercial firm to do the printing. But times had changed. There were labor difficulties in the printing industry and problems in the paper market. A more dependable arrangement was needed. The brothers prayed about the matter and watched for the Lord's leadings.

First of all, where should they locate the Society's offices? Should they move the headquarters back to Brooklyn? The Society's board of directors considered the matter, and a committee was appointed to check into the situation.

Brother Rutherford instructed C. A. Wise, the Society's vice president, to go to Brooklyn to see about reopening Bethel and renting premises where the Society could begin printing operations. Desirous of knowing what course God would bless, Brother Rutherford said: "Go and see whether it is the Lord's will for us to return back to Brooklyn."

"How will I determine as to whether it is the Lord's will for us to go back or not?" asked Brother Wise.

C. A. Wise made a test to see whether the Bible Students should reestablish headquarters in Brooklyn

"Let's make coal the test"

"It was a failure to get coal supplies in 1918 that drove us from Brooklyn back to Pittsburgh,"* Brother Rutherford replied. "Let's make coal the test. You go and order some coal."

"How many tons do you think I should order to make the test?"

"Well, make it a good test," Brother Rutherford recommended. "Order 500 tons."

That is exactly what Brother Wise did. And what was the outcome? When he applied to the authorities, he was granted a certificate to get 500 tons of coal—enough to care for their needs for a number of years! But where were they going to put it? Large sections of the basement of the Bethel Home were converted into coal storage.

The result of this test was taken as an unmistakable indication of God's will. By the first of October 1919, they were once again beginning to carry on their activity from Brooklyn.

Now, should they do their own printing? They endeavored to purchase a rotary magazine press but were told that there were only a few of these in the United States and that there was no chance of getting one for many months. Nevertheless, they were confident that if it was the Lord's will, he could open the way. And he did!

Just a few months after their return to Brooklyn, they succeeded in purchasing a rotary press. Eight blocks from the Bethel Home, at 35 Myrtle Avenue, they leased three floors in a building. By early 1920 the Society had its own printing shop—small, but well equipped. Brothers who had sufficient experience to operate the equipment offered to make themselves available to help with the work.

The February 1 issue of *The Watch Tower* that year came off the Society's own press. By April, *The Golden Age* was also being produced in their own printery. At the end of the year, it was a pleasure for *The Watch Tower* to report: "During the greater portion of the year all the work on THE WATCH TOWER, THE GOLDEN AGE, and many of the booklets, has been done by consecrated hands, but one motive directing their actions, and that motive being love for the Lord and his cause of righteousness. . . . When other journals and publications were required to suspend because of paper shortage or labor troubles, our publications went smoothly on."

The factory space was quite limited, but the amount of work done was amazing. Regular runs for *The Watch Tower* were 60,000 copies per issue. But *The Golden Age* was also printed there, and during the first year, the September 29 issue was a special one. It carried a detailed exposé of the

---

* This failure to get coal was not merely due to wartime shortage. Hugo Riemer, who was then a member of the headquarters staff, later wrote that it was principally because hatred for the Bible Students was so rampant in New York at that time.

perpetrators of the persecution of the Bible Students from 1917 to 1920. Four million copies were printed! One of the factory pressmen later said: 'It took everyone but the cook to get that issue out.'

In the first year of their use of the rotary magazine press, Brother Rutherford asked the brothers whether they could also print booklets on that press. Initially, it did not appear to be feasible. The makers of the press said that it could not be done. But the brothers tried and had good success. They also invented their own folder and thus reduced their need for workers for that aspect of the work from 12 to 2. What accounted for their success? "Experience and the Lord's blessing" is the way the factory manager summed it up.

It was not only in Brooklyn that the Society was setting up printing operations, however. Some of the foreign-language operations were supervised from an office in Michigan. To care for needs related to that work, in 1921 the Society set up a Linotype machine, printing presses, and other necessary equipment in Detroit, Michigan. There literature was printed in Polish, Russian, Ukrainian, and other languages.

In that same year, the Society released the book *The Harp of God*, which was written in a manner suitable for beginners in Bible study. As of 1921 the Society had not tried to print and bind its own books. Should they endeavor to undertake this work too? Again, they looked for the Lord's direction.

The Society's first rotary press was used to print 4,000,000 copies of the hard-hitting "Golden Age" No. 27

Dedicated Brothers Print and Bind Books

In 1920, *The Watch Tower* had reported that many colporteurs had been forced out of that service because printers and bookbinders had been unable to fill the Society's orders. The brothers at headquarters reasoned that if they could be free from dependence on commercial manufacturers with all their labor troubles, they would be in a position to accomplish a greater witness concerning God's purpose for humankind. If they printed and bound their own books, it would also be more difficult for opposers to interfere with the work. And in time they hoped to be able to save on the cost of the volumes and so be in a position to make them more readily available to the public.

But this would require more space and equipment, and they would have to learn new skills.

Could they do it? Robert J. Martin, the factory overseer, called to mind that in the days of Moses, Jehovah had 'filled Bezalel and Oholiab with wisdom of heart to do all the work' needed to construct the sacred tabernacle. (Ex. 35:30-35) Having that Bible account in mind, Brother Martin was confident that Jehovah would also do whatever was needed so that his servants could publish literature to advertise the Kingdom.

After much meditation and prayer, definite plans began to emerge. Looking back on what occurred, Brother Martin later wrote to Brother Rutherford: "Greatest day of all was the day when you wanted to know if there was any good reason why we should not print and bind all our own books. It was a breath-taking idea, because it meant the opening of a complete typesetting, electroplating, printing and binding plant, with the operation of more than a score of unfamiliar machines, mostly machines we never knew were made, and the necessity of learning more than a dozen trades. But it seemed the best way to meet the war prices charged for books.

"You leased the six-story building at 18 Concord Street (with tenants on two floors); and on March 1, 1922, we moved in. You bought for us a complete outfit of typesetting, electroplating, printing and binding machinery, most of it new, some of it second-hand; and we started work.

"One of the great printing establishments which had been doing much of our work heard of what we were doing and came, in the person of the president, to visit us. He saw the new equipment and sagely remarked, 'Here you are with a first-class printing establishment on your hands, and nobody around the place that knows a thing about what to do with it. In six months the whole thing will be a lot of junk; and you will find out that the people to do your printing are those that have always done it, and make it their business.'

"That sounded logical enough, but it left out the Lord; and he has always been with us. When the bindery was started he sent along a brother who has spent his whole life in the binding business. He was of great use at the time he was most needed. With his assistance, and with the Lord's spirit working through the brethren who were trying to learn, it was not long before we were making books."

R. J. Martin (right), first overseer of the Society's Brooklyn factory, conferring with Brother Rutherford

Since the factory on Concord Street had ample space, printing operations from Detroit were merged with those in Brooklyn. By the second year in this location, the brothers were turning out 70 percent of the books and booklets required, besides magazines, tracts, and handbills. The following year, growth in the work made it necessary to use the remaining two floors of the factory.

Could they speed up their book production? They had a print-

Typesetting

South Africa

United States

At first it was all done by hand, one letter at a time

From 1920 until the 1980's, Linotype machines were used

Japan

Germany

Now a computerized phototypesetting process is used

In some places the typesetting was done with Monotype equipment

ing press built in Germany, shipped to America, and put into operation in 1926 especially for that purpose. As far as they knew, that was the first rotary press used in America to print books.

However, the printing operations directed by the Bible Students were not all in America.

Early Printing Operations in Other Lands

Making use of *commercial firms,* Brother Russell had had printing done in Britain as early as 1881. It was being done in Germany by 1903, Greece by 1906, Finland by 1910, and even Japan by 1913. During the years following the first world war, a vast amount of such printing—of books, booklets, magazines, and tracts—was done in Britain, the Scandinavian lands, Germany, and Poland, and some was done in Brazil and India.

Then, in 1920, the same year that the Society undertook its own

Platemaking

From the 1920's to the 1980's, lead plates were made for letterpress printing

1. Lines of type for the pages of printed material were locked into metal frames called chases

2. Under pressure, an impression of the type was made on material that could be used as a mold

3. Hot lead was poured against the mat (or mold) to make curved metal printing plates

4. Unwanted metal was routed from the face of the plate

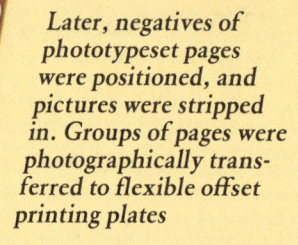

5. The plates were nickeled for durability

Later, negatives of phototypeset pages were positioned, and pictures were stripped in. Groups of pages were photographically transferred to flexible offset printing plates

printing of magazines in Brooklyn, arrangements got under way for our brothers in Europe to do some of this work too. A group of them in Switzerland organized a printing establishment in Bern. It was their own business firm. But they were all Bible Students, and they produced literature for the Society in European languages at very favorable rates. In time, the Society acquired title to that printing plant and enlarged it. To fill an urgent need in economically impoverished lands of Europe at that time, tremendous amounts of free literature were produced there. During the late 1920's, publications in more than a dozen languages were shipped from this factory.

At the same time, much interest in the Kingdom message was being shown in Romania. Despite severe opposition to our work there, the Society established a printing plant in Cluj, in order to lower the cost of the literature and make it more readily available to truth-hungry people in Romania and nearby countries. In 1924 that printery was able to turn out nearly a quarter of a million bound books, in addition to magazines and booklets, in Romanian and Hungarian. But one who had oversight of the work there proved unfaithful to his trust and committed acts that resulted in loss of the Society's property and equipment. Despite this, faithful brothers in Romania continued to do what they could to share Bible truths with others.

In Germany following World War I, large numbers of people were flocking to the meetings of the Bible Students. But the German people were suffering great economic distress. In order to hold down the cost of Bible literature for their benefit, the Society developed its own printing operations there too. At Barmen, in 1922, printing was done on a flatbed press on the staircase landing in the Bethel Home and on another in the woodshed. The following year the brothers moved to Magdeburg to more suitable facilities. They had good buildings there, more were added, and equipment for printing and bookbinding was installed. By the end of 1925, it was reported, the production capacity of this plant was to be at least as great as the one then being used at the headquarters in Brooklyn.

Most of the printing actually done by the brothers started on a small scale. That was true in Korea, where in 1922 the Society set up a small printing plant equipped to produce literature in Korean as well as Japanese and Chinese. After a few years, the equipment was transferred to Japan.

By 1924 printing of smaller items was also being done in Canada and in South Africa. In 1925 a small press was installed in Australia and another

One of the Society's first printeries in Europe (Bern, Switzerland)

one in Brazil. The brothers in Brazil were soon using their equipment to print the Portuguese edition of *The Watch Tower*. The Society's branch in England got its first equipment for printing in 1926. In 1929 the spiritual hunger of humble people in Spain was being satisfied by publication of *The Watch Tower* on a small press there. Two years later a press began running in the basement of the branch office in Finland.

Meanwhile, expansion was taking place at the world headquarters.

Their Own Factory at World Headquarters

Since 1920 the Society had been renting factory space in Brooklyn. Even the building used from 1922 on was not in good shape; the whole thing would shake badly when the rotary press was running in the basement. Besides that, more space was needed in order to care for the growing work. The brothers reasoned that the available funds could be put to better use if they had their own factory.

Some land within a few blocks of the Bethel Home seemed to be a very desirable location, so they bid on it. As it turned out, the Squibb Pharmaceutical Corporation outbid them; but when they built on that property, they had to sink 1,167 piles in order to have a solid foundation. (Years later, the Watch Tower Society purchased those buildings from Squibb, with that good foundation already in place!) However, the land that the Society purchased in 1926 had good load-bearing soil on which to build.

In February 1927 they moved into their brand-new building at 117 Adams Street in Brooklyn. It provided them almost twice the space they

In Magdeburg, Germany, the Society set up a printery during the 1920's

had been using up to that time. It was well designed, with the work moving from the upper floors down through the various departments until it reached the Shipping Department at ground level.

The growth was not finished, however. Within ten years this factory had to be enlarged; and there was more to come later. In addition to printing millions of copies of magazines and booklets yearly, the factory was turning out as many as 10,000 bound books per day. When complete Bibles began to be included among those books in 1942, the Watch Tower Society was again pioneering a new field in the printing industry. The brothers experimented until they were able to run lightweight Bible paper on rotary presses—something that other printers did not try until years later.

While such large-scale production was under way, groups with special needs were not overlooked. As early as 1910, a Bible Student in Boston, Massachusetts, and one in Canada were cooperating to reproduce the Society's literature in Braille. By 1924, from an office in Logansport, Indiana, the Society was turning out publications to benefit the blind. Because of very limited response at that time, however, the Braille work was terminated in 1936, and emphasis was placed on helping the blind by means of phonograph records as well as personal attention. Later on, in 1960, Braille literature again began to be produced—this time in greater variety, and gradually with better response.

> **'Evidence of Jehovah's Spirit'**
>
> *"The successful printing of books and Bibles on rotary presses by persons of little or no previous experience [and at a time when others were not yet doing it] is evidence of Jehovah's oversight and the direction of his spirit," said Charles Fekel. Brother Fekel knew well what was involved, for he had shared in the development of the printing operations at the Society's headquarters for over half a century. In his later years, he served as a member of the Governing Body.*

Charles Fekel

Meeting the Challenge of Severe Opposition

In a number of lands, the printing was done in the face of extremely difficult circumstances. But our brothers persevered, appreciating that the proclamation of the good news of the Kingdom was work that Jehovah God, through his Son, had commanded to be done. (Isa. 61:1, 2; Mark 13:10) In Greece, for example, the brothers had set up their printery in 1936 and operated it for only a few months when there was a change of government and the authorities shut down their plant. Similarly, in India, in 1940, Claude Goodman worked for months to set up a press and learn how to operate it, only to have police dispatched by the maharaja swoop in, truck away the press, and dump all the carefully sorted type into large tins.

In many other locations, laws governing imported literature made it necessary for the brothers to give the work to local commercial printers, even though the Society had a printing establishment in a nearby country that was equipped to do the work. That was true in the mid-1930's in such places as Denmark, Latvia, and Hungary.

In 1933 the German government, urged on by the clergy, moved to close down the printing activities of Jehovah's Witnesses in Germany. The police occupied the Watch Tower Society's factory at Magdeburg and shut it down in April of that year, but they could find no incriminating evidence, so they withdrew. Nevertheless, they intervened again in June. In order to continue the dissemination of the Kingdom message, the Society established a printery in Prague, Czechoslovakia, and considerable equipment was moved there from Magdeburg. With this, magazines in two languages and booklets in six languages were produced during the next few years.

Then, in 1939, Hitler's troops marched on Prague, so the brothers quickly dismantled their equipment and shipped it out of the country. Some of it went to the Netherlands. This was most timely. Communication with Switzerland had become more difficult for the Dutch brothers. So now they rented space and, with their newly acquired presses, did their own printing. This continued for only a short time, however, before the plant was seized by the Nazi invaders. But the brothers had kept that equipment in use just as long as possible.

When arbitrary official action in Finland forced a halt in publication of *The Watchtower* during the war, the brothers there mimeographed the main articles and delivered these by courier. After Austria came under Nazi domination in 1938, *The Watchtower* was printed on a mimeograph machine that constantly had to be moved from place to place in order to keep it out of the hands of the Gestapo. Similarly, in Canada during the time that the Witnesses were under wartime ban, they had to relocate their equipment repeatedly in order to continue to provide spiritual food for their brothers.

In Australia during the time that the work of Jehovah's Witnesses was under ban, the brothers printed their own magazines and even printed and bound books—something they had not done there even under more favorable circumstances. They had to move their bindery 16 times to prevent confiscation of the equipment, but they managed to turn out 20,000 hardbound books in time for release at a convention held in 1941 in spite of overwhelming obstacles!

Relying on Almighty God

An experience related by Hugo Riemer, former purchasing agent for the Watch Tower Society, reflects the way the Watch Tower Society carries out its business.

During World War II, printing paper was rationed in the United States. Appeal for supplies had to be made to a government-appointed committee. On one occasion one of the prominent Bible societies had lawyers, big-business men, preachers, and others there to represent them before the committee. They were granted far less than they wanted. After their request had been heard, the committee called for the Watchtower Bible and Tract Society. When Hugo Riemer and Max Larson stepped forward, the chairman asked: "Just the two of you?" The reply: "Yes. We hope that Almighty God is with us too." They were granted all the supplies they needed.

Hugo Riemer

Printing Presses

Presses of many varieties have been used by the Watch Tower Society in its printing operations

For many years flatbed presses of many descriptions were used (Germany)

Job presses have been used to print not only forms and handbills but also magazines (U.S.A.)

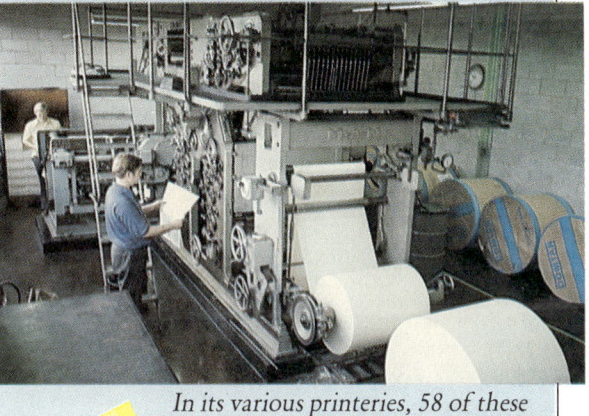

In its various printeries, 58 of these MAN rotary letterpresses from Germany were used (Canada)

Now, high-speed full-color web offset presses manufactured in various lands are used in the Society's principal printeries

Italy

Germany

Bookbinding

Some of the early bookbinding in Watch Tower factories was done by hand (Switzerland)

Large-scale production in the United States required many separate operations

1. Gathering signatures
2. Sewing them together 
3. Pasting on endsheets 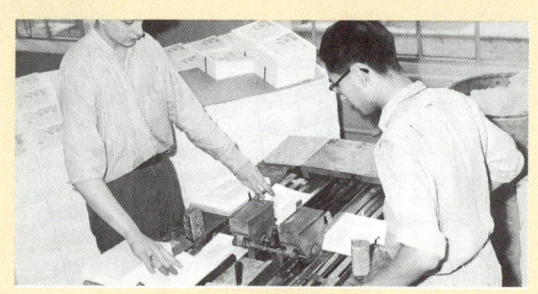
4. Trimming 

Expansion After World War II

After the war ended, Jehovah's Witnesses met in international assembly in Cleveland, Ohio, in 1946. There Nathan H. Knorr, then president of the Watch Tower Society, spoke on reconstruction and expansion. Since the outbreak of World War II, the number of Witnesses had increased by 157 percent, and missionaries were rapidly opening up the work in new fields. To fill the global demand for Bible literature, Brother Knorr outlined plans to enlarge the facilities of the world headquarters. As a result of the proposed expansion, the factory would have more than double the space that was in the original 1927 structure, and a greatly enlarged Bethel Home was to be provided for the volunteer workers. These additions were completed and put to use early in 1950.

The factory and office facilities at the world headquarters in Brooklyn

5. Embossing the covers

6. Putting covers on the books

7. Pressing the books until the paste set

Now, instead of sewing, burst binding is often used, and high-speed machines may each turn out 20,000 or more books per day

have had to be enlarged again and again since 1950. As of 1992 they covered about eight city blocks and included 2,476,460 square feet of floor space. These are not just buildings for making books. They are dedicated to Jehovah, to be used in producing literature designed to educate people in his requirements for life.

In some areas it was difficult to get the Society's printing operations under way again after the second world war. The factory and office complex that belonged to the Society in Magdeburg, Germany, was in the Communist-controlled zone. The German Witnesses moved back into it, but they were able to operate only briefly before it was again confiscated. To fill the need in West Germany, a printery had to be established there. The cities had been reduced to rubble as a result of bombing. However, the Witnesses soon obtained the use of a small printery that had been

Elandsfontein, South Africa (1972)

São Paulo, Brazil (1973)

Strathfield, Australia (1972)

Numazu, Japan (1972)

operated by the Nazis, in Karlsruhe. By 1948 they had two flatbed presses running day and night in a building that was made available to them in Wiesbaden. The following year they enlarged the Wiesbaden facilities and quadrupled the number of presses in order to meet the needs of the rapidly growing number of Kingdom proclaimers in that part of the field.

When the Society resumed printing openly in Greece in 1946, the electric power supply was far from dependable. Sometimes it was off for hours at a time. In Nigeria in 1977, the brothers faced a similar problem. Until the Nigeria branch got its own generator, the factory workers would go back to work at any time, day or night, when the power came on. With such a spirit, they never missed an issue of the *The Watchtower*.

Following a visit by Brother Knorr to South Africa in 1948, land was purchased in Elandsfontein; and early in 1952, the branch moved into a new factory there—the first actually built by the Society in South Africa. Using a new flatbed press, they proceeded to print magazines in eight languages used in Africa. In 1954 the branch in Sweden was equipped to print its magazines on a flatbed press, as was the branch in Denmark in 1957.

Lagos, Nigeria (1974)

Wiesbaden, Germany (1975)

Toronto, Canada (1975)

As the demand for literature grew, high-speed rotary letterpresses were provided, first to one branch and then another. Canada received its first one in 1958; England, in 1959. By 1975 the Watch Tower Society had 70 large rotary presses operating in its printeries worldwide.

A Global Network to Publish Bible Truth

In the late 1960's and thereafter, a concerted effort was made to achieve further decentralization of the Watch Tower Society's printing operations. Growth in the number of Jehovah's Witnesses was rapid. More factory space was needed to provide Bible literature for their own use and for public distribution. But expansion in Brooklyn was a slow process because of limited available property as well as legal red tape. Plans were made to do more of the printing elsewhere.

Thus, in 1969 work began on the design of a new printery to be built near Wallkill, New York, about 95 miles northwest of Brooklyn. This would augment and spread out the headquarters facilities, and eventually almost all the *Watchtower* and *Awake!* magazines for the United States would come from Wallkill. Three years later a second factory for Wallkill was on the drawing boards, this one much larger than the first. By 1977 the rotary letterpresses there were turning out upwards of 18 million magazines a month. As of 1992, large MAN-Roland and Hantscho offset presses (just 4 offset presses instead of the former 15 letterpresses) were in use, and the production capacity was well over a million magazines a day.

When plans for printing operations at Wallkill were first laid, *The Watchtower* was being published in Brooklyn in 32 of its then 72 languages; *Awake!* in 14 of its 26 languages. Some 60 percent of the total number of copies printed worldwide were being produced there at the world headquarters. It would be beneficial to have more of this work done in lands outside the United States and by our own brothers there instead of by commercial firms. Thus, if future world crises or governmental interference with the work of Jehovah's Witnesses should hinder operations in any part of the earth, essential spiritual food could still be provided.

So it was that in 1971, nearly two years before the first Watch Tower factory at Wallkill went into operation, work got under way to provide a fine new printing plant in Numazu, Japan. The more than fivefold increase in Kingdom proclaimers in Japan during the preceding decade indicated that much Bible literature was going to be needed there. At the same time, the branch facilities in Brazil were being enlarged. The same was true in South Africa, where Bible literature was being produced in more than two dozen African languages. The following year, 1972, the Society's publishing facilities in Australia were quadrupled in size, with a view to providing each issue of *The Watchtower* and *Awake!* in that part of the world without prolonged shipping delays. Additional factories were also erected in France and the Philippines.

Early in 1972, N. H. Knorr and the Brooklyn factory overseer, M. H. Larson, made an international tour to examine the work being done, in order to organize matters for the best use of these facilities and to lay the groundwork for more expansion to come. Their visits included 16 countries in South America, Africa, and the Far East.

Shortly thereafter, the branch in Japan was itself producing the Japanese-language magazines needed for that part of the field, instead of depending on a commercial printer. That same year, 1972, the branch in Ghana began to print *The Watchtower* in three of its local languages, instead of waiting for shipments from the United States and Nigeria. Next, the Philippines branch began to care for the composition and printing of *The Watchtower* and *Awake!* in eight local languages (besides printing English-language magazines that were needed). This represented a further major step in the decentralization of Watch Tower printing operations.

By the end of 1975, the Watch Tower Society was publishing Bible literature in its own facilities in 23 lands spread around the globe—books in three countries; booklets or magazines or both in all 23 locations. In 25 other lands, the Society was reproducing smaller items on its own equipment.

The Society's capacity for producing bound books was also being increased. Some bookbinding had been done in Switzerland and in Germany as early as the mid-1920's. Following World War II, in 1948 the brothers in Finland undertook the binding of books (at first, largely by hand) to care principally for the needs of that country. Two years later the branch in Germany was again operating a bindery, and in time it took over the bookbinding being done in Switzerland.

Then, in 1967, with over a million Witnesses worldwide and with the introduction of pocket-size books for use in their ministry, the demand for this type of Bible literature soared. Within nine years, there was more than a sixfold increase in bindery lines in Brooklyn. As of 1992 the Watch Tower Society had a total of 28 bindery lines operating in eight different countries.

In that same year, 1992, not only was the Watch Tower Society printing Bible literature in 180 languages in the United States but four of its major printeries located in Latin America were supplying much of the literature needed both domestically and by other countries in that part of the world. Eleven more printeries were producing literature in Europe, and all of these were helping to fill the literature needs of other lands. Of these, France was regularly supplying literature for 14 countries, and Germany, which printed in over 40 languages, was shipping large quantities to 20 countries and smaller amounts to many other lands. In Africa, six Watch Tower printeries were turning out Bible literature in a total of 46 languages. Another 11 printeries—some large, some small—were supplying the Middle East and the Far East, islands of the Pacific, Canada, and other areas with literature to use in spreading the urgent message about God's Kingdom. In yet another 27 lands, the Society was printing smaller items needed by the congregations in order to function smoothly.

New Methods, New Equipment

During the 1960's and 1970's, a revolution swept through the printing industry. At an amazing rate, letterpress was being discarded in favor of offset printing.* The Watch Tower Society did not quickly jump on

---

* Letterpress printing is done from a raised surface on which appears a mirror image of what will be on the printed page. This raised surface is inked and pressed against paper. Offset printing is done by making an inked impression from a plate onto a rubber-blanketed cylinder and then transferring that impression to the paper.

To Promote Knowledge of God's Kingdom

The Watch Tower Society has at various times produced literature in more than 290 different languages. As of 1992 they were publishing literature in some 210 languages. All of this was done in order to help people to know about God's Kingdom and what it means for them. Among their Bible study aids most widely distributed to date are the following:

"The Truth That Leads to Eternal Life" (1968): 107,553,888 copies, in 117 languages

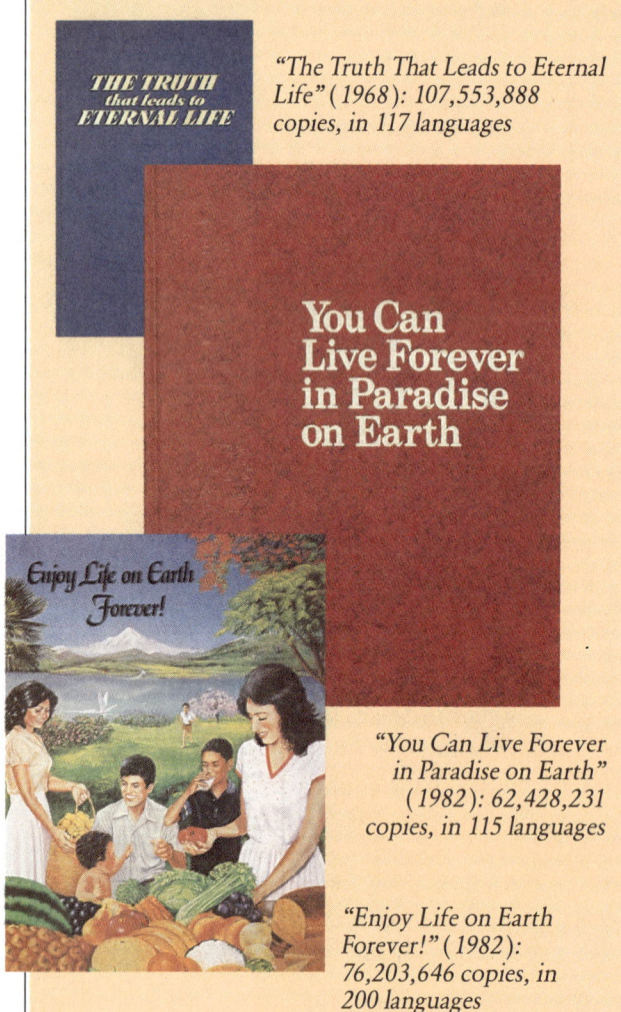

"You Can Live Forever in Paradise on Earth" (1982): 62,428,231 copies, in 115 languages

"Enjoy Life on Earth Forever!" (1982): 76,203,646 copies, in 200 languages

Figures given above are as of 1992.

---

the bandwagon. Plates that were available for offset presses were not well suited to the long runs that the Society needed for its literature. Furthermore, a change of this sort would require completely new modes of typesetting and composition. New printing presses would be needed. New technology would have to be learned. Virtually all the printing equipment in the Society's factories would have to be replaced. The cost would be staggering.

However, in time it became evident that supplies to support letterpress printing would not be available much longer. The durability of offset plates was rapidly improving. The change had to be made.

As early as 1972, because of their keen interest in developments in offset printing, three members of the Bethel family in South Africa purchased a small secondhand *sheetfed offset* press. Some experience was gained in doing small printing jobs on it. Then, in 1974, that press was used to print *The Truth That Leads to Eternal Life*, a pocket-size book, in the Ronga language. Their being able to do that quickly made it possible to get valuable Bible instruction to thousands of truth-hungry people before the work of Jehovah's Witnesses was again banned in the area where those people lived. Another sheetfed offset press, given to the Society's South Africa branch shortly after our brothers purchased the first one, was shipped to Zambia and was put to use there.

The Society's factory in Germany also got an early start in offset printing. In April 1975 the brothers there began to use a sheetfed press to print magazines on Bible paper for Jehovah's Witnesses in East Germany, where the Witnesses were then under ban. This was followed up, the next year, with production of books on that offset press for those persecuted brothers.

At about the same time, in 1975, the Watch Tower Society put its first *web offset* press for magazines into operation in Argentina. It ran for only a little more than a year, however, before the Argentine government banned the work of the Witnesses and sealed their printery. But offset printing operations in other countries continued to expand. Early in 1978, at the Watch Tower Society's headquarters plant in Brooklyn, New York, a web offset press began to turn out three-color printing for books.* A second press was purchased in that same year. Yet, much more equipment was needed in order to complete the changeover.

The Governing Body was confident that Jehovah would provide whatever was needed in order to accomplish the work that he wanted to have done. In April 1979 and January 1980, letters were sent out to congregations in the United States explaining the situation. Donations came in—slowly at first, but in time there was enough to equip the entire global network of Watch Tower factories for offset printing.

Equipping the entire global network of Watch Tower factories for offset printing

In the meantime, to make good use of existing equipment and to speed up the changeover, the Watch Tower Society contracted to have its late-model MAN presses converted for offset printing. Twelve countries were supplied with these presses, including six that had not previously printed their magazines locally.

Four-Color Printing

The branch in Finland was the first to do offset printing of each issue of its magazines in four colors, beginning in a simple way with issues in January 1981 and then progressively using improved techniques. Next, Japan used four-color printing for a bound book. Other Watch Tower printeries have followed suit as equipment has become available. Some of the presses have been purchased and shipped by the world headquarters. Others have been financed by Jehovah's Witnesses within the country where the factory is located. In yet other cases, the Witnesses in one country have made a gift of needed equipment to their brothers in another land.

During the era following World War II, the world became very picture oriented, and use of realistic color did much to make publications more visually appealing. This use of color has made the printed page

---

* From 1959 to 1971, the Society had used a sheetfed offset press at its Brooklyn plant to produce four-color calendars featuring themes related to the preaching of the good news.

more attractive and therefore encouraged reading. In many places it was found that the distribution of *The Watchtower* and *Awake!* increased considerably after their appearance was thus enhanced.

Developing Suitable Computer Systems

To support four-color printing, a computerized prepress system had to be developed; and the decision to go ahead with this was made in 1977. Witnesses who were experts in the field volunteered to work at the world headquarters to help the Society meet these needs quickly. (Shortly after this, in 1979, a team in Japan that eventually involved about 50 Witnesses began work on programs needed for the Japanese language.) Available commercial computer hardware was used, and programs were prepared by the Witnesses to help fill the Society's administrative and multilanguage publishing needs. To maintain high standards and have the needed flexibility, it was necessary to develop specialized programs for typesetting and photocomposition. There were no commercial programs available for entering and phototypesetting many of the 167 languages in which the Watch Tower Society was then printing, so the Witnesses had to develop their own.

At that time the commercial world saw no money in languages used by smaller populations or by people with very limited income, but Jehovah's Witnesses are interested in lives. Within a relatively short time, the typesetting programs that they developed were being used to produce literature in over 90 languages. Concerning their work the respected *Seybold Report on Publishing Systems* said: "We have nothing but praise for the enterprise, initiative and insightfulness of the Watchtower people. There are few today either ambitious enough or courageous enough to undertake such an application, especially virtually from scratch."—Volume 12, No. 1, September 13, 1982.

"We have nothing but praise for . . . the Watchtower people"

Printing operations and maintenance would be greatly facilitated if the equipment used worldwide was fully compatible. So in 1979 the decision was made for the Watch Tower Society to develop its own phototypesetting system. The team working on this was to make the principal hardware, instead of relying so heavily on commercial equipment.

Thus, in 1979 a group of Jehovah's Witnesses with their base of operations at Watchtower Farms, Wallkill, New York, began to design and build the Multilanguage Electronic Phototypesetting System (MEPS). By May 1986 not only had the team working on this project designed and built MEPS computers, phototypesetters, and graphics terminals but, more important, they had also developed the software required for processing material for publication in 186 languages.

PRODUCING BIBLE LITERATURE FOR USE IN THE MINISTRY

Coordinated with this software development was a large font-digitizing operation. This required intensive study of the distinctive characteristics of each language. Artwork had to be done for each character in a language (for example, each letter in capitals and lower case, as well as diacritical marks and punctuation—all in a variety of size ranges), with separate drawings for each typeface (such as, lightface, italic, bold, and extra bold), possibly in a number of distinctive fonts, or type styles. Each roman font needed 202 characters. Therefore, the 369 roman fonts have required a total of 74,538 characters. Preparation of Chinese fonts called for the drawing of 8,364 characters for each, with more characters to be added later.

After the artwork was done, software was designed that would make it possible to print the characters in clean, sharp form. The software had to be able to handle not only the Roman alphabet but also Bengali, Cambodian, Cyrillic, Greek, Hindi, and Korean as well as Arabic and Hebrew (both of which read from right to left) and Japanese and Chinese (which do not use alphabets). As of 1992 the software was available for processing material in over 200 languages, and programs for other languages used by millions of people were still being developed.

The implementation of the changeover in the branches required adopting new procedures and learning new skills. Personnel were sent to the world headquarters to learn how to erect, operate, and maintain large web offset presses. Some were taught how to do color separation work with a laser scanner. Additional personnel were trained in the use and the maintenance of computer equipment. Thus, production problems arising anywhere in the world could be quickly resolved so that the work would continue to move ahead.

The Governing Body realized that if Jehovah's Witnesses worldwide could study the same material in their meetings week by week and distribute the same literature in the field ministry, this would have a powerful

Intensive font digitizing has been done by the Witnesses to meet their need for Bible literature in many languages (Brooklyn, N.Y.)

Audiocassette Recordings

In addition to using the printed page in its evangelizing work, since 1978 the Watch Tower Society has produced audiocassettes—upwards of 65 million copies on its own equipment in the United States and Germany.

The entire "New World Translation" is on audiocassettes in English, French, German, Italian, Japanese, and Spanish. As of 1992 varying amounts of this Bible translation were also available on audiocassettes in eight other languages.

As an aid in teaching young children, tape recordings have been made of "My Book of Bible Stories" and "Listening to the Great Teacher," publications especially designed for young ones.

In addition, in some lands audiotapes are produced for use in radio broadcasts.

Recordings are produced by an orchestra made up entirely of Witnesses. These tapes are used as accompaniment for singing at conventions of Jehovah's Witnesses. Beautiful orchestral arrangements of this music are also available for home enjoyment.

Recorded dramas (both modern-day and Bible accounts) are used at conventions, where Witness actors help the audience to visualize events. Some of these are later used for instructive and enjoyable family entertainment.

Both the "Watchtower" and "Awake!" magazines are available on audiocassettes in English and Finnish. Also, "The Watchtower" is available in French, German, Danish, Norwegian, and Swedish. Originally intended for people who had poor eyesight, these tapes are appreciated by many thousands of others.

J. E. Barr in recording studio

---

unifying effect. In the past, literature published in English was not usually available in other languages until at least four months later; for many languages it was a year, or often years, later. But now a change was possible. Having *fully compatible* equipment in the printing branches was an important factor in being able to publish literature simultaneously in a variety of languages. By 1984, simultaneous publication of *The Watchtower* was achieved in 20 languages. In 1989, when the powerful message contained in the book *Revelation—Its Grand Climax At Hand!* was distributed to the public just a few months after its release, that book was available in 25 languages. By 1992, simultaneous publication of *The Watchtower* had broadened out to include 66 languages, those being used by a large proportion of the world's population.

Since the MEPS project was undertaken in 1979, the computer industry has made extraordinary advances. Powerful personal computers with great versatility are now available at a fraction of the cost of the earlier equipment. To keep pace with the needs of its publishing work, the Watch Tower Society decided to make use of these personal computers, along with its own software. This greatly speeded up the production process. It also made it possible to provide the benefits of the publishing programs to more of the Society's branches, and the number of branches using these quickly rose to 83. By 1992 the Watch Tower Society had, worldwide, over 3,800 terminals in which it was using its own computer programs. Not all the branches that are thus equipped do printing, but any branch that has a small computer and the Society's software, along with a small laser printer, has the capability for prepress work on tracts, magazines, books, and any other printing that needs to be done.

Increased Computer Support for Translators

Could computerization also be used to give greater support to those doing the work of translation? Translators of Watch Tower publications now do their work, in most cases, at computer terminals. Many of these are at the Society's branch offices. Others, who may translate at home and who have done their work for many years on typewriters or even by hand, have been helped to learn how to enter their translation at computer workstations or on laptop computers (ones that are conveniently small) purchased by the Society. Adjustments in the translation can easily be made right there on the computer screen. If the translating is done somewhere other than in the office of a branch where the actual printing will be done, all that is needed is to transfer the text to a thin, flexible disk and send it to the printing branch for processing.

During 1989-90, as rapid changes took place in the governments in many lands, international communication became easier. Quickly, Jehovah's Witnesses convened a seminar of their translators from Eastern Europe. This was designed to help them improve the quality of their work, to enable them to benefit from available computer equipment, and to make possible simultaneous publication of *The Watchtower* in their languages. Additionally, translators in Southeast Asia were given similar help.

But could the computer be used to speed up the work of translation or improve its quality? Yes. By 1989, powerful computer systems were being harnessed by Jehovah's Witnesses to assist in Bible translation. After extensive preliminary work, electronic files were provided that would enable a translator quickly to call up on the computer screen a visual display of any

Color computer workstations enable art designers to position, crop, and refine pictures electronically

Use of Videocassettes in Kingdom Proclamation

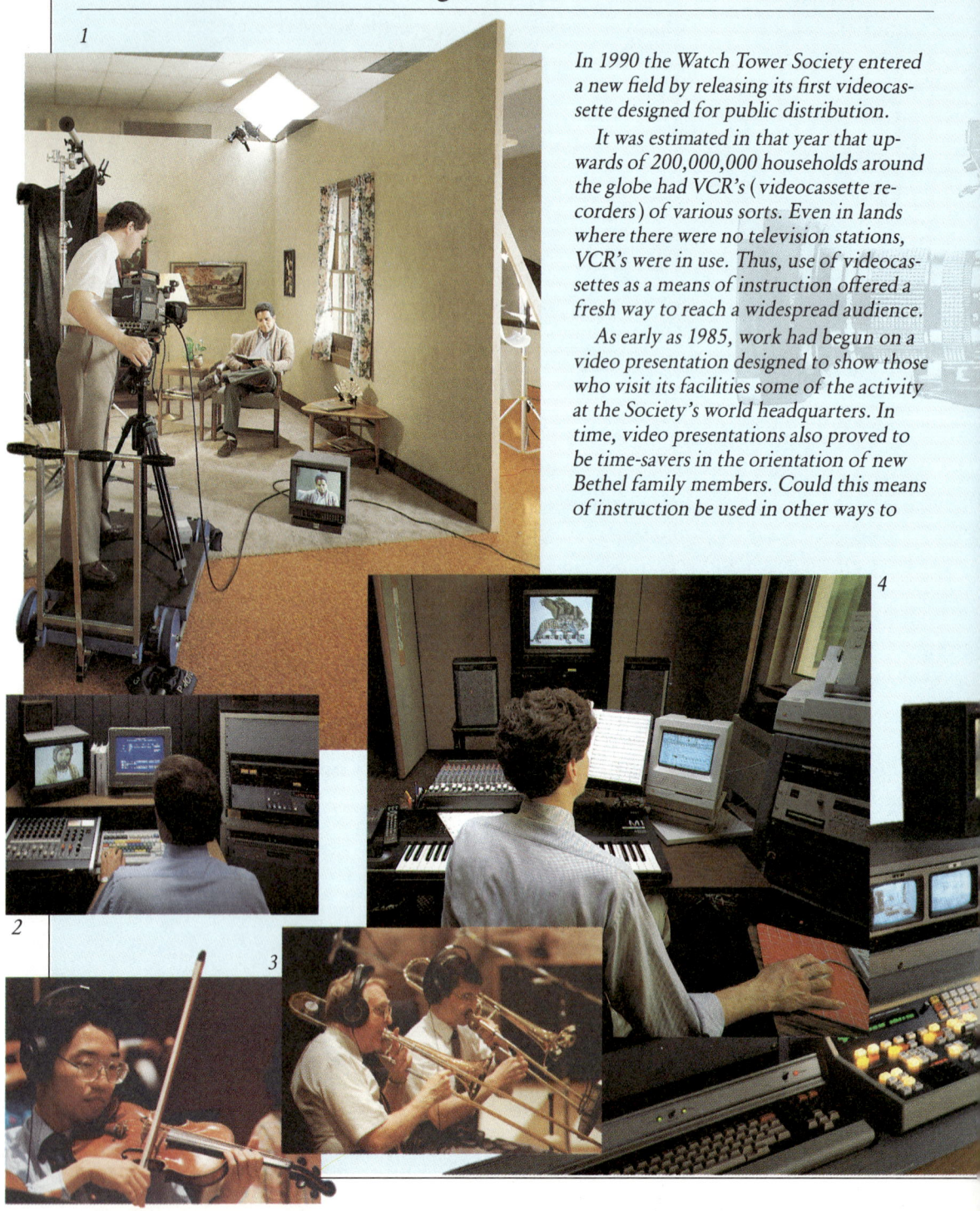

1

In 1990 the Watch Tower Society entered a new field by releasing its first videocassette designed for public distribution.

It was estimated in that year that upwards of 200,000,000 households around the globe had VCR's (videocassette recorders) of various sorts. Even in lands where there were no television stations, VCR's were in use. Thus, use of videocassettes as a means of instruction offered a fresh way to reach a widespread audience.

As early as 1985, work had begun on a video presentation designed to show those who visit its facilities some of the activity at the Society's world headquarters. In time, video presentations also proved to be time-savers in the orientation of new Bethel family members. Could this means of instruction be used in other ways to

4

2

3

assist in the global work of disciple making? Some of the brothers believed that it could.

As a result, in October 1990, the videocassette "Jehovah's Witnesses—The Organization Behind the Name" was released. The response was outstanding. A flood of requests for more of such programs was received. To fill the need, a new department called Video Services was established.

Witnesses who were experts in the field gladly offered their help. Equipment was obtained. Studios were set up. A camera crew began to travel to various lands to film people and objects that could be used in video presentations designed to build faith. The international all-Witness orchestra that had repeatedly helped with special projects provided music that would enhance video presentations.

---

1. After basic content is determined, videotaping proceeds as the script is being developed

2. Pictures are selected and their sequence is determined during off-line editing

3. Orchestral music that has been specially composed is recorded to enhance the presentation

4. Digital music and sound effects are merged with narration and pictures

5. Audio and visual features are given final editing

Plans were implemented to reach more language groups. By mid-1992, the video "Jehovah's Witnesses—The Organization Behind the Name" was being sent out in over a dozen languages. It had been recorded in 25 languages, including some for Eastern Europe. In addition, arrangements were under way to record it in Mandarin as well as Cantonese for the Chinese. The Society had also acquired the rights to reproduction and distribution of "Purple Triangles," a video about the integrity of a Witness family in Germany during the Nazi era. Within a two-year period, well over a million videocassettes had been produced for use by Jehovah's Witnesses in their ministry.

Special attention was given to the needs of the deaf. An edition of "Jehovah's Witnesses—The Organization Behind the Name" was produced in American Sign Language. And studies were undertaken with a view to providing videos that would be suitable for deaf people in other lands.

While this was being done, work was under way to produce a series that would help to build faith in the book that is the very foundation of Christian faith, the Bible. By September 1992, the first part of that program, "The Bible—Accurate History, Reliable Prophecy," was complete in English, and editions in other languages were being prepared.

Videocassettes are by no means taking the place of the printed page or personal witnessing. The Society's publications continue to fill a vital role in spreading the good news. The house-to-house work of Jehovah's Witnesses remains a solidly based Scriptural feature of their ministry. However, videocassettes now supplement these as valuable tools for cultivating faith in Jehovah's precious promises and stimulating appreciation for what he is having done on the earth in our day.

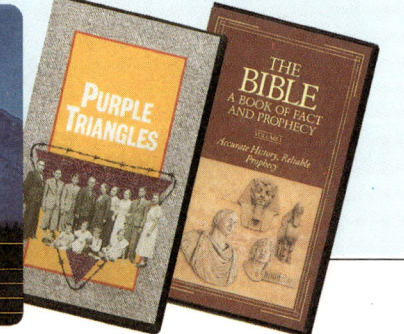

Jehovah's Witnesses use computer systems to speed up and refine the work of Bible translation (Korea)

given original-language word along with a record of all the ways it had, in accord with the context, been rendered into English in the *New World Translation*. He could also select a key English word and call up all the original-language words from which this (and possibly words of similar meaning) had been drawn. This would often reveal that a group of words were being used in English to convey the idea embodied in a single original-language term. It would quickly provide the translator with an in-depth view of what he was translating. It would help him to capture the distinctive sense of the basic original-language expression as well as the exact meaning required by the context and thus to express it accurately in his own language.

Using these computer files, veteran translators would examine all the occurrences of any given word in the Bible and assign local-language equivalents for each of these occurrences according to what was required by context. This would assure a high degree of consistency. The work of each translator would be reviewed by others working on the team so that the translation would benefit from the research and experience of all of them. After this was done, the computer could be used to display a given passage of Scripture, showing every word in the English text, a key to what appeared in the original language, and the local-language equivalent that had been selected. This would not complete the work. The translator still needed to smooth out the sentence structure and make it read well in his own language. But while doing this, it would be vital to have a clear grasp of the meaning of the scripture. To help him, he was given instantaneous computer access to published Watch Tower commentary on the Bible verse or any expression in it.

Research time could thus be held down, and a high degree of consistency could be achieved. With further development of this potential, it is hoped that more valuable publications can be made available quickly even in languages with limited staffs of translators. Use of this tool to provide literature in support of the proclamation of the Kingdom message has opened up a tremendous publishing field.

Thus, like their early Christian counterparts, Jehovah's Witnesses in modern times employ the latest means to spread God's Word. In order to reach as many people as possible with the good news, they have not been afraid to take on new challenges in the field of publishing.

CHAPTER 27

PRINTING AND DISTRIBUTING GOD'S OWN SACRED WORD

ON THE outside of the principal factory complex at their world headquarters, Jehovah's Witnesses have for decades displayed a sign that urges everyone: "Read God's Word the Holy Bible Daily."

They themselves are diligent students of God's Word. Over the years they have made use of scores of different Bible translations in an endeavor to ascertain the exact sense of the original inspired Scriptures. Every Witness is encouraged to have a personal program of daily Bible reading. In addition to their topical study of God's Word, they progressively read and discuss the Bible itself in their congregation meetings. Their objective is not to search out texts to support *their* ideas. They recognize the Bible as *God's* own inspired Word. They realize that it gives reproof and discipline, and they earnestly endeavor to conform their thinking and conduct to what it says.—2 Tim. 3:16, 17; compare 1 Thessalonians 2:13.

Because of their conviction that the Bible is God's own sacred Word and because they know the glorious good news that it contains, Jehovah's Witnesses are also zealous publishers and distributors of the Bible.

A Bible-Publishing Society

It was in 1896 that direct reference to the Bible was *officially* included in the name of the legal corporation then being used by the Bible Students in their publishing work. At that time Zion's Watch Tower Tract Society became legally known as Watch Tower *Bible* and Tract Society.* The Society did not immediately become a *printer* and *binder* of Bibles, but it was an active *publisher* of them, working out

---

* As shown by the *Watch Tower* of July 15, 1892 (p. 210), the name Watch Tower Bible and Tract Society had been used for a number of years before that name was legally registered. A tract published in 1890 in the *Old Theology* series identified the publishers as Tower *Bible* and Tract Society.

A Few of the Translations Used by Early Bible Students

Young's literal translation

Leeser's translation (English alongside Hebrew)

Tischendorf's "New Testament" (with variant readings from Greek MSS)

Murdock's translation (from Syriac)

"The Emphatic Diaglott" (Greek to English)

Variorum Bible (with various English renderings)

"The Newberry Bible" (with valuable marginal notes)

specifications, providing valuable supplementary features, and then arranging with commercial firms to do the printing and binding.

Even prior to 1896, the Society was doing much as a Bible distributor. Not for commercial gain but as a service to its readers, it drew attention to various Bible translations that were available, bought them in large quantities so as to obtain good rates, and then made them available for a price that was sometimes only 35 percent of the list price. Included among these were numerous editions of the *King James Version* that were easy to carry and use, also larger 'Teachers' Bibles' (*King James Version* with such helps as a concordance, maps, and marginal references), *The Emphatic Diaglott* with its Greek-to-English interlinear rendering, Leeser's translation that placed the English text alongside the Hebrew, Murdock's translation from ancient Syriac, *The Newberry Bible* with its marginal references that drew attention to occurrences of the divine name in the original language as well as other valuable details reflected in the Hebrew and Greek text, Tischendorf's *New Testament* with its footnote references to variant readings in three of the most complete ancient Greek Bible manuscripts (Sinaitic, Vatican, and Alexandrine), the Variorum Bible with its footnotes that set out not only variant readings of ancient manuscripts but also various translations of portions of the text by eminent scholars, and Young's literal translation. The Society also made available such helps as *Cruden's Concordance* and Young's *Analytical Concordance* with its comments on the original Hebrew and Greek words. In the years that followed, around the globe Jehovah's Witnesses frequently obtained from other Bible societies many thousands of Bibles in whatever languages were available and distributed these.

As early as 1890, according to available evidence, the Society arranged for a special printing, bearing its own name, of the Second Edition of *The New Testament Newly Translated and Critically Emphasised*, as prepared by the British Bible translator Joseph B. Rotherham. Why this translation? Because of its literalness and its endeavor to benefit fully from research that had been done to establish a more accurate Greek text and because the reader was helped by devices employed by the translator to identify which words or expressions were given special emphasis in the Greek text.

In 1902 a special printing of the Holman Linear Parallel Edition of the Bible was made by arrangement

Introduction to the edition of Rotherham's "New Testament" printed for Watch Tower Society c. 1890

JEHOVAH'S WITNESSES—PROCLAIMERS OF GOD'S KINGDOM

of the Watch Tower Society. It contained wide margins in which were printed references to places in Watch Tower publications where various verses were explained, also an index listing scores of subjects along with Scripture citations and helpful references to the Society's publications. This Bible contained the wording of two translations—the *King James* rendering above that of the *Revised Version* where there was any difference. It also included an extensive concordance that alerted the user to various meanings of original-language words.

That same year, the Watch Tower Society came into possession of the printing plates for *The Emphatic Diaglott*, which includes J. J. Griesbach's Greek text of the Christian Greek Scriptures (the 1796-1806 edition) along with an English interlinear translation. Alongside this was the rendering of the text by British-born Benjamin Wilson, who had taken up residence in Geneva, Illinois, U.S.A. Those plates and the sole right of publication had been purchased and then given as a gift to the Society. After copies already in stock had been sent out, arrangements were made by the Society for more to be produced, and those became available in 1903.

Four years later, in 1907, the Bible Students Edition of the *King James Version* was published. The "Berean Bible Teachers' Manual" was bound with it, as an appendix. This included concise comments on verses from all parts of the Bible, along with references to Watch Tower publications for fuller explanation. An edition with an enlarged appendix was published about a year later.

These Bibles were ordered from the printers and binders in lots of between 5,000 and 10,000 at a time, in order to keep the cost down. The Society was desirous of making a variety of Bible translations and related research tools readily available to as many people as possible.

Then, in 1926 the Watch Tower Society took a major step forward in its involvement in Bible publishing.

Printing the Bible on Our Own Presses

It was 36 years after it first undertook publishing Bibles that the Watch Tower Bible and Tract Society *printed* and *bound* a Bible in its own factory. The first one thus produced was *The Emphatic Diaglott*, the plates for which had been owned by the Society for 24 years. In December 1926 this Bible was printed on a flatbed press in the Society's Concord Street factory in Brooklyn. To date, 427,924 of these have been produced.

Holman Linear Parallel Edition of the Bible, as published by arrangement of Watch Tower Society in 1902

Watchtower edition of "King James Version," with specially designed concordance (1942)

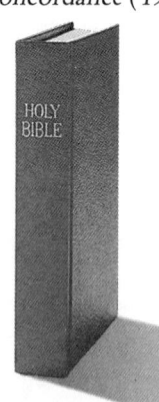

PRINTING AND DISTRIBUTING GOD'S OWN SACRED WORD

Sixteen years later, in the midst of World War II, the Society undertook the printing of the entire Bible. To this end, plates for the *King James Version* with marginal references were purchased in 1942 from the A. J. Holman Company, of Philadelphia, Pennsylvania. This translation of the complete Bible into English was produced, not from the Latin *Vulgate*, but by scholars who were able to compare earlier translations with the original Hebrew, Aramaic, and Greek. A concordance, prepared by more than 150 collaborating servants of Jehovah, was added. This was specially designed to help Jehovah's Witnesses find appropriate texts quickly when in the field ministry and thus use the Bible effectively as "the sword of the spirit," to cut away and expose religious falsehood. (Eph. 6:17) In order to make the Bible available to people everywhere at a low cost, it was printed on a web rotary press—something that had never been attempted by other Bible printers. As of 1992, a total of 1,858,368 of these Bibles had been produced.

The desire of Jehovah's Witnesses went beyond getting copies of the Bible, the book itself, into the hands of people. The Witnesses wanted to help people to get to know the personal name, as well as the purpose, of its divine author, Jehovah God. There was a translation in English—the *American Standard Version* of 1901—that used the divine name in the more than 6,870 places where it appeared in the sources from which the translators worked. In 1944, after a number of months of negotiations, the Watch Tower Society purchased the right to make a set of key plates for this Bible from plates and type supplied by Thomas Nelson and Sons, of New York. During the next 48 years, 1,039,482 copies were produced.

Steven Byington, of Ballard Vale, Massachusetts, U.S.A., had also made a modern-English translation of the Bible that gave the divine name its rightful place. The Watch Tower Society came into possession of his unpublished manuscript in 1951 and acquired the sole right of publication in 1961. That complete translation was printed in 1972. Down till 1992, there had been 262,573 produced.

In the meantime, however, another development was taking place.

Producing the *New World Translation*

It was early in October 1946 that Nathan H. Knorr, who was then the president of the Watch Tower Society, first proposed that the Society produce a fresh translation of the Christian Greek Scriptures. Actual work on the translation got under way on December 2, 1947. The complete text was carefully reviewed by the entire translation committee, all of them spirit-anointed Christians. Then, on September 3, 1949, Brother Knorr convened a joint meeting of the boards of directors of the Society's New York and Pennsylvania corporations. He announced to them that the New World Bible Translation Committee had completed work on a modern-language

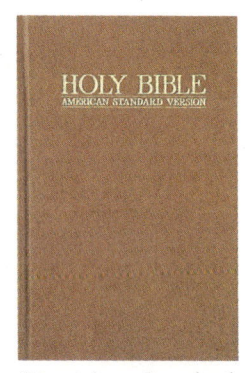

"American Standard Version," a translation that uses the divine name, Jehovah, over 6,870 times; Watchtower edition (1944)

Byington's translation (1972)

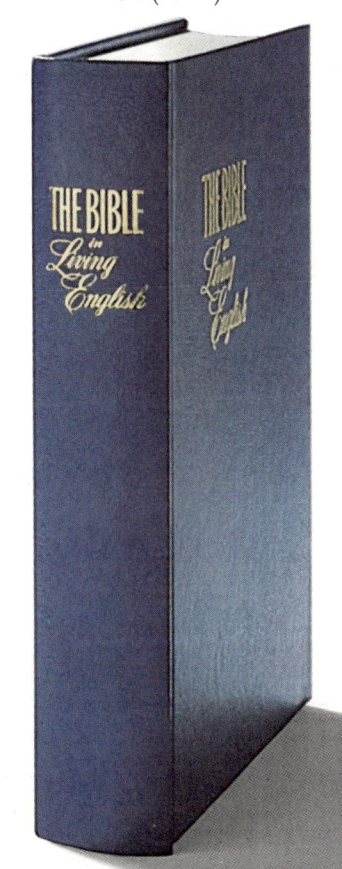

"New World Translation," first released in English in six volumes, from 1950 to 1960; later combined in a special students' edition

Published as a compact single volume in 1961

Large-print edition, with references for study, published in 1984

translation of the Christian Greek Scriptures and had turned it over to the Society for publication.* This was a fresh translation from the original Greek.

Was there really need for another translation? Already at that time, the complete Bible had been published in 190 languages, and at least part of it had been translated into 928 additional languages and dialects. Jehovah's Witnesses have at various times used most of these translations. But the fact is that most of these were made by clergymen and missionaries of Christendom's religious sects, and to varying degrees their translations were influenced by the pagan philosophies and unscriptural traditions that their religious systems had inherited from the past as well as by the bias of higher criticism. Furthermore, older and more reliable Bible manuscripts were becoming available. The Greek language of the first century was becoming more clearly understood as a result of archaeological discoveries. Also, the languages into which translations are made undergo changes over the years.

Jehovah's Witnesses wanted a translation that embodied the benefits of the latest scholarship, one that was not colored by the creeds and traditions

---

* This translation was assigned to the Watch Tower Bible and Tract Society of Pennsylvania for publication, with the request that the names of the translators never be published. They wanted all honor to go to Jehovah God, the Divine Author of his inspired Word.

of Christendom, a literal translation that faithfully presented what is in the original writings and so could provide the basis for continued growth in knowledge of divine truth, a translation that would be clear and understandable to modern-day readers. The *New World Translation of the Christian Greek Scriptures,* released in 1950, filled that need—at least for that part of the Bible. As Jehovah's Witnesses began to use it, many were thrilled not simply because they found its modern-day language easier to read but because they realized that they were getting a clearer understanding of the sense of God's inspired Word.

One of the outstanding features of this translation is its restoration of the divine name, the personal name of God, Jehovah, 237 times in the Christian Greek Scriptures. This was not the first translation to restore the name.* But it may have been the first to do it consistently in the main text from Matthew through Revelation. An extensive discussion of this matter in the foreword showed the sound basis for what was done.

Thereafter, the Hebrew Scriptures were translated into English and were released progressively, in five separate volumes, beginning in 1953. As had been done with the Christian Greek Scriptures, care was exercised to convey as literally as possible what was in the original-language text. Special attention was given to making the renderings uniform, conveying accurately the action or state expressed in the verbs, and using simple language that would be readily understood by modern-day readers. Wherever the Tetragrammaton appeared in the Hebrew text, it was appropriately rendered as the personal name of God, instead of being replaced by some other term as had become common in many other translations. Appendix articles and footnotes in these volumes enabled careful students to examine the basis for the renderings used.

On March 13, 1960, the New World Bible Translation Committee completed its final reading of the text of the portion of the Bible that was designated for the fifth volume. That was 12 years, 3 months, and 11 days after actual translation of the Christian Greek Scriptures had begun. A few months later, that final volume of the Hebrew Scriptures, in printed form, was released for distribution.

Rather than disband after that project was completed, the translation committee continued to work. A comprehensive review of the entire translation was

---

* Some earlier translations into Hebrew, German, and English restored the divine name in the Christian Greek Scriptures, as did many missionary versions.

A Fresh Translation

*When the first volume of the "New World Translation of the Hebrew Scriptures" was published, Alexander Thomson, a British Bible critic, wrote: "Original renderings of the Hebrew Scriptures into the English language are extremely few. It therefore gives us much pleasure to welcome the publication of the first part of the New World Translation [of the Hebrew Scriptures], Genesis to Ruth. . . . This version has evidently made a special effort to be thoroughly readable. No one could say it is deficient in freshness and originality. Its terminology is by no means based upon that of previous versions."
—"The Differentiator," June 1954, p. 131.*

> ### "A Text With Instant Vocabulary"
>
> In *"The Classical Journal,"* Thomas N. Winter of the University of Nebraska wrote a review of *"The Kingdom Interlinear Translation of the Greek Scriptures"* in which he said: "This is no ordinary interlinear: the integrity of the text is preserved, and the English which appears below it is simply the basic meaning of the Greek word. Thus the interlinear feature of this book is no translation at all. A text with instant vocabulary more correctly describes it. A translation in smooth English appears in a slim column at the right-hand margin of the pages. . . .
>
> "The text is based on that of Brooke F. Westcott and Fenton J. A. Hort (1881, repr.), but the translation by the anonymous committee is thoroughly up-to-date and consistently accurate."—April-May issue of 1974, pp. 375-6.

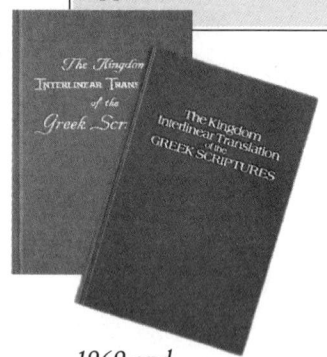

1969 and 1985 editions

made. Then, the complete *New World Translation of the Holy Scriptures,* a revised edition in one volume, was published by the Watch Tower Society in 1961. It was made available for distribution for just one dollar (U.S.) so that everyone, regardless of his economic situation, would be able to obtain a copy of God's Word.

Two years later a special students' edition was published. This combined under one cover all the original individual volumes, unrevised, with their thousands of valuable textual footnotes, as well as foreword and appendix discussions. It also retained the valuable cross-references that directed readers to parallel words, parallel thoughts or events, biographic information, geographic details, fulfillments of prophecies, and direct quotations in or from other parts of the Bible.

Since the one-volume edition of 1961 was published, four additional up-to-date revisions have been issued. The most recent of these was in 1984, when a large-print edition with an extensive appendix, 125,000 marginal references, 11,400 enlightening footnotes, and a concordance was published. The features of this edition help students to understand why various texts need to be rendered in a certain way in order to be accurate, as well as when texts can be correctly rendered in more than one manner. The cross-references also help them to appreciate the interlocking harmony between the various Bible books.

As part of the earnest effort of the New World Bible Translation Committee to help lovers of God's Word to get acquainted with the contents of the original Koine (common Greek) text of the Christian Greek Scriptures, the committee produced *The Kingdom Interlinear Translation of the Greek Scriptures.* This was first published by the Watch Tower Society in 1969 and then updated in 1985. It contains *The New Testament in the Original Greek,* as compiled by B. F. Westcott and F. J. A. Hort. At the right-hand side of the page appears the *New World Translation* text (the 1984 revision in the updated edition). But then, between the lines of Greek text, there is another translation, a very literal, word-for-word rendering of what the Greek actually says according to the basic meaning and grammatical form of each word. This enables even students who cannot read Greek to find out what is actually in the original Greek text.

Was this work on the *New World Translation* going to benefit only those who could read English? In many places Watch Tower missionaries were finding it difficult to obtain enough local-language Bibles to distribute to people who longed for a personal copy of God's Word. It was not uncommon, in some parts of the world, for these missionaries to be the principal distributors of Bibles printed by other Bible societies. But that was not always viewed favorably by religious personnel who represented those Bible societies. Further, some of these Bibles were not the best of translations.

Translation Into Other Languages

The year that the complete *New World Translation* first appeared in a single volume, that is, 1961, a group of skilled translators was assembled to render the English text into six other widely used languages—Dutch, French, German, Italian, Portuguese, and Spanish. Retranslation from English, supplemented by comparison with the Hebrew and the Greek, was possible because of the literal nature of the English translation itself. The translators worked as an international committee in association with the New World Bible Translation Committee, at the Society's headquarters in Brooklyn, New York. In 1963 the Christian Greek Scriptures was printed and released in all six languages.

By 1992 the complete *New World Translation of the Holy Scriptures* was available in 12 languages—Czech, Danish, Dutch, English, French, German, Italian, Japanese, Portuguese, Slovak, Spanish, and Swedish. The Christian Greek Scriptures was available in two more languages. That meant that this translation was available in the native tongues of some 1,400,000,000 persons, or upwards of one fourth of the world's population, and many more were benefiting from it through the translation of excerpts from it into 97 other languages in *The Watchtower*. Those reading these 97 languages, however, were anxious to have the full *New World Translation* in their own tongue. As of 1992, arrangements were already under way to produce this translation in 16 of those languages and to complete the Hebrew Scriptures in the 2 languages that had only the Christian Greek Scriptures.

Since the publishing of these Bibles was done in the Society's own factories by volunteer workers, it was possible to make them available at minimal cost. In 1972 when an Austrian Witness showed a bookbinder the *New World Translation* in German and asked him how much he thought it would cost, the man was amazed to learn that the suggested contribution was only one tenth of the price he named.

The Opinion of a Hebrew Scholar

Regarding the "New World Translation," Professor Dr. Benjamin Kedar, a Hebrew scholar in Israel, said in 1989: "In my linguistic research in connection with the Hebrew Bible and translations, I often refer to the English edition of what is known as the 'New World Translation.' In so doing, I find my feeling repeatedly confirmed that this work reflects an honest endeavor to achieve an understanding of the text that is as accurate as possible. Giving evidence of a broad command of the original language, it renders the original words into a second language understandably without deviating unnecessarily from the specific structure of the Hebrew.... Every statement of language allows for a certain latitude in interpreting or translating. So the linguistic solution in any given case may be open to debate. But I have never discovered in the 'New World Translation' any biased intent to read something into the text that it does not contain."

Progressively the "New World Translation" has been made available in more languages

JEHOVAH'S WITNESSES—PROCLAIMERS OF GOD'S KINGDOM

Some examples illustrate the impact of this translation. In France the Catholic Church had for centuries prohibited possession of the Bible by the laity. Catholic translations that had become available were relatively expensive, and few homes had these. The *New World Translation of the Christian Greek Scriptures* was released in French in 1963, followed by the complete Bible in 1974. By 1992 a combined total of 2,437,711 copies of the *New World Translation* had been shipped out for distribution in France; and the number of Jehovah's Witnesses in France increased 488 percent during that same period, reaching a total of 119,674.

The situation was similar in Italy. The people had long been forbidden to have a copy of the Bible. After the release of the Italian edition of the *New World Translation* and down till 1992, there were 3,597,220 copies distributed; the vast majority of these were the complete Bible. People wanted to examine for themselves what God's Word contains. Interestingly, during that same period, the number of Jehovah's Witnesses in Italy rose sharply—from 7,801 to 194,013.

When the *New World Translation of the Christian Greek Scriptures* was made available in Portuguese, there were just 30,118 Witnesses in Brazil and 1,798 in Portugal. During the following years, down till 1992, a total of 213,438 copies of the Christian Greek Scriptures and 4,153,738 copies of the complete Bible in Portuguese were sent out to individuals and congregations in these lands. What were the results? In Brazil, over 11 times as many active praisers of Jehovah; and in Portugal, 22 times as many. Tens of thousands of people who had never had a Bible were grateful to get one, and others appreciated having a Bible that used words they could understand. When the *New World Translation of the Holy Scriptures—With References* was made available in Brazil, the news media pointed out that it was the most complete version (that is, with more cross-references and footnotes) available in the country. It also noted that the initial printing was ten times as great as that for most national editions.

The Spanish edition of the *New World Translation of the Christian Greek Scriptures* was also released in 1963, followed in 1967 by the complete Bible. There were 527,451 copies of the Christian Greek Scriptures published, and thereafter, down to 1992, a total of 17,445,782 copies of the complete Bible in Spanish. This contributed to an outstanding increase in the number of praisers of Jehovah in Spanish-speaking lands. Thus, from 1963 to 1992, in predominantly Spanish-speaking lands where Jehovah's Witnesses carry on their ministry, their numbers grew from 82,106 to 942,551. And in the United States, in 1992, there were another 130,224 Spanish-speaking Witnesses of Jehovah.

It was not only in the realm of Christendom that the *New World Translation* was enthusiastically received. In the first year of publication of the Japanese edition, the branch office in Japan received orders for half a million copies.

As of 1992 the printing of the complete *New World Translation of the Holy Scriptures,* in the 12 languages then available, numbered 70,105,258 copies. In addition to that, 8,819,080 copies of portions of the translation had been printed.

Making the Bible Available in Many Forms

Computerization of the Watch Tower Society's operations, starting in 1977, has assisted in Bible production, as it has in other aspects of publishing activity. It has helped translators to achieve greater consistency in their work; it has also made it easier to print the Bible in a variety of forms.

After the full text of the Bible was entered into the computer, it was not difficult to use an electronic phototypesetter to print out the text

Growth of Witnesses Since Publication of "New World Translation"

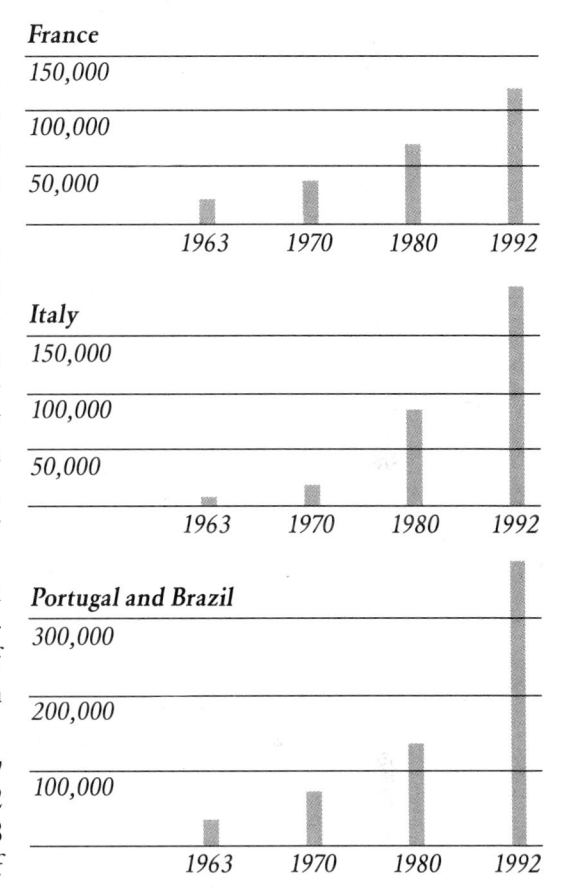

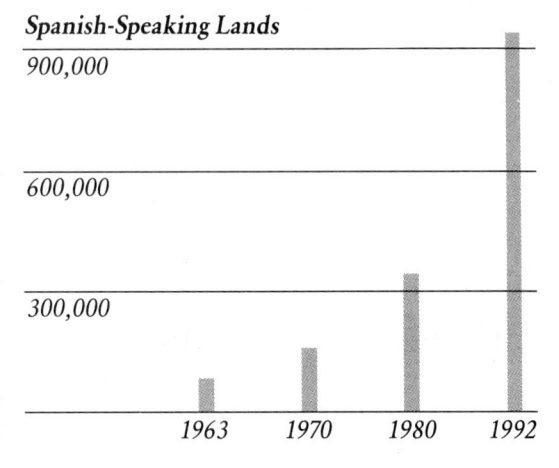

France

Italy

Portugal and Brazil

Spanish-Speaking Lands

"New World Translation"
in very large print

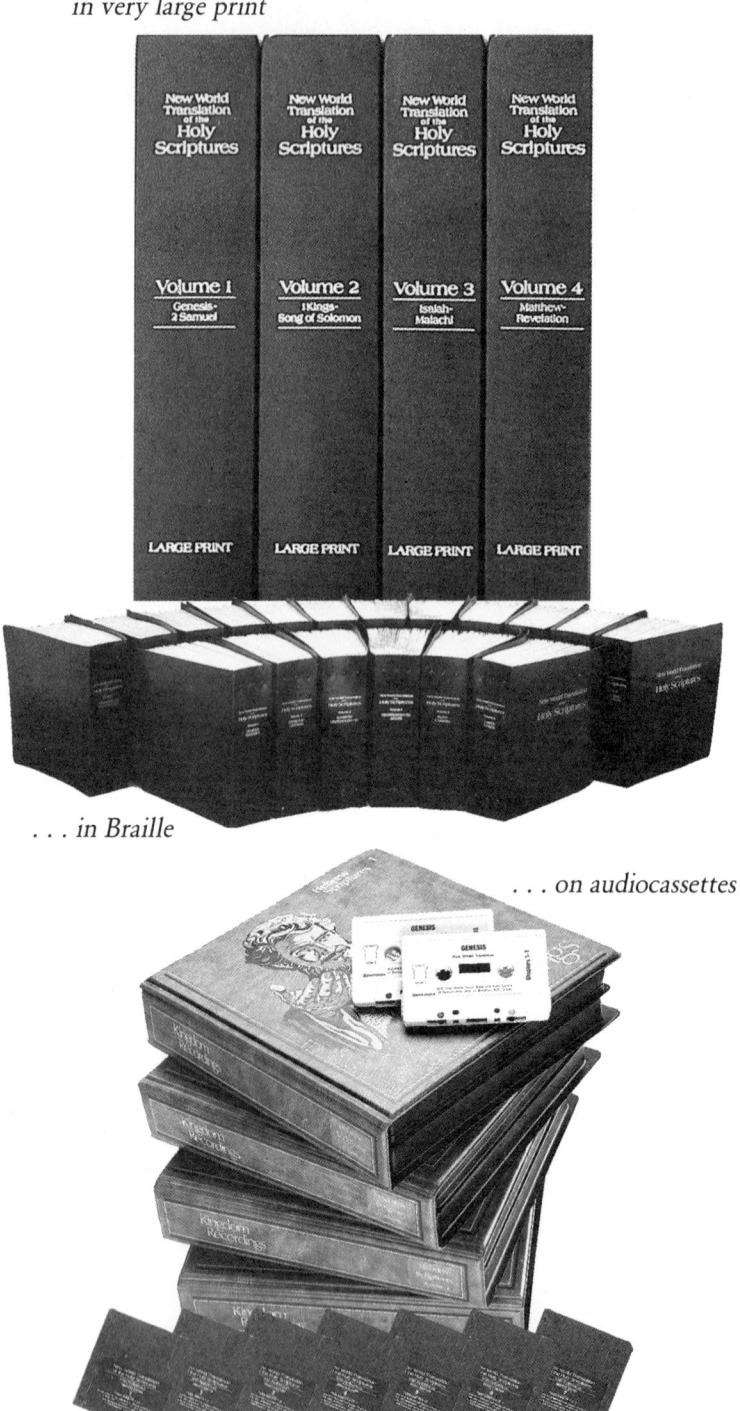

. . . in Braille

. . . on audiocassettes

. . . on computer diskettes

in a variety of sizes and forms. First, in 1981, came a regular-sized edition in English with a concordance and other helpful appendix features. This was the first edition to be printed by the Watch Tower Society on a web *offset* press. After the benefits of revision had been incorporated into the text stored in the computer, a large-print edition in English was issued in 1984; this included many valuable features for research. A regular-size English edition of that same revision was also made available that year; cross-references and a concordance were included, but not footnotes; and its appendix was designed for field ministry instead of for deeper study. Then, for the benefit of those who wanted a very small pocket edition, this was published in English in 1987. All these editions were quickly published in other languages too.

In addition, attention was given to assisting those with special needs. To help those who could see but who needed very large print, the complete English-language *New World Translation* in four large volumes was published in 1985. Soon that same edition was printed in German, French, Spanish, and Japanese. Before that, in 1983, the *New World Translation of the Christian Greek Scriptures,* in four volumes, had been made available in grade-two English Braille. Within another five years, the complete

New World Translation had been produced in English Braille in 18 volumes.

Would some people be helped if they could listen to a recording of the Bible? Definitely. So the Watch Tower Society undertook the production of this too. The first audiocassette recording was *The Good News According to John*, in English, released in 1978. In time the entire *New World Translation* in English was made available on 75 audiocassettes. What began as a small operation soon mushroomed into a major project. Quickly, it became available in other languages. By 1992 the *New World Translation*, the whole or part, was available on audiocassettes in 14 languages. At first, some of the branches had the work done by commercial companies. Down till 1992, on their own equipment, the Watch Tower Society had turned out over 31,000,000 of such audiocassettes.

The benefits from the Bible audiocassettes and the uses to which they were put far exceeded original expectations. In all parts of the earth, people were using cassette players. Many who could not read were helped in this way to benefit personally from God's sacred Word. Women were able to listen to the audiocassettes while doing their housework. Men listened to them on tape decks while commuting to work by automobile. The teaching ability of individual Witnesses was enhanced as they listened regularly to God's Word and took note of the pronunciation of Bible names and the manner in which passages of Scripture were read.

As of 1992, various editions of the *New World Translation* were being printed on the Society's presses in North and South America, Europe, and the Orient. A total of 78,924,338 volumes had been produced and made available for distribution. In Brooklyn alone, there were three huge high-speed web offset presses largely devoted to Bible production. Combined, these presses can produce the equivalent of 7,900 Bibles per hour, and at times it has been necessary for them to run an extra shift.

However, Jehovah's Witnesses offer people more than a Bible that might simply be put on the shelf. They also offer to anyone who is interested in the Bible—whether he obtains a copy from Jehovah's Witnesses or not—a free home Bible study. These studies do not continue indefinitely. Some students take to heart what they learn, become baptized Witnesses, and then share in teaching others. After some months, if reasonable progress is not made in applying what is learned, studies are often discontinued in favor of other people who are genuinely interested. As of 1992, Jehovah's Witnesses were providing 4,278,127 individuals or households with this free Bible study service, usually on a weekly basis.

Thus, in a manner unmatched by any other organization, Jehovah's Witnesses are publishers and distributors of the Bible and are teachers of God's sacred Word.

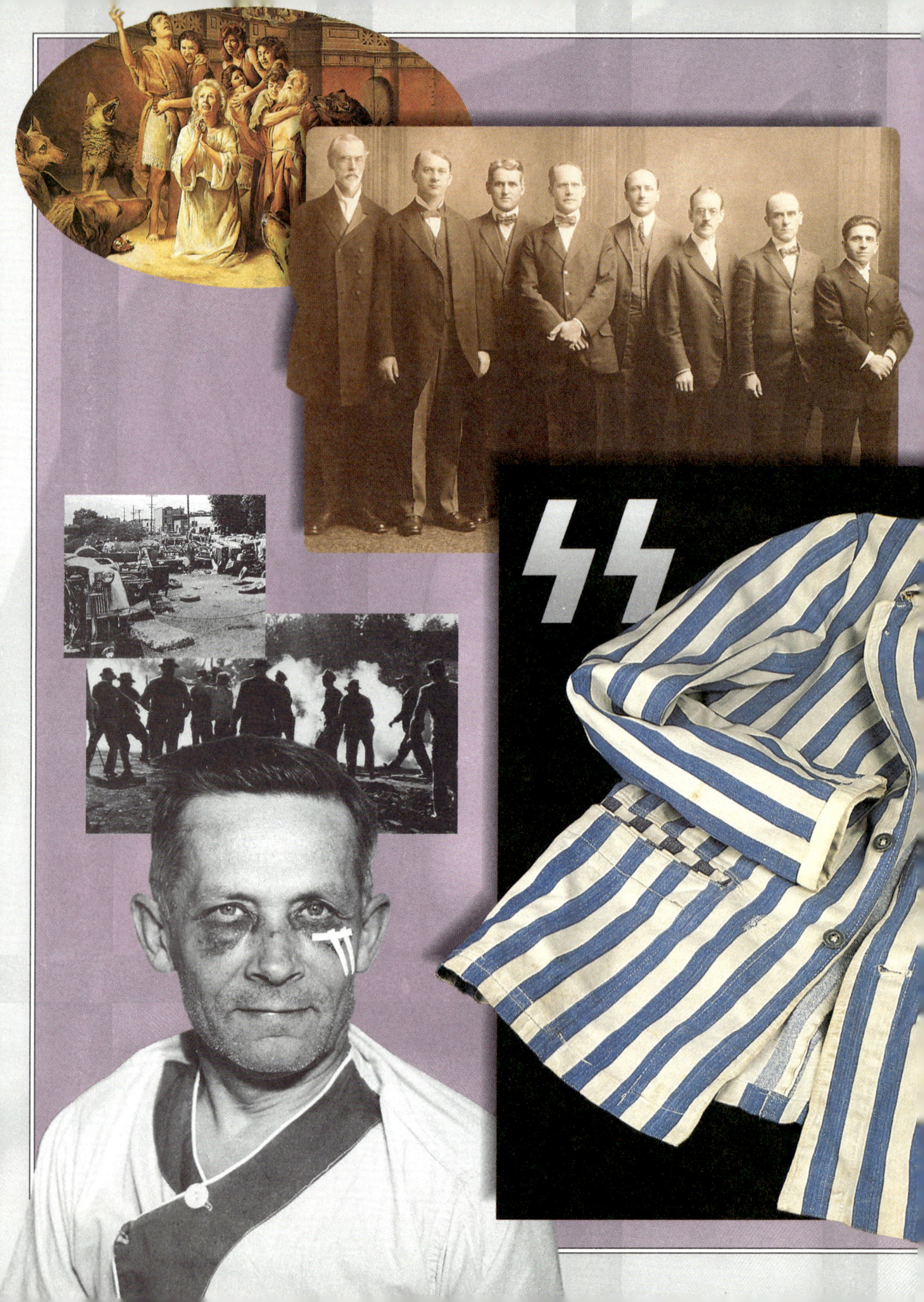

SECTION 6

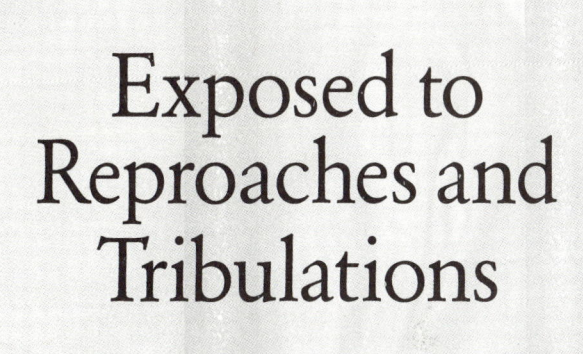

Exposed to Reproaches and Tribulations

Jesus Christ warned his followers that they would face trials—some because of human imperfection, others because of false brothers, and even more because of persecution at the hands of opposers. Chapters 28 to 30 vividly relate what Jehovah's Witnesses have experienced in modern times and how their faith has enabled them to come off victorious.

CHAPTER 28

TESTING AND SIFTING FROM WITHIN

THE development and growth of the modern-day organization of Jehovah's Witnesses has included many situations that have severely tested the faith of individuals. As threshing and winnowing separate wheat from chaff, so these situations have served to identify those who are real Christians. (Compare Luke 3:17.) People associated with the organization have had to manifest what was in their hearts. Were they simply serving for personal advantage? Were they merely followers of some imperfect human? Or were they humble, eager to know and to do God's will, complete in their devotion to Jehovah?—Compare 2 Chronicles 16:9.

First-century followers of Jesus Christ likewise experienced tests of their faith. Jesus told his followers that if faithful, they would share with him in his Kingdom. (Matt. 5:3, 10; 7:21; 18:3; 19:28) But he did not tell them *when* they would receive that prize. In the face of public apathy, even hostility, toward their preaching, would they loyally continue to make the interests of that Kingdom the first concern in their lives? Not everyone did.—2 Tim. 4:10.

The manner in which Jesus himself taught presented a test to some. The Pharisees were stumbled when he bluntly rejected their traditions. (Matt. 15:1-14) Even many who professed to be Jesus' disciples took offense at his manner of teaching. On one occasion, when he was discussing the importance of exercising faith in the value of his own flesh and blood offered in sacrifice, many of his disciples expressed shock at the figurative language that he used. Not waiting for further explanation, they "went off to the things behind and would no longer walk with him."—John 6:48-66.

But not all turned away. As Simon Peter explained, "Lord, whom shall we go away to? You have sayings of everlasting life; and we have believed and come to know that you are the Holy One of God." (John 6:67-69) They had seen and heard enough to be convinced that Jesus was the one through whom God was making manifest the truth concerning himself and his purpose. (John 1:14; 14:6) Nevertheless, the tests of faith continued.

After Jesus' death and resurrection, he used the apostles and others as shepherds of the congregation. These were imperfect men, and at times their imperfections were a trial to those around them. (Compare Acts 15: 36-41; Galatians 2:11-14.) On the other hand, there were individuals who became unbalanced in their admiration of prominent Christians and who said: "I belong to Paul," while others said: 'I belong to Apollos.' (1 Cor. 3:4) All of them needed to be on guard so as not to lose sight of what it meant to be a follower of Jesus Christ.

The apostle Paul foretold other serious problems, explaining that even within the Christian congregation men would "rise and speak twisted things to draw away the disciples after themselves." (Acts 20:29, 30) And the apostle Peter warned that false teachers among God's servants would seek to exploit others with "counterfeit words." (2 Pet. 2:1-3) Obviously, heart-searching tests of faith and loyalty lay ahead.

So, the testing and sifting that are part of the modern-day history of Jehovah's Witnesses have come as no surprise. But not a few have been surprised at *who* stumbled and *over what*.

Testing and sifting have come as no surprise

Did They Truly Appreciate the Ransom?

During the early 1870's, Brother Russell and his associates grew in knowledge and appreciation of God's purpose. It was a time of spiritual refreshment for them. But then, in 1878, they were confronted with a major test of their faith and their loyalty to God's Word. At issue was the sacrificial value of Jesus' flesh and blood—the very teaching over which many of Jesus' first-century disciples had stumbled.

It was just two years before this, in 1876, that C. T. Russell had entered into a working relationship with N. H. Barbour of Rochester, New York. Their study groups had become affiliated. Russell had provided funds to revive the printing of Barbour's magazine *Herald of the Morning*, with Barbour as editor and Russell as an assistant editor. They had also produced together a book entitled *Three Worlds, and the Harvest of This World*.

Then a bombshell exploded! In the August 1878 issue of *Herald of the Morning*, Barbour wrote an article in which he brushed aside such scriptures as 1 Peter 3:18 and Isaiah 53:5, 6, also Hebrews 9:22, and declared that the whole idea that Christ died to atone for our sins was obnoxious. Russell later wrote: "To our painful surprise, Mr. Barbour . . . wrote an article for the *Herald* denying the doctrine of the atonement—denying that the death of Christ was the ransom-price of Adam and his race, saying that Christ's death was no more a settlement of the penalty of man's sins than would the sticking of a pin through the body of a fly and causing it suffering and death be considered by an earthly parent as a just settlement for misdemeanor in his child."*

---

* *Zion's Watch Tower and Herald of Christ's Presence*, Extra Edition, April 25, 1894, pp. 102-4.

This was a crucial matter. Would Brother Russell hold loyally to what the Bible clearly said regarding God's provision for the salvation of humankind? Or would he fall prey to human philosophy? Although Russell was only 26 years old at the time and Barbour was a much older man, Russell courageously wrote an article for the very next issue of the *Herald* in which he strongly defended the sin-atoning value of Christ's blood, which he referred to as "one of the most important teachings of God's word."

Next, he invited J. H. Paton, the other assistant editor of the *Herald*, to write an article in support of faith in the blood of Christ as the basis for atonement for sin. Paton did write the article, and it was published in the December issue. After repeated unsuccessful efforts to reason on the matter with Barbour from the Scriptures, Russell broke off association with him and withdrew support from his magazine. In July 1879, Russell began to publish a new magazine—*Zion's Watch Tower and Herald of Christ's Presence*—which was from the start a special advocate of the ransom. But that was not the end of it.

Two years later, Paton, who was then serving as a traveling representative of the *Watch Tower,* also began to turn away, thereafter publishing a book (his second one entitled *Day Dawn*) in which he rejected belief in Adam's fall into sin and consequently the need for a redeemer. He reasoned that the Lord himself was an imperfect man who by his life simply showed others how to crucify their sinful propensities. In 1881, A. D. Jones, an-

A major test of faith involved recognition of the sin-atoning value of Jesus' sacrifice

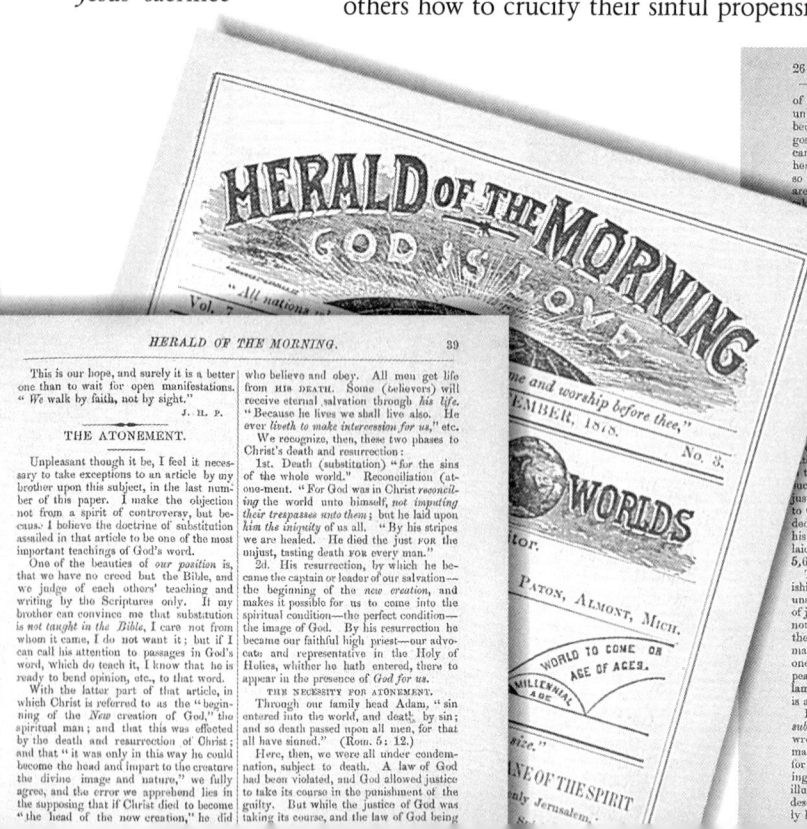

other associate, started a paper (*Zion's Day Star*) along the same lines as the *Watch Tower* but with the idea that it would set out simpler features of God's purpose. At first it seemed that all was well. Yet, within a year, Jones' paper had repudiated Christ's atoning sacrifice, and within another year, it had rejected all the rest of the Bible. What had happened to those men? They had allowed personal theories and fascination with popular philosophies of men to lead them astray from the Word of God. (Compare Colossians 2:8.) The paper published by A. D. Jones continued for only a short time and then faded from view. J. H. Paton decided to publish a magazine in which he set out the gospel as he saw it, but its circulation was quite limited.

Brother Russell was deeply concerned about the effect that all of this was having on readers of the *Watch Tower*. He realized that it put each one's faith to the test. He well knew that some construed his criticism of unscriptural teachings to be prompted by a spirit of rivalry. But Brother Russell sought no followers for himself. Concerning what was taking place, he wrote: "The object of this trial and sifting evidently is to select all whose heart-desires are unselfish, who are fully and unreservedly consecrated to the Lord, who are so anxious to have the Lord's will done, and whose confidence in his wisdom, his way and his Word is so great, that they refuse to be led away from the Lord's Word, either by the sophistries of others, or by plans and ideas of their own."

"They refuse to be led away from the Lord's Word"

Was God Using a Visible Channel?

There are, of course, many religious organizations, and a considerable number of teachers make some use of the Bible. Was God particularly using Charles Taze Russell? If so, did God cease to have a visible channel when Brother Russell died? These became critical issues, ones that led to further testing and sifting.

It certainly could not be expected that God would use C. T. Russell if he did not loyally adhere to God's Word. (Jer. 23:28; 2 Tim. 3:16, 17) God would not use a man who fearfully refrained from preaching what he saw clearly written in the Scriptures. (Ezek. 2:6-8) Nor would God use a person who exploited his knowledge of the Scriptures to bring glory to himself. (John 5:44) So, what do the facts show?

As Jehovah's Witnesses today review the work that he did, the things he taught, his reason for teaching them, and the outcome, they have no doubt that Charles Taze Russell was, indeed, used by God in a special way and at a significant time.

This view is not based solely on the firm stand that Brother Russell took with regard to the ransom. It also takes into account the fact that he fearlessly rejected creeds that contained some of the foundation beliefs of

> **W. E. Van Amburgh**
>
> In 1916, W. E. Van Amburgh declared: "This great worldwide work is not the work of one person. . . . It is God's work." Although he saw others turn away, he remained firm in that conviction right down till his death in 1947, at 83 years of age.

Christendom, because these clashed with the inspired Scriptures. These beliefs included the doctrine of the Trinity (which had its roots in ancient Babylon and was not adopted by so-called Christians until long after Bible writing was completed) as well as the teaching that human souls are inherently immortal (which had been adopted by men who were overawed by the philosophy of Plato and which left them open to such ideas as the eternal torment of souls in hellfire). Many of Christendom's scholars, too, know that these doctrines are not taught in the Bible,* but that is not generally what their preachers say from the pulpits. In contrast, Brother Russell undertook an intensive campaign to share what the Bible actually does say with everyone who was willing to hear.

Noteworthy too is what Brother Russell did with other highly significant truths that he learned from God's Word. He discerned that Christ would return as a glorious spirit person, invisible to human eyes. As early as 1876, he recognized that the year 1914 would mark the end of the Gentile Times. (Luke 21:24, *KJ*) Other Bible scholars had likewise perceived some of these things and had advocated them. But Brother Russell used all his resources to give them international publicity on a scale then unequaled by any other individual or group.

He urged others to check his writings carefully against God's inspired Word so that they would be satisfied that what they were learning was in full harmony with it. To one who wrote a letter of inquiry, Brother Russell replied: "If it was proper for the early Christians to prove what they received from the apostles, who were and who claimed to be inspired, how much more important it is that you fully satisfy yourself that these teachings keep closely within their outline instructions and those of our Lord; —since their author claims no inspiration, but merely the *guidance* of the Lord, as one used of him in feeding his flock."

Brother Russell claimed no supernatural power, no divine revelations. He did not claim credit for what he taught. He was an outstanding student of the Bible. But he explained that his remarkable understanding of the Scriptures was due to 'the simple fact that God's due time had come.' He said: "If I did not speak, and no other agent could be found, the very

---

* Regarding the Trinity, see the *New Catholic Encyclopedia*, Volume XIV, 1967, page 299; *Dictionary of the Bible*, by J. L. McKenzie, S.J., 1965, page 899; *The New International Dictionary of New Testament Theology*, Volume 2, 1976, page 84. Regarding the soul, see the *New Catholic Encyclopedia*, Volume XIII, 1967, pages 449-50, 452, 454; *The New Westminster Dictionary of the Bible*, edited by H. S. Gehman, 1970, page 901; *The Interpreter's Bible*, Volume I, 1952, page 230; *Peake's Commentary on the Bible*, edited by M. Black and H. H. Rowley, 1962, page 416.

stones would cry out." He referred to himself as being simply like an index finger, pointing to what is stated in God's Word.

Charles Taze Russell wanted no glory from humans. To readjust the thinking of any who were inclined to give excessive honor to him, Brother Russell wrote, in 1896: "As we have been to some extent, by the grace of God, used in the ministry of the gospel, it may not be out of place to say here what we have frequently said in private, and previously in these columns,—namely, that while we appreciate the love, sympathy, confidence and fellowship of fellow-servants and of the entire household of faith, we want no homage, no reverence, for ourselves or our writings; nor do we wish to be called Reverend or Rabbi. Nor do we wish that any should be called by our name."

"We want no homage, no reverence, for ourselves or our writings"

As his death neared, he did not take the view that there was nothing more to be learned, that there was no more work to be done. He had often spoken of preparing a seventh volume of *Studies in the Scriptures*. When asked about it before he died, he said to Menta Sturgeon, his traveling companion: "Some one else can write that." In his will he expressed the desire that *The Watch Tower* continue to be published under the direction of a committee of men fully devoted to the Lord. He stated that those who would thus serve were to be men "thoroughly loyal to the doctrines of the Scriptures—especially so to the doctrine of the Ransom—that there is no acceptance with God and no salvation to eternal life except through faith in Christ and obedience to His Word and its spirit."

Brother Russell realized that there was much work yet to be done in preaching the good news. At a question-and-answer session in Vancouver, B.C., Canada, in 1915, he was asked when Christ's spirit-anointed followers then living could expect to receive their heavenly reward. He replied: "I do not know, but there is a great work to be done. And it will take thousands of brethren and millions in money to do it. Where these will come from I don't know—the Lord knows his own business." Then, in 1916, a short while before he began the speaking tour on which he died, he called A. H. Macmillan, an administrative assistant, to his office. On that occasion he said: "I am not able to carry on the work any longer, and yet there is a great work to be done." For three hours he described to Brother Macmillan the extensive preaching work that he saw ahead, on the basis of the Scriptures. To Brother Macmillan's objections, he replied: "This is not man's work."

Change of Administration Brings Tests

Many of Brother Russell's associates were firmly convinced that the Lord had things well in hand. At Brother Russell's funeral, W. E. Van Amburgh stated: "God has used many servants in the past and He will doubtless use many in the future. Our consecration is not to a man, or to a man's work, but *to do the will of God,* as He shall reveal it unto us through His Word and providential leadings. God is still at the helm." Brother Van Amburgh never wavered from that conviction down till his death.

"God is still at the helm"

Sadly, however, there were some who professed to admire Russell but who manifested a different spirit. As a result, the changed circumstances after Russell's death resulted in a testing and sifting. Apostate groups broke away not only in the United States but also in Belfast, Ireland; in Copenhagen, Denmark; in Vancouver and Victoria, British Columbia, Canada; and in other places. In Helsinki, Finland, some adopted the view that after Russell's death there was no channel for further spiritual light. At the urging of certain prominent ones, 164 there left the organization. Did that have God's blessing? For a while they published their own magazine and held their own meetings. In time, however, the group split up, withered, and ceased to exist; and many of them gladly returned to the meetings of the Bible Students. However, not all returned.

The death of Brother Russell, along with subsequent developments, also presented a test to R. E. B. Nicholson, the secretary of the Australia branch, and caused him to make manifest what was in his heart. After Russell's death Nicholson wrote: "For over a quarter of a century I have loved him, not only for his works' sake, but also for his beautiful character, have rejoiced in the truths he has sent out as 'meat in due season,' and in his counsel, admiring the sympathetic, kind, loving nature so grandly blended with fortitude and strong determination to do and dare anything in order to accomplish what he believed to be the Divine will or the unfolding of His Word. . . . There is a sense of loneliness as one realizes that this strong stay is removed in person."

Joseph F. Rutherford, the new president of the Watch Tower Society, was not the sort of man Nicholson thought should have the position of oversight that Brother Russell had occupied. Nicholson became openly critical of the blunt manner in which new Bible study material denounced false religion. Before long he left the organization, and he took with him much of the Society's property (which he had registered in his own name) and those in Melbourne who, in turn, had been inclined to look up to him. Why did it happen? Evidently Nicholson had allowed himself to become the follower of a man; so, when that man was gone, Nicholson's honesty and zeal for serving the Lord grew cool. None of those that broke away at that time prospered. It is noteworthy, however, that Jane Nicholson, though frail in stature, did not join her husband in his defection. Her devotion was foremost to Jehovah God, and she continued to serve him full-time right down till her death in 1951.

TESTING AND SIFTING FROM WITHIN 625

Many discerned that what was taking place in the years after Brother Russell's death was accomplishing the Lord's will. One of Jehovah's servants in Canada wrote concerning this to Brother Rutherford, saying:

"Dear Brother, do not misunderstand me now when I write what I do. Your disposition and that of our dear Brother Russell's are as dissimilar as day is from night. Many, alas, very many, liked Brother Russell on account of his personality, disposition, etc.; and very, very few lifted up their finger against him. Many accepted the truth just because Brother Russell said so. Then, many got to worshiping the man . . . You remember the time when Brother Russell at a convention had a heart to heart talk about this failing of many well-intentioned brethren, basing his talk on John and the angel. (Revelation 22:8, 9) When he passed beyond we all know what happened.

Some who admired Russell found that their reaction to Rutherford's disposition brought to light whom they were really serving

"But you, Brother Rutherford, have a disposition which has no comparison with that of Brother Russell. Even your looks are different. It is not your fault. It was your birthday present, and you could not refuse it. . . . Ever since you have been placed at the head of affairs of the SOCIETY, you have been the object of unjust criticisms and slander of the worst kind, all this coming from the brethren. Yet in spite of all this you have been loyal and devoted to the dear Lord and to his commission as recorded in Isaiah 61:1-3. Did the Lord know what he was doing when he placed you at the head of affairs? He surely did. In the past we were all prone to worship the creature more than the Creator. The Lord knew that. So he placed a creature with a different disposition at the head of affairs, or I should say in charge of the work, the harvest work. You desire nobody to worship you. I know that, but you *do* desire that all of like precious faith should enjoy the light that is now shining on the pathway of the just, as the Lord sees fit for it to shine. And that is what the Lord wants done."

Clearing Up the Identity of the "Faithful and Wise Servant"

Many who were sifted out at that time clung to the view that a single individual, Charles Taze Russell, was the "faithful and wise servant" foretold by Jesus at Matthew 24:45-47 (*KJ*), which servant would distribute spiritual food to the household of faith. Particularly following his death, *The Watch Tower* itself set forth this view for a number of years. In view of the prominent role that Brother Russell had played, it appeared to the Bible Students of that time that this was the case. He did not personally promote the idea, but he did acknowledge the apparent reasonableness of the arguments of those who favored it.* He also emphasized, however, that whoever the Lord might use in such a role must be humble as well as zealous to bring glory to the Master, and that if the one chosen by the Lord failed, he would be replaced by another.

However, as the light of truth progressively shone even more brightly after Brother Russell's death, and as the preaching that Jesus had foretold became even more extensive, it became evident that the "faithful and wise servant" (*KJ*), or "faithful and discreet slave" (*NW*), had not passed off the scene when Brother Russell died. In 1881, Brother Russell himself had expressed the view that that "servant" was made up of the entire body of faithful spirit-anointed Christians. He saw it as being a collective servant, a class of persons who were united in doing God's will. (Compare Isaiah 43:10.) This understanding was reaffirmed by the Bible Students in 1927. Jehovah's Witnesses today recognize the *Watchtower* magazine and kindred publications to be the ones used by the faithful and discreet slave to dispense spiritual food. They do not claim that this slave class is infallible, but they do view it as the *one channel* that the Lord is using during the last days of this system of things.

When Pride Got in the Way

There have been times, however, when individuals in responsible positions came to view themselves as the channel of spiritual light, so that they

The "faithful and wise servant" had not passed off the scene when Brother Russell died

---

* According to Brother Russell, his wife, who later left him, was the first one to apply Matthew 24:45-47 to him. See the *Watch Tower* issues of July 15, 1906, page 215; March 1, 1896, page 47; and June 15, 1896, pages 139-40.

resisted what was provided by the organization. Others simply gave in to the desire to exercise greater personal influence. They sought to get others to follow them, or, as the apostle Paul put it, "to draw away the disciples after themselves." (Acts 20:29, 30) Of course, this tested the motives and spiritual stability of those whom they endeavored to entice. Consider some examples:

Special letters to the Bible Students in Allegheny, Pennsylvania, invited them to a meeting on April 5, 1894. Brother and Sister Russell were not invited and did not attend, but about 40 others were present. The letter, signed by E. Bryan, S. D. Rogers, J. B. Adamson, and O. von Zech, said that the meeting would involve things concerning their "highest welfare." It turned out to be a malicious effort on the part of these conspirators to poison the minds of others by divulging what they surmised to be evil in Brother Russell's business affairs (though the facts were to the contrary), by arguing that Brother Russell had too much authority (which they wanted for themselves), and by complaining because he favored use of the printed page to spread the gospel and Bible-class meetings instead of only giving discourses (in which they might more readily expound personal views). The congregation was greatly disturbed by what occurred, and many were stumbled. But those who turned aside did not as a result become more spiritual persons or more zealous in the Lord's work.

A malicious effort to poison the minds of others

Over 20 years later, prior to his death, Brother Russell expressed his intention to send Paul S. L. Johnson, a very capable speaker, to Britain to strengthen the Bible Students there. Out of respect for Brother Russell's wish, the Society dispatched Johnson to Britain in November 1916. However, once he was in Britain, he dismissed two of the Society's managers. Seeing himself as an important personage, he argued in speeches and correspondence that what he was doing was foreshadowed in the Scriptures by Ezra, Nehemiah, and Mordecai. He claimed to be the steward (or, man in charge) referred to by Jesus in his parable at Matthew 20:8. He tried to take control of the Society's money, and he instituted a suit in the High Court of London to achieve his aims.

Thwarted in his endeavors, he returned to New York. There he sought to elicit support from certain ones who were serving on the Society's board of directors. Those who were persuaded to side with him endeavored to achieve their aims by trying to pass a resolution to repeal bylaws of the Society that authorized the president to manage its affairs. They wanted authority for all decisions to rest with them. Legal action was taken by Brother Rutherford to safeguard the interests of the Society, and those who were seeking to disrupt its work were asked to leave the Bethel Home. At the annual meeting of the Society's shareholders early the following year, when the board of directors and its officers were elected for the year to come, those who had been agitators were overwhelmingly rejected. Perhaps some of them thought that they were in the right, but the vast majority of their spiritual brothers made it clear that they did not agree. Would they accept that reproof?

Thereafter, P. S. L. Johnson appeared at meetings of the Bible Students and made it seem that he was in agreement with their beliefs and activity. But after gaining the confidence of some, he would sow seeds of doubt. If anyone suggested a break with the Society, he hypocritically discouraged this—*until* the loyalty of the group had been thoroughly undermined. By correspondence and even by personal trips, he endeavored to influence the brothers not only in the United States but also in Canada, Jamaica, Europe, and Australia. Was this successful?

Perhaps it seemed so when the majority in a congregation voted to sever ties with the Society. But they were like a branch cut from a tree—green for a while, then withered and lifeless. When the opposers held a convention in 1918, differences surfaced, and a split occurred. Further disintegration followed. Some functioned for a while as small sects with a leader that they admired. None of them devoted themselves to the work of giving a public witness in all the inhabited earth concerning God's Kingdom, which is the work that Jesus assigned to his followers.

As these things took place, the brothers reminded themselves of what was recorded at 1 Peter 4:12: "Beloved ones, do not be puzzled at the burning among you, which is happening to you for a trial, as though a strange thing were befalling you."

Some allowed pride to undermine their faith

Those mentioned above were not the only ones who allowed pride to undermine their faith. Others also did so, including Alexandre Freytag, the manager of the Society's office in Geneva, Switzerland. He liked to attract attention to himself, would add his own ideas when translating the Society's publications into French, and even used the Society's facilities to publish his own material. In Canada, there was W. F. Salter, a branch manager of the Society who began to disagree with the Society's publications, let it be known that he expected to be the next president of the Watch Tower Society, and, after he was dismissed, dishonestly used the Society's letterhead to instruct congregations in Canada and abroad to study material that he personally had written. In Nigeria, there was, among others, G. M. Ukoli, who at first showed zeal for the truth but then began to see it as a means of material gain and personal prominence. Afterward, when thwarted in his aims, he turned to roasting faithful brothers in the public press. And there were others.

Even in recent years, some individuals who occupied prominent positions of oversight displayed a similar spirit.

Of course, these people certainly had the freedom to believe what they chose. But anyone who publicly or privately advocates views that are divergent from what appears in the publications of an organization, and who does so while claiming to represent that organization, causes division. How did Jehovah's Witnesses deal with these situations?

They did not launch a campaign of persecution against such persons (though the defectors often indulged in abuse of their former spiritual brothers), nor did they seek to do physical harm to them (as was practiced by the Catholic Church by means of the Inquisition). Rather, they followed the inspired advice of the apostle Paul, who wrote: "Keep your eye on those who cause divisions and occasions for stumbling contrary to the teaching that you have learned, and avoid them. For men of that sort are slaves, not of our Lord Christ . . . By smooth talk and complimentary speech they seduce the hearts of guileless ones."—Rom. 16:17, 18.

"Keep your eye on those who cause divisions . . . and avoid them"

As others observed what was taking place, they too were given opportunity to manifest what was in their hearts.

Doctrinal Views in Need of Refinement

Jehovah's Witnesses freely acknowledge that their understanding of God's purpose has undergone many adjustments over the years. The fact that knowledge of God's purpose is progressive means that there must be change. It is not that God's purpose changes, but the enlightenment that he continuously grants to his servants calls for adjustments in their viewpoint.

From the Bible the Witnesses point out that this was also true of God's faithful servants in the past. Abraham had a close relationship with Jehovah; but when he left Ur, that man of faith did not know the land to which God was leading him, and for many years he was not at all sure how God would fulfill his promise to make a great nation out of him. (Gen. 12:1-3; 15:3; 17:15-21; Heb. 11:8) God revealed many truths to the prophets, but there were other things that they did not then understand. (Dan. 12:8, 9; 1 Pet. 1:10-12) Likewise, Jesus explained much to his apostles, but even at the end of his earthly life he told them that there were yet many things for them to learn. (John 16:12) Some of these things, such as God's purpose to bring Gentiles into the congregation, were not understood until the apostles saw what was actually occurring in fulfillment of prophecy.—Acts 11:1-18.

As might be expected, when changes have required the setting aside of formerly cherished views, that has been a test for some. Furthermore, not all adjustments in understanding have come simply, in one step. Because of imperfection, there is at times a tendency to go to one extreme or another before the correct position is discerned. This may take time. Some who are inclined to be critical have stumbled over this. Consider an example:

As early as 1880, the Watch Tower publications discussed various details associated with the Abrahamic covenant, the Law covenant, and the new covenant. Christendom had lost sight of God's promise that through Abraham's seed all the families of the earth would certainly bless themselves. (Gen. 22:18) But Brother Russell was keenly interested in discerning how God would accomplish this. He thought he saw in the Bible description of the Jewish Atonement Day indications as to how it might be accomplished in connection with the new covenant. In 1907, when the same covenants were discussed again, with special emphasis on the role of Christ's joint heirs in bringing about for mankind the blessings foretold in the Abrahamic covenant, strong objections were raised by some of the Bible Students.

At that time there were certain obstacles to a clear understanding of matters. The Bible Students did not yet correctly see the position that natural Israel then occupied in relation to God's purpose. This obstacle was not moved out of the way until it became overwhelmingly evident that the Jews as a people were not interested in being used by God in the fulfillment of his prophetic word. Another obstacle was the inability of the Bible Students to identify correctly the "great crowd" of Revelation 7:9, 10. This identity did not become clear until the great crowd actually began to manifest itself in fulfillment of prophecy. Those who severely criticized Brother Russell did not understand these matters either.

Falsely, however, some who professed to be Christian brothers charged that *The Watch Tower* had denied that Jesus is the Mediator between God and men, that it had repudiated the ransom and denied the necessity and fact of the atonement. None of this was true. But some who said it were prominent individuals, and they drew others after themselves as disciples. They may have been right in some of the details that they taught in connection with the new covenant, but did the Lord bless what they were doing? For a time some of them held meetings, but then their groups died out.

Some falsely charged that "The Watch Tower" had repudiated the ransom

In contrast, the Bible Students continued to share in the preaching of the good news, as Jesus had commanded his disciples. At the same time, they continued to study God's Word and to watch for developments that would shed light on its meaning. Finally, during the 1930's, the principal obstacles to a clear understanding of the covenants were removed, and corrected statements of the matter appeared in *The Watchtower* and related publications.* What joy this brought to those who had patiently waited!

---

* *Vindication*, Book Two, pp. 258-9, 268-9; *The Watchtower*, April 1, 1934, pp. 99-106; April 15, 1934, pp. 115-22; August 1, 1935, pp. 227-37.

Were Their Expectations Correct?

At certain times the Bible Students had hopes and expectations that have been ridiculed by critics. Yet, all those hopes and expectations were rooted in a keen desire to see the fulfillment of what these zealous Christians recognized to be the unfailing promises of God.

From their study of the inspired Scriptures, they knew that Jehovah had promised blessings for all nations of the earth by means of the seed of Abraham. (Gen. 12:1-3; 22:15-18) They saw in God's Word the promise that the Son of man would rule as heavenly King over all the earth, that a little flock of faithful ones would be taken from the earth to share with him in his Kingdom, and that these would rule as kings for a thousand years. (Dan. 7:13, 14; Luke 12:32; Rev. 5:9, 10; 14:1-5; 20:6) They knew Jesus' promise that he would return and take with him those for whom he had prepared a place in heaven. (John 14:1-3) They were acquainted with the promise that the Messiah would also select some of his faithful forefathers to be princes in all the earth. (Ps. 45:16) They recognized that the Scriptures foretold the end of the wicked old system of things and realized that this was associated with the war of the great day of God the Almighty at Armageddon. (Matt. 24:3; Rev. 16:14, 16) They were deeply impressed by the scriptures that show that the earth was created to be inhabited forever, that those who lived on it were to have true peace, and that all who would exercise faith in Jesus' perfect human sacrifice could enjoy an eternity of life in Paradise.—Isa. 2:4; 45:18; Luke 23:42, 43; John 3:16.

It was only natural that they should wonder *when* and *how* these things would occur. Did the inspired Scriptures provide any clues?

Using Bible chronology that had first been laid out by Christopher Bowen of England, they thought that 6,000 years of human history had ended in 1873, that thereafter they were in the seventh thousand-year period of human history, and that they had surely approached the dawn of the foretold Millennium. The series of books known as *Millennial Dawn* (and later called *Studies in the Scriptures*), which were penned by C. T. Russell, drew attention to the implications of this according to what the Bible Students understood from the Scriptures.

Something else that was seen as a possible time indicator involved the arrangement that God instituted in ancient Israel for a Jubilee, a year of release, every 50th year. This came after a series of seven 7-year periods, each of which ended with a sabbath year. During the Jubilee year, Hebrew slaves were freed and hereditary land possessions that had been sold were restored. (Lev. 25:8-10) Calculations based on this cycle of years led to the conclusion that perhaps a greater Jubilee for all the earth had begun in the autumn of 1874, that evidently the Lord had returned in that year and was invisibly present, and that "the times of restitution of all things" had arrived.—Acts 3:19-21, *KJ*.

Based on the premise that events of the first century might find parallels in related events later, they also concluded that if Jesus' baptism and anointing in the autumn of 29 C.E. paralleled the beginning of an invisible presence in 1874, then his riding into Jerusalem as King in the spring of 33 C.E. would point to the spring of 1878 as the time when he would assume his power as heavenly King.* They also thought they would be given their heavenly reward at that time. When that did not occur, they concluded that since Jesus' anointed followers were to share with him in the Kingdom, the resurrection to spirit life of those already sleeping in death began then. It was also reasoned that the end of God's special favor to natural Israel down to 36 C.E. might point to 1881 as the time when the special opportunity to become part of spiritual Israel would close.#

In the lecture "Millions Now Living Will Never Die," delivered by J. F. Rutherford on March 21, 1920, at the Hippodrome in New York City, attention was directed to the year 1925. On what basis was it thought to be significant? In a booklet published in that same year, 1920, it was pointed out that if *70 full Jubilees* were calculated *from what was understood to be the date when Israel entered the Promised Land* (instead of starting after the last typical Jubilee *before the Babylonian exile* and then counting to the *beginning* of the Jubilee year at the end of the *50th* cycle), this could point to the year 1925. On the basis of what was said there, many hoped that perhaps the remaining ones of the little flock would receive their heavenly reward by 1925. This year also was associated with expectations for resurrection of faithful pre-Christian servants of God with a view to their serving on earth as princely representatives of the heavenly Kingdom. If that really occurred, it would mean that mankind had entered an era in which death would cease to be master, and millions then living could have the hope of never dying off the earth. What a happy prospect! Though mistaken, they eagerly shared it with others.

Later on, during the years from 1935 through 1944, a review of the overall framework of Bible chronology revealed that a poor translation of

---

* That 1878 was a year of significance seemed to be fortified by reference to Jeremiah 16:18 ('Jacob's double,' *KJ*) along with calculations indicating that 1,845 years had apparently elapsed from Jacob's death down till 33 C.E., when natural Israel was cast off, and that the double, or duplicate, of this would extend from 33 C.E. down to 1878.

Extending the parallels further, it was stated that the desolation of Jerusalem in 70 C.E. (37 years after Jesus was hailed as king by his disciples when he rode into Jerusalem) might point to 1915 (37 years after 1878) for a culmination of anarchistic upheaval that they thought God would permit as a means for bringing existing institutions of the world to their end. This date appeared in reprints of *Studies in the Scriptures*. (See Volume II, pages 99-101, 171, 221, 232, 246-7; compare reprint of 1914 with earlier printings, such as the 1902 printing of *Millennial Dawn*.) It seemed to them that this fitted well with what had been published regarding the year 1914 as marking the end of the Gentile Times.

Acts 13:19, 20 in the *King James Version*,* along with certain other factors, had thrown off the chronology by over a century.# This later led to the idea—sometimes stated as a possibility, sometimes more firmly—that since the seventh millennium of human history would begin in 1975, events associated with the beginning of Christ's Millennial Reign might start to take place then.

Did the beliefs of Jehovah's Witnesses on these matters prove to be correct? They certainly did not err in believing that God would without fail do what he had promised. But some of their time calculations and the expectations that they associated with these gave rise to serious disappointments.

Following 1925, meeting attendance dropped dramatically in some congregations in France and Switzerland. Again, in 1975, there was disappointment when expectations regarding the start of the Millennium failed to materialize. As a result, some withdrew from the organization. Others, because they sought to subvert the faith of associates, were disfellowshipped. No doubt, disappointment over the date was a factor, but in some instances the roots went deeper. Some individuals also argued against the need to participate in the house-to-house ministry. Certain ones did not simply choose to go their own way; they became aggressive in opposing the organization with which they had been associated, and they made use of the public press and television to air their views. Nevertheless, the number who defected was relatively small.

Although these tests resulted in a sifting and some blew away like chaff when wheat is winnowed, others remained firm. Why? Regarding his own experience and that of others in 1925, Jules Feller explained: "Those who had set their confidence in Jehovah remained steadfast and continued their preaching activity." They recognized that a mistake had been made but that in no respect had God's Word failed, and therefore there was no reason either to let their own hope grow dim or to slow down in the work of pointing people to God's Kingdom as mankind's only hope.

Some expectations had not been fulfilled, but that did not mean that Bible chronology was of no value. The prophecy recorded by Daniel regarding the appearance of the Messiah 69 weeks of years after "the going forth of

Jules Feller

When he was a young man, Jules Feller observed severe testings of faith. Some congregations in Switzerland shrank to half their former size or less. But he later wrote: "Those who had set their confidence in Jehovah remained steadfast and continued their preaching activity." Brother Feller determined to do that too, and as a result, down till 1992 he has enjoyed 68 years of Bethel service.

---

* Compare the rendering in *The Emphasised Bible*, translated by J. B. Rotherham; see also the footnote on Acts 13:20 in the *New World Translation of the Holy Scriptures—With References*.
· # See *"The Truth Shall Make You Free,"* chapter XI; *"The Kingdom Is at Hand,"* pages 171-5; also *The Golden Age*, March 27, 1935, pages 391, 412. In the light of these corrected tables of Bible chronology, it could be seen that previous use of the dates 1873 and 1878, as well as related dates derived from these on the basis of parallels with first-century events, were based on misunderstandings.

C. J. Woodworth

To one who forsook Jehovah's service because the anointed followers of Jesus Christ were not taken to heaven in 1914, C. J. Woodworth wrote as follows:

"Twenty years ago you and I believed in infant baptism; in the Divine right of the clergy to administer that baptism; that baptism was necessary to escape eternal torment; that God is love; that God created and continues to create billions of beings in His likeness who will spend the countless ages of eternity in the strangling fumes of burning sulphur, pleading in vain for one drop of water to relieve their agonies . . .

"We believed that after a man dies, he is alive; we believed that Jesus Christ never died; that He could not die; that no Ransom was ever paid or ever will be paid; that Jehovah God and Christ Jesus His Son are one and the same person; that Christ was His own Father; that Jesus was His own Son; that the Holy Spirit is a person; that one plus one, plus one, equal one; that when Jesus hung on the cross and said, 'My God, My God, why hast Thou Forsaken Me,' He was merely talking to Himself; . . . that present kingdoms are part of Christ's Kingdom; that the Devil has been away off somewhere in an unlocated Hell, instead of exercising dominion over the kingdoms of this earth . . .

"I praise God for the day that brought Present Truth to my door. It was so wholesome, so refreshing to mind and heart, that I quickly left the humbug and claptrap of the past and was used of God to also open your blinded eyes. We rejoiced in the Truth together, working side by side for fifteen years. The Lord greatly honored you as a mouthpiece; I never knew anybody who could make the follies of Babylon look so ridiculous. In your letter you ask, 'What next?' Ah, now comes the pity of it! The next thing is that you permit your heart to become embittered against the one whose labors of love and whose blessing from on High brought the Truth to both our hearts. You went out, and took several of the sheep with you. . . .

"Probably I look ridiculous to you because I did not go to Heaven, October 1st, 1914, but you don't look ridiculous to me—oh no!

"With ten of the greatest nations of earth writhing in their death agonies, it seems to me a particularly inopportune time to seek to ridicule the man, and the only man, who for forty years has taught that the Times of the Gentiles would end in 1914."

Brother Woodworth's faith was not shaken when the events of 1914 did not turn out as expected. He simply realized that there was more to learn. Because of his confidence in God's purpose, he spent nine months in prison in 1918-19. Later he served as editor of the magazines "The Golden Age" and "Consolation." He remained firm in faith and loyal to Jehovah's organization right down till his death in 1951, at 81 years of age.

the word to restore and to rebuild Jerusalem" was fulfilled right on time, in 29 C.E.* (Dan. 9:24-27) The year 1914 was also marked by Bible prophecy.

1914—Expectations and Reality

In 1876, C. T. Russell wrote the first of many articles in which he pointed to the year 1914 as the end of the Gentile Times referred to by Jesus Christ. (Luke 21:24, *KJ*) In the second volume of *Millennial Dawn*, published in 1889, Brother Russell set out in a reasoned manner details that would enable readers to see the Scriptural basis for what was said and to check it for themselves. Over a period of nearly four decades leading up to 1914, the Bible Students distributed millions of copies of publications focusing attention on the end of the Gentile Times. A few other religious papers took note of the Bible chronology that pointed to the year 1914, but what group other than the Bible Students gave it ongoing international publicity and lived in a manner that showed that they believed that the Gentile Times would end in that year?

As 1914 neared, expectations heightened. What would it mean? In *The Bible Students Monthly* (Volume VI, No. 1, published early in 1914), Brother Russell wrote: "If we have the correct date and chronology, Gentile Times will end this year—1914. What of it? We do not surely know. Our expectation is that the active rule of Messiah will begin about the time of the ending of the lease of power to the Gentiles. Our expectation, true or false, is that there will be wonderful manifestations of Divine judgments against all unrighteousness, and that this will mean the breaking up of many institutions of the present time, if not all." He emphasized that he did not expect the "end of the world" in 1914 and that the earth abides forever, but that the present order of things, of which Satan is ruler, is to pass away.

In its issue of October 15, 1913, *The Watch Tower* had stated: "According to the best chronological reckoning of which we are capable, it is *approximately* that time—whether it be October, 1914, or later. Without dogmatizing, we are looking for certain events: (1) The termination of the Gentile Times—Gentile supremacy in the world—and (2) For the inauguration of Messiah's Kingdom in the world."

How would this come about? It seemed reasonable to the Bible Students then that it would include the glorification of any still on earth who had been chosen by God to share in the heavenly Kingdom with Christ. But how did they feel when that did not occur in 1914? *The Watch Tower* of April 15, 1916, stated: "We believe that the dates have proven to be quite right. We believe that Gentile Times have ended." However, it candidly added: "The Lord did not say that the Church would all be glorified by 1914. We merely inferred it and, evidently, erred."

In this they were somewhat like Jesus' apostles. The apostles knew and

"We merely inferred it and, evidently, erred"

---

* See *Insight on the Scriptures*, Volume 2, pages 899-904.

thought they believed the prophecies concerning God's Kingdom. But at various times they had wrong expectations as to how and when these would be fulfilled. This led to disappointment on the part of some.—Luke 19:11; 24:19-24; Acts 1:6.

When October 1914 passed without the expected change to heavenly life, Brother Russell knew that there would be serious searchings of heart. In *The Watch Tower* of November 1, 1914, he wrote: "Let us remember that we are in a testing season. The Apostles had a similar one during the interim between our Lord's death and Pentecost. After our Lord's resurrection, He appeared to His disciples a few times, and then they did not see Him for many days. Then they became discouraged and said, 'There is no use waiting'; 'I go fishing,' said one. Two others said, 'We will go with thee.' They were about to go into the fishing business and leave the work of fishing for *men*. This was a testing time for the disciples. So also there is one now. If there is any reason that would lead any to let go of the Lord and His Truth and to cease sacrificing for the Lord's Cause, then it is not merely the love of God in the heart which has prompted interest in the Lord, but something else; probably a hoping that the time was short; the consecration was only for a certain time."

That evidently was the case with some. Their thoughts and desires had been fixed primarily on the prospect of being changed to heavenly life. When this did not occur at the anticipated time, they closed their minds to the significance of the amazing things that did take place in 1914. They lost sight of all the precious truths that they had learned from God's Word, and they began to ridicule the people who had helped them to learn these.

Humbly, the Bible Students examined the Scriptures again, to let God's Word readjust their outlook. Their conviction that the Gentile Times had ended in 1914 did not change. Gradually they came to see more clearly how the Messianic Kingdom had begun—that it was established in heaven when Jehovah bestowed authority on Jesus Christ, his Son; also, that this did not have to wait until Jesus' joint heirs were raised to heavenly life but that they would be glorified with him later. In addition, they came to see that the spreading of the influence of the Kingdom did not require that first the faithful prophets of old be resurrected, but that the King would use loyal Christians now living as his representatives to set before people of all nations the opportunity to live forever as earthly subjects of the Kingdom.

As this grand picture opened before their eyes, further testing and sifting resulted. But those who truly loved Jehovah and took delight in serving him were very grateful for the privileges of service that opened up to them. —Rev. 3:7, 8.

One of these was A. H. Macmillan. He later wrote: "Although our expectations about being taken to heaven were not fulfilled in 1914, that year did see the end of the Gentile Times . . . We were not particularly disturbed

Those who truly loved Jehovah were grateful for the privileges of service that opened up to them

that not everything took place as we had expected, because we were so busy with the Photo-Drama work and with the problems created by the war." He kept busy in Jehovah's service and was thrilled to see the number of Kingdom proclaimers increase to well over a million during his lifetime.

Looking back over his experiences during 66 years with the organization, he said: "I have seen many severe trials come upon the organization and testings of the faith of those in it. With the help of God's spirit it survived and continued to flourish." Regarding adjustments of understanding along the way, he added: "The fundamental truths we learned from the Scriptures remained the same. So I learned that we should admit our mistakes and continue searching God's Word for more enlightenment. No matter what adjustments we would have to make from time to time in our views, that would not change the gracious provision of the ransom and God's promise of eternal life."

During his lifetime, Brother Macmillan saw that, among the issues that resulted in tests of faith, willingness to witness and appreciation of theocratic organization were two that laid bare what was really in the hearts of individuals. How so?

A. H. Macmillan

"I have seen the wisdom of patiently waiting on Jehovah to clear up our understanding of Scriptural things instead of getting upset over a new thought. Sometimes our expectations for a certain date were more than what the Scriptures warranted. When those expectations went unfulfilled, that did not change God's purposes."

Field Service and Organization Become Issues

Beginning with its first issue, and with increasing emphasis thereafter, *Zion's Watch Tower* urged each and every true Christian to share the truth with others. Thereafter, readers of the *Watch Tower* were frequently encouraged to appreciate their privilege and responsibility to proclaim the good news to others. Many shared in limited ways, but relatively few were in the forefront of the work, calling from house to house so as to give everyone the opportunity to hear the Kingdom message.

However, beginning with the year 1919, participation in the field service came to the fore more strongly. Brother Rutherford forcefully emphasized it in a discourse at Cedar Point, Ohio, that year. In each congregation that requested the Society to organize it for service, arrangements were made for a service director, appointed by the Society, to care for the work. He was to take the lead himself and see to it that the congregation had the needed supplies.

In 1922, *The Watch Tower* published an article entitled "Service Essential." It pointed to the dire need for people to hear the good news of the Kingdom, directed attention to Jesus' prophetic command at Matthew 24: 14, and stated to elders in the congregations: "Let no one think that because he is an elder of the class all his service should consist of preaching by word of mouth. If opportunities offer for him to go among the people and place in their hands the printed message, that is a great privilege and is preaching the gospel, often more effectively than any other way of preaching it." The article then asked: "Can any one who is really consecrated to the Lord justify himself or herself in idleness at this time?"

> "Can any one who is really consecrated to the Lord justify himself or herself in idleness at this time?"

Some held back. They raised all sorts of objections. They did not think it appropriate to "sell books," though the work was not being done for profit and though it was through these same publications that they had learned the truth about God's Kingdom. When house-to-house witnessing with the books on Sunday was encouraged, beginning in 1926, some argued against that, although Sunday was the day that many people customarily set aside for worship. The basic problem was that they felt it beneath their dignity to preach from house to house. Yet, the Bible clearly says that Jesus sent his disciples to the homes of people to preach, and the apostle Paul preached "publicly and from house to house."—Acts 20:20; Matt. 10:5-14.

As emphasis on the field service increased, those whose hearts did not move them to imitate Jesus and his apostles as witnesses gradually withdrew. The Skive Congregation in Denmark, along with some others, was reduced to about half. Out of the hundred or so associated with the Dublin Congregation in Ireland, only four remained. There was a similar testing and sifting in the United States, Canada, Norway, and other lands. This resulted in a cleansing of the congregations.

Those who truly wanted to be imitators of God's Son responded favorably to the encouragement from the Scriptures. However, their willingness did not necessarily make it easy for them to begin going from house to house. Some had a hard time starting. But arrangements for group witnessing and special service assemblies were an encouragement. Two sisters in northern Jutland, in Denmark, long remembered their first day of field service. They met with the group, heard the instructions, started for their territory, but then gave way to tears. Two of the brothers saw what was happening and invited the sisters to work with them. Soon the sun was shining again. After having a taste of field service, most were filled with joy and were enthusiastic about doing more.

Then, in 1932, *The Watchtower* contained a two-part article entitled "Jehovah's Organization." (Issues of August 15 and September 1) This showed that the *elective* office of elder in the congregations was unscriptural. Congregations were urged to use in responsible positions only men who were active in the field service, men living up to the responsibility implied by the name Jehovah's *Witnesses*. These were to function as a service committee. One of their number, nominated by the congregation, was appointed by the Society to be service director. In Belfast, Ireland, this sifted out more of those whose desire was for personal prominence rather than for humble service.

When more emphasis was placed on field service, many withdrew; others showed increased zeal

By the early 1930's, most of those in Germany who were trying to put the damper on field service had withdrawn from the congregations. Some others fearfully withdrew when in 1933 the work was banned in many of the states in Germany. But thousands endured these tests of faith and showed themselves willing to preach regardless of the danger involved.

Around the earth the proclamation of the Kingdom gained momentum. Field service became an important part of the life of all of Jehovah's Witnesses. The congregation in Oslo, Norway, for example, rented buses on weekends to transport publishers to nearby cities. They met early in the morning, were in their territory by nine or ten o'clock, worked hard in the field service for seven or eight hours, and then joined the bus group for their homeward trip. Others traveled into rural areas by bicycle, with bookbags and cartons loaded with extra supplies. Jehovah's Witnesses were happy, zealous, and united in the doing of God's will.

In 1938, when attention was again given to the appointment of responsible men in the congregations,* the elimination of all local elections of servants was generally welcomed. Congregations gladly passed resolutions showing appreciation for theocratic organization and requesting "the Society" (which they understood to mean the anointed remnant, or faithful and discreet slave) to organize the congregation for service and to appoint all the servants. Thereafter, the visible Governing Body proceeded to make the needed appointments and to organize the congregations for united and productive activity. Only a few groups held back and withdrew from the organization at this point.

Devoted Solely to Spreading the Kingdom Message

For the organization to continue to have Jehovah's approval, it must be devoted exclusively to the work that his Word commands for our day.

---

* See Chapter 15, "Development of the Organization Structure."

As theocratic organization came to the fore, those seeking personal prominence were sifted out

That work is the preaching of the good news of the Kingdom of God. (Matt. 24:14) However, there have been a few instances in which individuals who worked hard in cooperation with the organization also endeavored to use it to promote programs that tended to divert their associates to other activities. When reproved, this was a test to them, especially when they felt that their motives had been noble.

This occurred in Finland during 1915, when some brothers founded a cooperative association called Ararat and used the columns of the Finnish edition of *The Watch Tower* to urge its readers to join this business association. The one who had initiated this activity in Finland responded humbly when Brother Russell pointed out that he and his associates were letting themselves be "led away from the important work of the Gospel." However, pride hindered another brother, one who had been active in Jehovah's service for over a decade in Norway, from accepting the same counsel.

During the 1930's, in the United States, a somewhat similar problem arose. A number of congregations were publishing their own monthly service instruction sheets, which included reminders from the Society's *Bulletin* as well as experiences and their local schedule of service arrangements. One of these, published in Baltimore, Maryland, gave enthusiastic support to the preaching activity but was also used to promote certain business ventures. Initially Brother Rutherford gave tacit approval to some of these. But when it was realized what could develop from involvement in such ventures, *The Watchtower* stated that the Society did not endorse them. This presented a severe personal test to Anton Koerber, for he had intended by these means to be of help to his brothers. In time, however, he again made full use of his abilities to further the preaching work being done by Jehovah's Witnesses.

A related problem arose in Australia starting in 1938 and escalated during the ban on the Society (January 1941 to June 1943). In order to care for what at the time seemed to be valid needs, the branch office of the Society got directly involved in a variety of commercial activities. Thus, a great mistake was made. They had sawmills, more than 20 "Kingdom farms," an engineering company, a bakery, and other enterprises. Two commercial printeries provided a cover for continued production of the Society's publications during the ban. But some of their business operations got them involved in violations of Christian neutrality, the work being done on the pretext of providing funds and supporting the pioneers during the ban. The consciences of some, however, were deeply disturbed. Although the majority stayed with the organization, general stagnation in the work of Kingdom proclamation set in. What was holding back Jehovah's blessing?

When the ban on the work was lifted in June 1943, the brothers then at the branch office appreciated that these enterprises should be disposed of, in favor of focusing on the all-important preaching of the Kingdom. In the space of three years, this was accomplished, and the Bethel family was reduced to a normal size. But it was still necessary to clear the air and thus restore complete confidence in the organization.

Nathan H. Knorr, the president of the Society, and his secretary M. G. Henschel visited Australia specifically to deal with this situation in 1947. In reporting on the matter, *The Watchtower* of June 1, 1947, said of the commercial activity that had been carried on: "It was not the every-day secular work of brethren engaged in making a living that was involved, but it was the fact that the Society's Branch office had obtained various kinds of industries and called in publishers from all parts of the country, particularly pioneers, to work in these industries rather than preaching the gospel." This had led even to indirect involvement in the war effort. At conventions in each of the provincial capitals, Brother Knorr spoke frankly to the brothers about the situation. At each assembly a resolution was adopted in which the Australian brothers acknowledged their error and asked Jehovah's mercy and forgiveness through Jesus Christ. Thus, vigilance has been required and tests have been confronted so that the organization would continue to be devoted solely to spreading the message of the Kingdom of God.

As Jehovah's Witnesses look back over their modern-day history, they see evidence that Jehovah has truly been refining his people. (Mal. 3:1-3) Wrong attitudes, beliefs, and practices have gradually been cleared out, and any who have chosen to cling to these have gone with them. Those who remain are not people who are willing to compromise Bible truth in order to accommodate human philosophy. They are not followers of men but are devoted servants of Jehovah God. They gladly respond to the direction of the organization because they see unmistakable evidence that it belongs to Jehovah. They rejoice in the advancing light of truth. (Prov. 4:18) They individually count it a grand privilege to be active Witnesses of Jehovah, proclaimers of the Kingdom of God.

Wrong attitudes, beliefs, and practices have gradually been cleared out

CHAPTER 29

"OBJECTS OF HATRED BY ALL THE NATIONS"

DURING the last evening that Jesus spent with his apostles before his death, he reminded them: "A slave is not greater than his master. If they have persecuted me, they will persecute you also; if they have observed my word, they will observe yours also. But they will do all these things against you on account of my name, because they do not know him that sent me." —John 15:20, 21.

It was not merely isolated instances of intolerance that Jesus had in mind. Just three days earlier, he had said: "You will be *objects of hatred by all the nations* on account of my name."—Matt. 24:9.

Yet, Jesus counseled his followers that when faced with persecution, they must not resort to carnal weapons. (Matt. 26:48-52) They were not to revile their persecutors or seek to retaliate. (Rom. 12:14; 1 Pet. 2:21-23) Might it not be that even those persecutors would someday become believers? (Acts 2:36-42; 7:58–8:1; 9:1-22) Any settling of accounts was to be left to God.—Rom. 12:17-19.

It is well-known that early Christians were cruelly persecuted by the Roman government. But it is also noteworthy that the foremost persecutors of Jesus Christ were the *religious leaders* and that Pontius Pilate, the Roman governor, had Jesus executed because they demanded it. (Luke 23:13-25) After Jesus' death it was once again the religious leaders who were in the forefront as persecutors of Jesus' followers. (Acts 4:1-22; 5:17-32; 9:1, 2) Has that not also been the pattern in more recent times?

The foremost persecutors of Jesus Christ were the religious leaders

Clergy Call for Public Debate

As the circulation of C. T. Russell's writings quickly escalated into tens of millions of copies in many languages, the Catholic and Protestant clergy could not easily ignore what he was saying. Angered by the exposure of their teachings as unscriptural, and frustrated by the loss of members, many of the clergy used their pulpits to denounce Russell's writings. They commanded their flocks not to accept literature distributed by the Bible Students. A number of them sought to induce public officials to put a stop to this work. In some places in the United States—among them Tampa, Florida; Rock Island, Illinois; Winston-Salem, North Carolina; and Scranton, Pennsylvania—they supervised public burning of books written by Russell.

Some of the clergy felt the need to destroy Russell's influence by exposing him in public debate. Near the headquarters of his activity, a group of clergymen endorsed as their spokesman Dr. E. L. Eaton, pastor of the North Avenue Methodist Episcopal Church in Allegheny, Pennsylvania. In 1903 he proposed a public debate, and Brother Russell accepted the invitation.

Six propositions were set forth, as follows: *Brother Russell affirmed,* but Dr. Eaton denied, that the souls of the dead are unconscious; that the "second coming" of Christ precedes the Millennium and that the purpose of both his "second coming" and the Millennium is the blessing of all the families of the earth; also that only the saints of the "Gospel age" share in the first resurrection but that vast multitudes will have opportunity for salvation by the subsequent resurrection. *Dr. Eaton affirmed,* but Brother Russell denied, that there would be no probation after death for anyone; that all who are saved will enter heaven; and that the incorrigibly wicked will be subjected to eternal suffering. A series of six debates on these propositions were held, each debate before a packed house at Carnegie Hall in Allegheny in 1903.

What was behind that challenge to debate? Viewing the matter from a historical perspective, Albert Vandenberg later wrote: "The debates were conducted with a minister from a different Protestant denomination acting as the moderator during each discussion. In addition, ministers from various area churches sat on the speaker's platform with the Reverend Eaton, allegedly to provide him with textual and moral support. . . . That even an unofficial alliance of Protestant clergymen could be formed signified that they feared Russell's potential to convert members of their denominations."—"Charles Taze Russell: Pittsburgh Prophet, 1879-1909," published in *The Western Pennsylvania Historical Magazine,* January 1986, p. 14.

Such debates were relatively few. They did not yield the results that the alliance of clergymen desired. Some of Dr. Eaton's own congregation, impressed by what they heard during the series of debates in 1903, left his church and chose to associate with the Bible Students. Even a clergyman who was present acknowledged that Russell had 'turned the hose on hell and put out the fire.' Nevertheless, Brother Russell himself felt that the cause of truth could be better served by use of time and effort for activities other than debates.

The clergy did not give up their attack. When Brother Russell spoke in Dublin, Ireland, and Otley, Yorkshire, England, they planted men in the audience to shout objections and false charges against Russell personally. Brother Russell deftly handled those situations, always relying on the Bible as authority for his replies.

Protestant clergymen, regardless of denomination, were associated in what is known as the Evangelical Alliance. Their representatives in many lands agitated against Russell and those who distributed his literature. In Texas (U.S.A.), as an example, the Bible Students found that every preacher, even in the smallest towns and rural districts, was equipped with the same set of false charges against Russell and the same distortions of what he taught.

However, these attacks against Russell sometimes had results that the clergy did not anticipate. In New Brunswick, Canada, when a preacher used his pulpit for a derogatory sermon about Russell, there was a man in the audience who had personally read literature written by Brother Russell. He was disgusted when the preacher resorted to deliberate falsehoods. About the middle of the sermon, the man stood up, took his wife by the hand, and called to his seven daughters who sang in the choir: "Come on, girls, we are going home." All nine walked out, and the minister watched as the man who had built the church and was the financial mainstay of the congregation departed. The congregation soon fell apart, and the preacher left.

Resorting to Ridicule and Slander

In their desperate efforts to kill the influence of C. T. Russell and his associates, the clergy belittled the claim that he was a Christian minister. For similar reasons, the Jewish religious leaders in the first century treated the apostles Peter and John as "men unlettered and ordinary."—Acts 4:13.

"The Pittsburgh Gazette" gave extensive publicity to the debates that resulted from Dr. Eaton's challenge to C. T. Russell

Brother Russell had not graduated from one of Christendom's theological schools. But he boldly said: "We challenge [the clergy] to prove that they ever had a Divine ordination or that they ever think of it. They merely think of a sectarian ordination, or authorization, each from his own sect or party. . . . God's ordination, or authorization, of any man to preach is by the impartation of the Holy Spirit to him. Whoever has received the Holy Spirit has received the power and authority to teach and to preach in the name of God. Whoever has not received the Holy Spirit has no Divine authority or sanction to his preaching."—Isa. 61:1, 2.

In order to impugn his reputation, some of the clergy preached and published gross falsehoods about him. One that they frequently employed —and still do—involves the marital situation of Brother Russell. The impression that they have sought to convey is that Russell was immoral. What are the facts?

In 1879, Charles Taze Russell married Maria Frances Ackley. They had a good relationship for 13 years. Then flattery of Maria and appeals to pride on her part by others began to undermine that relationship; but when their objective became clear, she seemed to regain her balance. After a former associate had spread falsehoods about Brother Russell, she even asked her husband's permission to visit a number of congregations to answer the charges, since it had been alleged that he mistreated her. However, the fine reception she was given on that trip in 1894 evidently contributed to a gradual change in her opinion of herself. She sought to secure for herself a stronger voice in directing what would appear in the *Watch Tower*.* When she realized that nothing that she wrote would be published unless her husband, the editor of the magazine, agreed with its contents (on the basis of its consistency with the Scriptures), she became greatly disturbed. He put forth earnest effort to help her, but in November 1897 she left him. Nevertheless, he provided her with a place to live and means of maintenance. Years later, after court proceedings that had been initiated by her in 1903, she was awarded, in 1908, a judgment, not of absolute divorce, but of divorce from bed and board, with alimony.

Having failed to force her husband to acquiesce to her demands, she put forth great effort after she left him to bring his name into disrepute. In 1903 she published a tract filled, not with Scriptural truths, but with gross misrepresentations of Brother Russell. She sought to enlist ministers of various denominations to distribute them where the Bible Students were holding special meetings. To their credit not many at that time were willing to

"God's ordination, or authorization, of any man to preach is by the impartation of the Holy Spirit to him"

---

* The Bible Students did not clearly understand at that time what the Witnesses now know from the Bible regarding men as teachers in the congregation. (1 Cor. 14:33, 34; 1 Tim. 2: 11, 12) As a result, Maria Russell had been associate editor of the *Watch Tower* and a regular contributor to its columns.

Gross falsehoods about the marital affairs of Charles and Maria Russell were widely circulated by opposers

be used in that way. However, other clergymen since then have shown a different spirit.

Earlier, Maria Russell had condemned, verbally and in writing, those who charged Brother Russell with the sort of misconduct that she herself now alleged. Using certain unsubstantiated statements made during court proceedings in 1906 (and which statements were struck from the record by order of the court), some religious opposers of Brother Russell have published charges designed to make it appear that he was an immoral man and hence unfit to be a minister of God. However, the court record is clear that such charges are false. Her own lawyer asked Mrs. Russell whether she believed her husband was guilty of adultery. She answered: "No." It is also noteworthy that when a committee of Christian elders listened to Mrs. Russell's charges against her husband in 1897, she made no mention of the things that she later stated in court in order to persuade the jury that a divorce should be granted, though these alleged incidents occurred prior to that meeting.

Nine years after Mrs. Russell first brought the case to court, Judge James Macfarlane wrote a letter of reply to a man who was seeking a copy of the court record so that one of his associates could expose Russell. The judge frankly told him that what he wanted would be a waste of time and money. His letter stated: "The ground for her application and of the decree entered upon the verdict of the jury was 'indignities' and not adultery and the testimony, as I understand, does not show that Russell was living 'an adulterous life with a co-respondent.' In fact there was no co-respondent."

Maria Russell's own belated acknowledgment came at the time of Brother Russell's funeral at Carnegie Hall in Pittsburgh in 1916. Wearing a veil, she walked down the aisle to the casket and laid there a bunch of lilies of the valley. Attached to them was a ribbon bearing the words, "To My Beloved Husband."

It is evident that the clergy have used the same sort of tactics that were employed by their first-century counterparts. Back then, they endeavored to kill Jesus' reputation by charging that he ate with sinners and that he himself was a sinner and a blasphemer. (Matt. 9:11; John 9:16-24; 10:

33-37) Such charges did not change the truth about Jesus, but they did expose those who resorted to such slander—and they expose those who resort to like tactics today—as having as their spiritual father the Devil, which name means "Slanderer."—John 8:44.

Seizing on War Fever to Achieve Their Aims

With the nationalistic fever that swept the world during the first world war, a new weapon was found for use against the Bible Students. The enmity of Protestant and Roman Catholic religious leaders could be expressed behind a front of patriotism. They took advantage of wartime hysteria to brand the Bible Students as seditious—the same charge that was leveled against Jesus Christ and the apostle Paul by the religious leaders of first-century Jerusalem. (Luke 23:2, 4; Acts 24:1, 5) Of course, for the clergy to make such a charge, they themselves had to be active champions of the war effort, but that did not seem to bother most of them, even though it meant sending young men out to kill members of their own religion in another land.

It was in July 1917, after Russell's death, that the Watch Tower Society released the book *The Finished Mystery*, a commentary on Revelation and Ezekiel as well as The Song of Solomon. That book roundly exposed the hypocrisy of Christendom's clergy! It was given extensive distribution in a relatively short time. Late in December 1917 and early in 1918, the Bible Students in the United States and Canada also undertook the distribution of 10,000,000 copies of a fiery message in the tract *The Bible Students Monthly*. This four-page tabloid-sized tract was entitled "The Fall of Babylon," and it bore the subtitle "Why Christendom Must Now Suffer—The Final Outcome." It identified Catholic and Protestant religious organizations together as modern-day Babylon, which soon must fall. In support of what was said, it reproduced from *The Finished Mystery* commentary on prophecies expressing divine judgment against "Mystic Babylon." On the back page was a graphic cartoon that showed a wall crumbling. Massive stones from the wall bore such labels as "Doctrine of the Trinity ('3 X 1 = 1')," "Immortality of the Soul," "Eternal Torment Theory," "Protestantism—creeds, clergy, etc.," "Romanism—popes, cardinals, etc., etc."—and all of them were falling.

"The Finished Mystery" book roundly exposed the hypocrisy of Christendom's clergy!

The clergy were furious at such exposure, just as the Jewish clergy had been when Jesus exposed their hypocrisy. (Matt. 23:1-39; 26:3, 4) In Canada the clergy reacted quickly. In January 1918, upwards of 600 Canadian clergymen signed a petition calling on the government to suppress the publications of the International Bible Students Association. As reported in the *Winnipeg Evening Tribune*, after Charles G. Paterson, pastor of St. Stephen's Church in Winnipeg, denounced from his pulpit *The Bible Students Monthly*, which contained the article "The Fall of Babylon," Attorney General

The clergy were furious when 10,000,000 copies of this tract were distributed exposing their doctrines and practices in the light of God's Word

Johnson got in touch with him to obtain a copy. Shortly thereafter, on February 12, 1918, a Canadian government decree made it a crime punishable by fine and imprisonment to have in one's possession either the book *The Finished Mystery* or the tract shown above.

That same month, on February 24, Brother Rutherford, the newly elected president of the Watch Tower Society, spoke in the United States at Temple Auditorium in Los Angeles, California. His subject was a startling one: "The World Has Ended—Millions Now Living May Never Die." In setting forth evidence that the world as known till that time really had ended in 1914, he pointed to the war then in progress, along with accompanying famine, and identified it as part of the sign foretold by Jesus. (Matt. 24: 3-8) Then he focused attention on the clergy, saying:

"As a class, according to the scriptures, the clergymen are the most reprehensible men on earth for the great war that is now afflicting mankind. For 1,500 years they have taught the people the satanic doctrine of the divine right of kings to rule. They have mixed politics and religion, church and state; have proved disloyal to their God-given privilege of proclaiming the message of Messiah's kingdom, and have given themselves over to encouraging the rulers to believe that the king reigns by divine right, and therefore whatsoever he does is right." Showing the result of this, he said: "Ambitious kings of Europe armed for war, because they desired to grab the territory of the other peoples; and the clergy patted them on the back and said: 'Go to it, you can do no wrong; whatsoever you do is all right.'" But it was not only the European clergy that were doing it, and the preachers in America knew it.

An extensive report of this lecture was published the next day in the

Los Angeles *Morning Tribune*. The clergy were so angered that the ministerial association held a meeting that very day and sent their president to the managers of the newspaper to make known their intense displeasure. Following this, there was a period of constant harassment of the offices of the Watch Tower Society by members of the government's intelligence bureau.

During this period of nationalistic fervor, a conference of clergymen was held in Philadelphia, in the United States, at which a resolution was adopted calling for revision of the Espionage Act so that alleged violators could be tried by court-martial and subjected to the death penalty. John Lord O'Brian, special assistant to the attorney general for war work, was selected to present the matter to the Senate. The president of the United States did not permit that bill to become law. But Major-General James Franklin Bell, of the U.S. Army, in the heat of anger divulged to J. F. Rutherford and W. E. Van Amburgh what had occurred at the conference and the intent to use that bill against the officers of the Watch Tower Society.

Official U.S. government files show that at least from February 21, 1918, onward, John Lord O'Brian was personally involved in efforts to build a case against the Bible Students. The Congressional Record of April 24 and May 4 contains memos from John Lord O'Brian in which he argued strongly that if the law allowed for utterance of "what is true, with good motives, and for justifiable ends," as stated in the so-called France Amendment to the Espionage Act and as had been endorsed by the U.S. Senate, he could not successfully prosecute the Bible Students.

In Worcester, Massachusetts, "Rev." B. F. Wyland further exploited the war fever by asserting that the Bible Students were carrying on propaganda

Newspapers fanned the flames of persecution of the Bible Students in 1918

for the enemy. He published an article in the *Daily Telegram* in which he declared: "One of your patriotic duties that confronts you as citizens is the suppression of the International Bible Students Association, with headquarters in Brooklyn. They have, under the guise of religion, been carrying on German propaganda in Worcester by selling their book, 'The Finished Mystery.'" He bluntly told the authorities it was their duty to arrest the Bible Students and prevent them from holding further meetings.

The spring and summer of 1918 witnessed widespread persecution of the Bible Students, both in North America and in Europe. Among the instigators were clergymen of Baptist, Methodist, Episcopal, Lutheran, Roman Catholic, and other churches. Bible literature was seized by officers without a search warrant, and many of the Bible Students were thrown into jail. Others were chased by mobs, beaten, whipped, tarred and feathered, or had their ribs broken or their heads cut. Some were permanently maimed. Christian men and women were held in jail without charge or without trial. Over one hundred specific instances of such outrageous treatment were reported in *The Golden Age* of September 29, 1920.

Charged With Espionage

The crowning blow came on May 7, 1918, when federal warrants were issued in the United States for the arrest of J. F. Rutherford, the president of the Watch Tower Bible and Tract Society, and his closest associates.

The previous day, in Brooklyn, New York, two indictments had been filed against Brother Rutherford and his associates. If the desired results did not come from one case, the other indictment could have been pursued. The first indictment, which laid charges against the greater number of individuals, included four counts: Two charged them with *conspiring* to violate the Espionage Act of June 15, 1917; and two counts charged them with attempting to carry out their illegal plans or actually doing so. It was alleged that they were conspiring to cause insubordination and refusal of duty in the armed forces of the United States and that they were conspiring to obstruct the recruiting and enlisting of men for such service when the nation was at war, also that they had attempted to do or had actually done both of these things. The indictment made particular mention of publication and distribution of the book *The Finished Mystery*. The second indictment construed the sending of a check to Europe (which was to be used in the work of Bible education in Germany) to be inimical to the interests of the United States. When the defendants were taken to court, it was the first indictment, the one with four counts, that was pursued.

Yet another indictment of C. J. Woodworth and J. F. Rutherford under the Espionage Act was at that time pending in Scranton, Pennsylvania. But, according to a letter from John Lord O'Brian dated May 20, 1918, members

Christian men and women were mobbed, thrown into jail, and held there without charge or without trial

"OBJECTS OF HATRED BY ALL THE NATIONS" 651

of the Department of Justice feared that U.S. District Judge Witmer, before whom the case would be tried, would not agree with their use of the Espionage Act to suppress the activity of men who, because of sincere religious convictions, said things that others might construe as antiwar propaganda. So the Justice Department held the Scranton case in abeyance, pending the outcome of the one in Brooklyn. The government also managed the situation so that Judge Harland B. Howe, from Vermont, whom John Lord O'Brian knew agreed with his viewpoint on such matters, would sit as judge in the case in the U.S. District Court for the Eastern District of New York. The case went to trial on June 5, with Isaac R. Oeland and Charles J. Buchner, a Roman Catholic, as prosecutors. During the trial, as Brother Rutherford observed, Catholic priests frequently conferred with Buchner and Oeland.

As the case proceeded, it was shown that the officers of the Society and the compilers of the book had no intent to interfere with the country's war effort. Evidence presented during the trial showed that plans for the writing of the book—indeed, the writing of most of the manuscript—had occurred before the United States declared war (on April 6, 1917) and that the original contract for publication had been signed before the United States had passed the law (on June 15) that they were said to have violated.

The prosecution highlighted additions to the book made during April and June of 1917, in the course of processing the copy and reading the proofs. These included a quotation from John Haynes Holmes, a clergyman who had forcefully declared that the war was a violation of Christianity. As indicated by one of the defense attorneys, that clergyman's comments, published under the title *A Statement to My People on the Eve of War,* was still on sale in the United States at the time of the trial. Neither the clergyman nor the publisher was on trial for it. But it was the Bible Students who referred to his sermon who were held liable for the sentiments expressed in it.

The book did not tell men of the world that they had no right to engage in war. But, in explanation of prophecy, it did quote excerpts from issues of *The Watch Tower* of 1915 to show the inconsistency of

During the trial here of members of the Society's headquarters staff, much attention was focused on the book "The Finished Mystery"

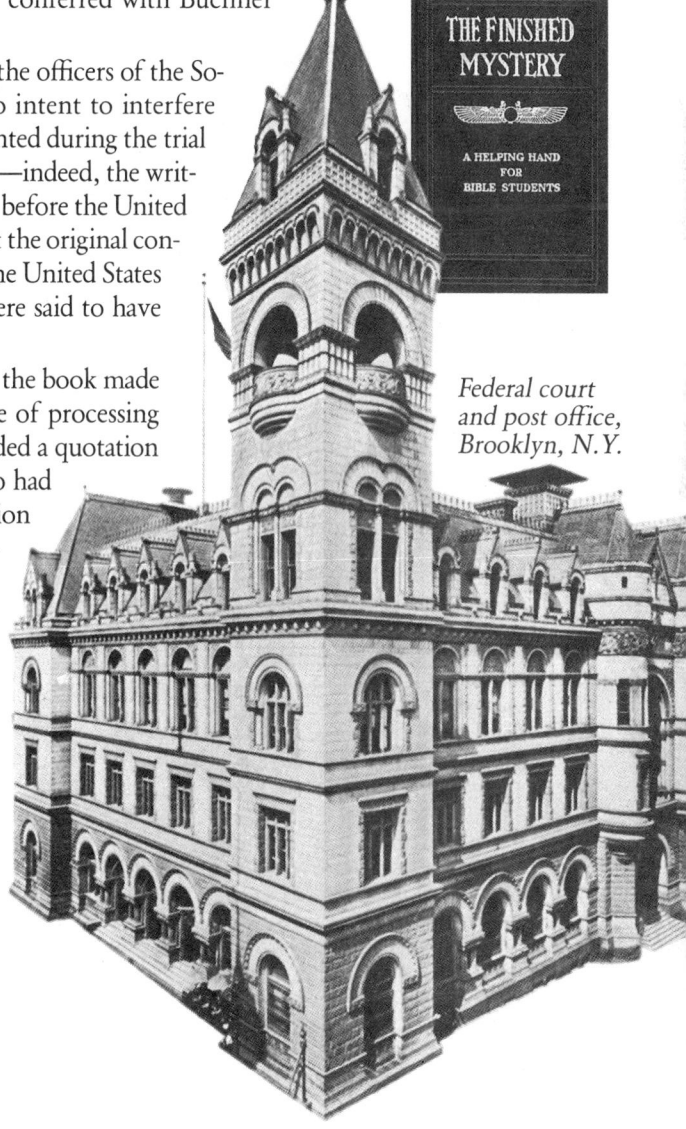

Federal court and post office, Brooklyn, N.Y.

clergymen who professed to be ministers of Christ but who were acting as recruiting agents for nations at war.

When it had been learned that the government objected to the book, Brother Rutherford had immediately sent a telegram to the printer to stop producing it, and at the same time, a representative of the Society had been dispatched to the intelligence section of the U.S. Army to find out what their objection was. When it was learned that because of the war then in progress, pages 247-53 of the book were viewed as objectionable, the Society directed that those pages be cut out of all copies of the book before they were offered to the public. And when the government notified district attorneys that further distribution would be a violation of the Espionage Act (although the government declined to express an opinion to the Society on the book in its altered form), the Society directed that all public distribution of the book be suspended.

Why Such Severe Punishment?

Regardless of all of this, on June 20, 1918, the jury returned a verdict finding each of the defendants guilty on each count of the indictment. The next day, seven* of them were sentenced to four terms of 20 years each, to be served concurrently. On July 10, the eighth# was sentenced to four concurrent terms of 10 years. How severe were those sentences? In a note to the attorney general on March 12, 1919, U.S. president Woodrow Wilson acknowledged that "the terms of imprisonment are clearly excessive." In fact, the man who fired the shots at Sarajevo that killed the crown prince of the Austro-Hungarian Empire—which incident triggered the events that plunged the nations into World War I—had not been given a more severe sentence. His sentence was 20 years in prison—not four terms of 20 years, as in the case of the Bible Students!

What was the motivation behind the imposing of such severe prison terms on the Bible Students? Judge Harland B. Howe declared: "In the opinion of the Court, the religious propaganda which these defendants have vigorously advocated and spread throughout the nation as well as among our allies, is a greater danger than a division of the German Army. . . . A person preaching religion usually has much influence, and if he is sincere, he is all the more effective. This aggravates rather than mitigates the wrong they have done. Therefore, as the only prudent thing to do with such persons, the Court has concluded that the punishment should be severe." It is also noteworthy, however, that before passing sentence, Judge

"The terms of imprisonment are clearly excessive"
—U.S. president Woodrow Wilson

---

* Joseph F. Rutherford, president of the Watch Tower Society; William E. Van Amburgh, secretary-treasurer of the Society; Robert J. Martin, office manager; Frederick H. Robison, a member of the editorial committee for *The Watch Tower;* A. Hugh Macmillan, a director of the Society; George H. Fisher and Clayton J. Woodworth, compilers of *The Finished Mystery.*

Giovanni DeCecca, who worked in the Italian Department in the Watch Tower Society's office.

Howe said that statements made by attorneys for the defendants had called into question and treated severely not only the law officers of the government but *"all the ministers throughout the land."*

The decision was immediately appealed to the U.S. circuit court of appeals. But bail pending the hearing of that appeal was arbitrarily refused by Judge Howe,* and on July 4, before a third and final appeal for bail could be heard, the first seven brothers were hastily moved to the federal penitentiary in Atlanta, Georgia. Thereafter, it was demonstrated that there were 130 procedural errors in that highly prejudiced trial. Months of work went into the preparation of required papers for an appeal hearing. Meanwhile, the war ended. On February 19, 1919, the eight brothers in prison sent an appeal for executive clemency to Woodrow Wilson, the president of the United States. Other letters urging the release of the brothers were sent by numerous citizens to the newly appointed attorney general. Then, on March 1, 1919, in reply to an inquiry from the attorney general, Judge

Sentenced to punishment more severe than was the assassin whose shot triggered World War I. From left to right: W. E. Van Amburgh, J. F. Rutherford, A. H. Macmillan, R. J. Martin, F. H. Robison, C. J. Woodworth, G. H. Fisher, G. DeCecca

---

* Circuit Judge Martin T. Manton, an ardent Roman Catholic, refused a second appeal for bail on July 1, 1918. When the federal court of appeals later reversed the judgment of the defendants, Manton cast the one dissenting vote. It is noteworthy that on December 4, 1939, a specially constituted appellate court upheld the conviction of Manton for abuse of judicial power, dishonesty, and fraud.

Howe recommended "immediate commutation" of the sentences. While this would have reduced the sentences, it would also have had the effect of affirming the guilt of the defendants. Before this could be done, the attorneys for the brothers had a court order served on the U.S. attorney that brought the case before the appeals court.

Nine months after Rutherford and his associates were sentenced—and with the war past—on March 21, 1919, the appeals court ordered bail for all eight defendants, and on March 26, they were released in Brooklyn on bail of $10,000 each. On May 14, 1919, the U.S. circuit court of appeals in New York ruled: "The defendants in this case did not have the temperate and impartial trial to which they were entitled, and for that reason the judgment is reversed." The case was remanded for a new trial. However, on May 5, 1920, after the defendants had appeared in court, on call, *five times*, the government's attorney, in open court in Brooklyn, announced withdrawal of the prosecution.* Why? As revealed in correspondence preserved in the U.S. National Archives, the Department of Justice feared that if the issues were presented to an unbiased jury, with the war hysteria gone, the case would be lost. U.S. attorney L. W. Ross stated in a letter to the attorney general: "It would be better, I think, for our relations with the public, if we should on our own initiative" state that the case would be pressed no further.

On the same day, May 5, 1920, the alternate indictment that had been filed in May 1918 against J. F. Rutherford and four of his associates was also dismissed.

Who Really Instigated It?

Was all of this really instigated by the clergy? John Lord O'Brian denied it. But the facts were well-known by those who lived at that time. On March 22, 1919, *Appeal to Reason*, a newspaper published at Girard, Kansas, protested: "Followers of Pastor Russell, Pursued by Malice of 'Orthodox' Clergy, Were Convicted and Jailed Without Bail, Though They Made Every Effort That Was Possible to Comply with the Provisions of Espionage Law. . . . We declare that, regardless of whether or not the Espionage Act was technically constitutional or ethically justifiable, these followers of Pastor Russell were wrongfully convicted under its provisions. An open-minded study of the evidence will speedily convince any one that these men

---

* That these men were unjustly imprisoned, and were not convicts, is demonstrated by the fact that J. F. Rutherford remained a member of the bar of the United States Supreme Court from his admission in May 1909 until his death in 1942. In 14 cases appealed to the Supreme Court from 1939 until 1942, J. F. Rutherford was one of the attorneys. In the cases known as *Schneider v. State of New Jersey* (in 1939) and *Minersville School District v. Gobitis* (in 1940), he personally presented oral argument before the Supreme Court. Also, during World War II, A. H. Macmillan, one of the men wrongly imprisoned in 1918-19, was accepted by the director of the federal Bureau of Prisons as a regular visitor to federal prisons in the United States to care for spiritual interests of young men who were there because of having taken a stand of Christian neutrality.

The Clergy Show Their Feelings

Reactions of religious periodicals to the sentencing of J. F. Rutherford and his associates in 1918 are noteworthy:

• *"The Christian Register"*: "What the Government here strikes at with deadly directness is the assumption that religious ideas, however crazy and pernicious, may be propagated with impunity. It is an old fallacy, and hitherto we have been entirely too careless about it. . . . It looks like the end of Russellism."

• *"The Western Recorder,"* a Baptist publication, said: "It is a matter of small surprise that the head of this cantankerous cult should be incarcerated in one of the retreats for recalcitrants. . . . The really perplexing problem in this connection is whether the defendants should have been sent to an insane asylum or a penitentiary."

• *"The Fortnightly Review"* drew attention to the comment in the New York *"Evening Post,"* which said: "We trust that teachers of religion everywhere will take notice of this judge's opinion that teaching any religion save that which is absolutely in accord with statute laws is a grave crime which is intensified if, being a minister of the gospel, you should still happen to be sincere."

• *"The Continent"* disparagingly styled the defendants as "followers of the late 'Pastor' Russell" and distorted their beliefs by saying that they contended "that all but sinners should be exempted from fighting the German kaiser." It claimed that according to the attorney general in Washington, "the Italian government sometime ago complained to the United States that Rutherford and his associates . . . had circulated in the Italian armies a quantity of antiwar propaganda."

• A week later *"The Christian Century"* published most of the above item verbatim, showing that they were in full agreement.

• The Catholic magazine *"Truth"* briefly reported the sentence imposed and then expressed the feelings of its editors, saying: "The literature of this association fairly reeks with virulent attacks on the Catholic Church and her priesthood." Endeavoring to pin the "sedition" label on any who might publicly disagree with the Catholic Church, it added: "It is becoming more and more evident that the spirit of intolerance is closely allied to that of sedition."

• Dr. Ray Abrams, in his book *"Preachers Present Arms,"* observed: "When the news of the twenty-year sentences reached the editors of the religious press, practically every one of these publications, great and small, rejoiced over the event. I have been unable to discover any words of sympathy in any of the orthodox religious journals."

not only had no intention of violating the law, but that they did not violate it."

Years later, in the book *Preachers Present Arms*, Dr. Ray Abrams observed: "It is significant that so many clergymen took an aggressive part in trying to get rid of the Russellites [as the Bible Students were derogatorily labeled]. Long-lived religious quarrels and hatreds, which did not receive any consideration in the courts in time of peace, now found their way into the courtroom under the spell of war-time hysteria." He also stated: "An analysis of the whole case leads to the conclusion that the churches and the clergy were originally behind the movement to stamp out the Russellites." —Pp. 183-5.

However, the end of the war did not bring an end to persecution of the Bible Students. It simply opened a new era of it.

Priests Put Pressure on the Police

With the war past, other issues were stirred up by the clergy in order to stop, if at all possible, the activity of the Bible Students. In Catholic Bavaria and other parts of Germany, numerous arrests were instigated in the 1920's under peddling laws. But when the cases came into the appeal courts, the judges usually sided with the Bible Students. Finally, after the courts had been deluged with thousands of such cases, the Ministry of the Interior issued a circular in 1930 to all police officials telling them to stop initiating legal action against the Bible Students under the peddling laws. Thus, for a short time, pressure from this source subsided, and Jehovah's Witnesses carried on their activity on an extraordinary scale in the German field.

The clergy also exercised powerful influence in Romania during those years. They succeeded in getting decrees published banning the literature and activity of Jehovah's Witnesses. But the priests were afraid that the people still might read the literature that they already had and as a result would learn about the unscriptural teachings and fraudulent claims of the church. To prevent this, priests actually went with the gendarmes from house to house looking for any literature that had been distributed by Jehovah's Witnesses. They would even ask unsuspecting little children whether their parents had accepted such literature. If any was found, the people were threatened with beating and prison if they ever accepted more. In some villages the priest was also the mayor and the justice of the peace, and there was very little justice for anyone who would not do what the priest said.

The record that some American officials made in doing the will of the clergy during this era is no better. Following the visit of Catholic Bishop O'Hara to La Grange, Georgia, for example, the mayor and the city attorney had scores of Jehovah's Witnesses arrested in 1936. During their incarceration, they were made to sleep alongside a manure pile on mattress-

There was very little justice for anyone who would not do what the priest said

When this assembly of Witnesses was held in New York in 1939, some 200 mobsters led by Catholic priests tried to break it up

es spattered by cow urine, were fed wormy food, and were forced to labor on road gangs.

In Poland too, the Catholic clergy used every means they could devise to hinder the work of Jehovah's Witnesses. They incited the people to violence, burned the literature of Jehovah's Witnesses publicly, denounced them as Communists, and haled them into court on the charge that their literature was "sacrilegious." Not all officials, however, were willing to do their bidding. The state attorney of the court of appeal of Posen (Poznan), for one, refused to prosecute one of Jehovah's Witnesses whom the clergy had denounced on the charge that he had referred to the Catholic clergy as "Satan's organization." The state attorney himself pointed out that the immoral spirit that spread throughout Christendom from the papal court of Alexander VI (1492-1503 C.E.) was, indeed, the spirit of a satanic organization. And when the clergy charged one of Jehovah's Witnesses with blasphemy against God by reason of distributing Watch Tower literature, the state attorney of the court of appeal in Thorn (Toruń) demanded acquittal, saying: 'The Witnesses of Jehovah take exactly the same stand as did the first Christians. Misrepresented and persecuted, they stand for the highest ideals in a corrupt and falling world organization.'

Canadian government archives reveal that it was in compliance with a letter from the palace of Catholic Cardinal Villeneuve, of Quebec, to the minister of justice, Ernest Lapointe, that Jehovah's Witnesses were banned in Canada in 1940. Other government officials thereafter called for a full explanation of the reasons for that action, but Lapointe's replies were not at all satisfying to many members of the Canadian Parliament.

On the other side of the globe, there was similar scheming by the clergy. The Australian government archives contain a letter from the Roman Catholic archbishop of Sydney to Attorney General W. M. Hughes urging that Jehovah's Witnesses be declared illegal. That letter was written on

August 20, 1940, just five months before a ban was imposed. After reviewing the alleged basis for the ban, Mr. Justice Williams of the Australian High Court later said that it had "the effect of making the advocacy of the principles and doctrines of the Christian religion unlawful and *every church service held by believers in the birth of Christ an unlawful assembly.*" On June 14, 1943, the Court ruled that the ban was not consistent with Australian law.

In Switzerland a Catholic newspaper demanded that the authorities seize literature of the Witnesses that the church viewed as offensive. They threatened that if this was not done, they would take the law into their own hands. And in many parts of the world, that is exactly what they did!

Religious Leaders Resort to Violence

The Catholic clergy in France felt that they still had a firm hold on the people, and they were determined not to let anything interfere with that monopoly. During 1924-25, the Bible Students in many lands were distributing the tract *Ecclesiastics Indicted.* In 1925, J. F. Rutherford was scheduled to speak in Paris on the subject "The Frauds of the Clergy Exposed." Regarding what took place at the meeting, an eyewitness reported: "The hall was packed. Brother Rutherford appeared on the stage, and there was warm applause. He began to speak, when suddenly about 50 priests and members of Catholic Action, armed with sticks, rushed into the hall singing *La Marseillaise* [the French national anthem]. They threw tracts from the top of the stairs. One priest got up onto the stage. Two young men threw him down. Three times, Brother Rutherford left the stage and then came back. Finally, he left for good. . . . The tables showing a display of our literature were overturned and our books thrown all around. It was utter confusion!" But it was not an isolated incident.

Jack Corr, while witnessing in Ireland, frequently felt the fury of the Catholic clergy. On one occasion a mob, instigated by the parish priest, pulled him out of bed at midnight and then burned all his literature in the public square. At Roscrea in County Tipperary, Victor Gurd and Jim Corby arrived at their accommodations only to find that opposers had stolen their literature, soaked it with petrol, and set it on fire. Around the bonfire stood the local police, the clergy, and children from the area, singing "Faith of Our Fathers."

Before Jehovah's Witnesses met in Madison Square Garden in New York in 1939, threats were made by followers of the Catholic priest Charles Coughlin that the assembly would be broken up. The police were notified. On June 25, Brother Rutherford spoke to the 18,000 or more in that auditorium, as well as to a large international radio audience, on the subject "Government and Peace." After the discourse had begun, 200 or more Roman Catholics and Nazis, led by several Catholic priests, crowded into the

"Objects of Hatred by All the Nations"

balcony. At a given signal, they set up a terrific howl, shouting *"Heil Hitler!"* and *"Viva Franco!"* They used all manner of vile language and threats and assaulted many of the ushers who took action to quell the disturbance. The mobsters did not succeed in breaking up the meeting. Brother Rutherford continued to speak forcefully and fearlessly. At the height of the tumult, he declared: "Note today the Nazis and Catholics that would like to break up this meeting, but by God's grace cannot do it." The audience gave support with round after round of vigorous applause. The disturbance became a permanent part of the sound recording made on that occasion, and it has been heard by people in many parts of the world.

Where possible, however, as in the days of the Inquisition, the Roman Catholic clergy made use of the State to suppress any who dared question the church's teachings and practices.

Brutal Treatment in Concentration Camps

In Adolf Hitler the clergy had a willing ally. During 1933, the very year that a concordat between the Vatican and Nazi Germany was signed, Hitler launched a campaign to annihilate Jehovah's Witnesses in Germany. By 1935 they were proscribed in the entire nation. But who instigated this?

A Catholic priest, writing in *Der Deutsche Weg* (a German-language newspaper published in Lodz, Poland), said in its issue of May 29, 1938: "There is now one country on earth where the so-called . . . Bible Students [Jehovah's Witnesses] are forbidden. That is Germany! . . . When Adolf Hitler came to power, and *the German Catholic Episcopate repeated their*

During World War II, thousands of Jehovah's Witnesses were thrown into these concentration camps

Skull insignia of SS guards (left)

> ### "Persecuted on Religious Grounds"
>
> "There existed a group of people in Mauthausen Concentration Camp who were persecuted on religious grounds only: members of the sect 'Earnest Bible Students,' or 'Witnesses of Jehovah'... Their rejection of the loyalty oath to Hitler and their refusal to render any kind of military service —a political consequence of their belief—were the reason for their persecution."—"Die Geschichte des Konzentrationslagers Mauthausen" (*The History of Mauthausen Concentration Camp*), documented by Hans Maršálek, Vienna, Austria, 1974.

request, Hitler said: 'These so-called Earnest Bible Students [Jehovah's Witnesses] are troublemakers; ... I consider them quacks; I do not tolerate that the German Catholics shall be besmirched in such a manner by this American Judge Rutherford; I dissolve [Jehovah's Witnesses] in Germany.'"—Italics ours.

Was it only the German Catholic Episcopate that wanted such action taken? As reported in the *Oschatzer Gemeinnützige,* of April 21, 1933, in a radio address on April 20, Lutheran minister Otto spoke about the "closest cooperation" on the part of the German Lutheran Church of the State of Saxony with the political leaders of the nation, and then he declared: "The first results of this cooperation can already be reported in the ban today placed upon the International Association of Earnest Bible Students [Jehovah's Witnesses] and its subdivisions in Saxony."

Thereafter, the Nazi State unleashed one of the most barbaric persecutions of Christians in recorded history. Thousands of Jehovah's Witnesses—from Germany, Austria, Poland, Czechoslovakia, the Netherlands, France, and other countries—were thrown into concentration camps. Here they were subjected to the most cruel and sadistic treatment imaginable. It was not unusual for them to be cursed and kicked, then forced to do knee-bending, jumping, and crawling for hours on end, until they fainted or dropped from exhaustion, while guards laughed with glee. Some were forced to stand naked or lightly clad in the courtyard in midwinter. Many were whipped until they were unconscious and their backs were covered with blood. Others were used as guinea pigs in medical experiments. Some, with their arms tied behind their back, were hung by their wrists. Though weak from hunger and inadequately clothed in freezing weather, they were forced to do heavy labor, working long hours, often using their own hands when shovels and other tools were needed. Both men and women were thus abused. Their ages ranged from the teens into the seventies. Their tormentors shouted defiance of Jehovah.

In an effort to break the spirit of the Witnesses, the camp commander at Sachsenhausen ordered August Dickmann, a young Witness, to be executed in the presence of all the prisoners, with Jehovah's Witnesses out front where they would get the full impact. After that, the rest of the prisoners were dismissed, but Jehovah's Witnesses had to remain. With great emphasis the commander asked them, 'Who is now ready to sign the declaration?'—a declaration renouncing one's faith and indicating willingness to become a soldier. Not one of the 400 or more Witnesses responded.

Then two stepped forward! No, not to sign, but to ask that their signatures given about a year earlier be annulled.

In the Buchenwald camp, similar pressure was brought to bear. Nazi officer Rödl notified the Witnesses: "If anyone of you refuses to fight against France or England, all of you must die!" Two fully armed SS companies were waiting at the gatehouse. Not a single one of the Witnesses gave in. Harsh treatment followed, but the officer's threat was not carried out. It came to be well recognized that, while the Witnesses in the camps would do almost any sort of work they were assigned, yet, even though punished with systematic starvation and overwork, they would firmly refuse to do anything in support of the war or that was directed against a fellow prisoner.

What they went through defies description. Hundreds of them died. After the survivors were released from the camps at the end of the war, a Witness from Flanders wrote: "Only an unswerving desire to live, hope and trust in Him, Jehovah, who is all-powerful, and love of The Theocracy, made it possible to endure all this and win the victory.—Romans 8:37."

Parents were torn away from their children. Marriage mates were separated, and some never heard from each other again. Shortly after he got married, Martin Poetzinger was arrested and taken to the infamous camp at Dachau, then to Mauthausen. His wife, Gertrud, was incarcerated in Ravensbrück. They did not see each other for nine years. Recalling his experiences in Mauthausen, he later wrote: "The Gestapo tried every method to induce us to break our faith in Jehovah. Starvation diet, deceitful friendships, brutalities, having to stand in a frame day after day, being hung from a ten-foot post by the wrists twisted around the back, whippings—all these and others too degraded to mention were tried." But he

---

Translation of Declaration That the SS Tried to Force Witnesses to Sign

Concentration camp . . . .
Department II

DECLARATION

I, the . . . .
born on . . . .
in . . . .
herewith make the following declaration:

1. I have come to know that the International Bible Students Association is proclaiming erroneous teachings and under the cloak of religion follows hostile purposes against the State.

2. I therefore left the organization entirely and made myself absolutely free from the teachings of this sect.

3. I herewith give assurance that I will never again take any part in the activity of the International Bible Students Association. Any persons approaching me with the teaching of the Bible Students, or who in any manner reveal their connections with them, I will denounce immediately. All literature from the Bible Students that should be sent to my address I will at once deliver to the nearest police station.

4. I will in the future esteem the laws of the State, especially in the event of war will I, with weapon in hand, defend the fatherland, and join in every way the community of the people.

5. I have been informed that I will at once be taken again into protective custody if I should act against the declaration given today.

. . . . , Dated . . . .
. . . .
Signature

Letters From Some Who Were Sentenced to Death

From Franz Reiter (who was facing death by guillotine) to his mother, January 6, 1940, from the detention center Berlin-Plötzensee:

"I am strongly convinced in my belief that I am acting correctly. Being here, I could still change my mind, but with God this would be disloyalty. All of us here wish to be faithful to God, to his honor. . . . With what I knew, if I had taken the [military] oath, I would have committed a sin deserving death. That would be evil to me. I would have no resurrection. But I stick to that which Christ said: 'Whosoever will save his life will lose it; but whosoever will lose his life for my sake, the same will receive it.' And now, my dear Mother and all my brothers and sisters, today I was told my sentence, and don't be terrified, it is death, and I will be executed tomorrow morning. I have my strength from God, the same as it always was with all true Christians away back in the past. The apostles write, 'Whosoever is born from God cannot sin.' The same goes for me. This I proved to you, and you could recognize it. My dear one, don't get heavyhearted. It would be good for all of you to know the Holy Scriptures better still. If you will stand firm until death, we shall meet again in the resurrection. . . .

"Your Franz
"Until we meet again."

From Berthold Szabo, executed by a firing squad, in Körmend, Hungary, on March 2, 1945:

"My dear sister, Marika!

"These one and one half hours I have left, I will try to write to you so that you will be able to let our parents know about my situation, immediately facing death.

"I wish them the same peace of mind that I experience in these last moments in this world fraught with disaster. It is now ten o'clock, and I will be executed at half past eleven; but I am quite calm. My further life I lay into the hands of Jehovah and his Beloved Son, Jesus Christ, the King, who will never forget those sincerely loving them. I know too that there will soon be a resurrection of those who died or, rather, who went to sleep, in Christ. I should also like to particularly mention that I wish you all Jehovah's richest blessings for the love you bestowed on me. Please kiss Father and Mother for me, and Annus too. They should not worry about me; we shall be seeing each other again soon. My hand is calm now, and I shall go to rest until Jehovah calls me again. Even now I shall keep the vow I took for him.

"Now my time is up. May God be with you and with me.
"With much love, . . .
"Berthi"

remained loyal to Jehovah. He was also among the survivors, and later he served as a member of the Governing Body of Jehovah's Witnesses.

Imprisoned Because of Their Faith

Jehovah's Witnesses were not in the concentration camps because they were criminals. When officers wanted someone to shave them, they trusted a Witness with the razor, because they knew that no Witness would ever use such an instrument as a weapon to harm another human. When SS officers at the Auschwitz extermination camp needed someone to clean their homes or care for their children, they selected Witnesses, because they knew these would not try to poison them or try to escape. When the Sachsenhausen camp was being evacuated at the end of the war, the guards positioned a wagon on which they had their loot in the midst of a column of Witnesses. Why? Because they knew that the Witnesses would not steal from them.

Jehovah's Witnesses were imprisoned because of their faith. Repeatedly they were promised release from the camps if they would only sign a declaration renouncing their beliefs. The SS did everything in their power to entice or force the Witnesses to sign such a declaration. Above all else, this was what they wanted.

All but a few of the Witnesses proved unbreakable in their integrity. But they did more than suffer because of their loyalty to Jehovah and their devotion to the name of Christ. They did more than endure the inquisitional torture that was inflicted on them. They maintained strong ties of spiritual unity.

Theirs was not a spirit of personal survival at all costs. They showed self-sacrificing love for one another. When one of their number became weak,

---

Noted for Courage and Convictions

• *"Against all odds, Witnesses in the camps met and prayed together, produced literature and made converts. Sustained by their fellowship, and, unlike many other prisoners, well aware of the reasons why such places existed and why they should suffer thus, Witnesses proved a small but memorable band of prisoners, marked by the violet triangle and noted for their courage and their convictions."* So wrote Dr. Christine King, in *"The Nazi State and the New Religions: Five Case Studies in Non-Conformity."*

• *"Values and Violence in Auschwitz,"* by Anna Pawełczyńska, states: *"This group of prisoners was a solid ideological force and they won their battle against Nazism. The German group of this sect had been a tiny island of unflagging resistance existing in the bosom of a terrorized nation, and in that same undismayed spirit they functioned in the camp at Auschwitz. They managed to win the respect of their fellow-prisoners . . . of prisoner-functionaries, and even of the SS officers. Everyone knew that no 'Bibelforscher' [Jehovah's Witness] would perform a command contrary to his religious belief."*

• Rudolf Hoess, in his autobiography, published in the book *"Commandant of Auschwitz,"* told of the execution of certain ones of Jehovah's Witnesses for refusal to violate their Christian neutrality. He said: *"Thus do I imagine that the first Christian martyrs must have appeared as they waited in the circus for the wild beasts to tear them in pieces. Their faces completely transformed, their eyes raised to heaven, and their hands clasped and lifted in prayer, they went to their death. All who saw them die were deeply moved, and even the execution squad itself was affected."* (This book was published in Poland under the title *"Autobiografia Rudolfa Hössa-komendanta obozu oświęcimskiego."*)

Part of a book for Bible study photographically reduced, put into a matchbox, and smuggled to Witnesses in a concentration camp

others would share their meager food ration. When deprived of all medical treatment, they lovingly cared for one another.

Despite all the efforts of their persecutors to prevent it, material for Bible study reached the Witnesses—concealed in gift packets from outside, through the mouths of newly arriving prisoners, even hidden in the wooden leg of a new inmate, or by other means when they were on work assignments outside the camps. Copies were passed from one to another; sometimes they were surreptitiously duplicated on machines right in the offices of camp officials. Although there was great danger involved, some Christian meetings were held even in the camps.

The Witnesses kept right on preaching that God's Kingdom is mankind's only hope—and they did it there in the concentration camps! Within Buchenwald, as a result of organized activity, thousands of inmates heard the good news. In the camp at Neuengamme, near Hamburg, a campaign of intensive witnessing was carefully planned and carried out early in 1943. Testimony cards were prepared in various languages spoken in the camp. Efforts were made to reach each internee. Arrangements were made for regular personal study of the Bible with interested ones. So zealous were the Witnesses in their preaching that some political prisoners complained: "Wherever you go, all you hear is talk about Jehovah!" When orders came from Berlin to disperse the Witnesses among the other prisoners in order to weaken them, this actually made it possible for them to witness to more people.

Regarding the 500 or more faithful female Witnesses in Ravensbrück, a niece of French General Charles de Gaulle wrote following her own release: "I have true admiration for them. They belonged to various nationalities: German, Polish, Russian and Czech, and have endured very great sufferings for their beliefs. . . . All of them showed very great courage and their attitude commanded eventually even the respect of the S.S. They could have been immediately freed if they had renounced their faith. But, on the contrary, they did not cease resistance, even succeeding in introducing books and tracts into the camp."

Like Jesus Christ, they proved themselves conquerors of the world that sought to make them conform to its satanic mold. (John 16:33) Christine King, in the book *New Religious Movements: A Perspective for Understanding Society*, says regarding them: "The Jehovah's Witnesses offered a challenge to the totalitarian concept of the new society, and this challenge, as well as the persist[e]nce of its survival, demonstrably disturbed the architects of the new order. . . . The time-honoured methods of persecution, torture, imprisonment and ridicule were not resulting in the conversion of any Witnesses to the Nazi position and were in fact back-firing against their instigators. . . . Between these two rival claimants on loyalty, the fight was bitter, even

"Objects of Hatred by All the Nations"

more so, since the physically stronger Nazis were in many ways less sure, less rooted in the firmness of their own conviction, less certain of the survival of their 1,000 year Reich. Witnesses did not doubt their own roots, for their faith had been evident since the time of Abel. Whilst the Nazis had to suppress opposition and convince their supporters, often borrowing language and imagery from sectarian Christianity, Witnesses were sure of the total, unbending loyalty of their members, even to death."—Published in 1982.

At the end of the war, over a thousand surviving Witnesses came out of the camps, with their faith intact and their love for one another strong. As the Russian armies neared, the guards quickly evacuated Sachsenhausen. They grouped the prisoners according to nationality. But Jehovah's Witnesses stayed together as one group—230 of them from this camp. With the Russians close behind them, the guards became excited. There was no food, and the prisoners were weak; yet, anyone who lagged behind or dropped because of exhaustion was shot. Thousands of such were strewed along the line of march. But the Witnesses helped one another so that not even the weakest was lying on the road! Yet some of them were between 65 and 72 years old. Other prisoners tried to steal food along the way, and many were shot while doing it. In contrast, Jehovah's Witnesses seized opportunities to tell people along the evacuation route about Jehovah's loving purposes, and some of these, out of gratitude for the comforting message, supplied them with food for themselves and their Christian brothers.

Some of the Witnesses whose faith endured the crucible of the Nazi concentration camps

Mauthausen

Wewelsburg

The Clergy Continue to Fight

Following World War II, the clergy in the eastern part of Czechoslovakia continued to instigate persecution of Jehovah's Witnesses. During the time of Nazi domination, they had charged that the Witnesses were Communists; now they claimed that the Witnesses were against the Communist government. At times, when Jehovah's Witnesses were making calls at the homes of the people, the priests urged teachers to let hundreds of children out of school to throw stones at the Witnesses.

Similarly, Catholic priests in Santa Ana, El Salvador, agitated against the Witnesses in 1947. While the brothers were having their weekly *Watchtower* Study, boys threw stones through the open door. Then came the procession led by priests. Some carried torches; others carried images. "Long live the Virgin!" they shouted. "May Jehovah die!" For some two hours, the building was pelted with stones.

In the mid-1940's, Jehovah's Witnesses in Quebec, Canada, were also subjected to horrible abuse, at the hands of Catholic mobs and officials alike. Delegations from the bishop's palace called daily at the police department to demand that the police get rid of the Witnesses. Frequently, before an arrest was made, the police were seen emerging from the back door of the church. In 1949, missionaries of Jehovah's Witnesses were driven out of Joliette, Quebec, by Catholic mobsters.

But not all the people in Quebec were in agreement with what was being done. Today, there is a fine Kingdom Hall of Jehovah's Witnesses on one of the main thoroughfares in Joliette. The former seminary there has been closed down, purchased by the government, and turned into a community college. And in Montreal, Jehovah's Witnesses have held large international conventions, with attendance running as high as 80,008 in 1978.

Nevertheless, the Catholic Church has used every means possible to maintain an iron grip on the people. By bringing pressure on government officials, they saw to it that Witness missionaries were ordered to leave Italy in 1949 and that, when possible, permits secured by the Witnesses for assemblies there were canceled during the 1950's. In spite of this, the numbers of Jehovah's Witnesses continued to grow, and by 1992 there were more than 190,000 Witness evangelizers in Italy.

As in the time of the Inquisition, the clergy in Spain did the denouncing and then left it to the State to do the dirty work. For example, in Barcelona, where the archbishop launched a crusade against the Witnesses in 1954, the clergy used their pulpits as well as the schools and the radio to advise people that when the Witnesses called on them, they should invite them in—and then quickly call the police.

The priests feared that the Spanish people might learn what was in the

The priests urged teachers to let children out of school to throw stones at the Witnesses

Violence frequently greets controversial Witnesses of Jehovah when they preach their interpretation of Scriptures. Here, Chateauguay Basin, Que., crowds, held back by police officers, threaten Witnesses Frank Roncarelli and son (R). Sect's most spectacular battleground is in Quebec province.

Bible and perhaps even show others what they had seen. When Manuel Mula Giménez was imprisoned in Granada in 1960 for the "crime" of teaching others about the Bible, the prison chaplain (a Catholic priest) had the only Bible in the prison library removed. And when another prisoner lent Manuel a copy of the Gospels, this was snatched from him. But the Bible has now reached the common people in Spain, they have had opportunity to see for themselves what it says, and by 1992, there were upwards of 90,000 who had taken up the worship of Jehovah as his Witnesses.

In the Dominican Republic, the clergy collaborated with Dictator Trujillo, using him to accomplish their aims even as he used them for his own purposes. In 1950, after newspaper articles written by priests denounced Jehovah's Witnesses, the Watch Tower Society's branch overseer was summoned by the Secretary of the Interior and Police. As he waited outside the office, the branch overseer saw two Jesuit priests enter and then leave. Immediately after that, he was called in to the Secretary's office, and the Secretary nervously read a decree banning the activity of Jehovah's Witnesses. After the ban was briefly lifted in 1956, the clergy used both radio and press in renewed slander of the Witnesses. Entire congregations were arrested and ordered to sign a statement renouncing their faith and promising to return to the Roman Catholic Church. When the Witnesses refused, they were beaten, kicked, whipped, and had their faces smashed with rifle butts. But they stood firm, and their numbers grew.

In Sucre, Bolivia, there was more violence. At the time of an assembly of Jehovah's Witnesses in 1955, a gang of boys from the Sacred Heart

Mob violence near Montreal, Quebec, in 1945. Such clergy-inspired violence against the Witnesses was frequent during the 1940's and 1950's

Catholic School surrounded the assembly place, yelled, and threw stones. From the church building across the street, a powerful loudspeaker urged all Catholics to defend the church and the "Virgin" against the "Protestant heretics." The bishop and the priests personally tried to disrupt the meeting but were ordered out of the hall by the police.

The previous year, when Jehovah's Witnesses were holding an assembly in Riobamba, Ecuador, their program featured a public talk entitled "Love, Practical in a Selfish World?" But a Jesuit priest had stirred up the Catholic populace, urging them to prevent that meeting. Thus, as the talk got under way, a mob could be heard shouting: "Long live the Catholic Church!" and, "Down with the Protestants!" The police commendably held them back, with swords drawn. But the mob hurled stones at the meeting place and, later, at the building in which the missionaries lived.

The Roman Catholic clergy have been in the forefront of the persecution, but they have not been the only ones. The Greek Orthodox clergy have been just as fierce and have used the same tactics, in their more limited area of influence. In addition, where they felt that they could do it, many of the Protestant clergy have demonstrated a similar spirit. For example, in Indonesia they have led mobs that broke up Bible studies in private homes and that savagely beat Jehovah's Witnesses who were present. In some African lands, they have endeavored to influence officials to exclude Jehovah's Witnesses from the country or to deprive them of freedom to talk about God's Word with others. Although they may differ on other matters, the Catholic and Protestant clergy as a whole are in agreement on their opposition to Jehovah's Witnesses. On occasion they have even joined forces in trying to influence government officials to stop the activity of the Witnesses. Where non-Christian religions have dominated life, they too have often used the government to insulate their people from any exposure to teachings that might cause them to question the religion of their birth.

At times, these non-Christian groups have joined forces with professed Christians in scheming to maintain the religious status quo. At Dekin, in Dahomey (now Benin), a juju priest and a Catholic priest conspired together to get officials to suppress the activity of Jehovah's Witnesses early in the 1950's. In their desperation they fabricated charges that were calculated to stir up all sorts of hostile emotions. They charged that the Witnesses were urging the people to revolt against the government, were not paying taxes, were the reason why the jujus did not give rain, and were responsible for the ineffectiveness of the prayers of the priest. All such religious leaders feared that their people might learn things that would free them from superstitious beliefs and a life of blind obedience.

Gradually, however, the influence of the clergy has diminished in many places. The clergy do not now find that the police are always behind

The clergy joined forces to oppose the Witnesses

"Objects of Hatred by All the Nations"

them when they harass the Witnesses. When a Greek Orthodox priest tried to break up an assembly of Jehovah's Witnesses by mob violence in Larissa, Greece, in 1986, the district attorney along with a large contingent of police intervened on behalf of the Witnesses. And at times the press has been quite blunt in its denunciation of acts of religious intolerance.

Nevertheless, in many parts of the world, other issues have led to waves of persecution. One of these issues has involved the attitude of Jehovah's Witnesses toward national emblems.

Because They Worship Only Jehovah

In modern times it was first in Nazi Germany that Jehovah's Witnesses were outstandingly confronted with issues involving nationalistic ceremonies. Hitler endeavored to regiment the German nation by making the Nazi salute *"Heil Hitler!"* compulsory. As reported by Swedish journalist and BBC broadcaster Björn Hallström, when Jehovah's Witnesses in Germany were arrested during the Nazi era, the charges against them usually included "refusal to salute the flag and to give the Nazi salute." Soon other nations began to demand that everyone salute their flag. Jehovah's Witnesses refused—not out of disloyalty but for reasons of Christian conscience. They respect the flag but regard the flag salute as an act of worship.*

After some 1,200 Witnesses had been imprisoned in Germany early in the Nazi era for refusal to give the Nazi salute and to violate their Christian neutrality, thousands were physically abused in the United States because they refrained from saluting the American flag. During the week of November 4, 1935, a number of schoolchildren in Canonsburg, Pennsylvania, were taken to the school boiler room and whipped for refusal to salute. Grace

Thousands of Jehovah's Witnesses (including John Booth, shown here) were arrested when they distributed Bible literature

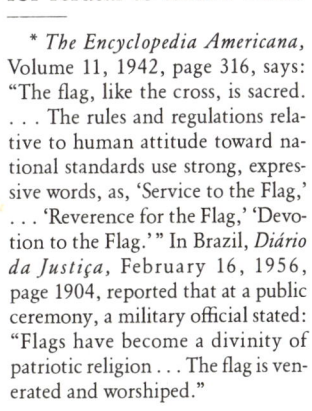

---

* *The Encyclopedia Americana*, Volume 11, 1942, page 316, says: "The flag, like the cross, is sacred. . . . The rules and regulations relative to human attitude toward national standards use strong, expressive words, as, 'Service to the Flag,' . . . 'Reverence for the Flag,' 'Devotion to the Flag.'" In Brazil, *Diário da Justiça*, February 16, 1956, page 1904, reported that at a public ceremony, a military official stated: "Flags have become a divinity of patriotic religion . . . The flag is venerated and worshiped."

Following a Supreme Court decision against the Witnesses in 1940, mob violence swept through the United States, meetings were disrupted, Witnesses were beaten, and property was destroyed

Estep, a teacher, was discharged from her position in that school for the same reason. On November 6, William and Lillian Gobitas refused to salute the flag and were expelled from school at Minersville, Pennsylvania. Their father sued to have his children readmitted. Both the federal district court and the circuit court of appeals decided the case in favor of Jehovah's Witnesses. However, in 1940, with the nation on the brink of war, the U.S. Supreme Court, in *Minersville School District v. Gobitis*, by an 8-to-1 decision, upheld compulsory flag saluting in public schools. This led to a nationwide outburst of violence against Jehovah's Witnesses.

There were so many violent attacks upon Jehovah's Witnesses that Mrs. Eleanor Roosevelt (wife of President F. D. Roosevelt) pleaded with the public to desist. On June 16, 1940, the U.S. solicitor general, Francis Biddle, in a coast-to-coast radio broadcast, made specific reference to the atrocities committed against the Witnesses and said these would not be tolerated. But this did not stem the tide.

Under every conceivable circumstance—on the streets, at places of employment, when Witnesses called at homes in their ministry—flags were thrust in front of them, with the demand that they salute—or else! At the end of 1940, the *Yearbook of Jehovah's Witnesses* reported: "The Hierarchy and the American Legion, through such mobs that have taken the law into their own hands, violently worked havoc indescribable. Jehovah's witnesses have been assaulted, beaten, kidnapped, driven out of towns, counties and states, tarred and feathered, forced to drink castor oil, tied together and chased like dumb beasts through the streets, castrated and maimed, taunted and insulted by demonized crowds, jailed by the hundreds without charge and held incommunicado and denied the privilege of conferring with relatives, friends or lawyers. Many other hundreds have been jailed and held in so-called 'protective custody'; some have been shot in the nighttime; some threatened with hanging and beaten into unconsciousness. Numerous varieties of mob violence have occurred. Many have had their clothes torn from them, their Bibles and other literature seized and publicly burned; their automobiles, trailers, homes and assembly places wrecked and fired... In numerous instances where trials have been held in mob-ruled communities, lawyers as well as witnesses have been mobbed and beaten while attending court. In almost every case where there has been mob violence the public officials have stood idly by and refused to give protection, and in scores of instances the officers of the law have participated in the mobs and sometimes actually led the mobs." From 1940 to 1944, more than 2,500 violent mobs assaulted Jehovah's Witnesses in the United States.

Mobs assaulted Jehovah's Witnesses in the United States

Because of the wholesale expulsion of the children of Jehovah's Witnesses from school, for a time during the late 1930's and early 1940's it was necessary for them to operate their own schools in the United States and Canada in order to provide education for their children. These were called Kingdom Schools.

Other countries too have harshly persecuted the Witnesses because they refrain from saluting or kissing national emblems. In 1959, children of Jehovah's Witnesses in Costa Rica who would not engage in what the law describes as 'worship of the National Symbols' were barred from the schools. Similar treatment was meted out to Witness children in Paraguay in 1984. The Supreme Court in the Philippines ruled in 1959 that, despite religious objections, children of Jehovah's Witnesses could be compelled to salute the flag. Nevertheless, school authorities there, in most cases, cooperated with the Witnesses so that their children could attend school without violating their consciences. In 1963, officials in Liberia, West Africa, charged the Witnesses with disloyalty to the State; they forcibly disrupted a Witness assembly at Gbarnga and demanded that everyone present—both Liberians and foreigners—pledge allegiance to the national flag. In 1976 a report entitled "Jehovah's Witnesses in Cuba" stated that during the previous two years, a thousand parents, both men and women, had been sent to prison because their children would not salute the flag.

Not everyone has agreed with such repressive measures against people who, for reasons of conscience, respectfully refrain from participating in patriotic ceremonies. *The Open Forum,* published by the Southern California Branch of the American Civil Liberties Union, stated in 1941: "It is high time that we came to our senses regarding this matter of flag-saluting. Jehovah's Witnesses are not disloyal Americans. . . . They are not given to law-breaking in general, but lead decent, orderly lives, contributing their share to the common good." In 1976 a newspaper columnist in Argentina, in the Buenos Aires *Herald,* frankly observed that Witness "beliefs are only offensive to those who think patriotism is chiefly a matter of flag-waving and anthem-singing, not a matter of the heart." He added: "Hitler and Stalin found [the Witnesses] indigestible, and treated them abominably. Lots of other dictators yearning for conformity have tried to suppress them. And failed."

It is well-known that some religious groups have supported armed violence against governments that they disapproved. But nowhere on earth have Jehovah's Witnesses ever engaged in political subversion. It is not because of disloyalty—because of supporting some other human government—that they refuse to salute a national emblem. They take the same stand in every country where they are found. Their attitude is not one of disrespect. They do not whistle or shout to disrupt patriotic ceremonies; they do not spit on the flag, trample on it, or burn it. They are not antigovernment. Their position is based on what Jesus Christ himself said, as recorded at Matthew 4:10: "It is Jehovah your God you must worship, and it is to him alone you must render sacred service."

In many places it was necessary to establish Kingdom Schools because Witness children had been expelled from the public schools

The stand taken by Jehovah's Witnesses is like that taken by the early Christians in the days of the Roman Empire. Regarding those early Christians, the book *Essentials of Bible History* states: "The act of emperor worship consisted in sprinkling a few grains of incense or a few drops of wine on an altar which stood before an image of the emperor. Perhaps at our long remove from the situation we see in the act nothing different from . . . lifting the hand in salute to the flag or to some distinguished ruler of state, an expression of courtesy, respect, and patriotism. Possibly a good many people in the first century felt just that way about it but not so the Christians. They viewed the whole matter as one of religious worship, acknowledging the emperor as a deity and therefore being disloyal to God and Christ, and they refused to do it."—Elmer W. K. Mould, 1951, p. 563.

Hated for Being "No Part of the World"

Because Jesus said that his disciples would be "no part of the world," Jehovah's Witnesses do not share in its political affairs. (John 17:16; 6:15) In this too, they are like the early Christians, concerning whom historians say:

"Early Christianity was little understood and was regarded with little favor by those who ruled the pagan world. . . . Christians refused to share certain duties of Roman citizens. . . . They would not hold political office." (*On the Road to Civilization—A World History,* A. K. Heckel and J. G. Sigman, 1937, pp. 237-8) "They refused to take any active part in the civil administration or the military defence of the empire. . . . It was impossible that the Christians, without renouncing a more sacred duty, could assume the character of soldiers, of magistrates, or of princes."—*History of Christianity,* Edward Gibbon, 1891, pp. 162-3.

This position is not viewed with favor by the world, especially not in lands where rulers require that everyone participate in certain activities as an evidence of support of the political system. The result is as Jesus stated: "If you were part of the world, the world would be fond of what is its own. Now because you are no part of the world, but I have chosen you out of the world, on this account the world hates you."—John 15:19.

In some lands, voting in political elections is viewed as an obligation. Failure to vote is punished by fine, imprisonment, or worse. But Jehovah's Witnesses support the Messianic Kingdom of God, which, as Jesus said, "is no part of this world." Therefore, they do not participate in the political affairs of the nations of this world. (John 18:36) The decision is a personal

---

"They Are Not Anti-Country"

"They are not anti-country; they are just pro-Jehovah." "They don't burn draft cards, rise up in rebellion . . . or engage in any form of sedition." "Honesty and integrity of Witnesses is a constant. Whatever one may think about the Witnesses—and a lot of people think a lot of negative things—they live exemplary lives."
—"*Telegram,*" Toronto, Canada, July 1970.

> ### Who Is in Charge?
>
> *Jehovah's Witnesses know that their responsibility to preach does not depend on the operation of the Watch Tower Society or any other legal corporation. "Let the Watch Tower Society be forbidden and its Branch offices in various lands be forcibly closed down by state interference! That does not nullify or lift the divine charge from the men and women who are consecrated to do God's will and upon whom He has put his spirit. 'Preach!' is written down plain in his Word. This order takes precedence over that of any men." ("The Watchtower," December 15, 1949) Recognizing that their orders come from Jehovah God and Jesus Christ, they persevere in proclaiming the Kingdom message regardless of the opposition they encounter.*

one; they do not force their views on others. Where religious toleration is lacking, government officials have seized on the Witnesses' nonparticipation as an excuse for vicious persecution. During the Nazi era, for example, this was done in lands under their control. It has also been done in Cuba. However, officials in many lands have been more tolerant.

Yet, in some places those in power have demanded that everyone indicate support of the controlling political party by shouting certain slogans. Because they could not conscientiously do that, thousands of Jehovah's Witnesses in eastern parts of Africa were beaten, deprived of their livelihood, and driven from their homes during the 1970's and 1980's. But Jehovah's Witnesses in all lands, though they are industrious and law-abiding, are Christian neutrals as to political issues.

In Malawi, there is only one political party, and possession of a party card indicates membership. Although the Witnesses are exemplary in paying their taxes, in harmony with their religious beliefs, they decline to buy political party cards. To do so would be a denial of their faith in God's Kingdom. Because of this, late in 1967, with the encouragement of government officials, gangs of youths throughout Malawi launched an all-out attack on Jehovah's Witnesses that was unprecedented in its obscenity and sadistic cruelty. Over a thousand devout Christian women were raped. Some were stripped naked before large mobs, beaten with sticks and fists, and then sexually assaulted by one person after another. Nails were driven through the feet of the men and bicycle spokes through their legs, and then they were ordered to run. Throughout the country their homes, furniture, clothing, and food supplies were destroyed.

Again, in 1972, there was a renewed outbreak of such brutality following the annual convention of the Malawi Congress Party. At that convention it was officially resolved to deprive Jehovah's Witnesses of all secular employment and drive them away from their homes. Even appeals of employers to keep these trusted workers availed nothing. Homes, crops, and domestic animals were confiscated or destroyed. Witnesses were prevented from drawing water from the village well. Large numbers were beaten, raped, maimed, or murdered. All the while, they were mocked and ridiculed for their faith. Upwards of 34,000 finally fled the country to avoid being killed.

But it was not over yet. First from one country and then from another, they were forced back over the border into the hands of their persecutors, only to experience more brutality. Yet, despite it all, they did not compromise, and they did not abandon their faith in Jehovah God. They proved to be like those faithful servants of God concerning whom the Bible says: "Others received their trial by mockings and scourgings, indeed, more than that, by bonds and prisons. They were stoned, they were tried, they were sawn asunder, they died by slaughter with the sword, they went about in sheepskins, in goatskins, while they were in want, in tribulation, under ill-treatment; and the world was not worthy of them."—Heb. 11:36-38.

Persecuted in All Nations

Is it only relatively few nations of the world that have betrayed their pretensions of freedom by such religious persecution? By no means! Jesus Christ warned his followers: "You will be objects of hatred *by all the nations* on account of my name."—Matt. 24:9.

During the last days of this system of things, since 1914, that hatred has become especially intense. Canada and the United States led off the attack by imposing bans on Bible literature during the first world war, and they were soon joined by India and Nyasaland (now called Malawi). During the 1920's, arbitrary restrictions were imposed on the Bible Students in Greece, Hungary, Italy, Romania, and Spain. In some of these places, distribution of Bible literature was forbidden; at times, even private meetings were prohibited. More countries joined in the assault during the 1930's, when bans (some on Jehovah's Witnesses, others on their literature) were imposed in Albania, Austria, Bulgaria, Estonia, Latvia, Lithuania, Poland, certain cantons of Switzerland, what was then Yugoslavia, the Gold Coast (now Ghana), French territories in Africa, Trinidad, and Fiji.

During World War II, there were bans on Jehovah's Witnesses, their public ministry, and their Bible literature in many parts of the world. This was true not only in Germany, Italy, and Japan—all of which were under dictatorial rule—but also in the many lands that came directly or indirectly under their control before or during that war. Included among these were Albania, Austria, Belgium, Czechoslovakia, Korea, the Netherlands, Netherlands East Indies (now Indonesia), and Norway. During those war years, Argentina, Brazil, Finland, France, and Hungary all issued official decrees against Jehovah's Witnesses or their activity.

Britain did not directly outlaw the activity of Jehovah's Witnesses during the war, but it deported the Watch Tower Society's American-born branch overseer and endeavored to strangle the activity of the Witnesses by a wartime embargo on shipments of their Bible literature. Throughout the British Empire and the British Commonwealth of Nations, outright bans on Jehovah's Witnesses or prohibitions of their literature were imposed. Australia, the Bahamas, Basutoland (now Lesotho), Bechuanaland (now Botswana), British Guiana (now Guyana), Burma (now Myanmar), Canada, Ceylon (now Sri Lanka), Cyprus, Dominica, Fiji, the Gold Coast (now Ghana), India, Jamaica, the Leeward Islands (B.W.I.), New Zealand, Nigeria, Northern Rhodesia (now Zambia), Nyasaland (now Malawi), Singapore, South Africa, Southern Rhodesia (now Zimbabwe), and Swaziland all took such action to express hostility toward Jehovah's servants.

After the end of the war, there was a letup in persecution from some quarters but an increase from others. During the next 45 years, in addition to the fact that Jehovah's Witnesses were refused legal recognition in many lands, outright bans were imposed on them or their activities in 23 lands in Africa, 9 in Asia, 8 in Europe, 3 in Latin America, and 4 in certain island nations. As of 1992, Jehovah's Witnesses were still under restrictions in 24 lands.

This does not mean that all government officials personally oppose the work of Jehovah's Witnesses. Many officials uphold religious freedom and recognize that the Witnesses are a valuable asset to the community. Such men do not agree with those who agitate for official action against the Witnesses. For example, before the Ivory Coast (now Côte d'Ivoire) became an independent nation, when a Catholic priest and a Methodist minister tried to influence an official to get Jehovah's Witnesses out of the country, they found that they were talking to officials who were not willing to become pawns of the clergy. When an official tried to shape the law of Namibia, in 1990, to discriminate against refugees who were known to be Jehovah's Witnesses, the Constituent Assembly did not allow it. And in many countries where Jehovah's Witnesses were at one time under ban, they now enjoy legal recognition.

In every part of the earth, Jehovah's Witnesses are persecuted

Yet, in various ways, in every part of the earth, Jehovah's Witnesses are persecuted. (2 Tim. 3:12) In some places, that persecution may come mainly from abusive householders, opposed relatives, or workmates or classmates who manifest no fear of God. Regardless of who the persecutors are or how they try to justify what they are doing, however, Jehovah's Witnesses understand what is really behind the persecution of true Christians.

The Issue

Watch Tower publications have long pointed out that in symbolic language the first book of the Bible foretold the enmity, or hatred, of Satan the Devil and those under his control toward Jehovah's own heavenly organization and its earthly representatives. (Gen. 3:15; John 8:38, 44; Rev. 12:9, 17) Especially since 1925, *The Watch Tower* has shown from the Scriptures that there are just two principal organizations—Jehovah's and Satan's. And, as 1 John 5:19 states, "the whole world"—that is, all mankind outside of Jehovah's organization—"is lying in the power of the wicked one." That is why all true Christians experience persecution.—John 15:20.

But why does God permit it? Is any good being accomplished? Jesus Christ explained that before he as heavenly King would crush Satan and his wicked organization, there would be a separating of people of all nations, as a Middle Eastern shepherd separates sheep from goats. People would be given opportunity to hear about the Kingdom of God and to take their stand on its side. When the proclaimers of that Kingdom are persecuted, the question is thrust even more prominently to the fore: Will those who hear about it do good to the "brothers" of Christ and their associates and thus show love for Christ himself? Or will they join with those who heap abuse on these representatives of God's Kingdom—or perhaps remain silent while others do so? (Matt. 25:31-46; 10:40; 24: 14) Some in Malawi saw clearly who were serving the true God and so threw in their lot with the persecuted Witnesses. Not a few prisoners as well as some guards in German concentration camps did the same.

Even though lying accusations are made against them and they are physically abused, even taunted for their faith in God, Jehovah's Witnesses do not feel forsaken by God. They know that Jesus Christ experienced the same things. (Matt. 27:43) They also know that by his loyalty to Jehovah, Jesus proved the Devil a liar and contributed to the sanctification of his Father's name. It is the desire of every Witness of Jehovah to do the same.—Matt. 6:9.

The issue is not whether they can outlive torture and escape death. Jesus Christ foretold that some of his followers would be killed. (Matt. 24:9) He himself was killed. But he never compromised with God's chief Adversary, Satan the Devil, "the ruler of the world." Jesus conquered the world. (John 14:30; 16:33) The issue, then, is whether worshipers of the true God will remain faithful to him in spite of whatever hardship they may undergo. Jehovah's modern-day Witnesses have given abundant evidence that they are of the same mind as the apostle Paul, who wrote: "Both if we live, we live to Jehovah, and if we die, we die to Jehovah. Therefore both if we live and if we die, we belong to Jehovah."—Rom. 14:8.

Like the Early Christians

• *"Jehovah's Witnesses have a religion they take far more seriously than the great majority of people. Their principles remind us of the early Christians who were so unpopular and who were persecuted so brutally by the Romans."* —*"Akron Beacon Journal,"* Akron, Ohio, September 4, 1951.

• *"They [the early Christians] lived quiet, moral, indeed model lives. . . . In every respect except that single matter of incense-burning they were exemplary citizens." "While sacrifice to the Genius of the emperor remained the test of patriotism, could the state authorities afford to wink at the contumacy of these unpatriotic Christians? The trouble in which the Christians consequently found themselves was not wholly unlike the trouble in which, during the war years, that aggressive sect known as Jehovah's Witnesses found itself in the United States over the matter of saluting the national flag."*—*"20 Centuries of Christianity,"* by Paul Hutchinson and Winfred Garrison, 1959, p. 31.

• *"Perhaps the most notable thing about the Witnesses is their insistence upon their primary allegiance to God, before any other power in the world."* —*"These Also Believe,"* by Dr. C. S. Braden, 1949, p. 380.

CHAPTER 30

'DEFENDING AND LEGALLY ESTABLISHING THE GOOD NEWS'

THE intense persecution brought upon Jehovah's Witnesses has resulted in their being haled before police officials, judges, and rulers earth wide. Legal cases involving the Witnesses have numbered many thousands, and hundreds of these have been appealed to higher courts. This has had a profound effect on the law itself and has often fortified legal guarantees of basic freedoms for people in general. But this has not been the main objective of Jehovah's Witnesses.

Their principal desire is to proclaim the good news of the Kingdom of God. Legal action that they take is not because they are social agitators or legal reformers. Their objective is to 'defend and legally establish the good news,' even as was true of the apostle Paul. (Phil. 1:7) Hearings before government officials, whether at the request of the Witnesses or because they are under arrest for their Christian activity, are also viewed as opportunities to give a witness. Jesus Christ told his followers: "You will be haled before governors and kings for my sake, for a witness to them and the nations."—Matt. 10:18.

An International Flood of Legal Action

Long before the first world war, the clergy, by putting pressure on local officials, endeavored to hinder distribution of literature by the Bible Students in their areas. Following World War I, however, opposition intensified. In one country after another, legal hurdles of every imaginable sort were put before those who endeavored to obey Christ's prophetic command to preach the good news of God's Kingdom for the purpose of a witness.—Matt. 24:14.

Stirred by evidence of the fulfillment of Bible prophecy, the Bible Students left their convention at Cedar Point, Ohio, in 1922, determined to let the world know that the Gentile Times had expired and that the Lord had taken his great power and was ruling from the heavens as King. "Advertise, advertise, advertise, the King and his kingdom" was their slogan. In that same year, the clergy in Germany agitated for the police to arrest

'Defending and Legally Establishing the Good News'

some of the Bible Students when they were distributing Bible literature. This was no isolated incident. By 1926, there were 897 of such cases pending in the German courts. So much litigation was involved that in 1926 it became necessary for the Watch Tower Society to establish a legal department at its branch office in Magdeburg. During 1928, in Germany alone there were 1,660 legal proceedings initiated against the Bible Students, and the pressure continued to mount year by year. The clergy were determined to put an end to the work of the Bible Students, and they rejoiced when any court decision indicated that they were having some measure of success.

In the United States, arrests of Bible Students for house-to-house preaching took place in 1928, in South Amboy, New Jersey. Within a decade the annual number of arrests in connection with their ministry in the United States was in excess of 500. During 1936 the number rose sharply —to 1,149. To provide needed counsel, it became necessary to have a legal department at the Society's headquarters also.

Intensive preaching activity in Romania likewise met with severe resistance from the authorities then in power. Jehovah's Witnesses who distributed Bible literature were often arrested and viciously beaten. From 1933 to 1939, the Witnesses there were confronted with 530 lawsuits. The law of the land, however, contained guarantees of freedom, so appeals to the Romanian High Court brought many favorable decisions. When the

In 138 cases involving Jehovah's Witnesses, appeals and petitions have been presented to the U.S. Supreme Court. For 111 of these, from 1939 to 1963, Hayden Covington (shown here) served as attorney

police began to realize this, they would confiscate literature and abuse the Witnesses but try to avoid court action. After the Society finally was allowed to register as a corporation in Romania, opponents endeavored to frustrate the purpose of this legal registration by obtaining a court order prohibiting distribution of Watch Tower literature. This ruling was overturned by a higher court, but then the clergy induced the minister of cults to take action to counteract that decision.

In Italy and Hungary, as in Romania, Bible literature used by the Witnesses was confiscated by the police under the governments that were then ruling. The same was done in Japan, Korea, and the Gold Coast (now called Ghana). Jehovah's Witnesses who had come from abroad were ordered to leave France. For many years none of Jehovah's Witnesses were granted permission to enter the Soviet Union to preach about God's Kingdom.

As the fever of nationalism swept across the world from 1933 on into the 1940's, government bans were placed on Jehovah's Witnesses in one land after another. Thousands of the Witnesses were brought before the courts during this period because of their conscientious refusal to salute flags and their insistence on Christian neutrality. In 1950 it was reported that during the preceding 15 years, Jehovah's Witnesses in the United States alone had suffered more than 10,000 arrests.

When upwards of 400 Witnesses were brought before the courts of Greece within a short period in 1946, this was not the beginning of such action there. It had been going on for years. In addition to imprisonment, heavy fines were imposed, draining the brothers financially. But as they viewed their situation, they said: "The Lord opened the way for the witness work to reach the officials of Greece, who heard about the establishment of the kingdom of righteousness; also the judges in the courts had the same opportunity." Jehovah's Witnesses clearly viewed the matter in the way that Jesus said that his followers should.—Luke 21:12, 13.

A Battle With Seemingly Impossible Odds

During the 1940's and 1950's, the Canadian province of Quebec became a veritable battleground. Arrests for preaching the good news had been taking place there since 1924. By the winter of 1931, some individual Witnesses were being picked up by the police every day, sometimes twice a day. Legal expenses for the Witnesses in Canada became heavy. Then, early in 1947 the total number of cases involving the Witnesses that were pending in the courts in Quebec Province soared to 1,300; yet, there was only a small band of Jehovah's Witnesses there.

This was an era when the Roman Catholic Church was a powerful influence with which every politician and every judge in the province had to reckon. The clergy were generally held in high esteem in Quebec, and oth-

Government bans were placed on Jehovah's Witnesses in one land after another ers were quick to obey the dictates of the local priest. As the book *State and Salvation* (1989) described the situation: "The cardinal of Quebec had a throne on the floor of the Legislative Assembly immediately beside the one reserved for the lieutenant-governor. One way or another much of Quebec was under direct church control... The mission of the church was, in fact, to make Quebec's political life conform to the Roman Catholic concept in which truth is Catholicism, error is anything non-Catholic, and liberty is the freedom to speak and live the Roman Catholic truth."

Humanly speaking, the odds against the Witnesses not only in Quebec but worldwide seemed impossible.

Charges of Every Conceivable Type

Opponents of the Witnesses combed the lawbooks to find any possible pretext for putting an end to their activity. Frequently they charged them with peddling without a license, thus claiming that the work was commercial. Contradicting this, elsewhere some of the pioneers were charged with vagrancy because it was contended that they were not gainfully employed.

For decades, officials in some cantons of Switzerland persistently endeavored to classify the distribution of Bible literature by Jehovah's Witnesses as commercial peddling. The state attorney in the French-speaking Canton of Vaud, in particular, was determined not to let stand any decisions from the lower courts that were favorable to the Witnesses.

In one place after another, Jehovah's Witnesses were told that they had to have permits to distribute their literature or to hold their Bible meetings. But was a permit really required? The Witnesses answered "No!" On what basis?

They explained: 'Jehovah God commands his witnesses to preach the gospel of his kingdom, and God's commandments are supreme and must be obeyed by his witnesses. No earthly law-making or law-enforcing body can properly interfere with Jehovah's law. Since no governing power of the world can properly *prohibit* the preaching of the gospel, no such worldly authority or power can grant a *permit* to preach the gospel. Worldly powers

Maurice Duplessis, premier of Quebec, publicly kneeling before Cardinal Villeneuve in the late 1930's and putting a ring on his finger as evidence of the close ties between Church and State. In Quebec, persecution of Jehovah's Witnesses was especially intense

have no authority in the matter one way or the other. To ask humans for permission to do something that God has commanded would be an insult to God.'

The charges laid against the Witnesses often gave strong evidence of religious animosity. Thus, when the booklets *Face the Facts* and *Cure* were circulated, the Society's branch overseer in the Netherlands was summoned to appear in court in Haarlem, in 1939, to answer the charge of insulting a group of the Dutch populace. The prosecutor argued, for example, that Watch Tower literature stated that the Roman Catholic hierarchy fraudulently extracted money from the people by claiming to free the dead from a place where they are *not*—from purgatory, the existence of which, the literature said, the Church could not prove.

On the stand the hierarchy's star witness, "Father" Henri de Greeve, wailed: "My biggest grievance is that an outsider could get the impression that we priests are just a bunch of villains and swindlers." When called to testify, the Society's branch overseer opened the Catholic Bible and showed the court that what the booklet said about Catholic teachings was in accord with their own Bible. When the Society's attorney then asked de Greeve if he could prove the doctrines of hellfire and purgatory, he answered: "I cannot prove it; I only believe it." The judge quickly realized that this is exactly what the booklet had claimed. The case was dismissed, and the priest rushed from the courthouse in a rage!

Agitated by increased activity of Jehovah's Witnesses in the eastern part of what was then Czechoslovakia, the clergy there charged the Witnesses with espionage. The situation was like that experienced by the apostle Paul when the first-century Jewish clergy accused him of sedition. (Acts 24:5) Hundreds of cases went to court in 1933-34, until the government became convinced that there was no valid basis for the accusation. In the Canadian province of Quebec, in the 1930's and the 1940's, Witnesses were also being brought to trial on the charge of seditious conspiracy. The clergy themselves—both Catholic and Protestant, but especially Roman Catholic—even went into court as witnesses against them. What had Jehovah's Witnesses done? The clergy argued that they had endangered national unity by publishing things that could cause disaffection toward the Roman Catholic Church. However, the Witnesses replied that, in reality, they had distributed literature that brought humble people comfort from God's Word but that this infuriated the clergy because unscriptural teachings and practices were being exposed.

What made it possible for Jehovah's Witnesses to keep going in the face of such persistent opposition? It was their faith in God and his inspired Word, their unselfish devotion to Jehovah and his Kingdom, and the strength that results from the operation of God's spirit. As the Scrip-

The case was dismissed, and the priest rushed from the courthouse in a rage!

tures state, "the power beyond what is normal [is] God's and not that out of ourselves."—2 Cor. 4:7.

Jehovah's Witnesses Take the Offensive in the Legal Arena

For decades before World War I, the Bible Students had engaged in extensive free distribution of Bible literature on streets near the churches and from house to house. But then many towns and cities in the United States passed ordinances that greatly hindered such "volunteer work." What could be done?

The Watch Tower of December 15, 1919, explained: "Believing it to be our duty to put forth every possible effort to witness to the Lord's kingdom and not to slack our hand because we see the door closing, and in view of the fact that there was such systematic effort against the volunteer work, arrangements were made for the use of a magazine, . . . THE GOLDEN AGE."*

As the intensity of house-to-house witnessing increased, however, so did attempts to apply laws to abridge or prohibit it. Not all lands have legal provisions that make it possible to secure freedoms for minorities in the face of official opposition. But Jehovah's Witnesses knew that the U.S. Constitution guaranteed freedom of religion, freedom of speech, and freedom of the press. So, when judges construed local ordinances in such a way as to hinder the preaching of God's Word, the Witnesses appealed their cases to the higher courts.#

In reviewing what took place, Hayden C. Covington, who had a prominent role in legal matters for the Watch Tower Society, later explained: "Had the thousands of convictions entered by the magistrates, police courts and other lower courts not been appealed, a mountain of precedent would have piled up as a giant obstacle in the field of worship. By appealing we have prevented the erection of such obstacle. Our way of worship has been written into the law of the land of the United States and other countries because of our persistence in appealing from adverse decisions." In the United States, scores of cases went all the way to the Supreme Court.

W. K. Jackson, who was on the Society's headquarters legal staff, served for ten years as a member of the Governing Body of Jehovah's Witnesses

---

* The first issue was dated October 1, 1919. Distribution of that magazine and its successors, *Consolation* and *Awake!*, has been extraordinary. As of 1992, the regular circulation of *Awake!* was 13,110,000 in 67 languages.

As a general policy, when taken to court because of witnessing, Jehovah's Witnesses appealed their cases instead of paying fines. If a case was lost on appeal, then, instead of paying the fine, they went to jail, if allowed to do so by law. The persistent refusal of the Witnesses to pay fines helped to discourage some officials from continuing to interfere with their witnessing activity. While this policy may still be followed under some circumstances, *The Watchtower* of April 1, 1975, showed that in many cases a fine could properly be viewed as a judicial penalty, so paying it would not be an admission of guilt, just as going to jail would not prove one's guilt.

Strengthening the Guarantees of Freedom

One of the first cases involving the ministry of Jehovah's Witnesses to reach the Supreme Court of the United States originated in Georgia and was argued before the Court on February 4, 1938. Alma Lovell had been convicted in the recorder's court of Griffin, Georgia, of violating an ordinance that prohibited the distribution of literature of any kind without a permit from the city manager. Among other things, Sister Lovell had offered people the magazine *The Golden Age*. On March 28, 1938, the Supreme Court of the United States ruled that the ordinance was invalid because it subjected freedom of the press to license and censorship.*

The following year J. F. Rutherford, as attorney for the petitioner, presented arguments to the Supreme Court in the case of *Clara Schneider v. State of New Jersey*.# This was followed, in 1940, by *Cantwell v. State of Connecticut*,△ for which J. F. Rutherford drafted the legal brief and Hayden Covington presented oral argument before the Court. The positive outcome of these cases buttressed the constitutional guarantees of freedom of religion, freedom of speech, and freedom of the press. But there were setbacks.

Severe Blows at the Hands of the Courts

The flag-salute issue as it related to the schoolchildren of Jehovah's Witnesses first reached the American courts in 1935 in the case of *Carlton*

---

* *Lovell v. City of Griffin*, 303 U.S. 444 (1938).
# *Schneider v. State of New Jersey* (*Town of Irvington*), 308 U.S. 147 (1939).
△ 310 U.S. 296 (1940).

A Witness to the U.S. Supreme Court

When appearing before the Supreme Court of the United States as legal counsel in the "Gobitis" case, Joseph F. Rutherford, a member of the New York Bar and the president of the Watch Tower Society, clearly focused attention on the importance of submitting to the sovereignty of Jehovah God. He said:

"Jehovah's witnesses are those who bear testimony to the name of Almighty God, whose name alone is JEHOVAH. . . .

"I call attention to the fact that Jehovah God, more than six thousand years ago, promised to establish through the Messiah a government of righteousness. He will keep that promise in due season. The present-day facts in the light of prophecy indicate that it is near. . . .

"God, Jehovah, is the only source of life. No one else can give life. The State of Pennsylvania cannot give life. The American Government cannot. God made this law [forbidding the worship of images], as Paul puts it, to safeguard His people from idolatry. That is a small thing, you say. So was the act of Adam in eating of the forbidden fruit. It was not the apple that Adam ate, but it was his act of disobeying God. The question is whether man will obey God or obey some human institution. . . .

"I remind this Court (it is hardly necessary that I do so) that in the case of 'Church v. United States' this Court held that America is a Christian nation; and that means that America must be obedient to the Divine law. It also means that this Court takes judicial notice of the fact that the law of God is supreme. And if a man conscientiously believes that God's law is supreme and conscientiously deports himself accordingly, no human authority can control or interfere with his conscience. . . .

"I may be permitted to call attention to this: that at the opening of every session of this Court the crier announces these words: 'God save the United States and this honorable Court.' And now I say, God save this honorable Court from committing an error that will lead this people of the United States into a totalitarian class and destroy all the liberties guaranteed by the Constitution. This is a matter that is sacred to every American who loves God and His Word."

B. *Nicholls v. Mayor and School Committee of Lynn* (*Massachusetts*).* The case was referred to the Massachusetts Supreme Judicial Court. The court ruled, in 1937, that regardless of what Carleton Nichols, Jr., and his parents said they believed, no allowance need be made for religious belief because, it said, "the flag salute and pledge of allegiance here in question do not in any just sense relate to religion. . . . They do not concern the views of any one as to his Creator. They do not touch upon his relations with his Maker." When the issue of compulsory flag salute was appealed to the U.S. Supreme Court in the case of *Leoles v. Landers*# in 1937, and again in *Hering v. State Board of Education*△ in 1938, the Court dismissed these cases because there was, in their opinion, no important federal question to consider. In 1939 the Court again dismissed an appeal involving the same issue, in the case of *Gabrielli v. Knickerbocker*.⊠ That same day, without hearing oral argument, they affirmed the adverse decision of the lower court in the case of *Johnson v. Town of Deerfield*.□

Finally, in 1940, a full hearing was given by the Court to the case styled *Minersville School District v. Gobitis*.+ An array of celebrated lawyers filed briefs in the case on both sides. J. F. Rutherford presented oral argument on behalf of Walter Gobitas and his children. A member of the law department of Harvard University represented the American Bar Association and the Civil Liberties Union in arguing against compulsory flag saluting. However, their arguments were rejected, and with only one dissenting vote, the Supreme Court, on June 3, ruled that children who would not salute the flag could be expelled from the public schools.

During the next three years, the Supreme Court ruled against Jehovah's Witnesses in 19 cases. Most significant was the adverse decision, in 1942, in *Jones v. City of Opelika*.◊ Rosco Jones had been convicted of engaging in distribution of literature on the streets of Opelika, Alabama, without payment of a license tax. The Supreme Court upheld the conviction and said that governments have the right to charge reasonable fees for canvassing and that such laws could not be challenged even if local authorities might arbitrarily revoke the license. This was a severe blow, because now any community, goaded by clergymen or anyone else who opposed

Rosco Jones, whose case involving the ministry of Jehovah's Witnesses went twice to the U.S. Supreme Court

---

* 297 Mass. 65 (1935). The case involved an eight-year-old schoolboy, whose name is correctly spelled Carleton Nichols.
  # 302 U.S. 656 (1937) (from Georgia).
  △ 303 U.S. 624 (1938) (from New Jersey).
  ⊠ 306 U.S. 621 (1939) (from California).
  □ 306 U.S. 621 (1939) (from Massachusetts).
  + 310 U.S. 586 (1940). Walter Gobitas (correct spelling), the father, along with his children William and Lillian, had gone to court to restrain the school board from refusing to permit the two children to attend the Minersville public school because the children would not salute the national flag. The federal district court and the circuit court of appeals both decided in favor of Jehovah's Witnesses. Then the school board appealed the case to the Supreme Court.
  ◊ 316 U.S. 584 (1942).

Justices of the U.S. Supreme Court who, by a vote of 6 to 3 in the "Barnette" case, rejected compulsory flag saluting in favor of freedom of worship. This reversed the Court's own earlier decision in the "Gobitis" case

Children involved in the cases

Marie and Gathie Barnette

Lillian and William Gobitas

the Witnesses, could legally exclude them and thus, the opposers might reason, stop the preaching activity of Jehovah's Witnesses. But a strange thing happened.

The Tide Turns

In *Jones v. Opelika,* the very decision that was such a blow to the public ministry of Jehovah's Witnesses, three of the justices stated that not only did they disagree with the Court majority on the case at hand but they also felt that they had helped to lay the foundation for it in the *Gobitis* case. "Since we joined in the opinion in the Gobitis case," they added, "we think this is an appropriate occasion to state that we now believe that it was also wrongly decided." Jehovah's Witnesses took that as a cue to present the issues anew to the Court.

A Motion for Rehearing was filed in the case of *Jones v. Opelika*. In that motion, strong legal arguments were presented. It also firmly declared: "This Court should reckon with the paramount fact, that it is judicially dealing with servants of Almighty God." Biblical precedents showing the implications of this were reviewed. Attention was directed to the advice given by the law teacher Gamaliel to the first-century Jewish supreme court, namely: "Do not meddle with these men, but let them alone; . . . otherwise, you may perhaps be found fighters actually against God." —Acts 5:34-39.

At last, on May 3, 1943, in the landmark case *Murdock v. Commonwealth of Pennsylvania*,* the Supreme Court reversed its earlier decision in *Jones v. Opelika*. It declared that any license tax as a precondition to exercising one's freedom of religion by distribution of religious literature is unconstitutional. This case reopened the doors of the United States to Jehovah's Witnesses and has been appealed to as authority in hundreds of cases since then. May 3, 1943, was truly a memorable day for Jehovah's Witnesses as regards litigation before the Supreme Court of the United States. On that one day, in 12 out of 13 cases (all of which were consolidated for hearing and opinion into four decisions), the Court ruled in their favor.#

About a month later—on June 14, the nation's annual Flag Day—the Supreme Court again reversed itself, this time as to its decision in the *Gobitis* case, doing so in the case styled *West Virginia State Board of Education v. Barnette*.△ It ruled that "no official, high or petty, can prescribe what shall

---
* 319 U.S. 105 (1943).

During the calendar year 1943, petitions and appeals in 24 legal cases involving Jehovah's Witnesses were submitted to the Supreme Court of the United States.

△ 319 U.S. 624 (1943).

Setting the Stage for a Reversal

When the American Supreme Court ruled, in 1940, in "Minersville School District v. Gobitis," that schoolchildren could be required to salute the flag, eight of the nine justices concurred. Only Justice Stone dissented. But two years later, when registering their dissent in the case of "Jones v. Opelika," three more justices (Black, Douglas, and Murphy) took the occasion to state that they believed that the "Gobitis" case had been wrongly decided because it had put religious freedom in a subordinate position. That meant that four of the nine justices were in favor of reversing the decision in the "Gobitis" case. Two of the other five justices who had downplayed religious freedom retired. Two new ones (Rutledge and Jackson) were on the bench when the next flag-salute case was presented to the Supreme Court. In 1943, in "West Virginia State Board of Education v. Barnette," both of them voted in favor of religious freedom instead of compulsory flag saluting. Thus, by a vote of 6 to 3, the Court reversed the position it had taken in five earlier cases ("Gobitis," "Leoles," "Hering," "Gabrielli," and "Johnson") that had been appealed to this Court.

Interestingly, Justice Frankfurter, in his dissent on the "Barnette" case, said: "As has been true in the past, the Court will from time to time reverse its position. But I believe that never before these Jehovah's Witnesses cases (except for minor deviations subsequently retraced) has this Court overruled decisions so as to restrict the powers of democratic government."

be orthodox in politics, nationalism, religion, or other matters of opinion or force citizens to confess by word or act their faith therein." Much of the reasoning set out in that decision was thereafter adopted in Canada by the Ontario Court of Appeal in *Donald v. Hamilton Board of Education,* which decision the Canadian Supreme Court refused to overrule.

Consistent with its decision in the *Barnette* case, and on the same day, in *Taylor v. State of Mississippi,** the Supreme Court of the United States held that Jehovah's Witnesses could not validly be charged with sedition for explaining their reasons for refraining from saluting the flag and for teaching that all nations are on the losing side because they are in opposition to God's Kingdom. These decisions also set the scene for subsequent favorable rulings in other courts in cases involving Witness parents whose children had refused to salute the flag in school, as well as in issues involving employment and child custody. The tide had definitely turned.#

Opening a New Era of Freedom in Quebec

Jehovah's Witnesses were also pressing the issue of freedom of worship in Canada. From 1944 to 1946, hundreds of Witnesses had been arrested in Quebec when they shared in their public ministry. Canadian law provided for freedom of worship, but mobs disrupted meetings where the Bible was discussed. The police obeyed demands of the Catholic clergy that Jehovah's Witnesses be stopped. Judges of the local recorders' courts heaped abuse on the Witnesses, though no action was taken against the mobsters. What could be done?

The Society arranged for a special assembly in Montreal on November 2 and 3, 1946. Speakers reviewed the position of Jehovah's Witnesses Scripturally and from the standpoint of the law of the land. Then arrangements were announced for a 16-day, coast-to-coast distribution—in English, French, and

---

* 319 U.S. 583 (1943).

From 1919 through 1988, petitions and appeals in a total of 138 cases involving Jehovah's Witnesses were made to the U.S. Supreme Court. One hundred thirty of these cases were submitted by Jehovah's Witnesses; eight, by their adversaries at law. In 67 cases the Supreme Court refused to review the cases because, as the Court viewed the matter at the time, no important federal constitutional or statutory questions were raised. In 47 of the cases that the Court did consider, the decisions were favorable to Jehovah's Witnesses.

> **"An Age-Old Form of Missionary Evangelism"**
>
> In 1943, in the case of "Murdock v. Pennsylvania," the Supreme Court of the United States said, among other things:
>
> "The hand distribution of religious tracts is an age-old form of missionary evangelism—as old as the history of printing presses. It has been a potent force in various religious movements down through the years. This form of evangelism is utilized today on a large scale by various religious sects whose colporteurs carry the Gospel to thousands upon thousands of homes and seek through personal visitations to win adherents to their faith. It is more than preaching; it is more than distribution of religious literature. It is a combination of both. Its purpose is as evangelical as the revival meeting. This form of religious activity occupies the same high estate under the First Amendment as do worship in the churches and preaching from the pulpits. It has the same claim to protection as the more orthodox and conventional exercises of religion. It also has the same claim as the others to the guarantees of freedom of speech and freedom of the press."

Ukrainian—of the tract *Quebec's Burning Hate for God and Christ and Freedom Is the Shame of All Canada*. It reported in detail the mob violence and other atrocities being committed against Jehovah's Witnesses in Quebec. This was followed by a second tract, *Quebec, You Have Failed Your People!*

Arrests in Quebec skyrocketed. To cope with the situation, the Canada branch of the Watch Tower Society set up a legal department with representatives both in Toronto and in Montreal. When news reached the press that Maurice Duplessis, the premier of Quebec, had deliberately ruined the restaurant business of Frank Roncarelli, one of Jehovah's Witnesses, simply because he provided bail for fellow Witnesses, the Canadian public protested loudly. Then, on March 2, 1947, Jehovah's Witnesses launched a nationwide campaign inviting the people of Canada to petition the government for a Bill of Rights. Over 500,000 signatures were obtained—the largest petition that had ever been presented to the Canadian Parliament! This was followed, the next year, by an even larger petition to reinforce the first one.

Meanwhile, the Society selected two test cases for appeal to the Supreme Court of Canada. One of these, *Aimé Boucher v. His Majesty The King*, dealt with the charge of sedition that had repeatedly been laid against the Witnesses.

The *Boucher* case was based on the part that Aimé Boucher, a mild-tempered farmer, had in distributing the tract *Quebec's Burning Hate*. Was it seditious for him to make known the mob violence directed against Witnesses in Quebec, the disregard for law on the part of officials who dealt with them, and evidence that the Catholic bishop and others of the Catholic clergy were instigating it?

In analyzing the tract that was distributed, one of the justices of the Supreme Court said: "The document was headed 'Quebec's Burning Hate for God and Christ and Freedom Is the Shame of All Canada;' it consisted first of an invocation to calmness and reason in appraising the matters to be dealt with in support of the heading; then of general references to vindictive persecution accorded in Quebec to the Witnesses as brethren in Christ; a detailed narrative of specific incidents of persecution; and a concluding appeal to the people of the province, in protest against mob rule and gestapo tactics, that, through the study of God's Word and obedience to its commands, there might be brought about a 'bounteous crop of the good fruits of love for Him and Christ and human freedom.'"

Aimé Boucher, acquitted by Canada's Supreme Court in a decision that rejected charges of sedition against Jehovah's Witnesses

The decision of the Court nullified the conviction of Aimé Boucher, but three of the five justices merely ordered a new trial. Would that result in an impartial decision in the lower courts? Application was made by counsel for Jehovah's Witnesses for the Supreme Court itself to rehear the case. Amazingly, this was granted. While the application was pending, the number of judges on the Court was increased, and one of the original judges changed his mind. The result in December 1950 was a 5-to-4 decision fully acquitting Brother Boucher.

At first, this decision was defied by both the solicitor general and the premier (who was also attorney general) of the province of Quebec, but gradually it was enforced through the courts. Thus the charge of sedition that had repeatedly been raised against Jehovah's Witnesses in Canada was effectively buried.

Yet another test case was appealed to the Canadian Supreme Court —*Laurier Saumur v. The City of Quebec.* This one confronted the licensing bylaws that were involved in a large number of convictions in the lower courts. In the *Saumur* case, the Society was seeking a permanent injunction against the city of Quebec to prevent the authorities from interfering with the distribution of religious literature by Jehovah's Witnesses. On October 6, 1953, the Supreme Court rendered its decision. The answer was "Yes" to Jehovah's Witnesses, "No" to the province of Quebec. That decision also brought victory in a thousand other cases where the same principle of religious liberty was the governing factor. This opened a new era for the work of Jehovah's Witnesses in Quebec.

> **"Equal Rights to All"**
>
> Under the above heading, in 1953 a Canadian columnist, well-known at the time, wrote: "A large bonfire on Parliament Hill should celebrate the Supreme Court of Canada's decision in the Saumur case [which was brought before the Court by Jehovah's Witnesses]; a bonfire worthy of a great occasion. Few decisions in the history of Canadian justice can have been more important. Few courts can have done better service than this to Canada. None has placed Canadians who value their inheritance of freedom more deeply in its debt. . . . The deliverance cannot be celebrated with the bonfires it deserves."

Education in Legal Rights and Procedure

As the number of court cases increased in the late 1920's and thereafter, it became necessary for Jehovah's Witnesses to be instructed in legal procedures. Since J. F. Rutherford was a lawyer and had himself served on occasion as a judge, he appreciated the need for the Witnesses to have direction in these matters. Particularly since 1926 the Witnesses had been emphasizing house-to-house preaching *on Sundays,* with the use of books explaining the Bible. Because of opposition to their Sunday distribution of Bible literature, Brother Rutherford prepared the pamphlet *Liberty to Preach* to help those in the United States to understand their rights under the law. However, he could not personally do all the legal work, so he arranged for other attorneys to serve as part of the Society's headquarters staff. In addition, others, spread across the country, cooperated closely.

The attorneys could not be present for all the

'Defending and Legally Establishing the Good News'

court appearances required in the thousands of cases involving the preaching activity of Jehovah's Witnesses, but they could provide valuable counsel. To that end, arrangements were made to train all of Jehovah's Witnesses in basic legal procedures. This was done at special assemblies in the United States in 1932 and, later, on the regular Service Meeting programs in the congregations. A detailed "Order of Trial" was published in the *1933 Year Book* of Jehovah's Witnesses (later as a separate sheet). These instructions were adjusted as circumstances required. In the November 3, 1937, issue of *Consolation,* further legal counsel was given regarding specific situations that were being encountered.

Using this information, the Witnesses usually handled their own defense in local courts, instead of securing the services of a lawyer. They found that in this way they could often give a witness to the court and present the issues squarely to the judge, instead of having their cases decided merely on legal technicalities. When any case was adversely decided, an appeal was usually filed, though some Witnesses served a jail term instead of hiring an attorney, whose services would be needed in an appellate court.

As new situations arose and precedents were set by decisions in the courts, more information was provided to keep the Witnesses up-to-date. Thus, in 1939 the booklet *Advice for Kingdom Publishers* was printed to aid the brothers in court battles. Two years later a more extensive discussion was set out in the booklet *Jehovah's Servants Defended*. It quoted or discussed 50 different American court decisions involving Jehovah's Witnesses, as well as numerous other cases, and explained how these legal precedents could be beneficially used. Then, in 1943, a copy of *Freedom of Worship* was made available to each Witness and was diligently studied at Service Meetings in the congregations. In addition to providing a valuable digest of legal cases, this booklet set out in detail the Scriptural reasons for handling matters in particular ways. This was followed, in 1950, by the updated booklet *Defending and Legally Establishing the Good News*.

All of this was a progressive legal education. The objective, however, was not to make the Witnesses lawyers but to keep the way open to preach the good news of God's Kingdom publicly and from house to house.

Like a Swarm of Locusts

Where officials viewed themselves as being above the law, their treatment of the Witnesses was sometimes ruthless. Regardless of the methods

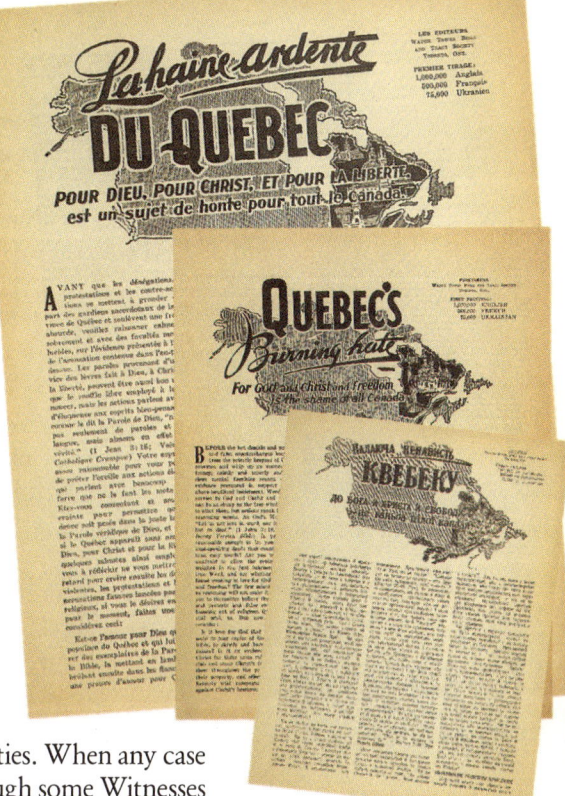

This tract, in three languages, informed all of Canada of atrocities committed against Jehovah's Witnesses in Quebec

It became necessary to teach Jehovah's Witnesses legal procedures so they could deal with opposition to their ministry; these are some of the legal publications they used

employed by their opponents, however, Jehovah's Witnesses knew that God's Word counsels: "Do not avenge yourselves, beloved, but yield place to the wrath; for it is written: 'Vengeance is mine; I will repay, says Jehovah.'" (Rom. 12:19) Nevertheless, they felt keenly obligated to give a witness. How did they do it when confronted with official opposition?

Although the individual congregations of Jehovah's Witnesses were usually rather small during the 1930's, there was a strong bond among them. When there was serious trouble in any location, Witnesses from surrounding areas were eager to help. In 1933 in the United States, for example, 12,600 Witnesses were organized into 78 divisions. When there were persistent arrests in an area, or when opposers succeeded in pressuring radio stations to cancel contracts for broadcasting programs prepared by Jehovah's Witnesses, the Society's office in Brooklyn was notified. Within a week, reinforcements were dispatched to that area to give a concentrated witness.

Depending on the need, from 50 to 1,000 Witnesses would rendezvous at an appointed time, usually in the countryside near the area to be worked. They were all volunteers; some came as much as 200 miles. Individual groups were given territory that could be covered in perhaps 30 minutes or possibly as much as two hours. As each car group began to work in its assigned section, a committee of brothers called on the police to notify them of the work being done and to provide a list of all the Witnesses who were working in the community that morning. Realizing that their own forces were overwhelmed by the sheer number of Witnesses, the officials in most places permitted the work to go on without hindrance. In some localities they filled their jail but then could do no more. For any that were arrested, the Witnesses had attorneys on hand with bail. The effect was like that of the symbolic swarm of locusts referred to in the Scriptures at Joel 2:7-11 and Revelation 9:1-11. In this way it was possible to continue preaching the good news even in the face of intense opposition.

Exposing Actions of High-Handed Officials to Public View

It was deemed beneficial to inform people in some areas as to what their local officials were doing. In Quebec, when the courts subjected Witnesses to procedures reminiscent of Inquisitional tribunals, a letter was sent to all the members of the Quebec legislature setting out the facts. When that brought no action, the Society forwarded a copy of the letter to 14,000 businessmen throughout the province. Then the information was taken to the editors of newspapers for publication.

In the eastern United States, the public was informed by radio broadcasts. At Brooklyn Bethel a number of trained actors, good at imitating, formed what was called The King's Theater. When high-handed officials put Jehovah's Witnesses on trial, a full stenographic record was made of the court proceedings. The actors were present in the court so as to become well acquainted with the tone of voice and manner of speech of the police, the prosecutor, and the judge. After extensive advertising to ensure a large radio audience, The King's Theater would reenact courtroom scenes with remarkable realism so that the public would know exactly what their officials were doing. In time, because of the floodlight of publicity upon them, some of these officials became more careful in their handling of cases involving the Witnesses.

Some officials became more careful in their handling of cases involving the Witnesses

United Action in the Face of Nazi Oppression

When the government of Nazi Germany put into operation a campaign to stop the activity of Jehovah's Witnesses in Germany, repeated efforts were made to gain a hearing with the German authorities. But no relief was forthcoming. By the summer of 1933, their work had been banned in the majority of German states. Therefore, on June 25, 1933, a declaration regarding their ministry and its objectives was adopted by Jehovah's Witnesses at an assembly in Berlin. Copies were sent to all the high government officials, and millions more were distributed to the public. Nevertheless, in July 1933 the courts refused to grant a hearing for relief. Early the following year, a personal letter regarding the situation was written by J. F. Rutherford to Adolf Hitler and delivered to him by special messenger. Then the entire worldwide brotherhood went into action.

On Sunday morning, October 7, 1934, at nine o'clock, every group of Witnesses in Germany assembled. They prayed for Jehovah's guidance and blessing. Then each group sent a letter to German government officials declaring their firm determination to keep on serving Jehovah. Before dismissing, they discussed together the words of their Lord, Jesus Christ, at Matthew 10:16-24. After this they went out to give a witness to their neighbors about Jehovah and his Kingdom under Christ.

That same day, Jehovah's Witnesses throughout the earth met and, after united prayer to Jehovah, sent a cablegram warning the Hitler government: "Your ill-treatment of Jehovah's witnesses shocks all good people of earth and dishonors God's name. Refrain from further persecuting

Jehovah's witnesses; otherwise God will destroy you and your national party." But that was not the end of it.

The Gestapo intensified their efforts to crush the activity of Jehovah's Witnesses. After mass arrests in 1936, they thought that perhaps they had succeeded. But then, on December 12, 1936, some 3,450 Witnesses who were still free in Germany blitzed the country with a printed resolution that clearly stated Jehovah's purpose and set forth the determination of Jehovah's Witnesses to obey God as ruler rather than men. The opposers could not understand how such a distribution was possible. A few months later, when the Gestapo belittled the charges made in the resolution, Jehovah's Witnesses prepared an open letter in which they unsparingly named the Nazi officers who had fiendishly abused Jehovah's Witnesses. In 1937, this letter too was given wide distribution in Germany. Thus the deeds of wicked men were laid bare for all to see. This also gave the public opportunity to decide what course they personally would pursue regarding these servants of the Most High.—Compare Matthew 25:31-46.

Global Publicity Brings Some Relief

Other governments too have dealt harshly with Jehovah's Witnesses, prohibiting their meetings and public preaching. In some cases these governments have caused the Witnesses to be forced out of secular employment and their children to be barred from the schools. A number of governments have also resorted to physical brutality. Yet, these same lands usually have constitutions that guarantee religious freedom. With a view to bringing relief to their persecuted brothers, the Watch

---

A Firm Declaration to the Nazi State

On October 7, 1934, the following letter was sent to the German government by every congregation of Jehovah's Witnesses in Germany:

"TO THE OFFICIALS OF THE GOVERNMENT:

"The Word of Jehovah God, as set out in the Holy Bible, is the supreme law, and to us it is our sole guide for the reason that we have devoted ourselves to God and are true and sincere followers of Christ Jesus.

"During the past year, and contrary to God's law and in violation of our rights, you have forbidden us as Jehovah's witnesses to meet together to study God's Word and worship and serve him. In his Word he commands us that we shall not forsake the assembling of ourselves together. (Hebrews 10:25) To us Jehovah commands: 'Ye are my witnesses that I am God. Go and tell the people my message.' (Isaiah 43:10, 12; Isaiah 6:9; Matthew 24:14) There is a direct conflict between your law and God's law, and, following the lead of the faithful apostles, 'we ought to obey God rather than men,' and this we will do. (Acts 5:29) Therefore this is to advise you that at any cost we will obey God's commandments, will meet together for the study of his Word, and will worship and serve him as he has commanded. If your government or officers do violence to us because we are obeying God, then our blood will be upon you and you will answer to Almighty God.

"We have no interest in political affairs, but are wholly devoted to God's kingdom under Christ his King. We will do no injury or harm to anyone. We would delight to dwell in peace and do good to all men as we have opportunity, but, since your government and its officers continue in your attempt to force us to disobey the highest law of the universe, we are compelled to now give you notice that we will, by his grace, obey Jehovah God and fully trust Him to deliver us from all oppression and oppressors."

Tower Society has frequently given worldwide publicity to details concerning such treatment. This is done by means of the *Watchtower* and *Awake!* magazines, and these reports are at times taken up by the public press. Many thousands of letters making appeals in behalf of the Witnesses then flood into the offices of government officials from all over the world.

As a result of such a campaign in 1937, the governor of Georgia, in the United States, received some 7,000 letters from four countries within a two-day period, and the mayor of La Grange, Georgia, was also deluged with thousands of letters. Such campaigns were likewise conducted in behalf of Jehovah's Witnesses in Argentina in 1978 and 1979, Benin in 1976, Burundi in 1989, Cameroon in 1970, the Dominican Republic in 1950 and 1957, Ethiopia in 1957, Gabon in 1971, Greece in 1963 and 1966, Jordan in 1959, Malawi in 1968, 1972, 1975, and again in 1976, Malaya in 1952, Mozambique in 1976, Portugal in 1964 and 1966, Singapore in 1972, Spain in 1961 and again in 1962, also Swaziland in 1983.

As a recent example of what is done by Jehovah's Witnesses worldwide to bring relief to their oppressed brothers, consider the situation in Greece. Because of the intensity of persecution of Jehovah's Witnesses at the instigation of the Greek Orthodox clergy there, in 1986 both the *Watchtower* and *Awake!* magazines (with combined international circulation of over 22,000,000 copies) reported details of the persecution. Witnesses in other lands were invited to write to officials of the Greek government in behalf of their brothers. They did; and as reported in the Athens newspaper *Vradyni*, the minister of justice was deluged with over 200,000 letters from upwards of 200 lands and in 106 languages.

The following year, when a case involving the Witnesses was heard in the appeals court in Hania, Crete, representatives of Jehovah's Witnesses were present from seven other lands (England, France, Germany, Italy, Japan, Spain, and the United States) as parties in the case and in support of their Christian brothers. Then, following an adverse decision in 1988 in the Supreme Court of Greece in yet another case involving the Witnesses, appeal was made to the European Commission of Human Rights. There, on December 7, 1990, 16 jurists from almost all parts of Europe were presented with a file of 2,000 arrests and hundreds of court cases in which Jehovah's Witnesses in Greece had been sentenced because they spoke about the Bible. (Actually, there were 19,147 of such arrests in Greece from 1938 to 1992.) The Commission unanimously decided that the case should be heard by the European Court of Human Rights.

In some instances such exposure of the violation of human rights brings a measure of relief. Regardless of what action is taken by judges or rulers, however, Jehovah's Witnesses continue to obey God as their Supreme Ruler.

Securing Legal Recognition

The *authorization* to carry on true worship obviously does not originate with any man or any human government. It comes from Jehovah God himself. In many countries, however, in order to secure the protection that is afforded by secular law, it has proved advantageous for Jehovah's Witnesses to be *registered* with the government as a religious association. Plans to purchase property for a branch office or to do extensive printing of Bible literature may be facilitated by the forming of local legal corporations. In harmony with the precedent set by the apostle Paul in ancient Philippi in 'legally establishing the good news,' Jehovah's Witnesses take appropriate action to accomplish this.—Phil. 1:7.

At times, this has been very difficult. For example, in Austria, where a concordat with the Vatican assures government financial support for the Catholic Church, the efforts of Jehovah's Witnesses were at first repulsed by officials, who said: 'Your intention is to form a religious organization, and an organization of that type cannot be constituted under Austrian law.' In 1930, however, they were able to register an association for distributing Bibles and Bible literature.

In Spain the 20th-century activity of Jehovah's Witnesses dates back to the time of World War I. But since the early years of the Inquisition in the 15th century, the Roman Catholic Church and the Spanish State had, with few exceptions, worked hand in glove. Changes in the political and religious climate led to allowance for individuals to practice another religion, but public manifestations of their faith were forbidden. In spite of these circumstances, in 1956 and again in 1965, Jehovah's Witnesses sought to gain legal recognition in Spain. Yet, it was not until the Spanish Parliament passed the Religious Liberty Law of 1967 that any real progress was possible. Finally, on July 10, 1970, when the Witnesses already numbered more than 11,000 in Spain, legal recognition was granted.

Application for legal registration of the Watch Tower Society was made to the French colonial governor of Dahomey (now known as Benin) in 1948. But it was not until 1966, six years after the country became an independent republic, that such legal registration was granted. Still, that legal recognition was withdrawn in 1976 and then restored in 1990 as changes occurred in the political climate and in the official attitude toward religious freedom.

Although Jehovah's Witnesses had enjoyed legal recognition in Canada for years, World War II provided an excuse for opposers to persuade a new governor-general to declare the Witnesses illegal. This was done on July 4, 1940. Two years later, when the Witnesses were granted opportunity to make representations to a select committee of the House of Commons, that committee strongly recommended that the ban on Jehovah's Witnesses and their legal corporations be lifted. However, it was not until there had been repeated and extended debate in the House of Commons and much work had been done to gather signatures on two nationwide petitions that the minister of justice, a Roman Catholic, felt compelled to remove the ban completely.

Basic changes in the outlook of governments in Eastern Europe were required before Jehovah's Witnesses could gain legal recognition there. Finally, after decades of appeals for religious freedom, the Witnesses were granted legal recognition in Poland and Hungary in 1989, in Romania and East Germany (before its unification with the Federal Republic of Germany) in 1990, in Bulgaria and what was then the Soviet Union in 1991, and in Albania in 1992.

Jehovah's Witnesses endeavor to work in harmony with the laws of any nation. They strongly advocate, on the basis of the Bible, respect for government officials. But when the laws of men conflict with clearly stated commands of God, they reply: "We must obey God as ruler rather than men."—Acts 5:29.

When Fear Causes People to Forget Basic Freedoms

Because of the increase in drug abuse on the part of many people and inflation, which has frequently forced both husbands and wives to take secular jobs, Jehovah's Witnesses in the United States have found themselves confronted with new situations in their ministry. Many neighborhoods are nearly empty during the day, and burglary is rampant. People are fearful. In the late 1970's and early 1980's, a new wave of solicitation-licensing ordinances were enacted in order to keep track of strangers in communities. Some towns threatened Jehovah's Witnesses with arrest if they did not obtain permits. But a sound legal foundation had already been laid, so efforts could be made to handle the problems out of court.

Where difficulties arise, local elders may meet with town officials to work out a solution. Jehovah's Witnesses firmly refuse to ask for *permission* to do work that God has commanded, and the U.S. Constitution,

---

Witnesses Under Ban Clearly State Their Position

The organization of Jehovah's Witnesses was put under government ban in Canada in 1940. There were over 500 prosecutions thereafter. What defense could the Witnesses offer? Respectfully but firmly, they made statements to the Court along the following lines:

'I have no apologies to offer for these books. They teach the way to eternal life. I sincerely believe them to explain the purpose of Almighty God to establish a Kingdom of righteousness in the earth. To me, they have been the greatest blessing of my life. In my opinion it would be a sin against the Almighty to destroy these books, and the message of God they contain, in the same way as it would be a sin to burn the Bible itself. Every person must choose whether he will risk the disapproval of men or the disapproval of the Almighty God. For myself I have taken my stand on the side of the Lord and His Kingdom, and I seek to honor the name of the Most High, which is Jehovah, and if I am to be penalized for that, then there is responsibility before God to be taken by those who impose the penalty.'

buttressed by Supreme Court decisions, guarantees freedom of worship and of the press that is not subject to the payment of any fee as a precondition. But Jehovah's Witnesses understand that people are fearful, and they may agree to *notify* the police before they start to witness in a certain area, if necessary. However, if no acceptable compromise can be reached, an attorney from the Society's headquarters will correspond with local officials explaining the work of Jehovah's Witnesses, the constitutional law that supports their right to preach, and their ability to enforce that right through federal civil rights damage actions against the municipality and its officials.*

In some lands it even proves necessary to go into court to reaffirm basic freedoms that have long been taken for granted. That was true in Finland in 1976 and again in 1983. Ostensibly to preserve peace for householders, a rash of local ordinances prohibited religious work that involved going from house to house. However, it was pointed out in court in Loviisa and in Rauma that house-to-house preaching is part of the religion of Jehovah's Witnesses and that the government had approved this method of evangelizing when it granted a charter to the religious association of Jehovah's Witnesses. It was also shown that many people welcome the calls of the Witnesses and that it would be an abridgment of freedom to ban such activity just because not everyone appreciates it. Following the successful conclusion of those cases, many towns and cities repealed their ordinance.

Shaping of Constitutional Law

The activity of Jehovah's Witnesses has, in some lands, been a major factor in shaping the law. Every American law student well knows the contribution made by Jehovah's Witnesses to the defense of civil rights in the United States. Reflecting the extent of this contribution are articles such as the following: "The Debt of Constitutional Law to Jehovah's Witnesses," which appeared in the *Minnesota Law Review,* of March 1944, and, "A Catalyst for the Evolution of Constitutional Law: Jehovah's Witnesses in

---

* *Jane Monell v. Department of Social Services of the City of New York,* 436 U.S. 658 (1978).

How Members of the Canadian Government Viewed It

Here are statements made by some of the members of the Canadian House of Commons in 1943 when urging the minister of justice to remove the ban on Jehovah's Witnesses and their legal corporations:

"No evidence was put before the committee by the department of justice which indicated that at any time Jehovah's witnesses should have been declared an illegal organization . . . It is a disgrace to the Dominion of Canada that people should be prosecuted for their religious convictions in the way in which these poor people have been prosecuted." "In my opinion it is clear, pure religious prejudice that is maintaining the ban."—Mr. Angus MacInnis.

"The experience of most of us has been that these are harmless people, devoid of any intent to do wrong to the state. . . . Why has the ban not been lifted? It cannot be because of any fear that this organization is detrimental to the welfare of the state, or that its actions are subversive to the war effort. There has never been even the slightest evidence that such is the case."—Mr. John G. Diefenbaker.

"It does make one wonder whether the action against Jehovah's Witnesses is largely on account of their attitude toward the Roman Catholics, instead of their attitude of a subversive nature."—Mr. Victor Quelch.

the Supreme Court," published in the *University of Cincinnati Law Review*, in 1987.

Their court cases make up a significant portion of American law relating to freedom of religion, freedom of speech, and freedom of the press. These cases have done much to preserve the liberties not only of Jehovah's Witnesses but also of the entire populace. In a speech at Drake University, Irving Dilliard, a well-known author and editor, said: "Like it or not, the Jehovah's Witnesses have done more to help preserve our freedoms than any other religious group."

And regarding the situation in Canada, the preface to the book *State and Salvation—The Jehovah's Witnesses and Their Fight for Civil Rights* declares: "The Jehovah's Witnesses taught the state, and the Canadian people, what the practical content of legal protection for dissenting groups should be. Moreover, the . . . persecution [of the Witnesses in the province of Quebec] led to a series of cases that, in the 1940s and 1950s, made their way to the Supreme Court of Canada. They too made an important contribution to Canadian attitudes about civil rights, and they constitute the bedrock of civil-liberties jurisprudence in Canada today." "One of the results" of the Witnesses' legal battle for freedom of worship, the book explains, "was the long process of discussion and debate that led to the Charter of Rights," which is now part of the fundamental law of Canada.

"Service to the Cause of Religious Freedom"

"It would not be fair to dismiss this brief survey of the troubles of Jehovah's Witnesses with the State without referring to the service to the cause of religious freedom under our Constitution which has been rendered as a result of their persistence. In recent years they have taken the time of the courts more than any other religious group, and they have appeared to the public to be narrow-minded, but they have been true to their conscientious convictions, and as a result the Federal courts have rendered a series of decisions which have secured and broadened the religious-freedom guarantees of American citizens, and have protected and extended their civil liberties. Some thirty-one cases in which they were involved came before the Supreme Court in the five years from 1938 to 1943, and the decisions in these and later cases have greatly advanced the cause of the freedoms of the Bill of Rights in general, and the protection of religious freedom in particular."—"Church and State in the United States," by Anson Phelps Stokes, Volume III, 1950, page 546.

Supremacy of God's Law

Primarily, however, the legal record of Jehovah's Witnesses has been a testimony to their conviction that divine law is supreme. At the root of the position they have taken is their appreciation of the issue of universal sovereignty. They recognize Jehovah as the only true God and the rightful Sovereign of the universe. They therefore firmly take the position that any laws or court decisions that would prohibit the doing of what Jehovah commands are invalid and that the human agency that has imposed such restrictions has exceeded its authority. Their stand is like that of the apostles of Jesus Christ, who declared: "We must obey God as ruler rather than men."—Acts 5:29.

With God's help Jehovah's Witnesses are determined to preach this good news of God's Kingdom in all the inhabited earth for a witness to all nations before the end comes.—Matt. 24:14.

Rejoicing in Their Freedom to Worship

In many lands where Jehovah's Witnesses did not have full religious freedom in the past, they now meet openly for worship and freely share with others the good news of God's Kingdom.

Quebec, Canada
During the 1940's, the few Witnesses here in Châteauguay were attacked by a mob. In 1992, more than 21,000 Witnesses in the province of Quebec were meeting freely in their Kingdom Halls

St. Petersburg, Russia
In 1992, a total of 3,256 presented themselves for baptism at the first international convention of Jehovah's Witnesses in Russia

Palma, Spain
After Jehovah's Witnesses in Spain were granted legal recognition in 1970, large signs on meeting places reflected their joy at being able to assemble openly

Tartu, Estonia
Witnesses in Estonia have been grateful to receive Bible literature without hindrance since 1990

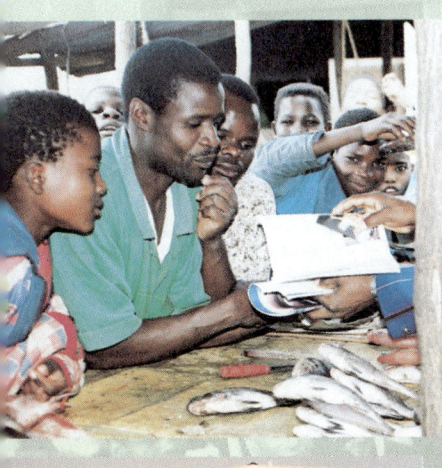

Maputo, Mozambique
Within a year after Jehovah's Witnesses were given legal status here in 1991, more than 50 congregations of enthusiastic Witnesses were carrying out their ministry in and around the capital city

Cotonou, Benin
On arrival at a meeting in 1990, many were surprised to see a banner publicly welcoming Jehovah's Witnesses. Here they learned that the ban on their worship had been lifted

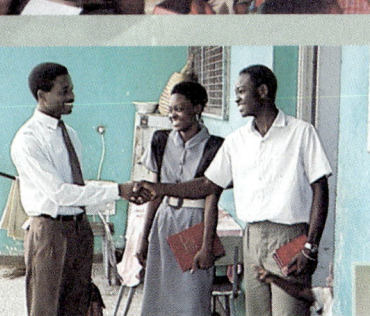

Prague, Czechoslovakia
Shown below are a few who served Jehovah under government ban for 40 years. In 1991, they rejoiced to be together at an international convention of Jehovah's Witnesses in Prague

Luanda, Angola
When the ban was lifted in 1992, over 50,000 individuals and families welcomed the Witnesses to study the Bible with them

Kiev, Ukraine
Meetings in this land (often in rented halls) are well attended, especially since Jehovah's Witnesses were granted legal recognition in 1991

JEHOVAH'S WITNESSES
PROCLAIMERS OF GOD'S KINGDOM

SECTION 7

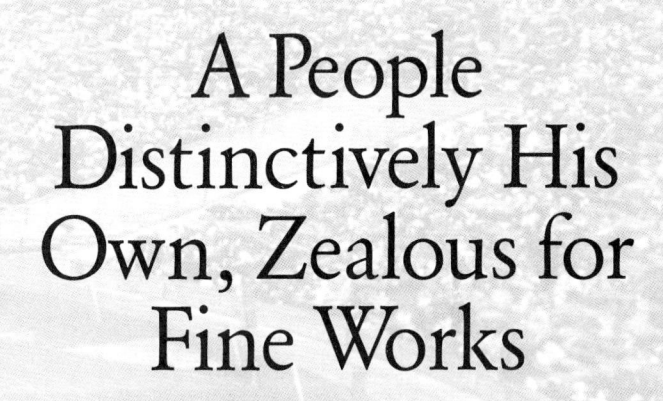

A People Distinctively His Own, Zealous for Fine Works

Why do Jehovah's Witnesses believe that they are being led by God? What identifies them as genuine disciples of Jesus Christ? Since they proclaim that God's Kingdom already rules from the heavens, for what further great event are they eagerly keeping on the watch? This final section (Chapters 31 to 33) answers these questions.

CHAPTER 31

HOW CHOSEN AND LED BY GOD

"IT IS only logical that there would be one true religion. This is in harmony with the fact that the true God is a God, 'not of disorder, but of peace.' (1 Corinthians 14:33) The Bible says that actually there is only 'one faith.' (Ephesians 4:5) Who, then, are the ones who form the body of true worshipers today? We do not hesitate to say that they are Jehovah's Witnesses," declares the book *You Can Live Forever in Paradise on Earth*.*

'How can you be so sure that you have the true religion?' some may ask. 'You do not have supernatural evidence—such as miraculous gifts. And through the years have you not had to make adjustments in your views and teachings? How, then, can you be so confident that you are being led by God?'

To answer those questions, it is helpful to consider first how Jehovah chose and led his people in ancient times.

God's Choosing in Bible Times

In the 16th century B.C.E., Jehovah gathered the Israelites at Mount Sinai and invited them to become his chosen people. First, though, Jehovah informed them that there were specific requirements that they would have to meet. He told them: "If you will strictly obey my voice . . . , *then* you will certainly become my special property." (Ex. 19:5) Through Moses, Jehovah clearly set out the requirements, after which the people responded: "All the words that Jehovah has spoken we are willing to do." Jehovah then concluded a covenant with Israel and gave them his Law.—Ex. 24:3-8, 12.

Chosen by God—what an awesome privilege! But that privilege brought upon Israel the responsibility to strictly obey God's Law. Failure to do so would result in their rejection as a nation. To instill in them a wholesome fear so that they would obey him, Jehovah caused spectacular supernatural signs—"thunders and lightnings began occurring," and "the whole mountain was trembling very much." (Ex. 19:9, 16-18; 20:18, 20) For about the next 1,500 years, the Israelites were in a unique position —they were God's chosen people.

---

* Published by the Watchtower Bible and Tract Society of New York, Inc.

In the first century C.E., however, the situation changed drastically. Israel lost its privileged status, being cast off by Jehovah because of rejecting his Son. (Matt. 21:43; 23:37, 38; Acts 4:24-28) Jehovah then brought forth the early Christian congregation, founded on Christ. At Pentecost 33 C.E., Jehovah poured out his holy spirit on Jesus' followers in Jerusalem, constituting them "a chosen race, . . . a holy nation, a people for special possession." (1 Pet. 2:9; Acts 2:1-4; Eph. 2:19, 20) They became "God's chosen ones."—Col. 3:12.

Membership in that chosen nation was conditional. Jehovah set strict moral and spiritual requirements that had to be met. (Gal. 5:19-24) Those who conformed to the requirements put themselves in line to be chosen by him. Once chosen by God, however, it was vital that they remain obedient to his laws. Only "those obeying him as ruler" would continue to receive his holy spirit. (Acts 5:32) Those who failed to obey him were in danger of being put out of the congregation and of losing their inheritance in the Kingdom of God.—1 Cor. 5:11-13; 6:9, 10.

Once chosen by God, it was vital that they remain obedient to his laws

But how would others know for sure that God had chosen that early Christian congregation to replace Israel as "the congregation of God"? (Acts 20:28) God's choice was evident. Following Jesus' death, He bestowed miraculous gifts on members of the early Christian congregation to show that they were now God's chosen ones.—Heb. 2:3, 4.

Were supernatural signs, or miracles, *always* necessary to identify those who were chosen and led by God in Bible times? No, not at all. Miraculous works were not a common occurrence throughout Bible history. Most persons living in Bible times never witnessed a miracle. The majority of the miracles recorded in the Bible took place during the days of Moses and Joshua (16th and 15th centuries B.C.E.), Elijah and Elisha (10th and 9th centuries B.C.E.), and Jesus and his apostles (1st century C.E.). Other faithful persons chosen by God for specific purposes, such as Abraham and David, observed or experienced demonstrations of God's power, but there is no evidence that they *performed* miracles themselves. (Gen. 18:14; 19: 27-29; 21:1-3; compare 2 Samuel 6:21; Nehemiah 9:7.) As to the miraculous gifts present in the first century, the Bible foretold that these would "be done away with." (1 Cor. 13:8) And this occurred with the passing of the last of the 12 apostles and those who had received the miraculous gifts through them.—Compare Acts 8:14-20.

What About God's Choosing Today?

After the first century, the foretold apostasy developed unrestrained. (Acts 20:29, 30; 2 Thess. 2:7-12) For many centuries the lamp of true Christianity burned very low. (Compare Matthew 5:14-16.) Yet, in an illustration Jesus indicated that at the 'conclusion of the system of things,' there would be a clear distinction between "the wheat" (true Christians) and "the weeds" (imitation Christians). The wheat, or "chosen ones," would be gathered into one true Christian congregation, as in the first century. (Matt. 13:24-30, 36-43; 24:31) Jesus also described the anointed members of that congregation as "the faithful and discreet slave" and indicated that in the time of the end, they would be dispensing spiritual food. (Matt. 24:3, 45-47) That faithful slave would be joined by "a great crowd" of true worshipers out of all nations.—Rev. 7:9, 10; compare Micah 4:1-4.

How would true worshipers living in the time of the end be identified?

How would true worshipers living in the time of the end be identified? Would they always be right, would their judgment be infallible? Jesus' apostles were not above the need for correction. (Luke 22:24-27; Gal. 2:11-14) Like the apostles, true followers of Christ in our day must be humble, willing to accept discipline and, when necessary, make adjustments, in order to bring their thinking into ever closer harmony with God's.—1 Pet. 5:5, 6.

When the world entered the last days in 1914, what group proved to be the one true Christian organization? Christendom abounded with churches that claimed to represent Christ. But the question is: Which, if any, among them was meeting the Scriptural requirements?

The one true Christian congregation would have to be an organization that *holds to the Bible as its foremost authority,* not one that quotes scattered verses but rejects the rest when these do not conform to its contemporary theology. (John 17:17; 2 Tim. 3:16, 17) It would have to be an organization whose members—not *some* but all—are truly *no part of the world,* in imitation of Christ. So how could they involve themselves in politics, as the churches of Christendom have done repeatedly? (John 15:19; 17:16) The true Christian organization would have to *bear witness to the divine name, Jehovah,* and do the work that Jesus commanded—*the preaching of the good news of God's Kingdom.* Like the first-century congregation, not just a few but all its members would be whole-souled evangelizers. (Isa. 43: 10-12; Matt. 24:14; 28:19, 20; Col. 3:23) True worshipers would also be known by their *self-sacrificing love for one another,* a love that would transcend racial and national barriers and unite them into a worldwide brotherhood. Such love would have to be manifested not merely in isolated cases but in a way that would truly set them apart as an organization.—John 13: 34, 35.

Clearly, when the time of the end began in 1914, none of the churches of Christendom were measuring up to these Bible standards for the one true Christian congregation. What, though, about the Bible Students, as Jehovah's Witnesses were then known?

A Fruitful Quest for Truth

As a young man, C. T. Russell came to the conclusion that the Bible had been grossly misrepresented by Christendom. He also believed that it was time for God's Word to be understood and that those who would sincerely study the Bible and *apply it in their lives* would get understanding.

A biography of Russell, published shortly after his death, explained: "He was not the founder of a new religion, and never made such claim. He revived the great truths taught by Jesus and the Apostles, and turned the light of the twentieth century upon these. He made no claim of a special revelation from God, but held that it was God's due time for the Bible to be understood; and that, being fully consecrated to the Lord and to His service, he was permitted to understand it. Because he devoted himself to the development of the fruits and graces of the Holy Spirit, the promise of the Lord was fulfilled in him: 'For if these things be in you and abound, they make you that ye shall neither be barren nor unfruitful in the knowledge of our Lord Jesus Christ.'—2 Peter 1:5-8."—*The Watch Tower,* December 1, 1916, p. 356.

"He made no claim of a special revelation from God"

The quest for Scriptural understanding by C. T. Russell and his associates was fruitful. As lovers of truth, they believed that the Bible is the inspired Word of God. (2 Tim. 3:16, 17) They rejected the evolutionary ideas of Darwin and the faith-destroying views of higher critics of the Bible. Accepting the Scriptures as supreme authority, they also rejected as unscriptural the teachings of the Trinity, immortality of the soul, and eternal torment—doctrines with pagan religious roots. Among the "great truths" that they accepted were that Jehovah is the Creator of all things, that Jesus Christ is the *Son* of God, who gave his life as a ransom for others, and that at his return Jesus would be invisibly present as a spirit creature. (Matt. 20:28; John 3:16; 14:19; Rev. 4:11) They also understood clearly that man is a mortal soul.—Gen. 2:7; Ezek. 18:20.

It is not that the Bible Students associated with Russell uncovered all these truths; many had been understood earlier by sincere persons professing to be Christians, some of whom even took a stand when such beliefs were not popular. But did such persons conform to all the Scriptural requisites for true worship? For example, were they truly no part of the world, as Jesus said his true followers would be?

In addition to their view of the Bible, in what other ways did the early Bible Students associated with Russell stand out as different? Certainly in the zeal that they manifested in sharing their beliefs with others, with special emphasis on proclaiming God's name and Kingdom. Though they were relatively few in number, they quickly reached out into scores of lands with the good news. Were they also truly no part of the world, as followers of Christ? In some respects, yes. But their awareness of the responsibility involved in this has grown since World War I, until now it has become an outstanding characteristic of Jehovah's Witnesses. It should not be overlooked that when other religious groups were hailing the League of Nations and, later, the United Nations, Jehovah's Witnesses proclaimed God's Kingdom—not any man-made organization—as mankind's only hope.

But have not some of the beliefs of Jehovah's Witnesses undergone adjustments over the years? If they were truly chosen and led by God and if their teachings were backed by Scriptural authority to begin with, why would such changes be necessary?

How Jehovah Leads His People

Those who make up the one true Christian organization today do not have angelic revelations or divine inspiration. But they do have the inspired Holy Scriptures, which contain revelations of God's thinking and will. As an organization and individually, they must accept the Bible as divine truth, study it carefully, and let it work in them. (1 Thess. 2:13) But how do they arrive at the correct understanding of God's Word?

The Bible itself says: "Do not interpretations belong to God?" (Gen. 40:8) If in their study of the Scriptures a certain passage is difficult to understand, they must search to find other inspired passages that shed light on the subject. Thus they let the Bible interpret itself, and from this they endeavor to understand "the pattern" of truth set forth in God's Word. (2 Tim. 1:13) Jehovah leads or guides them to such understanding by means of his holy spirit. But to get the guidance of that spirit, they must cultivate its fruitage, not grieve or work against it, and keep responsive to its proddings. (Gal. 5:22, 23, 25; Eph. 4:30) Moreover, by zealously applying what they learn, they keep building up their faith, as a basis for gaining clearer and clearer understanding of how they must do God's will in the world of which they are no part.—Luke 17:5; Phil. 1:9, 10.

They let the Bible interpret itself

Jehovah has always led his people to clearer understanding of his will. (Ps. 43:3) Just how he has guided them may be illustrated this way: If a person has been in a dark room for a long period of time, is it not best if he is exposed to light *gradually?* Jehovah has exposed his people to the light of truth in a similar manner; he has enlightened them *progressively.* (Compare John 16:12, 13.) It has been as the proverb says: "The path of the righteous ones is like the bright light that is getting lighter and lighter until the day is firmly established."—Prov. 4:18.

Jehovah's dealings with his chosen servants in Bible times confirm that clear understanding of his will and purposes often comes gradually. Thus, Abraham did not fully understand how Jehovah's purpose in connection with the "seed" would work out. (Gen. 12:1-3, 7; 15:2-4; compare Hebrews 11:8.) Daniel did not grasp the final outcome of the prophecies he recorded. (Dan. 12:8, 9) Jesus, when on earth, admitted that he did not know the day and hour that the present system of things would end. (Matt. 24:36) The apostles did not at first understand that Jesus' Kingdom would be heavenly, that it was not to be established in the first century, and that even Gentiles may inherit it.—Luke 19:11; Acts 1:6, 7; 10:9-16, 34, 35; 2 Tim. 4:18; Rev. 5:9, 10.

It should not surprise us that in modern times too, Jehovah has often led his people as a progressive organization, gradually enlightening them as to Bible truths. It is not the truths themselves that change. Truth remains truth. Jehovah's will and purpose, as outlined in the Bible, remain fixed. (Isa. 46:10) But their *understanding* of these truths gets progressively clearer "at the proper time," Jehovah's due time. (Matt. 24:45; compare Daniel 12:4, 9.) At times, because of human error or misguided zeal, their viewpoint may need to be adjusted.

For example, at various times in the modern-day history of Jehovah's Witnesses, their zeal and enthusiasm for the vindication of Jehovah's sovereignty have led to premature expectations as to *when* the end of Satan's wicked system of things would come. (Ezek. 38:21-23) But Jehovah has not revealed in advance the exact time. (Acts 1:7) Hence, Jehovah's people have had to adjust their views in this matter.

Such adjustments in viewpoint do not mean that God's purpose has changed. Nor do they suggest that the end of this system is necessarily a long way off. On the contrary, the fulfillment of Bible prophecies concerning "the conclusion of the system of things" confirms the nearness of the end. (Matt. 24:3) Well, does the fact that Jehovah's Witnesses have had some premature expectations mean that they are not being led by God? Not any more than the disciples' question about the imminence of the Kingdom in their day meant that they were not chosen and led by God! —Acts 1:6; compare Acts 2:47; 6:7.

Why are Jehovah's Witnesses so sure that they have the true religion? Because they believe and accept what the Bible says as to the identifying marks of true worshipers. Their modern-day history, as discussed in earlier chapters of this publication, shows that, not just as individuals but as an organization, they meet the requisites: They loyally advocate the Bible as God's sacred Word of truth (John 17:17); they keep completely separate from worldly affairs (Jas. 1:27; 4:4); they bear witness to the divine name, Jehovah, and proclaim God's Kingdom as mankind's only hope (Matt. 6:9; 24:14; John 17:26); and they genuinely love one another.—John 13: 34, 35.

Why is love an outstanding identifying mark of worshipers of the true God? What sort of love is it that identifies true Christians?

Jehovah has led his people as a progressive organization, gradually enlightening them as to Bible truths

CHAPTER 32

"BY THIS ALL WILL KNOW THAT YOU ARE MY DISCIPLES"

IT WAS Nisan 14, 33 C.E., the final night of Jesus' earthly life. He knew that his death was near, but he was not thinking of himself. Instead, he took advantage of this opportunity to encourage his disciples.

Jesus knew that it would not be easy for them after his departure. They would be "objects of hatred by all the nations" on account of his name. (Matt. 24:9) Satan would try to divide and corrupt them. (Luke 22:31) As a result of apostasy, imitation Christians would spring up. (Matt. 13: 24-30, 36-43) And 'because of the increasing of lawlessness the love of the greater number would cool off.' (Matt. 24:12) In the face of all of this, what would hold his genuine disciples together? Above all, their love for Jehovah would serve as a uniting bond for them. (Matt. 22:37, 38) But they would also have to love one another and do so in a way that would distinguish them from the rest of the world. (Col. 3:14; 1 John 4:20) What sort of love did Jesus say would clearly identify his true followers?

What sort of love did Jesus say would clearly identify his true followers?

That final evening, Jesus laid this command upon them: "I am giving you a new commandment, that you love one another; just as I have loved you, that you also love one another. By this all will know that you are my disciples, if you have love among yourselves." (John 13:34, 35) Jesus spoke of love more than 20 times that night. And three times he stated the command that they "love one another." (John 15:12, 17) Clearly, Jesus had in mind not just his 11 faithful apostles who were with him that evening but all others who would eventually embrace true Christianity. (Compare John 17:20, 21.) The command to love one another would be binding upon genuine Christians "all the days until the conclusion of the system of things."—Matt. 28:20.

But did Jesus mean that just any individual anywhere in the world who showed kindness and love to his fellowman would thereby be identified as one of Jesus' genuine disciples?

"Have Love *Among Yourselves*"

On that same evening, Jesus also had much to say about unity. "Remain in union with me," he told his disciples. (John 15:4) He prayed that his followers would "all be one," and added, "just as you, Father, are in union with me and I am in union with you, that they also may be in union with us." (John 17:21) In this context he commanded them: "Have love *among yourselves.*" (John 13:35) So their love would be expressed not simply toward a few close friends or within a single congregation. Echoing Jesus' command, the apostle Peter later wrote: "Have love for the whole association of brothers [or, 'the brotherhood']." (1 Pet. 2:17, *Kingdom Interlinear;* compare 1 Peter 5:9.) So they would be a close-knit, worldwide brotherhood. Special love would be due all within the global family of believers because they would be viewed as brothers and sisters.

They would be a close-knit, worldwide brotherhood

How would such love be manifest? What would be so distinctive, so different, about their love for one another that others would see in it clear evidence of true Christianity?

"As I Have Loved You"

"You must love your fellow as yourself," stated God's Law to Israel more than 1,500 years before Jesus lived on earth. (Lev. 19:18) Such love of neighbor, though, was not the kind of love that would distinguish Jesus' followers. Jesus had in mind a love that would go far beyond loving others as yourself.

The command to love one another was, as Jesus said, "a new commandment." New, not because it was more recent than the Mosaic Law, but new in the extent to which the love was to be carried out. Love one another "as I have loved you," explained Jesus. (John 13:34) His love for his disciples was strong, constant. It was a *self-sacrificing* love. He demonstrated it by doing more than just a few good deeds for them. He fed them spiritually and, when necessary, cared for their physical needs. (Matt. 15: 32-38; Mark 6:30-34) And in ultimate proof of his love, he gave his life for them.—John 15:13.

Such is the outstanding kind of love that the "new commandment" calls for, the love that Jesus' true followers would have for one another. (1 John 3:16) Who today give clear proof of obeying the "new commandment"? The evidence presented earlier in this publication unequivocally points to one worldwide association of Christians.

They are known, not by a peculiar form of dress or some unusual customs, but by the strong and warm attachment that they have to one another. They have a reputation for demonstrating a love that surmounts racial differences and national boundaries. They are known for refusing to fight against one another even when the nations in which they live go to war. Others have been impressed at how they reach out to one another in times of adversity, such as when natural disasters strike or when some members of their brotherhood are persecuted for maintaining integrity to

God. They are ready to endure hardship or encounter danger to help their brothers and sisters for whom Christ laid down his life. And, yes, they are willing to die for one another. The love that they demonstrate is unique in a world of increasing selfishness. They are Jehovah's Witnesses.*

An example of such love in action was seen following Hurricane Andrew, which hit the coast of Florida, U.S.A., in the early morning hours of Monday, August 24, 1992. In its wake some 250,000 people were left homeless. Among the victims were thousands of Jehovah's Witnesses. Almost immediately the Governing Body of Jehovah's Witnesses acted by appointing a relief committee and arranging to make relief funds available. Christian overseers in the stricken area quickly contacted individual Witnesses to assess their needs and render assistance. Already on Monday morning, the day of the storm, Witnesses in South Carolina, hundreds of miles away, dispatched to the disaster area a truck loaded with generators, chain saws, and drinking water. On Tuesday, along with more supplies that had been donated, hundreds of out-of-town volunteers arrived to assist the local brothers in repairing Kingdom Halls and private homes. Regarding the relief efforts, a non-Witness woman who lived near a Kingdom Hall remarked: "This truly has to be the Christian love the Bible speaks of."

Would such love subside after one or two acts of kindness? Would it be directed only toward people of the same race or nationality? Certainly not! As a result of unstable political and economic conditions in Zaire, during 1992 over 1,200 Witnesses there lost their homes and all their belongings. Other Witnesses in Zaire quickly came to their aid. Even though hard-pressed themselves, they also shared with refugees that came into Zaire from Sudan. Soon, relief supplies arrived from South Africa and France; these included cornmeal, salted fish, and medical supplies—items that they could really use. Again and again, help was provided, as conditions required. And while this was going on, similar help was being provided in many other lands.

Yet, their having such love does not make Jehovah's Witnesses complacent. They realize that, as followers of Jesus Christ, they must continue to keep on the watch.

"Witnesses Care for Their Own—And Others"

Under that heading, "The Miami Herald" reported on the relief efforts of Jehovah's Witnesses in South Florida following the devastation caused by Hurricane Andrew in August 1992. The article stated: "No one in Homestead is slamming doors on the Jehovah's Witnesses this week—even if they still have doors to slam. About 3,000 Witness volunteers from across the country have converged on the disaster area, first to help their own, then to help others.... About 150 tons of food and supplies have funneled through a command post at the Assembly Hall in western Broward County to two Kingdom Halls in the Homestead area. From the halls, crews fan out each morning to repair the battered homes of Witness brethren.... A field kitchen churns out meals for up to 1,500 persons, three times a day. And it's not just hot dogs and doughnuts. Volunteers are treated to home-baked bread, lasagna from scratch, tossed salads, stew, flapjacks and French toast—all from donated ingredients."—August 31, 1992, page 15A.

---

* See Chapter 19, "Growing Together in Love."

CHAPTER 33

Continuing to Keep on the Watch

"SINCE Jesus clearly stated that no man could know 'that day' or 'the hour' when the Father will order his son to 'come' against Satan's wicked system of things, some may ask: 'Why is it so urgent to live in expectation of the end?' It is urgent because practically in the same breath, Jesus added: 'Keep looking, keep awake . . . keep on the watch.' (Mark 13:32-35)" —*The Watchtower,* December 1, 1984.

Jehovah's Witnesses have been watching for decades now. Watching for what? For Jesus' coming in Kingdom power to execute judgment against Satan's wicked system of things and to extend the full benefits of his Kingdom reign earth wide! (Matt. 6:9, 10; 24:30; Luke 21:28; 2 Thess. 1:7-10) These watching ones know that the "sign" of Jesus' presence has been in evidence since 1914 and that the present system of things entered its last days in that year.—Matt. 24:3–25:46.

But, as yet, Jesus has not come as Executioner and Deliverer. So how do Jehovah's Witnesses view their present situation?

'Fully Assured' of Their Understanding

As a worldwide congregation, they have "the full assurance of their understanding." (Col. 2:2) It is not that they feel that they understand every detail of Jehovah's purposes. They keep searching the Scriptures with an open mind, and they keep learning. But what they learn does not change their basic viewpoint regarding the *fundamental truths* of God's Word. They are 'fully assured' of these foundation truths; they have recognized and accepted them for many decades now. What they learn does, however, continually improve their understanding of how certain scriptures fit into the overall pattern of Bible truth and how they can more fully apply the counsel of God's Word in their own lives.

Jehovah's Witnesses have "full assurance" also concerning *God's promises*. They have absolute confidence that none of his promises will fail even in the smallest detail and that all of them will be fulfilled in his appointed time. The fulfillment of Bible prophecy that they have both seen and experienced thus leaves them fully assured that the present world is in its "time of the end" and that God's promise of a righteous new world will soon be realized.—Dan. 12:4, 9; Rev. 21:1-5.

Fully assured that the present world is in its "time of the end"

What, then, should they be doing? "Keep looking, keep awake," commanded Jesus, "for you do not know when the appointed time is. Therefore keep on the watch . . . in order that when [the Master] arrives suddenly, he does not find you sleeping. But what I say to you I say to all, Keep on the watch." (Mark 13:33, 35-37) Jehovah's Witnesses are keenly aware of the need to keep on the watch.

The overeagerness that they have at times manifested regarding the fulfillment of certain prophecies does not alter the evidence piling up since World War I that we are in the conclusion of the system of things. Surely, it is far better to be zealous—even overzealous—to see God's will accomplished than to be spiritually asleep to the fulfillment of his purposes!—Compare Luke 19:11; Acts 1:6; 1 Thessalonians 5:1, 2, 6.

What does keeping on the watch involve?

Keeping on the Watch—How?

Watchful Christians do not just fold their arms and wait. Far from it! They must keep in fit condition spiritually so that when Jesus comes as Executioner, he will also prove to be their Deliverer. (Luke 21:28) "Pay attention to yourselves," Jesus warned, "that your hearts never become weighed down with overeating and heavy drinking and anxieties of life, and suddenly that day be instantly upon you as a snare. . . . Keep awake." (Luke 21:34-36) Thus, watching Christians must first 'pay attention to themselves,' being careful to live each day as a Christian should. They must stay wide awake to Christian responsibilities and avoid the unchristian conduct characteristic of a world "lying in the power of the wicked one." (1 John 5:19; Rom. 13:11-14) When Christ comes, they must be ready.

Being careful to live each day as a Christian should

Who have truly kept wide awake, in fit condition spiritually? The historical record presented in earlier chapters of this publication points to Jehovah's Witnesses. Clearly, they take seriously the responsibilities involved in being Christians. In time of war, for example, they have been willing to risk imprisonment and death because of being wide awake to the obligation to be no part of the world and to show self-sacrificing love for one another. (John 13:34, 35; 17:14, 16) Persons who observe them at their Kingdom Halls, at their large conventions, or even on their secular jobs are impressed by their 'fine conduct.' (1 Pet. 2:12) In this world that has "come to be past all moral sense," they have a reputation for leading honest, morally clean lives.—Eph. 4:19-24; 5:3-5.

Keeping on the watch, though, involves more than 'paying attention to yourself.' A watchman must announce to others what he sees. In this time of the end, watchful Christians who clearly see the sign of Christ's presence must proclaim to others the "good news of the kingdom" and must warn them that soon Christ will come and execute judgment against this wicked system of things. (Matt. 24:14, 30, 44) In this way they help others to put themselves in line for "deliverance."—Luke 21:28.

Who have proved to be on the watch by sounding the warning? Jehovah's Witnesses are known the world over for their zeal in proclaiming God's name and Kingdom. They do not reserve preaching for a select clergy class. They recognize that it is a responsibility of *all* believers. They view it as an essential part of their worship. (Rom. 10:9, 10; 1 Cor. 9:16) What have been the results?

They now constitute a growing congregation of millions of active members in over 220 lands throughout the earth. (Isa. 60:22; compare Acts 2:47; 6:7; 16:5.) Some of the most powerful governments in the history of mankind have banned their work, even rounding them up and putting them into prison. But Jehovah's Witnesses have continued to proclaim God's Kingdom! Their determination is like that of the apostles who, when ordered to stop preaching, declared: "As for us, we cannot stop speaking about the things we have seen and heard." "We must obey God as ruler rather than men."—Acts 4:18-20; 5:27-29.

"Keep in Expectation of It"

The situation of Jehovah's Witnesses today is similar to that of first-century Judean Christians. Jesus had given them a sign whereby they would know when it was time to flee from Jerusalem so as to escape its destruction. "When you see Jerusalem surrounded by encamped armies, . . . begin fleeing," Jesus said. (Luke 21:20-23) A little more than 30 years later, in 66 C.E., Jerusalem was surrounded by Roman armies. When the Roman forces suddenly withdrew for no apparent reason, Judean Christians followed Jesus' instructions and fled—not just from Jerusalem but from the whole land of Judea—to a city in Perea called Pella.

There, in safety, they waited. The year 67 C.E. came and went. Then 68 gave way to 69. Yet, Jerusalem remained free. Should they return? After all, Jesus had not said how long to wait. But if any did return, it was too bad, for in 70 C.E. the Roman armies came back in numbers that caused their impact to be like a flood that could not be stopped, and this time they did not withdraw. Instead, they demolished the city and killed more than a million people. How happy those Judean Christians in Pella must have been that they had kept waiting for Jehovah's appointed time to execute judgment!

It is similar with those keeping on the watch today. They fully realize that the deeper we get into this time of the end, the more challenging it will be to *keep* in expectation of Jesus' coming. But they have not lost faith in Jesus' words: "Truly I say to you that this generation will by no means pass away until all these things occur." (Matt. 24:34) The expression

Who have proved to be on the watch by sounding the warning?

"these things" refers to the various features of the composite "sign." This sign has been in evidence since 1914 and will culminate at the "great tribulation." (Matt. 24:21) The "generation" that was alive in 1914 is fast dwindling. The end cannot be far off.

Meanwhile, Jehovah's Witnesses are absolutely determined to keep on the watch, in full faith that God will carry out all of his promises *at his due time!* They take to heart Jehovah's words to the prophet Habakkuk. Concerning Jehovah's apparent toleration of wickedness in the kingdom of Judah during the latter part of the seventh century B.C.E., Jehovah told the prophet: "Write down the vision [concerning the end of the oppressive conditions], and set it out plainly upon tablets, in order that the one reading aloud from it may do so fluently. For the vision is yet for the appointed time, and it keeps panting on to the end, and it will not tell a lie. Even if it should [appear to] delay, keep in expectation of it; for it will without fail come true. It will not be late." (Hab. 1:2, 3; 2:2, 3) Similarly, Jehovah's Witnesses have confidence in Jehovah's righteousness and justice, and this helps them to keep their balance and to wait for Jehovah's "appointed time."

F. W. Franz, who was baptized in 1913, well expressed the feelings of Jehovah's Witnesses. In 1991, as president of the Watch Tower Society, he stated:

"Our hope is a sure thing, and it will be fulfilled fully to every last one of the 144,000 members of the little flock to a degree beyond what we have even imagined. We of the remnant who were on hand in the year 1914, when we expected all of us to go to heaven, have not lost our sense of value of that hope. But we are as strong for it as we ever were, and we are appreciating it all the more the longer we have to wait for it. It is something *worth* waiting for, even if it required a million years. I evaluate our hope more highly than ever before, and I *never* want to lose my appreciation for it. The hope of the little flock also gives assurance that the expectation of the great crowd of other sheep will, without any possibility of failure, be fulfilled beyond our brightest imagination. That is why we are holding fast down to this very hour, and we are going to hold fast until God has actually proved that he is true to his 'precious and very grand promises.'" —2 Pet. 1:4; Num. 23:19; Rom. 5:5.

The time is rapidly approaching when Christ's presence in Kingdom power will be made clearly manifest to all humankind. Then, the watching ones will "receive the fulfillment of the promise." (Heb. 10:36) Indeed, their expectations will be fulfilled beyond 'what they have ever imagined.' How happy and how thankful they will be that in the closing days of this wicked system of things, they were the ones who continued to keep on the watch, the ones who zealously proclaimed God's Kingdom!

> *"I evaluate our hope more highly than ever before, and I never want to lose my appreciation for it"* —F. W. Franz

Reports of Global Witnessing

Total Lands

Year	Lands	Year	Lands	Year	Lands
1920	46	1945	107	1970	208
1925	83	1950	147	1975	212
1930	87	1955	164	1980	217
1935	115	1960	187	1985	222
1940	112	1965	201	1992	229

The number of lands is calculated according to the way the earth was divided in the early 1990's, not according to political divisions that prevailed, for example, when former large empires ruled territory that now is divided among a number of independent nations.

Total Congregations

Year	Congs.	Year	Congs.	Year	Congs.	Year	Congs.
1940	5,130	1955	16,044	1970	26,524	1985	49,716
1945	7,218	1960	21,008	1975	38,256	1992	69,558
1950	13,238	1965	24,158	1980	43,181		

Before 1938 no consistent international record of the total number of congregations was kept.

Total Kingdom Publishers

Year	Pubs.	Year	Pubs.
1935	56,153	1965	1,109,806
1940	96,418	1970	1,483,430
1945	156,299	1975	2,179,256
1950	373,430	1980	2,272,278
1955	642,929	1985	3,024,131
1960	916,332	1992	4,472,787

The method of counting publishers underwent a number of changes during the 1920's and the early 1930's. Congregation reports were sent to the Society weekly, instead of once a month. (Monthly reports did not go into effect until October 1932.) To be counted as a class worker (congregation publisher), one had to devote at least 3 hours a week (or 12 per month) to the field service, according to the "Bulletin" of January 1, 1929. Sharpshooters (isolated publishers) were to devote at least two hours per week to witnessing.

Pioneers

Year	Pioneers	Year	Pioneers	Year	Pioneers
1920	480	1945	6,721	1970	88,871
1925	1,435	1950	14,093	1975	130,225
1930	2,897	1955	17,011	1980	137,861
1935	4,655	1960	30,584	1985	322,821
1940	5,251	1965	47,853	1992	605,610

The figures listed here include regular pioneers, auxiliary pioneers, special pioneers, missionaries, circuit overseers, and district overseers. Pioneers were formerly known as colporteurs, and auxiliary pioneers as auxiliary colporteurs. For most years the figures represent monthly averages.

Home Bible Studies

Year	Bi. St.	Year	Bi. St.
1945	104,814	1970	1,146,378
1950	234,952	1975	1,411,256
1955	337,456	1980	1,371,584
1960	646,108	1985	2,379,146
1965	770,595	1992	4,278,127

During the 1930's, some studies were conducted with individuals, but emphasis was on teaching people how to do it themselves, also on organizing studies that could be attended by other interested persons in the area. Later, when individuals showed genuine interest, studies were conducted with them until they got baptized. Still later, encouragement was given to continue the study until the person had been given substantial help toward becoming a mature Christian.

Total Hours

Years	Hours	Years	Hours
1930-35	42,205,307	1961-65	760,049,417
1936-40	63,026,188	1966-70	1,070,677,035
1941-45	149,043,097	1971-75	1,637,744,774
1946-50	240,385,017	1976-80	1,646,356,541
1951-55	370,550,156	1981-85	2,276,287,442
1956-60	555,859,540	1986-92	5,912,814,412

There was no general reporting of time until the late 1920's. The method of counting hours underwent a number of changes: In the early 1930's, only time devoted to house-to-house witnessing was counted—not what was spent on return visits. While the report shown here is truly impressive, it is really only an approximation of the vast amount of time devoted by Jehovah's Witnesses to the work of proclaiming God's Kingdom.

Literature Distributed

Years	Lit. Dist.	Years	Lit. Dist.
1920-25	38,757,639	1956-60	493,202,895
1926-30	64,878,399	1961-65	681,903,850
1931-35	144,073,004	1966-70	935,106,627
1936-40	164,788,909	1971-75	1,407,578,681
1941-45	178,265,670	1976-80	1,380,850,717
1946-50	160,027,404	1981-85	1,504,980,839
1951-55	237,151,701	1986-92	2,715,998,934

With some few exceptions, the figures for years before 1940 do not include magazine placements, although millions of copies were distributed. Figures since 1940 include books, booklets, brochures, and magazines, but not the hundreds of millions of tracts that have also been used to stimulate interest in the Kingdom message. The total of 10,107,565,269 pieces of literature distributed from 1920 to 1992 in more than 290 languages gives evidence of an extraordinary global witness.

Memorial Attendance and Partakers

Year	Att.	Part.	Year	Att.	Part.
1935	63,146	52,465	1965	1,933,089	11,550
1940	96,989	27,711	1970	3,226,168	10,526
1945	186,247	22,328	1975	4,925,643	10,550
1950	511,203	22,723	1980	5,726,656	9,564
1955	878,303	16,815	1985	7,792,109	9,051
1960	1,519,821	13,911	1992	11,431,171	8,683

Before 1932, available figures for Memorial attendance are often incomplete. At times, only groups of 15, 20, 30, or more were being included in totals published. Interestingly, most years for which any figures are available show that at least some of the attenders were not partakers. By 1933 the difference was about 3,000.

Noteworthy Events in the Modern-Day History of Jehovah's Witnesses

1870 Charles Taze Russell and a group from Pittsburgh and Allegheny, Pennsylvania, U.S.A., begin systematic study of the Bible

1870-75 Russell and his study associates learn that when Christ comes again he is to be invisible to human eyes and that the object of his return includes the blessing of all families of the earth

1872 Russell and his study group come to appreciate the *ransom price* that Christ provided for humankind

1876 C. T. Russell receives a copy of *Herald of the Morning*, in January; meets N. H. Barbour, the editor, that summer in Philadelphia, Pennsylvania

Article by C. T. Russell, published in October issue of *Bible Examiner*, in Brooklyn, New York, points to 1914 as the end of the Gentile Times

1877 The book *Three Worlds* is published, as a result of joint efforts of N. H. Barbour and C. T. Russell

C. T. Russell publishes the booklet *The Object and Manner of Our Lord's Return*, at the office of *Herald of the Morning*, in Rochester, New York

1879 Russell withdraws all support from *Herald of the Morning*, in May, because of Barbour's attitude toward the ransom

First issue of *Zion's Watch Tower and Herald of Christ's Presence*, dated July 1879

1881 First tracts published by Bible Students; before 1914, yearly tract distribution totals tens of millions of copies in 30 languages

Zion's Watch Tower Tract Society is organized; call goes out "Wanted 1,000 Preachers," some to be regular colporteurs, others to give whatever time they can to spreading Bible truth

Distribution of 300,000 copies of *Food for Thinking Christians* to churchgoers in principal cities in Britain

1883 *Watch Tower* reaches China; former Presbyterian missionary soon begins to witness to others there

1884 *Food for Thinking Christians* reaches Liberia, Africa; an appreciative reader writes to ask for copies to distribute

Zion's Watch Tower Tract Society is legally chartered in Pennsylvania; officially recorded on December 15

1885 Watch Tower publications are already being read by some truth-hungry people in North and South America, Europe, Africa, and Asia

1886 *The Divine Plan of the Ages* is published, the first volume of the series called *Millennial Dawn* (later known as *Studies in the Scriptures*)

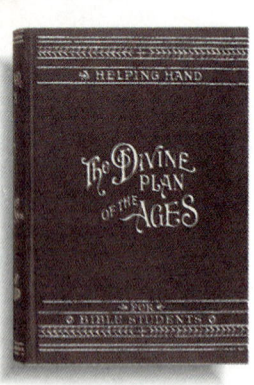

NOTEWORTHY EVENTS 719

1889 The Bible House is constructed on Arch Street, in Allegheny, Pennsylvania, as headquarters for the Society

1891 First gathering of Bible Students that they call a convention, in Allegheny, Pennsylvania (April 19-25)

1894 Traveling overseers that in time came to be known as pilgrims (today, circuit and district overseers) are sent out in connection with the Society's program for visiting congregations

1900 The Watch Tower Society's first branch office is opened, in London, England

Witnessing by the Bible Students has been done in 28 countries, and the message they preach has reached 13 other lands

1903 Intense house-to-house distribution of free tracts on Sundays; earlier, much of the tract distribution was done on streets near churches

1904 Sermons by C. T. Russell begin to appear regularly in newspapers; within a decade they are being printed by about 2,000 papers

1909 Headquarters of the Society is moved to Brooklyn, New York, in April

1914 First showing of the "Photo-Drama of Creation," in New York, in January; before the end of the year, it is seen by audiences totaling over 9,000,000 in North America, Europe, and Australia

On October 2, in the Bethel dining room at Brooklyn, C. T. Russell affirms, "The Gentile times have ended"

Bible Students are active preaching in 43 lands; 5,155 share in witnessing to others; reported Memorial attendance is 18,243

1916 Death of C. T. Russell at 64 years of age, on October 31, while on a train traveling through Texas

1917 J. F. Rutherford becomes president of Society on January 6, after an executive committee of three has administered the Society's affairs for about two months

The book *The Finished Mystery* is released to the Bethel family in Brooklyn on July 17; four who had been serving on the Society's board of directors become heated in their opposition; thereafter many congregations are split

1918 The discourse "The World Has Ended—Millions Now Living May Never Die" is first delivered, on February 24, in Los Angeles, California. On March 31, in Boston, Massachusetts, the talk is entitled "The World Has Ended—Millions Now Living *Will* Never Die"

J. F. Rutherford and close associates are named in federal arrest warrants issued on May 7; trial begins on June 5; they are sentenced on June 21 (one on July 10) to long terms in federal penitentiary

Brooklyn headquarters is closed in August, and its operations are transferred back to Pittsburgh for over a year

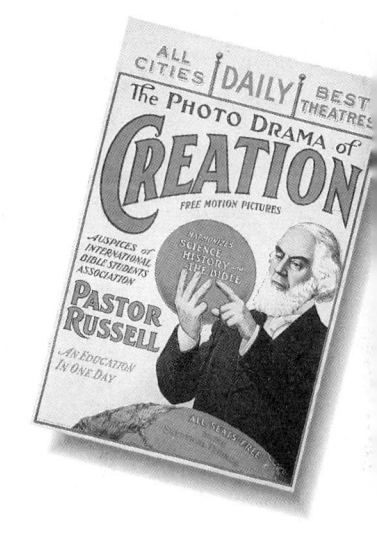

1919 The Society's officers and associates are released on bail, on March 26; on May 14 the court of appeals reverses the decision of the lower court, and a new trial is ordered; the next year, on May 5, the government withdraws from the case, declining to prosecute

As a test to see whether the work of the Bible Students can be revived, J. F. Rutherford arranges to give the public lecture "The Hope for Distressed Humanity," at Clune's Auditorium, in Los Angeles, California, on May 4; the crowd cannot all fit in, and the talk has to be given a second time

Bible Students hold convention at Cedar Point, Ohio, September 1-8; coming publication of the magazine *The Golden Age* (now known as *Awake!*) is announced

Bulletin (now known as *Our Kingdom Ministry*) is published as stimulus to field service

Report for the year shows 5,793 Bible Students actively preaching in 43 lands; reported Memorial attendance, 21,411

1920 Watch Tower Society undertakes its own printing operations, in Brooklyn

1922 Radio is first used by J. F. Rutherford, on February 26, in California, to broadcast a Bible discourse

Convention of Bible Students at Cedar Point, Ohio, September 5-13; the appeal is made "Advertise, advertise, advertise, the King and his kingdom"

Clergy in Germany agitate for police to arrest Bible Students when these engage in public distribution of Bible literature

1924 WBBR (first radio station owned by Watch Tower Society) begins to broadcast on February 24

1925 *Watch Tower* of March 1, in discussing the birth of God's Kingdom in 1914, shows that there are two distinct and opposing organizations —Jehovah's and Satan's

1926 House-to-house preaching with books on Sunday is encouraged

1928 Bible Students are arrested in New Jersey (U.S.A.) for distributing literature as part of their house-to-house preaching; within a decade, there are over 500 such arrests per year in the United States

1931 The name Jehovah's Witnesses is adopted by resolution at a convention in Columbus, Ohio, on July 26, and thereafter at conventions around the earth

1932 *Vindication*, Book 2, explains why Biblical restoration prophecies apply not to the natural Jews but to spiritual Israel

Arrangement for "elective elders" is terminated, in harmony with explanation in *Watchtower* issues of August 15 and September 1

1933 Jehovah's Witnesses are banned in Germany. During the intense persecution down to the end of World War II, 6,262 are arrested, and their combined time of imprisonment totals 14,332 years; 2,074 are sent to concentration camps, where their confinement totals 8,332 years

Transcription machines (some mounted on automobiles) are used by Witnesses to broadcast Bible lectures in public places

NOTEWORTHY EVENTS 721

1934 Portable phonographs are used by Witnesses to play short recorded Bible discourses for interested ones

1935 In convention discourse at Washington, D.C., on May 31, the "great multitude" is identified as an earthly class; 840 persons are baptized at this convention; greater emphasis is progressively given to hope of eternal life on a paradise earth for faithful servants of God now living

Meeting place is, for the first time, called Kingdom Hall, in Honolulu, Hawaii

1936 Advertising placards are first worn by Kingdom publishers to notify public of Bible lectures

Encouragement is given to start studies with interested people, using the Society's book *Riches* along with the Bible; these are frequently group studies

1937 Portable phonographs are used by Witnesses to play recorded Bible talks right on the doorsteps of homes

1938 Theocratic arrangements for selecting overseers in congregations replace democratic procedures, in harmony with *Watchtower* issues of June 1 and 15

Zone assemblies (now known as circuit assemblies) are arranged for groups of congregations

1939-45 Throughout British Empire and British Commonwealth, 23 nations ban Jehovah's Witnesses or place prohibitions on their Bible literature

1940 Street distribution of *Watchtower* and *Consolation* becomes a regular feature of the activity of Jehovah's Witnesses

Decision of U.S. Supreme Court, on June 3, upholding mandatory flag salute regardless of religious belief unleashes nationwide mob violence against Jehovah's Witnesses

1941 Active Witnesses pass the 100,000 mark, reaching a peak of 109,371 in 107 lands, in spite of the fact that World War II has engulfed Europe and is spreading in Africa and Asia

1942 J. F. Rutherford dies on January 8, in San Diego, California.

N. H. Knorr becomes third president of Society on January 13

Total printing of *Watchtower* for the year in all languages is 11,325,143

An Advanced Course in Theocratic Ministry is inaugurated for the Society's headquarters staff, on February 16

Watch Tower Society prints the complete Bible, *King James Version,* on its own press (a web rotary)

1943 First class of Watchtower Bible School of Gilead begins its studies on February 1

Course in Theocratic Ministry (now called Theocratic Ministry School) for congregations of Jehovah's Witnesses introduced at assemblies in April

U.S. Supreme Court renders decisions favorable to Jehovah's Witnesses in 20 out of 24 cases; High Court in Australia lifts ban on Witnesses there, on June 14

1945 As of October 1, the Society's board of directors is no longer selected by voters who qualify because of monetary donations

Average number of free home Bible studies being conducted each month is now 104,814

1946 During the preceding seven years, over 4,000 of Jehovah's Witnesses in the United States and 1,593 in Britain have been arrested and sentenced to prison terms ranging from a month to five years because of their Christian neutrality

In this first year after World War II, 6,504 are sharing in full-time service as pioneers

Awake! magazine (successor to *The Golden Age* and *Consolation*) begins publication; total printing of 13,934,429 copies for the year

Over 470 Witnesses are taken before the courts in Greece because of sharing Bible teachings with others

1947 In Quebec, Canada, 1,700 cases involving the evangelizing work of Jehovah's Witnesses are pending in the courts

Number of congregations now exceeds 10,000, reaching a total of 10,782 worldwide

1950 *New World Translation of the Christian Greek Scriptures* is released in English, on August 2, at convention in New York

1953 An extensive program of training of Jehovah's Witnesses in house-to-house preaching gets under way, September 1

1957 In 169 lands, 100,135,016 hours are devoted by Jehovah's Witnesses to proclaiming God's Kingdom and conducting Bible studies with newly interested persons

1958 Divine Will International Assembly, in New York, draws attendance of 253,922 from 123 lands; 7,136 baptized

1959 First sessions of Kingdom Ministry School, starting March 9, at South Lansing, New York, designed for congregation overseers and traveling overseers

1961 First group of the Society's branch overseers attends special ten-month training course at Brooklyn, New York, with a view to further unification of the work of Jehovah's Witnesses worldwide

New World Translation of the Holy Scriptures, the complete Bible in one volume, is released in English

1963 *New World Translation of the Christian Greek Scriptures* is released in six more languages (Dutch, French, German, Italian, Portuguese, and Spanish), with more to come in later years

Over a million of Jehovah's Witnesses are now active in 198 lands; peak of publishers for the year is 1,040,836; 62,798 more baptized

1965 First Assembly Hall, a renovated theater, is put to use by Jehovah's Witnesses in New York

1967 Waves of prolonged and savage persecution of Jehovah's Witnesses sweep across Malawi and continue for years thereafter

NOTEWORTHY EVENTS

1969 Home Bible studies exceed a million; report shows average of 1,097,237

1971 Governing Body is enlarged; on October 1, chairmanship begins to rotate among its members on an annual basis

1972 Congregations of Jehovah's Witnesses come under local supervision of body of elders, instead of one person, as of October 1

1974 Peak publishers worldwide reach 2,021,432; pioneers increase from 94,604, in 1973, to 127,135

1975 Governing Body is reorganized; on December 4, responsibility for much of the work is assigned to six committees, which begin to function on January 1, 1976

1976 Branch offices of Watch Tower Society each come under supervision of a committee of three or more spiritually mature men, instead of one overseer, as of February 1

1977 Pioneer Service School begins to provide specialized training for tens of thousands of pioneers worldwide

1984 Home Bible studies being conducted by Jehovah's Witnesses now average 2,047,113

1985 Arrangement for international volunteers is initiated, coordinating from headquarters the Society's worldwide construction work

Report shows 3,024,131 sharing in the work of Kingdom preaching in 222 lands; pioneers now average 322,821; 189,800 baptized this year

1986 Regional Building Committees appointed to help coordinate building of Kingdom Halls

1987 Disciple-making work continues to expand, as Bible studies are now being conducted with 3,005,048 individuals and family groups, many on a weekly basis; baptisms for the year total 230,843

Ministerial Training School goes into operation on October 1, with first class at Coraopolis, Pennsylvania

1989 Changing conditions in Eastern Europe help to make possible three large international conventions in Poland, and then in other lands in following years

1990 Lifting of restrictions on Jehovah's Witnesses in lands in Africa and Eastern Europe facilitate evangelizing among an additional 100,000,000 people

Kingdom publishers reach new peak of 4,017,213; pioneer ranks swell to 536,508; total of 895,229,424 hours are devoted to urgent work of Kingdom proclamation

1991 Bans lifted in Eastern Europe and Africa make it easier to reach 390,000,000 more people with the good news of God's Kingdom

1992 *Watchtower* has average printing of 15,570,000 in 111 languages; *Awake!*, available in 67 languages, has an average production of 13,110,000

Greatest witness ever given, as 4,472,787 share in Kingdom proclamation in 229 lands; monthly average of 605,610 pioneers; 1,024,910,434 hours devoted to public witnessing; 4,278,127 Bible studies conducted; 301,002 new disciples baptized

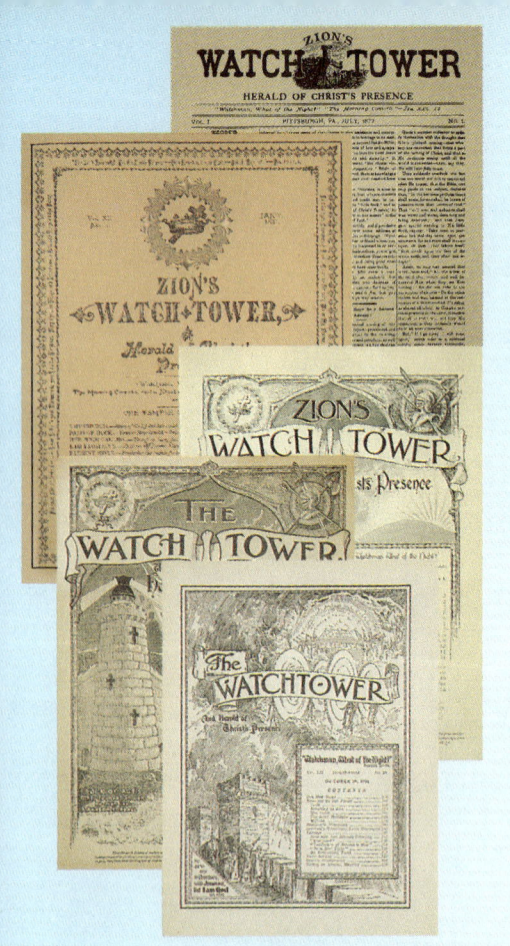

PUBLISHING *THE WATCHTOWER*

When first produced, in July 1879, it was called *Zion's Watch Tower and Herald of Christ's Presence*. This magazine, which was a champion of the ransom sacrifice of Jesus Christ, was published to serve spiritual food to the household of faith. On January 1, 1909, the title was changed to *The Watch Tower and Herald of Christ's Presence*, in order to focus attention more clearly on the objective of the magazine. As of January 1, 1939, putting increased emphasis on the fact that Christ was already ruling from heaven as King, the title was altered to read *The Watchtower and Herald of Christ's Kingdom*. Then on March 1, 1939, by changing the title to *The Watchtower Announcing Jehovah's Kingdom*, attention was directed more prominently to Jehovah as the Universal Sovereign, the one who gave ruling authority to his Son.

When first published, the *Watch Tower* was an eight-page paper, produced once a month. The size was increased to 16 pages in 1891, and it became a semimonthly magazine in 1892. A 32-page format was adopted for many languages in 1950.

Translation of the *Watch Tower* into other languages began slowly. A single sample issue was published in Swedish in 1883 for use as a tract. From 1886 to 1889, a small-sized edition of the mag-

AWAKE!—A MAGAZINE WITH BROAD PUBLIC APPEAL

This magazine originally bore the title *The Golden Age*. The first issue was dated October 1, 1919. This was a magazine that reported on many fields of human endeavor. It alerted people to what was going on in the world and showed them that the real solution to mankind's problems is Christ's Millennial Reign, which will truly usher in a "golden age" for humankind. The cover design of the magazine underwent changes, but the message remained the same. *The Golden Age* was designed for public distribution, and for many years its circulation was far in excess of that for *The Watch Tower*.

Beginning with the issue of October 6, 1937, the title was changed to *Consolation*. This was very appropriate in view of the oppression that many were experiencing and the turmoil in which

azine was printed in German. But it was not until 1897 that the *Watch Tower* appeared again in German and continued to be published on a consistent basis. By 1916 it was being printed in seven languages—Dano-Norwegian, English, Finnish, French, German, Polish, and Swedish. When the preaching of the good news took on greater momentum in 1922, the number of languages in which the magazine was published was increased to 16. As of 1993, however, it was being regularly produced in 112 languages—those used by a large proportion of earth's population. This included not only languages such as English, Spanish, and Japanese, in which millions of copies per issue were printed, but also Palauan, Tuvaluan, and others in which only a few hundred were being distributed.

For many years *The Watchtower* was viewed as a magazine largely for the "little flock" of consecrated Christians. Its circulation was somewhat limited; by 1916 only 45,000 copies were being printed. But beginning in 1935, repeated emphasis was placed on encouraging "the Jonadabs," or "great crowd," to obtain and read *The Watchtower* regularly. In 1939, when the cover of the magazine began to highlight the Kingdom, subscriptions for *The Watchtower* were offered to the public during a four-month international subscription campaign. As a result, the subscription list rose to 120,000. The following year *The Watchtower* was being regularly offered to people on the streets. Circulation increased rapidly. By early 1993 the printing per issue in all languages was 16,400,000.

the world became embroiled in World War II. The consolation that the magazine offered, however, was the sort that appeals only to those who have genuine love for truth.

As of the issue of August 22, 1946, the title *Awake!* was adopted. Emphasis was placed on awakening people to the significance of world events. The magazine used conventional news sources, but it also had its own correspondents around the globe. The balanced, practical in-depth articles in *Awake!* that discuss a wide range of subjects encourage readers to give consideration to this magazine's most important message, namely, that world events fulfill Bible prophecy, which shows that we live in the last days and that soon God's Kingdom will bring eternal benefits to those who learn and do God's will. This magazine has been an effective instrument in the global proclamation of the good news of the Kingdom of God and a bridge to deeper study material as set forth in *The Watchtower* and bound books.

By early 1993, *Awake!* was being printed in 67 languages, 13,240,000 copies per issue.

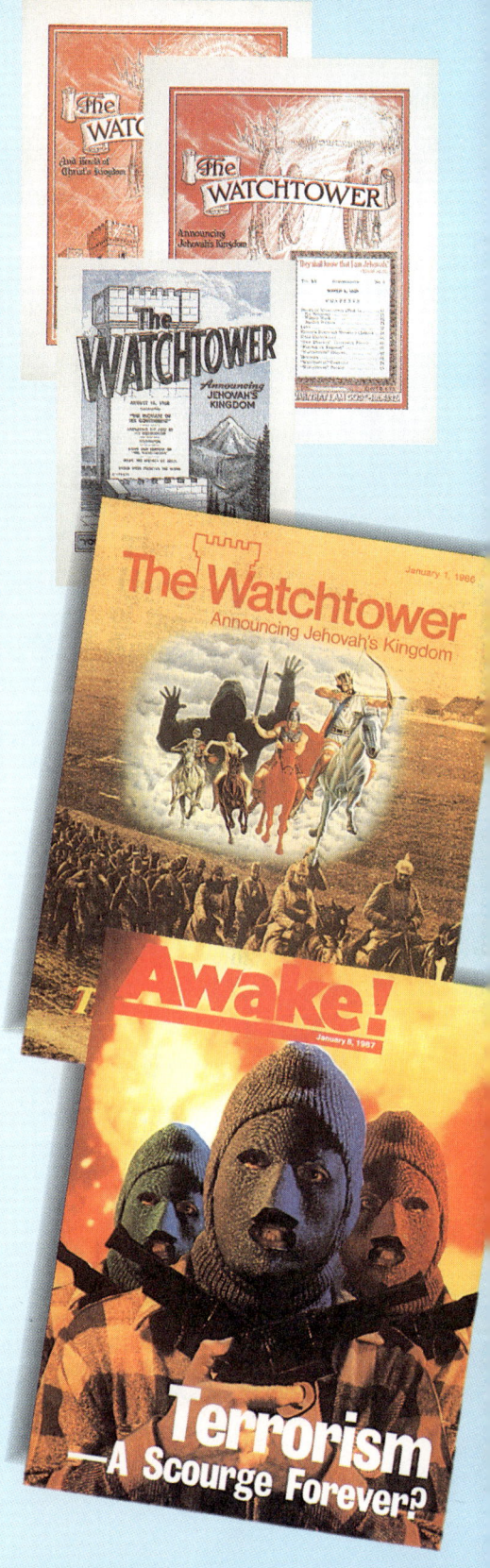

INDEX

*Page numbers set in italics refer to locations where pictures accompany the text.
Subject headings in italics usually are the names of publications*

A

Aaron: 15, *16*
Abbott, Eva: 158
Abel: 13
Abortion
   view of Witnesses: 183
Abrahamson, Richard E.: 91
Abrams, Ray: 191, 552, 655-6
Abt, Harald and Elsa: *453*
Ackley, Maria Frances (See Russell, Maria)
Adamson, J. B.: 627
"Address to Co-laborers"
   convention discourse, 1919: 258
ADV
   convention banner, 1922: 260
Advanced Course in Theocratic Ministry: 94, 568, 721
Adventists, Second: 45, 60
   Christ's return: 132
   influence on Russell: 43-4, 122
'Advertise the King and the Kingdom'
   convention, 1922: 72, 77-8, 138, 213, *259, 260*, 678, 720
Advertising
   newspapers: *560*, 561-2
   placards: 266, 567, *568*, 721
Advice for Kingdom Publishers
   legal procedures: 691, *692*
Afghanistan: 430, 469
Africa
   animism: 483
   bans: 675-6
   countries, number preached in, 1975: 488
   countries, number preached in, 1992: 518
   countries, number reached by 1945: 518
   early witnessing: 521, 548
   film showings: *481*
   how truth spread: 475, *477*
   literacy classes: 480
   local customs: 531
   Memorial attendance, 1992: 518
   persecution: 10
   polygamy: 176-7
   publishers, number: 435, 488, 501, 518
Agbetor, Akakpo: 477
Aid to Bible Understanding: 233
Aimé Boucher v. His Majesty The King
   court case: 689
Akintoundé, Nouru: 484
Akpabio, Asuquo: 176
Alaska
   branch office: *357*
   early witnessing: 440
   reaching remote areas: 357, 499
Albania
   bans: 675
   early witnessing: 429, 432
   legal recognition: 505, 697
Albu, Pamfil: *453*
Alcoholic beverages
   view of Witnesses: 181-2

Algeria: 430, 475
Allegheny, Pennsylvania
   early conventions: 55, 254
   headquarters of Bible Students: 54, 208, 719
   place of Russell's birth: 42
   place of Russell's burial: 64
"All Scripture Is Inspired of God and Beneficial": 103, 122
Amazon: 465
American Bar Association
   flag salute: 685
American Legion
   flag salute: 671
American Standard Version: 607
American Telephone and Telegraph Company
   radio network, 1931: 267
Amis: 536
Analytical Concordance: 605
Ancient worthies (See Princes)
Andersen, Anna: 559
Anderson, Andrew: 419
Anderson, C. H.: 68
Angels
   role in preaching work: 549-51
Angola
   Bible studies: 510, 701
   counterfeit Watchtower movements: 481-2
   early witnessing: 430, 437, 528
   freedom of worship: 510, 701
   publishers, number: 481-2, 488, 510
   relief received: 312
Anointed (See **144,000**)
Anointing
   purpose of: 51, 159
Antigua (See Leeward Islands)
Apostasy: 33-41
   early developments: 33-6
   Greek word: 33
   modern-day: 111
Appointments
   deacons, early views: 206-9
   elders, adjustments: 106, 233-4
   elders, early views: 206-9, 638-9
   elders, theocratic procedure: 218-19, 721
   Governing Body: 233, 639
   ministerial servants: 233-4
   service committee: 212, 214, 638
   service director: 212, 214, 637-8
   theocratic, benefits of: 220-1
   traveling speakers: 222-3
   V.D.M. Questions: 215
Ararat
   business association in Finland: 640
Argentina
   assemblies and conventions: 281, 467, *468*, 502-3
   attending meetings (experience): 253
   bans: 467, 502, 595, 675
   letter campaigns: 316, 695

   branch office: *366*
   web offset printing: 595
   early witnessing: 366, 412, 428, 436-8, 521
   flag salute: 672
   missionaries: 366, 539
   publishers, number: 366, 463
   reaching remote areas: 444-5, 466
Argyrós, Nicolás: 437, *438*, 444
Armageddon
   destruction: 170
   early view: 139-40
   later view: 140-1
Armenians: 428
Arnold, Adolphe, Emma, and Simone: *451*
Arnott, Harry: 537
Arrests
   Britain: 722
   Canada: 680, 689
   China: 490
   divisional campaigns: 82, 692
   Germany: 194, 451-2, 553, 678-9, 694, 720
   Greece: 680, 695
   Japan: 452, 455
   Netherlands: 267
   paying fines: 683
   Romania: 679-80
   Spain: 494
   United States: 194, 679-80, 683-4, 692, 720, 722
Aruba: 463
Asia and islands of the world
   preaching activity, 1992: 519
Assemblies (See also **Conventions**)
   circuit (zone): 226, 281, 721
   despite obstacles: 467-8
   efforts to attend: 281
   special assembly days: 281
Assembly Halls: *330*
   construction: 328-32
   court cases: 331-2
   donations: 347
   first: 328, *329*, 722
Associated Bible Students: 151
Atonement (See Ransom)
"Atonement, The": 47
At-one-ment Between God and Man, The: 53
Audiocassettes: *356*, 598, 615
Augustine: 36, *38*
Auschwitz concentration camp: 179, 452, 663
Australia
   Assembly Hall: 329
   ban: 10, 456-7, 586, 640-1, 658, 676
   lifted, 1943: 721
   printing operations: 586
   branch office: *400*
   area served in the past: *400*

construction: 335-6, 347
languages printed: 400
printing: 583, *590*, 592
Regional Engineering Office: 332, *400*
when established: 210, 419
clergy opposition: 447-8, 657
convention, 1941: *456*, 457
early witnessing: 418-19
field ministry, World War II: 457
Knorr's visit, 1947: 98, 641
missionaries sent out: 541
Pacific islands, help in witnessing: 470-1
"Photo-Drama of Creation": 60

radio station 2HD: *81*
reaching remote areas: 445
Rutherford visits, 1938: 246
sound cars: 567
tests of faith: 624, 640-1
Austria
bans: 675
providing literature: *450*, 454, 586
branch office: *373*
clergy opposition: 441, 543
congregations, number, 1992: 373
early witnessing: 373, 430
legal recognition: 696

"Millions Now Living Will Never Die,"
discourse: 426
persecution, World War II: 448
relief received and sent out: 308-9
Russell's visit, 1891: 406
Awake!
audiocassettes: 598
begins publication: 722
circulation: 683, 722-3, 725
languages, number: 592, 683, 723, 725
purpose: 724-5
replaces *Consolation:* 97

B

Babylon (ancient): 189
Babylon the Great
identity, early view: 52, 84, 189, 647
identity, later view: 84, 147-8
letter of withdrawal: 189
"Babylon the Great Has Fallen!" God's Kingdom Rules: 148
Back-calls: 85
Bahamas
ban: 676
branch office: *357*
Watch Tower literature reaches Bahamas: 357
Bangladesh: 537
Bans: 503, 505, 509-10, 657-9, 675-6, 680
assemblies: 468
countries, number: 117, 519, 676
lifting of restrictions in Africa and Eastern Europe, 1990-92: 723
list by country:
Africa, French territories: 675
Albania: 675
Argentina: 467, 502, 595
Australia: 10, 640-1, 676
Austria: 675
Bahamas: 676
Basutoland (Lesotho): 676
Bechuanaland (Botswana): 676
Belgium: 675
Brazil: 502
Britain: 721
British Guiana (Guyana): 676
Bulgaria: 675
Burma (Myanmar): 676
Canada: 10, 69-70, 498, 675, 696-8
Central African Republic: 477
Ceylon (Sri Lanka): 676
Cyprus: 676
Czechoslovakia: 675
Dahomey: 484
Dominica: 676
Estonia: 675
Fiji: 675-6
Germany: 442, 639, 675, 693-4, 720
Gold Coast (Ghana): 675-6
India: 675-6
Italy: 675
Jamaica: 676
Japan: 675
Korea: 675
Latvia: 675
Leeward Islands (British West Indies): 676

Lithuania: 675
Netherlands: 675
Netherlands East Indies: 675
New Caledonia: 471
New Zealand: 676
Nigeria: 486, 676
Northern Rhodesia (Zambia): 676
Norway: 675
Nyasaland: 675-6
Poland: 381, 503, 675
Portugal: *494*
Singapore: 676
South Africa: 676
Swaziland: 676
Switzerland: 675
Tahiti: 471
Trinidad: 675
United States: 675
Yugoslavia: 675
Zimbabwe: 392, 676
meetings: *494*
World War I: 675
World War II: 455, 457-8, 675-6, 720-1
Baptism
immersion: 145
Jonadabs: 83
number: 105, 107, 722-3
screening baptismal candidates: 186, 479
Baptist Church
origin of name: 150
Barbados
branch office: *358*
early witnessing: 358, 413, 461
Barber, Carey W.: *116, 226, 227*
Barber, Norman: 546
Barber, R. H.: 199
Barbour, Nelson H.: *48*
association with Russell: 120, 133-5, 575, 718
beliefs: 46-8, 133-5
death: 48
rejects ransom: 47, 131, 619-20
Russell severs ties: 47-8, 131
Three Worlds: 718
Barnette, Gathie and Marie: *686*
Barr, John E.: *116*, 598
Barry, Bill: 419
Barry, Mrs. Thomas: 419
Barry, W. Lloyd: *116*, 419, *491*
Basutoland (See **Lesotho**)
Battle of Armageddon, The: 53, 140
Beams, Captain: 440

Bechuanaland (See **Botswana**)
Beecher, Henry Ward: 59
Behannan, Harry: 485
Belarus: 506
Belgian Congo (See **Zaire**)
Belgium
ban: 675
branch office: *373*
clergy opposition: 448
early witnessing: 409-10, 429
Knorr's service tour: 96
languages in which literature is distributed: 373
persecution: 448, 492
relief provided: 308
Belize
branch office: *358*
early witnessing: 461
Kingdom Hall construction: 325
reaching remote areas: 358
Bell, Major-General James Franklin: 649
Bender, J. J.: 405, 561
Benedek, Andrásné: 430
Bengel, J. A.
Christ's return: 40
Benin
ban: 484
letter campaign: 695
branch office: *385*
clergy opposition: 385, 668
convention, 1990: *385*
early witnessing: 433, 483
legal recognition: 510, 696, *701*
literacy classes: 480
missionaries: 541
polygamy (experience): 176
publishers, number, 1948: 484
religious beliefs: 483-4
Bennecoff, Ethel: 78
"Be of Good Courage"
Watch Tower article, 1921: 563
"Berean Bible Study Helps": 238
Berean Circles for Bible Study: 237
"Berean Questions": 252
Bergen-Belsen concentration camp: 452
Berner, Alice: 298
Bethel (world headquarters)
Advanced Course in Theocratic Ministry: 94, 568, 721
Bethel family, growth worldwide: 113-14
buildings, early: *216-17*
buildings, 1992: *352-6*, 589

closed and relocated, 1918: 71, 577, 719
expansion: 98-9, 270-1, 336, 584, 588-9
financing the work: 345
factories: *354-6, 603*
   Bible printing: 606-7, 611, 613-15
   bindery: 580, 593
   leased factory space: 578, 580
   magazines, production capacity: 592
   web offset printing: 595
instruction programs: 112-13
literature, number of languages printed in Brooklyn: 355
morning worship: 112-13, 234
moved to Brooklyn: 59, 719
name: 59
rebellion at, after Russell's death: 66-8
reopened in Brooklyn, 1919: 76, 577-8
Watchtower Study: 234
Bethel service: 295, *296-7*, 298
faithful examples: 295, *298*
number:
   1896: 295
   1976: 114
   1992: 114, 295, *297*
vow of poverty: 351
Beth-Sarim: *76*, 89
sold: 76
"Beyond the Grave"
convention discourse, Russell: 257
Bhutan
early witnessing: 513
Bible
American Standard Version, Watchtower edition: 607
Byington translation: 607
commercial printers: 605
Emphatic Diaglott: 606
first, published under name of Watch Tower Society: 605
King James Version, Watchtower edition: 93, 606-7
languages, number, 1950: 608
New World Translation: 607, *608,* 609-15, 722
printing and distribution, Society's role: 603-15
various translations used by Witnesses: 604-8, 609-11
Bible, The—Accurate History, Reliable Prophecy
videocassette: 601
Bible, The—God's Word or Man's?: 112, 122
"Bible Brown" (See Brown, W. R.)
Bible Examiner: 45-6, 575
article by Russell: 134-5, 718
Storrs, editor: 45-6, 127, 135
Bible House (Allegheny, Pennsylvania): *208-9*
built, 1889: 54, *719*
outgrown: 59
typesetting and composition: 576
Bible Students: 149, 156
adjustments in understanding of God's purposes: 630, 637
character development: 292, 294
congregations, early: *239*
conventions: 254-61
   attendance: 255-9
   local assemblies: 255-6
   love feasts: 257
   prayers: 257
   program for colporteurs: 255
   resolutions, 1922-28: 260, *261*
   singing: 256-7
   travel arrangements: 255-6
meetings: 236-41
   Berean Circles for Bible Study: 237
   Cottage Meetings: 238, 241
   Dawn Circles for Bible Study: 237
   literature used: 237-8, 240-1, 252
   meeting places: 251, 318-19
   no collections: 237
   Prayer, Praise and Testimony Meetings: 238, 247
   prayers: 238
   public speakers: 248-9
   singing: 238, 240-1
   Sunday meetings: 238
   use of Bible: 238, 241
   Workers' Meetings: 247
   youths: 244-5
Memorial: 242-3
number: 404, 422, 425
persecution: 423-4, 552, 644, 647-56, 658, 678-9
preaching work: 404-43, 556-64
   all encouraged to share: 51, 562-4
   colporteurs: 405-6, 558-60
   hired assistants to distribute literature: 405
   tract distribution: 557
tests resulting from—
   adjustments in understanding: 629-30
   attitude toward ransom: 619-21
   business ventures: 639-41
   change of administration: 623-6
   expectations based on dates: 631-7
   field ministry and organization: 637-9
   pride: 626-9
Tower Tract Fund: 342-3, 348
view on "faithful and wise servant": 626
voluntary donations: 340-3
Bible Students Monthly, The
"Fall of Babylon, The": *189,* 647, *648*
1914, end of Gentile Times: *135,* 635
Bible Students' Tracts: 51
Bible studies
completing two books: 115
correspondence course, 1921: 560
development of Bible study activity: 572-4
Mexico: *363*
model studies: 85
1945-92 (chart): 717
1950-92 (chart): 574
number:
   1945: 461, 722
   1950: 574
   1969: 723
   1975: 501
   1984: 723
   1987: 723
   1992: 574, 615, 723
   Asia and islands of the world, 1992: 519
   North America, 1992: 517
   South America, 1992: 518
publications used: 105, *571,* 574, 721
Bible Vs. Tradition: 48
Bill of Rights: *679,* 699
Birthdays: 199, 201
"Birth of the Nation"
Watch Tower article, 1925: 78-9, 138-9
Bishops: 35-6
Blackwell, Victor: 92, 523
"Blessed Are the Fearless"
Watch Tower article, 1919: 212, 563
"Blest Be the Tie That Binds Our Hearts in Christian Love"
sung at love feasts: 257
Blindheim, Rasmus: 408
Blood
God's law: 145
Blood, Medicine and the Law of God: 183
Blood transfusions
view of Witnesses: 183-6
Board of directors (Watch Tower Society)
at Russell's death: 65
four members oppose Rutherford: 66-8, 627, 719
members, mid-1950's: *100*
members voted in, 1918: 68
Bogard, Kathryn: *298*
Böhmermann, Gerrit: 307
Bohnet, J. A.: 68, *79*
Bolivia
branch office: *367*
clergy opposition: 666-8
early witnessing: 367, 436, 438
missionaries: 463-4, 535
reaching isolated publishers: 540
Bookbinding: *588*
Booth, John C.: *116, 226, 669*
Booth, Joseph: 418, 521
Botswana
ban: 676
early witnessing: 435
missionaries: 485, 539
reaching remote areas: 485
Boucher, Aimé: *689,* 690
Bowen, Christopher: 134, 631
Braille: 585, 614
Branch offices (Watch Tower Society): 271, *357-401*
Branch Committees: *109,* 235, 544, 723
early branches: 210, 719
expansion of facilities: 114, 332-5, *338*
financing: 346-7
missionaries assist in oversight: 541, 544
number:
   1942: 97
   1946: 97
   1955: 101
   1976: 97
   1992: 210, 332
printing branches, 1992: 347
Branch overseers
training: *230,* 533, 544, 722
Brathwaite, Joseph: 413
Brazil
ban: 502, 675
baptisms, number: 368
branch office: 368-9, *590*
   expansion: 333-4, 592
   printing: 584
clergy opposition: 457-8
conventions: 281, *369,* 460, 502, *503*
early witnessing: 413, 436, 457-8, 548
hours, increase: 334
local customs: 531
meeting attendance: 253
missionaries: 461, *530*
New World Translation: 612

Pioneer Service School: 300
publishers:
  1945: 463
  1945/46: 460
  1950-92 (chart): 369
  1963-92, increase: 612
  1992: 368
serving where the need is greater: 470
Brenisen, Edith: 238
Brenisen, Edward (Brenneisen): 64, 222-3
Brickell, Ben: 288, *289*
Britain
Assembly Halls: 328-9, *330*
bans: 675, 721
branch office: *374*
  established: 210, 719
  literature, languages printed: 374
  printing: 584
clergy opposition: 643
congregations:
  1900: 406
  1992: 374
conventions: 260, 267, 275, 495
early witnessing: 405, 411, *412*
embargo on Society's literature: 675
Food for Thinking Christians, distribution, 1881: 561, 718

IBSA House: *374*
imprisonments: 194, 722
Kingdom Hall construction: 324
Knorr's service tours: 96, 98
military exemption, World War I: 192
military exemption, World War II: 194
missionaries sent out: 541
"Photo-Drama of Creation": 422
publishers:
  1900: 406
  1938-45, increase: 455
  1992: 374
relief efforts: 305, 308
Russell's visits: 406-7
service assemblies: 266
use of commercial printers: 581
use of placards: 447, 567-8
Watch Tower House: *374*
British Commonwealth
bans, World War II: 457, 675, 721
British East Africa (See **Kenya**)
British Guiana (See **Guyana**)
British Honduras (See **Belize**)
British West Indies: 423
Brooklyn, New York
headquarters moved to: 59, 719
headquarters reopened, 1919: 76, 577-8

Brooklyn Tabernacle: 59, 71, 75, 251
Brown, John A.: 134
Brown, W. R.: 414, 433, *434,* 485-6, 488, 521, 549
Bruch, Victor: *452*
Bryan, E.: 627
Buchenwald concentration camp: 452, 661, 664
Buchner, Charles J.: 651
Bulgaria
ban: 675
early witnessing: 430, 432
legal recognition: 505, 697
relief provided: 308
Bulletin: 246, *247,* 348, 563, 720
Burford, Hazel: 86, 89, *460*
Burgess, A. E.: 64
Burkina Faso: 478, 529, 541
Burma (See **Myanmar**)
Burt, Don: *460*
Burundi
early witnessing: 476, 535
letter campaign: 695
missionaries: 542
Byington, Steven: 607

C

Caamano, Maria: 514
Cain, Gerald: 500
Callaway, Neal: 540
Calvin, John: *39*
Cambodia: 535
Cameroon: 433, 539, 695
Campanus, Johannes: 44
Campbell, Merton: 88
Canada
Assembly Halls: 329, *330,* 331
bans: 10, 498, 586, 648, 657, 675-6, 680, 688-90, 696-8
  "Fall of Babylon, The": *648*
  Finished Mystery, The: 69-70, *648*
  printing operations: 586
blood transfusions: 184-6
branch office: *360-1, 591*
  expansion: 333-4
  legal department: 689
  printing: 583
clergy opposition: 644, 647, 657, 666, 667, 680-2, 688-90
congregation, 1912: *239*
conventions: 255, *256,* 260, 265-6, 282
court cases: 498, 688-90
  advance cause of religious freedom: 690, 699
  literature distribution: 690, 697
  sedition: 682, 689-90
  total pending in 1947: 722
"Ecclesiastics Indicted," distribution: 427
field ministry:
  reaching remote areas: *360-1,* 439
  World War II: 456-7
flag salute: 688
Kingdom Hall construction: 324
Kingdom Schools: 671
legal recognition: 696-7
missionaries sent out: 541

persecution:
  mobs: 498, 700
  World War I: 424, 552
  World War II: 456-7
petitions for Bill of Rights: 689, 699
public meetings: 249
publishers:
  increase, 1938-45: 457
  number, 1992: 360
radio station CHCY: *81*
relief efforts: 308
Russell's visit, 1891: 406
tests resulting from—
  field ministry: 638
  Russell's death: 624
Cantwell, Henry A.: 97
Cantwell, Jesse L.: 100, 527, *530*
Cantwell v. State of Connecticut
court case: 684
Cape Verde, Republic of: 437, 510
Capito, Wolfgang Fabricius: 44
Caribbean
missionary work: 462-3
publishers, 1945: 461
Carpenter, Sadie: 84
Carter, Stanley: *462,* 463
Carvajalino, Antonio: 525
Catholic Action: 85, 471, 658
Catholic Church: 38
concordats with—
  Fascist Italy: 442
  Nazi Germany: 659
involvement in politics: 195, 680-1, 696
opposition to Jehovah's Witnesses: 379, 384, 492-4, 512, 682
Cedar Point, Ohio (See **Conventions,** 1919, 1922)
Cellarius, Martin: 44

Celsus: 548
Central African Republic
ban: 477
branch office: *385*
early witnessing: 385, 476-7
Central America
congregations, 1975: 470
missionary work: 463-5
publishers, number: 461, 470
Ceylon (See **Sri Lanka**)
Chad: 476, 510, 513
Chairman's Committee
Governing Body: 117, 234
"Challenge to World Leaders, A"
resolution, 1922: *261,* 426, *427*
Character development: 172-3, 292
"Character or Covenant—Which?"
Watch Tower article, 1926: 172-3, 292
"Character or Integrity—Which?"
Watchtower article, 1941: 172
Charles, Cyril: 536
"Chart of the Ages": 161, *162*
Charuk, John: 316, 542
Children: 86, *88*
"Children of the King"
discourse, 1941: 86
Chile
branch office: *367*
  financing construction: 346
congregations, 1945: 463
early witnessing: 367, 436-8
missionaries: 461
publishers, number: 366, 460
reaching remote areas: 367
China
convention, 1936: 454
early witnessing: 418, 421, 423-4, 441, 455-7, *489*

missionary work: 489-90, 535
persecution: 490
publishers, 1956: 490
relief, after World War II: 308
Russell's visit, 1912: 420, 489
Watch Tower first reaches China: 718
Choi, Young-won: 491
Christendom: 157, 189
beginning: 38
Christianity Goes to Press: 575
Christians (early)
adjustments in understanding God's purposes: 629
attitude toward—
birthdays: 199
military service: 192, 673
national emblems: 673, 677
politics: 190, 673
world: 200
common people: 547-8
congregations:
elders: 218, 233
ministerial servants: 233
oversight: 29, 106
exemplary lives: 677
financial support of congregations: 341-2
first called Christians: 149-50
house-to-house preaching: 571
identifying features: 29-32
loving brotherhood: 304, 710-11
meetings: 236
modern-day Witnesses patterned after: 234
persecution: *32,* 642, 644, 646-7, 677
"The Way": 30, 149, 172
traveling overseers: 222
unity: 28-9
witnesses of Jehovah and of Jesus: 26, 32
world's attitude toward: 200
"Christians in the Crucible"
convention discourse, 1946: *268*
"Christians' Mission on Earth"
Watch Tower article, 1927: 563
Christmas
celebration discontinued: 79, *200*
early view: 199
Chronology
expectations:
adjustments: 635-7, 709
1873: 631, 633
1874: 47, 631-2
1878: 632-3
1881: 632
1914: 60-3, 134, *135,* 136-9, 635-7
1915: 632
1925: 78, 632-3
1975: 104, 633
1914, Russell's announcement at Bethel: 61, 719
1914, Russell's article in *Bible Examiner:* 134-5, 718
Russell's view: 46-7, 49, 60, 136
Church
Bible Students' use of term: 206
Circuit overseers (servants) (See also **Traveling overseers**): 223
Civil Liberties Union
flag salute: 672, 685
Clara Schneider v. State of New Jersey
court case: 684

Clarke, H. P.: 413
Class
Bible Students' use of term: 206
Class workers: 560
Clergy
instigate government opposition: 69-70, 384, 423, 434, 450, 455, 458, 472, 477-8, 484, 494, 498, 552, 666-9, 676, 678-82, 688-9, 695
opposed Russell: 642-6
opposed *The Finished Mystery:* 69-70
opposition by: 189, 379, *380,* 384-5, 447-8, 458, 474-5, 502, *512,* 566, 573, 644, 647-50, 654-60, 666-9, 678-9
persecuted early Christians: 642, 644, 646-7
political involvement: 680-1, 696
some seek truth: 474
supported war effort: 191, 647-8, 651-2
Clergy-laity distinctions
development: 35-7, 40
view of early Christians: 29
view of modern-day Witnesses: 144
Clune's Auditorium
discourse by Rutherford, 1919: 76, 720
Cobb, Mildred: 84
Colombia
branch office: *370-1*
expansion: 333-4, 337-8
clergy opposition: 468, 542-3
convention: 468
early witnessing: 371, 424, 438, 521
Kingdom Halls: 322, *327*
missionaries: 461, 464, *530,* 535
publishers, number: 463, 470
relief efforts: 314
Witnesses come to serve where need is greater: 469-70
Colporteurs: *412,* 558-60
direction from Society: 211
experiences: 284-91, 408, 421
number:
1885: 210, 284
1909: 559
1914: 284
1917: 66
service instituted: 210, 284, 405-6, 558
Comfort for the Jews: 141
Comoros: 513
Company
Witnesses' use of term: 206
Computers
use in printing: 596-8
use in translation: 599, 602
Concentration camps
commendation of Witness inmates: 179, 663-4
declaration renouncing one's faith: 660-1, 663
executions: 660, 663
love among Witnesses: 663-5
number of Witnesses confined, World War II: 720
preaching work: 663-4
prisoners become Witnesses: 677
receiving Bible literature: *664*
treatment of Witnesses: *659,* 660-1
Concordats
Catholic Church with—
Fascist Italy, 1929: 442
Nazi Germany, 1933: 659

Congregation Book Study: 237-8
Congregations
early Bible Students: *239*
early Christian: 28-9, 106
early terms used: 50, 206
increase in number, 1972-92: 234
meetings: 236-53
singing: 240-1
number:
1916: 239
1940-92 (chart): 717
1976-92 (chart): 114
1992: 234
number formed, 1976-92: 115
oversight: 218-19, 234, 723
rate of increase: 318, 322
service organization: 212
Conley, W. H.: 576
Consolation (See also *Awake!*): 683, *724, 725*
Construction
Assembly Halls: 328-32
branches: 114, 332-6
international volunteers: 336-9
Kingdom Halls: 115, *320-1,* 322-8
Conventions: 254-82
accommodations: 267, 269, *272,* 275, 277, 279
baptisms: *273,* 274, 277, *280,* 479
conduct at, serves as witness: 281-2
convention tours: *255,* 256-7
delegates from foreign lands: 270-1, 275-82, 504, 506-7, 509
dramas: 276, 598
efforts to attend: 267, 269, 276
expressions of appreciation: 255-6
field ministry: 258-60, 262, *265,* 266-7, 276-7, 569
financial assistance to attend: 282
food service: *272,* 275, 277
foreign-language sessions: 259, 270, *273, 277, 279-80,* 282
international gatherings: 270-5
key cities tied together: 270, 278
list by year:
1880's: 55
1891: 254, 719
1892: 254-5
1893: 255
1898: 255
1900: 93, 255
1903: 256
1905: 257
1909: 255-7
1911: 256-7
1917: 256
1919: 72-4, 76-7, 257, *258,* 259, 425, 637, 720
1922: 72, 77-8, 138, 246, *259,* 260, 265, 678, *720*
1922-28: 260
1925: 265
1927: 266
1928: 266
1931: 79, 82, 155-6, 261, *262-3,* 266-7, 720
1935: 83-4, 166, *167,* 261, 266, 267, 721
1936: 447

INDEX 731

1937: 84-5
1938: 267, 447
1939: *265*
1941: 86, 88, 220-1, 262
1942: 92-3
1943: 94
1945: 267, *488,* 489
1946: 97-9, *268,* 270
1950: 99, 262-3, 274, *526*
1951: 275, 470
1952: *269*
1953: 99-100, 263, *273,* 274-5
1955: 275-6, 495, *496*
1957: 468
1958: 101, *102,* 264, *270-1,* 274, 282, 722
1962: 264
1963: 103, 264, 276, *277,* 282, 397-8, 536, 542
1964: 264
1965: 496
1966-67: 276
1969: 264, 278, 398, *493,* 495-6
1970-71: 277-8, *279, 479*
1971: 106, 233, 264
1972: 264
1973: *387,* 398
1974: 269
1977: 264
1978: 282, *383,* 387, 397-8, 510
1983: 278, 344
1985: 282, *381,* 387, 397, 502, *503,* 504
1988: 264, 278, 282
1989: 278-9, *280, 504,* 723
1990: 280-1, *369, 385, 389,* 502, 506-7
1991: 281, *397, 506,* 507
1992: 281, *392,* 509, *511*
media coverage: 495, 502, 504-5, 510
one-day, served by Russell: 130
orchestras: 260, 275
organizing: *272-3,* 278
pilgrims: 255-6
radio and telephone hookups: 260, *266,* 267, 278
resolutions: 260, *261,* 426
service assemblies: 266
singing: 241, 269
special sessions for colporteurs: 285
themes: 264-5, 274-6, 282
trailer and tent cities: *273,* 275
travel arrangements: 255-6, 267, 272, 275-6, 457

unity: 254, 269, 278
volunteers: *272,* 275
Cooke, Eric: *430*
Cooke, John: *430,* 481-2, 537
Cook Islands: 282, 440
Corby, Jim: 658
Cormican, Hugh and Carol: 534
Corporations
used by Witnesses: 229
Corr, Jack: 658
Costa Rica
branch office: *358*
financing construction: 346
early witnessing: 413
flag salute: 671
missionaries: 461
relief efforts: 311
Côte d'Ivoire
branch office: *386*
early witnessing: 386
government officials uphold Witnesses: 478, 676
missionaries: 386, 478, *532,* 535
relief sent out: 309
Cottage Meetings: 238, 241
Cotterill, Richard: 540
Couch, George: *274*
Coughlin, Charles: 658
Countries
number already reached by Witnesses:
by 1900: 719
by 1914: 422
by 1935: 443, 550
by 1939, South America: 518
by 1945: 461
by 1945, Africa: 475, 518
by 1945, Asia and islands of the world: 519
by 1945, North America: 517
by 1975: 501
by 1975, Africa: 475
by 1992: 520
by 1992, Asia and islands of the world: 519
by 1992, North America: 517
number in which Witnesses were preaching:
1914: 719
1919: 425, 720
1920-92 (chart): 717
1922: 260, 425
1931: 566
1935: 443

1938: 458
1939: 461
1941: 721
1943: 544
1945: 461
1945, Africa: 475
1957: 722
1963: 722
1975: 501
1975, Africa: 488
1985: 723
1992: 520, 544, 723
1992, Africa: 518
Course in Theocratic Ministry (See also **Theocratic Ministry School**): 94
Covington, Hayden C.: 89, 91-2, *679,* 683-4
Coward, E. J.: *414,* 423, 521
Croatia: 281, *506*
Cross and crown symbol: *200*
Cruden's Concordance: 605
Cuba
conventions: *458,* 459
early witnessing: 458
first baptisms: 459
Knorr's service tour: 97
missionaries: 458-9, 524
persecution: 671-2, 674
publishers, number: 459
radio broadcasts: 459
Russell's visit: 414, 421, 458
Cuminetti, Remigio: *191,* 192
Curaçao (See **Netherlands Antilles**)
Cure
clergy reaction in Netherlands: 682
Cutforth, John: 527-8, *529*
Cyprian: *35,* 36
Cyprus: *376,* 676
Cyranek, Ludwig: 454
Czechoslovakia
ban: 195, 675
clergy opposition: 666, 682
conventions: 281, 432, *506,* 507, *701*
delegates attend Poland conventions: 279, 504
early witnessing: 410, 429, 430-2
literature distributed: 432
"Photo-Drama of Creation": 432
printery: 586
publishers, number, 1935: 432
relief efforts: 308-9
visit by member of Governing Body: 506

D

Dachau concentration camp: 452, 661
Dahomey (See **Benin**)
Daily Manna: 201
Davison, John: 474
Dawn Circles for Bible Study: 237
Day, Frank: 440
Day of Vengeance, The: 53, 140
Deacons
appointment: 206-9
V.D.M. Questions: 215
Deane, Eldon: 88

Death
belief of Witnesses: 145
Debates
Eaton-Russell: 129-30, 643
DeCecca, Giovanni: 75, 652, *653*
DeCecca, Grace: 298
"Decently and in Order"
Watch Tower article, 1895: 205-6
"Declaration Against Satan and for Jehovah"
resolution, 1928: 261

Defending and Legally Establishing the Good News
legal procedures: 691, *692*
Deliverance: 140
Demut, Margarethe: 410
Denmark
Assembly Halls: 332
blood transfusion (experience): 184
branch office: *377*
construction: 335
languages printed: 377

printing operations: 586, 590
conventions: 265, 495-6
court cases: 494-5
early witnessing: 377, 407, 548
meeting attendance: 253
missionaries sent out: 541
relief efforts: 308-9
Russell's visit, 1891: 406
service assemblies: 265-6
tests resulting from—
　field ministry: 638
　Russell's death: 624
witnessing to Turkish people: 497
Deschamp, Clem and Jean: *287*
Dewar, Frank: 446, *447*
Dickmann, August: 660
Director: 247
Disciple
Greek word: 27

Disfellowshipping
discussion: 186-7
number, 1960's: 103
District overseers (servants) (See also **Traveling overseers**): 223
Divine Name That Will Endure Forever, The: 124
Divine Plan of the Ages, The: 52, 122, 161, *576*, *718*
translations: 408
Divisional campaigns: 82-3, 692
Divorce
view of Witnesses: 177-8
Djibouti: *387*
Dochow, Carl: 464
Dodote, Eric: 515-16
Dominica: 414, 676
Dominican Republic
ban: 667
letter campaign: 695

branch office: *359*
clergy opposition: 667
early witnessing: 359, 438
missionaries: *359*, 461, 535
Dos Santos, Joseph: 440-1, *453*, 488, 521
"Do the Scriptures Teach That Eternal Torment Is the Wages of Sin?"
Old Theology, The, 1889: 128
Downing, Miss C. B.: 418
Dramas: 276
audiocassettes: 598
Drug abuse
view of Witnesses: 180-1
Dulchinos, John: 83
Duncan, W. B.: 70
Duplessis, Maurice: *681*, 689
Dutch Guiana (See **Suriname**)
Dwenger, Heinrich: *298*
Dyer, Lois: 534

E

Early, Sister: *284*
Earnest Bible Students (See **International Association of Earnest Bible Students**)
Earth
conditions under Kingdom: 162-3, 168
God's original purpose: 168
East Pakistan (See **Bangladesh**)
Eaton, Dr. E. L.: *128*, 129, 643, *644*
Ebersohn, Frans: 418
Ecclesia
Bible Students' use of term: 206
"Ecclesiastics Indicted"
resolution, 1924: *261*, 427
tract distributed: 658
Ecuador
branch office: *367*
　financing construction: 339, 346-7
clergy opposition: 502, 543
　mob violence: 668
early witnessing: 438
field ministry, bus terminals: 513-14
missionaries: 463-5
publishers, number, 1992: 367
Witnesses from abroad assist with preaching: *367*, 469
Edgar, John: 64, 130
Editorial Committee: 146
Russell's will: 64-5
Eisenhower, Charles: *366*, *460*, 528
Eisenhower, Lorene: *460*
"Ekklesia, The"
Watch Tower article, 1881: 204-5
Elders
adjustments, 1972: 106, 234, 723
alcohol, use of: 182
appointment, early views: 206-9, 213-14, 638-9, 720

appointment, theocratic: 218-19, 221, 721
body of elders: 105-7
early Christian: 106, 218, 233
field ministry: 212-14, 564, 637-8
Greek word: 35-6
service committee: 212, 214, 638
service director: 212, 214, 637-8
serving in areas that have greater need: 500, 508-10
V.D.M. Questions: 215
Ellis, Aaron: 48
El Refugio
boat used in Peru: *465*
Elrod, William A.: 89
El Salvador
branch office: *359*
　construction: 339
clergy opposition: 666
early witnessing: 359, 424
first baptism: *359*
missionaries: 461, 463, 535
relief efforts: 311
Witnesses from abroad assist with preaching: 469
Emphatic Diaglott, The: 604, 605-6
parousia translated "presence": 46, 133
Enemies: 84
Engel, Mick: 455
England (See **Britain**)
Enjoy Life on Earth Forever!: 112, 574, *594*
Enoch: 14
Equatorial Guinea: 477-8
"Equipped for Every Good Work": 97
Erler, Brother: 410
Ernste Bibelforscher (See **International Association of Earnest Bible Students**)

Errichetti, John: 526, *528*
Espionage Act: 649-52, 654
Estelmann, Otto: 457-8
Estep, Grace A.: 101, 669-70
Esterwegen concentration camp: 453
Esther
boat used in Norway: 440
Estonia
ban: 675
Bible literature being received: *700*
convention: *506*, 507
early witnessing: 429
radio broadcasts: *81*, 429
visit by member of Governing Body: 506
Ethiopia
ban: 510, 695
early witnessing: 428
missionaries: 476, 535
Watch Tower mission: *476*
"Eureka Drama": 60
Europe: *428*
hours, number, 1992: 518
Knorr's service tours: *96*, 98
publishers, number, 1975: 501
publishers, number, 1992: 518
Evangelical Alliance: 644
Evolution
undermined faith in Bible: 41
Ewins, Eric: 446
Executions
concentration camps: 663
　letters from some sentenced to death: 662
Executive Committee: 65, 70-1, 719
"Exposed"
recording by Rutherford, 1937: 573

F

"Face the Facts"
convention discourse, 1938: *80*, 267, 447
reaction to booklet, in Netherlands: 682
Facey, Louis: 413

Faeroe Islands: 441
Faithful and discreet slave
identity: 142-3, 146, 218-19, 626, 706
legal agencies used: 228

Russell viewed as: 143
"The Society": 219
Faithful and wise servant (See **Faithful and discreet slave**)

INDEX

Faith on the March: 61
"Fall of Babylon, The"
  ban, Canada: 648
  distribution: 189, 211, 647, *648*
Family life
  among Witnesses: 175, 178
"Fascism or Freedom"
  discourse by Rutherford, 1938: 85
"Fearless Despite World Conspiracy"
  discourse, 1946: 268
Federal Council of the Churches of Christ in America: 191-2
Fekel, Charles: *585*
Feller, Jules: *633*
Ferguson, Bellona: *413,* 436
Fergusson, Ian: 537
Ferrie, Sarah: 411
Field ministry (See also **Bible studies**)
  advertisements in magazines and newspapers: 405, 409, 418, 425, *560,* 561-2
  airplanes: 299, *357,* 499, 514
  angels' role: 549-51
  Awake!: 725
  balance: 294
  Bible studies: 85, 105, 460, 463, *571, 572-4,* 615, 717
  bicycles: 284, *564*
  billboards: 425
  Bulletin: 246, *247,* 563, 720
  bus terminals: 513-14
  Christian responsibility: 51, 63, 145, 212-14, 637-8
  clergy opposition: 447-8, 474-5, 484, 492-4, 542-3, 551-2, 566, 573, 656-9, 666-9
  commission: 26-7, 556
  concentration camps: 451-4, 664
  defending right to distribute literature: 678-88, 690, 697
  defending right to preach publicly and from house to house: 494-5, 498-9, 679-81, 683, 688, 697-8
  Director: 247
  divisional campaigns: 82-3, 692
  early Christians: 26-8, 32
  early methods: 411-12, 419, 557-65
  early-morning witnessing: 516
  1870's-1914: 404-22
  elders: 212-14, 564, 637-8
  emphasis, 1919 convention: 77, 258-9, 425
  emphasis, 1919 onward: 212-14, 562-3, 637-9
  emphasis, 1922 convention: 77-8, *259,* 260, 265, 678, *720*
  evening witnessing: 516
  government opposition: 490
  handbills: 249, 266, 447, 460
  high-security buildings: 516
  hired assistants: 405, 561
  holy spirit: 547-53
  hours:
    1930-92 (chart): 717
    1935: 443
    1936-45: 461
    1946-75: 501, 520
    1957: 722
    1975: 517
    1976-90: 520
  1982: 302
  1990: 723
  1990-91: 520
  1992: 302, 517, 520, 723
  1992, Asia and islands of the world: 519
  1992, Europe: 518
  house to house: 82, 559, 570-1, *572-3*
  identity of great crowd, effect on work: 84, 170, 261
  importance, Russell's view: 51, 209
  informal witnessing: 514
  Informant: 247
  Jonadabs (Jehonadabs): 83-4, 292
  lands, number: 422, 443, 461, 501, 517-20, 717
  letter writing: *495*
  literature, distribution, 1920-92 (chart): 717
  literature, use of: 559
  marketplaces: 513-14
  missionaries: 462-6, 521, 525-6, 535-7
  multilingual territory: 496-7
  newspapers, use of: 58-9
  1914-35: 423-43
  1935-45: 444-61
  1945-75: 462-501
  1975-92: 502-20
  objective: 159-60, 515
  organizing, early: 210-12
  Our Kingdom Ministry: 247
  phonograph: 85, *87,* 565, *566, 721*
  placards: 249, 266, 447, 460, 567, *568,* 721
  qualifications to participate: 293-4
  radio: *80-1,* 249, 447-8, 562, *563,* 573, 720
  reaching everyone in household: 516
  reaching remote areas: *357-8, 360-1,* 367, *368, 370, 398, 439-40,* 441, 444, *445,* 446-7, 455, *465,* 466, 485, 499-500, 519, 551, 562
  recordings: 249
  regional service director: 223
  reporting: 212, 717
  return visits: 66, 85, 460
  seaports: 513, *514*
  service assemblies: 266
  service committee: 212, 214, 638
  service director: 212, 214, 637-8
  Service Meeting: 247, *248*
  service organization: 212
  serving where need is greater: 300-1, *367, 369,* 374, 378, 399-400, 468-72, 499-500
  sound cars: *87,* 267, 566, *567*
  street witnessing: 456-7, 567, 721, *569*
  Suggestive Hints to Colporteurs: 246
  Sunday witnessing: 66, 82, 564, 638, 690, 720
  telephone witnessing: 516
  territory assignments: 499-500
    frequency of coverage: 515-17
  testimony cards: 564, *565*
  tests resulting from: 637-8, *639*
  tract distribution: 210, 557-8
  training program: 99-100, 568-9, 722
  transcription equipment: *87,* 448, 566, 573, 720
  traveling overseers: 223-7
  unassigned territory: 499-500
  using every opportunity: 301-2
  using secular work assignments in foreign lands: 476, 478
  variety of methods: 574
  Watchtower, The: 725
  Watch Tower articles highlight importance: 563-4
  why Witnesses make repeated calls: 570
  window signs: 561, *568*
  witnessing:
    to government officials: 486-8
    to prisoners: 514-15
    to relatives: 514
    while in prison: 424, 490, *495*
  Workers' Meetings: 247
  World War I, effect on preaching work: 423-5
  World War II, effect on preaching work: 448-58
Fiji
  bans: 675-6
  branch office: *398*
  conventions: 398
  early witnessing: 441
"Filling the House With Glory"
  convention discourse, 1953: 263
Financial support
  voluntary donations:
    early Christian congregation: 341-2
    modern-day organization: 340-51
Finished Mystery, The: 88, 148
  distribution: 69, 211
  distribution suspended: 652
  how compiled: 67
  objectionable pages cut from book: 652
  opposed by some on Society's board of directors: 66-8, 719
  opposition: 69-70, 423-4, 648-50, *651,* 652
  released, 1917: 66-7, 647, 719
"'Finished Mystery' and Why Suppressed, The": 70
Finland
  ban: 675
  branch office: *378*
    bindery: 593
    printing operations: 584, 586
    printing with four colors: 595
  commercial printers, use of: 581
  defending right to go from house to house: 698
  early witnessing: 378, 408-9
  missionaries: 539, 541
  publishers, increase, 1938-45: 455
  relief received and sent out: 308-9
  tests resulting from—
    business venture: 640
    Russell's death: 624
Fisher, George H.: 64, 67-8, 652, *653*
Flag salute: 196-8, 669-73, 684-8
  comments by Rutherford: 196-7
  court cases: 670, 680, 684-8, 721
  persecution: 669-72, 721
  school expulsions: 670-2, 685
  Witnesses' attitude: 669, 672-3
  Witnesses like early Christians: 677
Flores, Juan: 438

Food for Thinking Christians: 123
  distribution: 210, 348, 404-5, 561, 718
Fornication
  definition: 174
  ground for divorce: 177
  view of Witnesses: 173-5
Fourie, Stoffel: 418
France
  ban: 675
  branch office: *375*
    literature shipped out: 375
    printing: 592
  clergy opposition: 658
  conventions: 495, *496*
  early witnessing: 409-10, 429-30, 548
  "Ecclesiastics Indicted," resolution: 427
  field ministry in high-security buildings: 516
  Knorr's service tour: 96
  New World Translation: 612
  persecution: 448
  publishers:
    increase, 1938-45: 455
    increase, 1963-92: 612
    number, 1940: 95
  number, 1945: 95
  number, 1992: 510, 612
  relief received and sent out: 308, 313, 712
  tests resulting from expectations regarding 1925: 633
France Amendment to the Espionage Act: 649
Franke, Charles: 70
Franke, Max, Konrad, and Gertrud: 451
Franks, Leslie: 534
Franske, F. J.: *439*
Franz, Frederick W.
  association with Knorr: 91, *99*
  background: 111, 130, *131*
  baptism: 111
  Bethel service: 295, *298*
  board of directors: *100*
  convention, 1950: 263
  convention, 1958: *264*
  death: 111
  Governing Body: *116*
  president: 109, 111
  remarks about 1975: 104
  remarks about value of Christian hope: 716
  service tours, 1945-46: 459-61
  vice president: 91
  with Rutherford before his death: 89
"Frauds of the Clergy Exposed, The"
  discourse, 1925: 658
Fredianelli, George: 533
"Freedom for the Peoples"
  convention discourse, 1927: 266
Freedom of Worship
  legal procedures: 691, *692*
French
  number of French-speaking people worldwide: 375
French, Edward: 70
French Indochina (See Cambodia; Laos; and Vietnam)
French Togo (See Togo)
French West Africa (See Senegal)
Freytag, Alexandre: 628
Friend, Irma: 298
Friend, Maxwell: 523, *525*
From Paradise Lost to Paradise Regained
  release: 101
Frost, Erich: *268*
Furgala, John: 301

G

GA (Golden Age): 258
Gabon: 695
Gambia, The: 433, 535
Gambling
  view of Witnesses: 179-80
Gangas, George D.: *260*
  first talk: 94
  Governing Body: *116*
"Gathering the Multitude"
  Watchtower articles, 1936: 170
Gavette, Penny: 465-6
Gentile Times
  end of: 135-6, 138
  expectations of Bible Students: 61-3, 134-8
  Russell's announcement: 61, 719
  views of commentators before 1914: 134
"Gentile Times: When Do They End?"
  Russell's article in *Bible Examiner:* 134-5
German Democratic Republic (East)
  legal recognition: 280, 505, 697
Germany
  Assembly Hall: *330*
  bans: 442, 552, 639, 659-60, 675, 693-4, 720
    arrests: 194, 553, 694, 720
    imprisonment: 194
    letters to German government, 1934: 315, 693-4
    providing literature: 450, 454
  branch office: 376-7
    audiocassettes: 598
    bindery: 593
    established: 210
    expansion: 334-5, 508
    financing construction: 346
    languages printed: 376-7
    legal department: 679
    literature to Eastern Europe: 508
  printing: 583, *584*, 586, 589-90, *591*, 594-5
  clergy opposition: 656, 659-60, 678-9, 720
  commercial printers, use of: 581
  concentration camps: 452-3, 659-65, 720
    Memorial: 243
  conventions:
    1946: *268*
    1951: 275
    1955: 275-6, *496*
    1969: 495-6
    1990: 280, 506
  court cases:
    defending right to distribute literature: 679
    number, 1926: 679
    number, 1928: 679
  early witnessing: 410-11, *432*
  field ministry:
    after many arrests in Bavaria: 442
    during Nazi era: 448-9, 694
    effect of World War I: 423
    hours, 1946-92: 376
    seaports: 513
  Gilead Extension School: 533, 545
  Juvenile Bible Class: 244
  Knorr's service tour: 98
  literature distributed, 1919-33: 442
  meeting attendance: 253
  "Millions Now Living Will Never Die," discourse: 425
  missionaries:
    assist local Witnesses: 539
    sent out: 541
  multilingual territory: 497
  nationalism: 196, 669
  Nazi salute: 669
  opposition of Nazi government: 10, 448-9, 552-3, 659-60, 693-4
  "Photo-Drama of Creation": 422
  publishers, number: 315, 443
  relief received: 308
  resolutions distributed:
    "Challenge to World Leaders, A": 426-7
    "Ecclesiastics Indicted": 427
    protest against mistreatment of Witnesses: 448-9, 693-4
  Russell's visit, 1891: 406
  tests resulting from field ministry: 639
  tract distribution: 561
  Watch Tower literature reaches Germany: 410
Ghana
  bans: 675-6
  branch office: *386-7*
    financing construction: 346
    languages printed: 386
    printing: 592
  congregations, number, 1992: 386
  early witnessing: 386, 433
  restrictions removed, 1991: 510
  screening baptismal candidates: 479
Gibbard, Marie: 93
Gilboa
  boat used in preaching: *439*
Gilead Cultural School of Mexico: 533, 545
Gilead Extension School: 533, 545
Gilead School: 300, 533
  assignments, 1943-45: 460
  campus, South Lansing, New York: *95*, *527*
  classes, number: 533
  courses for those entrusted with branch oversight: 533, 544
  curriculum: 523
  Extension Schools: 533

first class: 95, 458, *522,* 523, 721
graduations: *526*
Knorr's opening address: 523-4
lands from which students came: 524, 538
lands in which graduates served: 524
locations of school: 533
Ministerial Training School: 533, *545,* 546
recognized by U.S. Office of Education: 538
students, number: 524, 533
traveling overseers: 231
Giménez, Manuel Mula: 667
Goas, Kate and Marion: 521
Gobitas, Walter: 685
Gobitas, William and Lillian: 670, 685, 686
Gobitis case (See *Minersville School District v. Gobitis*)
"God Be With You Till We Meet Again" song: 256
God Cannot Lie
film: 481
"God's Kingdom Rules—Is the World's End Near?"
convention discourse, 1958: 264, 270-1
God's Way Is Love: 574
Gog of Magog: 263
Gold Coast (See Ghana)
Golden Age, The (See also *Awake!*)
convention, 1919: *258*
discussion: *724*
exposé on persecution of 1917-20: 70, 578-9, 650
first issue: 683
release: 77, 577, 720
use in field ministry: 212, 246
Golden Age ABC, The: 245
Gölles, Peter: *450,* 454
Goodman, Claude: 287, *288,* 446, 521, 566, 585
Gott, Tarissa P.: 68-9
Governing Body
appointment of overseers: 544, 639
chairmanship: 106, 233-4

combined years of full-time service, 1992: 233
committees: 109, 234-5, 723
early Christian: 29, *31,* 143, 222
enlarged, 1971: 108, 723
members: *116,* 228-9, 233
modern-day: 146
morning worship, Brooklyn Bethel: 234
relationship to Society board of directors: 228, 233
reorganized, 1975: 723
vow of poverty: 351
"Government"
convention discourse, 1935: *266,* 267
"Government and Peace"
convention discourse, 1939: 658
Governments
attitude of modern-day Witnesses toward: 147, 190, 195-6, 672
church support: 189
Jesus' attitude toward: 189-90
officials show impartiality toward Witnesses: 676
Graham, Alexander M.
letter from Russell: 210
Great crowd
faithfulness required: 167
gathering: 170, 214
Rutherford's comment about: 171
identified: 84, 169-70, 261, 444, 630, 721
effect on preaching work: 170, 444
identity, early view: 161, 166
location "before the throne": 167
Memorial: 243
Newton's view: 160
one flock with 144,000: 171
role in congregation: 214, 216
Greatest Man Who Ever Lived, The: 111
Great multitude (See Great crowd)
Greece
arrests: 680, 695
ban: 675
branch office: *380*
construction: *338*
printing: 585, 590
clergy opposition: *380,* 450, 668-9, 695
commercial printers, use of: 581
early witnessing: 429

field ministry:
court cases, 1946: 722
World War II: 450
military service: 194
persecution: 680, 695
effort to bring relief: 695
letter campaigns: 315, 695
publishers:
increase, 1938-45: 455
number, 1992: 380
relief received: 308
Greek philosophy
effect on early Christians: 36-7
Green, Alexander B.: 500
Greenlees, Alfred and Minnie: 411-12
Grenada: 414
Grew, Henry: 44-5, *125*
Griffin, S. H.: 70
Groh, John: *274*
Gross-Rosen concentration camp: 452
Grove, Frank: *418,* 419
Gruber, Kurt: 446
Guadeloupe
Assembly Hall: 328, *329*
branch office: *359*
frequently worked territory: 515
relief received: 313
Guam
branch office: *398*
Guatemala
branch office: *360*
early witnessing: 424
missionaries: 461, 535
publishers, number, 1945: 463
relief efforts: 310, *313*
Guinea-Bissau: 510
Gurd, Victor: 658
Guyana
ban: 676
branch office: *368*
financing construction: 346
congregations:
1915: *239*
number, 1945: 463
early witnessing: 413
reaching remote areas: 368

H

Haidostian, Sona: 541
Haiti
Assembly Hall: 329
branch office: *361*
financing construction: 346
missionaries: 461, 535
Hallström, Björn: 669
Hammer, Knud Pederson: 407
Handbills: 249, 266, 447, 460
Hannan, Mary: 298
Happiness of the New World Society, The
film: 481
Harp of God, The: 88, 560, 573, 579
Harrub, James: 319
Hart, Tom: 411
Harteva, Kaarlo: 408-9
Haslett, Don and Mabel: 75, *490,* 491

Hatzakortzian, Krikor: 428
Hawaii
branch office: *399*
early witnessing: 441
first "Kingdom Hall": *318,* 319, 721
missionaries sent out: 541
telephone witnessing: 516
Heaven
hope of early Christians: 159
number who go there: 159, 169
Heide, Richard: 426
Hell: 437
Hellfire
doctrine exposed by Russell: 126, 128-30
doctrine exposed from 18th century onward: 48
"To Hell and Back!": 130

Henschel, Milton G.
board of directors: *100*
conventions:
1953, Argentina: 468
1963, Liberia: 542
1992, Russia: *511*
delegation to Liberia, 1963: 316
Governing Body: *116*
secretary to Knorr: 96
service tours: 271, 459, 641
Herald of the Morning: 46-8, 131, 575, 619, *620,* 718
Heritage
film: 481
Herkendell, Hermann: *411,* 560
Hersee, William: 222
Heuse, Ernest, Jr.: *483*

Higher powers (See Superior authorities)
Himm, Lew Ti: 489
Hippodrome, New York City: 632
Hirsh, Robert: 64
"His Unspeakable Gift"
  convention discourse, 1945: 308
Hitler, Adolf: 552-3
  clergy instigation to ban Witnesses: 659-60
  letter from Rutherford: 693
  nationalism: 196
Hoffman, Zola: 534
Holidays
  Witnesses adjust view: 79, 199
Holland (See Netherlands)
Hollister, Robert R.: 421, *423*, 521
Holman, A. J., Company: 607
Holman Linear Parallel Edition of the Bible: 605, *606*
Hombach, Maria: *451*
Homosexuality
  view of Witnesses: 174-5

Honduras
  branch office: *362*
    financing construction: 346
  early witnessing: 424
  hours, number, 1916-92: 362
  missionaries: 463, 535
  relief sent out: 311
Honesty
  view of Witnesses: 145, 178-9
Hong Kong
  branch office: *393*
    translation: 393
  family pressure on young Witnesses: 473
  missionaries: 535
  pioneers from the Philippines assist with preaching: 473
  Russell's visit, 1912: 393
"Hope for Distressed Humanity, The"
  convention discourse, 1919: 76, 258, 720
Hort, F. J. A.: 610
Horton, Bert and Vi: 549, 566
Hospital Liaison Committees: 185
House-cars: *286, 445*, 465

House-to-house preaching: 556, 570-2
  divisional campaigns: 82-3
  phonograph: 85, *87*
  Scriptural basis reaffirmed: 110-11
  Sunday witnessing: 82, 720
  testimony cards: 564, *565*
  tract distribution: 66
  training program: 100, 722
How Can Blood Save Your Life?: 184
Hubler, John and Ellen: *471*
Hudgings, W. F.: 73
Hughes, A. Pryce: *191*, 192, *451*
Hungary
  ban: 675
  commercial printers, use of: 586
  conventions: 281, *506*, 507
  early witnessing: 413, 430
  Governing Body members visit: 506
  legal recognition: 505, 697
  persecution: 680
  publishers, number, 1935: 431
  relief received: 308-9
Hunter, Bill: 287
Hymns of the Millennial Dawn: 240

I

Iceland
  branch office: *379*
  early witnessing: 379, 441
  literature distributed: 379
  missionaries: 441
  publishers, number, 1992: 379
  Witnesses from abroad assist with preaching: 469
Immortality of the soul
  conditional immortality: 45
  effect of belief on Kingdom hope: 37-8
  exposed by Russell: 127
  exposed from 18th century onward: 48
  origin of belief: 127
  Plato: 36
Imprisonment (See Arrests)
India
  bans: 675-6
  branch office: *393*
    financing construction: 346
    printing: 585
    translation: 393
  commercial printers, use of: 581
  congregation, 1915: *239*
  early witnessing: 420-1, 430, 521
  Gilead classes: 545
  Knorr's service tour: 98
  public meetings: 430
  publishers, number: 512-13
  Russell's visit, 1912: 419-21
  traveling overseer (experience): 540
Indonesia
  ban: 675
  clergy opposition: 668
  early witnessing: 441, 445-7, 521
  pioneers from the Philippines assist with preaching: 473
Industrial revolution: 41
Informant: 213, *247*

Insight on the Scriptures: 111, 122
Integrity (See Issues)
"Integrity"
  convention discourse, 1941: 86, 262
Interfaith
  view of Witnesses: 145
International Association of Earnest Bible Students: 660
  banned in Germany: 442
International Bible Students Association (See also Bible Students): 229
  world tour by committee of seven: 419, *420*, 421
International Bible Students' Association: 151
International construction program: 336-9
"International Sunday School Lessons"
  Watch Tower: 245
Inthaphan, Chomchai: *447*
Iran: 430
Ireland
  branch office: *380*
  clergy opposition: 492, 643, 658
  convention, 1965: 496
  early witnessing: 430
  Kingdom Hall: *327*
  missionaries: *530*
  publishers, increase: 510
  Russell's visit, 1891: 406
  tests resulting from—
    field ministry: 638
    organizational changes: 638
    Russell's death: 624
  Witnesses from abroad assist with preaching: 469
  witnessing to relatives (experience): 514

Irofa'alu, Shem: *474*
Ishii, Jizo and Matsue: 157, *452*, 491
Israel (ancient)
  chosen and led by God: 704
  festivals: 254
  nation of witnesses: 17-18
  replaced by Christian congregation: 28
Israel (modern)
  early witnessing: 413
  restoration prophecies: 141
Israel (spiritual)
  identified: 141, 720
Issues
  godship: 15-18
  God's name: 124, 153, 167
  integrity: 11, 18, 22
  universal sovereignty: 10-11, 18, 21-2, 699
Is the Bible Really the Word of God?: 122
Italy
  Assembly Halls: *330*, 332
  ban: 675
  blood transfusion (experience): 184
  branch office: *378-9*
    bookbinding: 378
  clergy opposition: 493, *512*, 666
  congregations:
    first formed: 406
    number, 1949: 493
    number, 1975: 501
    number, 1992: 512
  conventions: 276, *493*, 496
  early witnessing: 409, 429, 443
  "Ecclesiastics Indicted," resolution: 427
  hours, 1946-92: 379, 512
  literature, amount distributed: 512
  meeting attendance: 253
  military service, World War I: 192
  missionaries: *530*

Index

New World Translation, distribution: 612
Pioneer Service School: 300
publishers, number:
  1946: 493, 512

1963: 612
1963-92: 613
1975: 493-4
1989: 253

1992: 379, 512, 612, 666
relief efforts: 308-9, 312, 315
Russell's visit, 1891: 406
Ivory Coast (See **Côte d'Ivoire**)

J

Jackson, W. K.: *683*
'Jacob's double' (See **Chronology**, 1878)
Jamaica
  ban: 676
  branch office: *362*
  early witnessing: 413
  missionaries: 461, 463, 530
  publishers, number, 1945: 463
Japan
  Assembly Halls: 329, *330*
  ban: 675
  branch office: *394, 590*
    expansion: 334-5, *338*
    printing: 394, 583, 592, 595-6
    Regional Engineering Office: 332, *394*
  commercial printers, use of: 581
  congregations, number, 1975: 501
  convention, 1963: *277*
  early witnessing: 418, 421, 423-4
  hours, number, 1992: 394
  Kingdom Halls: *327,* 344
  literature distribution: 349
  local customs: 531
  missionaries: 490-1, 530, 535
    number that have served: 540
  New World Translation: 613
  persecution of Witnesses: 443, 455, 490, 680
  pioneers:
    number, 1975-92: 394
    number, 1992: 540
    percentage: 303, 394, 540
  Pioneer Service School: *300*
  publishers:
    increases following World War II: 491
    1950-92 (chart): 513
    1972: 334
    1989: 334
    1992: 512, 534
  relief efforts: 311-12
  Russell's visit, 1911: 420
Jaracz, Theodore: *116, 280*
Java (See **Indonesia**)
Jehovah
  beliefs of Witnesses: 144
  Jesus revealed: 21
  restoration of name in *New World Translation:* 609
  use of name by Bible Students: 123-4
    Isaiah 43:10, 12 never discussed in detail in *Watch Tower* in first 40 years: 152
Jehovah: 124
"Jehovah's Organization"
  Watchtower article, 1932: 213, 638, *640*
Jehovah's Servants Defended
  legal procedures: 691, *692*
Jehovah's Witnesses
  all evangelizers: 548, 569-73

attitude toward—
  abortion: 183
  blood transfusions: 183-6
  gambling: 179-80
  God's name: 123-4
  government: 681-2, 697, 699
  preaching: 291-5
beliefs: 144-5, 709
  adjustments in understanding: 121, 132-3, 146-7, 629-30, 708-9
called Bible Students: 149, 151
chart of noteworthy events, 1870-1992: 718-23
clergy opposition: 656-60, 666-9, 676, 680-2, 688-9, 695
commendation by others: 179, 195-6, 467, 663, 673, 677
compared with early Christians: 234, 677
conventions: 254-82
court cases: 678-99
faithful and discreet slave, identity: 142-3, 626
first century: 26-32
fulfilling Jesus' commission to preach: 404-520, 547-53, 556-74, 674
honesty, reputation: 179
how chosen and led by God: 704-9, 711
how viewed by others: 152, 158, 182
Israel (ancient): 17-18
Jesus, greatest witness: 19-21
love, distinguishing characteristic: 304-17, 712
  assistance in building projects: 320-39
  care for others in congregation: 304-6
  prayers for one another: 315, 317
  relief efforts: 307-9, *310,* 311-12, *313,* 314-17
meetings: 236-53
name:
  adopted: 82, 151-2, 155-6, 213, 261, 720
  applies also to other sheep: 83
  in various languages: 151, 153-4
  reaction to: 156-8
percentage of anointed: 501
percentage of other sheep: 501
pre-Christian: 13-18
publishers and distributors of the Bible: 603-15
seek Kingdom first: 283-303
students of the Bible: 603
tests resulting from—
  adjustments in understanding: 629-36
  business ventures: 639-41
  change of administration: 623-6
  expectations based on dates: 631-7
  field service: 637-8
  organizational changes: 638-9
  pride: 626-9
  ransom: 619-21
unified instruction: 252-3
unity: 232, 254, 269, 278

voluntary donations: 340-51
willingness to help non-Witnesses: 315
witnesses of Jehovah and of Jesus: 26
Jehovah's Witnesses and the Question of Blood: 184
Jehovah's Witnesses—The Organization Behind the Name
  videocassette: *601*
Jehovah's Youth
  magazine in Switzerland: 245
Jerusalem
  in prophecy: 142
Jesus Christ: 19-22, *23,* 24-5
  beliefs of Witnesses: 144
  dates projected for return: 40
  Head of congregation: 29, 218
  Leader: 204
  ministry: 20-2, 248
  persecuted by religious leaders: 642, 646
  presence:
    Barbour's view: 46
    results of apparent delay: 38
    sign of: 24-5
  purpose in coming to earth: 20-2
  ransom: 22
  theme of preaching: 21
  trained disciples to preach: 247-8
Jewish Antiquities: 32
Jews (modern)
  restoration prophecies: 141
  Russell spoke to: 141
Johansson, P. J.: 408
Johnson, Carl: *452*
Johnson, Emmanuel: 478
Johnson, Freida: 289
Johnson, Paul S. L.: 627-8
Johnson v. Town of Deerfield
  flag salute: 685, 687
Johnston, William: 521
Joly, Brother and Sister: 539
Jonadabs (Jehonadabs)
  baptism encouraged: 83
  great crowd identified with: 84, 169-70
  identified with sheep class: 165-6
  invitation to 1935 convention: 83, 166
  Memorial: 243
Jones, Rosco: *685*
Jones, Stanley: *489,* 490
Jones, Thomas: *451*
Jones v. City of Opelika
  court case: 685-7
Jordan: 695
Joseph, A. J. and Gracie: 420, *421*
Joseph, Alfred: 424
"Junior Witnesses"
  group in United States: 245
"Juvenile Bible Study"
  Golden Age feature: 245

K

Kaelin, Sara C.: 73
Kallio, Leo: 170
Kattner, Erich: 457-8, *459*
Kazakhstan
 convention, 1991: *506*, 507
Keefer, Malinda: 256-7, *285*
Keim, Kasper: 565
Keith, B. W.: 46
Keller, Eduardo: 523
Kelsey, Richard and Peggy: 88
Kenya
 branch office: *387*
 convention, 1973: *387*
 early witnessing: 387, 435
 government restrictions removed: 510
 meetings, efforts to attend: 253
 missionaries: 485, 535, 541
 Witnesses from abroad assist with preaching: 485
Kim, Bong-nyu: *453*
King, Harold: *243*, 244, *489*, 490
Kingdom
 Christendom's hope fades: 37-8
 purpose: 21-2
 view of—
  Augustine: 38
  early Bible Students: 138
  Witnesses: 139, 144
"Kingdom"
 phonograph record: 565
"Kingdom, The"
 convention discourse, 1922: 77, 260
"Kingdom, the Hope of the World, The"
 convention discourse, 1931: 79, 137, 139, 155, 267
Kingdom, the Hope of the World, The
 booklet: 139, *158*, 438-9, 443, 565-6
Kingdom Halls: 251, 318-26, *327*, 328
 churches converted into Kingdom Halls: 474
 early Kingdom Halls: *318-19*
 financial support: 343-4
 name: 251, *319*, 721
 quick construction: 115, *320-1*, 322-5
 Regional Building Committees: 325-6, 328, 723
 Society Kingdom Hall Fund: 344

Kingdom Hymns: 240
Kingdom Interlinear Translation of the Greek Scriptures, The: 610
"Kingdom Is at Hand, The": 133
Kingdom Melodies: 241, 598
Kingdom Ministry School: 102, 113, *231*, 232, 305, 722
Kingdom Ministry School Course: 294
Kingdom News: 69-70
Kingdom Schools: 671, *672*
Kingdom Service Song Book: 241
King James Version: 605
 Bible Students Edition: 606
 Holman Linear Parallel Edition: *606*
 Watchtower edition: 93, *606*, 607, 721
King's Theater, The: 693
Kirk, Robert: 528
Kiss, József: 431
Kitto, Tom and Rowena: *471*
Klein, Karl F.: *116*, 220, *240*
Klein, Ted and Doris: *535*
Klukowski, Jennie: 88
Knorr, Nathan H.
 background: 91
 baptism: 91
 Bible printing: 93
  proposes a fresh translation: 607
 board of directors: *100*
 conventions:
  1938, Britain: 447
  1942: 262
  1945, Brazil: *459*
  1946: 270-1, 588
  1950: *264*
  1951, Australia: 470
  1952: 269
  1953, Argentina: *468*
  1974: 269
 course in theocratic ministry: 568
 death: 108-9, 111
 Franz as close associate: 91, *99*
 Gilead School: 522-4, *526*
  personal interest in missionaries: 524-5
 president of Society: 91, 227-8, 721
  Bethel family's letter of support: 91-2

service tours:
 Cuba: 97
 1945: 96, 308
 1945-46: 459-61
 1945-56 (maps): *96*
 1947: 98, 271
 1947, Australia: 641
 1972: 592
 with Rutherford before his death: 89
 zone visits: 227-8
Koerber, Anton: 640
Koivisto, George: 542-3
Königer, Margarita: 541, *542*
Korea (See also Korea, Republic of)
 ban: 675
 branch office:
  printing: 583
 early witnessing: 418, 421, 423-4
 field ministry, World War II: 455
 persecution: 443, 455, 680
Korea, Republic of (South)
 Assembly Hall: 329
 Bible studies, number, 1975: 492
 branch office: 395
  expansion: 334
  literature produced: 395
 congregations, number, 1975: 501
 full-time service: 302, 395, 540
 Kingdom Hall: *327*
 missionaries: 491-2, 538
 pioneers from the Philippines assist with preaching: 473
 publishers, number:
  1950-92: 513
  1975: 492
  1992: 395, 512
 relief efforts: 314
Korean War: 98
Kosrae: 513
Kovalak, Nicholas, Jr.: 83
Kozhemba, Stepan: *511*
Kraft, August: *450*, 454
Krebs, LaVonne: 88
Kusserow family: *449*
Kwazizirah, Gresham: 434-5

L

Labrador: 325
Laos: 473, 535
Larson, Max H.: 586, 592
Larson, Norman: 86
La Torre del Vigía de México: 466
Latvia
 ban: 675
 commercial printers, use of: 585-6
 early witnessing: 429, 561
Lauper, Samuel: 410
Laurier Saumur v. The City of Quebec
 court case: 690
League of Nations: 258
 clergy support: 192

formation: 77, 192
 Witnesses' attitude toward: 192, *193*, 258
Lebanon
 local customs: 531-2
 relief efforts: 309
 sound cars: 566
Leeser's Bible translation: *604*, 605
Leeward Islands (Antigua)
 ban: 676
 branch office: 362
 early witnessing: 362, 463
 missionaries: 537
Leffler, Ralph: 55
Legal cases: 678-99
 Covington, H. C.: 91

damage suits: 185-6
fines: 683
global publicity: 694-5
instructions on legal procedures: 690-2
issues contested:
 commercial peddling: 681
 compulsory flag salute: 680, 684-8
 distributing literature without a permit: 684, 690, 697
 espionage: 682
 license tax for privilege of distributing literature: 685, 687
 permits to build Assembly Halls: 331-2
 sedition: 682, 688-9
legal department: 82, 679

INDEX

letter campaigns: 695
number of cases:
  Canada: 680
  Germany: 679
  Greece: 680
  Romania: 679-80
  United States: 680, 688
Witnesses' court cases advance cause of freedom for everyone: 678, 683-4, 688, 690, 698-9
Leoles v. Landers
  flag salute: 685, 687
Lesotho: 322, 435, 676
"Let God Be True": 97, 475, 574
"Let Your Kingdom Come": 111
"Let Your Name Be Sanctified": 124
"Let Your Will Come to Pass"
  convention discourse, 1958: 102
Leydig family: 465
Liberia
  branch office: *388*
  early witnessing: 414, 433, 485, 718
  Kingdom Hall, funds for building: 344
  missionaries: 485-6, 535
  publishers, number, 1975: 486
  relief efforts: 309
  Witness assembly disrupted: 542, 671
Liberty to Preach: 692
  legal procedures: 690
Libya: 476
Life Everlasting—In Freedom of the Sons of God: 104
Life—How Did It Get Here? By Evolution or by Creation?: 112
Light
  books: *88*, 148
  boat used in West Indies: 463

Lightbearer
  boat used in Southeast Asia: *440,* 441, 446
Lindal, Georg: *379,* 441
Listening to the Great Teacher: 246
  audiocassette: 598
Literacy classes: *362*
  Africa: 480
  Mexico: 466, *467*
Literature
  bans: 455, 457-8, 471, 477, 484, 486, 586, 680
  Braille: 585, 614-15
  commercial printers, use of: 576-7, 579, 581, 585-6, 592
  distribution:
    1915: 348
    1920-92: 520, 717
    1936-45: 461
    street work: 557, 567, 721
    World War II: *450,* 454
  effect of four-color printing on distribution: 595-6
  free of charge: 343, 348-50
  house-to-house distribution: 557-60, 564, 719
  languages: 576-7, 579, 583, 586, 592-3, *594, 596-9, 602*
  paper rations, World War II: 586
  pocket-size books: 593
  published simultaneously, 1992: *250*
  suggesting a specific contribution: 348-9
  tracts: *50,* 348, *557,* 558, 576-7
  translation: 112, *391,* 599, *602*
  use at meetings: 237-8, 240-1, 252-3
  Watch Tower Society's printing operations: 575-615
  writers, reason not named: 146

Lithuania
  ban: 675
  early witnessing: 410, 429
Little flock (See **144,000**)
Liverance, Wallace: 540
Logan, Harvey and Kathleen: 536
Löhr, Elfriede: 543, *450*
London Tabernacle: 251
  renamed, 1937-38: 319
"Look! I Am Making All Things New": 574
Lord's Evening Meal (See **Memorial**)
Lord's Supper (See also **Memorial**): 242
Love
  early Christians: 304
  how demonstrated: 304-17, 711-12
  identifying mark of true Christians: 709-12
Lovell, Alma: 684
Lovell v. City of Griffin
  court case: 684
Lovini, William: 472
Loyalty: 197
Lublin concentration camp: 452
Lundborg, August and Ebba: 408
Lunstrum, Elwood: 85
Luther, Martin: *39,* 51
Lutheran Church
  name: 150
Luxembourg
  branch office: *382*
  literature, number of languages: 497-8
  early witnessing: 430

M

Macedonia: 406
MacGillivray, Alexander: 411-12, 445, *446*
Mackenzie, Fanny: *423,* 424
Macmillan, Alexander H.
  announces Russell's death to Bethel family: 63
  annual meeting, 1919: 72-4
  arrest and sentencing: 652, *653*
  board of directors: 68
  convention, 1919: 257
  expectations, 1914: 61-2, 636-7
  name Jehovah's Witnesses: 152
  Palestine: 142
  pilgrim: 222
  Russell's view on preaching: 63, 623
  visiting Witnesses in prison: 654
Madagascar: 435, 541
Madeira: 437
Madison Square Garden
  violent attempt to disrupt meeting, 1939: 658-9
Magyarosi, Martin: *453*
"Make Sure of All Things"
  release: 99-100
Maki, Gust: *462,* 463
Making Your Family Life Happy: 110
Makore, Isaiah: 227

Malawi
  bans: 675-6
  confusion as to identity of Bible Students: 418, 434
  early witnessing: 434, 436, 521
  persecution: 195, 674-5, 722
  letter campaigns: 317, 695
Malaya: 441, 695
Malaysia: 430, 469, 473
Mali: 475
Mama, Emmanuel: 478
Mancoca, João and Mary: 481, *482,* 528
Manera, Angelo C., Jr.: 94
Mankind's Search for God: 36, 39, 112
Marquesas Islands: 513
Marriage
  view of Witnesses: 174-7
Martin, Helmut: 505
Martin, Robert J.: 91, 257, *580,* 652, *653*
Martinique
  branch office: *364*
  construction: 333
  early witnessing: 364
  publishers, number, 1992: 364
  relief sent out: 313
Martyr
  Greek word: 13
Marx, Karl: *40*

Mauritania: 476
Mauritius
  branch office: *389*
  early witnessing: 389, 435
  missionaries: 535
Mauthausen concentration camp: 308, 452, 660-1, 665
Mayer, J. L.: 424
McGrath, Joseph: 536
McKay, Ruth: 529
McLuckie, Bert and Bill: 434
Meetings: 236-53
  attendance: 253
  ban: 449, *494,* 694
  Bible, basis for instruction: 238, 241
  Congregation Book Study: 237-8
  Cottage Meetings: 238, 241
  Dawn Circles for Bible Study: 237
  early Bible Students: 50, 54-5, 205, 236-41
  early Christians: 28, 236, 251
  Kingdom Hall: 251
  literature used: 237-8, 240-1, 252-3
  no soliciting for money: 340, 343
  Prayer, Praise and Testimony Meetings: 238, 247
  Public Meetings: 249, 251
  Schools of the Prophets: 247
  Service Meetings: 247

singing: 240-1
Sunday meetings: 238
Theocratic Ministry School: 94, 248, *249*, 568-9, 721
training in field ministry: 246-8
unified instruction: 252-3
unity: 237, 246
Watchtower Study: 252-3
Workers' Meetings: 247
youths: 244-6
Memorial (Lord's Evening Meal): 242-4
  active Witnesses compared with attendance, 1935-92 (chart): 242
  annual observance: 242
  attendance:
    1883: 242
    1914: 719
    1919: 720
    1935-92 (chart): 717
    1938: 243
    1992, Africa: 518
  attending despite difficult circumstances: 243-4
  conventions: 55, 254
  date of celebration: 242
  early Bible Students: 55, 242-3
  great crowd: 243
  "little flock": 243
  partakers: 501
    1935-92 (chart): 717
    1938: 243
    1992: 243
  partakers compared with attendance, 1935-60 (chart): 171
Menazzi, Armando: 444, *445*
Men of old (See Princes)
MEPS (Multilanguage Electronic Phototypesetting System): 114, 596-8
Meredith, Martha: 71
"Message of Hope"
  resolution, 1925: 261
Messiah: 19
Metcalfe, Fred: *492*
Methodist Church
  name: 150
Mexico
  Bible studies: 303, *363*, 503
  branch office: 334, *363*
  clergy opposition: 502-3
  congregations, number, 1975: 470
  early witnessing: 414
  Gilead Cultural School of Mexico: 533, 545

Knorr and Franz visit: 459
literacy classes: 466, *467*
missionaries: 461
pioneers, number, 1992: 303
Pioneer Service School: 300
publishers, number:
  1945: 461, 463
  1975: 470, 503
  1992: 503
relief efforts: 312, *313*
Michalec, Edward: *464*
Military service
  Bible Students during World War I: 191-2
  clergy support, World War I: 191, 647-8, 651-2
  Czechoslovakia: 195
  early Christians: 192, 673
  exemption: 192, 194
  Greece: 194
  Italy, World War I: 191-2
  view of Witnesses: 194, 198, 662
Millennial Dawn (See also *Studies in the Scriptures*): 52, 406, 631-2, 635
  Dano-Norwegian: 407
  effect on readers: 53-4
  German: 410
  name change: 42, 53
  use at meetings: 237-8
  writer: 52-3
"Millennial Hopes and Prospects"
  discourse by Russell, 1903: 406
Miller, William: 40, 60, 62
"Millions Now Living Will Never Die"
  discourse by Rutherford: 259, *425*, *426*, 632, 719
Millions Now Living Will Never Die
  booklet, 1920: 78, *163*, 425
Minersville School District v. Gobitis
  compulsory flag salute: 654, 670, 684-7
Minister
  V.D.M. Questions: 215
Ministerial servants
  appointment: 233-4
  early Christians: 233
  qualifications: 182
Ministerial Training School: 113, 300, 350, 533, *545*, 546, 723
Missionaries: 521-46
  adjusting to new living conditions and customs: 528-9, 531-2
  appearing before government officials: 539
  branch oversight: 541, 544

conventions:
  1950: 271
  1966-67: 276-7
Gilead School: 522-5, *527*, 533
  extension schools: 533, 544-5
  total students, 1992: 524
intensifying the preaching work: 462-6, 535
new languages: 532-4
number: 101, 521
number of lands in which they have served: 524
objectives: 523-8, 537-9
obtaining residence visas: 527
opening new fields: 535
persecution: 541-3
pre-Gilead missionaries: 521
stimulate full-time service: 540-1
traveling overseers: 539-40
Witness missionaries contrasted with Christendom's: 525-8
Miura, Katsuo: *452*, 491
Model studies: 85
Model Study
  booklets: 574
Moldova: 406, 507-8, 511
Morality
  view of Witnesses: 145, 173-5
Morocco: 475, 487, 541
Morris, Harold: *464*
Morrison, Donald: 526
Morton
  schooner used in Canada: 439
Moser, Alois: *451*
Moses: 15, *16*, 17
Motion pictures: 480, *481*
Mozambique
  early witnessing: 430, 437
  legal recognition: 510, 701
  letter campaign: 695
  relief received: 309
Muñiz, Juan: 436, *437*, 521
Murdock's Bible translation: *604*, 605
Murdock v. Commonwealth of Pennsylvania: 349
  court case: 687-8
Myanmar: 430, 456
  ban: 455, 676
  branch office: *395*
  clergy opposition, 455
  publishers, number: *395*
My Book of Bible Stories: 110, 246
  audiocassettes: 598

N

Namibia
  early witnessing: *439*
  Kingdom Hall: 319, 322
  missionaries: 535
  officials show impartiality toward Witnesses: 676
Nationalism
  early Christians: 673, 677
  emblems: 669-73, 677
  patriotic ceremonies: 196-7
  under Hitler: 196
  Witnesses attitude: 196-8, 677

"Nations Shall Know That I Am Jehovah, The"—How?: 124
Nauru: 513
Nelson, Ed: *418*, 419
Nelson, Thomas, and Sons: 607
Netherlands
  ban: 675
  branch office: *382*
    construction, donations: 347
    printery seized by Nazis: 586
  printing: 586
  translation: 382

  videocassettes: 382
  clergy opposition: 682
  convention, 1945: 267
  early witnessing: 430
  field ministry:
    seaports: 513, *514*
    World War II: 449-50
  Knorr's service tour: 96
  meetings, World War II: 449
  missionaries sent out: 541
  persecution, World War II: 267, 448
  publishers:
    increase, 1938-45: 455

number, 1940: 95
number, 1945: 95
number, 1992: 382
number, pre-World War II: 267
relief efforts: 307-9
Netherlands Antilles (Curaçao)
branch office: *364*
missionaries: 364, 529
Netherlands East Indies (See **Indonesia**)
Neuengamme concentration camp: 664
Neutrality: 189-98, 495
benefits: 195
Bible Students during World War I: 191-2
early Christians: 190
Jesus' example: 189-90
Witnesses commended: 195
Witnesses during World War II: 193-4
Newberry Bible, The: 604, 605
New Britain: 474
New Caledonia
Assembly Hall: 331
ban: 471
branch office: *399*
early witnessing: 441
first congregation: 399
publishers, number, 1992: 399
Witnesses from other lands help with preaching: 471
New Creation, The: 52, 53, 186, 190, 207-8, 342, 559
Newell, Earl E.: 79
Newfoundland
Knorr's service tour: 98
"New Heavens and a New Earth": 156
New Hebrides (See **Vanuatu**)
Newlands, Bill: *445*
"New Light" Church: 319
"New Name, A"
resolution, 1931: 82, 155-7
Newspapers
advertising literature: 409-10, 561
Russell's sermons: *58,* 59, 421-2, *561,* 719
"New Systems of Things"
convention discourse, 1950: 263
Newton, Sir Isaac: 46, *125,* 160
New World Bible Translation Committee: 607-10
"New World Society Attacked From the Far North"
convention discourse, 1953: 263
New World Society in Action, The
film: 480-1
New World Translation of the Christian Greek Scriptures
Braille: 614
release: 99, 262-3, *264,* 607, *722*
restored divine name: 99
translations into other languages: 611-13, *722*

New World Translation of the Hebrew Scriptures
comments by A. Thomson: 609
New World Translation of the Holy Scriptures: 607-15
audiocassettes: 598, *614,* 615
comments by Hebrew scholar Kedar: 611
computer diskettes: *614*
editions:
Braille, 1988: *614,* 615
Kingdom Interlinear Translation of the Greek Scriptures, The: 610
large print with references, 1984: 111, *608,* 610, 614
one volume, 1961: *608,* 609-10, *722*
pocket size, 1987: 614
regular size, 1981: 614
regular size, 1984: 614
six volumes, 1950-60: *608,* 609
special students', 1963: 610
very large print, 1985: *614*
languages: 507, 612-13
New World Bible Translation Committee: 607-10
number printed, as of 1992: 613, 615
translation, use of computers: 599, 602, 613-14
New Zealand
ban: 676
branch office: *399*
translation: *399*
clergy opposition: 447
conventions:
1963: 277
1978: 282
early witnessing: 418-19
Kingdom Hall construction: 325
Knorr's service tour: 98
missionaries sent out: 541
"Photo-Drama of Creation": 60
Nicaragua
branch office: *364*
missionaries: 461, 463, 535
publishers, number: 364, 463
relief efforts: 311
Nichols, Carleton and Flora: *197*
Nichols, Carleton B., Jr.: *685*
flag salute: 196-7
Nicholson, Jane: 624
Nicholson, R. E. B.: 624
Niger: 475-6, 510
Nigeria
Assembly Halls: 332
ban: 486, 568, 676
Branch Committee: *109*
branch office: 333, *388-9, 591*
financing construction: 346
literature distributed: 388
printing: 590
congregations, number, 1975: 475

conventions:
1970: 277-8, *279, 479*
1990: *389*
early witnessing: 388, 433, 486
government official comments on Witnesses: 488
literacy classes: 480
polygamy (experiences): 176-7
publishers, number:
1950: 486
1970: 486
1975: 488
1992: 388
relief efforts: 309
1914
comment of *The World:* 60
expectations of Bible Students: 60-3, 134-5, 635
pointed to by others: 134
reaction of Bible Students after 1914: 136-7, 636-7
Russell's announcement in Bethel dining room: 61, 719
Russell's article in *Bible Examiner:* 718
view of Witnesses: 139, 144
Nisbet, Robert: 435
Nisbet family: 487
Niue: 472
Nkounkou, Etienne: 477
Noah: 14, *15*
"Noah's Day"
Watchtower article, 1941: 174
Noll, Xavier and Sara: *364*
Norman, David: 435
North America
publishers, number:
1945: 517
1992: 517
Northern Rhodesia (See **Zambia**)
Norway
ban: 675
branch office: *383*
congregation, 1915: *239*
conventions:
1905: 257
1911: 257
early witnessing: 383, 407-8
field ministry:
gains momentum: 639
reaching remote areas: 440
Kingdom Halls: 325, *327*
meetings of early Bible Students: 237-8
"Millions Now Living Will Never Die," discourse: 426
relief received: 308
Russell's visit, 1891: 406
tests resulting from—
business ventures: 640
field ministry: 638
Nuremberg trials
sentencing: 268
Nyasaland (See **Malawi**)

O

Oates, Hector: 455-6
Object and Manner of Our Lord's Return, The: 47, 132-3, 557, 575, 718

Øiseth, Andreas: *408*
Ojeda, Rosendo: 466
Older men (See also **Elders**)

Greek word: 35-6, 233
Old Theology, The
tract: 128, 343

Old Theology Quarterly
  tract: *50,* 51
Oleszynski, Brother: 413
Olson, Olaf: *460,* 525, 546
144,000: 38, 145
  called by God: 162, 170
  early Christians: 159
  kings in heaven: 159, 169
  not only natural Jews: 159, 169
  one flock with great crowd: 171
  work on earth: 159
"Only Light, The"
  convention discourse, 1942: 92-3
"Opportunities for Service"
  Watch Tower article, 1919: 212
Opposition (See Persecution)
Orchestras
  convention: 260, 275
"Order of Trial"
  legal procedures: 691, *692*
Organization
  appointments:
    elders, adjustments, 1972: 106, 233-4, 723
    elders, early views: 206-9, 638-9
    ministerial servants: 233-4

service director: 212, 214, 637-8
speakers, V.D.M. Questions: 215
theocratic: 218-21, 721
traveling speakers: 204, 222-3
branch offices established: 210
branch overseers, training: *230*
expansion of headquarters and branch facilities: 332-9
financial support: 340-51
Governing Body: 106, *116,* 228-9, 233-5
Jehovah's and Satan's: 78-9, 676, 720
Leader is Christ: 29, 117, 204, 674
legal corporations: 210, 229, 234
meetings, early: 205
no clergy class: 204-5
organization instructions: *232*
pastoral workers: 211, 560
"Photo-Drama of Creation," showings: 211
purpose: 210
response to organizational changes of 1930's: 638-9
Russell's view: 204-5
service organization: 212
theocratic procedure: 218-19, 223, 228-9, 638-9, 721
  effect on meetings: 252

traveling overseers: 222-7
  training: 231
unified instruction: 252-3
Watchtower article, 1932: 213, *640*
Watchtower article, 1938: 218-19, *640*
zone visits: 227
"Organization": 218-19, *640*
Watchtower article, 1938:
  reactions: 219, 221
Organization Instructions: 219
Organization Method: 212
Orient: 418, 518-19, 521
Origen: 36
Origin of Species, The: 40, 41
Orphanidis, George: 194
Österman, Emil: 408-9
Ott, Carlos: 437
Ott, Gertrud: *452*
Our Kingdom Ministry: 247
Out Islands, Bahamas
  boat used to reach islands: 463
Ovbiagele, Ezekiel: 480
Overseers
  Greek word: 35

P

Paas, Gottlieb: 410
Page, William E.: 64
Pakistan: 531
Palm, Kathe: 289, *290,* 438
Panama
  branch office: *365*
    construction, donations: 347
  early witnessing: 365, 413
  missionaries: 461
Paniagua, Trinidad: 461
Papua New Guinea
  Assembly Hall: 329
  branch office: *400*
    construction: 339, 346
  languages spoken: 400, 497
  Witnesses from abroad assist with preaching: 400, *471*
Paraguay
  branch office: *369*
  congregations, 1945: 463
  early witnessing: 369, 413, 437
  missionaries: 369
  Witnesses from abroad assist with preaching: 369
Park, Ock-hi: *453*
Parker, John and Adda: *460*
Parkin, Ronald: *462,* 463
Parousia (See Presence of Christ)
Parsons, Julia: 543
"Passing Over From Death to Life"
  convention discourse, 1964: 264
Pastor
  why Russell called: 54
Pastoral work: 66, 211, 560
Paterson, Gabriel and Florence: 478
Paton, Fred: 455-6
Paton, J. H.: 620

"Peace—Can It Last?"
  convention discourse, 1942: 93, 95, 193, 262
Pele, Fuaiupolu: *473*
Peloubet, F. N.: 245
Peoples Friend, The: 439
Peoples Pulpit Association: 73, 91, 229
Persecution: 642-77
  bans: 675-6
  clergy incite: 69-70, 434, 441, 551-2, 642, 644, 647-50, 654-6, *657,* 658-60, 666-9, 676, 678-82, 688-9, 695
  concentration camps: *659,* 660-4, *665*
  early Christians: 30-1, *32,* 642, 646-7
  examples of faith: *451-3,* 677
  family and community pressure: 473
  flag salute: 669-72, 721
  letter campaigns: 315-17, 694-5
    cablegrams: 552
  missionaries: 541-3
  mob violence: *667,* 668, *670,* 671, 721
  politics, nonparticipation: 673-5
  printing operations shut down: 585-6, 589
  Satan behind persecution: 676
  school expulsions: 670-2
  why Jehovah permits: 677
  World War I: 423-5, 647-56
  World War II: 448-58
Persia (See Iran)
Personnel Committee: 114, 235
Peru
  branch office: *370*
    expansion: 333
  early witnessing: 370, 436, 438
  first congregation formed: 370, 459
  Kingdom Hall: *327*
  missionaries: 532

publishers, number, 1992: 370
reaching remote areas: 465
relief efforts: *311,* 312
Peters, August: *452*
Petersen, Anna (Later Rømer): 285
Petition
  for release of Society's officers, 1919: 74-5
Pfannebecker, Brother: 260
Philbrick, Herman L.: 77
Philippines
  branch office: *396*
    expansion: 333, 339
    financing construction: 346
    languages printed: 396
    printing: 592-3
    translation: 489
  congregations, number, 1992: 396
  conventions: 281, *488,* 489
  early witnessing: 441, 521
  field ministry:
    hours, total to 1992: 396
    World War II: 455
  flag salute: 671
  Kingdom Ministry School: *231*
  pioneers, number, 1992: 302
  publishers:
    number, 1992: 510
    increase after World War II: 489
  relief efforts: 308, 315
  Russell's visit, 1912: 396, 419-20
  strengthening congregations after World War II: 488-9
Phillips, George: *298,* 521
Phillips, Llewelyn: 486
Phonograph: 85, *87,* 565, *566,* 721
"Photo-Drama of Creation": *56-7,* 60, 561
  Drama Committees: 211

INDEX

intensive witness: 422, *562*
no admission fee: 249, 340-1
number of viewers, 1914: 422, *562*, 719
"Scenario": *56*
showings: 56, 423
    Czechoslovakia: 432
    Spain: 437
    Yugoslavia: 432
Piccone, Domenick and Elsa: 541-2
Pierson, A. N.: 65
Pilgrims (See also **Traveling overseers**):
66, 222-3, 237, 252, 255-6
Pioneers
auxiliary pioneers: 299-300, 302, 717
colporteurs: 66, 717
experiences: 285-91, 444-7
number:
    1920-92 (chart): 717
    1946: 722
    1973: 723
    1974: 723
    1975: 517
    1976-92 (chart): 112
    1978: 113
    1985: 723
    1990: 723
    1992: 113, 300, 517, 723
percentage increase, 1982-92: 302-3
regular pioneers: 299-300
special pioneers: 85, 299, 350
training: 300, 723
Pioneer Service School: 113, *300*, 723
Pittsburgh, Pennsylvania
early meetings: 49
first headquarters: 54, *208-9*
headquarters returned to: 71, 577, 719
Pittsburgh Gazette, The
Russell-Eaton debates: *644*
Placards: 249, 266, 447, 460, 567, *568*, 721
Plymouth Bethel: 59
Poelmans, Brother: 566
Poems and Hymns of Millennial Dawn: 240
Poetzinger, Gertrud: *291, 452,* 661
Poetzinger, Martin
comments about the name Jehovah's Witnesses: 158
concentration camp: *452,* 661
full-time service: 290, *291*
Governing Body: 663
Poland
assemblies and conventions: 278-9, *280, 381,* 503, *504,* 723
bans: 381, 503, 675
branch office: *181*
clergy opposition: 657
commercial printers, use of: 581
early witnessing: 413
Governing Body members
    visit: 506
government officials defend Witnesses: 657
hours, number, 1992: 505
legal recognition: 504, 697
Memorial attendance, 1992: 115

publishers, number: 115, 381, 429, 503, 505
relief received: 308
Politics
attitude of Witnesses: 673-4
early Christians: 190, 673
Polygamy
view of Witnesses: 176-7
Porneia: 177
Portugal
branch office: *383*
conventions: 269, *383,* 510
early witnessing: 430, 436-7
legal recognition: 269, 383, 494
missionaries: 537, 539, 541
New World Translation, distribution: 612
persecution:
    Catholic clergy incite: 494
    letter campaigns: 695
    meetings while under ban: *494*
publishers, number: 269, 383, 494, 510, 612
Portuguese East Africa (See **Mozambique**)
Portuguese West Africa (See **Angola**)
Powell, Grover: 92
"**Prayer**"
phonograph record: 565
Prayer, Praise and Testimony Meetings: 238, 247
Preachers Present Arms: 191, 552, 655-6
Preaching (See **Field ministry**)
Presbyteros: 35, 233
Presence of Christ
Adventists' views: 45, 60, 132
Barbour's views: 46-7
invisible: 45-6, 132-4
parousia: 46, 133
sign: 24-5
Presidents (Watch Tower Society)
Franz: 109, 111
Knorr: 91, 227, 721
Russell: 576
Rutherford: 65, 68, 719
Priests
origin of term: 36
Princes: 76, 138, 161
convention, 1950: 263
Printing
Bible printing and distribution: 603-15
bookbinding: 579-81, *588-9,* 593
Braille: 585
commercial printers: 576-7, 581, 585-6, 592, 605
computer systems, development and use: 596-9, 602
expansion, after World War II: 588-91
foreign languages: 576-7, 579, 583, 586, 592-4, 596-8
    early operations in Michigan: 579-80
    simultaneous publications: 598-9
    translation: 112, 375, 391, 599, *602*
four-color printing: 595-6
photocomposition: 375, 596
platemaking: *582*
presses:
    flatbed: *587,* 590
    job: *587*

sheet offset: 594-5
web offset: *587,* 592, 595, 597, 614-15
web rotary: 578, *579,* 585, *587,* 591-2
Society in forefront of printing industry: 575, 579, 581, 584-5, 596-7, 607
Society begins its own printing operations: 577-81, 720
Society's printing operations outside the United States: 583, 585-93
    printing branches: *590-1,* 593
three-color printing: 595
typesetting: *581,* 594, 596
Prisons
witnessing to inmates: 514-15
"**Problems of Reconstruction and Expansion, The**"
convention discourse, 1946: 97-8
Proclaiming "Everlasting Good News" Around the World
film: 481
Prohibition
view of Bible Students: 182
Prophecy: 88, 124
Protection: 573
Public Meeting: 248-9, 251
Publishers
increase:
    during World War II: 98
    following World War II: 230
    France: 95
    Holland: 95
    1928, United States: 564
    1938-45: 455, 457
    1939-46: 229-30, 588
    1947-52: 98
    1975-92: 517
    1976-92 (chart): 115
    1980-85: 111
    1982-92: 302
    1982-92 (chart): 303
    1985-92: 111
number:
    early 1880's: 404
    1914: 422, 719
    1919: 425, 720
    1920: 259
    1922: 260, 425
    1922, United States: 563
    1924, United States: 563
    1926, United States: 564
    1935: 443
    1935-92 (chart): 242, 717
    1939: 461
    1941: 721
    1942: 108
    1943: 544
    1945: 461, 501, 517
    1953: 100
    1963: 722
    1967: 593
    1968: 104
    1974: 723
    1975: 488, 498, 501
    1976: 108
    1977-78, decrease: 110
    1985: 723
    1990: 723
    1992: 117, 243, 517-19, 544, 723

number of countries with a population less than total Witnesses worldwide: 519
percentage:
 anointed 1935: 501
 anointed 1975: 501
 "other sheep," 1945: 501
Publishing Committee: 113-14, 235

Puerto Rico
 blood transfusion (experience): 184
 branch office: 365
 translation: 365
 early witnessing: 438-9
 literature distributed, 1930-92: 365
 missionaries: 461, 535

relief efforts: 313
return visits, 1930-92: 365
"Purgatory"
 phonograph record: 565
Purple Triangles
 videocassette: *601*
Pyramid of Gizeh: *201*

Q

Quebec, Canada
 arrests: 498, 689
 exposing high-handed judges: 692-3
 mob violence: 498, *700*

persecution of Witnesses: 682, 688-90
Quebec, You Have Failed Your People!
 tract: 689
Quebec's Burning Hate for God and Christ

and Freedom Is the Shame of All Canada
 tract: 689, *691*
Questions Young People Ask—Answers That Work: 110, 175, 246

R

Radio
 chain broadcasts: 79, *137,* 139, 158
 clergy opposition: 447-8, 573
 number of stations carrying Society's broadcasts: 80, 562
 Society begins using radio: 562, 720
 stations owned or operated by Society: *80*
  CHCY: *81*
  2HD: *81*
  WBBR: *80,* 562, 572, 720
  WORD: *81*
 value in proclaiming the Kingdom: 249, 562
Raibe, Seremaia: 472
Randle, Horace: 418
Ransom: 22
 Barbour's view: 47-8, 131, 619-20
 test involving belief: 619-21
 view of Russell and associates: 45, 47-8, 131-2, 620, 718
 Watch Tower, advocate of ransom: 620
Raunholm, Unn: *543*
Ravensbrück concentration camp: 179, 452, 551, 661, 664
Raymond Street jail, Brooklyn: *69*
Recordings
 audiocassettes: 598, 615
 discourses for the public: 87, 249, 565-6
 Kingdom songs: 241
 videocassettes: 600-1
Reformation, Protestant: 38-40
Regan, Michael: 514
Regional Building Committees: 325-6, 328, 723
Regional Engineering Offices: 332, 394, 400
Regional servants (See also **Traveling overseers**): 223
Regional service directors (See also **Traveling overseers**): 223
Reiter, Franz: 662
Religion
 early view of the term: 447, 567
 "Religion and Christianity"
  recording by Rutherford: 573
Resolutions: 261, 426-7
"Resolution to the Peoples of Christendom": 261

Restoration prophecies: 141-2, 720
Return of Christ (See **Presence of Christ**)
Return visits: 66, 85, 299, 460
 number made, 1945-76: 501
 number made, Puerto Rico, 1930-92: 365
Réunion: 469
Reusch, Lyle: 103
Revelation—Its Grand Climax At Hand!: 111, 148, 598
Revised Version: 606
Rice, Frank: 286, *287,* 447, 521
Riches: 84, *88, 571,* 573, 721
Riemer, Hugo H.: *100,* 578, *586*
Ritchie, A. I.: 65
Robison, Frederick H.: 64, 652, *653*
Rockwell, Henry C.: 64
Roe, Webster: 169
Rogers, S. D.: 627
Rollwald Camp: 451
Romania
 ban: 675
 clergy opposition: 656, 680
 conventions: *506,* 507
 early witnessing: 431
 Governing Body member visits: 506
 lawsuits, 1933-39: 679
 legal recognition: 505, 697
 literature placements, 1924-35: 431
 publishers, number: 431
 relief received: 308-9, *310*
 Society's printing operations: 583
Roncarelli, Frank: 667, 689
Roosevelt, Eleanor: 670
Rosam, Eugene and Camilla: 88
Rosario, Ana Paz de: 184
Rota: 513
Rotherham, Joseph B.: 605
Royal Albert Hall: *80,* 422, 447
"Ruler for the People"
 convention discourse, 1928: 262, 266
Russell, Ann Eliza: 42
Russell, Charles T.: *42, 53, 625*
 acknowledged indebtedness to others for assistance in Bible study: 43-9, 120
 announces "Gentile Times have ended": 61, 719
 associates, early: 45-6, 120, 127

Barbour, N. H.: 46-8, 131, 620, 718
begins systematic study of Bible: 44, 718
Bible discourses: 53, 55, *405*
biography: 64
clergy opposition: 642-6
conventions: 130, 256-7
death: 63, *64,* 719
 reactions of Bible Students: 63, 624, *625, 626*
debates: *128,* 129-30, 643, *644*
description: *53,* 55, 228-9, 284
early life: 42-5
evangelizing trips: *405*
 Austria: 406
 Britain: 406
 Canada: 406, 421
 Caribbean: 405
 China: 420, 489
 Cuba: 414, 421, 458
 Denmark: 406
 Europe: 406, *407,* 421
 Germany: 406
 India: 419-21
 Ireland: 406
 Italy: 406
 Jamaica: 414, 421
 Japan: 420
 Middle East: 406
 North America: 405
 Norway: 406
 Orient: 419-21
 Panama: 414, 421
 Philippines: 419-20
 Russia: 406, 507-8
 Scotland: 406
 Sweden: 406
 Switzerland: 406
 Turkey: 406
 world tour, 1911-12: 419-21
"faithful and wise servant": 143, 626
finances: 47, 351
Herald of the Morning: 46-8, 131, 575, 718
infallibility, no claim of: 207
inspiration never claimed: 622
marriage: 645, *646*
meetings: 236-8
newspapers carried sermons: *58,* 59, 421-2, *561,* 719
Object and Manner of Our Lord's Return, The: 47, 132-3, 557, 575, 718

Pastor, why called: 54, 560
president of Watch Tower Society: 576
refusal to solicit financial support: 340, 342, 350
religious background: 42-3, 122, 126
spoke to Jews: 141
Three Worlds published with N. H. Barbour: 47, 135, 575, 718
Tower Publishing Company: 576
turned "hose" on hell: 130
views on—
  alcohol: 181-2
  Armageddon: 139-40
  Bible and study helps: 133, 238, 240
  Christ's presence: 133
  Christ's return: 45, 132-3, 622, 718
  chronology: 46-7, 133-5
  covenants: 630
  eternal life on earth: 161-2
  "faithful and wise servant": 142-3, 626
  government: 190
  hellfire: 43, 126-9, *130*, 622
  his role: 48-9, 143, 707
  Jehovah, the name: 123-4
  Lord's work: 211
  1914: 60, 135-6, 622, 635-6, 718
  ordination: 645
  preaching work: 51, 63, 556-7, 559, 623
  progressive truth: 121, 133
  ransom: 45-8, 131-2, 620-1, 623, 718
  selection of elders: 206-7
  soul: 44, 127, 622
  Trinity: 124-6, 622
visited early *Watch Tower* readers: 50, 205, 222, 404
writings: *52*, 53, 404
Russell, Joseph L.: 42, *43*
Russell, Maria: 143, 645, *646*
"Russellites": 150, 156
Russia
  baptisms: *700*
  conventions: 281, *506*, 509, *511, 700*
  early witnessing: 411, 454, 507-8
  Governing Body members visit: 506
  Russell's visit, 1891: 406, 507-8
Rutherford, Joseph F.
  arrest and sentencing: 69, 650-2, *653*
  background: 67
  conventions:
    1919: 257, *258,* 259
    1922: 260
    1927: 266
    1931: 266-7
    1935: 261, *266,* 267
    1938: 447
    1941: 262
  court cases: 684
  death: 89-90, 227, 721
  discourses: 84, 86, 155, 258-62
    "Face the Facts," 1938: *80,* 447
    "Frauds of the Clergy Exposed, The" 1925: 658
    "Government and Peace," 1939: 658
    "Millions Now Living Will Never Die": 425, 632, 648, 719
  Editorial Committee: 64
  Executive Committee: 65, 67
  field service: 260, 637
  illness: 75-6, 89
  imprisonment: *69,* 70
    release: 75, 654
  instructions for Witnesses on legal procedures: 690
  Judge, why called: 67
  lawyer for Society: 59, 67, 654
  leadership, comments on: 220, *221*
  letter expressing support: 625-6
  letter to Adolf Hitler: 693
  member of New York Bar: 684
  name Jehovah's Witnesses: 151-2, 155-6
  not a convict: 654
  opposition toward, at headquarters: 66-8
  personal characteristics: 66, 220, 624, *625, 626*
  president of Watch Tower Society: 719
    elected, 1917: 65
    reelected, 1918: 68
    reelected, 1919: 74
  radio discourses: 447-8, 458, 562, *563*
    first broadcast: *80*
    recordings: 249, 573
  Russell's funeral: 284
  Supreme Court cases: 684-5
  test in Los Angeles: 75-6
  wintered in California: *76*
Rutherford, Malcolm: 89
Rutherford, Mary: 89
"Rutherfordites": 150
Rwanda: *387,* 510

S

Sabbath: 144
Sachsenhausen concentration camp: 453, 660, 663, 665
St. Croix
  relief received: 313
St. Helena: 435
St. Kitts: 414
St. Lucia: 414, 469
St. Maarten
  Sibia, Society's schooner: 463
St. Thomas: 413
Salgar, Ramón: 424
Salter, W. F.: 628
"Saluting a Flag"
  radio discourse by Rutherford: 196-7
Samoa: 441
Sandwich signs (See **Placards**)
Santo Domingo (See **Dominican Republic**)
Sargent, Melvin: *574*
Satan: 144
Scheider, Wilhelm: *453*
Schenck, Agnes: 471
Schmidt, Victor: 92
Schneider v. State of New Jersey
  court case: 654, 684
Schools
  flag salute: 684-8
Schools, Watch Tower Society
  Gilead School: *95*, 522-4, *527,* 721
  Kingdom Ministry School: 102-3, 113, 231, 722
  Ministerial Training School: 113, 300, 533, 545, 723
  Pioneer Service School: 113, *300,* 723
  Theocratic Ministry School: 94, 248, *249,* 721
Schools of the Prophets: 247
Schreiber, Therese: *450,* 454
Schroeder, Albert D.
  branch overseer, Britain: 522
  convention, 1938, Britain: 447
  Gilead School: 95, 522-3, *524*
  Governing Body: 95, *116,* 522
Schurstein, Karl: *452*
Scotland
  convention, 1909: 257
  early witnessing: 405, 411-12, 447, 567
  Russell's visit, 1891: 406
Scott, Edwin: 427
Sedition
  charge against Witnesses: 682, 688, 690
Second Adventists: 45, 60
  Christ's return: 132
  influence on Russell: 43-4, 122
Seegelken, Hermán: 549
Seeley, Robert
  comments about Gentile Times: 134
Seiss, Joseph
  comments about Gentile Times: 46, 134
Seliger, Ernst and Hildegard: *452*
Senegal
  branch office: *390*
  early witnessing: 476, 535
  Witnesses from abroad assist with preaching: 469
Servants to the brethren (See also **Traveling overseers**): 93, 223
Service Committee: 114, 234-5
Service committee (congregation)
  1919: 212
  1932: 214, 638
Service director
  1919: 212, 637
  1932: 214, 638
"Service Essential"
  Watch Tower article, 1922: 563, 637-8, *639*
Service Meeting: 247, *248*
Sessi, Ayité: 477
Sewell, John E. (Ted): *445,* 446
Sexton, E. D.: 73-4
Sheep and goats
  Jesus' illustration: 163-4
Shepherd, Sydney: 440
Shooter, Alfred: 478
Shuster, Eugene and Delia: 500
Siam (See **Thailand**)
Siberia
  convention, 1991: 507
Sibia
  Society's schooner: *462,* 463

Sierra Leone
 branch office: *391*
 early witnessing: 391, 424, 433
 relief received: 309
Simonsen, Theodor: 408
Singapore
 bans: 676, 695
 early witnessing: 412, 430-1, 445-6, 535
 Lightbearer, Society's boat: 441
Singing
 early conventions: 256-7
 songbooks: *240-1*
"Singing and Accompanying Yourselves With Music in Your Hearts": 241
Sing Praises to Jehovah: 241
Six Sermons: 45
Sjoberg, Hilma: 438
Skinner, Edwin: 430, *431,* 521
Slide showings: 481
Smets, Brother: 566
Smith, Frank and Gray: *435*
Sobhuza II, King: 435, 487
"Society, the"
 identity: 219, 639
Sodaemun Prison
 Korea: 453
Solomon Islands
 branch office: *401*
 early witnessing: 401
 religious leader accepts truth: *474*
Somalia: 535
Songs of Praise to Jehovah: 241
Songs of the Bride: 240
Songs to Jehovah's Praise: 241
Soul (See also **Immortality of the soul**):
 36-8, 127, 145
 serving whole-souled: 294
Sound cars: *87, 156, 267, 566, 567*
South Africa
 "A Challenge to World Leaders," distribution: *427*
 ban: 676
 branch office: *390-1, 590*
  construction, donations: 346-7
  expansion: 334
  printing: 583, 590, 592, 594
  translation: *391*
 congregation, 1915: *239*
 convention, 1985: 282
 early witnessing: 418, 430, 521
 "Millions Now Living Will Never Die," discourse: 426
 racial unity of Witnesses: 322
 reaching remote areas: 439
 relief efforts: 312, 712
South America: 413
 Bible studies, number, 1992: 518
 congregations, number: 470, 518
 early witnessing: 521
 missionaries: 463-6
 publishers, number: 439, 461, 470, 518
Southern Rhodesia (See **Zimbabwe**)
South-West Africa (See **Namibia**)
Sovereignty (See **Issues**)
Soviet Union (See **U.S.S.R.**)
Sozoñiuk, Alejandro: 466

Spain
 Assembly Halls: 329
 bans: 675
  letter campaigns: 315, 695
 branch office: *384*
  financing construction: 346-7
  printing: 584
 clergy opposition: 494, 666
 congregations, number: 384, 501
 early meeting place: 318
 early witnessing: 384, 424, 430, 436-7, 521
 Kingdom Halls: 384
 legal recognition: 384, 494, 696, *700*
 missionaries: 537-8, 541
 persecution: 494
 publishers, number: 384, 494, 510, 667, 696
 witnessing while in prison: 495
Spanish
 number who speak, worldwide: 365
 publishers, number: 613
Speakers
 certificates: 204
 meetings, early Bible Students: 237
 Public Meetings: 249, 251
 Schools of the Prophets: 247
 Theocratic Ministry School: 94, 248, *249*
 traveling: 222-3
 V.D.M. Questions: 215
Special pioneers (See **Pioneers**)
Spill, W. E.: 68
Spiritism
 view of Witnesses: 144
Sri Lanka
 ban: 676
 branch office: *397*
 congregation, 1915: *239*
 early meetings: 240
 early witnessing: 397, 412, 430, 535
Stanley Theater: 331-2
Steele, Don and Earlene: *491*
Stephanoff, Basil: *406*
Stephenson, F. de P.: 414
Stetson, George W.: 45, 120
Storrs, George: *46,* 575
 associate of Russell: 45-6, 120, 127
 beliefs: 44-6, 48
Street witnessing: 456-7, *567, 569,* 721
Stubbs, Louise: *460*
Studies in the Scriptures (See also ***Millennial Dawn***): 42, 53, 66-7, 111, 135, 175, 406, 577, 623, 631-2
 name change: 42, 53
 use at meetings: 240, 252
Sturgeon, Menta: *63, 623*
Subjection
 superior authorities: 145, 147, 190-2, 198, 264
"Subjection to Superior Authorities"
 convention discourses, 1962: 264
Sudan
 early witnessing: 476, 535
 relief received: 712
Suggestive Hints to Colporteurs
 pamphlet: 246
Suiter, Grant
 board of directors: *100*

 comments about great crowd: 166
 convention, 1950: *274*
 Schools of the Prophets: 247
Sullivan, Thomas J.: *71,* 424
 board of directors: *100*
 convention, 1922: 77
Sunal, Rudolph: *453*
Sunday meetings: 238
Sunday witnessing: 82, *564,* 720
Sunderlin, J. C.: *405,* 561
Superior authorities: 145, 147, 190-1, 198, 264
Supreme Court
 Canada: 689-90
 United States: 197, 349, 499, 654, 670, *679,* 684-8, 697-9, 721
Suriname: 344, 465
 attending meetings (experience): 253
 branch office: *371*
 congregations, number, 1945: 463
 early witnessing: 413
Swaziland
 ban: 676
  letter campaign: 695
 early witnessing: 435
 witnessing to king: 435, 487
Sweden
 Assembly Hall: 331
 branch office: *383*
  construction: 334, 347
  languages: 383
  printing: 590
 early meeting place: 318
 early witnessing: 407-8
 field ministry, total hours, 1983-92: 383
 missionaries sent out: 541
 relief sent out: 308-9
 Russell's visit, 1891: *406*
Swingle, Lyman A.: *91, 100, 116*
Switzerland
 ban: 675
 branch office: *384*
  bindery: 593
  printing: 583
 clergy opposition: 658
 court cases: 494, 681
 early witnessing: 409, 548
 "Jehovah's Youth": *244,* 245
 Knorr's visit: 96
 literature distribution: 349, 583
 meeting the challenge of language differences (experience): 497
 "Photo-Drama of Creation": 422
 publishers, increase: 455
 relief sent out: *306,* 308-9
 Russell's visit, 1891: 406
 tests resulting from expectations based on 1925: 633
Sydlik, Daniel: *116*
Syria
 clergy opposition: 566
 missionaries: 541
Szabo, Berthold: 662
Szabó, Károly: 431
Szinger, Ádám: *453*

INDEX 747

T

Tahiti
  ban: 471
  branch office: 333, *401*
  early witnessing: 401, 440, 471
  legal recognition: 471
Taiwan
  Amis tribesmen: *536*
  branch office: *397*
  convention, 1991: 281
  early witnessing: 397, 473
  pioneers from the Philippines assist with preaching: 473
Tanganyika (See Tanzania)
Tanzania: *387*, 435, 480
Taylor v. State of Mississippi
  flag salute: 688
Teaching Committee: 112, 234
Temple Auditorium, Los Angeles, California: 648
Templeton, Ramon: 88
Tertullian: 304, 341-2
Testimony cards: 93, 564, *565*
"Testimony to the Rulers of the World, A"
  resolution, 1926: 261, 437
Thailand
  conventions: 281, *397*
  early witnessing: 397, 418, 430, 446-7
  Kingdom Ministry School: *231*
  office: *397*
  pioneers from the Philippines assist with preaching: 473
"Then Is Finished the Mystery of God": 107, 148
Theocracy
  definition: 217
"Theocracy's Increase"
  convention theme, 1950: 99, 274
Theocratic Ministry School
  beginning: 94, 721
  benefits: 94, 568-9
  Brooklyn Bethel: 248
  development: 247-8, 568
  sisters invited to enroll: 569

Thérond, Elie: 409
"Thief in Paradise, the Rich Man in Hell, and Lazarus in Abraham's Bosom, The"
  discourse, 1909: 257
Thomas, Hans: 446
Thompson, Adrian: *451*
Thorn, Walter J.: 79
"Thorns and Traps Are in the Way of the Independent One"
  Bible drama, 1969: 175
Thousand Year Reign: 104, 162-3
Three Worlds, and the Harvest of This World: 47, 135, 575, 619, 718
Thy Kingdom Come: 52, 53
Tilmant, Jean-Baptiste, Sr.: 409-10
Time Is at Hand, The: 52, 53
Time prophecies (See Chronology)
Tippin, Ronald: 287-8, 521
Tischendorf's *New Testament*: *604*, 605
Tobacco
  view of Witnesses: 180-1
Tobago: 325
Toco, Simão Gonçalves: 481-2
Togo: 477, 510, 532
"To Hell and Back!"
  discourse: *130*, 433
Tonga: 472
Tornow, Nikolaus von: 411
Toutjian, Herald: 78
Tower Bible and Tract Society (See also Watch Tower Bible and Tract Society of Pennsylvania): 603
Tower Publishing Company: 576
Tower Tract Fund: 342-3
Tower Tract Society representatives: 223
Tracts: 50, 51, 66, 69-70
  distribution: 576, 718-19
  protected under First Amendment in United States: 688
  first tracts published by Bible Students: 348, *557*, 576, 718

languages, number, 1881: 718
Tracy, Robert: *530*
Transcription equipment: *87*, 448, 566, 573, 720
Translators: *391*
  computer support: 599, *602*, 613-14
  number, 1992: 112
Traub, Richard: 438
Traveling overseers (See also Circuit overseers; District overseers; Zone overseers): 93, 222-3, *224-5*, 226-7, 298, 719
  early: 222, 719
  financial support: 350-1
  missionaries: 539-40
  number: 115, 298
  supervision of: 234-5
  training: 102, 223, 231, 722
Trinidad
  branch office: *365*
  early witnessing: 365, 414, 462
  missionaries: *365*, 462-3, 538
  persecution: 675
Trinity
  early antitrinitarians: 44, 125
  exposed by Russell: 124-6, 622, 707
  origin of doctrine: 36
"Trinity"
  phonograph record: 565
"Triumphant Kingdom"
  convention, 1955: 276
"Truth Shall Make You Free, The": *107*, 133
Truth That Leads to Eternal Life, The: 105, *107*, 571, 574, *594*
Tsukaris, John: 194
Tuček, Alfred and Frieda: *433*
Tunisia: 475
Turkey: 406
"Two Great Battles Raging—Fall of Autocracy Certain"
  tract: 70
Tyndale, William: 44

U

Ubangi-Shari (See Central African Republic)
Uganda
  early witnessing: 435
Ukoli, G. M.: 628
Ukraine
  conventions, 1991: *506*, 507-8
  Governing Body member visits: 506
  legal recognition: 701
  meetings: *701*
  relief received: 309
Uncovered
  booklet: 573
Unglaube, Willy: *429*, 430, 446
United in Worship of the Only True God: 293
United Nations
  beginning: 95
  clergy support: 193
  State of Israel becomes member: 141
  Witnesses' attitude: 192, *193*

United States
  arrests: 552, 669
  divisional campaigns: 82, 692
  house-to-house work: 679
  neutrality: 194, 722
  number: 82, 679-80, 720
  Assembly Halls:
    first: 328, *329*, 722
    Stanley Theater: 331-2
  ban: 552, 675
  clergy opposition: 70, 642-6, 648-50, 654-7
  congregations:
    number: 500
    number formed 1985/86: 325
  court cases:
    defending right to distribute literature: 683-8, 697
    defending right to preach publicly and from house to house: 683, 697-8

  effect of Witness cases on American law: 698-9
  exposing high-handed officials to public view: 693
  Supreme Court: 197, 349, 499, 654, 670, 679, 684-8, 721
  field ministry:
    reaching night workers: 514
    telephone witnessing: 516
    training: 569
    World War II: 456-7
  flag salute: 196-7, 669-72, 680, 684-8, 721
  "Junior Witnesses": 245
  Kingdom Hall construction: 320-4, 326
  literature distribution: 349-50
  meetings, efforts to attend (experience): 253
  military exemption, World War II: 194
  missionaries sent out: 541
  persecution: 10, 69-70, 82

World War I: 423-5, 552, 649-56
World War II: 456-7, 721
Prohibition: 182
public meetings: 249
publishers: 457
  number: 443, 564
  Spanish-speaking, 1992: 613
relief efforts:
  after natural disasters: 313-15, 712
  after World War II: *306*, 308
  assistance to Cuban refugees: 316
  in wartime: 309
tests resulting from—
  business ventures: 640
field ministry: 638
  Russell's death: 68, 624
  unassigned territories: 499
Universal sovereignty (See **Issues**)
Unterdörfer, Ilse: *450,* 543
Upper Volta (See **Burkina Faso**)
Uruguay
  branch office: *372*
  early witnessing: 437
  missionaries: 372, 461, *530*
  pioneer helped over 100 into truth: 276
  publishers, number: 372
U.S.S.R. (See also **Russia**)
  conventions: 507
  delegates attend Poland conventions, 1989: 279, *280,* 504
  early witnessing: 507-8
  government opposition: 508, 680
  legal recognition: 505, 697
  Memorial attendance, 1992: 117
  publishers, number, 1946: 508
  radio broadcasts: 429
  Russell visits: 406, 507-8
  witnessing after World War II: 454, 508, 551

V

Values and Violence in Auschwitz: 663
Van Amburgh, William E.
  announces Knorr's presidency: 91
  arrest and sentencing: 652, *653*
  board of directors: 65, 68, 74
  convention, 1942: 93
  Editorial Committee: 64
  Executive Committee: 65, 68
  reaction to Russell's death: 622-4
  visits Cuba, 1944: 459
  Way to Paradise, The: 245
Van Daalen, Emil: *460*
Vandenberg, Albert
  Russell-Eaton debates: 643
Vanderhaegen, Peter: 525
Van Hoesen, Mrs. D.: 70
Van Twest, Mr.: 412
Vanuatu: 440
Variorum Bible: *604,* 605
V.D.M. Questions: 215
Venezuela
  Assembly Hall: *330*
  branch office: *372*
  early witnessing: 372, 521
  first congregation: 459
  missionaries: 465-6, 535
  publishers, number: 372, 463
Videocassettes: 600-1
Video Services: *600-1*
Vietnam
  early witnessing: 447
  language: 532
  missionaries: 531, 535
  pioneers from the Philippines assist with preaching: 473
Vigo, Malcolm and Linda Louise: *530*
Vindication: 88, 141, 165, 720
Virgin Islands, U.S.: 535
Voices From the Holocaust: 179

W

Wagner, Charles E.: 90
Walder, Thomas: 521
Wallis and Futuna Islands: 513
Wandres, Albert: *450*
"Wanted 1,000 Preachers"
  Watch Tower article, 1881: 210, 284, 718
"Warning From Jehovah"
  resolution, 1931: 82, 565
"Warning to All Christians, A"
  resolution, 1923: 261
"Watch Tower"
  background of expression: 48
Watchtower, The (Formerly called *Zion's Watch Tower; The Watch Tower*): 42, 724-5
  advocate of the ransom: 47, 132, 620
  audiocassettes: 598
  benefits: 230
  "Berean Questions": 252
  commercial printers: *576,* 592
  distribution figures:
    1879: 48
    1914: 48
    1914-18: 71
    1916: 725
    1920: 578
    1942: 721
    1992: 723
    1993: 725
  duplication and distribution, World War II: 454
  Editorial Committee: 64, 146
  first issue: 47-8, *121,* 122, 718, 724
  for persons who are poor: 343, 348
"International Sunday School Lessons": 245
languages:
  German: 410
  number, 1922: 725
  number, 1938: 252
  number, 1969: 592
  number, 1976: 110, 112
  number, 1992: 110, 112, 723
  number, 1993: 725
  simultaneous, 1992: 114, 253, 598-9
  Spanish: 436
  Swedish: 407
name changes: 724-5
never begs for money: 340
purpose: 557, 724
street distribution: 567, 721, 725
subscriptions: 348, 558, 725
use at meetings: 252-3
writers: 146
Watchtower Bible and Tract Society of New York, Inc. (Formerly called Peoples Pulpit Association): 91, 229
Watch Tower Bible and Tract Society of Pennsylvania (Formerly called Zion's Watch Tower Tract Society)
  annual meetings: 65, 68, 72-4, 229
  arrest and sentencing of administrative staff: 69, 70, 424, 552, 650, *651,* 652, *653,* 654-6, 719
  appeal of case: 653-4
  comments in religious periodicals: 655
  judgment reversed: 654, 720
  release: 75, 257, 425, 654, 720
  Bibles: 606-7
board of directors: 65, *100,* 228-9, 722
  relationship to Governing Body: 233
charter: 228-9, 576
financial support: 340-51
legally incorporated: 210, 229, 234, 576, 718
membership: 228-9
name changes: 229, 576, 603
officers: 228-9
opposition on board of directors, 1917: 66-8, 627, 719
outside the United States: 583, 585-93
president: 67, 91, 111, 234, 576, 719, 721
printing operations: 575-81, 585, 596-7, 607, 720
publisher and distributor of the Bible: 603-15
purpose: 576, 603
relief efforts: 308-13, 317
shareholder-voters: 228-9
Tower Publishing Company: 576
Watchtower Bible School of Gilead (See **Gilead School**)
Watchtower Educational Center: 336, *352*
Watchtower Farms: *354,* 356
  developing computer systems: 596-7
  factory complex: 591-2
  magazine printing: 356, 592
Watchtower movements (Africa): 434
Watchtower Study: 252-3
Waterfall, Edna: 532
Watkins, George and Willa Mae: 529
Watson, Claud: 70
"Way to Life"
  phonograph record: 565

INDEX

Way to Paradise, The: 245
WBBR radio station: 80, 341, 562, 720
   why sold: 572
Weber, Adolf: *409,* 410, 521, 561
Weeds
   Jesus' illustration: 44, 121, 706
Wendell, Jonas: 43-5, 120
Wesley, John
   followers called Methodists: 150
West Africa: 521
Westcott, B. F.: 610
Western Samoa: *401,* 473
West Indies: *462,* 463
West Virginia State Board of Education v. Barnette: 197, 686-8
Wewelsburg concentration camp: 665
What Do the Scriptures Say About "Survival After Death"?: 127
What Say the Scriptures About Hell?: 129
Wheat
   Jesus' illustration: 44, 121, 706
"Where Are the Dead?"
   discourse by Russell: 396
Where Are the Dead?
   booklet: 130
"Where Are the Nine?"
   tract, 1928: *288*
White, Victor: *540*
Whittington, Mary: *485*
Whittington, Warigbani: 176-7
"Who Will Honor Jehovah?"
   Watch Tower article, 1926: 124, 152

"Why Clergy Oppose Truth"
   phonograph record: 565
Wiederkehr, Rudolf: 497
Williams, Arthur, Sr.: 419
Willis, Arthur: *445*
Wilson, Benjamin: 606
   Emphatic Diaglott: 46
Wilson, Gladys: *460*
Wilson, Woodrow: 652-3
Window signs: 561, *568*
Windward Islands: 463
Winkler, R. Arthur: *453,* 454
Winter, Sophus: 407-8
Winter, Thomas N.
   comments about *Kingdom Interlinear:* 610
Winton, George: 440
Wise, Brian and Elke: 529
Wise, C. A.: 74, *577,* 578
Witness
   Greek words: 12-13, 20
   Hebrew words: 12
Wittig, Karl
   Witnesses in concentration camps: 553
Wohlfahrt, Franz: *451*
Wolfgramm, David: 472
Woodard, Hermon: 526, *528*
Woodworth, C. James: 93-4
Woodworth, Clayton J.
   arrest and sentencing: 650-2, *653*
   editor of *The Golden Age* and *Consolation: 634*

Finished Mystery, The: 66-7
   reaction to disappointed expectations: *634*
WORD radio station: *81*
Workers' Meetings: 247
World
   attitude of Witnesses: 673
   early Christians: 198, 200, 673
   hatred of Christians: 200, 673
   invisible ruler: 190, 193
   maps: *415-17*
   "no part of" (John 17:16): 188-201
World Council of Churches
   political involvement: 195
World War I: 61, 77
   effect on preaching work: 423-5
   newspaper comment: 60
   persecution of Bible Students: 647-54
World War II: 89, 95
   bans on Witnesses: 455-8
   effect on preaching work: 448-58
   imprisonments: 451-3
   paper rations: 586
Worldwide Security Under the "Prince of Peace": 171
"World-wide Witness"
   Watch Tower article, 1927: *639*
Worsley, Arthur: 89, *462,* 463
Wozniak, André: 227
Wright, George: 430, 521
Wright, J. D.: 65
Writing Committee: 110, 234
Wycliffe, John: 44

Y

Yankee Stadium
   conventions: 99-102, 106, *270-1,* 274
Yeatts, Russell: 529
You Can Live Forever in Paradise on Earth: 112, *571,* 574, *594*
Young, George: *436,* 521
Young's literal Bible translation: *604,* 605
"Your Will Be Done on Earth": 102
"Your Word Is a Lamp to My Foot": 479

Your Youth—Getting the Best Out Of It: 110, 175, 246
Youths
   donations to Kingdom work: 345, 347
   "Jehovah's Youth": *244,* 245
   "Junior Witnesses": 245
   juvenile classes: *244,* 245
   literature: *244,* 245-6
   meetings: 244-6
   Theocratic Ministry School: 249

   training: 244
Yuen, Nancy: 490
Yugoslavia
   ban: 675
   conventions: 507
   early witnessing!: 430, 432
   "Photo-Drama of Creation": 432
   relief efforts: 309-10
Yuille, Maud: 221

Z

Zaire
   Bible studies, number, 1992: 510
   congregations, number, 1975: 483, 501
   counterfeit Watchtower movements: 482-3
   Kingdom Halls reopened: 509-10
   missionaries: 483
   polygamy (experience): 176-7
   publishers, number: 482-3, 510
   relief efforts: 712
   repressive measures by colonial officials: 482-3, 486-7
Zambia
   bans: 509, 676
   branch office: *392*
      financing construction: 346-7
   congregations, number: 475, 537
   conventions: *269, 392*
   early witnessing: 436
   film *The New World Society in Action:* 480
   Memorial, 1992: 509

   printing: 594
   publishers, number: 392
   relief efforts: 317
   return visits, number, 1936-92: 392
Zanzibar (See **Tanzania**)
Zech, O. von: 627
Zeppelinwiese
   convention, 1946: 268
Zimbabwe
   ban: 676
   branch office: *392*
   circuit assembly, effort to attend (experience): 281
   early witnessing: 430, 436
   legal recognition: 486
   meetings (experience): 251
   Memorial (experience): 243
   missionaries: 526, *530*
   publishers, number: 392, 486
   traveling overseers: 227

Zimmerman, Harold and Anne: *469, 470*
"Zionism in Prophecy"
   discourse by Russell: 141
Zion's Day Star: 621
Zion's Glad Songs: 240
Zion's Glad Songs of the Morning: 240
Zion's Watch Tower and Herald of Christ's Presence (See also *Watchtower, The*): 47-8, 252, 718, 724-5
Zion's Watch Tower Tract Society (See also **Watch Tower Bible and Tract Society of Pennsylvania**)
   colporteurs: 284
   legally chartered: 229, 718
   organized: 718
Zone assembly (See **Assemblies**)
Zone overseers (servants): 101, 223, 226
Zwingli, Ulrich: 39

PICTURE CREDITS

Page 35, Cyprian: ICCD E 1588. *Page 36*, Plato: Vatican Museum photograph. *Page 38*, Augustine of Hippo: ICCD E 52787. *Page 39*, Calvin: Courtesy of the Trustees of The British Museum. Zwingli: Courtesy of the Trustees of The British Museum. *Page 40*, Marx: New York Times, Berlin—33225115. Communist Manifesto: By permission of the British Library. *The Origin of Species:* By permission of the British Library. Darwin: Courtesy of the Trustees of The British Museum. *Page 41*, Electric light: U.S. Department of the Interior/National Park Service; Edison/National Historic Site. Telephone: Courtesy of AT&T Archives. Linotype: Division of Graphic Arts, National Museum of American History, Smithsonian Institution. Phonograph: U.S. Department of the Interior/National Park Service; Edison/National Historic Site. *Page 46*, Storrs: *Six Sermons*, by George Storrs (1855). *Page 48*, Barbour: Based on a sketch from the Rochester *Union & Advertiser*. *Page 96*, Airplane: Boeing Company Archives. *Page 125*, Grew: Courtesy of The New-York Historical Society, NYC. *Page 128*, Carnegie Hall: Carnegie Library of Pittsburgh. *Page 142*, Ship: Courtesy of the American Merchant Marine Museum. *Page 193*, Former League of Nations headquarters: UN photo. UN General Assembly: UN photo/Milton Grant. *Pages 208-9*, Map: Carnegie Library of Pittsburgh. *Pages 216-17*, Brooklyn Bridge: *New York in the Nineteenth Century*, by John Grafton, Dover Publications, Inc. *Page 288*, Cow: The Bettmann Archive. *Pages 402-3*, Map: *The Pictorial History of the World*, Volume 1, by James D. McCabe and Henry Davenport Northrop (1907). *Page 611*, Manuscript: Courtesy of the Shrine of the Book, Israel Museum, Jerusalem. *Page 651*, Brooklyn Federal Court and Post Office. The Brooklyn Historical Society. *Page 659*, Concentration camp (center): Oświecim Museum. Insignia: Courtesy of Regimentals, London. *Page 667*, Mob: Courtesy Canada Wide. *Page 669*, Jail: *Chicago Herald-American*. *Page 670*, Mob (top): AP/Wide World Photos. *Page 679*, U.S. Supreme Court building: Photo by Josh Mathes, Collection of the Supreme Court of the United States. *Page 681*, Duplessis and Cardinal Villeneuve: Photo by W. R. Edwards. *Page 686*, U.S. Supreme Court justices: Collection of the Supreme Court of the United States.

CHIEF OFFICE AND OFFICIAL ADDRESS OF
WATCH TOWER BIBLE AND TRACT SOCIETY OF PENNSYLVANIA
WATCHTOWER BIBLE AND TRACT SOCIETY OF NEW YORK, INC.
INTERNATIONAL BIBLE STUDENTS ASSOCIATION
25 COLUMBIA HEIGHTS, BROOKLYN, NEW YORK 11201, U.S.A.
ADDRESSES IN OTHER COUNTRIES:

ALASKA 99507: 2552 East 48th Ave., Anchorage. **ALBANIA:** Kutia Postare 118, Tiranë. **ARGENTINA:** Elcano 3820, 1427 Buenos Aires. **AUSTRALIA:** Box 280, Ingleburn, N.S.W. 2565. **AUSTRIA:** Postfach 67, A-1134 Vienna [13 Gallgasse 42-44, Vienna]. **BAHAMAS:** Box N-1247, Nassau, N.P. **BARBADOS:** Fontabelle Rd., Bridgetown. **BELGIUM:** rue d'Argile-Potaardestraat 60, B-1950 Kraainem. **BELIZE:** Box 257, Belize City. **BENIN, REP. OF:** BP 06-1131, Cotonou. **BOLIVIA:** Casilla No. 1440, La Paz. **BRAZIL:** Caixa Postal 92, 18270-970 Tatuí, SP. **BULGARIA:** P.K. 353, Sofia 1000. **CANADA:** Box 4100, Halton Hills (Georgetown), Ontario L7G 4Y4. **CENTRAL AFRICAN REPUBLIC:** B.P. 662, Bangui. **CHILE:** Casilla 267, Puente Alto [Av. Concha y Toro 3456, Puente Alto]. **COLOMBIA:** Apartado Aéreo 85058, Bogotá 8, D.E. **COSTA RICA:** Apartado 10043, San José. **CÔTE D'IVOIRE (IVORY COAST), WEST AFRICA:** 06 B P 393, Abidjan 06. **CROATIA:** p.p. 417, 41001 Zagreb. **CYPRUS:** P. O. Box 33, Dhali, Nicosia. **CZECH REPUBLIC:** P.O. Box 90, 198 00 Praha 9. **DENMARK:** Stenhusvej 28, DK-4300 Holbæk. **DOMINICAN REPUBLIC:** Apartado 1742, Santo Domingo. **ECUADOR:** Casilla 09-01-4512, Guayaquil. **EL SALVADOR:** Apartado Postal 401, San Salvador. **ENGLAND:** The Ridgeway, London NW7 1RP. **ETHIOPIA:** P.O. Box 5522, Addis Ababa. **FIJI:** Box 23, Suva. **FINLAND:** Postbox 68, FIN-01301 Vantaa 30. **FRANCE:** B.P. 63, F-92105 Boulogne-Billancourt Cedex. **FRENCH GUIANA:** 15 rue Chawari, Cogneau Larivot, 97351 Matoury. **GERMANY:** Niederselters, Am Steinfels, D-65618 Selters. **GHANA:** Box 760, Accra. **GREECE:** P.O. Box 112, GR-322 00 Thiva. **GUADELOUPE:** Monmain, 97180 Sainte Anne. **GUAM 96913:** 143 Jehovah St., Barrigada. **GUATEMALA:** 17 Calle 13-63, Zona 11, 01011 Guatemala. **GUYANA:** 50 Brickdam, Georgetown 16. **HAITI:** Post Box 185, Port-au-Prince. **HAWAII 96819:** 2055 Kam IV Rd., Honolulu. **HONDURAS:** Apartado 147, Tegucigalpa. **HONG KONG:** 4 Kent Road, Kowloon Tong. **HUNGARY:** Cserkut u. 13, H-1162 Budapest. **ICELAND:** P. O. Box 8496, IS-128 Reykjavík. **INDIA:** Post Bag 10, Lonavla, Pune Dis., Mah. 410 401. **IRELAND:** 29A Jamestown Road, Finglas, Dublin 11. **ISRAEL:** P. O. Box 961, 61-009 Tel Aviv. **ITALY:** Via della Bufalotta 1281, I-00138 Rome RM. **JAMAICA:** Box 180, Kingston 10. **JAPAN:** 1271 Nakashinden, Ebina City, Kanagawa Pref., 243-04. **KENYA:** Box 47788, Nairobi. **KOREA, REPUBLIC OF:** Box 33 Pyungtaek P. O., Kyunggido, 450-600. **LEEWARD ISLANDS:** Box 119, St. Johns, Antigua. **LIBERIA:** P.O. Box 10-0380, 1000 Monrovia 10. **LUXEMBOURG:** B. P. 2186, L-1021 Luxembourg, G. D. **MADAGASCAR:** B. P. 511, Antananarivo 101. **MALAYSIA:** 28 Jalan Kampar, Off Jalan Landasan, 41300 Klang, Sel. **MARTINIQUE:** Cours Campeche, Morne Tartenson, 97200 Fort de France. **MAURITIUS:** Clairfond No. 2, Box 54, Vacoas. **MEXICO:** Apartado Postal 896, 06002 Mexico, D. F. **MOZAMBIQUE:** Caixa Postal 2600, Maputo. **MYANMAR:** P.O. Box 62, Yangon. **NETHERLANDS:** Noordbargerstraat 77, NL-7812 AA Emmen. **NETHERLANDS ANTILLES:** P.O. Box 4708, Willemstad, Curaçao. **NEW CALEDONIA:** B.P. 787, Nouméa. **NEW ZEALAND:** P.O. Box 142, Manurewa. **NICARAGUA:** Apartado 3587, Managua. **NIGERIA:** P.M.B. 1090, Benin City, Edo State. **NORWAY:** Gaupeveien 24, N-1914 Ytre Enebakk. **PAKISTAN:** 197-A Ahmad Block, New Garden Town, Lahore 54600. **PANAMA:** Apartado 6-2671, Zona 6A, El Dorado. **PAPUA NEW GUINEA:** Box 636, Boroko, N.C.D. **PARAGUAY:** Díaz de Solís 1485 esq. C.A. López, Sajonia, Asunción. **PERU:** Apartado 18-1055, Lima 18 [Av. El Cortijo 329, Monterrico Chico, Lima 33]. **PHILIPPINES, REPUBLIC OF:** P. O. Box 2044, 1099 Manila [186 Roosevelt Ave., San Francisco del Monte, 1105 Quezon City]. **POLAND:** Skr. Poczt. 13, PL-05-830 Nadarzyn. **PORTUGAL:** Apartado 91, P-2766 Estoril Codex [Rua Conde Barão, 511, Alcabideche, P-2765 Estoril]. **PUERTO RICO 00970:** P.O. Box 3980, Guaynabo. **ROMANIA:** Str. Parfumului 22, RO-74121, Bucharest. **RUSSIA:** ul. Tankistov, 4, Solnechnoye, Sestroretzky Rayon, 189640 St. Petersburg. **SENEGAL:** B.P. 3107, Dakar. **SIERRA LEONE, WEST AFRICA:** P. O. Box 136, Freetown. **SLOVAKIA:** P.O. Box 17, 810 00 Bratislava 1. **SLOVENIA:** Poljanska cesta 77a, SLO-61000 Ljubljana. **SOLOMON ISLANDS:** P.O. Box 166, Honiara. **SOUTH AFRICA:** Private Bag X2067, Krugersdorp, 1740. **SPAIN:** Apartado postal 132, E-28850 Torrejón de Ardoz (Madrid). **SRI LANKA, REP. OF:** 711 Station Road, Wattala. **SURINAME:** P. O. Box 49, Paramaribo. **SWEDEN:** Box 5, S-732 21 Arboga. **SWITZERLAND:** P.O. Box 225, CH-3602 Thun [Ulmenweg 45, Thun]. **TAHITI:** B.P. 518, Papeete. **TAIWAN:** No. 3-12, 7 Lin, Shetze Village, Hsinwu Hsiang, Taoyuan County, 327. **THAILAND:** 69/1 Soi Phasuk, Sukhumwit Rd., Soi 2, Bangkok 10110. **TOGO:** B.P. 4460, Lome. **TRINIDAD AND TOBAGO, REP. OF:** Lower Rapsey Street & Laxmi Lane, Curepe. **UKRAINE:** Glavposhtamt Box 246, 290000 Lviv. **UNITED STATES OF AMERICA:** 25 Columbia Heights, Brooklyn, NY 11201-2483. **URUGUAY:** Francisco Bauzá 3372, 11600 Montevideo. **VENEZUELA:** Apartado 20.364, Caracas, DF 1020A [Av. La Victoria; cruce con 17 de diciembre, La Victoria, Edo. Aragua 2121A]. **WESTERN SAMOA:** P. O. Box 673, Apia. **YUGOSLAVIA, F.R.:** Milorada Mitrovića 4, YU-11 000 Belgrade. **ZAIRE, REP. OF:** B.P. 634, Limete, Kinshasa. **ZAMBIA:** Box 33459, Lusaka 10101. **ZIMBABWE:** 35 Fife Avenue, Harare.